Alberta's North

*A History, 1890–1950*

ALBERTA
REFLECTIONS

# Alberta's North

## A History, 1890–1950

DONALD G. WETHERELL AND IRENE R.A. KMET

Canadian Circumpolar
Institute Press

The University of
Alberta Press

Alberta Community
Development

First published by the Canadian Circumpolar Institute Press, The University of Alberta Press and Alberta Community Development

Canadian Circumpolar Institute Press
Old St. Stephen's College
8820 – 112 Street
Edmonton, Alberta Canada   T6G 2P8

The University of Alberta Press
Ring House 2
Edmonton, Alberta, Canada   T6G 2E1

ISBN 1–896445–17–9 (Canadian Circumpolar Institute Press)
Occasional Publication No. 48
Northern Alberta Research Series No. 5

ISBN 0–88864–342–X (The University of Alberta Press)

CANADIAN CATALOGUING IN PUBLICATION DATA

Wetherell, Donald G. (Donald Grant), 1949-
Alberta's north

(Northern Alberta research series ; no. 5) (Occasional publication / Canadian Circumpolar Institute ; no. 48) (Alberta reflections)
   Copublished by: Canadian Circumpolar Institute Press, and Alberta Community Development.
   Includes bibliographical references and index. ISBN 0-88864-342-X (University of Alberta Press) — ISBN 1-896445-17-9 (Canadian Circumpolar Institute Press)

   1. Alberta, Northern—History. 2. Northwest Territories—History—1870-1905.*
   I. Kmet, Irene, 1950- II. Canadian Circumpolar Institute. III. Alberta. Alberta Community Development. IV. Title. V. Series: Northern Alberta research series ; no. 5.
   VI. Series: Occasional publication (Canadian Circumpolar Institute) ; no. 48. VII. Series: Alberta reflections.
   FC3694.4.W47 2000    971.23    C00-910503-4 F1078.W47 2000

∞ Printed on acid-free paper.
Photographs scannned by Screaming Color.
Printed and bound in Canada by Friesens, Altona, Manitoba.

The University of Alberta Press gratefully acknowledges the support received for its publishing program from The Canada Council for the Arts. In addition, we also gratefully acknowledge the financial support of the Government of Canada through the Book Publishing Industry Development Program for our publishing activities.

# Contents

*Alberta 2005*  /IX

*Acknowledgements*  /XI

*Abbreviations*  /XIII

Introduction  /XV


PART I **Canada Takes Control, 1890–1899**

⎯ 1 Region and Place: *Northern Alberta in the Late 1800s*  /3

⎯ 2 The 1890s: *The Beginnings of Canadian Control*  /29

⎯ 3 Treaty and Scrip in Northern Alberta  /49


PART II **Transitions, 1900–1920**

⎯ 4 A Foundation for Development:
*The State and Northern Alberta, 1900–1915*  /77

⎯ 5 Northern Life and Society to 1916  /107

⎯ 6 Changing Course, 1912–1921  /151


PART III **The Decline of Regional Unity, 1920–1950**

⎯ 7 Getting In, Getting Out:
*Transportation Development in Northern Alberta*  /185

⎯ 8 The Evolution of Separate Societies:
*Towns and Social Services*  /215

9 Farm Settlement: *The Peace River Country* /239

10 Farming in the Peace River Country /259

11 Society and Social Life: *The Peace River Country* /285

12 Natives, Land and Power /305

13 Development of Northern Resources /333

14 Crisis Upon Crisis: *Trapping in Northern Alberta* /363

**PART IV Conclusion**

15 Diverging Paths /397


*Notes* /411

*Bibliography* /469

*Index* /485


*List of Tables*

Table 5–1
*Boarding School Enrolment versus Treaty Population, Treaty 8, 1910* /145

Table 10–1
*Farm Size, and Acreage in Wheat and Oats, Peace River Country,*
*1921–1946* /262


*Maps*

Northern Alberta /2

Major Transportation Routes 1880 /16

Major Transportation Routes 1890 /17

NAR Lines in Northern Alberta 1930 /150

*For Noah, Jasper and River*

**ALBERTA REFLECTIONS**

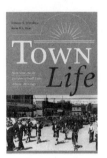

**Town Life**
*Main Street and the Evolution of Small Town Alberta, 1880–1947*
Donald G. Wetherell and Irene R.A. Kmet

**The Literary History of Alberta, Volume One**
*From Writing-on-Stone to World War Two*
George Melynk

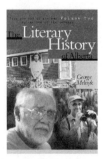

**The Literary History of Alberta, Volume Two**
*From the End of the War to the End of the Century*
George Melynk

# Alberta 2005

*Alberta Reflections*

THE YEAR 2005 WILL MARK the centennial of the Province of Alberta. In 1988, a group of Albertans from various backgrounds met in Red Deer to discuss the possibility of producing a multi-volume history of the province in time for its hundredth anniversary. The result was the creation of the Alberta 2005 Centennial History Society, a nonprofit association devoted to producing a history that is both accurate and accessible. The principal work of the Society since 1991 has been to identify areas of Alberta's past most in need of further research and to sponsor a series of studies aimed at filling the blanks.

Our intention has been to commission specialized studies for publication in the series that we call Alberta Reflections. We are pleased to add *Alberta's North: A History, 1890–1950*, by Donald G. Wetherell and Irene R. A. Kmet, to the series. This team has been especially productive in recent years with excellent research leading to a range of publications about topics in Alberta history. Drawing attention to the northern focus in Alberta's heritage is a particularly valuable contribution, given its unique character and the more recent escalation in northern development and interest in the northern environment. Alberta's first century includes strong northern themes.

A large portion of the funding for the Alberta 2005 project has come from the Alberta Historical Resources Foundation, and we gratefully acknowledge this support.

CARL BETKE
*President, Alberta 2005*
*Centennial History Society*

# Acknowledgements

AUTHORS ACCUMULATE MANY DEBTS when writing a book. We owe thanks to Frits Pannekoek and Les Hurt of Historic Sites Service, Alberta Community Development, who recognized the need for a study of the modern history of northern Alberta. Historic Sites was soon joined by the Canadian Circumpolar Institute, University of Alberta, which was equally committed to encouraging historical understanding of northern Alberta in the period since Treaty 8 in 1899. We are grateful to Cliff Hickey for his initiative, commitment and support of the project, and we also wish to thank Elaine Maloney for facilitating the project and assisting with its publication. At Historic Sites, special thanks are owed to Michael Payne, who not only administered the project on behalf of his department, but, as a colleague, offered insight and discussion. Dave Leonard and Patricia Myers of Historic Sites Service also kindly read the manuscript and provided thoughtful comments. Fruitful conversations with Bob Irwin, Brian Calliou, Cora Voyageur, and, at Fort Chipewyan, Mary Bourque, made this a better book. Two anonymous reviewers made helpful and instructive comments. We also thank the staff of archives and libraries that we consulted across the country, especially those at the Provincial Archives of Alberta in Edmonton, the Glenbow Library and Archives in Calgary and the National Archives of Canada, Ottawa.

Mary Mahoney-Robson and Alan Brownoff at the University of Alberta Press were—as always—helpful and professional. We thank them sincerely. Thanks also to Eduard Wiens who drew the maps.

Despite the contributions of so many, any faults that this book possesses are ours alone.

DONALD G. WETHERELL

IRENE KMET

# Abbreviations

| | |
|---|---|
| A&GW | Alberta and Great Waterways Railway |
| APP | Alberta Provincial Police |
| AP | Anglican Papers, Provincial Archives of Alberta, Edmonton |
| CCR | Central Canada Railway |
| CNoR | Canadian Northern Railway |
| CNR | Canadian National Railway |
| ED&BC | Edmonton, Dunvegan and British Columbia Railway |
| GAI | Glenbow Alberta Institute Library and Archives, Calgary |
| GTP | Grand Trunk Pacific Railway |
| MLA | Member of the Legislative Assembly |
| NAC | National Archives of Canada, Ottawa |
| NAR | Northern Alberta Railway |
| NWMP | North West Mounted Police |
| NWT | Northwest Territories |
| PAA | Provincial Archives of Alberta, Edmonton |
| P&GE | Pacific and Great Eastern Railway |
| PP | Premiers' Papers, Provincial Archives of Alberta, Edmonton |
| RCMP | Royal Canadian Mounted Police |
| SABS | Saskatchewan Archives Board, Saskatoon |
| UAA | University of Alberta Archives, Edmonton |
| UCAT | United Church Archives, Toronto |

# Introduction

*Tell how familiar features, long known by heart, may while*
*We watch them, be transfigured in one short moment's space.*

FAIZ AHMED FAIZ[1]

ONE OF THE FIRST DISCOVERIES of an inquiry by the Canadian Senate on the Mackenzie basin in 1888 was that "very little more was known" about it than "the interior of Africa or Australia."[2] While the Senators' findings accurately reflected the general state of Canadian knowledge, the territory drained by the Peace and Athabasca Rivers—a major portion of the Mackenzie basin—had engaged the interests of fur traders, at times violently but more often profitably, since the 1700s. By the late nineteenth century, these old passions had faded, but by then the fur trade had helped to reshape the Peace and Athabasca drainage basin into a distinct region in western Canada. Although politically isolated from the rest of Canada, this region was united by the 1890s by a transportation network using steamboats and other water craft, common economic activities and, among other things, a regional urban system made up of small settlements. This region would later become northern Alberta, and in the 60 years after 1890, it was integrated into the Canadian economy. As Euro-Canadian interest and activity grew in northern Alberta, its economy and society, as well as its coherence as a functional region, were transformed.

The groundwork was laid for these new political and economic relationships in northern Alberta in the single decade between 1890 and 1900. During this expansionary time, the federal government asserted control over the region by sending in the North-West Mounted Police (NWMP) and establishing rudimentary government services. The decade closed with the signing of Treaty 8 with the First Nations people in 1899. After 1905, the new province of Alberta entrenched and expanded the integration of northern Alberta with Canada. In 1916 a railway, subsidized by the province, linked the Peace River country with Edmonton, and slightly later another line connected Edmonton with Fort McMurray. Although steamboats continued to be important in some areas, railway development was critical. In a staple economy dependent on outside capital, railways assisted in the development of new economic and social activity and the integration of distant places into the national economy. Subsequently, Euro-Canadian farm communities tied to Canadian and foreign markets grew up around centres like Grande Prairie, Peace River and Fort Vermilion in the Peace River country. New economic activity also began in the Fort McMurray district in the wake of its rail connections with Edmonton.

By the 1920s Canadian expansion and new economic activity had split the older and larger regional unit of the 1890s into two smaller and distinct units— in the west, the Peace River country, and in the east, the lower Athabasca River district between Fort McMurray and Fort Smith.[3] The character of these districts subsequently diverged, with their populations differentiated by class, race and occupation. These changes intensified during the interwar years and led to the emergence of separate transportation and urban networks in each district. Along with these developments came the expression of different social and economic priorities, ambitions and concerns. By 1939, a mere 40 years after the treaty was signed, older patterns of regional life had been transfigured, and as elsewhere in Canada, World War II brought further change and a transition to a new era.

As part of the revamping of northern Alberta's relationship with Canada, the authority and concerns of the Native cultures were replaced by those of outsiders and recent arrivals. Pressure on First Nations and Metis people was most intense in areas of farm settlement, but new economic and social conditions were also emerging in areas where fur remained central. Native people remained active participants in the society, yet residential schools, reserve policy and legal distinctions between treaty and nontreaty people brought directed cultural change as a part of public policy. Broader economic and social change had an equally powerful impact by affecting the ways that Native peoples made their living, how they used natural resources such as fur and game, and their place in the region's changing settlement and communications networks.

The rise of northern Alberta as a region, and its transformation because of national expansion, is part of the evolving character and definition of the "north" in Canada. In a mythology parallel to that of the American "frontier," Canada has often been said to be a nation whose northerness was not merely a geographical and political reality but an emotive part of its history and its future. The romance of a wild northern landscape has ebbed and flowed in Canada, forming at times a part of the definition of the nation's character and destiny. Indeed, this myth of northerness was sometimes thought to offer the possibility of transcending the country's regional and ethnic divisions.[4]

Yet this ideal of northerness was rarely capable of serving the demands placed on it. As a place, the north was continually in a state of flux, and as historian Morris Zaslow observed, "northern Canada" was a relative place, one with an undefined and constantly shifting boundary.[5] While Canadians in the mid 1800s saw the whole of the prairie west as a northern place, by 1900 they no longer viewed it as such; by then, the north was understood to be that area lying north of settled prairie agricultural lands.[6] This shifting boundary of what is the north in Canada also arose from a deep ambiguity in how Canadians viewed their northerness. While they have often been flattered by a mythology depicting them as a resourceful "northern" people able to survive a rigorous climate, they have not been entirely comfortable in such winter garb. Rather, Canadians have preferred to see farms and industrial cities—not wilderness—as the true measure of national accomplishment. Places that could not support this preferred lifestyle and economy were often disparaged. This perhaps contributed to unique attitudes and views in Canada about people's place in nature, but, most obviously, it forced Canadians to attempt to transcend their geography, or their "northerness." In a candid expression of this tension, Reverend Robertson, the superintendent of Presbyterian missions, told an Edmonton audience in 1884 that he had heard of the fine agricultural prospects of the Peace River country. He urged his listeners "to assist in the settling of that country, for if it became known that the country further north...was settled [by Euro-Canadians], people elsewhere would begin to look upon Edmonton as being far south."[7]

Within such attempts to transcend the north lay concerns about nation-building and the territorial expansion of Euro-Canadian society. Efforts after 1867 to tie the nation together and adapt its economy to industrial capitalism were important issues for the new Canadian nation. The annexation of the prairies in 1870 further required the integration of this new territory into the national economy and a revamping of the (often restricted) economic and social relationships that had existed between Canada and the old North-West. These objectives became additional elements in Canada's post-Confederation nation-building concerns. At first, this partly involved the reproduction of cultural, economic and political institutions and attitudes to cement the connections between the two parts of Canada. While this stimulated massive changes in Canada from which new provinces would emerge, it also eventually led to a new regional consciousness on the prairies. As political scientist Peter McCormick has phrased it, "regionalism in Canada is not a single story" and the elements that have contributed to its development have varied by location, time and circumstance. Indeed, by the late 1880s, a number of small "regions" had developed on the prairies as part of the changing environment. Geographer John Warkentin has identified at least seven such regions in prairie Canada in 1886 whose economic activities and coherent transportation networks made them into functional regions. Among these were the Edmonton-St. Albert district, the Saskatchewan district (Prince Albert-Batoche-Battleford), and the Bow River region comprised of the ranching country of southern Alberta. While traces of these regions endured, they were later absorbed into the larger prairie regional unit. Nation-building on the prairies, like province-building, thus spawned and then absorbed smaller regional units.[8]

Although Warkentin did not study the unorganized northern districts that did not yet have Euro-Canadian agrarian settlement, northern Alberta formed another of the distinctive regions in late nineteenth century prairie Canada.[9] How and why this region was integrated into Canada, the mechanisms that were applied to promote its integration and the consequences of these developments are central issues in its history. These have been persistent themes in the writing of prairie history, and as historians Kenneth Coates and William Morrison have noted, they have also been recurring issues in the history of the "middle north" (the northern districts of the provinces) as well as the far north of Canada.[10] So too, Canadians have increasingly recognized that regions and their constituent parts are not static or self-contained, nor is their evolution merely national history writ small or local history writ large. Historian Chad Gaffield theorizes that while it is well understood that regions exist within regions, their historical evolution within provincial and national life, and the definitions, changes and even dissolution of their boundaries provide new insights into the process of nation-building, regionalism and the evolution of Canadian society.[11] This also applies to northern Alberta, a region that existed on the cusp of the prairies. Although some local identities persisted and new forms emerged as part of the reorientation of northern Alberta's economy and society, parts of the region, such as the Peace River country, were largely absorbed into provincial and prairie agrarian life, while other parts, such as the lower Athabasca River district, which retained earlier economic characteristics, were marginalised within the larger Alberta and prairie unit.

— ✦ —

There has been extensive historical writing about parts of northern Alberta, especially the Peace River country, and to a lesser extent Fort Chipewyan. Earlier writers have focussed on the history of the fur trade and Christian missions before the treaty, as well as the Euro-Canadian settlement of the Peace River country after about 1910. *Alberta's North: A History, 1890 to 1950* is the first study that examines the history of the whole of the region after the end of the nineteenth century. The geographical area we study includes all of the territory in Alberta north of 55 degrees. This latitude was the southern boundary of the North-West Territories District of Athabaska (which was created in 1882) and also broadly formed the southern limit of Treaty 8. As well, it is the approximate edge of most of the Hudson's Bay and Mackenzie watersheds in Alberta. More recently, the interpretation of northern Alberta as the territory north of 55 degrees was demonstrated by the use of this boundary by the Alberta Royal Commission on the Development of Northern Alberta in 1958.

While this boundary is used to define northern Alberta, we do not adhere to it rigidly. Created by the Hudson's Bay Company as the centre of northern Alberta's transportation network, Athabasca is also included, even though it lies slightly south of 55 degrees, because it served as northern Alberta's southern portal between 1887 and the end of World War I. Areas beyond the province's boundaries that were connected to the economic and social life of northern Alberta are also studied. Direct reference is made to the Peace River block of British Columbia, which was economically and socially linked to Alberta. Similarly, reference is made to Fort Smith, located on the Alberta-Northwest Territories (NWT) border and the northern terminus of the Athabasca River system, and to Fond du Lac at the east of Lake Athabasca, which now lies in Saskatchewan. Northern Alberta was also related historically to the Mackenzie River valley, and other towns and settlements in western and northern Canada are mentioned in a similar effort to identify their relationship and interaction with northern Alberta. Yet detailed discussion of the Lac La

Biche and Cold Lake districts is not included, even though they, like Athabasca, lie close to the 55th parallel. By the 1890s, their primary orientation was southwards, having been included in Treaty 6 in 1876. Moreover, Lac La Biche lost many of its northern linkages in the 1880s when Athabasca replaced it as the focus for northern transportation. Edmonton is treated in a similar fashion. Although some people still saw it as a "northern" place as late as the 1930s, we do not define it as a part of northern Alberta. Edmonton's political and social life was primarily oriented south and eastwards. And while the city was enriched by northern trade (which it increasingly dominated), Edmonton's economic life was far more complex than simply that of a northern service centre.[12]

The flexibility that characterizes this loosely defined boundary of "northern" Alberta is one indication that historical change is never tidy. Social change over time involves both interfaces and discontinuities in the impact of events, geography, technology and economic and social structures and forces. While fundamental social forces (such as class and legal status), as well as basic conditions (such as technology, geography and transportation), can be isolated as important determinants in historical change, they are significant as part of a process. Each is an element in a range of developments that constantly shift relative to one another over time. In northern Alberta, the discontinuities these relative developments produced were especially sharp. The penetration of the region by expanding outside cultural, economic and political agencies was rapid, and the change this brought was not uniform in all parts of the region, nor did it affect all people in the same way. The new options this created for some people altered social relationships, social status and employment opportunities for others.[13]

This understanding of historical change has shaped the structure of *Alberta's North*, which is laid out in three parts. Part I is chronological and examines the beginnings of Canadian control in the 1890s. It ends with the signing of Treaty 8 in 1899. Part II, which deals with the subsequent extension of Canadian control until the end of World War I, is also chronological overall, but contains some thematic elements. Part III looks thematically at the period from 1920 until the end of World War II. This structure is not merely a literary device. The gradual shift from chronological to topical formats in the book reflects— just as the framing of a building reveals its structure and purpose—the transformation of northern Alberta after 1890 and the breakdown of its regional unity, the diverging economic and social life of its various districts, and the changing relationship between Aboriginal and Euro-Canadian people. Because of these diverging paths, a single narrative or perspective does not adequately explain northern Alberta's history. In this connection, we have also attempted to avoid the language and literary forms that have traditionally been vehicles for expressing Euro-Canadian notions about "progress" and the view that Canada's historical development has been inevitable.

Contemporary place names and spelling are used, except for administrative districts, constituencies and other official names. With respect to Aboriginal people, we have been conscious that the terms used in the past to describe them have often been ones that were invented as part of Euro-Canadian priorities and world view. Often, these terms bore little or no relationship to Aboriginal views of their own identity. This is a complex and sensitive issue, and as anthropologist Joe Sawchuk has observed, even though some of these terms (such as Native, Indian and nonstatus Indian) were invented as part of government policy, they now possess "considerable emotional and cultural significance" for Aboriginal people themselves. We use these terms conscious of their historical origins and their limits. We use the word Metis, for example, to describe people of First Nations-white ancestry, even though it is unlikely that its contemporary use to express cultural, legal and political identity can be applied to all such people before World War II.[14] Although some people believe that the term "Indian" has negative connotations, there is no precise alternative that is historically accurate. We therefore use this term only when discussing those people who were defined as "Indians" under the *Indian Act*. The terms Native and Aboriginal refer both to First Nations and Metis people.

# PART I

*Oxen were used to carry freight for the Hudson's Bay Company at the Fort Smith Portage. Photo taken about 1901–1903.* B2939 PAA.

# Canada Takes Control
## 1800–1899

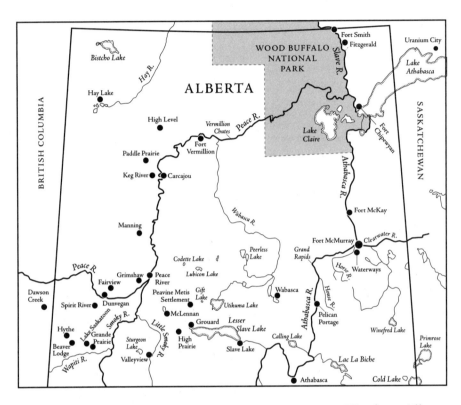

**Northern Alberta**

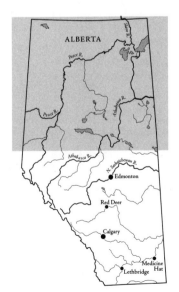

# Region and Place

*Northern Alberta in the Late 1800s*

IN THE 1780S, the fur trade brought northern Alberta into the economic orbit of distant metropolitan centres in eastern Canada and Europe and began to stimulate significant social and economic change in the area. By the mid 1800s, missionaries had also appeared in northern Alberta. Building upon existing patterns of settlement and life, fur traders and missionaries had by the 1890s contributed to the creation of a regional geography of communications and economic life in parts of the Peace and Athabasca River drainage basin. This region included all of the present-day Alberta north of 55 degrees, and extended beyond the current boundaries of the province to include the areas surrounding Lake Athabasca (most of which lies in present-day Saskatchewan) and the Peace River block of British Columbia. Although intimately connected with northern Alberta, the district between Fort Smith and Fort Resolution along the Slave River formed a transition zone more directly tied to the Mackenzie River and the far north.

## ⸺ People and Place

The Peace, Athabasca and Slave rivers and their tributaries formed ancient corridors of movement in the north. In the late 1700s, these were adopted by fur traders who moved goods over Portage La Loche (also called the Methy Portage), a route used by the Montreal trader Peter Pond in 1778 to cross from the Hudson's Bay to the Mackenzie watershed. From Lake Winnipeg (which the Hudson's Bay Company reached from York Factory and the Canadians reached from Montreal through Lake Superior), trade moved along the North Saskatchewan and Churchill rivers as far as Portage La Loche. Once across the portage, traders followed the Clearwater River about 115 kilometres westward to its juncture with the Athabasca River at the site of present-day Fort McMurray. While the Athabasca River was blocked south-west of Fort McMurray by a long series of rapids, it provided an unobstructed passage northwards as far as the Peace-Athabasca delta.[1] A crucial junction in the communications network, the delta was connected by water in all directions. To the west, it gave access to the Peace River, obstructed by rapids only at the Vermilion Chutes east of Fort Vermilion. From there lay a clear passage for about 650 kilometres as far as Hudson's Hope. To the east, the delta opened into Lake Athabasca, and to the north it gave access to Great Slave Lake and the Mackenzie River via the Slave River, broken only by the rapids just above Fort Smith.

Most of the Peace and Athabasca River basins was covered by boreal forest, broken in places by muskeg, swamps and occasional lakes and creeks stained the colour of copper by the muskeg. This vast forest was largely made up of spruce, aspen and birch and sheltered deer, moose, woodland caribou, bears and a small number of wood buffalo. Small mammals were limited overall, with beaver, muskrat and rabbit most common. A very different landscape characterized the Peace River country, where relatively small areas of park-land—or "prairies"—were separated by deep river valleys, hills and swamp lands. Although a rich environment in many respects, a scarcity of lakes some-what limited its natural wealth, while over-hunting had seriously reduced animal populations in some places by the late 1800s.[2]

Resources were more plentiful in some areas than in others. Fort Vermilion in the northern Peace country was one pocket of wealth, as was the area around Lesser Slave Lake, especially along the low-lying southern shore with its rich fish and waterfowl resources. But the greatest abundance was found in the Peace-Athabasca delta. During most of the year, water from Lake Athabasca drained into the Peace River. In the spring, however, the waters of the river were pushed back. During this reverse action, water spilled into the delta, filling its many sloughs. Like the Nile, this annual inundation created an environment of great richness, and the area abounded in fish, timber, large mammals, fur-bearing animals, and waterfowl that stopped there on their annual migrations.[3]

The distribution of people in the region reflected the importance of these pockets of natural wealth. By 1899, the Native population of present day northern Alberta stood at about 3,650. Not surprisingly, the great majority— about 80 percent—lived in the Lesser Slave Lake (including Wabasca) district, in the Fort Vermilion area, and around Fort Smith-Fort Chipewyan.[4] Most of the others lived in the Fort McMurray and Peace River districts, and a few lived around what have come to be called the "isolated settlements" around Peerless, Loon and Trout lakes north of Wabasca. North of this lay a huge, largely unpopulated wedge in the centre of the region.

The ancestry of these people is ancient—land-based hunting societies took shape in the boreal forest areas of northern Alberta at least 10,000 years ago. By the late nineteenth century, most of these First Nations people were either Athapaskan speaking, including Beaver (who called themselves Dunne za), Chipewyan and Slavey (who called themselves Dene), or Algonkian speaking, primarily Cree. Chipewyan people mainly lived around the west and north sides of Lake Athabasca and south along the Athabasca River. Slavey people lived west and north of the Slave River and the Beaver mainly lived in the Peace River country. Cree lived in many areas, including along the Athabasca River as far north as Fort Chipewyan, around Lesser Slave Lake, and on the lower Peace River.[5]

There were also a few white fur traders, missionaries and a handful of white trappers and prospectors. White traders had been present in northern Alberta since 1778 when Peter Pond established a short-lived trading post about 50 kilometres above Lake Athabasca on the Athabasca River. Fort Chipewyan was established a decade later further north on the lake shore as the trade centre for the Mackenzie basin. Fort Vermilion was established at about the same time on the lower Peace River. Direct trade and excessive competition had by the early 1800s depleted meat and fur-bearing animals in parts of northern Alberta. The monopoly of trade enjoyed by the Hudson's Bay Company after its amalgamation with the North West Company in 1821 lasted until the 1860s when competition from free traders emerged in the Peace River country. While such rivals did not appear in the richer Athabasca River districts until some-what later, they were operating year round as far north as Great Slave Lake by 1888.[6] Missionaries had by then also added to the white presence in the region. A Roman Catholic order, the Missionary Oblates of Mary Immaculate, constructed a mission building at Fort Chipewyan in 1851 and expanded its activities into the Peace River country in 1867 when it opened a permanent mission at Dunvegan. Anglican missionaries were also active from the early 1870s, and by the 1890s they too had established a number of missions and schools in what is now northern Alberta and the North-West Territories.[7]

Far more numerous than these few white people were the northern Metis who originated from relationships between white traders and Native women. An indigenous Metis population, for example, had developed by 1821 at the west end of Lesser Slave Lake. Anthropologist Trudy Nicks notes that while there were direct relationships between these Metis and local Cree people, the Metis at Lesser Slave Lake kept themselves separate on the whole and tended to marry other Metis. This remained the pattern at least until the early 1900s. In the lower Athabasca, Slave and Mackenzie River districts, the same pattern was apparent, although there are suggestions that ongoing interaction between Metis and First Nations people was more common there than Nicks found at Lesser Slave Lake.[8]

At the same time that this indigenous mixed blood population was forming in northern Alberta, similar ones were also developing in other parts of western Canada. Especially important was the Metis population at Red River. Some of these Metis and their descendants began to appear in northern Alberta by at least 1800. Some lived in northern Alberta only temporarily, in conjunction with fur trade operations, while others settled there permanently. Still more Red River Metis moved west in uneven waves of migration after their defeat by the Canadians at Red River in 1870 and at Batoche in 1885. Most of these migrants settled in what is now Saskatchewan and Alberta, including the Edmonton, Lac La Biche and St. Paul districts. Subsequent economic and social change and the hostility of incoming Euro-Canadian settlers led some of these people to move again, and a number from the Edmonton region moved further north in the late 1880s. Many Metis on the plains had worked at freighting, but the expansion of white settlement and rail networks after the early 1880s had cost them their livelihood. After the late 1880s, displacement and a search for new economic opportunities contributed to the migrations to northern Alberta, where freighting jobs could be had and opportunities for trapping, hunting and small-scale trading were better.[9] In 1896, Sergeant Hetherington of the NWMP wrote from Athabasca that "a general exodus" of Metis from the Edmonton district was about to take place. Already a number of families from Beaver Lake, Battle River and St. Albert had moved north, and "nearly all gave me to understand that they had friends who were to follow later." By the late 1890s Red River Metis and their descendants were widely distributed in northern Alberta, especially in the Athabasca, Lesser Slave Lake, Wabasca and Grande Prairie areas, while others moved as far north as Fort Smith. This was the first major movement of settlers to northern Alberta in the late nineteenth and early twentieth centuries.[10]

In prairie Canada, English-speaking Metis often identified with their English-speaking fathers, while French-speaking ones generally tended to identify themselves as Metis and adopted a more nomadic lifestyle. Yet, as historian Heather Devine cautions, a variety of social and economic factors shaped "personal identity" among Metis. Her study of one western Canadian Metis family demonstrates that children within the same nuclear family sometimes adopted "widely divergent social, economic and political responses" to changing social and economic environments. The same complexity characterized both the Red River Metis and those in northern Alberta. Certainly, the current associations of the term "Metis," and its implied cultural and political uniformity, cannot be applied coherently to the mixed race population of northern Alberta in the late nineteenth century. Confirming Heather Devine's conclusions, anthropologist Joe Sawchuk has argued that historically the categories that made up the prairie mixed race population were continually reformulated as their economic functions and social relationships evolved with a changing economy. Metis people thus viewed themselves in different ways and were defined by outsiders in various ways over time.[11] By the 1890s some of the northern Metis were economically and socially assimilated into First Nations societies, and it was this group that Bishop Grouard referred to in 1900 when he commented that there was a "class of people whom we have always considered as Indians," even though they had a small amount of "white blood." But, "for all purposes, they are pure Indians, having the same language, the same mode of living, shifting camps, hunting, fishing etc., in fact no difference at all can be made and they form an homogenous population."[12] In other cases, Metis people lived a somewhat more separate lifestyle and were differentiated by class, language and history. At Fort Chipewyan most of the local Metis population was French-speaking and Roman Catholic and occupied lower positions in the fur trade, while a few were English-speaking Anglicans with closer ties to the local fur trade establishment.[13] Although there were cases of intermarriage between the Metis and Cree and Chipewyan people at Fort Chipewyan, oral history reveals that the Metis did not generally mix with either group (who were in turn estranged from each other). These cultural distinctions also appear to have reflected economic specialization. At Fort Chipewyan, almost all Natives trapped, but Cree and Chipewyan did so on a full time basis, while many Metis trapped only between jobs or when there was no work on the river boats or with the fur trade companies or the missions.[14]

Despite distinctions within this northern Metis population and between them and First Nations people, these Metis created certain linkages within the region. Metis kin groups in the Mackenzie basin kept in touch and these ties "formed a web along the trade routes." Moreover, in communities like Fort Chipewyan (with its Cree, Chipewyan and Metis population), French served as a common language. The same pattern was found in other parts of northern

Alberta where French had made inroads as a common language because of the activities of French-speaking Metis, fur traders and Oblate missionaries. Nonetheless, Cree was another common language in many parts of northern Alberta, although anthropologist Patricia McCormack cautions that the extent of its use as a general language should not be overestimated at Fort Chipewyan. Nonetheless, in 1899 in northern Alberta, Cree was considered "the chief language of trade, and some of the Beavers and Chipewyans speak it in addition to their own tongues." English was less common overall, although it was used by the Hudson's Bay Company, Anglican missionaries and some northern Metis.[15]

The common experience of people in northern Alberta in the 1800s was directly shaped by the region's physical environment. Climatic variations such as heavy snowfall or unusually cold or warm weather, along with animal population cycles and their limited distribution and variety, affected the availability and type of animals used for food and trade. Northern Chipewyans hunted migratory caribou on the barrens and wood buffalo in the western part of the Lake Athabasca district, and took fish, waterfowl, muskrat and beaver in the Peace-Athabasca delta. The Dene and Beaver in the Peace River country and in areas further north hunted moose, birds, beaver and small game but often had less fish and muskrat than the Chipewyan. The Cree and Metis used all of these resources because they were widely distributed through most parts of northern Alberta by the 1890s.[16] Among First Nations people in northern Alberta, land and resources were governed within tribal units, where use, rather than ownership, was the primary consideration. Although these societies tended to place a high value on individual autonomy, use of resources was regulated communally through formal and informal techniques. Although fur and other provisions produced for sale belonged to the individual, items produced for immediate consumption were often shared among all band members. This was reinforced by traditions where the "more skilful or more fortunate shared their plenty with those in need."[17] People had "an undivided interest in the land" and all members of the group had "the right to the whole." Rights to land use also belonged to past and future generations as well as to all living things. Thus, there could be no claim by the living to absolute ownership of land or resources.[18]

Although tribal boundaries protected resources for use by individual tribes to a certain extent, the cyclical nature of animal populations necessitated arrangements with neighbouring tribes so that individuals and bands could move to the traditional territories of others to hunt during times of want. The same flexibility also generally characterized political organization. As the commissioners who negotiated Treaty 8 in 1899 commented, First Nations people in northern Alberta were "held together mainly by the language bond. The chiefs and headmen are simply the most efficient hunters and trappers." Hunting in small groups best accommodated the nature and extent of animal resources, although there were larger seasonal gatherings at fishing lakes and trading centres. Among the Cree and Chipewyan, nuclear and extended families were the basic economic units. Populations tended to be dispersed because small, mobile bands were "best suited to the pursuit of widespread, solitary and sedentary prey." The largest ongoing social entity was the hunting band, made up of two or more families, which "functioned independently of each other" during the winter when they lived in bush camps and ran trap lines from there. In the summer, a number of hunting bands would come together to form a regional band at a location good for fishing and hunting.[19] Within this broad cycle of life, people visited the settlements in spring, fall and early winter for social and religious events and to trade for goods needed in the coming season. These seasonal movements took place over relatively small areas which people used for specialized purposes year after year. Inspector Jarvis of the NWMP observed in 1897 that people (presumably Dene) in the Fort Smith district were not only relatively sedentary when in their winter bush camps, but their movements during the rest of the year were also limited. Although a few had recently travelled as far as Edmonton to sell fur, most of these people "hardly ever move from their homes, excepting to visit their lines of traps. I understand that this has been the custom for generations and there are many old Indians hereabouts who have not been even to [Fort] Chipewyan, which might be styled the metropolis of the district. I found this to be the custom of many of the northern Indians up to and along the Peace River."[20]

Despite such common patterns, there were differences in how resources were used. As sociologist Bennet McCardle has noted, wildlife allocation and exploitation in the 1890s in northern Alberta "were apparently not of a single type, since conflict occurred between native groups" about methods of resource use. Metis, and perhaps Cree as well, "rotated" their hunting grounds over a wide territory. When an area was depleted, people moved elsewhere and the area was not used again for years. In keeping with their more sedentary bush life, Dene tended to conserve fur resources in their home district to ensure future supply, and trapping grounds were changed mainly when disease, fire or varying water levels had affected the population and distribution of animals. When these groups operated in isolation, each of these different methods of resource use allowed "successful long-term adaptation" to a boreal forest environment. When the two approaches overlapped, however, conflict could occur.

Yet, as McCardle concludes, both responses reflected common economic conditions. "Ultimately, the choice between strategies—whether to clear out or conserve—may have been related to the need for a bare subsistence, in relation both to fluctuating game supplies and to the equally variable nature of the fur market."[21]

Material and social life in northern Alberta in the 1890s was also influenced by a shared environment, resources and history. Changes in material life had taken place because of the fur trade and missionary influences. Traditional materials and practices continued to be used alongside certain elements of Euro-Canadian material life. Iron tools had commonly been used since the mid 1850s and no doubt improved material standards of life. Guns were more convenient than spears and bows and arrows for some purposes, although people apparently retained a proficiency with traditional weapons well into the nineteenth century.[22] After the 1860s, and at an increasing pace after the 1880s, changes in material life became more pronounced. By the 1870s, free traders in parts of the Peace River country sold flour and other groceries, indicating declining local food resources as well as acculturation. After the 1880s more efficient transportation allowed traders to import more and different types of trade goods, including steel traps, cloth and repeating rifles. Indeed, by 1899 it was reported that people throughout northern Alberta largely wore clothes of Anglo-Canadian design. So too, the use of houses in winter had become common in many parts of northern Alberta, with tents principally in use during the summer.[23]

While the fur trade was a powerful force in changing material life, missionaries were also influential. Although Anglican and Roman Catholic missionaries were often gripped by an unseemly rivalry, both assumed that conversion to Christianity involved remaking Aboriginal people in a Euro-Canadian mould. As anthropologist Jean-Guy Goulet notes, the missionaries assumed that a Euro-Canadian lifestyle and its material standards were integral to Christianity. Consequently, they did not try to adapt Christian traditions to the Aboriginal cultural experience. Rather, they preached the virtues of such things as farming, Euro-Canadian housing forms and other material standards of life. Although we cannot now with certainty judge how Aboriginal people perceived these messages, it is apparent that their response was often complex. While outside observers in the 1890s described most Aboriginal people in northern Alberta as Christian, the missionaries did not, as Jean-Guy Goulet concludes, entirely succeed in driving out aboriginal religious belief systems. Among Aboriginal people, religion and culture tended to be unified, and changes in one area brought changes in other aspects of life. Among the Dene, for example, historian Kerry Abel notes that initial enthusiasm for Christianity came about for a variety of reasons, but attention then waned. Nonetheless, "the missionaries gradually became accepted as part of life in the north" and Christian "rituals and practices became widely known and almost as widely performed." Yet, Abel concludes, "it is still not clear whether the Dene were becoming assimilated into Euro-Canadian culture and whether they had completely accepted the Christian value system." Indeed, the missionaries were cautious about making such claims. The Dene were not, she concludes, passive recipients of European teaching about morality and culture. Many people believed that their traditional spiritual beliefs could co-exist with Christianity. Historian Martha McCarthy agrees with this interpretation overall, and she argues that conversions were often "dual"—both the old and new could be utilized in particular places, times or circumstances, and/or were "syncretic," that is, the old and new combined to form a new reality.[24]

The conclusion that spiritual life expressed a varied range of reactions is also helpful in understanding the social and economic impact of the early fur trade, a topic on which historical interpretation is divided. While there has been overall agreement that the fur trade involved a "partnering" between trader and Native, there are divergent viewpoints about whether the "partnership" implied equality or dependence, interdependence or autonomy. Obviously there was considerable continuity with pre-contact land use and social patterns. It is also clear that trader and Native were linked by commodities (the fur that the traders needed and the trade goods that the Natives wanted), by social relations (family or other ties) and by the commercial arrangements (such as credit and the use of local labour) of the trade. Nonetheless, there is a lack of agreement on the extent of change the fur trade brought in social structure, land use and personal relationships.[25] Even so, it is logical to assume that neither Native nor trader acted out of altruism but responded to economic and social needs within the myriad of practical problems created by a cyclical resource economy. A new economy with its own dynamic was thus created. However, the dual and/or syncretic nature of the relationships it brought is perhaps suggested by the observation that a century of direct fur trade had not by the 1890s reshaped Native society and economy into the Euro-Canadian pattern in which work and leisure were firmly separated, a distinction that was then becoming more rigid in Canadian society. Clearly, the changes that had taken place in material and social life by the 1890s had come without the use of money. Most furs were bartered, not sold, and labourers were often paid in goods, not cash. This practice was even more pronounced in areas further north. The Roman Catholic missionary, Isidore Clut, noted in 1888 that he had lived in the Fort Chipewyan-Fort Providence area for 13 years "without seeing any money at all." The fur trade used a debt system in which traders provided trappers with goods on credit, which was repaid with the next year's production. This also incorporated the economic support of trappers by the Hudson's Bay Company during hard economic times and during sickness and helped stabilize an economy dependent on fluctuating resources. Moreover, the fur trade had not led northern Alberta's Aboriginal people to accept Euro-Canadian assumptions that the accumulation of specie, land and durable goods marked economic success, social status and security. Further, while they may have been reshaped in some ways, Aboriginal communal arrangements in economic life and resource use had not been supplanted by Euro-Canadian individualism and social autonomy. Nor had it formalized a distinction between subsistence and commercial use of resources. Yet the fur trade offered opportunities beyond trapping, such as work for women as interpreters, domestics, food gatherers and gardeners at fur trade posts while men found jobs as hunters, freighters and labourers. Such labour had often become an integral part of local economic life and society by the 1890s. More significantly, the cash nexus was beginning to appear. Free traders sometimes competed with the Hudson's Bay Company by paying cash for furs, and along with other practices, the values and approaches of the Euro-Canadian market economy were beginning to be evident by the late 1890s.[26]

## ___ The Contribution of Transportation to Regional Unity

Both Roman Catholic and Anglican missionaries initially viewed the whole of the Mackenzie basin—the Peace and Athabasca drainage basins as well as the areas drained by the Slave and Mackenzie rivers in the present-day NWT— as a single unit. They soon found, however, that its size and internal distinctions required a narrower focus. While the Anglicans established the huge diocese of Mackenzie River in 1873, they divided it into two parts a decade later, restricting the diocese of Athabasca to the Peace and Athabasca River basins, with the northern boundary at the 60th parallel, the present boundary of Alberta and the NWT. The Roman Catholics too divided their equally large vicariate of Athabaska-Mackenzie in 1901, and like the Anglicans, made the Peace and Athabasca River basins into the vicariate of Athabaska.[27] These

*Before 1917, thousands of scows were built at Athabasca from local spruce. After the trip with freight to Fort McMurray, most were broken up and the lumber was reused. Not dated (ca. 1915)* A 11,517 PAA.

changes echoed those made earlier in the fur trade. Traders had initially viewed the whole of the Mackenzie basin as a single unit they called the Athabasca country. In 1823, the Hudson's Bay Company reorganized its operations by creating two districts—Mackenzie River and Athabasca. While this no doubt reflected administrative needs, it also confirmed distinctions between the Athabasca and Peace River basins and the far north along the Mackenzie River.

Changing views of northern Alberta were confirmed and expanded in the 1880s when the use of Portage La Loche declined. This was part of a general reorganization of the Hudson's Bay Company operations in the wake of the loss of its monopoly in 1870. Hudson's Bay Company management was also grimly determined to increase profits and reduce expenses. This required that the customs of the trade be reformed and that the company's transportation system be upgraded to increase efficiency and lower labour costs. Steamboat service, the construction of wagon roads and the upgrading of portages began almost immediately in some parts of western Canada, and by the early 1880s such projects were underway in northern Alberta as well.[28]

Various trails north of Edmonton had long offered alternatives to Portage La Loche, but none were serious challengers because Edmonton's link with the national economy was weak. But steam navigation on the North Saskatchewan River after 1875 and the construction of the Canadian Pacific Railway (CPR) across the southern prairies in the early 1880s changed this dynamic by

*The scow brigades sometimes worked in water up to their chests. In early spring, they also had to dodge floating ice.* B2895 PAA.

providing more effective communications between Edmonton and metropolitan centres in both eastern and western Canada. The shift became apparent in
1876 when the Hudson's Bay Company began shipping its goods by steamer on
the North Saskatchewan to Fort Edmonton. From here, they were taken north
about 160 kilometres over the newly built Athabasca Trail to the banks of the
Athabasca River where a small settlement called Athabasca Landing (now the
town of Athabasca) was created. Here, the Hudson's Bay Company constructed
a storage house and built boats and scows (large flat-bottomed barges about 15
metres long and 3 metres wide) to ship goods in both directions along the
Athabasca River.[29]

The growing use of the Athabasca Trail foretold Edmonton's role as the
metropolitan centre of northern Alberta, which was entrenched when the
Hudson's Bay Company abandoned Portage La Loche in 1887. The creation of
Athabasca as the portal to the north shifted the region's southern boundary
from the Clearwater-Athabasca River junction further to the south. While the
watersheds of the Peace and Athabasca rivers were confirmed as the core of the

region, the focus on Athabasca created a self-contained communications network within northern Alberta.

While freight had previously reached the Peace River country via Portage La Loche and the Peace-Athabasca delta, or (in the case of some free traders) from Quesnell, British Columbia, it now arrived from the south through Athabasca. Scows moved goods westward from Athabasca along the Athabasca River, then along the Lesser Slave River (which connected the Athabasca River and Lesser Slave Lake), and across Lesser Slave Lake to Grouard, a settlement node that then went by various names, including Lesser Slave Lake Settlement and Slave Lake Post. From here, it was moved by carts and wagons along a number of trails (mostly built by the Hudson's Bay Company in the late 1870s) to various points in the Peace River country. From Peace River Crossing (now the town of Peace River), goods could be shipped by scow down river to Dunvegan and Hudson's Hope, or upriver to Fort Vermilion and, after the portage at the Vermilion Chutes, to Fort Chipewyan.[30] In winter, the same system operated, but in a more limited way. Freight brought by sleighs from Edmonton to Athabasca was immediately shipped over winter trails or was stored for shipment in the spring by boat. Winter was in many respects the best time to travel; the frozen trails made travel easy and there were no mosquitoes and flies—the "frightful curse" of northern summer travel.[31] Dogs were the cheapest and best cartage animals for winter travel, although horses and sleighs were also used when trails and feed were available. By the mid 1890s, goods were being freighted in winter in all directions from Athabasca, mostly to closer-in centres like Wabasca, but also as far as Grouard and Fort McMurray.

Despite the advantages of winter freighting, water remained the only practical method of shipping long distances. Most freight for the Peace-Athabasca delta or the Mackenzie River was shipped east from Athabasca along the river as far as the Grand Rapids. There, the river drops over nine metres in about one kilometre, and freight and passengers had to be portaged. When the Hudson's Bay Company opted to use the Athabasca River as its principal route to the north, the Grand Rapids, like those interspersed beyond them for 145 kilometres as far as Fort McMurray, were uncharted and largely unknown. Even so, it was apparent that while scows loaded with freight had to be portaged around the Grand Rapids, skilled boatmen could run most of the rapids further down river.[32]

At the Grand Rapids, goods were portaged along an island about one kilometre in length, while the empty scows were coaxed across the rapids and reloaded at the other end of the island. In the 1880s the Hudson's Bay

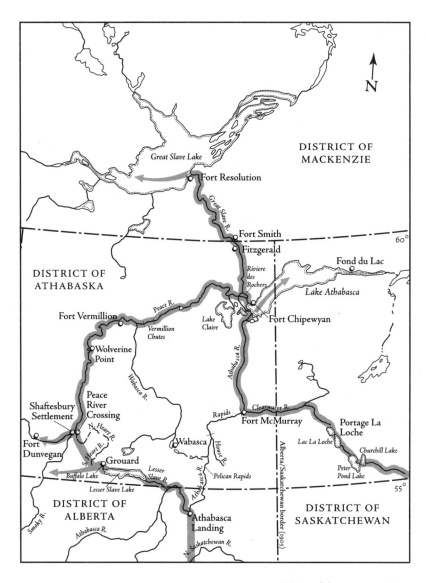

**Major Transportation Routes 1880**

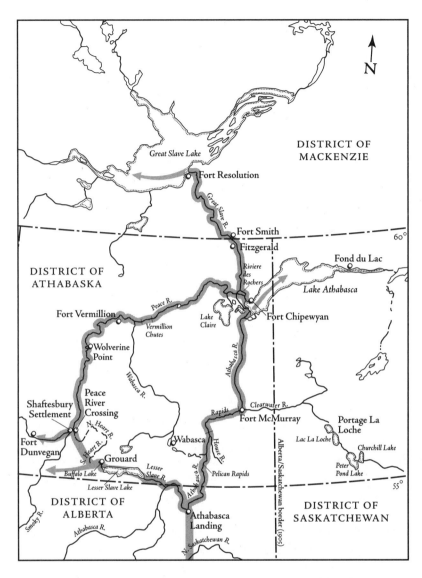

N

DISTRICT OF
MACKENZIE

Great Slave Lake

Fort Resolution

Great Slave R.

Fort Smith

Fitzgerald

60°

Riviere
des
Rochers

Fond du Lac

DISTRICT OF
ATHABASKA

Peace R.

Lake Athabasca

Fort Vermillion

Vermillion
Chutes

Lake
Claire

Fort Chipewyan

Wolverine
Point

Athabasca R.

Wabasca R.

Peace
River
Crossing

Rapids

Clearwater R.

Shaftesbury
Settlement

N. Heart R.

Fort McMurray

Portage La
Loche

Lac La Loche

Churchill Lake

Fort
Dunvegan

S. Heart R.

Grouard

Buffalo Lake

Lesser
Slave R.

Wabasca

House R.

Pelican Rapids

Peter
Pond Lake

Lac La Loche

Alberta/Saskatchewan border (1905)

Lesser Slave Lake

DISTRICT OF
ALBERTA

Smoky R.

Athabasca R.

Athabasca R.

Athabasca
Landing

N. Saskatchewan R.

DISTRICT OF
SASKATCHEWAN

55°

**▬ Major Transportation
Routes 1890**

Company constructed a tramway with push-carts across the island. Aside from the iron wheels on the trucks and the iron strapping on the runways, it was built of local timber, and its low capital cost added to its reputation as "the most profitable railway in the world." Its true value, however, lay in the power it gave the Hudson's Bay Company over northern transportation. The company often refused competing traders use of the railway, forcing their boatmen to carry everything across on their backs.[33]

The rest of the river down to Fort McMurray was dangerous. Although navigable in high water, guides were essential and scows were commonly damaged and sometimes sunk in the rapids. While many of the scows were broken up at Fort McMurray and goods were transferred to larger ones for the trip north, some went on to Fort Chipewyan and a few returned to Athabasca loaded with outgoing fur. Since no draught animal could navigate the slippery banks or work in water up to its knees, crews of Metis and Cree workers harnessed to tow ropes hauled (or "tracked") the scows against the current through the rapids. The federal public servant, Charles Camsell, recalled that on return trips, "apart from the bowman and the steersman the crews walked every step of the way harnessed to a tow rope." It was "rough, arduous work" wrote Arthur Robertson of the Hudson's Bay Company in 1887, "more suited to a canal horse than for human beings."[34]

The immense transportation network operating west of Athabasca to the Peace River country and east to the Lower Athabasca River gave northern Alberta an economic and geographical unity that was regional in character. Similar to the small regions that geographer John Warketin has identified on the southern prairies at about the same time, this regional character grew from the intersection of local conditions and history with broader change brought by an expanding Canadian economy. In 1882, as part of this emerging regional network in northern Alberta, the Hudson's Bay Company built a steamer, the *Grahame*, to operate on the Athabasca River below Fort McMurray. Some of the components were shipped in over Portage La Loche and the ship was assembled at Fort Chipewyan. At 45 metres in length, it was the largest craft on the river and carried goods and passengers between Fort McMurray and Fitzgerald (then Smith's Landing) at the head of the rapids on the Slave River. It also operated along the Clearwater River to Portage La Loche, and along the Peace River as far as the Vermilion Chutes. While canoes had customarily run parts of the rapids between Fitzgerald and Fort Smith, steam boats could not navigate any portion of them. This led to the upgrading of the trail around the rapids for the transhipment of freight by ox or horse-drawn carts. This increased emphasis on the Slave River portage subtly reconfirmed that Fitzgerald and Fort Smith marked the boundary of northern Alberta; a distinction that was further entrenched in 1885 when the Hudson's Bay Company built another steam ship, the *Wrigley*, to service the far north. Based at Fort Smith, it served points along the Mackenzie River to the Arctic Ocean. In a portent of coming change, rather than shipping them through Portage La Loche, the components for the *Wrigley* were shipped from Edmonton to Athabasca and taken over the Grand Rapids by scow.[35]

A further step in mechanizing the communications network on the Athabasca River took place in 1888 when the Hudson's Bay Company constructed yet another steamer. As part of the reorientation brought by the abandonment of Portage La Loche the year before, the ship was based at Athabasca and was used to carry freight and passengers down river as far as the Grand Rapids. It was anticipated that the ship would also operate westward from Athabasca to Grouard, where goods would then be shipped to the Peace River country over the Hudson's Bay Company wagon road. However, while the ship could get through the Lesser Slave River in occasional years of high water, goods usually had to be transhipped at its mouth to shallower craft.

While steamboats on the Athabasca River replaced labour formerly needed for scows and York boats, they also created some new opportunities. Scow brigades were still needed for the stretch between Grand Rapids and Fort McMurray and labourers were now needed as deck hands, stevedores and for cutting the huge amounts of wood that fuelled the ships. Some skilled work was also created for pilots and in boat construction and repair. [36] Thus mechanization, in its early stages at least, appears not to have been socially or economically disruptive. At the same time, however, mechanization had social implications that reinforced the public authority of those who owned and controlled it. The Roman Catholic mission at Fort Chipewyan began operating its own steamer on the Athabasca River, and the Oblates soon put a small steam boat on the Mackenzie River as well. While this aimed to circumvent the Hudson's Bay Company's high freight rates, the missionaries were conscious of how mechanization contributed to the church's dignity and social place. As Bishop Grouard remarked about the church's new steamer in 1895, the Natives keenly observed that the English were not the only ones able to own and operate new technology such as steam ships and that the "French were also capable of holding up their heads."[37]

*By about 1900, when this photograph was taken, the Hudson's Bay Company post at Fort Vermilion produced the highest fur returns in northern Alberta. B5461 PAA.*

## ▬ Northern Alberta's Urban System in the 1890s

While it may at first seem exaggerated to describe many of the settlements of northern Alberta, with their small populations and loose urban form, as "urban centres," they did serve obvious urban functions. They helped organize trade and markets, focussed ongoing economic and social activity, and rationalized and formalized interactions within the region. Responding to both local conditions and outside events and factors, the connections and interactions among the settlements reflected their place in an interlocked urban system.[38] Some of them, such as Fort Chipewyan and Fort Vermilion, were the oldest Euro-

Canadian settlements in Alberta. Many of them had also been important economic and population centres for thousands of years. Most were located near areas with plentiful resources and with easy access to important water routes. As archaeologist John Ives notes, "the very existence of the fur trade was inextricably tied to an ancient history of land use that took shape over the last ten thousand years." One such centre was Fort Resolution. Located in the region's transitional zone north of Fort Smith, it was the heart of a "land of plenty" with abundant fish and meat. Also in an area with a strategic relationship with the river and a fur rich hinterland, Fort Vermilion in the 1890s was the main Hudson's Bay Company post on the Peace River and produced the company's highest fur returns in the Athabasca District. Fort Chipewyan, the next largest fur producer, was another important settlement. As the headquarters of the Hudson's Bay Company Athabasca District, it received all the fur from the vast territory around Lake Athabasca and along the Athabasca River, the lower Peace River and the Slave River for reshipment to outside markets.[39]

While such dynamics continued to be central, the development of steam transportation brought changes in the siting, function and relative importance of some settlements. The most obvious example of this process was the development of the settlement of Athabasca. Located in a district with a small indigenous population and poor fur resources, Athabasca's purpose had little reference to the land—its place in the regional economy arose entirely from the corporate strategy of the Hudson's Bay Company. The company's domination of northern shipping meant that its choice of the Athabasca-Fort McMurray route to the Peace River country, the Peace-Athabasca delta, and the Mackenzie River District further north made it the primary highway to the north. No matter which direction goods moved, they passed through Athabasca. In 1884, Hudson's Bay Company staff were stationed there permanently and two years later the Company built stables and a staff residence on river front land it had purchased from the government of Canada. As the centre that linked the region with the national economy, Athabasca crowned the hierarchy of northern Alberta's settlements. Even though its population by 1889 was small—around 100 at the high point when the river brigades were in the settlement—it had become Canada's portal to northern Alberta, the Mackenzie River and the western Arctic.[40]

Athabasca's creation as a central place was the most obvious change in northern Alberta's network of settlements in the late 1800s. In most cases, new technology and corporate needs tended to confirm existing settlement patterns, although subtle changes took place in many districts. The use of steam ships led to the construction of a new settlement at Mirror Landing at the mouth of the Lesser Slave River where goods were transhipped to Grouard. Little Red River, an older settlement at the foot of the Vermilion Chutes, also gained new advantage because it was the furthest point that steam ships could travel westward on the Peace River from the Peace-Athabasca delta. In both cases, these places were seasonal settlements with little economic purpose aside from their transhipment function. Similarly, Fort McMurray's location at the end of the rapids and as the southern terminus of the *Grahame* made it into a "fairly busy place" in the summers by the 1890s. But its population was almost entirely seasonal and the "settlement" consisted only of a Hudson's Bay Company post built in 1870, made up of "five small log shacks." The transhipment of goods from scows to the steamer required no permanent infrastructure or staff, and by 1903 Fort McMurray was still "a place in name only." Although a free trader was operating there by then, it must have been a poor life. The area's hinterland lacked food resources and fur-bearing animals because of recent forest fires, and in 1898 the Hudson's Bay Company had moved all of its local operations to Fort McKay (then also called Little Red River), an area with more plentiful resources about 55 kilometres north along the Athabasca River.[41]

More significant growth because of steam transportation took place at Fitzgerald and Fort Smith. Lying about 40 kilometres apart on either end of the Slave rapids, both centres were located in rich fur and meat-producing country. As well, there were surface salt deposits near Fort Smith. By at least 1840 salt was gathered by a Metis family, the Beaulieu's, to supply the fur brigades. But the development of Fort Smith and Fitzgerald as local population centres owed more to their role in the transportation system than to local resources. The first important development took place in the 1840s when the Hudson's Bay Company adopted York boats on the Mackenzie River. This meant longer and heavier portages around the Smith Rapids, and a permanent population developed there to handle freight. To avoid taking heavy boats around the rapids, the Hudson's Bay Company had by the 1870s stationed one fleet of boats at Fort Smith for the northern Mackenzie River route, and another at Fitzgerald for the Athabasca River. The use of steamboats in the 1880s confirmed this pattern. By 1897 Fitzgerald had a Hudson's Bay Company post, two free traders (including a branch operation of Colin Fraser of Fort Chipewyan) and about 12 Metis families who hunted, fished and trapped in winter and portaged goods and ran boats over the rapids in summer. Similarly, Fort Smith's importance was enhanced when the steamer that served the Great Slave Lake and Mackenzie River districts was stationed there in 1885.[42]

In the western parts of northern Alberta, the same connection between urban growth and transportation was evident. In the Lesser Slave Lake district, Grouard was the terminus for river and lake traffic from Athabasca, as well as for trails from Athabasca, Edmonton and the Peace River country. The district headquarters of the Hudson's Bay Company for the Peace River was transferred there from Dunvegan in the 1880s, and a free trader was also operating in the settlement by 1894. The Oblates and the Anglicans established missions there in 1872 and 1886 respectively. In the late 1890s, the district experienced rapid growth, and by 1899, there were about 300 people living in scattered locations within about 15 kilometres of the posts and missions. By then, Grouard had eight free traders plus the Hudson's Bay Company operations. About 55 kilometres away was another settlement node at Utikuma Lake (then called Whitefish Lake), a largely Metis settlement where the Anglicans had established a mission in 1892. Further east was Wabasca, a Cree and Metis centre located in an area with good fishing and hunting resources. Many of these people had moved from Lac La Biche and other southern settlements in the 1890s, and Wabasca served as the trade centre for small settlements further north, such as those at Peerless, Loon and Trout lakes. At most of these settlements—especially at the west end of Lesser Slave Lake—some people cultivated small gardens consisting of potatoes, barley and some wheat, although the mainstay of their economies was fishing, hunting and freighting.[43]

Grouard was linked to the Peace River country by various trails. The most important by the 1890s was a 160 kilometre wagon trail to Peace River Crossing built by the Hudson's Bay Company. A trail from Peace River Crossing led north to Notikewin (then called Battle River), a small Hudson's Bay Company post with a few Native residents. More important was the cart road that ran along the north bank of the river to Dunvegan, about 90 kilometres upriver. An old fur trade centre, Dunvegan had fallen on hard times by the 1880s because of resource depletion, social change and the reorientation of trade. Indeed, by 1894 it was said to be "a place of no importance." The nearby small settlement of Spirit River had earlier been the site of a Hudson's Bay Company ranch and now had about six Metis families who raised cattle and horses. Reflecting its past importance, several trails led from Dunvegan west to Hudson's Hope and Fort St. John, and south and east to Grouard and Sturgeon Lake. The latter had been a Hudson's Bay Company outpost since at least the early 1880s, but by the late 1890s the area was suffering because of the depletion of fur-bearing animals.[44]

Along the Peace River between Fort Vermilion and the site of the present day town of Peace River was a scattering of small settlements of Metis and

*The original Roman Catholic church in Fort Chipewyan was built in the late 1840s. With paintings by Father Grouard, who used dyes manufactured from local natural materials, this new building was consecrated in 1909.*
OB7621 PAA.

Indians living together in relatively permanent centres. Showing their place in the trade network, some of these settlements featured small seasonal trading outposts. Some residents kept cattle, but most people were moose hunters, and many of these "settlements" were likely only winter hunting camps. The same pattern of small settlements occurred along the Athabasca River north of Fort McMurray. Often focussed around a small trading outpost, most had between five and ten Metis, Cree or Chipewyan families who hunted and trapped, supplementing these resources with fish when local conditions permitted.[45]

While these small centres focussed economic exchange at a local level, the major posts were most important in this respect. Here, people might find employment as freighters, labourers or hunters. Equally important, as central places that attracted people seasonally, the major settlements provided nontrading interests with a beachhead for organizing their activities. Missionaries almost immediately used the settlements as permanent locations from which to seek converts. Since Natives regularly visited the major posts at least seasonally, missions and schools were built nearby.[46] By the 1890s, the Roman Catholic mission at Fort Chipewyan included a church, convent, mission school (with a printing press where prayer books in Native languages were printed and bound) and a sawmill. This large establishment offered some local employment putting up hay for the mission livestock, catching and dressing fish (the mainstay of the mission diet) or in the sawmill. While the Anglicans were also active at Fort Chipewyan, their largest operation was at Fort Vermilion. Here, they had a church, small school, sawmill, gristmill and a farm and ranch operated by the Lawrence Brothers who had 130 acres under cultivation and several hundred head of livestock. The Catholic mission at Fort Vermilion, with two priests and two lay brothers, also had a school, large garden and gristmill. Missions were also located, among other places, at Fort Resolution, Fort Smith and at the Shaftesbury settlement, near present-day Peace River town.[47]

Some of these settlements also served as administrative centres for the church. Grouard had been a mission centre since 1846, and in 1891 it was made the seat of the Roman Catholic vicariate of Athabaska. At about the same time, the headquarters of the Anglican diocese of Athabasca was moved to Athabasca from Fort Vermilion. Showing the effect of the southward shift of northern Alberta's regional limits because of the creation of Athabasca as the region's transportation centre, the boundary of the Anglican diocese was also extended slightly southward to accommodate this change. While Athabasca's small Native population made it a poor place for missionary work, Bishop Young noted that as the hub of northern Alberta, it was "the only place from which a supervision can be effectively maintained of the Diocese."[48]

All of these northern settlements were loosely laid out and activity was focussed around fairly discrete nodes. In 1898 Inspector Routledge of the NWMP described Fort Chipewyan as "a quite respectable village." Strung out along the shore of the lake, its most important buildings were those of the Hudson's Bay Company and the Roman Catholic mission, each located at opposite ends of the settlement. A prominent local free trader, Colin Fraser, had his operation near the Roman Catholic mission, while the Anglican church was relatively close to the Hudson's Bay Company post. While the post was described in 1898 as "resembling a military barracks more than an Indian trading post," the company was well integrated into the local community, and outside the fort were a number of small log buildings occupied by company employees. Showing a similar integration with its community, the post at Fort Vermilion in the late 1890s was not stockaded and served as an open retail centre. The settlement's buildings were clustered at various points along both banks of the river. Similarly, the population around present-day Peace River town was also strung out along the river. On the south bank was Peace River

Crossing, basically the transhipment point at the end of the trail from Grouard. The Shaftesbury Settlement across the river, with 60 to 80 permanent residents whose houses were scattered along the river, was the important centre of the district. It also included the Hudson's Bay Company post, the Anglican and Roman Catholic missions, and a trading post run by the Brick Brothers.[49] Athabasca and Grouard also had a similarly loose urban form, and at Grouard most people lived on the nearby open prairie lands.

Despite their significant economic and social function, all of these settlements had small populations. In the 1890s, it was estimated that Fort Chipewyan had between 150 and 200 permanent residents, while the number of people making it their seasonal trading centre was reckoned in two different estimates in 1897 and 1898 at between 400 and 700. By the late 1890s Fort Vermilion had a population of about 168 people, Fort Smith had about the same number, and the population of Grouard and its surrounding districts was estimated at about 1,000. Fort Resolution had a winter population of about 108, but in summer it swelled to between 600 to 700. And even though fur was scarce at Sturgeon Lake, fishing remained good, and during the winter about 120 Cree lived there in about 40 houses.[50] While these were small places by any measure, their size relative to the region's population was notable. The total population (Native and white) of northern Alberta in the mid 1890s was about 3,700, and the residents of the three settlements of Forts Vermilion, Chipewyan and Smith alone accounted for about 14 percent of this population—marking the significant degree of urbanization that characterized the fur-based economy of northern Alberta.

By the end of the 1800s, the social life and culture of people in northern Alberta had a number of shared characteristics. Almost all people were touched, either directly or indirectly, by the fur trade. By then, the "traditional" economy of many Native people also included labour on the boats or at the missions or the fur trade posts. These common social practices and economic activities contributed to the region's distinctive character. Its network of settlements reflected ancient patterns of settlement and the river network. Fur traders and missionaries also adopted this outline as their own and modified it to meet the needs of the particular transportation technology they used. Thus, the settlements were points of mediation between outsiders and Natives, and focal points for development and change. With Athabasca as the portal of a vast transportation network that funnelled trade in and out of the region, a regional unity was created in northern Alberta. Nonetheless, while this regional character showed the importance of northern Alberta's river system, it was not a mere expression of geographical imperatives. The Hudson's Bay Company had developed its transportation network in the same way that it had created settlements such as Athabasca—as an evolving set of relationships that organized and focussed its northern operations. In this process, the commercial objectives of the region's most powerful corporate player contributed to the development of regional unity and coherence.

# The 1890s

## 2

### The Beginnings of Canadian Control

CANADIAN EXPANSION in northern Alberta in the late nineteenth century was driven and shaped by a mix of regional and national perceptions, events and forces. While the adoption of steamships on the Athabasca River in the 1880s had tightened the region's focus and increased the possibilities of exploiting a wider range of resources, new technology alone was insufficient to reorient its economy. Expanding Euro-Canadian activity needed a revised attitude towards the future, and scientific and geographical reconnaissances, travel accounts and the ambition of Canadian expansionists sparked interest in northern Alberta, as they had elsewhere on the prairies. Northern Alberta's integration into the national economy was also driven by western Canadian ambitions to take advantage of the possibilities offered by the new Canadian nation state. The federal government provided the most effective instrument for this expansion, since its administrative system (including the NWMP), its power to make treaties with Aboriginal people and its land and geological surveys provided mechanisms for establishing an orderly environment favouring the realization of Canadian control.[1]

For most of the 1880s, Canadian interest and activity in northern Alberta had been halting and indecisive. In 1882, northern Alberta was officially organized as the "unorganized" District of Athabaska. At almost 316,000 square kilometres, it was the largest district in the North-West Territories and included all the land between 55 and 60 degrees in the present day provinces of Alberta and north-west Saskatchewan. Even so, both public and private agencies in Canada saw it as something of a backwater. The decision in 1882 to push the CPR across the southern plains instead of a more northerly route had shifted the attention of both federal and territorial governments to the promotion of southern prairie settlement. Thus, in practical terms, the Hudson's Bay Company and the missionaries remained the only formal agencies looking after such matters as social welfare, roads and mail delivery in northern Alberta. Indeed, the federal government contended that it had no responsibility for social needs in the district because a treaty with the Aboriginal people had not been signed. Nonetheless, federal government survey crews began calculating the meridians and base lines in the upper Peace River country in 1883.[2] While this presumed future agricultural settlement, it was only an anticipatory gesture. This was also evident in efforts to gain knowledge about northern Alberta's mineral and petroleum resources. The oil sands in the Fort McMurray area had been described by the earliest Euro-Canadian travellers, but preliminary assessment of them and other mineral resources in the Athabasca River basin only began in 1882–83 under Robert Bell of the Geological Survey of Canada. Robert McConnell, also from the Geological Survey, conducted further surveys in 1887–88 and predicted huge petroleum reserves in the region. While these forays expressed part of the Geological Survey's mandate to ascertain the extent of Canada's resources, they were mainly "explorations that yielded descriptions and maps to assist future development" rather than an "overt exercise of authority or control."[3]

McConnell's findings about northern petroleum reserves nonetheless stimulated public interest about the potential of northern resources. They also contributed to the establishment in 1888 of an inquiry by the Canadian Senate into the resources of the Mackenzie basin. The first real official expression of government interest in the region, the inquiry reflected Canadian expansionist sentiments, such as those of Senator John C. Schultz. Schultz had been an adventurer in Red River in the 1860s and 1870s and had been one of the leaders of the "Canadian Party" that had antagonized the Metis with its chauvinism and demands for annexation to Canada. He continued to promote and boost western Canada, urging governments and corporations to invest there. For him, the Mackenzie basin was only an extension of the prairie regions to the south.

Chaired by Schultz, the Senate committee held extensive hearings. People familiar with Canada's northern regions were interviewed about transportation, resources, climate and land quality. While committee members concluded that fur would continue to be an important source of wealth, they anticipated broad economic expansion through development of northern timber, minerals and petroleum. Moreover, fine agricultural land in the Peace River country was said to be waiting for southern Canadians to exploit, and samples of wheat, rye, oats and barley were sent to various points in the Mackenzie basin for testing.[4] When the Committee's report was printed in 1888, it excited the imagination of many Canadian expansionists, and as historian Morris Zaslow comments, the enthusiastic predictions it spawned would "echo in publicity releases during the next forty years." Confirming public interest in the Mackenzie basin, a number of travel and exploration accounts were published in the next decade. In combination, these reports and books demonstrate Edward Said's contention that the objectification of people and places implicit in much of this expansion, collation and categorization of knowledge was integral to European imperialism and formed part of the connective tissue of cultural and economic expansion.[5]

Despite the Senate report, the federal government remained apathetic about northern development. Earlier projects were continued more as ongoing exploratory projects of individual departments than as reflections of a new national purpose. In 1890, apparently judging the region to be of little economic importance, Canada rejected a request for a treaty by Natives in the Lesser Slave Lake and Peace River districts. Revived interest in northern petroleum as a result of a further geological survey by Robert McConnell the same year, however, brought a quick reversal in federal policy.[6] By early 1891, the Canadian government, in a report of the Privy Council, asserted that northern Alberta's mineral and agricultural potential now made a treaty "advisable" for the territory between 55 degrees (the northern boundary of Treaty 6) and 63 degrees (the north shore of Great Slave Lake). Although plans were drawn up, they were quickly shelved. As Rene Fumoleau observed in his history of Treaties 8 and 11, Ottawa's eagerness evaporated when it was concluded that mining development, despite McConnell's forecasts, lay far in the future. Along with this growing uncertainty, the political drift and confusion caused by the death of Prime Minister John A. Macdonald in mid 1891 further contributed to Ottawa's abandonment of plans for a treaty.[7]

Even so, the Geological Survey of Canada undertook exploratory drilling for oil at two sites along the Athabasca River between Athabasca and Grand Rapids to follow up McConnell's 1890 survey. Some Geological Survey of Canada geologists postulated that the oil sands were part of an "upwelling" of huge pools of oil which could be tapped directly by conventional drilling. The test wells, however, found only natural gas. At Pelican Rapids in 1898, the well blew out of control and it was not capped until 1919. For over two decades, the roar of the burning gas could be heard two kilometres away, and when Charles

Mathers, the Edmonton photographer, passed it on his way to the Arctic in 1901, the flare was still about 9 metres high. By 1907 the volume of gas was declining. The wastefulness of the wildcat well drew sharp criticism from a number of observers, but such squandering of resources reflected its relative value. Natural gas was used largely for heating and lighting, and since methods of transporting it long distances were rudimentary, its value in remote districts was not great and the Geological Survey turned its attention to the more immediately valuable coal fields in western Canada. Nonetheless, the northern drilling experiments received widespread attention, and hopes remained high among mining promoters that oil would be found. A similar search for minerals, especially gold, was also underway. Prospectors were active on the Peace and Smoky rivers as early as 1892, and by 1895 the Macleod River and the Athabasca River between Fort Assiniboine and the Grand Rapids had been fully prospected, although with little success. As the NWMP reported in 1895, of those prospectors who went north that year, not more than 50 "made expenses, and not more than a dozen made wages." In any case, the federal government was unwilling to see extensive prospecting in the Athabasca country. The Department of Mines ruled that southern gold prospectors should be discouraged from exploring the Mackenzie basin since it was unlikely they would find paying quantities of gold and they would only antagonize the Native population by competing for already scarce game.[8]

Like its petroleum and mineral resources, the region's agricultural potential remained largely untested and subject to conflicting views. The bounty of northern gardens had been known since the early fur trade, and survey parties scouting possible routes for the CPR in 1872 wrote glowing reports about the fertility of the Peace River country. Nonetheless, these views, like other similarly positive ones over the next three decades, were challenged by critics who claimed that the winters were too severe, the summers too short and the top soil too thin for successful grain or livestock farming. By the mid 1890s, farming in northern Alberta still consisted of cultivating potatoes, root crops and small amounts of grain in "garden patches." Attempts to settle the uplands near the present day towns of Fairview and Peace River were short-lived and agricultural operations remained restricted to the bottom lands of the Peace River, mostly in conjunction with missionary or fur trade establishments. Nonetheless, Alex Mackenzie, a retired Hudson's Bay Company employee, had 40 acres in crop as well as 60 acres broken near Peace River town, and a number of other people also had small farms on the bottom lands where they raised horses and cattle and cultivated gardens. But most of these farmers were "miserably poor" and left in the fall to trap and hunt along "different points on the river," returning to their farms in the spring.[9]

Despite conflicting views about northern farming, the Senate Committee concluded in 1888 that the climate and soil in large areas of the Peace River district made it the most important arable portion of the Mackenzie basin. But this large pocket of farm land was separated by about 400 kilometres of nonarable land from the major settled areas to the south, and the lack of local markets for farm produce or transportation facilities to get it to outside markets ensured that the development of an export-based agricultural economy remained remote. The arrival of the railway in Edmonton in 1891 was the farthest north that rail lines extended in Canada, which still left the Peace River country distant from export markets. Under these conditions, the Department of the Interior discouraged settlement in the Peace River district, preferring instead that southern land be settled first to prevent the dispersal of settlement beyond areas already served by existing or planned transportation and administrative networks.[10]

Expansionist interests naturally opposed this policy. As Frank Oliver, the editor of the Edmonton *Bulletin*, wrote in 1898, the federal government could disapprove "of this northern country being opened up," but while it could delay, it could not prevent development.[11] Moreover, other agencies of the federal government were increasingly forced—as much by happenstance as by design—to become more active in northern Alberta. By the mid 1890s, the federal government provided small annual grants to support mission schools in the north; an indication of some interest in promoting cultural change in the region. More importantly, the government became more active as the Hudson's Bay Company finally began, as it had wanted to since the 1870s, to stop providing occasional relief to Native trappers. In addition to the benefits that it would bring to the company's balance sheet, this retreat was also related to growing competition from free traders who did not provide equivalent support. McDougall and Secord of Edmonton, for example, had developed interests in a number of posts in northern Alberta during the 1880s, while Hislop and Nagle had posts at Forts Rae and Resolution by 1893–94.[12] The erosion of its monopoly in northern Alberta persuaded Hudson's Bay Company management that its paternalistic policies could now be safely abandoned without harm to its commercial interests. Although the company continued to use limited relief to keep its trade advantage, it was eager to be rid of the task. In the face of actual and anticipated starvation in the 1890s, the federal government was forced on several occasions to distribute relief (through the Hudson's

*The NWMP seasonal barracks at the Grand Rapids was part of the effort by Canada to extend its control in northern Alberta. Photographed in 1899. Walker Album, SABS.*

Bay Company) at various northern posts. It did so grudgingly, and from fear of future demands, it insisted that the source of the assistance be kept secret. This meant, some critics charged, that the Hudson's Bay Company was able to take the credit, but bear none of the costs, for relief during hard times.[13]

This retraction by the Hudson's Bay Company occurred in other matters as well. In 1895, it stopped delivering mail to northern settlements. While this delivery task was becoming more onerous because the volume of mail was increasing, the company also judged that its postal services aided its competitors.[14] While the government was compelled to assume this task, it remained impassive when the company stopped maintaining trails. By the 1890s, for example, the wagon road between Grouard and Peace River Crossing received relatively heavy use. While it had always been a very rough trail, it was increasingly impassable in wet weather, having been "worn into very deep holes from traffic." But the Company refused to maintain it any longer since it benefited its competitors.[15] Despite these deteriorating conditions, the government refused to assume the maintenance of the road or to construct other roads and bridges. While the territorial government occasionally petitioned the federal government to build and improve trails to the Peace River country, such demands were neither consistently expressed nor pursued. By the end of the 1890s, the only significant developments were the construction of several ferries between Edmonton and the Peace River country and designation of the Athabasca Trail as a public road in 1898.[16]

While happenstance sometimes forced the federal government to take a more active role in northern Alberta, its own legislation for the control of the liquor trade directly compelled it to greater action. Canada's administration of justice had been almost nonexistent in northern Alberta until the early 1890s because the whole of the North-West Territories operated under a permit system in which public sale of liquor was illegal and only whites could obtain a permit to import it for personal use. This ended in 1892 when the federal government passed legislation permitting the public sale of liquor in the organized districts but not in the District of Athabaska where the permit system was maintained. The need to enforce this new liquor legislation, and to meet growing demands by free traders for protection of their goods from theft, forced the NWMP to establish a seasonal detachment at Athabasca. While liquor could legally be sold in the settlement since it lay slightly south of 55 degrees and was not part of the District of Athabaska, patrols in the district and sub-detachments at the Grand Rapids and Lesser Slave River portages were initiated to control the flow of liquor into the prohibition territory. But neither patrols nor permits could stem the traffic. In 1897, Inspector Jarvis of the NWMP noted that "permits are said to be fraudulently obtained by traders and others in the name of the boatmen and employees, who are in great measure paid for their summer's work in liquor." As well, intoxicating extracts such as ginger (also called "essences") could be legally sold in most parts of the region notwithstanding their high alcohol content.[17]

Despite such problems, the enforcement of liquor laws established a precedent for further police activity when the federal government passed legislation for game preservation in the region. Although game depletion had periodically occurred during the nineteenth century, new hunting practices appearing by the 1890s caused growing concern. The most significant of these new practices was the use of poison baits. Apparently a method most commonly used by white and Metis hunters, meat laced with strychnine was laid out to kill fur-bearing animals. More convenient and easier than running a trap line, this practice had long been used in the Peace country. It was also common in other parts of prairie Canada—it was, for example, a widely used method to kill wolves in ranching areas of southern Alberta and Saskatchewan. A wasteful practice that led to an overall decline in fur-bearing animals, it also killed valuable domestic dogs used by Natives as pack animals and retrievers. This caused much bitterness, and as the NWMP reported in 1895, many First Nations people in the Athabasca and Peace River districts resented "the indiscriminate use of poison by trappers." Two years later, the police again noted that the "Indians complain bitterly about the use of this poison put out by white men and half-breed trappers with whom they are unable to compete and think it hard that people who are not owners of the country are allowed to rob them of their living."[18]

Game legislation in the region was also encouraged by growing concerns about the future of the wood buffalo. By the late 1880s, nearly a century of over-hunting and a series of natural disasters had brought to near extinction the last of a species that had roamed "in countless thousands" before the arrival of Europeans. The Toronto *Mail* took up the cause, urging the federal government to obtain precise information about the buffalo and establish a reserve for their protection. This expressed an emerging conservation sentiment in Canada.[19] By the early 1890s it was increasingly evident that other animals were also in danger, especially beaver, which were nearing critically low levels. Since the northern unorganized districts were exempted from territorial game legislation, the federal government passed *An Act for the Preservation of Game in the Unorganized Portions of the Northwest Territories of Canada* in 1894. The legislation came into force in early 1896. It banned the use of poison baits and established annual closed seasons for hunting by nonresidents, except for buffalo and musk oxen, which could not be hunted at all for a period of five years. While nonresidents could not employ anyone to take game or birds' eggs out of season, residents were allowed to hunt for both subsistence and trade (with the exception of buffalo and musk oxen) as before 1896. The total hunting ban of endangered animals indicated that the federal government intended to regulate hunting regardless of Aboriginal claims or the absence of a treaty. Yet Natives were part of the motivation behind this legislation. Concern was expressed that game depletion might bring demands for government relief, or would force northern Natives to migrate to the southern parts of the prairies. If game in the north could be protected for Native hunters, various social problems and expense for government could be avoided.[20] Like the liquor laws, the enforcement of this legislation provided further incentive for the establishment of permanent police posts in northern Alberta and justified a more active role for Canada in the region's life.

Even though Canada's commitment was uneven, halting and lacking in political focus and will, its liquor and game legislation revealed a growing willingness to be involved in northern affairs and to integrate the region into the fabric of national life. This commitment broadened after the election of the Liberals in June 1896. The Liberals were then the party of national expansion, and one of the most vocal and prominent of these expansionists was the journalist, Frank Oliver, who had been elected in Edmonton to represent the Liberals. Oliver had well-honed skills as a promoter of northern development, which he believed was crucial for Edmonton's future. He had founded the Edmonton *Bulletin* in 1880 and from this base had rapidly built an impressive political career. Beginning as a member of the North-West Territories Assembly, he moved to federal politics in 1896, becoming one of western Canada's most powerful Liberals. The promise of a bright political future was confirmed in 1905 when he was appointed Minister of the Interior.

Four months after the 1896 election, Oliver wrote to the new Prime Minister, Wilfrid Laurier, warning him that parts of the Peace-Athabasca River basin were becoming socially destabilized. Native people were showing growing resentment over the use of poison baits by outsiders. Forest fires caused by travellers' carelessness with camp fires further destroyed fur-bearing animals and valuable timber and provided another "grievance against the white man which might at any moment culminate in serious trouble." Oliver argued that permanent NWMP detachments were needed at Athabasca, as well as at Grand Rapids, Fort McMurray and Fort Chipewyan in the unorganized District of Athabaska. Since this latter district lacked public infrastructure, Oliver noted that one police officer should have the powers of a Justice of the Peace to give prompt attention to charges laid by the police. He warned, however, that the number of police stationed in the north should be kept to a minimum to prevent Natives from assuming that the police were "there to overawe them." Like a Victorian boy's adventure story, he suggested that "someone should be employed in the guise of a trapper who would act as a detective to keep the Police advised of what is going on." [21]

Behind these concerns about northern instability lay a belief that the federal government should more actively encourage Euro-Canadian settlement in northern Alberta and regulate its economy and society to preserve natural resources for future development. Northern commerce, most of which originated in Edmonton or passed through the town, was increasing rapidly. Staff Sergeant Hetherington of the NWMP detachment at Athabasca reported that traffic through Athabasca during the 1896 navigation season had been much higher than in previous years and he predicted that it would increase further in 1897 since "the fur trade seems to be attracting general attention." As well, an Edmonton company was said to be planning to build a steamer at Athabasca to carry passengers and freight to Lesser Slave Lake "at a cheap rate." If this happened, Hetherington anticipated that Metis immigration would also increase. Further, the "large numbers of traders, trappers and others" now living north of Athabasca required that the seasonal detachment at Athabasca be made a permanent one.[22]

A.H. Griesbach, the Superintendent of "G" Division and responsible for the Edmonton and Athabasca areas, endorsed the expansion of the force's jurisdiction northwards. Other high ranking police officials also agreed. The NWMP Comptroller noted that while the police had occasionally gone further north during shipping season to control the liquor traffic, their "general instructions" were that "they were not to go beyond the northerly limits of the Electoral Districts of Saskatchewan and Alberta in the ordinary performance of their duty." Citing reports of murders in the north, the concerns outlined by Oliver about fires and the use of poison bait, and the obligation to enforce the new federal game legislation, the Comptroller agreed that "regular police supervision" should be extended about 650 kilometres north. He endorsed the immediate dispatch of a small patrol to visit Fort Chipewyan, Fort Vermilion and other points "with a view to gaining such general information as will enable the Police to establish themselves in the District next year without incurring unreasonable expense."[23] In other words, the decision to expand northwards had been taken. It now only needed to be implemented.

The patrol was put together in the fall of 1896. It was not meant merely as a foray into a new land but was designed to extend Canadian law and authority. Officials recognized that Inspector Jarvis, who had been selected to make the patrol, would have to act delicately in achieving this objective. As the NWMP Comptroller advised, "we have no authority to instruct him with regard to his duties as Justice of the Peace, but it would do no harm" to suggest to him that since there had so far been "no administration of justice of any kind in the Northern Districts," people were likely unaware of the game legislation and "may have offended unwittingly." Thus, he should "lose no opportunity of making known the laws and regulations on the various subjects so that there may be no excuses in future years."[24] This advice was incorporated into the detailed instructions that governed the patrol. L.W. Herchmer, the Commissioner of the NWMP, instructed Jarvis "to obtain an exhaustive report on the condition of affairs there generally, and particularly to collect information likely to be useful to the government in their future dealings with that territory." In particular, Jarvis was to report on the "use or abuse of liquor," forest fires, fish and wildlife resources and the use of poison baits. Beyond such fact-finding efforts, he was also to reconnoitre the best locations "for the police to work from," inventoring lumber and hay supplies, and identifying "districts suitable for settlement." He was also to instruct people he encountered about game legislation. Further, he was to investigate rumours of murders in the unorganized territories and, "if necessary, to take immediate action" and arrest the accused. As it was "impossible at present to imprison in that territory," Herchmer advised that time for collection of fines should be allowed since, by the time the fines were due, the police would doubtless be able to administer "the usual imprisonment" to enforce the conviction.[25]

These instructions, along with Jarvis's detailed report of his patrol, were printed the next year in the *Annual Report* of the NWMP. Together, they formed a public statement on the work of the force and of Canadian intentions in the north. Jarvis's patrol report was only the first of several that appeared in the NWMP's annual reports over the next few years, and collectively they provided official Euro-Canadian descriptions of northern Alberta before the signing of Treaty 8 in 1899. More than simple narratives describing the country and its people, they played an integral part in the incorporation of this northern region into Canada. They simultaneously contributed to a mental mapping of the region by Euro-Canadians and helped justify and explain the country's northward expansion. By framing questions about what was important and needed to be known about the north, these reports helped channel and focus the extension of Canada's authority and priorities in the region. They provided details on settlements, buildings and the distribution of population; about resources and the economy; the activities of white traders, settlers and missionaries; transportation routes; and certain aspects of social life, such as the racial make-up of the population. As such, they built upon the knowledge gathered by the Senate's committee in 1888 and a growing number of published travel accounts about northern Canada. On some issues, however, the reports were often silent. Native land use patterns, for example, were seemingly of limited interest, and social relationships were rarely noted.

The patrol, consisting of Jarvis, Staff Sergeant Hetherington, James Gullion (interpreter and guide) and P. Lutit (dog driver), set out from Fort Saskatchewan on January 4, 1897. With three dog trains of four dogs each, plus two spare dogs and all the necessary equipment, they travelled north by the winter trail from Edmonton through Lac La Biche. For Jarvis, leaving Lac La Biche was the true starting point for the expedition since he was then leaving the jurisdiction of 'G' Division. Lacking the familiar structure, it was apparent that for him the north had now begun.[26]

The patrol visited all the major settlements along the Athabasca and Slave rivers as far north as Fort Resolution on Great Slave Lake, which was reached in the middle of February. After a short rest, Jarvis returned to Fort Chipewyan, then struck westwards to the lower Peace River. While he had been instructed to travel south from Fort Vermilion to Wabasca, this was impossible since the country was "nearly unknown" and contained extensive tracts of muskeg and heavy bush. Since no one could be found to guide him, he instead followed the Peace River upstream as far as Peace River Crossing, returning to Fort Saskatchewan through Grouard and Athabasca. He reached home on April 15, having covered over 3,200 kilometres.[27]

In his report, Jarvis studiously replied to his instructions. All attempts at farming and each cluster of population were dutifully noted since all were potential sites for police posts or government centres. Along his route, Jarvis paid particular attention to the use of poison bait. While he found most north-erners unaware that its use was illegal under the 1894 game legislation, he confirmed that it was a source of conflict between newcomers (including Metis) and Natives. Jarvis also found that wood buffalo were extinct between Forts McMurray and Chipewyan, the last one having been killed by a Native hunter near Fort McKay in 1895. Although unable to estimate their number, Jarvis found that the remaining animals were largely in two herds near Fort Smith. Here, Jarvis encountered a party of Natives heading out to hunt buffalo, and he reported that they "had never heard of a game law, and were much surprised on hearing of it, but willingly gave up their hunt when I explained to them the necessity of complying with this law." As well, George Hanbury, an English sportsman and author was in Fort Smith, having just returned from an unsuc-cessful hunt accompanied by the local Hudson's Bay Company manager. Jarvis pointedly observed that Hanbury showed little respect for the game regula-tions and intended to return later in the year to hunt buffalo, whatever the law, and "the fear of a $200 fine will hardly prevent his hunt." As Jarvis noted, if Canada intended "to protect these nearly extinct animals," it could only do so by "placing officials on the spot." And as the Edmonton *Bulletin* reported the same year, Natives apparently were willing to stop killing wood buffalo if the ban applied to everyone, and whites thus had to be "absolutely prohibited" from hunting them.[28]

Forest fires were also of related significance for wildlife. Although Jarvis was unable to report accurately about northern timber resources since he travelled only along the rivers, it was nonetheless clear that "enormous damage has been done, and on the Upper Peace River these vast fires have driven off the game and consequently impoverished many of the Indians." In fact, fires everywhere in northern Alberta had ravaged huge tracts of land and killed many moose and bears, both important local sources of food. While Jarvis fined a number of people for carelessness with fires, he discovered that the issue was more complex than was usually assumed by southern commentators. Forest fires indeed represented a loss of timber and fur, but controlled burning to encourage a succession of plant and animal resources was also part of Native resource management. Between Lac La Biche and Fort McMurray, for example, Jarvis found the country "comparatively open" because it had been burnt off in the past by Natives to make "a moose range, which is done by burning off the timber which encourages the second growth on which the moose feed."[29]

On social issues, Jarvis confirmed that liquor was readily available in many parts of the north despite the permit system, and he advised that prohibition be enforced.[30] This conclusion supported one commonly held view about northern conditions, but a general social instability in the region as previously expressed by Frank Oliver and others was not so evident. While Jarvis encountered considerable unhappiness about the use of poison baits, he did not find a region on the edge of revolt. Indeed, other issues that concerned the NWMP appeared not to be a major concern for most northerners. Liquor appeared to have been more an issue among missionaries and other whites than among Native northerners, and while conservation of fur resources was at the heart of Native concerns about poison baits, conservation of the wood buffalo and other animals apparently was not a concern. Indeed, talk about game conservation and regulation often created alarm in northern hunting and trapping communities.

Jarvis's patrol asserted for the first time the authority of the state and gave notice that Canada now intended to administer more actively its interests in the region. Jarvis explained the laws regarding fire, poison and game to all he met, and although he posted written notices about the laws, their effect is questionable in a society that was overwhelmingly nonliterate. He also laid 20 charges in total, most for putting out poison, but a few also for liquor offences, setting fires and assault. While he allowed time "for payment of these fines," he urged that they be enforced when due to prevent "a bad precedent for further action in that country." His experience also revealed that northern police work could not be patterned solely on southern methods. He had covered over 3,200 kilometres in about four months, but this extraordinary pace, in combination with periodic shortages of food, had worn out his dogs. As well, some of the equipment issued by the police was inadequate, and Jarvis concluded that local equipment, such as Northern or Mackenzie River snowshoes, native-made moose hide moccasins and "caribou capotes" would be better than regular police issue.[31]

Jarvis's patrol was viewed in official circles as a success. He had shown the flag and had sketched a plan for permanently establishing the NWMP in the north.[32] Simultaneously, Edmonton commercial interests seized the opportunity to confirm the need for increased police activity to protect their trading activities. Frank Oliver argued throughout 1897 that police were essential at the Grand Rapids and Smith Rapids portages to protect traders' goods from theft. Edmonton businessman Richard Secord, for example, wrote to Oliver in early 1897 complaining that police were needed at Fort Smith because the portage required several trips "and [we] have to leave our goods piled on the beach for some time and frequently we have things stolen." At the same time that Oliver was arguing for these security needs, he was also furthering other interests of Edmonton's business community. In 1898, the NWMP requested his advice on where to place further detachments. Oliver gave points of commercial value the highest priority and also recommended that the police use Edmonton suppliers for its northern operations. "The firms to which I allude," he told the Comptroller, "are McDougall and Secord, Ross Brothers, and Larue and Picard." That same year, he also intervened with the police to defend the interests of McDougall and Secord in their quarrel with the Hudson's Bay Company over access to the waterfront at Athabasca.[33] For Oliver, northern expansion was directly connected to the interests of Edmonton's political and economic elite.

In contrast to the positive reaction of southern Euro-Canadians to Jarvis's tour, northern Native opinion was ambiguous. While many people welcomed efforts to stem the use of poison bait, they also recognized that the patrol was more than a casual reconnaissance and had the potential to change northern life by bringing enforcement of game laws and other regulations. While in Fort Chipewyan, Jarvis received a letter from Alicksand Levillot who lived about 50 kilometres from the settlement. Levillot's opening sentences were unequivocal: "Who told you to come out here. I would like to know that. [I] am sure it isn't God. God let this country [be] free, and we like to be free in this Country. I don't want any of you people to come a[nd] bother us in this country. We don't care how miserable we are in this Country. The Company was here from long ago and can stay as much [as] they like." Assuring Jarvis that this held nothing personal, Levillot observed:

> I think myself a man same as you, and I would not step back for your gun. Not [sic] you will scare me. It is not because [I] am down on you. I suppose you want to hear about our Country. If [you] want to see the People you should come here in the Spring not in the Winter and it is no use to stop us to kill anything in this Country. It is not you that grows anything in this Country. I don't care if I don't have a cent in my hand. God never made money for me, anything alive, that is my money in this Country for just now.[34]

Clearly, Levillot's suspicions arose because Jarvis had come in winter when most people were in the bush trapping rather than in the settlements. He was obviously concerned about the extension of Canadian wildlife conservation laws—in this case, probably the hunting ban on wood buffalo—but he also wondered what other restrictions were in store. But Levillot went further in his rejection of the expansion of the Canadian state. His assertion that his wealth came from the common use of the land and its resources, not from an individual's ownership of money or land, was a rejection of private property and the cash nexus and a defence of the existing economy.

The police dismissed Levillot's letter as "insolent," but it was soon evident that his fears were not unique. By the summer of 1897 there were similar reactions to the police elsewhere in the north, especially among the Metis at Grouard and district. In July 1897, Sergeant Hetherington reported that a recent patrol had been "very cooly received by Half-breeds and Indians" at Grouard, in the districts north of the settlement and at Peace River. This antagonism arose in part from fear of future enforcement of fish and game laws. Indeed, Hetherington noted that fish and game were coming under increasing pressure because of rapid population growth due to Metis migration, and he concluded that game and fish regulations could not be enforced "until some provision is made for the sustenance of these people." He also credited his poor reception to "the bad influence of a number of tough half-breeds, some of whom have been in the hands of the police." This may have been an euphemism for the 1885 Rebellion, for as he carefully noted, the Metis were "from nearly all parts of the North-West Territories," and "a large majority are much opposed to the Police being established in the Peace River District, especially at Lesser Slave Lake." The Metis had held meetings at Peace River, Grouard, Sturgeon Lake and Utikuma Lake to organize petitions demanding that the police withdraw from the district. Hetherington contended that the Metis had "so incited the Indians that a great number have also signed the petitions in question, and the reason given is that no treaty having been made with the Indians the Police have no right in the District." While he noted in his patrol report that there were "rumours that Police detachments at Lesser Slave Lake will be forcibly ejected," by the time he submitted his summary report two months later, he commented only that "no open hostility was shown but it was plain to be seen we were not welcome." He urged that a Justice of the Peace be appointed immediately and that the police detachment be strengthened to deal with the Metis since the people around Grouard "have no idea of Law and Order and will have to be handled firmly."[35]

These observations were reinforced by Corporal Macdonald after a patrol in the fall of 1897. While he contended that the hostility to the police in the Grouard area was due to the police restricting the sale of liquor, he also noted that people were anxious "about their hunting grounds, and they want to know what the government is going to give them for opening up the country" between Grouard and Peace River "which they claim to be theirs." While he believed that a handful of local people wanted the police to enforce the laws against setting fires, sale of liquor and use of poison baits, "there are very few." One local chief had been deposed by his people for welcoming the police, and the Hudson's Bay Company manager at Grouard believed that there would be trouble "with the Slave Lake Indians and those farther north if the government opens up the country."[36]

## ▬ The Klondike Gold Rush

Justifications for expanded Canadian control of northern Alberta culminated with the Klondike gold rush. In August 1896 an important gold strike was made in the Yukon. While communications with the Yukon were slow, news spread quickly once it reached the south because of modern systems of printing and photography, and by the spring of 1897 the gold rush was on. Although most prospectors travelled to the Yukon from the Pacific coast, a small number also went overland through Edmonton and northern Alberta. James MacGregor, in his history of the gold rush through Edmonton, estimated that nearly 300 prospectors used this route to the Yukon in 1897 alone. Although the numbers grew dramatically in early 1898, by the end of the year they were falling, and by the end of 1899 the rush was virtually over.[37]

*A few prospectors travelled through Athabasca in hopes of reaching the Klondike gold fields. This group was photographed at Athabasca in 1898.* B2588 PAA.

The gold rush prompted a number of proposals for a railway through Edmonton to the Yukon, but the short duration of the frenzy ensured that none was built. Instead, prospectors going through northern Alberta travelled along trails and rivers to reach the gold fields. From the terminus of the railway at Edmonton there were a number of routes to the Yukon. All were very long and brutally difficult, and many travellers, unprepared for the distances and nearly impassable trails, were forced to winter over on the trail. One such route followed the Athabasca Trail to Athabasca, then westward to the Peace River country and north-west to the Yukon. Another route involved travelling along the Athabasca and Mackenzie rivers to Fort Macpherson and then inland and southward (largely by river) through the Mackenzie Mountains to Dawson City. While roundabout and expensive, this was the best of the overland passages. To service this river traffic, a local entrepreneur and fur trader, Jim Cornwall, began operating a river boat on the Athabasca River in 1898.[38]

Although a few prospectors continued to travel through until 1899, ones straggling back from the north were more common. Many were financially bankrupt and physically broken. For the missionaries, this held the most important lesson of the gold rush, and they eagerly pointed out that these were the fruits of lust for material things. Bishop Grouard recalled meeting a party of miners returning from the Klondike in 1899, and with the feeling of an Old Testament prophet, he observed that they were "returning home discouraged, ruined [and] exhausted," resembling "a mirage that had been misled into our vast wilderness." Similarly, George Holmes, the Anglican missionary at Grouard, wrote that "the delusive spectre of a large fortune" had brought only misery and poverty.[39]

In the longer term, the Klondike rush had important but indirect influences on northern Alberta. Athabasca was confirmed as the gateway to the north, and the settlement of a few returning Klondikers in the Peace River country and around Athabasca added to the handful of white settlers in the region. As well, the Klondikers brought cash into the north and created a temporary economic boom. In Athabasca, new businesses opened to serve them, and boat building and freighting were stimulated. At the same time, local wages were inflated. In 1898 Hudson's Bay Company officials at Grouard complained that cash spent by Klondikers had pushed up local wages and had led Native labourers to demand cash instead of trade for their labour. So too, Inspector Routledge reported that Klondikers complained about the "excessive charges" levied by Native guides and pilots at the Grand and Smith Rapids, who, he surmised, looked upon the portages "as their 'Klondyke.'" He thought that their fees should be regulated by the government, as was the case with pilots elsewhere in Canada.[40] The NWMP also immediately stepped up its northern patrols in 1897, especially through the Peace River country. The next year, further patrols went north, including a famous trek by Inspector Routledge from Fort Saskatchewan to Fort Simpson.

Most importantly, the Klondike rush confirmed in Canadian official circles that, in addition to control of the north by the NWMP, a treaty with the Native people of northern Alberta was now needed. The Klondikers were often an unruly lot, and their relations with Natives were generally poor. At Fort St. John, Natives were on the verge of revolt in 1898, and it was widely feared that conflict would spread throughout the Peace River country. George Holmes observed that this conflict could hardly be unexpected "after the shameful way these white heathens have treated these poor harmless Indians—stealing and shooting their horses, robbing their caches, which until the white man came were always as safe as in the Bank." While the prospect of a Native rebellion at Fort St. John was unwelcome in itself, it was also worrying because NWMP forces were stretched to the limit since so many police were needed in the Yukon due to the influx of gold seekers and associated border tensions with the Americans.[41] At the same time, many Klondikers on the Mackenzie River route (especially around Great Slave Lake) prospected for gold as they moved along, hoping to find a new "Klondike." It was evident that if they made a strike, prospectors would quickly swarm into the area and bring conflict with the Native people. More generally, however, the gold rush renewed Euro-Canadian interest in northern resources. As an official with Indian Affairs recalled in 1900, while there had been no large influx of white settlers, the Klondike gold rush had increased its possibility since "the knowledge of the country obtained and diffused, if only by people passing through it, could hardly fail to attract attention to it as a field for settlement." In combination with Native resentment of white behaviour and the alarming prospect of a gold strike occurring in some part of the unceded territories, this further persuaded the federal government of the need for a treaty.[42]

— ✦ —

The tensions caused by the Klondike gold rush only compounded those already existing because of the activities of the NWMP, which had also arisen from growing Canadian interest in northern Alberta. By the time of Jarvis's patrol in 1897, this interest had been building, in fits and starts, for nearly a decade. Although Frank Oliver had contended in 1896 that the region was becoming destabilized, Jarvis's report showed that these claims were exaggerated. If anything caused worry among northerners, the sudden appearance of the police was most important. Some of the issues that Oliver noted, especially the use of poison bait, were of genuine concern, and police action with respect to them was welcomed. But between 1897 and 1898, police patrols and fears about the future created greater tension. The Metis clearly resented the police and played a major part in resisting the assertion of Canadian control over the north. Upcoming preparations for the treaty that would be signed in 1899 would intensify these concerns, and as would be demonstrated, Canadian control of the north would often bring tensions and uncertainty for the region's Aboriginal people.

# 3 Treaty and Scrip in Northern Alberta

TREATY NEGOTIATIONS with the Aboriginal peoples were critical in Canada's control over northern Alberta and its efforts to promote the region's integration with Canada. Preparations for the treaty with northern Native people began in 1898. Plans were also made to extinguish Metis claims by distributing scrip for land. While treaty and scrip would free land for white settlement and economic development, they also gave Canada legal authority to make laws for social order and the regulation of natural resources.[1]

Reflecting these motives, Canada's treaty commissioners were instructed to define the boundaries of the treaty area to include lands north of Treaty 6 (the 55th parallel) likely to be used by agricultural settlers or miners, or through which they might pass. At the same time, the government wanted to restrict the size of the treaty area to minimize future costs and obligations. Initially, it was thought that the treaty would extend only to Fort Smith, but in early 1899 the boundary was pushed further north to the southern shore of Great Slave Lake where mining development was anticipated. As a result, the area of Treaty 8 was large, including all of the Arctic watershed north of 55 degrees in what is now British Columbia and Alberta, and parts of present day NWT and Saskatchewan. These were the areas farthest north in which mining or other economic activity was anticipated.[2]

The government hoped that the treaty would be signed in 1898, but this did not allow sufficient time to notify all concerned and to have them meet, discuss and sign the document. Consequently, notices were distributed in 1898 by police, traders and missionaries informing people that treaty and scrip would be offered the following year and that they should make arrangements to meet the treaty commissioners at the appointed times. These notices created apprehension everywhere in the north. At Fort Smith, Colonel Trotter of the NWMP reported that "the Indians of this locality are very jealous of whitemen, trappers and miners coming into their country and want them forbidden to do so." Many also feared that they would be forced to live on reserves, and Trotter asserted that "they do not seem to understand the nature of the treaty at all" and foretold that the government would have "a great deal of trouble" before the Native people accepted it. He blamed "whitemen and half-breed traders" for "telling them that they will be put on a reserve and kept there, and not be allowed to go off it, nor to hunt, and that if they have to depend on the amount of provisions that they get from the Government that they will die of hunger." He attended "some of their meetings" to explain the treaty, telling people that they would not be forced to take it and "that their freedom would in no wise be interfered with so long as they obeyed the laws." This assurance, he wrote, somewhat lessened people's fears.[3]

Given the strong reaction to the establishment of police detachments the year before in the Peace River and Lesser Slave Lake districts, it was not surprising that reaction to the proposed treaty was particularly sharp in this area. NWMP Constable Phillips reported that it had been unanimously agreed at public meetings in Grouard that neither treaty nor scrip should be accepted "in any shape or form" since "the settlement of the country would surely follow." Apparently, it was believed that both Metis and Indian rights could best be secured in the face of advancing white settlement by refusing any negotiations with the government. Phillips contended that this opinion was general throughout the area, but he noted that "these meetings have always been very orderly and nothing of a hostile spirit has appeared amongst any of them." Similarly, George Holmes reported in April 1899 that people at Grouard were "at present determined to refuse either treaty or scrip and to oppose any European settlement in the country." A month later, he wrote that the brutal behaviour of Klondikers and then the announcement of the upcoming treaty negotiations had made people at Utikuma Lake "very sulky and awkward." They had pulled their children out of the Anglican school, "fearing that we would trade them to the Government." Both Holmes and Father Desmarais, the Catholic priest at Grouard, were "suspected" by the people at Utikuma Lake "to have invited all these people to come—as they say, opened the door into this country." Although Holmes believed that most would refuse treaty, he thought they would accept scrip.[4] The missionaries tried to counter these fears and urged the people to take treaty, which, in the circumstances, likely only added to the tensions in the community.

In addition to such open resistance, rising tensions over the treaty may also have been a factor in a number of reports of Windigos in the Sturgeon Lake and Grouard districts in the spring of 1899. In most Algonkian, as well as in some Athapaskan cultures, it was popularly believed that a human could be transformed into a Windigo, a creature that craved human flesh. As Inspector Jarvis noted in 1897, "Indians of unsound mind, styled 'We'h-ti-koo,' and reported to become cannibals, are frequently made away with to prevent them from killing and eating other members of their family or tribe." He believed that this accounted for the few "alleged murders" in the north, but he "was unable to locate any recent practice" other than a couple of cases at Grouard.[5]

If Jarvis was correct, the Windigo phenomenon had not been common in the period immediately before 1897. Charles Mair, one of the secretaries with the scrip commission in 1899, also observed that the Windigo "was not common among the Lesser Slave Lake Indians" but "was said to be on the increase." Indeed, in the late winter and early spring of 1899, the Lesser Slave Lake district had been filled with rumours of people with Windigo symptoms. Thus a story of a Windigo at Sturgeon Lake in April was dismissed as just another in a series of rumours. This time, however, a man suspected of becoming a Windigo was murdered. Three men were arrested and charged with his murder. Over the objections of Sam Cunningham, a local Metis leader (and a former MLA for St. Albert in the North-West Territories Assembly), the police rounded up witnesses and took them to Edmonton for trial. One of the accused died on the way to Edmonton, and one of the remaining two was found guilty of manslaughter and received a sentence of two months hard labour. While George Holmes called the murder "another of those heathen tragedies," he also noted that "I am afraid that in this sad case heathen fear and superstition are not altogether to blame." Holmes hated liquor, and he pointedly observed that people had been drinking ginger extract, which had contributed to the violence. But, he significantly added, "the Indians both here and at Sturgeon Lake are, as you may suppose, considerably excited over this and the proposed Treaty." Several months later, he noted once again that the Windigo murder caused "great excitement amongst the Indians here who were already in a fever of alarm about the approaching treaty."[6]

Tensions in the community about the prospect of the treaty, the Windigo murder, as well as the widespread and swirling rumours of other Windigos at

Sturgeon Lake and Grouard in the late winter and spring of 1899 were indications of a society enduring tremendous strain. Perhaps fear of outsiders and their intentions, and new concerns about the future, found expression through a cultural tradition related to a fear of the unknown. Windigos were traditionally connected with the forest; with places lying beyond human society and civilization. Moreover, they manifested an upset in nature and the social order.[7] Thus, while the Windigo incidents at Sturgeon Lake might have reflected social tension, they perhaps also manifested a fear of the unknown created by an imbalance in the world and by divisions in the community. As Holmes observed, the community was divided about accepting treaty, and "'Pow-wows' and counsel meetings became every week more frequent until the Indian Commissioners arrived" and the treaty was concluded.[8]

The government's response to news of resistance to the treaty was casual. While admitting that game and fish laws would be enforced, it initially argued people's livelihood would not be affected since widespread white settlement was unlikely and people would be free to live as before. Given the level of anxiety about the treaty's implications, this could hardly have satisfactorily calmed apprehensions about the future. The government did, however, change one aspect of its policy on reserves. In earlier treaties, reserves had been created where a number of families would live as a single community on land held by the Crown in trust. While such reserves were provided for in Treaty 8, its members were also allowed to hold land in severalty—in other words, land was allocated to individual families, although it was treated like reserve land and could not be sold without the permission of the Department of Indian Affairs. It was reasoned that since northern hunting was organized on an individual or family basis, rather than communally as in plains bison hunting, a rigid application of the conventional reserve system would be unsatisfactory. More directly, however, Natives in northern Alberta were reluctant to sign the treaty at all, and clearly many were apprehensive about settling on reserves. It was therefore hoped that the severalty provisions would allay such fears.[9]

The provision for reserve land in severalty in Treaty 8 was the only significant change from earlier treaties. Clifford Sifton, the minister of the Interior and Superintendent General of Indian Affairs, instructed the treaty commissioners that land could be granted in severalty to meet Native concerns but that other terms could be altered only if they did not exceed those in other treaties in the North-West Territories. Thus, as Richard Daniel notes in his history of Treaty 8, there was no "attempt to formulate a radically different sort of treaty for the area." The only other attempt to alleviate Native fears about hunting rights and white settlement was to recruit local missionaries and police officers to explain in advance the benefits of treaty. As well, Father Lacombe was taken on as an advisor to the treaty party. The most famous missionary of the Northwest, Lacombe was 72 years old and agreed to participate only after extracting a promise from Sifton that "the doctor of the Commission will be always in the party where I would be, in account of my infirmities."[10]

In addition to the many legal, economic and social concerns raised by the treaty, another difficulty arose because insufficient time had been allowed for discussion. To keep to their schedule, the commissioners had to travel quickly through a huge territory where travel was difficult. Estimating that almost 540 Indians and about 200 Metis would gather to meet the treaty party at Fort Chipewyan alone, Inspector Routledge anticipated that discussions would be lengthy. Even though the police were trying to counter negative "talk" about the treaty, Routledge noted that Native worries remained extensive.[11] The government's solution, however, was simply to rush the process along.


## ──Negotiating Treaty 8

Treaty negotiations opened at Grouard on June 20, 1899—later than first planned because of a cold spring, late break-up and heavy rain. The treaty commissioners were instructed to sign there before going further north in order to establish a precedent that would help persuade other Natives to sign. Because the treaty party was already behind schedule, discussions at Grouard were kept to a minimum and took only two days, with the annuities paid on the third day. The platform party consisted of commissioners David Laird (former Minister of the Interior and Lieutenant Governor of the North-West Territories), James Ross (the North-West Territories Minister of Public Works), James McKenna (the Private Secretary to the Superintendent General of Indian Affairs), Albert Tate (an interpreter) and several clerks. A NWMP escort provided a symbolic affirmation of the authority of the state and guarded the treaty chest containing $320,000. The commissioners were flanked on the left side by Fathers Lacombe and Grouard, and on the right by Revs. Holmes and White. Revelling in the Christian symbolism of left and right, Holmes remarked that the Anglicans were to "the right of the Government for once at any rate."[12]

In his opening address, Laird told the crowd that "it is not alone that we wish to prevent Indians from molesting whites, it is also to prevent the whites from molesting or doing harm to the Indians. The Queen's soldiers are just as

*This photograph shows the Treaty Commissioners' party leaving Edmonton for the north.* B783 PAA.

much for the protection of the Indians as for the white man." Further, despite "stories" to the contrary, he promised that "you will be just as free after signing the treaty as you are now." He then set out the terms the government was offering: an annuity of $12 per person for the first year and $5 per person per year thereafter with higher amounts for chiefs and headmen; clothes and other symbols of rank for chiefs; 640 acres of land for a family of five on a reserve or 160 acres per person in severalty; agricultural equipment, breeding livestock, and agricultural implements for those who wanted to take up farming; ammunition for those who wished to hunt and twine for nets for those who wanted to fish; schools; and, among other things, axes and construction tools for each band to assist in constructing houses. Returning to one of the central concerns, Laird observed that "Indians have been told that if they make a treaty they will not be allowed to hunt and fish as they do now. This is not true. Indians who take treaty will be just as free to hunt and fish all over as they now are." The Crown promised friendship and justice, and Laird concluded by explaining that Metis were being offered scrip because of their Indian ancestry.[13]

Debate then began. The treaty commissioners had earlier asked the Natives to elect Chiefs, and these elections took place on the eve of the negotiations. Debate during the negotiations was restricted to these leaders, and many people spoke about the need to protect their freedom to hunt, trap and fish. Many also stressed that they did not want to be forced to live on a reserve. While one of the leading figures, Moostoos, was favourable to the treaty, others were wary. Questions continued to be raised about the need for the treaty, and worries were voiced about its implications for their freedom. Commissioner Ross tried to meet these concerns by promising that people had nothing to lose "as all the rights you now have will not be interfered with, therefore anything you get in addition will be clear gain." Moreover, he argued that many whites would soon come, whether the treaty was signed or not, and the treaty would establish and protect Native rights. This was apparently a persuasive argument. Father Lacombe added his voice in urging people to accept the treaty, and by day's end, it seemed that agreement had been reached.[14]

The Commissioners then drew up the actual treaty document for presentation and signature the next day. The text was patterned on Treaty 7 (which Laird had negotiated), although there were differences that seemed to reflect "a recognition that the Indians of the North might wish to continue traditional economic activities, such as hunting, fishing, and trapping, and to resist being restricted to reserve land." As well, educational provisions were not restricted (as they had been in Treaty 7) to those Indians who had taken up reserve land. The treaty also gave options in the types of equipment, such as nets, ammunition and agricultural tools, that would be granted to accommodate the livelihood that particular people might follow.[15]

This document was presented the second day. Discussions among the Natives the previous evening, however, had raised fresh concerns about the future. While the Edmonton *Bulletin* reporter downplayed the discussions of the second day, it is apparent that genuine concerns about hunting and fishing rights had weakened the consensus reached the first day. Although transcripts of the second day's discussions have not survived, the commissioners noted in their official report that they were forced to promise that game regulations would not compromise Native livelihood and that they would continue to be free to hunt and fish. As well, they further reiterated that no one would be forced to live on a reserve.[16]

The discussions on the second day also reflected the rivalry that existed among missionaries in the region. Government support of schools had been promised in the treaty discussions on the first day, and the denomination of those running these schools now became an issue. This was a crucial concern for the missionaries who tried to persuade their adherents to stipulate that only one of either the Roman Catholics or Anglicans would run the schools. Father

At Fort Vermilion, the Beaver and Cree met with Treaty
Commissioner David Laird. Walker Album, SABS.

Grouard recalled with gratification that most Natives had spontaneously indi-
cated that they would choose Catholic instruction for their children, but
George Holmes charged that the Catholics had persuaded one of their adher-
ents to demand that all schooling would be run exclusively by the Catholics.
Later that evening, Holmes and White walked over to the Native camp to
persuade them to retract this request. Accordingly, the next day one of the
Indians asserted that "both [Protestants and Roman Catholics] are welcome."
Lacombe and Grouard, Holmes reported, "looked as though they had been
struck by a bullet."[17] Thus, in addition to concerns about their livelihood,
Natives became entangled in partisan debates about denominational advan-
tage.

Because the treaty party was behind schedule, it split into two after the
signing at Grouard. One group went to Peace River Crossing and the other set
out for Fort St. John. Few written records exist about the negotiations after
Grouard. Because the treaty had been finalized at Grouard, subsequent
changes were not allowed, and the "negotiations" at other places thus only
involved "adhesions" to the treaty already signed. At Peace River, the Cree led
by Duncan Tustawits signed after being assured that they would not be

conscripted into the army, but the Beaver refused to sign because not all of the band members were present. The treaty party travelling to Fort St. John abandoned the trip and turned back towards Peace River when it discovered that the Beaver people there had given up waiting and had gone hunting. On their way back to Peace River, however, they negotiated adhesions to the treaty with the Beaver at Dunvegan. The two treaty parties then travelled down the Peace River to Fort Vermilion and nearby Little Red River, each taking adhesions at various locations. Fort Chipewyan was the next stop and the Treaty Commissioners appointed Alexandre Lavilotte (a Metis married to a Chipewyan woman) as Chipewyan "chief," a new position in the community. This creation of a new political structure in Fort Chipewyan was among the first of the changes that would be stimulated by the treaty. Native concerns here, as elsewhere in the north, were primarily focussed around protecting hunting, fishing and trapping rights, and both the Cree and Chipewyan spokesmen demanded complete freedom to fish, hunt and trap. They also asked that their children be educated in Catholic schools. The Chipewyan spokesman had "a long list of demands including a Railway link with the south," which he said would increase the value of local produce and decrease the costs of imported goods. People at Fort Chipewyan did not want to be confined to a reserve, and Roman Catholic Bishop Breynat noted that "it was essential to them to retain complete freedom to move around."[18]

The Commissioners then travelled (in separate parties) to Fond du Lac, Smith's Landing (now Fitzgerald), Fort Smith, Fort McMurray and Wabasca, securing adhesions to the treaty at these points. Almost all of the territory included in the treaty was thus accounted for, although a good number of people still remained outside the treaty. Many of these were treated with the next year when the Beaver at Fort St. John, the Cree at Sturgeon Lake, the Dene (Slavey) band at Upper Hay River, and various peoples at Fort Resolution signed the treaty. About 2,400 people in northern Alberta entered treaty in 1899 and 1900, and more people (mainly in British Columbia) were admitted to treaty in the following years.[19]

## —— Metis Scrip

Because of the Canadian practice of defining who was "Indian" on the basis of legal qualities, the racially mixed population of northern Alberta did not create major problems for treaty-making. The appointment of a Metis, Alexandre Laviolette, as the Chipewyan Chief at Fort Chipewyan was one striking example of this. Anyone who was accepted as having an Aboriginal title in the land could take treaty and be defined as "Indian," or could refuse to take treaty and in law be defined as nontreaty (or "white"). Natives living in northern Alberta were thus free to take treaty and be defined as "Indian," or to receive scrip and be treated in law as "white" (that is, as no longer possessing Aboriginal title). The Metis Commissioners in Treaty 8 endorsed the definition earlier used in Treaty 6 that "it was lifestyle, more than biology, that distinguished Indians from other natives." But as anthropologist Trudy Nicks has noted, in light of the cultural mixing that had taken place in northern Alberta, "the clear distinction drawn between an Indian and white lifestyle was a fiction which probably only the government believed."[20] In any case, the government seems to have had little real concern about what people took as long as the Aboriginal title was extinguished, which it believed both treaty and scrip equally accomplished.

Metis Aboriginal claims were dealt with immediately after the treaty was signed. The important difference between the two negotiations was that Indian claims were dealt with collectively while those of the Metis were handled individually. The extinguishment of Metis Aboriginal title was premised on the signing of a treaty. As the deputy minister of the Department of the Interior explained in 1898, a Metis' rights arose because of his Indian ancestry and "but for this he would have no claim to be recognized. The Indian gives up his right for the benefits assured him by Treaty. If the Half-breed goes into Treaty he then loses his status as a Half-breed, becomes an Indian and has his claims satisfied in that way. If he does not accept Treaty, his right—because of his Indian blood—is satisfied by an issue of scrip."[21] Thus, the connection between settling Metis claims and Treaty 8 was clear and direct.

This successive staging of negotiations was also intended to meet several other goals. It was hoped that it would lessen the number of people who would refuse treaty in favour of scrip and that it would help gain the support of the Metis for the treaty. It was thought that the Metis, out of self-interest, would encourage Indians to sign the treaty so that their claims could in turn be settled. Further, the Metis in the Lesser Slave Lake and Peace River areas were agitating for recognition of their rights, and it was feared that delaying action on their demands might create political unrest and impede northern development. This reasoning led the scrip commissioners to congratulate themselves that their success meant "that the whole population of Indian and Half-breeds throughout the district of Athabasca are perfectly satisfied with the liberal manner in which they have been dealt with by the Government of Canada, and that in consequence no trouble or friction whatever need to be apprehended in bringing the country under government control."[22]

In northern Alberta, Metis scrip, was either a certificate for $240 "redeemable at its face value" in the purchase of homestead land, or a certificate that entitled its owner to 240 acres of land in areas still open to homesteading. The first type of scrip was popularly known as "cash" or "money" scrip, while the second type was called "land" scrip. While all scrip was a valuable commodity, land scrip was treated as real property and thus had a number of conditions attached to its sale. Since money scrip was personal property, it was easy to sell.[23]

When Manitoba was created in 1870, 1.4 million acres of land were set aside for the Metis to extinguish their aboriginal claims in the new province. Yet, as historian David Hall has noted, "indifferent politicians, changing governments and frequently altered regulations" forced many Metis to wait several years for their land. Some, especially those who were French-speaking, gave up and moved further west. Following the Rebellion of 1885, additional Metis claims were recognized in the North-West Territories through scrip distribution during 1885–87. As in Manitoba, the government handled it poorly and in a highly restrictive fashion, leaving "a continuing legacy of discontent" that was exported further west and north by Metis migrants leaving the Saskatchewan country. The necessity of a successful treaty in northern Alberta finally led the federal government to set out a blanket policy in respect to Metis claims. Unless they or their ancestors had already received it elsewhere, all Metis permanently residing in the treaty area in 1899 were allowed to receive scrip. As well, Metis born in the North-West Territories outside the boundaries of the original province of Manitoba between 1870 and 1885, and who had not received scrip elsewhere, were offered scrip.[24]

The scrip commissioners followed a few days or weeks behind the treaty party. Although scrip distribution at Grouard took over two weeks instead of the few days anticipated, the commissioners decided to keep to the schedule set by the treaty commissioners. Thus they visited "all the points advertised this year" because they feared that Indians might not sign the treaty if it became known that the Metis in northern Alberta "were not to be dealt with this year." Consequently, the commissioners were not able "to make as complete an examination of the squatters claims here [Grouard]" as they first intended, but by "working long hours and hard travelling," they believed they could "accomplish it and get out to Edmonton before winter sets in." Issuing scrip was time-consuming because each claim had to be verified. Charles Mair, one of the commission's two secretaries, wrote that there was "a never-ending stream of applicants, a surprising evidence of the growth of population in this remote wilderness." Each application was checked in "five elephant folios containing the records of the bygone issues of scrip in Manitoba and the organized Territories."[25]

There was no single reason why some people rejected treaty in favour of scrip. In some locations, identity and pride seem to have played a part. George Holmes noted that only a small number at Grouard accepted treaty, opting instead for scrip. "They regarded the term 'Indian Treaty' as much below their dignity," he wrote, "though they saw that the Treaty would be of the most practical and lasting benefit, both to themselves and their children. Pride of origin and not the future welfare of their families decided their choice."[26] Morris Zaslow also contends that many Metis in northern Alberta refused treaty because "of the stigma of inferiority they felt the Indian Act carried." But if Metis belief in their superiority sometimes accounted for their rejection of treaty, it was only one motivation among several. The Metis in northern Alberta were not a cohesive group and had different priorities depending on location and individual and community history. Given the restrictions that Indians then lived under on reserves, some Metis feared the loss of their independence if they took treaty. In yet other cases, they likely wanted the immediate cash that they could get by selling their scrip.[27]

Selling and buying scrip was a big business on the prairies in the late 1800s. Itinerant traders and scrip "hunters" followed the scrip commissioners, and like carpet baggers, moved through the north buying land and money scrip at greatly discounted prices. Chartered banks, lawyers and businessmen, among others, bought scrip in Western Canada, often making a career of it. In northern Alberta, the most important scrip hunters included Richard Secord of Edmonton and the Winnipeg bankers, Alloway and Champion. At Grouard, Alloway and Champion paid $75 for a $240 scrip note, but at Peace River, where competition was more intense, such scrip notes sold for $130. These prices were lower than those paid on the southern prairies during earlier scrip distributions. Thus, scrip in northern Alberta—as on the rest of the prairies—helped to enrich some of western Canada's leading families.[28]

By 1899, speculation had become an integral part of the working of the scrip system. In their history of Metis land rights in Alberta, Joe and Patricia Sawchuk and Theresa Ferguson observe that "speculation in Half-breed scrip was conducted with the government's knowledge and frequently with government assistance." Advertisements for scrip, "quoting the latest prices, were displayed in Dominion Land's offices," while the Department of the Interior ran "a banking service" that enabled scrip speculators "to apply their scrips as payment for land in the various Dominion Lands Agencies. Scrip could be deposited by the speculators and drawn upon when required for the payment of lands."[29] Nonetheless, the government theoretically tried to lessen speculation in some ways. Given past experience, it proposed restricting the transferability of money scrip in the case of adult Metis in northern Alberta. Additionally, it planned to make scrip issued to minors nonnegotiable until the child reached the age of majority. Father Lacombe at first vigorously supported this ruling and urged the Metis to accept these restrictions. The Metis refused to do so, arguing that their scrip had to be made payable to the bearer and that parents had to be able to "make use of their children's scrip for their benefit during their minority."[30]

While Lacombe's position was based upon experience and principle, the Metis received considerable support from other whites in opposing these restrictions. The scrip hunters flatly declared that they would not purchase such scrip except at an even greater discount. The scrip hunters had at least the virtue of honesty; other white participants deluded themselves by arguing that the Metis would not sell their children's scrip but, in contrast to earlier distributions of scrip in the West, would use it to become settled farmers, traders and ranchers. The Half-Breed Commissioners also used this argument, but admitted that "the strongest consideration" that prompted them to change the form of the money certificate

was the fact that if the wishes of the Half-breeds in this relation had not been complied with, the success of the Indian Treaty Commission in coming to terms with the Indian bands of the north would have been seriously compromised, as the dissatisfaction of the Half-breeds, who are in a great number of cases allied and in immediate touch with the Indians, would at once have spread amongst the latter and possibly prevented them from coming into treaty.

Thus, when the Metis opposition became clear, the Commissioners acquiesced almost immediately and persuaded Lacombe to support the change. Lacombe finally agreed that it was unlikely that the Metis in the north would be bilked as they had been on the prairies in 1870 and 1885. But Lacombe's fears were well founded. The scrip soon passed into the coffers of the traders and scrip hunters, and the cash went quickly. George Holmes noted in the autumn of 1899 that illegal importation and sale of liquor had skyrocketed "since the

Treaty" and drinking had "nearly emptied both Roman Catholic and Protestant churches alike. We were never so discouraged as now."[31]

The speculation surrounding this system was heightened because very few Metis in northern Alberta opted for land scrip. In the Treaty 8 area, 1,243 scrip notes were issued in 1899, of which 1,195 were money scrip (totalling $286,800) and 48 were land scrip (totalling 11,250 acres). A smaller number were also issued in 1900. Reflecting its place as a major Metis centre, about 47 percent of all money scrip and 68 percent of all land scrip issued in 1899 was in the Grouard area.[32] The tendency for Metis to favour money over land scrip was no doubt related to the greater complexity of selling land scrip. Additionally, while it could be applied to any available homestead land, such land was often in a different location than that in which the scrip holder lived. Moreover, few Metis were, or had a desire to become farmers, even if they had the capital.[33] Nonetheless, given the variations and complexities of northern Metis society, there were exceptions. It is evident that at Peace River (and probably at other points in northern Alberta as well), some Metis took advantage of broader land policies to obtain land. All squatters, whether Metis or white, who had settled and improved land before the signing of the treaty were given a free grant of the land, up to 160 acres. Title was issued when the land was surveyed, which at Peace River was almost a decade later. But squatters' rights were nonetheless recognized and protected, and among those claiming land under this system were a number of Metis who lived on the river bottoms.[34] For such individuals, it would have been advantageous to take money scrip in 1899 and sell it, and then obtain land under the free grant provisions.

The willingness to take money instead of land scrip was also encouraged by the Anglican missionaries at Grouard. While it probably had a minor effect on people's decisions, Anglican religious partisanship and a belief that the Roman Catholic church was conspiratorial and self-serving led George Holmes to endorse the taking of money scrip. As he wrote to Bishop Young, his opposition was only another skirmish in the great war with Catholicism:

> In connection with the Half breed Scrip, Pere LaCombe and his colleague had a great scheme that was of inducing the people here to take land instead of money scrip and to go out to Saddle Lake or some where near where Pere LaCombe had a large tract of country on which he hopes to settle Half breeds in order to keep them out of the way of Protestant contamination, and in the end, secure the land for the Church having the poor half breeds as their tenants. I did all in my power to warn the

people against being caught in this snare and, thank God, the whole scheme fell thru. I don't think they have succeeded in one single case. Since then Pere LaCombe and the priests here will not notice me in the road. The old gentleman was very genial before the treaty began, and they are all the same until you meet them on the battlefield.[35]

It has been held that illiteracy, unfamiliarity with English, fraud and other causes led the Metis to sell their scrip at greatly discounted prices to speculators. While fraud certainly existed, it should also be observed that for many Metis the practices of scrip speculators were hardly novel.[36] Since many northern Alberta Metis, especially in the Lesser Slave Lake area, had recently migrated from the Edmonton district, earlier scrip distributions in the North-West Territories must have been familiar, and the consequences of selling scrip at a discounted rate would not have been unknown. Whatever the case, because most Metis took money instead of land scrip, many were eventually socially and economically marginalised. The Euro-Canadian takeover of northern Alberta would make land a central pillar of political and social power, and in such an environment those who did not own land were powerless and vulnerable to economic change. As land was taken up for agricultural settlement, Metis in some parts of the north were deprived of hunting and trapping lands. The coming of the railway would also lead to a loss of freighting jobs, and many Metis would be pushed aside by white settlement. Customarily, Metis in such circumstances had moved to new locations. While some Metis did move further north after 1900, for most, the southern reaches of northern Alberta proved to be their last frontier. The Metis could not foresee the future, and for years many had moved steadily west and north to find new economic opportunities and to escape the changes and restrictions that had come with white settlement. Perhaps believing that there would be yet another frontier to move to, they may not have realized that this was the last one they would enjoy. Like characters in a drama by Chekhov, misfortune came from the intersection of class, history and circumstances beyond personal control.

**▬ Treaty 8**
The reasons why Natives finally agreed to Treaty 8 were varied and can probably now only be imperfectly understood. Generally, the pattern in northern Alberta resembled that seen elsewhere on the prairies where Indians seem to have assumed that the treaties would help them to meet changing conditions.

Moreover, the Crown's negotiators left the impression that the Indians were "getting something for nothing" and that the treaty would not threaten or impair their current social life and ways of making a living.[37] The legal text of the treaty itself is of minor significance in explaining this acceptance. As sociologist Richard Daniel notes, it was written in "legalistic language and presented to illiterate people unfamiliar with legal agreements based on written documents." Although the treaty was read and translated to the Indians, "this was only a small part of the exchange between the parties, not only during the treaty meetings, but in the months of preparation for those meetings." Thus, Daniel notes that one must look at "the entire negotiating process to determine the commitments made by both parties." These verbal promises and discussion are often called the "spirit" of the treaty.[38]

Of central significance in the negotiations were the promises that the Commissioners made and the appeal of their logic. Also significant was that each of the parties understood the agreement within their own context and priorities. This is not to suggest that each side heard only what it wanted to hear. The process was more complex because the needs and objectives of each party differed fundamentally in a number of important respects, leading each to their own interpretation of what had been negotiated. For its part, the Crown approached the treaty as a legal exercise. Following discussions, a binding agreement was signed. If disputes later arose about its meaning, reference would be made to the legal text or interpretation would be rendered by the courts. The government also assumed that white settlement, mining, lumbering and other activity would inevitably occur. This was not only a pragmatic understanding of the economy, but also reflected social Darwinist assumptions about "progress" and a belief that Euro-Canadian expansion was inevitable because of its supposed social and economic superiority.

How Natives saw this process is less clear, but there is evidence that they viewed the treaty as a friendship pact. Historian John Foster argues that this had its origins in the "partnering" between Natives and traders in the fur trade and that promises of protection, justice and friendship made during the treaty negotiations were seen by Natives as marking the beginning of a similar partnership. Certainly, the rituals of the treaty negotiations echoed the ceremonies of the fur trade where trade negotiations had been prefaced with smoking, eating and the firing of salutes to honour the leaders of the trading parties. These rituals had endured—although in diminished form—at least into the mid nineteenth century at Dunvegan, and presumably elsewhere in northern Alberta.[39] Similar rituals were used at the treaty negotiations; food and tobacco

*A decade after the signing of Treaty 8, Moostoos (left) and Kinoosayo (wearing his treaty medal) were still prominent Cree leaders. Photograph dated 1910.*
A7072 PAA.

were distributed and salutes were fired. As well, chiefs were singled out for higher annuities, medals and suits of clothing to show their rank and the special status ascribed to them by the Crown. Natives may have interpreted this as evidence that the treaty was a partnership similar to that experienced in the fur trade. In contrast, from the point of view of the treaty commissioners, these rituals were intended to impress the Natives with the majesty of the state.[40] Yet, Chief Commissioner Laird did characterize the treaty as a pledge of protection and friendship, and Indian oral history also clearly records that the Indians did not see it as a surrender of rights but as a treaty of peace, friendship and protection. Such objectives directly met Native concerns in districts that had already suffered from the depredations of Klondikers, white trappers and prospectors. Father Breynat also saw the treaty as "primarily a friendship Treaty,"[41] and Chief Commissioner Laird too described the treaty as bringing mutual obligations and the rule of law to guarantee peace and protection for Indians and whites alike; a relationship that the state pledged to mediate.[42]

Differing cultural assumptions in connection with land use and ownership also played a part in how Natives viewed the treaty. Before the treaty, "the Indians had no direct experience with land as a commodity to be bought and sold" or with a concept of land ownership that conferred rights on the owner to the exclusion of others. From the vantage point of Euro-Canadians, the text of Treaty 8 was clear—it asserted that the "Indians DO HEREBY CEDE, RELEASE, SURRENDER AND YIELD UP to the Government of the Dominion of Canada, for Her Majesty the Queen and her successors for ever, all their rights, titles and privileges whatsoever" in the lands dealt with by the treaty. Yet, some Natives, such as the Cree headman at Little Red River, had concerns about this right to "sell" the land. As he argued, he could not sell it since God alone owned it. Father Grouard persuaded him that the treaty payments were more in the nature of compensation for loss of exclusive use than a sale. As Richard Daniel notes, "Grouard attributed this 'case of conscience' to the man's recent acceptance of Christianity," but it more likely indicated "the difficulties the commissioners must have faced trying to explain what they meant by the surrender of land rights to a people for whom land had great religious significance, and little, if any, significance as a saleable commodity."[43]

While land ownership was the central justification for the treaty in the eyes of the government, Natives were more concerned with protecting their freedom of movement and their ability to hunt, trap and fish. In the matter of free movement, the Treaty Commissioners reported that negotiations would have collapsed "if we had not assured them that there was no intention of confining them to reserves. We had to very clearly explain to them that the provision for reserves and allotments of land were made for their protection, and to secure to them in perpetuity a fair portion of the land ceded, in the event of settlement advancing." While this suggested that the reserves were inviolable, in practical terms it established a new Euro-Canadian category of land tenure in northern Alberta that was part of the replacement of Aboriginal common use of land. As geographer Frank Tough notes, while this land classification provided Indians with some protection, it did not codify their use of other land. Reserve size was based on land then needed for an individual farm, not for trapping or other resource use. As such, it was poor compensation for the loss of systems of land use in which hunting territories had been restricted largely by tribal and social arrangements.[44]

With respect to the freedom to hunt, fish and trap, the text of the treaty provided that Indians would "have the right to pursue their usual vocations of hunting, trapping and fishing throughout the tract surrendered...subject to such regulations as may from time to time be made by the Government of the country...and saving and excepting such tracts as may be required or taken up from time to time for settlement, mining, trading or other purposes." While this affirmed the government's existing wildlife conservation programmes, it was also important because it allowed for the prohibition of Indian hunting, trapping and fishing on land subsequently alienated by the crown (as homesteads, for example) and because it asserted that all lands would be subject to game regulations. Initially, the Crown speciously argued that hunting rights would not be limited since there would be little or no white settlement. Of course, Natives did not accept this argument—by the Crown's own admission, one of the reasons for the treaty was to ensure peace between Natives and the whites who would soon be arriving in increasing numbers. Thus, when Natives continued to question the assurances that the government would not limit their freedom to hunt, trap and fish, the Commissioners argued that it was illogical for the government to provide ammunition and twine as part of the treaty if it intended to limit their traditional livelihood. The logic of this rebuttal was powerful. The treaty commissioners reported, with apparent pride in their cleverness, that the Indians "admitted that it would be unreasonable to furnish the means of hunting and fishing if laws were to be enacted which would make hunting and fishing so restricted as to render it impossible to make a livelihood by such pursuits." Yet, "over and above" this logic, the treaty commissioners still "had to solemnly assure them that only such laws as to hunting and fishing as were in the interest of the Indians and were found necessary in order to protect the fish and fur-bearing animals would be made, and that they would be as free to hunt and fish after the treaty as they would be if they never entered into it."[45]

These assurances were accepted by the Natives. The official report of the Treaty Commission carefully stipulated that the commissioners had stressed that the right to hunt, trap and fish was constrained by the need for wildlife regulation. Yet, the nuances of this qualification would have been lost among the bald statements that nothing would be done to restrict traditional livelihood and that people would be as free to hunt, trap and fish after the treaty as before it. Jim Cornwall, the Edmonton free trader and entrepreneur, stated in a 1937 affidavit that he had been present at the signing of the treaty at Grouard where "much stress was laid on one point by the Indians as follows: They would not sign under any circumstances, unless their right to hunt, trap and fish was guaranteed and it must be understood that these rights they would never surrender." Cornwall further recalled that the Commissioners admitted that Native arguments on this matter were "only fair and right but that they had no authority to write it into the Treaty." However, they made promises that "they felt sure" the Government would honour, pledging that "nothing would be allowed to interfere" with people's "traditional way of making a living." Only after the missionaries, Hudson's Bay Company and free traders "had given their word that they could rely fully" on these promises did the Indians agree to the treaty.[46]

As political scientists Richard Price and Shirleen Smith note, this evidence squares with the oral history handed down by elders that the commissioners "promised that only those regulations which would benefit conservation of game and fish would be introduced, and only for Indian benefit."[47] The key to this promise was, of course, who would define the "interest of the Indians" and what was meant by "hunting" and "fishing" in terms of wildlife conservation measures. For the Natives, this was almost wholly new territory. The treaty made no distinction between hunting and fishing for food or for trade, and this would become a major source of conflict in the future. The commissioners stated clearly that the treaty would not infringe people's economic life, and for northern Natives this meant that their right to hunt, trap and fish for trade, as well as for food, would not be limited. The treaty commissioners reinforced such assumptions by warning that Natives were expected to live as before the treaty and not on government handouts. As Richard Daniel has concluded, "there is every indication that commercial activities comprised such a large segment of the native economy that they would have refused to sign the Treaty had they been given any indication that they would be restricted to hunting, fishing and trapping for food" only. Yet it is apparent that the federal government has since the 1880s interpreted Aboriginal rights to hunt, trap and fish to include only food gathering and not commercial undertakings. This perspective may have been logical on the southern prairies where it was anticipated that Indians would take up farming and would hunt only to supplement their food supply. In many parts of northern Alberta where farming was impossible, however, the government had no reason to anticipate such a future. As geographer Arthur Ray has observed, it ignored "the Indians' historical circumstances. At the time the treaties were signed, the commercial and subsistence sectors of Indian hunting economies were interdependent."[48]

Other factors were also relevant in how Natives viewed the game conservation provisions of the treaty. On the positive side, efforts to suppress use of poison baits by the NWMP since Jarvis's patrol in 1897 had been welcomed, and in this instance people likely saw wildlife protection measures as benefiting and promoting their lifestyle.[49] Their only other experience with wildlife regulations had been with the prohibition of hunting wood buffalo in the Fort

Smith area. While Native reaction had been negative, the ban was geographically limited and was scheduled to expire in 1901. When the commissioners were at Fort Chipewyan, however, they received word that the ban on killing wood buffalo would be extended for another year. Commissioner McKenna noted that he and his colleagues did not "take the responsibility of telling the Indians that the prohibition was to be extended" because the news would guarantee the failure of the treaty negotiations at Forts Chipewyan and Smith. As McKenna noted, "the chief difficulty in dealing with the Indians in this country arose from the fact that they believed that the making of the treaty would lead to interference with their hunting upon which they must depend for a living." Noting that "we fear it is too late now to offer an opinion," all the commissioners agreed "that it would be better not to make the extension. There is very little in the talk about the public interest to be served by such a measure. It originates in the main with people who know nothing about local conditions." Indeed, McKenna argued that there "should be as little interference as possible with hunting and fishing" in order to preserve the Indians' economic independence and avoid future demands for government relief.[50]

An additional incentive for Indian agreement to the treaty was the promise that the government would provide medical assistance and care in times of need. Such pledges were especially persuasive at Fort Chipewyan where starvation had occurred in 1897 because of fur shortages. But Natives everywhere were concerned that they would receive assistance in times of distress (just as they had historically received it from fur traders). In their official report, the Commissioners stated that "we pointed out that the Government could not undertake to maintain the Indians in idleness," but that it would assist in times of need. Reinforcing the negotiators' contention that Native use of wildlife would not be limited, Laird argued that since "the same means of earning a livelihood would continue after the treaty as existed before it," Natives would only need relief in times of extreme want, and the government would "always" be ready to give assistance in such cases. Medicines and medical care as practicable were also promised.[51]

The acceptance of the treaty by Natives was also influenced by other interested but unofficial parties. The missionaries were at times significant players in persuading people to agree to the treaty, although their impact was not overwhelming. Certainly the Anglicans at Utikuma Lake were unable to persuade people there to take treaty rather than scrip. Nonetheless, the missionaries did exercise some influence and generally believed that the treaty would benefit the Natives. As Rene Fumoleau suggests in his history of Treaty 8, while the missionaries were "not naive enough to believe that the treaty would solve all of the Indians' problems," they hoped "that things would not get worse." Fumoleau further notes that in later years some missionaries, such as Constant Falher and Bishop Breynat, believed they had been manipulated and were "greatly disappointed to see that the Indians were not treated as well as had been promised."[52]

This reading of the missionaries' motives recognizes the sincerity with which most approached their role in the treaty negotiations. Although a number of promises made during the negotiations were later denied by the government, individuals like Bishop Breynat fought strenuously to force the government to honour its promises and meet its responsibilities. Yet the missionaries were not disinterested players in the negotiations. The Oblates had supported earlier treaties (such as Treaty 6) based on the belief that the treaties would promote their evangelization efforts by concentrating the Indian population on reserves and by making them sedentary and weaning them from hunting.[53] Similar anticipations influenced Oblate support for Treaty 8, and Father Lacombe characterized the treaty as a means for church and state to work together to "open officially this great Northern district to civilization and to brotherly relations and harmony between the white man and the Indian."[54] Bishop Grouard later recalled that he had been worried about the future of the missions if a treaty was signed because the government would begin to meddle in matters that the church had previously worked out alone. Thus, he saw Lacombe's nomination as the Commission's advisor as a sign of friendliness by the government towards the Roman Catholic church.[55] Of most direct and immediate importance was the future of the mission schools. The squabbling between Anglicans and Catholics during the negotiations at Grouard was intensified because each knew that after the treaty the federal government would pay school grants only for treaty children. Schools in areas where most of the children's parents took scrip instead of treaty would earn no grants, which naturally predisposed missionaries to see treaty, rather than scrip, in a positive light. George Holmes frankly told Bishop Young that the "most serious and discouraging point" in the crisis over the treaty was that most of the parents of children in the Anglican boarding school either refused treaty and took scrip, or did neither. As a result,

> we shall, with the exception of about 6 children, be deprived of the Government support grant. If we are to take in the same number of boarders, it means that we must turn adrift nearly all our present

number as boarders and endeavour to make up the number from the treaty end of the Lake. But what will our own people think of this? Especially those who have so recently joined us from the R.C. church. I shall have to tell them that they are responsible for the support of their own children but I fear they will never understand it.[56]

Holmes's recognition that government grants would be paid only for treaty children was one of the most immediate and telling indications of the way that Indians and Metis would henceforth be differentiated in the north. Rene Fumoleau charges that Metis scrip and Indian Treaty effectively divided "the native people into two groups, Treaty and non-Treaty Indians."[57] This may be accurate in many instances, but not in all. Some Metis, especially in the Lesser Slave Lake and Peace River districts, appear to have refused treaty out of a sense of superiority over Indians, which indicates that the treaty alone did not destroy an earlier, pristine unity in northern Alberta. Nonetheless, the resulting legal distinction between status and nonstatus people created a framework that brought future difficulties because Indians and Metis often continued to follow the same way of life but now had different relationships with the state. This would become important, for example, with respect to hunting rights and schooling, among other matters. The reserve system also effectively removed "Indians" from society by segregating them in particular locations where they were subjected to government controls not applied to other Natives.

Such matters were not apparent to many Natives at the time of the treaty. They did not appreciate the future implications of the region's integration with Canada because their experience was highly localized. The observation by anthropologists Trudy Nicks and Kenneth Morgan that elderly informants among Grande Cache Metis in the 1970s, "though quite conscious of the racial diversity of their background, generally did not dwell on the question of their identity vis-a-vis the outside world" applies equally well to conditions in northern Alberta in the 1890s. And as interviews with elders in the "isolated districts" north of Wabasca reveal, people tended to identify with "the community of his birth and other community members," even though everyone was "aware of who has Indian Status (as defined in the Indian Act) and who does not."[58] Nonetheless, in 1899 many people wanted to be recognized either as Metis or Indian, and to receive either scrip or treaty. This preference had a long history on the prairies, and by 1899 it was too late for the state to take a different course even had it wanted to. The Euro-Canadian population seems not to have cared which route was taken, as long as claims were settled so that development could proceed. But the treaty was a part of significant change. As George Holmes wrote from Grouard in late 1899, "it is hard to realize that we are living in the same place and amongst the same people" as three years earlier. The changes, he reflected, were "sufficient to make the strongest stagger."[59]

# PART II

*These well dressed people at Grouard were celebrating Dominion Day in 1907.*
A2321 PAA.

# Transitions
## *1900–1920*

# A Foundation for

## 4 Development

*The State and Northern Alberta, 1900–1915*

TREATY 8 PAVED THE WAY for Euro-Canadian expansion in northern Alberta. In the next 15 years, the federal and provincial governments built upon this base to promote white settlement and control of northern Alberta. By 1915 the federal and Alberta governments had created institutional and legal infrastructure in northern Alberta to assist economic growth, integration with the rest of Canada, and the implanting of Euro-Canadian society. The federal government implemented policies to facilitate the efficient distribution of land, created structures to enforce social order through civil and criminal administration, and encouraged scientific and geographical research about northern resources and conditions. After 1905, when most of the old District of Athabaska was incorporated into the new province of Alberta, the Alberta government made similar contributions to development by building roads, assisting railway construction and supporting the creation of local government and civic services. Although the provincial and federal governments disagreed about aspects of Indian hunting rights, both officially endorsed individualism as a social and economic ideal. Accordingly, they created conditions through regulation that favoured the private use of timber, fish and other resources in place of Aboriginal common use practices.

The Canadian tendency to use the state to lead and accommodate the territorial expansion of the nation was apparent in northern Alberta. While the federal government remained the primary agency for national expansion, after 1905 the province of Alberta acted as a supplementary, and sometimes even the

77

primary, vehicle for such expansion. While both federal and provincial governments espoused the view that private interests should take the risks and reap the benefits of investment, frontier economic development necessitated a broader and more complex approach. State policies met needs relative to time and place, the priorities of the governments of the day and the expected benefits, both in national and private terms. While the federal government was willing to make limited investment in transportation infrastructure in northern Alberta, the provincial government's road building programmes and subsidies for railway construction showed a stronger and more active commitment. Private interests, such as political parties, churches, farmers seeking land and business and industrial interests, acted in conjunction with both levels of government to rationalize and realize political, economic and social objectives. This interdependence of public policy and private interest was manifested in many ways, including political pressure, private initiatives and connections, and shared values and ideals. Consequently, development policies in northern Alberta did not reflect a single vision or objective, nor did they necessarily lead or follow development. While they generally aimed to sustain capitalist development and create conditions favouring the private accumulation of capital, state policies and programmes also expressed more independent concerns about national and provincial life and destiny and about community and morality.[1]

Capitalism was not, in any case, just a matter of developing appropriate economic structures; it was also an assertion of particular cultural values. Underlying and reinforcing the creed of private investment was a belief that people were by nature economic creatures who pursued and accumulated capital and possessions out of self-interest. In some respects, these beliefs challenged the attitudes of Natives in northern Alberta, whose civilization did not accept so uncritically that an individual's accumulation of capital or the pursuit of wealth was a "natural" or inevitable state of affairs. But since free will was integral to the theory that people naturally pursued wealth, those who did not show a commitment to capital accumulation, especially Natives, were accused by the dominant culture of wilful laziness, indolence and inertia. This tone was set from an early point. While Inspector Jarvis of the NWMP remarked in 1897 "that the farther north I went the better off I found the Indians, particularly in dress," he was generally critical of their lack of worldliness and acquisitiveness for material things. As he remarked at Fort Smith, the Natives there had "no ambition and little knowledge of the outer world, and as long as they have enough to fill themselves they are happy." Without power or influence to counter the hegemony of free market ideology, however, Natives would soon find themselves marginalised. In any society dominated by a belief in the market system, as economist Robert Wright phrased it, "everyone must become materialistic if only to reduce one's vulnerability to aggression by others. The market *makes* people self-centred."[2]

These assumptions were applied in northern Alberta against a backdrop of exaggerated anticipations throughout Canada about the wealth of natural resources that could be exploited everywhere in the nation's northland. Before World War I, there was much excitement among business interests about northern riches, especially agricultural, timber and mineral resources in northern Ontario and Quebec. Northern mineral deposits tantalized many in Ontario, and the exploitation of the nickel resources at Sudbury after the late 1880s and the development of Sault Ste. Marie as a pulp and industrial centre by the late 1890s provided solid evidence of the wealth that could be had in the north. This was intensified by the discovery of extremely rich and accessible silver deposits at Cobalt after 1904–05 and the beginning of Ontario's support for northern railway development. Farming in northern Ontario was seen to have a great future and while some settlement took place in the Clay Belt in the 1890s, it only began in earnest with the arrival of the first train at Cochrane in 1908. This settlement was accompanied by exaggerated estimates of the district's potential and by provincial government programmes to encourage the development of a "new Ontario" in the north.[3]

In prairie Canada, the greatest attention was focussed on northern Alberta where extensive arable land offered an irresistible draw and timber and mineral resources provided additional attractions. As the historical route to the Mackenzie valley and the western Arctic, northern Alberta held additional allure for expansionists. In contrast, development pressure remained less intense in northern Saskatchewan where mineral and agricultural resources did not attract widespread attention until the end of World War I. Northern Manitoba also failed to attract significant attention before 1914. The boundaries of the province were only extended to the 60th parallel in 1912, and while fish and timber resources in the interlake district provided a field of opportunity for Euro-Canadians, more remote areas remained less well known. Only the discovery of minerals at Flin Flon in 1915 marked the beginning of industrial expansion that would take place in northern Manitoba after 1930.[4]

In Alberta, as elsewhere in Canada, it was assumed that northern development would bring the replacement of the existing economy with one more in tune with Euro-Canadian precedents and interests. While the fur trade had never been separate from Euro-Canadian economic interests, in areas with agricultural, mineral or forestry potential, it was assumed that the fur trade would give way to activities more in keeping with the modern financial and technological systems that served the expanding ambitions of Canadian business. This was commonly believed to be a mark of "progress." Canada's willingness to sign a treaty in 1899 (one was not signed in the Mackenzie Valley of the North-West Territories for another two decades) reflected this early assumption about northern Alberta's potential. But expansionary rhetoric and the programmes and policies it brought primarily asserted the needs and rights of Euro-Canadians, leaving Natives with only diminished economic influence and minimal capability to influence the development of the region.

Native society was increasingly challenged, most directly in the Lesser Slave Lake district and the Peace River country, by the arrival of Euro-Canadian settlers. The region's potential to offer a better material and social life drew these settlers, but their migration was also prompted by the view that northern Alberta was a part of Euro-Canadian destiny. In this connection, its climate was said to be ideal for Euro-Canadians. The Rev. J.A. Ouellette, a promoter of French Canadian settlement, claimed in 1909 that many illnesses were cured or relieved by northern Alberta's climate. Similarly, the Grande Prairie newspaper editorialized in 1913 that local people were healthier than most; in part because "only the more rugged seek this distant country," but health and longevity were also preserved by the "health-giving qualities" of the climate. As the editorial concluded, "we have the finest climate for health."[5]

Such idealization of northern climes had been voiced since the early fur trade, but theories linking race, climate and national character became increasingly common in early twentieth century Canadian nationalist thinking.[6] The naturalist and author, Ernest Thompson Seton, described the Peace River country in 1912 as "a white man's climate, one of the most salubrious in the world, and all that its detractors can say is—it is too far north, it is too cold." But this related precisely to the question, "what is the ultimate race of the region to be?" For Seton, it was clear:

There is a zoological maxim that suggests the answer: An animal finds its highest development in the coldest part of its range where its food is abundant. How true this is of mankind…the dwarf races the world over are from the tropics, where they are overhot, or the poles, where they are underfed. The highest product of civilisation we believe to have been the white man of northern Europe—a product indeed of the snow. This should help us forecast the future of the north.[7]

Such notions were endorsed by early settlers and promoters, many of whom believed that development would only proceed when northern Alberta was settled by people of European ancestry, especially those from northern Europe. Fred Lawrence, the son of the Anglican missionary at Fort Vermilion and a local farmer-businessman and promoter, argued in 1907 that many people had long assumed that northern Alberta was "a wilderness, a country entirely unsuited for settlement, suitable only for Indians." Revealing an assumption that "civilization" and cereal cropping were connected, Lawrence claimed that the region's suitability for wheat proved that it was not a "wilderness" but "a fine country for white people to live in." It was popular to contend that the obstacles settlers faced on northern homesteads guaranteed a rugged class of people. As one Methodist minister remarked in 1910, "hundreds of people have started for this country [the Grande Prairie] but never reached their destination. They have 'taken cold feet' and turned back." As a result, those who reached their goal were "very superior." Moreover, it was popularly recognized that the alterations to the landscape that this vanguard would bring would change the region forever. Tillage—one of the central definitions of "civilization" according to Euro-Canadian thinking—would moderate the climate because clearing trees and breaking the land would allow the soil to absorb and retain more heat from the sun. For one, Ernest Thompson Seton asserted that southern Ontario and Manitoba had proven that "in all wheat countries, summer frost has fled before the plough, and it would similarly raise "the summer temperature" of the Peace River country, "this new Land of Promise."[8]

Such assumptions about climate and race did not encourage Euro-Canadian settlers to develop ties with the Native people in the region. The fur trade had found such relationships logical and useful, and white settlers in the late nineteenth century had not been isolated from the Native population. In the early twentieth century, however, white agriculturalists were increasingly self-reliant and many neither wanted nor needed ongoing contact with Natives. The creation of a new economy and landscape in which people could prosper with little reference to indigenous traditions and people marked a changing dynamic in the social and economic marginalising of the Native population in the Lesser

Slave Lake and Peace River areas. Views such as those of George Bredin, the first white settler on the Grande Prairie, were becoming typical. When asking A.M. Bezanson in 1907 to find him a wife in the south, Bredin added that he did not "mean a squaw either."[9]

Attitudes such as these indicated that firmer racial boundaries were emerging as part of the Euro-Canadian agricultural settlement of the Peace River country. Indeed, some saw this racial exclusivity and lack of integration as a mark of the region's "progress." The travel writer, Agnes Deans Cameron, made reference to a range of contemporary assumptions about race and culture in her 1910 book about her northern journeys. After travelling on the Athabasca and Mackenzie rivers, she noted that Fort Vermilion had a familiar and welcome difference:

> Here, in a nutshell, you have the difference between the Mackenzie River today and the Peace River. On the Mackenzie, swarthy forms are in evidence, Cree and French is [sic] spoken on all sides, there are no great fields of waving grain and the dog is the only domestic animal. On the Peace is an essentially white race, cows, chickens, trustworthy old nags, porridge for breakfast [and] "the tongue that Shakespeare spake."

While Cameron must have been thinking of the Athabasca River where Cree was more widely spoken than along the Mackenzie, her list of virtues and comforts and her admiration of a pastoral life indicated contemporary assumptions and biases in the English-speaking world. And she assumed that history was on her side—what she found appealing and comforting she believed would soon be replicated in the rest of the Peace River country.[10]

## ▬ The State and Northern Development

While the rhetoric of development often became entangled in assertions of Euro-Canadian racial superiority, the approach and language of capitalist development in northern Alberta took more direct reference from a "booster" attitude that saw economic growth as an end in itself and as a mark of social progress. Consequently, the development framework applied in northern Alberta did not build on unique policies or special approaches to suit the region's geography, history or indigenous traditions. Instead, the formal techniques used to regulate the use of natural resources, encourage railway construction and guide white settlement and other economic development were indistinguishable from those used elsewhere in western Canada. While this faith in existing methods in part indicated a failure of imagination, it also revealed that the ideology and preoccupations of many Canadians led them to view the north as no different than any other part of the country. Buttressed by their beliefs about the sources of economic growth and their confidence in their ability as colonisers, public and private interests eager to participate in the development of northern Alberta felt assured that they had the necessary tools to assert their values and aspirations.

While the creation of this infrastructure for a new society in northern Alberta was a complex process involving both private and public participation, state activity was at first of central importance. Because the territorial government's restricted jurisdiction and resources gave it little scope to promote northern development, such initiatives rested mainly with the federal government until the creation of the province of Alberta in 1905. The most important federal department in this respect was the Department of the Interior that was responsible for public lands, natural resources, land surveys and Indian affairs.

Federal policies responded to both political priorities and departmental objectives, although the two were not always in agreement. Boosterism often pervaded federal political attitudes towards northern development. As historian David Leonard has noted, while debate continued about the sort of development that was possible, promotional rhetoric that characterized the Peace River country as North America's "last great west" and lauded the economic potential of other parts of northern Alberta had received extensive national coverage by 1910.[11] Such views were reflected in the political arena. Frank Oliver continued to agitate for northern development, first from his vantage point as the Member of Parliament for Edmonton (a riding that included the Peace River country) and after 1905 as Minister of the Interior. Oliver assumed that the federal government and its employees should uncritically support northern development—especially the settlement of the Peace River country—and he became vitriolic when anyone disagreed. In 1903, James Macoun, a Geological Survey of Canada naturalist, made a three-month reconnaissance of the Peace River country. In a report published by the Geological Survey, Macoun argued that existing (and largely positive) evidence about the Peace River country's agricultural potential was based largely on surveys of river bottom lands. He surmised, however, that the more extensive uplands were less promising, and he questioned the wheat growing capacity of the region. While Macoun admitted that agriculture could be carried on, he argued that the Peace River country would never become a wealthy farm community because its cold climate and poorer soils ensured that it would always be "a poor man's country."[12]

These statements and their publication by a government agency would resonate for decades in northern Alberta. William Pearce, who worked in the CPR's land department and who had earlier surveyed parts of the Peace River country in his former role as a federal government surveyor, told a correspondent that Macoun's report, as well as other unnamed reports, had been "suppressed" because of their negative views. Pearce did not favour immediate settlement of the Peace River country, and he noted that "while I do not go as far as Macoun, I think he was more nearly correct than most people who have reported on that northern country." But Frank Oliver was outraged and responded with a campaign against Macoun in the pages of the Edmonton Bulletin, on the floor of the House of Commons and in the Commons' Select Committee on Agriculture and Colonization. Oliver impugned Macoun's competence and professional judgement and attacked his employer, the Geological Survey. It was a pattern familiar since the late nineteenth century in which the survey was periodically assailed by politicians and business leaders for being more concerned with science than with the "practical" exploration and promotion of Canada's resources. As historian Bill Waiser comments, these critics demanded that the Geological Survey "provide positive, practical information of immediate economic value."[13]

More in tune with Frank Oliver's thinking, Senator Davis, a Liberal from Prince Albert, Saskatchewan, spearheaded the formation in 1907 of a Senate Select Committee to hold hearings on northern resources. By 1905, officials in the Department of the Interior were beginning to worry that insufficient land remained on the southern prairies for homesteading. They concluded that more northerly lands would have to be opened for settlement. Davis believed that the Senate committee should follow up these conclusions as well as to try and correct "the black eye" that James Macoun had given the Peace River country three years earlier. Further, he hoped that the Committee would update the findings of the 1888 Senate inquiry, which, he contended, had done "a great deal of good" in promoting northern development. Yet Davis's attempt to invigorate and expand support for northern development was more than mere propaganda. It constituted a significant effort by a high-ranking political figure to promote northern development by increasing Euro-Canadian knowledge about the north. In 1907, as with the 1888 Senate inquiry, a central concern was to determine the nature and extent of resources that could be developed.

And as a resource hinterland, an integral part of this concern was to determine how northern Canada's geography would influence the transportation facilities needed to export a range of resources and import consumer goods. As Davis asserted, expanded knowledge and interest about the north would lead to investment, without which "the natural wealth of the country will be of no use."[14]

Under pressure from non-Western Senators, the Senate committee looked into conditions in Ungava, but it was primarily concerned with northern Saskatchewan, the Mackenzie basin and the navigability of Hudson's Bay. To publicize its findings, the Senate published a promotional booklet, *Canada's Fertile Northland*. It consisted of transcripts of some of the hearings that featured well known and colourful northern promoters and adventurers. Its preface endorsed the view, first given political expression by Senator Schultz in 1888, that the Mackenzie basin would soon experience a settlement boom similar to the one then occurring on the prairies. The booklet received extensive newspaper coverage and it was reissued in 1910, under a new title, *The New Northwest: Canada's Fertile Northland*.[15] This change was perhaps an effort to qualify the "northerness" of the Mackenzie basin in the public mind by implying that the history of the "old" northwest (that is, the southern prairies) was about to be replayed in northern Canada, especially northern Alberta. In other words, northern Alberta soon would no longer be a northern place, but one filled with farms, cities and industry.

The 1907 Senate inquiry demonstrated one dimension of the federal government's response to demands for northern development and the expanding opportunities it offered. More direct federal government support came from the creation of infrastructure to assist the development of Euro-Canadian society in the north. The establishment of permanent NWMP detachments after 1897 and the signing of Treaty 8 in 1899 had been preliminary steps in this process, and in 1900 the North-West Territories government appointed Justices of the Peace in the major settlements in the District of Athabaska.[16] Canadian commercial, property and criminal law shaped and structured the new society that was emerging and introduced and sustained new social and economic structures in the north. Although control of the Native population was an important aspect of NWMP activity, of greater significance was the creation of a climate of orderliness in which development could proceed.[17] While earlier detachments had been placed to protect trade, the new ones were located in areas of greatest potential for settlement and in those important for communication with these districts. By 1915, the NWMP had nine detachments in the Peace River country, five in the Athabasca-Grouard corridor, but only four—at Fort McMurray, Fitzgerald, Fort Chipewyan and Fort Resolution—along the lower Athabasca and Slave rivers.[18]

In addition to the significant role that they played in the direct control of the region, the police also promoted and encouraged economic development and white settlement. Since the 1890s, NWMP *Annual Reports* had provided extensive information about northern Alberta, but after about 1904 they became overtly promotional, a pattern that endured until 1917 when the Alberta government established its own police force, the Alberta Provincial Police (APP).[19] Typically, NWMP reports featured claims that modern transportation and communications networks would reinforce the accumulation of private property and the expression of self-initiative. As the NWMP Superintendent at Grouard reported in 1905, "I know of one Swede who came in here a few years ago without a cent, who now has $2,500 in the bank, besides stock etc." This had been earned with "hard work" and frugality, and "others can do the same." In another typical comment, Superintendent G.E. Sanders explicitly promoted northern development when he noted in 1910 that northern Alberta was "fast emerging from a little known country" dominated by the fur trade to one of "great importance" because of its good farm land, mineral resources and "great possibilities as regards water power." Once rail connections were established, he believed this economic potential would be realized.[20]

Such promotional efforts indicate an assumption that northern development was part of the mandate of the NWMP. Other federal government agencies and departments were also significant in this process. The Dominion Experimental Farms established a substation at Fort Vermilion in 1908 to keep meteorological records and test varieties of wheat, forage crops, vegetables and fruit trees for their suitability in northern areas. By 1914, similar experiments were underway at other points, including seed tests on behalf of the Dominion Experimental Farms by Donald Albright on his farm near Beaverlodge. As well, the surveyor's field notes and reports that were frequently published in the annual reports of the Department of the Interior provided the public with information and findings about climate, soils and the economic potential of farm land and mineral deposits. As the deputy minister of the Department of the Interior remarked in 1915, such promotion of knowledge about northern resources and conditions would help stimulate northern development.[21]

Such government activity did not occur in isolation. While the state sometimes initiated development, it also responded to public and private pressure.

This was especially clear in respect to farm settlement. While it represented deeply held social values and beliefs about character, initiative and national destiny, homesteading was also underpinned by the view that public land was a subsidy for the private accumulation of wealth and the stimulation of general economic growth. In the early 1900s, the federal government remained content to postpone the settlement of the Peace River country until suitable transportation facilities were in place and land in "older districts" elsewhere on the prairies had been taken up for farming. But even though Euro-Canadian settlement in the Peace River country was then very limited, the Dominion Lands Agent at Edmonton noted in 1904–05 that public inquiries were increasing so quickly that the territory "should be surveyed into townships as soon as possible." While base lines had been surveyed in the Peace River country in the 1880s, township surveys only began in 1905 and surveys of quarter sections in 1909. By 1912 large portions of the arable land in the Peace River country (including some areas around Fort Vermilion) had been surveyed. Ottawa's retreat after 1905 from its earlier reluctance to facilitate farm settlement in the Peace River country was part of the department's concern about the need to open new areas for homesteading. This also matched the thinking of Frank Oliver, the new minister of the Interior, and the general upswing in optimism about northern settlement and resources among potential homesteaders and commercial groups in Edmonton and other western cities.[22]

Land surveys were an essential step in economic development on the prairies. Indian reserves could then be set aside to free all other land for homesteading. In addition, settlers who had squatted on land could usually obtain legal title following formal survey of the land. And once surveying was completed, further development was encouraged in northern Alberta by establishing local land offices to relieve homesteaders of the long and costly trip to Edmonton to register their holdings.[23] Partly because of public pressure, land offices had been opened in Grouard, Grande Prairie and Peace River by 1915. By World War I, the Department of the Interior was fully involved in promoting the Peace River country to settlers. It distributed information about soils, climate and communications, and maintained immigration halls that provided free short-term accommodation to newly arrived settlers. When immigration was transferred from the Department of the Interior to the new Department of Immigration and Colonization in 1917, many immigration halls were closed, with the exception of those in "unsettled districts," which in Alberta included those in Edmonton, Athabasca and five towns in the Peace River country.[24]

State provision of communications networks also furthered development and the integration of northern Alberta into Canadian society and the national economy. While the NWMP continued to deliver mail in isolated areas, Athabasca gained regular mail service in 1901, and by 1908 a year-round monthly mail service was extended to most settlements in the Peace River country. In contrast, Fort Chipewyan, Fort Smith and Fitzgerald received only two or three mail deliveries by steamer in summer and three in winter by dog team from Lac La Biche or Athabasca. Telegraph service also expanded. In 1904 a government telegraph line was built to Athabasca from Edmonton and was extended to Lesser Slave Lake in 1909. By World War I, it had reached the main settlements in the Peace River country, while another line reached Fort McMurray in 1915.[25]

## ▬ The Province of Alberta and Northern Development

While federal politicians and government departments were actively promoting northern development, a new force emerged in 1905 with the creation of the province of Alberta. Considerable support had grown in Calgary and southern Alberta for the division of the North-West Territories into two strong provinces, each of which could then act as a powerful lever to promote economic growth within its territory.[26] In a similar vein, David Leonard argues that the creation in 1905 of two northern Alberta provincial ridings ("Athabaska" and "Peace River") gave promoters a new and influential public platform and the chance to marshal the resources of the provincial government for northern development. Indeed, regardless of party affiliation, the most clearly shared characteristic of northern Alberta's Members of the Legislative Assembly (MLAs) was their commitment to economic growth. Although there was some debate about the extent or economic potential of particular resources, all agreed that railways and Euro-Canadian settlement were essential for the development of northern resources. Most had lived at least intermittently in northern Alberta and had commercial interests there, and all recognized the usefulness of the state for promoting northern development. Alie Brick, the first MLA for the Peace River constituency and a resident of the Shaftesbury settlement, eagerly supported northern economic development and repeatedly drew attention to his riding's resources in the legislature. One of his pet concerns was to have the Vermilion Chutes cleared for navigation, but he also acted as "an advisor on the prospects of the Peace Country."[27]

*Jim Cornwall was nicknamed Peace River Jim for his commitment to northern development.*
GAI–NA969–2.

Brick's northern counterpart in the assembly, Fletcher Bredin, was elected by acclamation as the first MLA for the riding of Athabaska. Bredin was born in Ontario and had moved west to find new opportunities. In the late 1890s he had various business interests in northern Alberta, including a fur trade company at Athabasca in partnership with Jim Cornwall. Typical of Bredin's views was his testimony at the 1907 Senate inquiry that northern Alberta was "as good a place for a man to settle in as the Saskatchewan valley was 25 years ago" and that its climate was "no worse" than that of Manitoba and Saskatchewan. In 1909, Bredin was defeated by Jean Coté, a Dominion Land Surveyor from Athabasca. Coté too saw his role in the legislature as a promoter of northern resource development, especially petroleum resources in the Fort McMurray area. When named minister of Mines and Railways in 1918, he encouraged the creation of the Scientific and Industrial Research Council of Alberta to expand scientific knowledge and enable the development of northern Alberta's petroleum, salt and other mineral resources. Another MLA, William Rae, represented the Peace River constituency from 1917 to 1921. Rae had been one of the founders of the town of Grande Prairie and secretary of the company that developed it. As his obituary in 1943 stated, he was "always a believer in the future of the Peace River country" and had "worked tirelessly to promote its development."[28]

Of these MLAs, the most influential was Jim Cornwall. Born in Ontario in 1869, Cornwall arrived in Alberta in 1893. He was a river pilot on the Athabasca River for a time, and, in addition to his fur trading business with Fletcher Bredin, he continually created and sold businesses from his headquarters in Edmonton. A member of Alberta's entrepreneurial class, Cornwall was involved in a number of ventures in northern Alberta, one of the most important being his partnership in the Northern Transportation Company, a river boat company founded in 1904 in Athabasca. In 1905, he stood for election in the Peace River constituency. He was defeated by Alie Brick, but won by acclamation when he ran again in 1909.[29]

Reflecting his promotional activities, Cornwall was nicknamed "Peace River Jim." He has been referred to as the "empire builder of the north," who made "a tangible contribution to the northland, and people loved him for it." Historian J.G. McGregor provides a more balanced portrait in his observation that Cornwall was "probably the greatest booster the North, and particularly the Peace River country, ever had. A man of tremendous talents and a flare for salesmanship, he aroused mixed feelings in his contemporaries, many regarded him as a sham, but the majority fell under his spell." Like his political colleagues and rivals, Cornwall's primary concern during his tenure as MLA from 1909 to 1913 was northern development, but unlike many others, he had a measure of sympathy, even empathy, with Native northerners. His promotional efforts included tours of Canada, so he could speak to boards of trade and Canadian clubs about northern Alberta. In 1910, he also organized a month long promotional junket to the Peace River country for United States and Canadian journalists.[30]

Despite the efforts of political figures like Cornwall, the province's role in northern development was constrained before 1930 by federal control of public lands and natural resources. Even so, this did not prevent Alberta from colonizing its northern territories, and Edmonton initially had few substantive quarrels over the direction of federal resource policies in northern Alberta. In 1905, with Liberals in power in both Edmonton and Ottawa, partisanship mitigated federal-provincial conflict. One of the first departures from this accommodation came in 1910 when A. Bramley Moore (an Edmonton MLA) made a motion in the provincial assembly that Alberta should seek control of its natural resources. Seconded by Jim Cornwall, the motion received unanimous support but was withdrawn when the government revealed a plan to make representation to Ottawa on the subject.[31] The province, in any event, was then fully occupied, given its limited resources and nascent administrative ability, with matters already within its jurisdiction.

One such concern was road construction. Federal and territorial efforts in this respect had been limited, and the province too made a slow start. As was noted in Grouard in 1906, "with the exception of a few grants of money to be spent on the roads," and a ferry at Peace River, "we hear but little of the provincial government." Nonetheless, these grants indicated the province's interest, and while trails remained in poor condition and bridges and other infrastructure were, as it was phrased in 1907, "picturesque in their decay," trails such as the one between Grouard and Peace River were gradually improved. The province also built a winter trail west of Athabasca, although it was little used because freighters preferred to travel on the ice rather than along bush trails. More ambitious undertakings were also planned and implemented. In 1909 the province installed ferries at Dunvegan and Peace River, and between 1912 and 1916 it built roads in the south Peace River country to connect growing settlements.[32] In 1910 it announced plans to build a trail between Athabasca and Fort Vermilion. Given the optimism that then imbued most pronouncements about northern development, it was said to be "remarkable" that such a road had not been built "years ago." What was truly remarkable was that such a trail was even proposed, given the difficulties its construction and upkeep promised. More sober counsel apparently prevailed, and the province instead undertook a somewhat more modest road between Peace River and Fort Vermilion, and by 1915 a trail had been cut out as far as Keg River. Local governments too were responsible for roads, and in late 1912 two rural municipalities were formed by settlers in the Grande Prairie area to provide for local needs. While concerned with a number of local government issues, both gave primary attention to building local roads and bridges that connected with the more extensive road system gradually being built by the provincial government.[33]

—— Railways
*Alberta's Northern Policy*
Although some Euro-Canadian settlement took place before the arrival of the railway, extensive farm settlement in northern Alberta—as elsewhere on the

prairies—was viable only with rail connections. Defined by a commitment to progress and economic growth, railway construction was a central element in creating the framework for modern industrial capitalism. In northern Alberta, railways directed change by permitting economic activity that was difficult or impossible to carry out when only using steamboats and trails. Railways also helped to bias the economy in certain directions, such as towards the export of low value, bulky products like grain, lumber and fish. The function of railways in integrating outlying areas into the national economy was particularly important for the Peace River country which lay so far from other areas of continuous farm settlement. Thus, railways quickly became the central plank of Alberta's northern development policies. By 1910, promotional rhetoric had created a general perception that the only impediment to the migration of great numbers of settlers to the Peace River country was the lack of rail connections. Even though future benefits could not be estimated precisely, faith was firm in the elasticity and self-perpetuating quality of the market economy. The northern real estate promoter, A.M. Bezanson, recalled that sceptics commonly asked how settlers in the Peace River country would find a market for their produce before a railway came. His reply was disarmingly simple: "the first settlers will sell to new arrivals, [and] on and on as long as new arrivals keep coming in appreciable numbers. Some railway company will take notice by that time and build in."[34]

Despite Bezanson's faith, private railway construction was not so simply driven by demand. Railways were profit-making ventures involving private capital, and while the needs of pioneers had strong emotional appeal in Canada, those of a few settlers were never sufficient to shape railway policy. Instead, the primary contribution advance settlers made to the construction of a railway was to demonstrate an area's potential for future traffic. Even then, the whole system was financially tenuous. While the high capitalization of railways could be supported in densely populated regions with high value production (such as parts of eastern North America and western Europe), it was difficult to attract capital for railways in areas such as northern Alberta where future production was unproven or would involve low-value products like wheat. Consequently, railway construction depended on state support, and in Canada, an alliance between the state and railway developers had a long history. The railway that opened the prairies to white settlement had been built only with massive public financial support, and most observers recognized that this would also be necessary in northern Alberta. Railways in Canada had often found such support through grants of public land or cash, but government guarantees of railway company debt were also common. The latter approach nicely met prairie conditions, where newly established provincial governments had neither cash nor public lands with which to subsidize construction.

Despite considerable public cynicism about the motives of railway promoters and their political allies, railways were the object of collective desire in Canada. After 1900 the country became drunk on forecasts of the economic growth that railway construction would bring. The creation of the province of Alberta in 1905 thus occurred at a juncture when the public mood strongly supported railway development. In the early 1900s, planning for the Grand Trunk Pacific (GTP) had foreseen a line through Edmonton to the Peace River country and then through the mountains to a terminus on the north Pacific coast. The Canadian Northern Railway (CNoR) also planned a branch line from Edmonton to the Grande Prairie district. When it was apparent that these lines would not be built and that Ottawa would not subsidize new railways in Alberta, the provincial Liberal government of A.C. Rutherford committed the province to guarantee the bonds of a number of railway companies, including several to northern "pioneer" districts. While this represented a major commitment by the new province, an activist commitment to economic development led the provincial government to reason that Alberta's progress depended on railways, which could not be built without public assistance. Thus, it felt obligated to subsidize construction through guarantees of railway company debt. This became one of the planks of the Rutherford government in the 1909 election campaign, which featured the slogan "Rutherford, Reliability and Railways." The Liberals contended that Rutherford's policy was iron clad because it involved no expenditure of public money unless the companies failed, which was said to be highly remote given the province's great future.[35] Few found it relevant to ask why lenders were so insistent on state loan guarantees if the lines would be so profitable.

By 1911, a number of railway companies had obtained charters to build lines to northern Alberta. Indeed, there was a rail line for any fancy. By 1912, four railways had been chartered that would have passed through or originated in Athabasca alone. If constructed, they would have provided connections to Vancouver, Battleford, Fort Smith, Fort McMurray, Peace River and Lac La Biche. Like Athabasca, every aspiring town saw itself as a railway hub and a distribution point for commerce. Moreover, it was widely believed that a rail line to the south-west of the Peace River country with a terminus on the Pacific—the coast outlet of which so much would be heard 20 years later—was essential.[36] Of these lines, only four were built in northern Alberta. The

Edmonton, Dunvegan and British Columbia Railway (ED&BC) was chartered in 1907 to build from Edmonton through the Peace River country to Prince George, British Columbia. Track laying began in 1912, and although the ED&BC never made it as far as its charter allowed, it eventually connected Grande Prairie and the south Peace River country with Edmonton. A second line, the Central Canada Railway (CCR), was essentially a branch line that connected Peace River and the ED&BC mainline. A third line, from Edmonton to Athabasca, was completed in 1912. The fourth line, the Alberta and Great Waterways (A&GW), was chartered in 1909 by promoters from Kansas City and Winnipeg to provide connections between Edmonton and the head of navigation on the lower Athabasca River at Fort McMurray. Construction of this line began in 1914. In 1911 and 1913, J.D. McArthur, a Winnipeg railway promoter with close Liberal connections, acquired the charters of the ED&BC and the A&GW respectively.

Although it was assumed that these lines were important for the future of the whole province, they particularly met the expectations of the government's supporters in Edmonton and northern Alberta.[37] A line to the Peace River country was especially significant for Edmonton's business class, whose demands intensified in 1912 when the British Columbia government provided bond guarantees for construction of the Pacific and Great Eastern (P&GE) between Vancouver and the Peace River country through Prince George. The physical difficulties and the scandals that surrounded its construction—not to mention the distances involved (the line only reached Quesnel almost a decade after construction began)—did not temper the paranoia of Edmonton's business lobby that Vancouver was scheming to steal Edmonton's crown as the metropolitan centre of the Peace River country. These and other similar concerns provided further justification for the province's guarantee of $8 million of the ED&BC's bonds, even though the company had no capitalized stock to meet construction costs.[38]

The wishes of Edmonton's business lobby were also met when the province guaranteed the bonds of the A&GW. Relations between the early owners of the A&GW and the Rutherford government were especially close, and following allegations of corruption, Premier Rutherford resigned in 1910. The aftermath of the scandal was complicated, drawn-out, and of lasting importance in Alberta's political life.[39] But railways were central in province-building and the ideology of progress and capitalist development that it rested on. Thus, Arthur Sifton's Liberal government that followed continued to provide bond guarantees. But unlike Rutherford's emphasis on rail lines to unsettled regions, Sifton's railway policy went further and promised rail service "to every part of the province." While support for these railways continued to reflect sectional interests and priorities, the northern lines also demonstrated the general commitment of the Alberta government to develop its northern territory. After 1915, the government retreated from this policy in face of complaints from Calgary and other parts of southern Alberta that their interests were being ignored in provincial railway policy. Yet while there was dissent about where railways would be built, there was almost no public criticism of the principle of subsidizing their construction. The Conservative opposition endorsed it, and as historian L.G. Thomas wrote, "few dared to question the need for an indefinite expansion of railway facilities, fewer still the capacity for the province to bear the burden such an extravagant programme of construction involved."[40] As would be apparent by the end of World War I, such questions would not have been amiss.

## ▬ Assuring Equal Access
### The State and Resource Regulation, 1900–21

Regulations for controlling use of natural resources were an important part of the framework that the state provided to help integrate northern Alberta into Canada before 1916. Existing Canadian regulations for lumbering, fishing, trapping and hunting were applied in the region, and earlier justifications for wildlife regulation, such as those articulated in the mid 1890s regarding wood buffalo, were elaborated and expanded. After 1905, the regulation of wildlife became a provincial responsibility, but the philosophy that underlay earlier game policies endured. Although sometimes phrased in terms of northern needs, these conservation efforts were designed around the priorities and preoccupations of Euro-Canadians and promoted their cultural values and economic objectives. While licencing and regulatory fees raised revenues for government, this was a relatively minor objective in resource regulation. If anything, state regulation tended to enhance private sector profits by conserving resources for economic development and by creating parameters of development that favoured certain groups over others and purely commercial undertakings in place of combined subsistence-commercial ones. It officially promoted a system of open access in which resources on crown land were regulated by the state and made available to all citizens. Everyone had the right to hunt or to take lumber on crown land if they obtained the appropriate licences and adhered to pertinent regulations, but access (subject to applicable restrictions) to resources on private land was treated as a benefit of owing the land. This move away from Aboriginal patterns of common use of resources was a profound change. As historian Irene Spry has argued, it lay at the heart of the changes that came throughout western Canada with Euro-Canadian ascendancy.[41]

Regulation of natural resources emerged within the framework of a burgeoning conservation movement in Canada. By the early 1900s, public concern about endangered animals was intensifying as yet more species fell before the European invasion of the Americas. By World War I, the last passenger pigeon had died in a Cincinatti zoo; on the great plains the buffalo that remained had been put into protected areas; and fish in southern prairie lakes were being depleted by overfishing and pollution. These developments had immense symbolic and emotional resonance and helped confirm the rightness of efforts by government to conserve wildlife.[42] As George Altmeyer has argued, the Canadian conservation movement in the early twentieth century emerged from a recognition that the nation's natural resources were not the "bottomless horn of plenty" that Canadians had so wantonly exploited in the late 1800s. Instead, natural resources came to be seen as a "limited storehouse" that had to be managed to achieve a sustainable balance between conservation and production. Scientific planning was said to be a key in achieving this equilibrium. These pragmatic objectives were often combined with a related concern that earlier destruction of wildlife, timber and land was evidence of national moral failure. This view further held that mankind and nature were spiritually linked and that appreciation and interaction with nature were antidotes for the ills of an increasingly urbanized industrial society. "Conservationists" thus presumed a need to regulate access to resources as part of an effort to maintain them for all users, present and future, while "preservationists" tended to support protection of resources out of social and moral concerns with less attention to economic issues.[43] While there was some tension in Canada between the two views, they tended to merge and define the outlines of Canadian resource regulation. Thus, an economically-oriented conservation rationale for government regulation was most powerful in Canada, and, in contrast to the United States, there was less debate about whether "conservation" or "preservation" should guide state policy.[44]

The conservation bias in Canadian natural resource regulation was evident in efforts to preserve and regenerate timber resources in northern Alberta. As the director of Forestry noted in 1914, most of Alberta north of Red Deer had been "repeatedly swept by fires, until at the present time but a small proportion of the timber retains its virgin state." Careful protection of new growth would restore forest cover to help stabilize the flow of streams and rivers and ensure a future "bountiful supply of forest products." Permits were required to cut timber on crown land, but this requirement was enforced in northern Alberta only near Grouard and Athabasca. Timber on private land was treated as a private asset, and the Department of the Interior (whose Forestry Branch looked after timber regulation) allowed settlers to use crown timber for private use as if it was a common resource, although that "taken for barter or sale or used in commercial enterprises should be paid for."[45] Thus, while subsistence use was freely permitted, commercial production was regulated.

In keeping with its policy of protecting new growth trees, the government's central concern was to prevent forest fires. Northern Alberta was divided into several fire districts, each with fire guardians. Although fires were usually blamed on travellers' carelessness with camp fires or settlers using fire to clear land, Native controlled burning to renew hunting environments was also criticized. In areas where lumbering had taken place, the threat of fire was greater because the land was strewn with slash. While posters warning people to put out camp fires were posted in settlements and at popular camping spots along the rivers, people continued to be careless, and the size of the territory ensured that arrests occurred only by chance. The only practical policy was to try and reach a fire as quickly as possible to prevent its spread, and eventually patrol boats equipped with water pumps for fighting fires were used. This system was extended to the Fort McMurray district in 1913 when growing economic activity and prospects of petroleum development brought increased concern about forest fires. To assert more direct control of forestry resources, a fire ranger was stationed in the settlement the following year.[46]

While early timber regulation respected settlers' needs by making timber on public land available for noncommercial use, the regulation of fishing restricted Native subsistence use to preserve fish stocks for commercial purposes. Fishing was an ancient part of the Aboriginal economy and provided essential food for people as well as their dogs. Indeed, dogs consumed as much fish as people did. Although it provided an essential resource for early fur traders, fishing had apparently been more a subsistence than a commercial activity. While people fished "more or less all the year round for food," most fishing took place in the fall during spawning season and whole undressed fish were then "hung" to dry for winter dog food.[47] Given the importance of fish in their economy and lives, Natives were concerned about depletion. Early commercial fishing on Lesser Slave Lake in 1904 prompted local Native worries about depletion, while

Indians living around Sturgeon Lake asked for an exclusive right to fish in the lake. Indian Affairs Inspector Conroy supported this request, but his reasoning revealed an attitude that would become prevalent in the future: Sturgeon Lake fronted on the reserve, and was "unimportant" for commercial fishing.[48] In other words, Natives were free to maintain common use of a resource that was not wanted by whites or which did not yet figure in provincial or national economic needs.

Such views were confirmed when the prospect of railway connections to Lesser Slave Lake quickened efforts to regulate fishing. As the Department of Marine and Fisheries reported in 1913, while traditional Native fishing during spawning season had not caused depletion, it now needed to be curbed to guarantee commercial catches. Local needs and customs were made subservient to provincial and national ones. As the fisheries inspector noted, "if a supply of fish for the benefit of other parts of the province" was to be obtained from Lesser Slave Lake, "of necessity the lake must receive full protection in spawning time." Thus the government announced its intention to license all fishing and to enforce a closed season during spawning because "within a year or two this district will have railway service" and "an excellent market will be available." While Indian and Metis fishing would be allowed for personal use, such provisions were "concessions granted by the government and not rights." These regulations officially sanctioned a shift in emphasis from subsistence to commercial fishing.[49]

The same trends became apparent in efforts to regulate fur and game resources. Until the creation of the province, wildlife regulation in northern Alberta operated under the federal wildlife legislation passed in the 1890s for the unorganized districts of the North-West Territories. The new province adopted the two territorial ordinances respecting game and the protection of useful birds in 1906, and the next year it reworked this legislation into Alberta's first comprehensive game statute. In both cases, conservation programmes employed closed seasons and bag limits (except for most fur-bearing animals) to maximize use without causing depletion. While completely closed seasons were applied to some animals, open seasons, in which hunting was permitted, were set on the basis of reproductive cycles and periods when pelts were prime. The 1906 provincial game legislation did not apply north of 55 degrees except to prohibit hunting elk, buffalo and beaver. Under the 1907 game statute, however, while residents and travellers in northern Alberta were allowed to hunt freely for food throughout the year, closed seasons for most fur-bearing animals were established and the killing of beaver, elk and buffalo was entirely banned. Provisions such as those prohibiting unsportsmanlike behaviour and hunting on Sundays applied to the whole province. Licences were also required to kill big game. This legislation formalized the principle of regulated open access to wildlife on crown lands at the same time that it sustained property rights by banning all hunting on private land without the consent of the owner or occupant.[50]

Only minor dissent was voiced over this legislation. It did not offend the interests of farmers, the most influential political group in the province, because it respected property rights. More compelling, however, was the view that the economic importance of wildlife could be enhanced and protected through regulation. As Alberta's Chief Game Guardian phrased it in 1907, wildlife was one of the province's "greatest assets" and needed to be protected. It created tourist opportunities and income for trappers, hunters and retailers. Consistent with this economic rationale, market hunting (which was often credited with game depletion) was permitted under the 1907 game legislation. Wild ducks, geese, moose and deer were all commonly sold as meat for construction and lumber camp crews as well as to town and city consumers. So too, fur-bearing animals were treated as an open access resource that all residents— regardless of race or prior claim—could exploit for their own benefit and the general economic good of the province. Although licences in the period before World War I were required only to hunt big game, the province reasoned that wildlife conservation measures could be had at little public cost because they could in the future be self-supporting through licence fees and special taxes.[51]

Embedded in the broad objectives of protecting species threatened by extinction and the regulation of wildlife as an open access resource for the economic benefit of all users were interrelated assumptions about sport and legitimate hunting. Approved hunting behaviour set out in this early game legislation evolved from traditions of sportsmanship. As a sport, hunting was one possible use of the great outdoor playground where Canadians could revive their depleted energies. From this perspective, hunting was a leisure, rather than a subsistence, activity and concepts borrowed from sport were applied. "Fairness," for example, was commonly invoked to define sportsmanship. To establish a "fair" relationship between the hunter and his prey, practices such as using lights and hunting at night were banned. While these provisions helped to limit over hunting, they also suggested that proper conduct, as much as accomplishment, was an objective. This belief marked the social and economic gulf between people who had to capture game or starve, and those for whom failure had little more consequence than loss at a game.

Concepts such as open access to wildlife resources and hunting as sport were especially relevant for Natives since their lives were increasingly affected by provincial game legislation. These regulations were applied to Native people from the vantage point of Euro-Canadian assumptions about Native character rather than actual conditions relating to their specific economic and social needs or their legal rights. Presuming that Natives could not understand their own interests, some people charged that Native hunting had to be controlled to protect the food resources of all Native people. Another stream of thought idealized Natives as "natural conservationists" who killed only for need and pragmatically ensured that sufficient resources were left to regenerate to guarantee future supply. In reality, such idealization could not accommodate the nature of most subsistence hunting, in which people sometimes killed more than was immediately necessary, or during breeding season and regardless of age or sex of animal. This apparent contradiction was resolved by arguing that Natives had lost their "natural conservationist" habits because they had been corrupted by the fur trade and the market economy. In other cases, the idea that all humans, whatever their race, were greedy and brutal steadily gained strength in the conservation movement in the early 1900s, and Native hunting practices that did not accord with the idealization of the natural conservationist were cited as only further examples of universal human character. In yet another view, it was suggested that Natives were by their nature vicious hunters whose love of killing led them to wipe out whole populations of animals. This played upon the assumption of Native as "savage" and presumably was contrasted with the idealized Euro-Canadian sports hunter whose pleasure in the chase came from restraint and self-control.[52]

Whatever the case, it remained that Treaty 8 had dealt with the hunting rights of the Indian portion of the Native population, and this soon became an issue between Indians and government generally, and between federal and provincial governments in particular. As Chief Seenum of Utikuma Lake pointed out in 1912, "hunting and inland fishing is a pastime with most of our white brothers, but our very existence depends upon being allowed to exercise the right which has been ours by heredity and Imperial Treaty." This reference to treaty was crucial in Indian views of hunting regulations. Like everyone else, Indians were prohibited from hunting on private land without the permission of the owner or occupier, but a belief that the treaty gave them special rights to hunt on unoccupied crown land for food and income was a common Indian interpretation of the treaty's provisions.[53] The government of Alberta, however, like most Euro-Canadian settlers, refused to recognize such Aboriginal hunting rights. Usually couched in the assertion that all residents of the province were "equal" and had an equal access to wildlife, this view masked a deep hostility to Indian hunting rights. In some instances this probably arose from racism, but in other cases it reflected a competition between white and Native hunters. In yet other instances, it perhaps expressed a cultural anxiety—the granting of unique rights to the people who Euro-Canadians had displaced implicitly challenged the legitimacy of white occupation of the land. Whatever the underlying reason, Alberta's game commissioner noted in 1912 that "the Indian question throughout the province, as far as game protection is concerned, is a very sore one with many of the settlers."[54] Provincial politicians, political groups and the fish and game associations that were then being formed throughout the province were insistent that Indians had no special rights, a view that became a mantra in the debates about provincial game legislation.

Such provincial claims had long been the subject of federal-provincial disagreement. While the federal government had asserted that it had jurisdiction over Indian hunting because of the treaties and its responsibility for Indian welfare, developments in the late nineteenth century in Manitoba and Ontario challenged its powers. The provinces argued that they were not obligated to make special provisions for Indians—whatever the treaties negotiated by the federal government had stated. Consequently, the provinces argued that game laws applied to all residents of the provinces. Alberta's subsequent game statute therefore did not allow exemptions for Indians, nor did it acknowledge (as did Saskatchewan's game legislation) any jurisdiction by Indian Affairs over hunting by Indians. Alberta's Deputy Attorney General argued in 1908 that Alberta's game statute was "binding upon all persons, irrespective of 'race, creed or previous conditions of servitude' within the Province." Nonetheless, the game statute allowed residents and travellers in northern Alberta to hunt most animals and birds for food at any time of the year, thus recognizing northern Alberta as a unique region where hunting was an essential part of people's daily life. This did not, however, protect commercial hunting as part of Aboriginal (as distinguished from resident) common use of resources. Nor did it lead to provincial efforts to curb the activity of white trappers who were spreading into Native trapping areas and threatening the Native economy. Most particularly, it did not recognize treaty-protected hunting rights. While Indian Affairs noted in 1912 that Alberta did not act "very generously towards the Indians who were the original owners of their country" since it placed them "in no better position than that of farmers residing on their land," the province argued that its policy respected the equality of all Albertans to trap and hunt. This assumed that trapping and hunting was simply an "industry" for northern Natives and not also a way of life, a cultural tradition and an activity that, for some at least, possessed a spiritual context.[55]

Despite the federal government's expressed concern for Indian hunting rights, its motives were often ambiguous and contradictory, and its willingness to defend its jurisdiction over Indian hunting rights progressively weakened after about 1910. Richard Price and Shirleen Smith have argued that this arose because Ottawa's growing concerns about game depletion made it more willing to accept some controls over Indian hunting. Moreover, Indian hunting rights were increasingly seen as a transitory issue because it was popularly assumed that Aboriginal people would disappear because of disease or assimilation. As well, it was believed that the importance of the fur trade was fading as agriculture and industry became dominant in the Canadian economy. Nonetheless, hunting rights remained important in areas where agriculture was impossible. The federal government thus urged the provinces to relax game enforcement in such areas "for humanitarian, rather than legal or constitutional, reasons." In stating this objective, Frank Pedley, the Deputy Superintendent General of Indian Affairs, informed the Alberta Deputy Attorney General in 1908 that the federal government was reluctant to open debate on the constitutionality of provincial efforts to regulate Indian hunting, but he starkly noted that, in Ottawa's view, constitutional questions were secondary to those about welfare. As he noted,

This interest on the part of the Department [of Indian Affairs] in the preservation of game is mainly connected with its relation to protecting what constitutes, at any rate in certain districts, the main source of the food supply necessary for the preservation of the lives of its wards, and if it has good grounds for supposing that the ultimate supply is being insured unnecessarily at the danger of an immediate or intervening sacrifice of life, it would certainly appear to be its duty to intervene to the extent of its ability.[56]

Such reasoning indicated Ottawa's willingness to confront the provinces to defend the welfare of Indians rather than their hunting rights. In conjunction with adverse court rulings, this view was further enhanced when Frank Oliver (who as minister of the Interior was in charge of Indian Affairs) demanded that Indians observe Alberta's game legislation. As he argued in 1909, Indian Affairs could "do nothing…to save Indians from the consequences of disregarding the

provisions of the Provincial Game Ordinances" since exclusive provincial jurisdiction over game seemed to be upheld by the courts. The province in turn
made a minor concession by amending its game statute in 1912 so that Indians
could obtain required licences without charge. This was the only concession
that Alberta made to Treaty Indians—all other provisions applied to all residents of northern Alberta, regardless of status. While the federal government
continued to defend the rights of Indians in nonagricultural areas to hunt for
food—and in some instances to make a living from commercial hunting—the
province had clearly come out on top in the dispute over Indian hunting. And
although Indian Affairs still insisted on its right to defend Indian subsistence
hunting rights, by 1912 it typically replied to Indian complaints about provincial
restrictions by quoting those provisions of the treaty which stated that hunting
rights were subject to government regulations.[57]

These debates about treaty hunting rights were not rarefied political and
constitutional issues but had direct impact on daily life. Natives had been
brought within the orbit of state regulation of hunting, and while enforcement
of game legislation in northern Alberta was patchy, its impact on commercial
life was immediate because it made the sale of certain furs and types of fur
(such as unprime pelts) illegal. The fur trade was gradually forced to respect
these distinctions because of government inspection and export controls. More
directly, fire rangers began to act as game guardians, and volunteer guardians
were also appointed in many areas. Enforcement generally depended on the
police, however, and was consequently most stringent in areas with police
detachments. While officers apparently did not initially require Indians to have
big game licences, enforcement gradually became more comprehensive. By
World War I, direct attempts to enforce closed seasons were being made in the
Lesser Slave Lake and Fort Chipewyan districts.[58]

Native response to these developments was immediate. Police reports indicate resentment and resistance by Indians in most parts of northern Alberta to
the enforcement of provincial game legislation. One particular concern related
to the trapping of beaver. In the early 1900s, the federal government had considered banning their catch because of a concern about possible extinction. It
concluded, however, that this would be difficult to enforce and too disruptive
of people's livelihood. Moreover, the Department of Indian Affairs argued that
this would violate the treaty promises that Indian hunting would not be regulated "prior to the advent of settlers into their country."[59]

The province, however, had no such qualms and it banned beaver hunting
in 1906. Indians argued that this violated treaty rights and interfered with their
livelihood because it made the sale of beaver pelts illegal. In particular, Indians

at Fort Chipewyan found the law "very awkward" and the Chipewyan Chief noted that Indians did not kill beaver "to play with." In response, Indian Affairs Inspector Conroy told Treaty 8 Indians that they could kill beaver for food as long as they did not sell the pelts. Since the pelts could not be sold, he believed this would adequately protect beaver populations because people would "only as a last resort kill beaver for food." A series of poor trapping seasons culminated in 1909 with widespread hardship. Consequently, the province temporarily lifted its ban in the winter of 1908–09 so that Indians could hunt beaver for food, especially in the Peace-Athabasca delta where conditions were most severe. Apparently, the ban had been respected in some cases, even at great personal cost. As the police reported in 1909, "the Indians between [Fort] Chipewyan and [Fort] Resolution did not learn of the authority to kill beaver until the end of December and at that time many were sick from actual starvation." In another report, however, it was noted that people killed beaver for food, regardless of the law. And those living close to Saskatchewan or the NWT (where beaver hunting was legal) simply crossed the border to sell the pelts.[60] As NWMP officers in the field tirelessly reported, if the province wanted to preserve beaver populations, an open season was needed so animals would be trapped when their pelts were prime and could be sold legally, leaving the animals alone to breed at other times of the year.[61]

Under pressure from Indian Affairs, Alberta declared temporary open seasons for beaver in the next several years to prevent hardship. But the province remained determined to control such hunting. In 1913, the Chipewyan Chief, Alexander Laviolette, was charged and fined a token amount of $1 for hunting beaver. This caused outrage in Fort Chipewyan where it was seen as a violation of the promises made by the treaty commissioners barely a decade before that people would not be "interfered with in any way regarding their killing food or fur animals."[62] In light of court rulings and the new accommodation between Ottawa and Edmonton over game legislation, however, Indian Affairs was now less sympathetic to Indian claims. Inspector Conroy told people at Fort Chipewyan that the closed season was "imposed as much in the interests of the Indians as in those of the beaver" and that the law had to be respected. Although the province extended the ban on killing beaver until 1915, a special open season was declared in the winter of 1914–15 to prevent starvation during a time of low fur prices.[63]

In contrast to beaver preservation efforts, provincial and federal governments saw eye to eye on a total ban on hunting buffalo. Wood buffalo protection remained a federal responsibility, but the province assisted by including a ban on killing buffalo in its game legislation. In 1911, responsibility for wood buffalo protection was transferred from the NWMP to the Department of the Interior. Until 1922 when Wood Buffalo National Park was established, buffalo protection relied on police patrols that tried to prevent illegal hunting. As well, wolf bounties were paid in an attempt to reduce one of the buffalo's natural predators and the province also issued permits to use poison baits since wolves were so difficult to hunt or trap.[64] These policies gave rise to an often acrimonious debate about what actually endangered the buffalo. Some people, such as Inspector Jarvis of the NWMP and the naturalist and author, Ernest Thompson Seton, blamed Native hunters. As Jarvis wrote, "the constant cry of 'wolf' is a mere ruse to divert attention from the two-legged predators who are really doing the mischief." Jarvis contended that if the buffalo were to be protected, their range had to be made into a national park. Others, such as Inspector Conroy of Indian Affairs, blamed wolves for buffalo depredation. When the first detailed survey of the buffalo country around Fort Smith was made in 1911, no signs of significant wolf kills were found. Yet, the population of the herds remained unknown, and as historian Janet Foster noted, there was no way of "determining if, indeed, the herds were declining, much less what the cause of the decline could be."[65]

Some critics have argued that ongoing government efforts to protect buffalo "appear bizarrely out of proportion" in contrast to the lack of attention paid to the human residents of the region.[66] The occasional permits issued by the provincial government to sport hunters to kill buffalo caused "considerable resentment on the part of settlers and Indians in the north" and added to the incongruity of government policies.[67] But buffalo protection was primarily a response to broader Euro-Canadian thinking about nature and how the state should respond to concerns about depletion. Even though debate took place in the absence of scientific knowledge about the distribution and population dynamics of the buffalo, this ultimately was unimportant because buffalo protection was an emotional commitment to wildlife preservation in general. Euro-Canadians could support it with no personal inconvenience or cost; a gesture that also seems to have served as a painless compensation for the destruction brought about by prairie settlement, where the buffalo and other animals and birds had been nearly exterminated. As such, it was easy to blame low buffalo populations on wolves that had been demonized for centuries. Indeed, the use of wolf bounties in early buffalo protection policies became, in the logic of the time, an affirmation of Euro-Canadian commitment to wildlife preservation. These developments were further indications of how concerns and preoccupations relevant to Canadians living outside northern Alberta were translated to the region as part of its integration with the rest of the nation.

— ✦ —

The expansion of Canadian control in northern Alberta in the first decade and a half following the signing of Treaty 8 was facilitated and led by the state. Before the creation of the province in 1905, the federal government largely acted alone in this respect by extending political, legal and administrative structures to guide the distribution of land, conserve and control the use of natural resources, and publicize and expand knowledge about northern resources. These tactics differed little from those that Canada had successfully applied when opening the prairies to settlement after 1870, and their wholesale application to northern Alberta revealed an assumption that local needs and priorities were either irrelevant or identical to those of the dominant groups in the rest of Canada. This view was accompanied not only by popular notions about Euro-Canadian racial superiority and an exclusive definition of "progress," but by the more significant assumption that state policy should promote capitalist development and liberal individualism. In this context, the principles that underlay Native subsistence-commercial use of resources were considered to be worthless, or at least as a barrier, to the commercial development by Euro-Canadians of northern resources. Natives were thus bypassed, less because of their race than because their practices and traditions were seen as antithetical to the expansion of a market economy.

Similar assumptions guided the provincial government after 1905 and both federal and provincial governments agreed on a philosophy of expansion. Where differences appeared almost immediately was in regard to Aboriginal hunting rights. This arose in part from provincial demands for exclusive jurisdiction over hunting, and thus was an early expression of Alberta's province-building initiatives. It also belied, however, a narrower view on the part of the provincial government of the rights of some of its citizens. While appeals to equality slipped effortlessly from the lips of provincial politicians and spokesmen, such claims in practice served only the Euro-Canadian population. In a similar fashion, the needs of the province's business groups (especially those in Edmonton) and land seekers found ready encouragement from Alberta's willingness to finance and support railway development and the attendant expansion of the farming and resource frontier in northern Alberta. Such province-building initiatives would be pursued and expanded in the coming years; provoking yet further tensions between Aboriginals and whites and between federal and provincial governments.

# Northern Life and
# 5 Society to 1916

CHANGING ATTITUDES and ambitions on the part of government and private interests made the period between 1900 and 1916 a transitional one in northern Alberta. Regional life continued to be expressed within economic and technological structures important since the 1880s. The major rivers continued to focus transportation and communications; the urban system retained its earlier form; social life was reportedly stable; and life continued to revolve around trapping, fishing, hunting and seasonal labour on the river. At the same time, the new foundations that were being laid for northern development set the stage for significant change. During these years, the transportation network began to be reorganized; the trapping economy underwent significant change; farm settlement tentatively began; the economic potential of northern mineral and other resources was tested and explored; the first Indian reserves were established; and Indian schooling was put on a more centralized basis. New forces and expectations— sometimes connected, at other times disparate—revealed changing conditions arising from the revamping of the region's interaction with the rest of Canada.

## ▬ Northern Society After the Treaty

Despite the tensions that preceded treaty and scrip negotiations, there was little social conflict after both were concluded. While some Natives were confused about, or even resisted, the new legal systems being imposed, this seems to have been more a reaction to unfamiliar concepts than a rejection of

*The use of fashionable architectural styles promoted corporate identity and symbolized the expansion of Euro-Canadian activity independently of local traditions. Here, the mail team leaving Athabasca for Calling River in 1915 posed in front of the Imperial Bank of Canada. The building featured the style used by the bank across Canada. Aca36 PAA.*

the new order. J. Hurssell, a free trader who served as Justice of the Peace in Fitzgerald, wrote in 1903 that law enforcement in the district was problematical because there were too few police to lay informations. But he noted as well that the local community was reluctant to become involved in the administration of justice. Natives generally resisted laying informations about crimes, preferring "to suffer in silence rather than to procure redress from the white man." Further, many did not accept the Euro-Canadian distinction between civil and criminal law and could not see why, when an offender was fined under the Criminal Code, "the fine should not go to the party aggrieved." This view was one that most whites also accepted. As Hurssell pointed out, many were still connected in some way with the fur trade and the laying of informations would have been "inimical to business interests."[1]

In any case, northern Alberta was, from all reports, a law abiding society. In 1900, the District of Athabaska was said to enjoy "almost complete immunity from crime." The people were "self-supporting and content" and respect for property was widespread. In 1907 the NWMP reported that Indians in the

Lesser Slave Lake and Peace River areas were "exemplary in their conduct always, and whenever one does get into trouble he is almost always sure to be the victim of others." The Metis, "by far the largest" part of the population, were equally law abiding and "an occasional brush with them over illicit liquor is about all we have to complain about." Indeed, the enforcement of prohibition continued—as it had in the 1890s—to be the major law enforcement issue. Some people, such as Superintendent Routledge, thought that Natives had a "hereditary fondness for intoxicants of any kind," but enforcement problems were more often blamed on the failure of the permit system. One particularly vexing problem involved intoxicating essences, which were sold widely until their importation without a permit was banned in 1904.[2] By the early 1900s, disputes over liquor were becoming almost a northern tradition for whites and Natives alike. For Euro-Canadian males, liquor was apparently part of the freedom of the frontier. As a NWMP officer observed in 1912, drunkenness was prevalent in Athabasca (which lay slightly south of the prohibition territory), and "men who would be ashamed of being seen drunk on the streets of any large city" thought "it rather a joke" to stagger around the streets of the town.[3]

Settlements continued to provide a focus both for economic exchange and social interaction. As well as visiting for trading purposes, Natives often returned to the settlements from their bush camps for special occasions. Roman Catholic missionaries encouraged Natives to alter their seasonal routines and visit the missions at Christmas and Easter to participate in the religious celebrations. How widespread this practice was in the early 1900s is unclear, but the NWMP at Fort Chipewyan reported in October 1904 that people had just left for the winter hunt and would "not return to the settlement again until Christmas or New Years." A 1915 report from Fort Smith indicated the same pattern: many people had gathered in the settlement "to celebrate New Years Day. During the night they wasted a lot of ammunition shooting to welcome the New Year as they do every year."[4]

The annual treaty payments added to the draw of the settlements. Annuities were usually paid at a prearranged time during summer, although they were not always paid yearly in hard-to-reach districts. These occasions supplemented the century-old custom of seasonal trips to trading centres. While they confirmed the centrality of the settlements in Native life, treaty was paid in June or July when many people were on provision hunts or at work on the rivers. Indians at Lesser Slave Lake asked in 1901 that annuities be paid in winter so as not to interfere with their summer work. Similarly, in 1905 people at Fitzgerald were "all working in the rapids with Hislop and Nagle's boats" and the treaty party had to wait two days until the work was finished and the annuities could be paid. But Indians elsewhere in the agency apparently liked summer payments, and it was the best time for Indian Affairs officials to travel in the north.[5]

Throughout northern Alberta, treaty payment time was a festive occasion. In some cases, the treaty gatherings were large—in 1905, for example, about 200 to 300 people gathered at Fort Chipewyan. They had cash from their annuities, and it was a time for dancing, gambling, shopping and visiting. Following the payment of the annuity at Wabasca in 1916, people enjoyed horse and foot races and concluded the day with "a dance and feast" that lasted most of the night. In 1914, treaty was paid at Fort McMurray on June 15, and people stayed in the settlement until July 1 for Dominion Day when a picnic attended by most of the settlement's residents was held. During the sports events, typical of those at Dominion Day celebrations everywhere in Canada, Natives and whites competed in running, jumping and horse racing. Following the celebrations, the Natives left for their fishing and hunting camps along the river.[6]

As geographer Arthur Ray has noted with respect to the cash poor prairies in the 1870s and 1880s, annuity payments placed Indians among the few people with cash to spend. To a lesser extent, this was also the case in northern Alberta in the early 1900s. Although barter remained dominant, annuity payments helped boost the cash nexus and added to the forces contributing to the erosion of barter in the northern economy and the separation of fur trading and merchandising. Yet, by the early 1900s many northern Alberta Natives already operated in a highly mixed economy, albeit one in which cash was still unusual. They continued to follow traditional seasonal patterns, running trap lines or fishing in winter, and hunting and fishing during the rest of the year. For many, seasonal labour in freighting, cutting wood for steamboats, putting up hay and general labour at missions and fur trade posts complemented this activity. Around Grouard, a few Metis farmed and raised stock year round, but in late summer most people put up fish for the winter, or left the settlement to hunt moose or bears or to work on the boats on the Peace or Athabasca rivers. As it was noted, they were "little seen at this time of the year."[7] This economy depended on a number of activities and options that fit within an unevenly cyclical economy. People seemed comfortable with this way of life, and with an economy in which subsistence fishing, trapping and hunting could be accommodated relatively easily with wage labour.

Until the CNoR reached Athabasca in 1912, all transportation in northern Alberta continued by trail or river. Although the Peace River country could be reached by trail from Lac Ste. Anne via Sturgeon Lake, the Athabasca Trail remained dominant. By 1910, the CNoR and GTP transcontinental main lines running west from Edmonton had created new access routes, and in 1911 a trail between the Edson district on the GTP main line and Grande Prairie was opened. Partly built by the province, the Edson Trail appreciably shortened the distance between a rail head and the Peace River country, but the swamps and hills along it ensured travellers a difficult time. In the summer that it opened, the NWMP reported that the trail was "practically impassable," and as Superintendent Wroughton observed in 1912, all along it were "scattered pianos, organs, furniture, dead horses and oxen, broken-down wagons and sleighs and discouraged men." In contrast to the mythology of bravery and initiative that would later develop about the Edson Trail, Wroughton reported one man to remark that "I'll stay here [the Peace River country] and starve before I'll go on that trail again."[8]

Despite such problems, the Edson Trail was important for white settlement in the southern Peace River country before the railway arrived in 1916. While it created an illusion of greater accessibility, especially in winter when it was somewhat easier to use, its difficulties in all seasons underlined that large-scale farm settlement had to wait for rail connections. It also demonstrated that the economic advantage of urban centres was relative to regional transportation networks. Although the Edson Trail offered a shorter and more direct access to the southern Peace River country, the Athabasca-Grouard route remained dominant as long as steamboats were used on the Athabasca River and Lesser Slave Lake and trails provided winter connections. By 1912, teams going in various directions left Athabasca and Grouard most days in winter carrying passengers and freight. A return trip in winter could be made in 14 days between Athabasca and Grouard, and forage and provisions were available at stopping places along this "old travelled road." Travellers' comfort was often enhanced by a caboose—a "little house" built on sleigh runners. Like "a minia-ture Noah's ark," it was often equipped with a stove, and provided a warm place where travellers could also sleep.[9]

The communications system created in the 1880s continued to frame the regional economy. On the Peace River, service increased in 1903 when the

*This crew was waiting at Athabasca in 1913 for the departure of a scow to the north. Aca33 PAA.*

Oblates at Fort Vermilion built a small steamer. Although it offered faster transportation, the missionaries reportedly "charged exorbitant prices for both freight and passengers." These profitable days ended in 1905 when the Hudson's Bay Company built a rival steam ship. Other operators also provided service with scows, and in 1911 steam ship service expanded when the Peace River Trading and Land Company put a ship on the river.[10] This added further shipping capacity on the Peace River; anticipation of growth had exceeded the needs of the economy, bringing over-investment and excess capacity. On the lower Athabasca and Slave rivers, older patterns also endured. Scows built at Athabasca continued to carry goods and passengers over the Grand Rapids. By mid 1911, 70 scows had already set out downstream from Athabasca, carrying freight and passengers including traders, missionaries, surveyors, federal civil servants and police. So too, traffic continued to move in the opposite direction. In the late summer of 1913, the Hudson's Bay Company transport from the north manned by 100 boatmen passed through Fort McMurray and worked its way up the 140 kilometres of rapids with 65 passengers and 25 tons of fur valued at $1 million. Such activity expanded employment opportunities, and about 300 to 400 men, almost all Native, found work each season on the scow brigades.[11]

The river transport system ensured that the Smith Rapids remained one of the focal points in the region's transportation network, and the importance of

Fitzgerald and Fort Smith at either end of the portage continued to grow. This was confirmed in 1907 when the Hudson's Bay Company moved its northern operations from Fort Simpson to Fort Smith and augmented its Mackenzie River service with a second steamer based at Fort Smith. The Smith Portage was gradually upgraded—by 1901 the Hudson's Bay Company had installed a telephone line between Fitzgerald and Fort Smith, and the provincial government built bridges and culverts along the portage in 1906. New operators also emerged, and by 1907 most traders used the portage trail. To avoid the costs and difficulties of the portage, some still ran goods down the dangerous rapids by scows, even though they often lost 10 or 15 percent of their freight. Hislop and Nagle, which usually followed this practice, hired "white men" in 1906 to take its freight through the rapids. Apparently, many of these workers were Metis from Edmonton and St. Albert who formed part of a floating workforce in northern Alberta. Hired under contract and paid at the end of the season, they were said to be preferable to local workers who demanded higher wages and often quit work, "thereby causing considerable delay and extra expense." Indeed, in 1906 the NWMP proposed putting a detachment at Fitzgerald to "put a stop to these breaches of contract."[12]

While it is unclear if the police regulated labour at the Smith Portage, it would not have been unusual if they had. In 1909 the NWMP assigned a constable to the area between Fort McMurray and Athabasca "to maintain order generally," to arrest workers who deserted or refused to work, and to watch for smuggled liquor.[13] But police regulation was only a stop-gap measure in overcoming the limitations of northern transportation. Suggestions for circumventing the rapids with canals, trails or tramways were proposed from time to time. The Hudson's Bay Company considered building a tramway (like the one at Grand Rapids) along the Smith Portage, but it soon concluded that efforts to monopolize it would only create enforcement problems and improved conditions for rival traders.[14]

In any case, northern promoters had set their sights on alternatives to river shipping. Even the inveterate promoter, Jim Cornwall, remarked in 1907 that the high cost of making northern rapids navigable or constructing canals around them was unwarranted. This ensured that demand for higher shipping capacity turned attention to improving land transportation. In 1912 the Hudson's Bay Company began constructing a large warehouse in Fort McMurray as part of a plan to bypass the rapids with a winter trail from House River, about 130 kilometres upriver.[15] Two warehouses were also built at the mouth of the House River to store hay imported from Edmonton for the

*The boiler for the steamship of the Northern Transportation Company was laboriously hauled from Edmonton to Athabasca. Not dated, ca. 1902–1904. 70.297/53b, PAA.*

teams. As there were no stopping places along the trail, freighters carried their own supplies. How extensively this trail was used is unclear.[16] In any event, proposals for overland communications were now stressing railways, which were more in keeping with contemporary technology and its investment opportunities. As early as 1907, promoters such as Cornwall were lobbying for the development of a railway between Edmonton and Fort McMurray to bypass the Grand Rapids and put goods and passengers directly at the head of the great northern river system. Illustrating the mix of personal ambition and public advocacy that characterized booster thinking, Cornwall owned a charter for such a railway.[17]

While there was little prospect that river shipping north of Fort McMurray would be challenged by alternative methods, the potential for change was greater on the section of the river served by the settlement of Athabasca. In 1897 the Hudson's Bay Company steamer there was damaged, and the company opted to use scows instead of repairing the ship. While this decision was supported by rumours that a transcontinental railway would soon be built through the southern Peace River country, it proved to be a tactical error. The value of the company's dominance of shipping on the Athabasca River had come less from the direct profits earned by complex machine technology than the power to limit competition, and its failure to maintain this advantage allowed competition to emerge. In 1902 a steam ship hull built earlier at Athabasca by McDougall and Secord was purchased by Jim Cornwall and several partners. After installing an engine and boiler, it went into service in 1904. This was the start of the Northern Transportation Company, the first serious challenge to the Hudson's Bay Company on the Athabasca River.[18]

The Northern Transportation Company planned to operate nonstop service between Athabasca and Grouard. It was found, however, that even shallow draft ships could not get through the rapids of the Lesser Slave River. The company could thus use its ship only between Athabasca and Mirror Landing, and scows manned by Metis crews continued to carry goods and passengers along the Lesser Slave River and across Lesser Slave Lake. In an important development, however, the company began operating a steam ship on Lesser Slave Lake in 1907. This left the 35 kilometre portage around the rapids on the Lesser Slave River as the only bottleneck in the system. Charles Barber, one of the company's owners, persuaded the federal government to build small "wing" dams along the shallow rapids to force the river into a narrower channel and make it deeper. By 1908 the federal government had spent almost $35,000 on this project without any success, and in 1910 it dredged the river to open a channel for steam ships. Even then, only the construction of a small shallow draft steamer made it possible to travel, but only during high water, directly from Athabasca to Grouard.[19]

These developments helped make the Northern Transportation Company a major carrier in the Athabasca-Lesser Slave Lake district. In the summer of 1908, about 915 tonnes of freight passed through Athabasca, of which one-third—almost all the cargo moving to Lesser Slave Lake—was carried by the Northern Transportation Company.[20] The Hudson's Bay Company attempted to meet this competition by putting steamers on the same routes. This whole-sale replacement of scows by steam ships on the Athabasca-Grouard corridor revolutionized transportation. Although it did not bring basic economic change (such as export-based agriculture or mining), greater speed and convenience stimulated increased traffic throughout the network. This was further enhanced in 1909 when the Northern Transportation Company began operating two autos twice a week between Edmonton and Athabasca to connect to the boats. All along the Athabasca-Grouard corridor, the urban system expanded. While intermediate points like Slave Lake (then called Sawridge) increased in size, most growth occurred at Athabasca, the portal to the system, and at Grouard, the transhipment point for the Peace River country.[21] These changes enhanced the authority and wealth of the ascendant groups in northern Alberta by stimulating trade and by making communication easier. As NWMP Superintendent Constantine wrote in 1907, "it is wonderful what a difference there is already." It was now possible to get freight to Grouard in one or two weeks, "whereas in the old state of things, one was lucky to get anything through in three or four months." Moreover, it was now "comparatively easy" to get mail to Athabasca, the nearest telegraph station.[22]

These developments were seen as evidence of progress, but the economic change they brought had an uneven impact on people in the region. Almost overnight, steam ships made "the old time-honoured scows with their crews" obsolete in the Lesser Slave Lake district, but they did not bring equivalent replacement work. Winter jobs were also lost because easier shipping in summer led to a decline in winter freighting. In the winter of 1907–08 a poor fur catch along with rising unemployment brought hard times to the Lesser Slave Lake district. The "big traders" were "now carrying so much of their freight on the steamers, instead of the old time teaming on the ice," that a "large portion of the inhabitants" were unemployed, including Natives who kept stopping places on Lesser Slave Lake.[23]

Such change was integral to the technological expansion that accompanied the region's growing integration within Canada. As historian Michael Adas has shown, by the nineteenth century technology had become a basic element in Europeans' domination of the world economy, in their ability to occupy new territory, and in their view of themselves as a historical and cultural vanguard. This was the case in northern Alberta as it was in Africa, Asia and other parts of the Americas. Attributed to Jim Cornwall, the following slogan was mounted over the gates of the yards of the Northern Transportation Company in Athabasca:

> Of all invention, that of printing excepted, those which contributed to the course of transportation have done the most in the promotion of civilization. This is the Gateway to the Northern Transportation Company's shipping yards.[24]

## The Fur Trade After 1900
### Ongoing Changes

The restricted nature of the transportation system and a lack of local markets ensured that fur remained dominant in the regional economy before World

War I. Fur exports continued to benefit from a communications network that suited the character of the commodity and the type of trade goods that northern people purchased. After 1907, the enforcement of closed seasons on beaver began to change the fur trade by restricting the legal sale in Alberta of certain types of fur. But the trade also continued to be shaped by the variability of catches and the world fur market. The scarcity of fur in some districts in 1908–09, for instance, led traders to give credit only to the best hunters; a development that quickly rippled through the economy. Shipments of goods dried up, and Metis freighters suddenly found themselves "in very poor circumstances." Price changes had an equivalent effect. In 1906, for example, rumours that fur prices had fallen by 50 percent created alarm in the Lesser Slave Lake district. "No one up here," it was reported, was "altogether independent," and most people were "only just able to live and pay their way." Such problems were more severe in cases where trappers had stopped hunting or gathering most of their food and were instead purchasing it from traders. In 1914, as was noted at Fort Vermilion, "the Indians year after year have been buying more flour and other supplies, especially lard, and with fur a good price they kept themselves from the danger of starvation."[25]

After 1900, lifestyles were also increasingly affected by the expansion of the fur trade and growing competition. Such changes took place in all of northern Canada, and northern Alberta was only one example of the wider trend. In 1899 Revillon Frères, a French wholesale fur buyer with over a century of experience in Canada, opened a warehouse in Edmonton and soon expanded into retail fur buying. While it opened new posts elsewhere in northern Canada, it entered the northern Alberta market in 1906 by purchasing Bredin and Cornwall's string of fur trade posts. It also had a post in Athabasca from which it supplied its Lesser Slave Lake and Peace River operations. By 1907 Athabasca had become an important fur trade supply centre with a number of trading concerns, including the Hudson's Bay Company, Revillon, Hislop and Nagle and smaller operators such as John Secord and James McKinley.[26]

By 1909, competition among traders in northern Alberta was "very stiff." The old practice of "tripping"—in which a trader travelled from a main post to winter bush settlements to buy fur—expanded. The Hudson's Bay Company had posts in all the principal centres, although Revillon was still operating only in the Lesser Slave Lake and Peace River districts (including Fort Vermilion). As it had since the 1880s, Hislop and Nagle concentrated on the Slave and Mackenzie River districts, and smaller traders, such as Colin Fraser at Fort Chipewyan and Fond du Lac, Saskatchewan, and J. Hurssell at Fitzgerald,

*Before World War I, the Northern Trading Company competed for trade with the Hudson's Bay Company at various locations, including Fort McMurray. The individual in the left foreground is Jim Cornwall, one of the company's owners.* A7385 PAA.

provided more localized challenges. By 1914, competition had expanded throughout the region. Revillon, for example, was now operating in the lower Athabasca and Slave River districts as well as around Lesser Slave Lake and in the Peace River country. The Hudson's Bay Company also faced another well organized competitor, the Northern Trading Company, which had purchased Hislop and Nagle in 1913. Indicating some of the corporate interconnections important in the trade, the Northern Trading Company used the shipping services of the Northern Transportation Company, whose co-owner, Jim Cornwall, was also a partner in the Northern Trading Company. Even in this environment, however, the wealth of the Athabasca district ensured that it remained the Hudson's Bay Company's richest fur producing area in Canada.[27]

The fur trade before World War I not only featured greater competition among traders. European and American furriers now looked for cheaper substitutes for luxury furs (such as beaver and marten) that were becoming scarce. Previously low value furs such as mink, muskrat and ermine were now dyed and prepared in new ways to meet demand and create new fashions. By 1914

*Demand for types of fur shifted in tandem with changing fashions.*
*In the early 1900s, silver fox was a fashionable fur and prices*
*were high. This catch was photographed at Grouard in 1904.*

B10014 PAA.

muskrat had replaced beaver in volume of production in Canada. While always important in the Peace-Athabasca delta, muskrat now became dominant. It was a low-priced fur and muskrat populations, unlike beaver, fluctuated cyclically. This meant, as Arthur Ray has noted, that "muskrat-oriented economies offered only a marginal and very uncertain rate" of long-term return to trappers.[28]

The cycles of animal populations had always made the fur trade an unstable industry, but commercial speculation in the years leading up to World War I added to its volatility. Cash trading and consignment buying, in which a commission agent marketed a trader's furs, expanded. Consignment buying was "a boon to trappers and small independent traders" who could now sell their returns quickly. This reduced the amount of capital they needed and made it easier for newcomers to enter the business.[29] These changes made the trade more utilitarian and mercenary. Prices for fur and consumer goods—previously set for a entire trading year—now changed within the year. Formerly, news of price changes had been slow to reach the north, but price volatility increased as telegraph connections spread northwards; reaching Athabasca in 1904, Lesser Slave Lake in 1909, Peace River and Grande Prairie in 1912, and Fort McMurray in 1915. Moreover, while game depletion was already serious in some districts, high prices attracted an increasing number of white trappers, bringing even greater pressure on fur resources.

Changing conditions were masked because fur prices were generally strong before World War I and competition among traders helped sustain a seller's market. In Fort Chipewyan in 1902, the Hudson's Bay Company and three other traders competed for furs, and "all the young men of the place [have] been running for fur...Fur is everything this winter." Competition also brought lower consumer prices in some districts. At Peace River in 1911, for example, goods at the Peace River Trading and Land Company store were fresher and cost about 20 percent less than at the Hudson's Bay Company and Revillon stores. And though wage work was scarce, trapping in good years allowed people to avoid the hard labour of working on the boats. Simultaneously, high fur prices affected fur production because necessities—tea, tobacco, flour, ammunition and cloth—could be bought for fewer furs, while goods formerly considered to be luxuries became more affordable. In this expanding economy, increased goods were shipped north. In the earlier times of the Hudson's Bay Company monopoly, it was noted at Fort Chipewyan in 1905 that "a few scow loads of dry goods, tea, [and] tobacco, was all that was brought into the country, [but] now there are hundreds of tons of provisions, dry goods and hardware going in yearly." These increased shipments in turn created more freighting jobs. Yet expansion of this consumer market was limited because more wealth allowed more leisure. In contrast to the "laws" of the Euro-Canadian market economy where an individual's desire for capital and material goods (and the security and status they brought) were said to be practically unlimited, Natives in northern Alberta did not usually purchase more consumer goods merely because their incomes had risen. Instead, they often curtailed trapping and took time off once basic needs were satisfied. In addition, people often reduced demand instead of increasing production when the costs of consumer goods rose. After a disastrous fall in prices in 1914, for example, Chipewyan trappers near Fitzgerald set only a few traps, arguing that because of low prices, they would trap only to buy sugar, tea and tobacco.[30]

There were, of course, times when trappers tried to play the market to find higher returns. In 1915 when prices were low, some trappers north of Fort McMurray held their furs off the market hoping that prices would rise later in the year. As they had often done in the previous century, most trappers tried to realize the best price for their fur by bargaining or by selling when prices were higher. But while their wants and needs were increasing and people were becoming more dependent on imported goods, Natives remained reluctant to revamp their economic and personal lives entirely. For the most part, they refused to make the necessary adaptations to a market economy by accumulating capital and stockpiling consumer goods to weather economic cycles or take advantage of market swings. As NWMP Inspector West reported in 1901, while Natives in the Peace River country refused to accept less than "the market price" for their furs, they equally refused to increase production beyond that needed to buy necessities for the coming year. He believed that this partly accounted for a 50 percent reduction in the amount of fur marketed in 1901 from 20 years before.[31]

Although such trends had long been noted by observers and participants in the fur trade, most Euro-Canadians continued to see such economic behaviour as immature and foolish. Failing to recognize this behavior's cultural and social context, many whites appealed to racial stereotypes. In 1906—a year of high prices and plentiful fur—NWMP Superintendent Constantine stated that trappers had "done too well." Rather than acquiring goods and capital, "the Indian, as a general rule, has no thought or idea of saving or preparing for a bad season." Euro-Canadian needs also figured in this equation. As Constantine noted, prosperity had made Natives "utterly indifferent" to wage employment and "the freighting and boating interests" had consequently suffered. The next year, similar views were expressed at Lesser Slave Lake where the NWMP reported that the Natives seemed to be "a fairly industrious and prosperous lot." They lived on game and had "but little food to buy really, but their naturally improvident natures leave them from year to year in much the same position and they don't get appreciably better off."[32]

*Timber, Mining and Fishing*

For many observers, the continued importance of fur in northern Alberta's economy did not obscure the considerable future development potential of the region's other natural resources. Timber was a case in point. Spruce was the commonest tree, and it and other wood were used as fuel for home heating and cooking and for firing steamships. Most buildings were constructed with logs, but local demand for milled lumber increased steadily after 1900. Most was produced locally by both stationary and portable mills. Among the earliest commercial operations was the Roman Catholic mission at Grouard, where as early as 1898 a steam-powered mill produced milled lumber for local sale.[33] By 1908 similar sawmills produced "sufficient good lumber" to meet demand in most of the major settlements. At Athabasca, frame buildings were taking the place of log structures, and large quantities of lumber were used to build scows.[34] Such demand for milled lumber increased with advance settlement in the Peace River country. In 1912 two sawmills operating near Grande Prairie could not keep up with demand, and the next year another mill opened to produce finished lumber and shingles. By then, about seven sawmills were also operating around Lesser Slave Lake. Although the production of these mills was small in provincial terms, there was hope that once railway connections had been established, production for export would develop. But even as purely local manufacturing concerns, the mills provided winter jobs for local people, and, by manufacturing basic products from local resources, were said to contribute "towards the general development of the country."[35]

The view that economic diversification could be achieved by substituting locally produced goods for imported ones and by developing export markets was widespread in Alberta before 1914. Such prospects often focussed on the development of mineral resources. Although there was much fanciful speculation about gold and other mineral deposits, optimism arising from the Geological Survey of Canada's earlier reports about oil in northern Alberta drove most prospectors.[36] This was further encouraged by federal government mining regulations which permitted a prospector who had discovered petroleum in paying quantities to buy 640 acres of land (including the mineral rights) around his discovery at $1 per acre.[37]

In the Peace River country, natural gas springs and "tar springs" about 25 kilometres from Peace River indicated petroleum reserves, and hopes were high that oil would be found. Lord Rhondda and J.D. McArthur began drilling for oil near Peace River town in 1915, and 181 petroleum leases were applied for on nearby lands in 1915–16. Reports of an oil discovery in 1915 created "a mad rush for the lands office" to file claims. Over 200 men lined up at the office, some sleeping overnight in the line. Despite the failure to strike oil, enthusiasm remained high in the Peace River country. In 1907, Alfred von Hammerstein, an ex-Klondiker who had stayed in northern Alberta (where he became an ostentatious and shady oil promoter), told the Senate inquiry that there was "no doubt" that petroleum would be found "from the Athabasca River to the Peace River." But the resources of the Fort McMurray area garnered the most attention, and Hammerstein painted a picture of oil wealth waiting to be gathered up. As he told the Senators, petroleum at Fort McMurray had "broken through the surface and soaked the ground for miles around." This drew on the theory that the oil sands resulted from an "upwelling" of huge pools of oil. Much like famous oil strikes in the 1800s at Petrolia, Ontario and in Pennsylvania, which had occurred in areas with surface oil seepage, the dream persisted that the Fort McMurray petroleum deposits could be tapped by conventional drilling. Alfred von Hammerstein as well as a number of other oil exploration outfits (including one involving Jim Cornwall) drilled for oil between 1906 and 1913 near Fort McMurray. By 1912, there was "hardly a foot of land without a claims notice on it" on both sides of the river between Fort McMurray and Fort McKay. Adding to the drama and the aura of frontier struggle, all of the heavy equipment was taken in by scow from Athabasca. These projects encouraged much speculative fervour, which declined not because of failure but because of the discovery of crude oil at Turner Valley near Calgary in 1913. The accessibility of these deposits to markets was a sober reminder of the disadvantages of production in northern Alberta which was so distant from markets. The speculative binge that accompanied the discovery at Turner Valley and its more immediately profitable fields close to Calgary helped divert attention and capital from northern oil exploration.[38]

Of greater long term importance for northern Alberta was the recognition by some observers that the bitumen in the oil sands at Fort McMurray could be processed into asphalt for roofing, paving and similar uses. A small sidewalk paving experiment in Edmonton in 1911 using raw oil sands showed early interest in potential uses for the material, but scientific knowledge about the size of oil sands reserves and extraction methods was rudimentary. In 1913, J.L. Coté, the MLA for the constituency of Athabasca (which included Fort McMurray), requested technical information about the extent and potential of the oil sands deposits from the federal Mines Branch in Ottawa. Sidney Ells, a mining engineer with the branch, discovered that little more than promotional platitudes was known about the resource. The need for detailed scientific surveys was obvious, and at his own request, Ells was assigned to the project.[39]

Hiring a scow and four men in Athabasca, Ells travelled down the Athabasca River to Fort McMurray in the spring of 1913. During the summer he surveyed a number of locations and selected an area on the Horse River at Fort McMurray as an oil sands reserve where experiments might be carried out and from which material for possible paving projects in Canada's national parks could be mined. The creation of such a reserve also served wider objectives. At the time, recognition of the strategic military importance of oil was growing in Britain. Out of Imperial obligations and a recognition of its own dependence on imported oil, Canada responded by placing reserves over two areas with significant petroleum resources—Turner Valley and the Fort McMurray area—and stipulated that only British or Canadian firms could take out leases. Thus, Canada's commitment to survey and study the oil sands was not, as historian Barry Ferguson notes, merely a response to provincial agitation for immediate economic development, but part of broader national policies.[40]

In the fall, Ells and his crew strenuously tracked about eight tonnes of equipment and samples upstream to Athabasca from where it was shipped to Ottawa. There, Ells prepared a report on the potential of the oil sands at Fort McMurray. Although he recognized that commercial development was possible only if there was adequate transportation to markets, he concluded that the most practical use for the oil sands was for paving asphalt; a focus that dominated federal research efforts until about 1930. Demand for this product was developing on the prairies because of expanding settlement and an increased need for smoothly surfaced highways for a growing number of automobiles and trucks. Moreover, Ells concluded that new methods for extracting commercial quantities of petroleum products from the oil sands needed to devised and that the value of the deposits could be determined only through systematic surveys using core drilling techniques. Ells returned to Fort McMurray in 1914 and again in 1915, and also supervised an experimental paving project in Edmonton. He spent the next two years in Pittsburg at the Mellon Industrial Research Institute carrying out experiments on methods of separating bitumen from the sand. By this time, Ells had also concluded that the Mines Branch alone should be responsible for federal experimental work on the oil sands. As historians Jim Parker and Ken Tingley observe, this "proprietorial attitude" was characteristic of Ells's position on oil sands research, and along with an often unyielding, strong and sometimes quirky personality, soon embroiled him in conflict with other researchers.[41]

Although the often rambling character of Ells's reports also led to criticism by other scientists, his conclusions proved to be the indispensable basis for future development. As Barry Ferguson notes, they were "a critical check" on federal government hopes for development at Fort McMurray because they established that the oil sands were the important resource, not mythical pools of oil below them. This forced an entirely new approach by establishing that the oil sands were similar to other such deposits in North America and that "the separation of the bitumen from the mineral matter constituted the only way that petroleum would be recovered." With this conclusion, Ells helped establish the correct geological and engineering parameters for future oil sands research.[42] This did not, however, bring immediate changes in approaches to the oil sands. Promoters ignored these findings and continued to drill for pools of oil, and other boosters, including many of Edmonton's business class, disregarded the developmental difficulties that Ells's conclusions outlined. But business groups nonetheless welcomed efforts to expand knowledge and assess the commercial potential of the oil sands. From his vantage point as an Alberta MLA, J.L. Coté promoted Ells's findings, and Frank Oliver praised them and the work of the Mines Branch in the House of Commons. This was exactly the sort of positive, practical government research that Oliver and Canadian business favoured. But without adequate transportation to the Fort McMurray area, development was impossible, and only after the completion of the A&GW and its further extension in the mid 1920s did industrial development of the oil sands become feasible.[43]

Despite ongoing research about the oil sands, fish resources were of greater immediate potential in northern Alberta. The finest fishing lakes were Lesser Slave Lake, Lake Athabasca and numerous small lakes in the eastern parts of the region. The first commercial fishing in northern Alberta took place in the winter of 1904–05 when the Dominion Fish Company, an "eastern Canadian" concern, fished Lesser Slave Lake. Employing about 25 imported workers, about 32,000 kilograms of whitefish were caught with gill nets through the ice. Since the local population met all of its own needs itself, there was no local market and the catch was shipped over winter trails to Edmonton. Such slow and costly transportation made production of a low priced and perishable commodity unprofitable, and as was noted in 1906, "the weather is often very mild and the fish taints before it can be marketed." Moreover, the fish trade in Alberta was a tough business. The Euro-Canadian population in settled areas did not consume much fish, and small merchants disliked handling it. In this environment, wholesale buyers were willing to handle only carload shipments.[44]

While there was some further commercial fishing during the next winter at Lesser Slave Lake, it operated only intermittently during the next eight years. Local Natives apparently did not find commercial fishing attractive. Winter fishing conflicted with trapping and fur was easier to market and more profitable. It was also an unfamiliar activity and required capital for equipment and marketing. Most commercial fishing remained focussed near Edmonton, where the resources of relatively small lakes (such as Lake Wabamum) were sufficient for provincial demand. But the wealth of fish in northern lakes remained tantalizing, and in the winter of 1908–09 a Mr. Moore of Edmonton began commercial fishing on Calling Lake, about 80 kilometres north of Athabasca. Said to be a profitable operation, about 1,000 whitefish per day were caught and hauled to Edmonton. Moore employed Swedish and Native workers, who were relatively well paid for the time, receiving $60 per month plus room and board. Even so, still less than one-half of the whitefish caught in the province came from northern lakes by 1912–13. Almost as much fish was marketed from Lake Wabamum as from Lesser Slave Lake. Other lakes, especially Cold and Primrose lakes, also produced significant amounts. By 1912, however, the start of track laying for the ED&BC changed prospects for commercial fishing on Lesser Slave Lake. As well, a plant for smoking fish was set up in 1913 near Slave Lake (then called Sawridge), which it was said would become "a great industry" because of Lesser Slave Lake's abundant lake trout and whitefish.[45]


## ▬ Limited Enterprise

### Farming Before the Arrival of the Railway

In the same way that limited transportation and markets restricted lumbering, mining and fishing, agricultural development also remained tentative. Almost no grain was grown at Fort Chipewyan or Fitzgerald because of poor soil and a short growing season, and only a few cattle and horses were raised by the Hudson's Bay Company, the NWMP and the Catholic mission. Farming was limited even in parts of the Peace River country and Lesser Slave Lake districts where it was feasible. In 1901, for example, the settlers at the Shaftesbury settlement, consisting of about 20 families plus the staff of the two missions, produced only sufficient grain and vegetables for their own needs. Although a few hogs were kept, game was usually the only meat consumed in the settlement.[46]

Such limited farming was inevitable because local markets could only absorb small-scale agricultural production and the transportation system could not handle exports. Indeed, as the Alberta Department of Agriculture confessed in 1907, its knowledge about northern farming was slight. But as was demonstrated at Fort Vermilion—the largest and most important farm community in northern Alberta before 1910—when markets were available, northern agriculture was successful. Wheat, oats, barley and vegetables had been commercially grown there since the late 1800s to supply northern fur trade posts, including those along the Mackenzie River. In this sense, the northern Peace River country was still a larder of the fur trade. In 1902, the Hudson's Bay Company constructed a 50 barrel-a-day steam-powered gristmill at Fort Vermilion to produce flour for its northern posts. This flour cost about 40 percent less than that imported from Edmonton, even though farmers at Fort Vermilion and Shaftesbury settlement (which was easily accessible by river) apparently demanded exorbitant prices for their wheat. While the Hudson's Bay Company circumvented these demands by planting some wheat on its own land at Fort Vermilion, it calculated that a more efficient way to lower prices was to promote increased private production. Accordingly, it sold farm implements at cost to local farmers, reasoning that if production expanded because of mechanization, prices would fall. This policy apparently worked; by 1908, 1,200 acres of grain, mostly wheat and barley, were planted. The Fort Vermilion district had about 60 farmers and ranchers and a population of about 370, and the settlement boasted four threshers (two of them steam-powered), 15 binders, 250 horses and about 1,000 cattle and hogs. Farming activity had also expanded at Shaftesbury settlement and in 1908 most of the grain grown there was shipped to Fort Vermilion. Increased numbers of hogs and cattle were also kept at both places, especially at Fort Vermilion where the Hudson's Bay Company encouraged hog raising to supply meat to its northern posts.[47]

For some observers, developments at Fort Vermilion demonstrated northern Alberta's agricultural future. As Agnes Deans Cameron noted in 1910 during her travels in the north, "Vermilion farmers boast sulkies and gang-ploughs and the latest geared McCormick, Massey Harris, and Deering farm implements—self-binders and seeders. Everything is up-to-date." But appearances were deceptive; Fort Vermilion's modernity and growth relied on limited fur trade markets, not the larger national and international ones available to prairie farmers close to rail lines. And it was apparent that agriculture in northern Alberta—as in the rest of prairie Canada—would depend on foreign markets for the extensive (rather than intensive) agriculture that would be practised. Thus, despite Fort Vermilion's agricultural potential, trapping was "still the main occupation of the settlers" and "the principal trade of the country" by 1915.[48]

The practical testing of northern Alberta's agricultural potential nonetheless expanded with increased settlement in advance of the railway. The earliest sizeable movement of Euro-Canadian settlers to northern Alberta before the railway occurred around Athabasca between 1900 and 1905. Homesteading entries increased further following land surveys in 1905–06. In the Peace River country, this anticipatory period began later. Settlement spread westward from Lesser Slave Lake, and by 1908 the district around Peace River town had about 200 settlers while Grouard had about 250 residents. About 50 settlers had also established themselves around High Prairie (then called Prairie River), a short distance south-west of Grouard. Agricultural development was also beginning further west on the Grande Prairie—the fertile district stretching west from the Smoky River—and near Spirit River. By 1911, the Euro-Canadian population of the Peace River country was about 1,200, up from about 750 five years before. As prospects for rail connections increased, settlement expanded and between 1911 and 1916 the population grew to just over 6,100. In 1914 it was noted that the Peace River country "was filling fast with settlers."[49] Most settlement continued to take place south of the Peace River on the relatively open lands near Grande Prairie and Beaverlodge. While the most important settlement node was Grande Prairie, settlers were also attracted to the Spirit River, High Prairie, McLennan and Pouce Coupe (British Columbia) areas south of the river. Waterhole and Friedenstal (both near present day Fairview), as well as Berwyn and Grimshaw north of the Peace River also drew some settlers.[50]

As geographer P. L. McCormick has noted in his study of settlement in Saskatchewan, such developments showed that the pace of railway construction and settlement "did not always coincide." While settlers counted on the rails reaching their land in the foreseeable future, trails, not railways, "were the forerunners of development."[51] But while advance settlement in an area such as the Peace River country was not a unique pattern in prairie Canada, it was noteworthy. It was the furthest north that farm settlement had penetrated in Canada, and the district was separated from the edge of continuous settlement at Edmonton by a long stretch of nonarable land.

Why then did advance settlement in the Peace River country happen when it did? After all, there had been times of excitement and anticipation before, but only a handful of people had moved north. Indeed, in 1910 the agricultural potential of the Grande Prairie was still unproven and some observers surmised that the land along the Peace River between Dunvegan and Fort Vermilion would prove to be better farm land. There were only a few hundred acres in crop on the Grande Prairie, wage work was scarce and successful settlers required independent means. Moreover, proposals for a railway to the region remained—as the Dominion Lands Agent in Edmonton remarked in 1910—as tentative and rumour-filled as before. While he hoped that settlers would "not be forced to abandon their homesteads" because of the lack of a railway, he was not convinced that construction would begin soon.[52] Despite these apparent drawbacks, settlers going to the Peace River country by 1911 assumed that permanent settlements with railway connections were likely. Alberta was by then committed to supporting railway connections to northern Alberta, while Edmonton newspapers proffered stories and banner headlines about imminent railways to the north. As well, the CNoR was building towards Athabasca by 1910, which held promise of further connections to the Peace River country.[53] Such views were strengthened in 1912 with the inauguration of train service to Athabasca and the start of track-laying on the ED&BC between Edmonton and Peace River.

The prospect of rail communications was, however, only one factor among several that stimulated advance settlement. Although the settlement boom was slowing on the southern prairies, many Canadians remained as emotionally and economically committed to the promise of a new start and free land as before, prompting interest in the northern frontier. While some critics noted that between 25 and 30 percent of the land in the Grande Prairie, Dunvegan and Peace River districts was timbered, as was about 60 percent in the Spirit River and Fort Vermilion districts, it was popularly believed that there was plenty of open "prairie" land in the Peace River country.[54] While much forested homestead land remained in accessible areas in all three prairie provinces, by 1909 the amount of "open prairie" homestead land was comparatively small. This helped turn prospective settlers towards the Peace River district where it was said there were large stretches of open land. So too, there was now little reluctance to settle on uplands. Settlers in the Peace River country before 1911, like settlers on the southern prairies in the 1870s and 1880s, had strongly favoured river-bottom land out of fear of early frosts and a belief that uplands were dry and inhospitable.[55] By 1911 such concerns had diminished. Open prairie lands had by then been farmed successfully for several decades on the southern plains, while confidence about the Peace River country had also grown because of the introduction there in about 1910 of the high quality and

*Agricultural exhibitions, like the first one at Peace River town in 1911, provided an opportunity to showcase the agricultural bounty of the land.* A2557 PAA.

earlier maturing Marquis wheat. South African scrip for two quarter sections each also became available in 1908, the same year that homestead regulations were changed to allow larger farm units (160 acres of arable land for each homestead, rather than a total of 160 acres) in the Peace River country. Although knowledge about climate, soils and precipitation remained sketchy, real estate promoters seized on all of these developments, extolling the beauty and fertility of the Peace River country, often exaggerating the extent of its open grasslands that could be obtained at little cost as a homestead and put into production quickly.[56]

Once word spread that settlement in the Peace River country was about to take off, a self-fulfilling dynamic developed. From Calgary, William Pearce rather disdainfully watched the beginnings of advance settlement in the Peace River country and commented that he still believed the value of the district was overestimated. But "it is difficult to prevent people shoving to the front, there seems to be a fascination about it." This pushing to the front brought further settlement and encouraged the expansion of government infrastructure to support it. Settlers could now register their land holdings in local land offices, and further land surveys were undertaken after 1912 to keep up with settlement. As was noted in 1910, even though surveying was ongoing in the Grande Prairie district, settlers were "squatting beyond the survey."[57] Other developments, such as the expansion of postal and telegraph communications and road construction, created further optimism about the region's imminent integration with the national economy.

Most of these settlers had "mixed" farms where they raised livestock and grew some oats, wheat, barley and forage crops. Mixed farming was widely supported by farm experts who believed that it provided the best base for a rural economy. Indeed, some observers predicted that this period of isolated development would be beneficial in the long term for establishing mixed farming on a sound basis in northern Alberta. As was noted in 1913, the lack of a railway prevented the shipment of grain from the Grande Prairie district, forcing settlers "to go in for more stock raising, to use up the grain grown." Indeed, it was confidently forecast that since "this district is an ideal one for mixed farming, those who have adapted themselves to conditions will be in good shape to profit once a railway comes." Other ideas and institutions familiar to prairie farmers—such as agricultural societies—were also introduced. A greatly praised institution among rural reformers and agricultural experts, agricultural societies were designed to promote scientific farming and self-help by sponsoring lectures, agricultural fairs and demonstration projects. Such a society was organized at High Prairie in 1910 with 102 founding members (including a number of Metis) from Grouard, High Prairie and district. By 1912, others had been established at Spirit River, Peace River and Grande Prairie.[58]

The social institutions these settlers implanted were the familiar ones "imprinted with the technical, governmental, social, religious, and cultural features of the nation at large."[59] Elementary schools supported by local property taxes and administered by locally elected school boards were established in some districts, and places like Grande Prairie, Peace River, Lake Saskatoon and Falher offered settlers a range of services, including newspapers (started in Grande Prairie in 1913 and in Peace River in 1914). A hospital was established in Grande Prairie in 1911 by the Presbyterian Church, while one funded by local charitable donations was opened in 1914 in Peace River. In 1914 Grande Prairie consisted of 25 buildings, while Peace River grew from 125 to about 700 people between 1913 and 1914. Both settlements were incorporated as villages in 1914.[60]

At the local level, this emerging settlement pattern indicated the shift in farming from the Fort Vermilion district, and its connection with the fur trade, to the southern Peace River country, and its potential orientation to the export-oriented prairie farm economy. In 1915, gristmills were operating at Lake Saskatoon and Grande Prairie, and when the Hudson's Bay Company grist mill in Fort Vermilion burned that year, it was not rebuilt; likely because grain farming was then expanding more rapidly in the southern Peace River country. Despite these developments, few of these advance settlers enjoyed easy conditions. The limits of agricultural development and the nature of the northern economy forced them into the same economic patterns followed by many Native people in northern Alberta. It was an economy of "makeshifts"—of wage work when (and wherever) available, subsistence farming, trapping and hunting that together brought in enough income.[61]

Reinforcing this makeshifts economy, the Peace River country's deep river valleys and broken topography created barriers to continuous settlement and made communication among the small farm settlements difficult. This also added to the customary isolation and difficulties of pioneering. As one woman wrote from Dunvegan in 1913, "our country is beautiful to look upon," but she did not like "living out here." Travel was slow and difficult, medical help was far away, mail was infrequent, furniture was crude, and food was limited, especially in winter. People did little other than look after essentials. "You cannot buy lumber for building purposes. You must cut and skid and haul and hew logs for all your buildings," obtain food and water, and put up hay for the horses. The farm economy was tentative, and in 1914 settlers in the southern Peace River country had large amounts of unsold grain from the previous year. Most people were short of cash, and the outbreak of war that year put most commercial business on a cash basis, foretelling further problems for people already finding it difficult to make ends meet.[62]

## ▬ Settlers

As a northward extension of prairie settlement, the ethnicity of the Euro-Canadian settlers who reached northern Alberta before the railway was similar to that found elsewhere in prairie Canada. In the Athabasca area before 1912, most settlers were British and Canadian (especially French Canadian). A greater number of Americans and Europeans arrived subsequently. In 1913, the Dominion Lands Agent at Grouard reported that most settlers in the southern Peace River country were from eastern Canada and the United States. While statistics on the national and ethnic origin of settlers in the Peace River country are scarce before 1931, people's origins can be surmised from the 1931 Canadian census figures because ethnic composition remained relatively stable in settled agricultural districts. Thus, it appears that people of British origin formed about one-half the population in 1913, while Germans and Scandinavians formed the next largest group. Relatively few people were from central or southern Europe. This was the same population mix as in the rest of Alberta, except that the Scandinavian population was somewhat higher, and the central European population lower, than was typical elsewhere in the province.[63]

Single men were most prominent among these early settlers. In 1911, the first year for which statistics are available, there were 194 males to every 100 females in the southern Peace River country. This ratio had increased further by 1916, but then began to decline, signalling increased settlement by families. While gender imbalance was common in periods of rapid migration in western Canada, the bachelor homesteader was a historical discontinuity. The fur trade had depended on significant participation by women, as would the later settled agricultural period. The predominance of men over women in the initial stage of settlement was thus a historical anomaly in western Canada, but one that accommodated the transitional economy of the region at the time. As a Dominion Lands surveyor suggested in 1904, most single men in the Peace River country seemed "perfectly satisfied" with their lives. Indeed, he thought that only they could be successful, for a man with a family to support "would have many trials before him." In the Bluesky district, for example, poor crops in 1916 promised a difficult winter, but bachelor farmers had greater flexibility than those with families. Most single men joined the army, shipped out to the United States or the southern prairies to work as harvest labourers, or went north to trap. For families, conditions were more difficult. Although married men commonly worked away from home for wages in the winter, family obligations lessened mobility. Women with children had even less ability to move, making their lives more isolated and hard.[64]

While each settler no doubt had personal motives for coming north, together they shared a desire for land, independence and greater personal and economic freedom. A few came to escape persecution, such as a group of African-Americans from Oklahoma who settled north-east of Athabasca at Amber Valley between 1910 and 1912. Although they moved to Canada to escape growing racism in the United States, they also came up against it, albeit in not as virulent a form, in northern Alberta. The NWMP reported that some whites in Athabasca, like some homesteaders near Amber Valley, were antagonistic to these migrants. These views were especially common among settlers of American origin, many of whom had "very little use for a negro." The Calgary and Edmonton boards of trade also protested, while Frank Oliver too weighed in against them and, as minister of the Interior, approved regulations restricting further Afro-American immigration. Indeed, historian Harold Troper attributes the ending of Black immigration to Canada in late 1912 to this discriminatory legislation, although others have argued that Oklahoma Blacks had by then also shifted their sights from western Canada to northern U.S. cities. Even so, around 300 Blacks were living on 95 homesteads at Amber Valley by 1913. While it is unclear why they chose the area, its isolation was perhaps part of its attraction—given their experience in the United States, they wanted to live away from white people. As well, the north was being heavily promoted, and once a nucleus of people had settled there, others were drawn by friends and family.[65]

Religious and cultural motives in combination with a hunger for land brought others to northern Alberta.[66] The popular prairie view of pioneering as a new start in a new land obscures that many settlers saw the new land as a place for preserving old ways or distinctive beliefs. This was the case with the "Bull Outfit" (sometimes called the "Burnsites" after the name of their leader), a small group of break-away Methodists from Ontario who settled on the uplands near present day Beaverlodge between 1909 and 1911. A number of German Catholics also settled in the Friedenstal and Waterhole area, near present-day Fairview. Another religiously inspired settlement was a group of Norwegians who purchased Metis scrip land in 1912–13 and created a community they optimistically called Valhalla. They came from Norway, the United States and the Camrose area, where homestead land was no longer available. But their quest was not just for land. Scattered throughout North America, Norwegians were rapidly assimilating and losing their religious cohesion as a people. Halvor Ronning, a minister in the Norwegian Lutheran Church of America near Camrose, saw group settlement in the Peace River country as one solution. As he wrote, "it was the Lord who called me and sent me, I never doubted. As Abraham was commanded to get out of his country to go unto a land the Lord would show him, so sounded in my heart an inner call to me."[67]

Similar religious and cultural motives also prompted group settlement by French Canadian Roman Catholics from other parts of the prairies, Quebec and New England.[68] In Alberta, such settlements were initially in the Edmonton and St. Paul areas, but several were also set up around McLennan after 1912. While the leaders of the movement stressed the good agricultural prospects of the area, they also urged people to preserve their language and faith and not merely to pursue wealth. Led by Father Giroux, the sixth party of these settlers landed at Grouard in 1913. Even so, migration from Quebec failed to reach the levels its most optimistic supporters anticipated because of the indifference of the Quebec French-Canadian elite and, among other factors, a perception that the west was a hostile environment for French Canadians.[69]

While advance settlement by whites in northern Alberta was heralded by many Euro-Canadians as proof of their daring and pluck, many Natives recognized it as a threat to their way of life. The Treaty Commissioners had remarked in 1899 that the vast size of the country and Native reluctance to take up reserves allowed "quite time enough" to lay out reserves "as advancing settlement" required. And in 1906, similar sentiments were expressed in the observation that northern Alberta was truly a Native "Paradise," where there were "but few reserves and no resident agents at all," and the whole country was "one immense reserve."[70]

But change came more quickly than expected. In 1908 the first Indian Agency was established in northern Alberta. Headquartered in Grouard, the Lesser Slave Lake agency supervised a huge territory containing all the bands in the western parts of northern Alberta and north-eastern British Columbia. In 1911 another agency was opened at Fort Smith for the Athabasca country. Both were more a symbol of Indian Affairs' intentions than the actual exercise of control over the Indian population—the agents' influence over the daily lives of Indians was minimal because of slow communications and limited staff.[71] More important in signalling changing conditions and perceptions was the waning of earlier Indian opposition to reserves. Many Indians, especially in areas where white settlement was beginning or imminent, began to see reserves as a protective measure in a time of rapid change. As elsewhere on the prairies, Indian demands for the assignment of reservations in northern Alberta was often part of an effort to protect and enhance particular needs. As geographer Frank Tough noted, Indians in northern Manitoba "selected reserves based on their prior occupation of sites that offered a favourable combination of available resources."[72]

While reserves offered one means of protecting Indian interests, they had other far-reaching effects. For one, they helped codify legal distinctions between Indian and Metis and created an "ethnic division of space" by establishing areas where only Indians or their relatives lived. At first, the process was fluid. People who had been missed in the negotiations in 1899 and 1900 continued to be admitted to treaty or were issued scrip. Other people moved in and out of treaty as long as applications for scrip or treaty were heard by the federal government. The decisions people made in this respect remain imperfectly understood. While the process ostensibly involved self-definition as a treaty Indian, a non-Indian or as Metis, it also seems to have sometimes simply been a matter of jockeying for relative advantage and immediate gain. Father Grouard contended in 1900 that some Indians, encouraged by traders and scrip hunters, were "tempted to call themselves HalfBreeds and repudiate their treaty agreements in order to ask for scrip." This was also the conclusion of NWMP Inspector West, who made the observation in 1903 that most Metis were such only "because they were issued with scrip, whereas in reality they have just as much Indian blood in them as any that are in Treaty."[73]

The distinctions brought by Canadian legal practice and by the treaty created a situation in which identity came to involve a relationship among the individual, his or her legal status, and rights to land use. These distinctions were formalized further in 1912 when the option of scrip was withdrawn and all Aboriginal claims were henceforth dealt with solely by admission to treaty.[74] As a result, crossovers between the two communities became more difficult, and while reserves brought one part of the Native community (Treaty Indians) under more direct government control, they in practical terms also established that Metis had no special legal status.

At the request of the respective bands, two small provisional reserves were laid out in 1901 on the south shore of the west end of Lesser Slave Lake. One was for Kinoosayo's band at Sandy Bay and the other was for Moostoos's band at Sucker Creek. Other reserves were also laid out along the southern shore of the lake, and a number of applications for land in severalty were also registered. At Shaftesbury settlement in 1901, Indians selected separate places on the river flats where farming was possible. Since it was difficult to find farm and hay land together, separate lands for each activity were temporarily staked out where some of the Indians (such as Duncan Tustawits) had farmed for a number of years. Tustawits took his land in severalty. Other reserves were surveyed north of Dunvegan and in two large parcels south of Bear Lake (now Lac Cardinal). At Sturgeon Lake, surveying was held up because the Indians were said to have "the most inflated idea of the amount of land they are entitled to." This was not a dispute over the assignment of a reserve, only about its size, and by 1908 the Sturgeon Lake Cree had accepted a reserve.[75]

Indian demands for reserves, and the government's willingness to survey them in districts where white pressure on land was either mounting or fore-seeable, recognized the possibility of conflict. Many Indians found themselves in a contest for land with incoming or prospective white settlers. At Shaftesbury settlement, the reserves selected in 1901 were finally surveyed in 1905 because tensions were rising between Indians and incoming whites, some of whom were claiming the same land.[76] Even at Wabasca in 1909, which was well away from areas of growing white settlement, people "staked out two reserves for themselves" and demanded immediate surveys to secure the land "from the intrusion of the white settler, who, they say, are already looking over the country with a view to settling." Although local Indian Affairs officials urged haste in meeting this request, reserves were only surveyed at Wabasca in 1913. During a speculative real estate boom at Fort McMurray before World War I, a similar desire to preempt white newcomers prompted Indians there to settle on land they wanted as a reserve. Again, Ottawa was urged to survey the reserve immediately because "white squatters have been coming into the district in great numbers, and the longer this matter is postponed, the more difficult it will be to set aside reservations without a considerable amount of friction and trouble." Thus the surveying of a reserve by 1916 was welcomed because there would be "no further cause of annoyance from white settlers squatting on Indian locations."[77]

The situation at Fort McMurray indicated that haste on such matters was often crucial. Everyone involved was well aware that white squatters would try and oust Indians from unsurveyed land. In 1913 the Department of the Interior agreed to record Indian occupation of unsurveyed land "in the same way as the claims of white squatters." While white squatters could later file for a homestead patent for such land, Indians could not because they were excluded from the homestead system. However, since Treaty 8 allowed the holding of land in severalty, small plots of land could later be granted as a reserve, and the Department of the Interior confirmed that "the proper recording of their claims in our registers" would "sufficiently protect" Indian occupation of designated lands.[78]

Despite such provisions, Indian Affairs was reluctant to set aside reserves in areas with little real or prospective potential for white farmers. By 1909, members of the Beaver band at Fort Vermilion had selected land they wanted for a reserve, but Indian Affairs officials told them that "there was no immediate hurry" to have it surveyed "as it would be some years before any white settlers would be coming in." Such delays were also experienced by Indians at Fort Smith. By 1916, the Department of Indian Affairs had asked the Department of the Interior to prevent squatters from occupying two parcels of land that had been assigned as reserves near Fort Smith, but the land was not surveyed because of World War I and the failure to resolve conflicts over setting up Wood Buffalo Park.[79] Similarly, land was set aside at Fort Chipewyan following a land survey in 1913–15, but it was not reserve land as promised by the treaty and it merely specified that only Indians could build houses there. A reserve near Fort Chipewyan was not surveyed for a number of years.

## Reserve Farming

While the emphasis on establishing reserves in areas of actual or potential white settlement met the needs of Euro-Canadian settlers, it was also consistent with federal government policies that ostensibly encouraged Indians to farm when possible. This approach, however, was constrained in northern Alberta by its vast stretches of nonarable land where many Indians continued to have other opportunities, especially trapping. As Indian Affairs reported in 1900, many Indians in Treaty 8 were not inclined to take up farming because "the more congenial occupations of hunting and fishing are still open, and agriculture is not only arduous to those untrained to it, but in many districts it as yet remains untried." Thus, with almost a sigh of relief, the department concluded that expenditures for agricultural development as promised in the treaty would not be required in many locations for years to come. Nonetheless, farming remained part of the long-range plan for those northern Alberta Indians living on reserves. Like the missionaries, Indian Affairs officials saw farming as a way of recasting the Indian economy and lifestyle in a Euro-Canadian mould. Farming presumed a sedentary way of life—a full-time job that gave security and long-term prosperity. As historian Sarah Carter observes, the prevailing attitude held that "the Indian had to be taught to make his living from the soil. No other occupation could so assuredly dispossess the Indian of his nomadic habits and the uncertainties of the chase, and fix upon him the values of a permanent abode and the security of a margin of surplus." Moreover, it would teach thrift, an appreciation of private property, "impart a will to own and master nature," and teach "the necessity of habitual toil, systematic work, and attention to detail."[80]

While farming opportunities varied by location, it is apparent that some Indians in northern Alberta, as elsewhere on the prairies, did want to farm. On a number of occasions, Indian Affairs reported that Indians in the Peace River country and along the southern shore of Lesser Slave Lake were eager to farm because they saw their economy changing with the appearance of white settlers.[81] This was consistent with the Indians' view that reserves would help protect their economic interests, but it did not mean that they sought a drastic revamping of their lifestyle. Few Indians lived on the reserves year round, using them instead as a seasonal base for hunting, fishing and work on river crews. This was the case near Fort McMurray in 1916, and Indians in the Lesser Slave Lake district in 1907 did not "live on the reserve much, but are scattered in small encampments, hunting and fishing for their livelihood."[82] These patterns suggest that those Indians who farmed did so within the context of their individual economic needs and the nature of the regional economy. Farming offered an opportunity to supplement an already highly mixed personal economy, and perhaps a chance to provide some insurance for the future once white settlement had increased. As Frank Tough found in Indian communities in northern Manitoba, interest in farming rose and fell along with other economic conditions such as fur prices and the availability of freighting or other work.[83] Nonetheless, by 1910, there were a few horses and cattle and a few acres of garden crops on most reserves in the Peace River country and around Lesser Slave Lake. Some also had a few acres in oats, and most produced hay for winter feed for reserve livestock or for sale to Euro-Canadian settlers. In some cases, as with the Swan River band in 1910, the Indians sold their hay in the stopping places they operated along the lake. Band members also had gardens, a few livestock, cut firewood for sale, fished, hunted, trapped and worked for wages on the boats or elsewhere as available. Their annuity payments also provided a small yearly financial cushion.[84]

But subsistence farming was not commercial agriculture. All farming in northern Alberta before 1916 was constrained by limited markets, but while the failure of Euro-Canadian farming was invariably said to be proof of why a railway was needed, identical subsistence farming on reserves was said to be a sign of personal failure. In its annual reports, Indian Affairs continually blamed the Indians, claiming that they were "easily discouraged," careless with farm equipment and inattentive to the routines of farming because they preferred hunting and trapping.[85] But these stereotypes about Natives obscured more than they revealed because they ignored the economic context of the region and the department's own neglect in fulfilling treaty promises to assist those Indians who wanted to farm. Indeed, although Indian and white observers recognized that a shift from subsistence to commercial farming required equipment and training, such assistance was limited and slow to appear. At Peace River in 1900, Duncan and David Tustawits had broken 30 acres while Xavier and Modishe Mooswah had broken 10. Several other band members had also broken a few acres. Because they had no farm implements, they had to borrow them from neighbours. As NWMP Sergeant Butler advised Indian Affairs, "if the implements are here for them for the Spring work, they will have quite a crop." They needed to break as much land as soon as possible "if they are going to farm and get as good a start as possible." The same pattern was seen elsewhere. By 1902, the year in which the reserve was provisionally surveyed, the Indians at Sucker Creek had built 13 houses but had planted only three acres of wheat and oats because they had insufficient seed grain. The same situation existed on the neighbouring reserve at Sandy Bay. The Indians there had broken a few patches of land for potatoes, but they complained that they could not till the land without hoes and rakes. Apparently they had a plough for breaking, but their ponies were not strong enough to pull it. Draught horses or oxen were needed, and while the government had arranged for the delivery of 6 cows and a bull (an "ox") the previous year, the bull died on the long overland trail from Edmonton. In any case, the Indians had never used ploughs and did "not know anything about them." Nor did Indian Affairs provide advice on farming or the use of equipment because it did "not approve of sending an [farm] Instructor to the Indians of Treaty No. 8 at present." Consequently, Chief Kinoosayo took matters into his own hands and hired a man (who had been taught how to operate a mower by a neighbouring Metis) from the nearby Sucker Creek reserve to cut the hay.[86]

Despite these problems, farming on the reserves along Lesser Slave Lake was described three years later as relatively successful. Cattle, potatoes, oats, barley and hay were produced and the Indians were described as "enterprising and trying to get along."[87] While Indian Affairs officials in the field sent a constant stream of requests to Ottawa for farm instructors and better and more equipment, their requests were ignored. By 1915, on the eve of the arrival of the railway and the beginning of a new phase in Peace River agriculture, Indians in the Lesser Slave Lake Agency were unprepared to take advantage of new economic opportunities. Indian Affairs admitted that, "with the exception of a few mowers and rakes, there is no farm machinery in this agency" and less than half the reserves had any equipment at all. In 1908 the department justified its failure to provide equipment and training by stating that, despite a solid start, progress in farming on the Lesser Slave Lake reserves was held back because "the country is good for hunting, and fur being high, it pays them better than farming." In 1915 a similar justification appeared in the department's annual report when it was noted that "these Indian have enough for their needs, as farming is not one of their chief occupations." These claims were doubtless true in some cases; it would have been remarkable if people had abandoned familiar and accepted ways of life for something new and largely unknown. Even so, Indian Affairs recognized with a cruel logic the implications of the changing local economy. In 1908, it noted that Indians in areas where white settlement was imminent would soon have to earn their livelihood as farmers because hunting would soon be "a thing of the past."[88]

Such conditions support Sarah Carter's argument that government failure to provide the equipment and technology needed for western farming ensured the failure of reserve agriculture on the southern prairies. Although it had not been explained as such during the treaty negotiations in 1899, farm implements and stock for reserve farms granted under Treaty 8 were treated as "once-for-all" provisions and not as a pledge for economic development. With a few exceptions, such as a short-lived attempt to establish a farm colony at Salt River near Fort Smith in 1911–12, Indian Affairs' overall policy amounted to letting things slide until increased Euro-Canadian activity had destroyed trapping and hunting and forced the Indians to farm or take up other work.[89] Given this strategy, the department's commitment to enhancing Indian economic security was minimal. Instead, it allowed resource depletion to form the heart of its policies. As the Secretary of Indian Affairs, J.D. McLean, phrased it in 1902, the department did not wish to bring Natives in remote or unceded territories into what it called "premature contact" with Euro-Canadian economy or society. The department was content "to follow the natural order of events and wait until advancing civilization has so interfered with their natural resources as to convince them of the absolute necessity for turning for their maintenance to industrial pursuits, with which they have in the meantime become more or less familiar." Thus, as Frank Tough phrases it, Indian policy perceived Indians "in terms of their relationship to land and their role in labour markets." Cultural assimilation was thus a result both of direct government policies and an intention to let general economic forces take their course. As Tough notes, while there has been a recent tendency by historians to see cultural assimilation as a product of schools, missions and similar agencies, this view ignores the economic context and makes capitalism an "invisible historical force."[90]

## ━━ Schools and Northern Indian Policy

Indian schooling did not exist apart from the culture of Euro-Canadian expansionism, Indian Affairs' policies, or the desire by Aboriginal people to meet new conditions. As Indian Affairs Inspector MacRae noted in 1900, the department believed schooling for Indians in northern Alberta was necessary because its benefits would accrue to "both the industrial occupants of the country covered by the Treaty and to the Indians by weaning a number from the chase and inclining them to industrial pursuits." He further noted that schooling could prevent crime, ensure "peaceful conditions" during white settlement and help meet future demands for "intelligent labour" as development took place.[91] These long range considerations were offset, however, by more immediately practical ones. Since hunting, trapping and fishing would likely remain the major source of employment, MacRae emphasized that too much schooling would make the pupils unfit "to earn their living in the surroundings in which they would be placed on leaving school." The most likely alternative to a hunting lifestyle was to find work with a fur trading company or to join one of the churches. But there were relatively few permanent jobs for Natives with the companies, and almost none joined the church.[92]

The contradictions that lay beneath official policy on schooling gave rise to what has been called the Native-wilderness equation. As Robert Carney has noted in his studies of northern schooling, it was assumed that while reading, writing and arithmetic were not essential for a hunting and fishing life, they gave Natives certain advantages. This assumption was supported by government, missionaries and traders in the north, all of whom "saw the wilderness— where traditional beliefs had been tempered by the promise of the gospel, and the vagaries of the hunt had been lessened by the benefits of trade—as the best, if only, environment for the areas' aboriginal population." According to this view, bush life kept Natives law abiding, self-sufficient, and away from the temptations of the settlements and the evils of "civilization." Despite some misgivings, many Roman Catholic missionaries were drawn to this idealized image of a law abiding, religious and sober "Christian trapper."[93]

Native reaction to these issues was equally complicated. Many Indians wanted their children to attend school—they recognized that literacy was important in the new order and that their children would benefit by being able to read and write. Thus, they had specified during treaty negotiations that schooling be a treaty right. Historian Raymond Huel observes that Indians saw it as an opportunity "to borrow and adapt" elements of Euro-Canadian culture "to suit their own needs and ensure their own identity and survival." Joe Dion, a school teacher during the interwar years and a prominent Cree leader, recalled in his memoirs that Indians wanted their children to be educated and were "looking for the best that the white man had to teach us...The Indians were endeavouring to work out their own plans and their own self determination." Such hopes were not realized. Instead, Indian schooling in northern Alberta relied on existing Indian Affairs school policies, which, as elsewhere in Canada, ultimately met few of the needs of Aboriginal people.[94]

The Euro-Canadian system of funding public schools through local taxes could not be applied in most Native communities with their small population and low or nonexistent property assessments. In areas with higher population, public schooling was not in any case an option for Indian children under the

*Many of the Roman Catholic missions in northern Alberta were sizeable operations. This photograph shows the church and school at Fort Vermilion. Not dated.* OB796 PAA.

jurisdiction of Indian Affairs. While most Indian children in Canada attended day schools on their reserves, there were few such schools in northern Alberta. Treaty 8 did not contain provisions guaranteeing day schools, and Indian children in northern Alberta who attended school usually went to boarding schools funded by the federal government and operated by missionaries. These residential schools were in part justified as the best way of meeting the practical problems of providing schooling to a widely scattered small population. They also met the national objective of assimilating Indians since removing children from their culture and parental control was believed to assist in reshaping them in a Euro-Canadian mould. In northern Alberta, instruction was in English, although the Oblates also taught in French, and in Native languages in some cases. The curriculum stressed subjects such as religion, reading, writing and mathematics. Manual work at the school and learning trades or "industries" theoretically prepared students for farming or wage employment, while the schools' rigid routines and strict discipline were expected to contribute to the creation of industrial-style work habits and conventional Euro-Canadian attitudes towards money and time.[95]

In general, incomplete statistics make it difficult to judge attendance at these schools. In 1900, only a few Native children attended school; St. Bernard's, the

Roman Catholic school at Grouard, for example, had between 30 and 40 pupils boarding at the school, while the Anglican school at nearby Utikuma Lake had about 34 boarding and day pupils.[96] Although attendance at these schools had not increased substantially by 1910, the opening of additional schools allowed more Indian children in northern Alberta to be enrolled in school. Most pupils were from districts close by the schools while those living further away were less likely to attend school. As Table 5–1 indicates, the total number of pupils in the schools at any time was never a majority of the population aged 6 to 21 in the two agencies making up Treaty 8, and only rarely was it even a majority of such people in the area immediately adjacent to the schools. Nonetheless, these statistics are not entirely satisfactory because they overstate the school age population—pupils were not kept in school for such a long period, and almost never beyond age 18. It does, however, indicate that the number of Indian children having direct contact with schools had increased significantly by 1910. Indeed, the ratio was not far from the national average—about 54 percent of Indian children in Canada between 6 and 15 years of age were in some sort of school. At the same time, most non-Treaty Native children did not attend the schools. While Indian Affairs occasionally paid per capita school grants for Metis pupils, especially for those living on reserves, it more often insisted, despite the entreaties of the missionaries, that they were not a federal responsibility.[97]

Other aspects about schooling for Indian children in northern Alberta before World War I are also now difficult to gauge. Personal consequences may well have been grave. Although no evidence has been published about sexual abuse of children (both by adults and by other pupils) in schools in northern Alberta in these early years, it is apparent that it did exist at this time in a number of schools in western Canada, and it may have been a factor in northern schools as well.[98] Certainly, school discipline—which was often so severe that it was physically and emotionally abusive—was a concern to Native parents. Such discipline was justified by contemporary theories propounding that character and personality were shaped (and could therefore be remade) by the environment in which a person lived. This view integrated discipline into the acculturation objectives of the schools and likely made the discipline imposed in these schools even more severe than that practised in Euro-Canadian schools. As historian Jim Miller has noted, first Nations cultures generally favoured the tools of watching, listening and personal instruction to educate children. Community disapproval was also applied to socialize children and control adults. From this vantage point, the rigid discipline and

— Table 5–1

*Boarding School Enrolment Versus Treaty Population*

*Treaty 8, 1910*

| | Total enrolled in school** | Treaty population of immediate area aged 6–21* | Treaty population of agency aged 6–21* |
|---|---|---|---|
| **Northern District** | | | 404 |
| Fort Chipewyan | 44 | 113 | |
| Fort Resolution, NWT (R.C.) | 22 | n/a | |
| Fort Vermilion (R.C.) | 26 | 74 | |
| Hay River, NWT (Anglican) | 41 | 95 | |
| Total | 133 | 282 | 404 |
| | | | |
| **Lesser Slave Lake Agency** | | | 511 |
| Grouard (R.C.) | 40 ⎤ | | |
| Grouard (Anglican) | 13 ⎦ 105 | | |
| Sturgeon Lake (R.C.) | 32 | 62 | |
| Wabasca (R.C.) | 27 ⎤ | | |
| Wabasca (Anglican) | 21 ⎦ 86 | | |
| Whitefish Lake (Anglican) | 24 | 27 | |
| Peace River Crossing (Anglican) | 10 | n/a | |
| Total | 167 | 280 | 511 |

* Estimated

**While most of these pupils were Indian, a few were likely nontreaty. In addition, an unknown number of children attended the boarding schools at Grouard and Peace River town as day pupils.

Source: Compiled from Annual Report, Indian Affairs for the Year Ended March 31, 1910, 76–79, 324–25.

frequent use of corporal punishment in the residential schools were considered to be cruel, retributive, demeaning and evidence that the schools were more concerned with acculturation than with imparting skills such as literacy.[99]

For their part, the missionaries often believed that Native behaviour was motivated by laziness and opportunism. They observed that Native parents put their children in school when times were hard and food was scarce and pulled them out to help with tasks such as running trap lines or putting up fish or meat for winter when times were good. The schoolmaster at Utikuma Lake made this charge in 1913, while Reverend Robinson at Wabasca claimed that such practices proved that the Indians were "not prompted by a sincere desire" for their children's welfare. The depth of misunderstanding between the two parties was shown in Robinson's denunciation of Indian parents, who, he claimed, were not sufficiently grateful or respectful for what the schools were doing. As he wrote, the children were clothed, fed and educated free of cost, but "curiously enough," their parents had "the impression that we are under a great obligation to them for allowing their children to be with us. The natural result of this frame of mind is that they do not hesitate to come and dictate to us regarding their children and the treatment they wish them to receive." In one case, he noted, a mother pulled her daughter from the school because the teacher had sent the girl away from dinner "for a direct act of disobedience."[100] An evident case of cultural conflict in the context of Aboriginal attitudes to discipline, the incident demonstrated the gap in motives, behaviour and culture that already existed between some missionaries and the Native community.

Other educational and acculturative consequences of these school programmes are also now difficult to judge. Children, especially boys, were not kept long in school since too lengthy an education was considered unnecessary and undesirable. Residential schools in northern Alberta also did not usually provide practical training suited to the region. Girls were taught domestic skills like dressmaking, cooking and sewing, "in a word, everything that a good housekeeper should know," while boys were taught "farming" on the mission farms and gardens. But this prepared the children for few practical responsibilities and did not provide an education equivalent to that received by children attending public schools. The school farms were usually small and poorly equipped, and in places such as Fort Chipewyan, they were further limited by a shortage of arable land. In many cases, most of the work at the schools consisted of cleaning, housekeeping chores and chopping huge piles of wood needed for the school stoves in winter. As historian Martha McCarthy concluded in respect to the Dene, residential schools did not go far enough to acculturate the pupils, but went beyond a rudimentary education. Although girls could possibly adopt some of their training in household skills to everyday life, boys were not given any training that would help them in making their way in an economy dominated by hunting and trapping. In any event, religious conversion, not vocational training, was often the true objective of most of the schools. The Anglican Bishop noted in 1910 that he believed that the mission farms in northern Alberta should be abolished or reorganized because the financial worries they brought had "a strong tendency to secularize the minds and interest of the clergy" and had "proved to militate against rather than to help the spiritual interests of our work."[101]

Although the federal government was usually enthusiastic about such assimilationist endeavours because it saw them as a way of achieving economic self-sufficiency for Indians, it was less eager to fund them. In general, Euro-Canadians tended to criticise any public expenditure on Natives, and cutting public spending on Indians was almost always politically popular. As a result, the school system was chronically underfunded. The government was content to let the churches run the schools because this was less costly than operating them directly; a policy that was further justified by an assumption that the missionaries were skilled in acculturating Aboriginal people.[102] The schools also enabled the government to minimize its social welfare costs. If Holy Angels school (which began as a convent and later evolved into a school) in Fort Chipewyan was typical, a substantial number of the students were either orphaned or handicapped.[103] While the fiscal benefits to government of this church-state alliance were clear, the churches also gained significant advantage. They acquired state sanctioned authority in northern communities through their domination of the school system, which they could not otherwise have been able to fund. In this respect, the Roman Catholics were better placed since priests and nuns, unencumbered by families or financial concerns, could deliver low cost programmes. Still, finances were an ongoing problem even for the Catholic schools, although they were far more serious for the Anglicans.

Despite the benefits that both government and church gained from the relationship, their alliance was often uneasy. Everywhere in Canada there was rivalry between Roman Catholic and Protestant schools, and since Treaty 8 allowed parents to chose Roman Catholic or Protestant schools for their children, competition was probably even more intense in northern Alberta. While a few schools in northern Alberta received government grants before the treaty, the promise of free education under the treaty encouraged the churches to try and obtain grants for existing schools as well as those they hoped to construct.

Since school expansion was being driven by sectarian competition, Indian Affairs tended to see such requests as an attempt to have government underwrite Roman Catholic and Anglican competition for converts. Although Indian Affairs had brokered a neutrality pact in the 1890s whereby different denominations would behave cordially and respect each other's "territory," the churches showed little respect for this entente. The Anglicans bitterly decried Catholic success and accused Ottawa of playing favourites, while the Roman Catholics saw the Indian Affairs department as a scion of a hostile Anglo-Canadian Protestant establishment.[104]

The philosophy and intent behind Indian schools, the rivalry among denominations and the lack of adequate funding all combined to limit the possibility that schools for Indian children in northern Alberta, as in other parts of Canada, would respect their pupils' cultural and emotional needs or provide relevant training to help them make a living in a changing economy. The whole system was riven with conflict, including the resentments and rivalries among denominations and the tensions between state and church and between the schools and the Native community. Later historical evidence indicates that most Indian children living in remote areas in northern Alberta were bypassed by the school system until after World War II—before then, children living on reserves and closest to schools or Indian Agency offices were most likely to go to school. Those in districts closest to white settlements and who were most vulnerable to Euro-Canadian economic policies were thus also most vulnerable to assimilationist school policies. The practical effect of Euro-Canadian legal distinctions among Aboriginal peoples was also most immediately apparent in these districts where "Indian" and "Metis" were beginning to diverge in their access to schooling and where land holding took different forms for each group.

The divide that was emerging in northern Alberta was thus not only between white and native, but in some cases extended older distinctions within the Native community or created new ones. Although such divisions among Natives, and between Natives and whites, were not uniformly found in the region before World War I, they did indicate how the definitions, priorities and culture of the nationally dominant groups would be applied. White farm settlement rested on a similar foundation of integrative forces and beliefs, working in conjunction with the pursuit of individual benefit. While French Canadian, Norwegian and other block settlements indicated collective cultural motives, they nonetheless remained an expression of economic individualism.

— ✦ —

The migration of white farm settlers and trappers to northern Alberta in the early 1900s was not in itself a radical change. For over a century the region had received migrants—fur traders, Red River Metis and missionaries—connected in some way with Euro-Canadian culture and economy. The difference between them and their twentieth century counterparts was that the latter found few reasons to integrate with or accommodate Native society. Farm settlers, as independent commodity producers, could operate independently of the region's past and its Native population because they were part of a new economy whose technology and production did not generally rely on anyone outside the farm family. So too, the success of white town settlers depended on linkages with Canadian manufacturers, distributors and governments rather than local connections. Like many white trappers, these new migrants possessed a degree of cultural and economic autonomy that did not bring about a mingling with local culture and traditions. Thus, white children went to public schools, Indian children went to segregated residential schools, and Metis children often went to neither. Euro-Canadian farm and business interests were based on the private ownership of land, but Indian land ownership was increasingly circumscribed in the form of reservations, and many Metis began to find themselves operating outside both the common property of the reserve and the private property of farm and town. As with the Native community, Euro-Canadian society in northern Alberta was far from uniform—religion, ethnicity, place of origin and class were all dividing forces—but two largely separate worlds were appearing; that of the Native community and that of the Euro-Canadian. Both increasingly responded to each other across a divide defined by economic role, legal status, property and class.

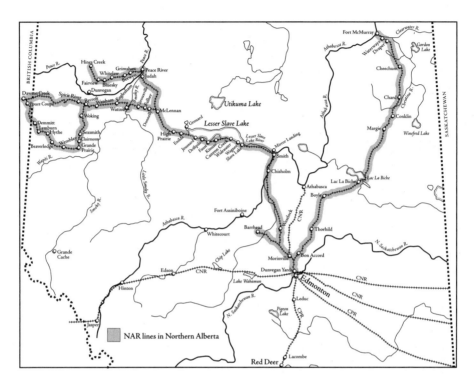

NAR lines in Northern Alberta

—— **NAR Lines in Northern Alberta 1930**

# Changing Course,
# 6
## 1912–1921

Between 1912 and 1917, different parts of northern Alberta were linked to Edmonton by rail. These lines did not have a linear impact on the northern economy because they reached different parts of northern Alberta at different times. Moreover, once service was established, it was so variable among the different lines that it did not immediately create uniform conditions in the region. Athabasca received rail connections when the CNoR reached the village in 1912, while the east end of Lesser Slave Lake was connected by a separate line in 1914 when the ED&BC reached the area. This line was then pushed westward along the south shore of the lake towards the Peace River country, reaching both Peace River and Grande Prairie in early 1916. In the eastern parts of the region, the Fort McMurray area had a rail line in 1917, but service was at first so chaotic that effective connections only came later.

These rail lines helped refashion the northern economy by bringing increased population and expanding markets. They brought significant change to the districts they reached, but their impact also rippled outwards, influencing events in areas that they did not touch directly. The replacement of river by land transportation shattered the coherence of the transportation network that had operated in northern Alberta since the 1880s and encouraged the growth of two distinct economic and social units in the region. In the western districts, the way was opened for the development of an export-driven agricultural economy in the Peace River country. To the east, the railway made Fort McMurray the portal to the lower Athabasca River and the far north, supplanting the town of Athabasca. Although the river remained the only method of communication with the Athabasca-Peace delta, the proximity of the railway at Fort McMurray indirectly brought social and economic change.

## ___ The Coming of the Railway

The first district in northern Alberta to be affected by the expansion of railways was around the town of Athabasca. As the railway was slowly constructed north of Edmonton, settlers were drawn to the areas through which it passed or through which it would pass. By 1909, as the railway neared Athabasca, settlement picked up and about 1,500 farm settlers were drawn to the area, occupying most of the fertile land. While Athabasca still had a "deserted appearance" when the river crews were not in town, its character soon changed. For at least a year before the CNoR arrived, economic activity expanded. By mid 1911, land prices in the town were rising quickly and farms three kilometres away were selling for $250 per acre "for the purpose of being subdivided" into lots. The year closed with feverish speculation when the Hudson's Bay Company offered most of its town lots for sale. "A number of real estate men from Edmonton and Saskatoon" came for the sale in mid December, and all the lots were sold for high prices on the first day.[1]

When it reached the town in 1912, the railway brought exaggerated growth and a massive land boom, while wages rose "out of all reason." Faith in the future was so great that lots worth $300 the year before now fetched $3,000, and "outlying homesteads" were rapidly subdivided and sold to outsiders for "big prices." Extensive building was underway and in 1913 the federal government built an immigration hall to assist incoming settlers. Between 1911 and 1913 Athabasca grew from about 450 people to about 2,000. Although its economy remained dependent on river freighting, piloting, boat building and lumbering, grand predictions about other possibilities were broadcast and it was said that Athabasca's "many natural advantages" ensured its future as a distributing centre. Such forecasts in the early phase of town life were typical on the prairies, as was the eager participation in land speculation by railway companies. The Hudson's Bay Company, which had earlier bought river-front land in Athabasca from the federal government, gave the CNoR valuable land concessions so that it would locate its station on the river front—costs the Hudson's Bay Company quickly recovered when land values around the station skyrocketed.[2] In 1913, the town changed its name from Athabasca Landing to Athabasca, a symbolic act demonstrating that it was no longer just a spot on the way to somewhere else. Local merchants even boldly proposed changing the name of the principal street from Skinner Street to Main Street. This too was a symbolic act; the older name had honoured Sir William Skinner of the Hudson's Bay Company. Showing that its power was not yet so remote, the company challenged this diminution of its corporate elite and the town council retreated, assuring the company that it meant no "disrespect" and promised to retain the name out of a desire "to work in harmony with the Company."[3]

By June 1913 Athabasca enjoyed daily train connection with Edmonton. By intensifying use of the Athabasca-Grouard corridor to the Peace River country, the railway confirmed the town's central place in northern transportation and led to increased business outfitting settlers and building and servicing boats. Similarly, commercial fishing operations at nearby Calling Lake expanded. Fish were still taken over a winter trail to Athabasca but then were shipped quickly to Edmonton by train. In 1913–14 more whitefish were taken commercially from Calling Lake than from the much larger Lesser Slave Lake, and fish populations in the smaller lake quickly came under pressure. As a result, Calling Lake was closed to commercial fishing in 1916, and fishing companies moved to other lakes, including Lesser Slave Lake where rail connections (through the ED&BC) had just been established.[4]

The railway's arrival at Athabasca also affected the whole of the town's hinterland. One observer called 1913 a year "of great development and progress" in northern Alberta. In 1912, the Edmonton *Bulletin* had foretold that rail connections with Athabasca would bring general economic expansion in the north because a

> navigable water system which gives communication throughout a region 2,000 miles long by 500 miles wide cannot be brought in touch with railways without arousing curiosity, cupidity and enterprise on an ever-increasing scale, to say nothing of the constantly increasing pressure because of constantly increasing population and wealth which compels men to go into waste places to look for wealth and opportunity.

Rail travel was obviously more efficient than the rough Athabasca trail, and "under the new conditions," heavy machinery, especially for mining, could be loaded directly from the train onto scows and taken "without transhipment" as far as Lake Athabasca. While the Grand Rapids were conveniently ignored in this rosy picture, the Smith Portage remained, but was characterized as a gateway, not a barrier, to "the riches of the Mackenzie Basin."[5]

Although there was no realistic prospect that it would soon have rail connections, increased optimism and speculation all along the upper Athabasca River combined with purely local prospects to create a minor land boom in Fort McMurray. By June 1912 there were 40 or 50 white settlers in the district, many squatting along the Clearwater River. Six townships were being surveyed, and it was anticipated that they would soon be opened for home-steading. Optimism was sustained by forecasts about local oil resources and future railway connections. By this time, an "enormous townsite" had been laid out and lots were sold "at very large prices." While one NWMP constable judged that the oil sands ensured Fort McMurray's future as "a town of some importance," he saw the boom as "inflated and fictitious." Even so, by early 1913 Fort McMurray had grown to include a free trader and the Hudson's Bay Company (which that year had moved back to Fort McMurray from Fort McKay to participate in the boom), plus a sawmill, oil exploration outfits, Roman Catholic and Presbyterian missions, a NWMP detachment and a public school. Despite its speculative character, the boom lasted into 1913–14. In 1914 the NWMP at Fort McMurray noted that local oil companies, "unde-terred by some years of failure," planned to expand their exploration efforts. The boom was also sustained by the start of construction of a government tele-graph line from Athabasca. The beginning of construction of the A&GW and fantastically optimistic forecasts of when it would arrive added to the specula-tive binge. Even though homestead land in the area had still not been opened for entry by 1915, the settlement's population vacilated between 250 and 400, and it had a number of retail outlets plus two poolrooms, a restaurant, a hotel and three boarding houses. While lumber salvaged from scows continued to be used for building, construction materials were also now produced by three portable sawmills. But the boom soon deflated, and World War I further stymied growth. As was soberly remarked in 1915, "Fort McMurray is only a village, and it is certainly not yet the CITY some newspapers attribute it to be."[6]

In contrast to conditions at Fort McMurray, the economic boom along the transportation corridor between Athabasca and Peace River rested on a some-what more solid foundation. Increased movement of settlers stimulated trade and the start of construction of the ED&BC in 1912 confirmed the area's future. In late 1911 a new townsite was surveyed and laid out at Peace River Crossing, which was on the south side of the river and more accessible for a railway. Lots went on the market for the relatively high price of $200 each. This was the beginning of the present-day town of Peace River and it marked the start of the decline of the older Shaftesbury settlement across the river. General

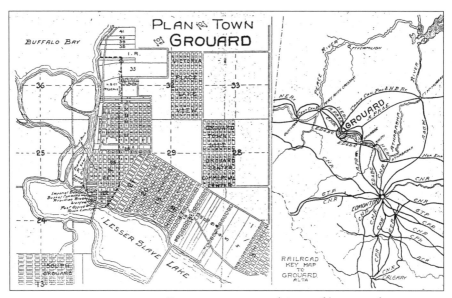

*Promoters were eager to persuade investors of the prosperous future of northern towns. A popular claim was that a town, such as Grouard, had incomparable geographical advantages that would soon make it a major urban centre. Grouard News, July 11, 1914.*

expansion in the area led to much speculation. The NWMP officer at Athabasca observed in 1912 that land was being taken up and subdivided in all the settlements between Athabasca and Peace River town. "In fact," he remarked, "everybody wants to get a section or two, subdivide it, put it on the market and get rich."[7]

In 1913, the population of Slave Lake (Sawridge) grew to about 200, and by 1913 Mirror Landing had expanded to include three or four stores and several poolrooms, restaurants and warehouses. Grouard grew especially quickly. In 1911 it was incorporated as a village and by 1912 its population had reached about 500. Residents were gripped by "a boom such as Athabasca Landing had a year ago" and promoters were calling Grouard the "Edmonton of the North." It had two banks, stores, telegraph service, three churches, the only newspaper north of Athabasca and even a town band. Despite the stumps and ruts on the main street, 25 buildings were put up in the first six months of 1912. Building was so rapid that local sawmills could not keep up with demand. In 1913, boat service to Athabasca increased to four trips a week, creating a system that was over-confidently said to be "almost equal to having a railway." In winter, about 250 teams freighted tons of goods from the town, and its land office served part of the north Peace River country. By early 1914, Grouard had a population of just over 1,400.[8]

In 1909 Metis had made up a clear majority of Grouard's population. When the fur trader, Philip Godsell, passed through in 1911, he described it as a "picturesque" village of widely spaced whitewashed houses, a police barracks, Hudson's Bay Company and Revillon trading posts, and "a pretentious Catholic hospital and mission." But when Godsell returned in 1912, he was struck by the "remarkable transformation" that had taken place in a single year: "frame 'hotels,' tawdry cafes and dance halls had sprung into existence along with the inevitable real estate offices." Land for miles around was being surveyed, and close-in property was selling for high prices. In this process, Grouard's social make-up changed. While the Metis presence was still significant, Euro-Canadians who had come to profit from the town's growth now formed the majority. As the NWMP Superintendent reported in late 1913, Grouard had "changed from a half-breed hamlet to a white town."[9]

The cultural changes taking place at Grouard were also demonstrated by the development of a new urban form in the town. By 1913 the widely dispersed collection of buildings focussed around the missions and the trading posts had been absorbed into an urban form much like that found elsewhere in prairie Canada. Buildings were aligned along relatively straight streets with economic functions concentrated on a main street lined with stores and other businesses. Such a "main street town" revealed changing urban functions. While the main street's importance as a focus for social life represented a continuation of the settlement's role as a meeting place, it was now a more overtly commercial entity. In addition to asserting a commercial rationale and the preeminence of the town's business class, such formal segregation by economic and social function asserted the value of land as capital. Concentrated business development along the main street made property there more valuable, while noncommercial property of lower value, usually for housing, was located away from the downtown. This commodification of land and the concentration of highly-valued property in the business core often created unstable conditions, especially as real estate values rose ever higher. In Grouard, as in Peace River, speculation in anticipation of the railway drove land prices so high that by late 1913 town growth and business began to suffer, and settlement began to disperse outside the town core as people sought out less expensive property off main street.[10]

*This group of buildings stretched on either side of the Anglican Church in Fort Chipewyan. Not Dated (ca. 1912)*

A2340 PAA.

*Although Grouard soon all but disappeared, in 1915 new construction was still underway along parts of the town's main street. A10,187 PAA.*

In contrast to the events at Grouard, older patterns persisted in places such as Fort Smith and Fort Chipewyan. By 1913, when Grouard had emerged as a prairie town like any other, buildings in Fort Chipewyan were still not grouped on the basis of property values. The settlement had about 70 buildings, the majority of which were houses owned by Metis. One of the newest buildings was the NWMP barracks, sited near the Hudson's Bay Company post. Here and there, people grew vegetables on pockets of soil, and houses were linked to the rest of the community by footpaths. While this urban form, and the social organization it implied, endured, more buildings began to appear each year and by 1922 the town, which was now about 2.5 kilometres long, presented an observer from the lake with a more regular townscape.[11]

Despite this growth, Fort Chipewyan was largely immune from the speculative activity that was reshaping life in northern Alberta's more southerly communities. Some observers claimed that the changes taking place in the latter centres proved their permanence and future prosperity. With reference to the Lesser Slave Lake and Peace River districts, Jim Cornwall wrote in 1913 that it amused him "to hear people dubious of the rise of great cities along the waterways of this country." Large Russian cities were similarly located, and one could not "pooh-pooh" what would develop in northern Alberta with its milder climate and greater fertility.[12] Yet the network of existing northern towns and their fortunes were directly tied to the river-based transportation system, and the first example of what would become commonplace occurred when the ED&BC reached the banks of the Athabasca River across from Mirror Landing in 1914. Here, the ED&BC created a divisional point called Smith, and Mirror Landing soon disappeared when businesses moved across the river to the new town. By spring 1914, the line reached Slave Lake and goods were now shipped here from Edmonton on the train and taken by boat across Lesser Slave Lake to Grouard. The elimination of shipments through Athabasca gave the ED&BC command of traffic to the Peace River country and destroyed Athabasca's "natural advantage" as a central place for the Lesser Slave Lake and Peace River areas. While these developments challenged the region's unity, they initially brought further growth at Grouard, whose place as the "business centre" of the Peace River country expanded. Rail service between Edmonton and Slave Lake, in combination with steamer connections across the lake, brought Grouard within a day and a half of Edmonton under ideal conditions. Peace River town lay two days by trail beyond Grouard, and a traveller from Edmonton could now reach it—a distance of over 550 kilometres—in three and-one-half days, and "all but the last 90 miles in all the comfort and conven-ience of railway and steamboat travel."[13]

Although Grouard's civic leaders ran extensive advertisements about the town's great future, Grouard's glory was short-lived. As the ED&BC built westward along the southern shore of Lesser Slave Lake in 1914, it was learned that the track would pass about 10 kilometres south of the town. While some bravely predicted that its "natural advantages" as the hub of the Peace River country would ensure that the town could not be bypassed, others claimed that the railway was "running a bluff," presumably to extract the highest possible concessions from the town. But Grouard's leaders knew that the town was doomed without a railway. Numerous other pre-railway prairie towns had been destroyed when they had been bypassed by railways. In many cases, this was a deliberate railway policy: by eliminating existing towns, they concen-trated economic activity in centres that they built and owned. The ED&BC naturally protested that it had no such motives, arguing that the area around Grouard was prone to flooding and that engineering difficulties made it too costly to build into the town.[14]

In response, Grouard hired an engineer to prove that it was feasible for the line to pass closer to the town, and a delegation met with the Board of Railway Commissioners to press the town's case. Because of indications that legislation might be enacted to prevent railways from bypassing existing towns for merce-nary reasons, it was also hoped that the provincial government would stop the railway from trying to make more money from real estate manipulation than from "legitimate transportation."[15] But the Board of Railway Commissioners sided with the ED&BC, and although the outcry from Grouard and pressure by the provincial government forced the ED&BC to promise a spur line into the town, the pledge went unfilled when bonds for the line could not be sold. By mid 1915, after spending $15,000 to secure rail connections, Grouard had been "completely side-tracked." Without railway connections it could not participate in the new economy emerging in the Peace River country. In the same year, rail competition ended steam boat navigation on Lesser Slave Lake. Grouard's population fell to about 300 and within a year it had reverted to its economic functions and urban form of 20 years earlier. Marking its decline, the Dominion Lands office was moved to Peace River in 1915, and many of Grouard's buildings were dismantled or moved to other towns on the rail line.[16]

Whether Grouard was simply the victim of railway profit-seeking is unclear. While the engineering difficulties involved in building into the town made other routes logical, the ED&BC was not always so particular about avoiding such problems. Its line along the south shore of Lesser Slave Lake was built through an area of unstable soil and was prone to flooding. Whatever the case, many people in Grouard believed that their town had been bypassed so the ED&BC could profit by building its own town—a suspicion that was confirmed when the divisional point of McLennan (then called Round Lake) was created 40 kilometres away. This wholly new town owned by the ED&BC was built in an area that the railway erroneously claimed had good and abundant water for steam engines. Nonetheless, McLennan rapidly grew into a regional centre, becoming the "gateway" to the Peace country that Grouard had once been. McLennan, and to a lesser extent, High Prairie, now dominated the areas around the west end of Lesser Slave Lake and the territory east of the Smoky River and north to the Peace River.[17]

McLennan's rise and Grouard's collapse were only one aspect of the railway's impact on town development. Some people believed that they could anticipate the railway and build towns at locations through which it had to pass. A.M. Bezanson was certain that the geography of the Smoky River would force any railway to the southern Peace River country to cross it below the mouth of the Simonette River. He obtained land there and built a town he named after himself. Carpenters from Grande Prairie constructed buildings and by early 1915 the settlement boasted a general store, blacksmith, livery barn and restaurant. Several other stores were also under construction. While many freighters passed through the settlement and small boats carried goods up from Peace River, its promise faded as quickly as it had developed when the ED&BC crossed the Smoky River at a different location.[18]

In other cases, the prospect of a railway brought the imaginative boosting of areas that had only the remotest possibility of benefiting from rail connections. Often fraudulent, this boosterism was one mark of the speculative nature of settlement in a market economy. Although promotional efforts before 1914 were intense at Grouard, the most lavish campaign took place at Dunvegan, which Edmonton real estate speculators advertised as a potentially important point on the ED&BC. Although it was then only the site of a fur trade post fallen on hard times, extravagant claims were broadcast about Dunvegan's future, and unwitting purchasers bought lots, sight unseen, on the precipitous hills above the fort. The literature churned out by Dunvegan's promoters

left nothing to the imagination. There were business streets, long avenues of prosperous homes, crowded street cars, bustling hotels, and golf courses for the relaxation of the tired business men in the thriving north. Men bought eagerly; they were allowed to get in on the ground floor. Lots on streets neither paved nor even laid out, were bought and sold. In distant Edmonton and other cities this thriving metropolis in the land of the midnight sun looked like a new Eldorado.[19]

Another aspect of the social side of railway construction was the temporary towns set up to serve railway construction crews. While some people were willing to wager that these would become permanent towns, most were abandoned once the line moved on. This process was most evident 65 kilometres west of McLennan at the point where the railway crossed the Smoky River. Overcoming the unstable banks and steep grades in the 200 metre deep valley made this a major engineering feat. In preparation for the crossing, a little settlement, later to be known as Smoky Crossing, sprang up in early 1915. Built in one or two months, it soon had a population of about 300, with 18 log buildings sheltering a railway station and a range of businesses catering to the work crews. "Train loads" of people arrived each week. It was anticipated that the town would be the end of steel for between 12 and 18 months, and it temporarily drew much of the population away from McLennan. The NWMP saw such settlements as natural gathering places for "the rough and criminal classes." Controlling these locations was thus important for maintaining order on the frontier and a NWMP detachment was placed in Smoky Crossing. A steel jail cell was ordered for the barracks and an "able bodied" constable was put in charge as "there may be rough characters to handle." But the frontier was more peaceable than anticipated. Little serious crime occurred—the only reported concern was the use of cocaine and morphine, said to be evidence of "an ever increasing prevalence of the drug habit in the north country."[20]

By May 1915 the end of steel was about 12 kilometres from Smoky Crossing. By then, there were several population clusters: about 150 people lived at the end of steel and slowly moved towards the second more developed, and somewhat more permanent, town of Smoky Crossing, which now had grown to about 500 people. A third, but smaller town developed across the river. From there, the west end of the bridge was built and the rails were laid westward in advance of the line crossing the river. Although the local NWMP constable predicted that Smoky Crossing would develop into a town of "considerable size" once the bridge was completed, the reason for his optimism is unclear. The rugged surrounding area contained almost no settlers, and without other

*After 1916, when this photograph of the main street was taken,*
*Peace River town benefited economically by being the end of steel.*
A9862 PAA.

economic activity to sustain it, the town's population fell quickly as the bridge neared completion. By July, when the river was crossed, it had only 15 people, almost one-half of whom planned to leave soon. The ED&BC closed the station (which also meant that the telephone office disappeared), and postal service was scheduled to end in August. It was expected that the town would soon contain "no one except one restaurant that figures on keeping open through the summer." Police patrols were unnecessary because there was no nearby rural population and there were "no disturbances of any kind" since "all the bootleggers and parties of questionable character" had left the area.[21] By the time the detachment closed in September 1916, Smoky Crossing had disappeared.

After the crossing of the Smoky River, the line reached Spirit River in early 1916. Still largely a Metis settlement, the town had developed as the trading centre for the recently settled Pouce Coupe prairie straddling the British Columbia border. Initially, the railway was surveyed to run directly west to this district, but fortunately for Spirit River's future, it was instead built south from Rycroft (the railway station near Spirit River) to Grande Prairie which had a larger population. This preserved Spirit River's role as the metropolis for the large area to the west not served by the railway. When the ED&BC reached Grande Prairie in early 1916, this marked, for the time being, the last of the rail connections in the south Peace River country.[22]

Access to the area north of the Peace River was provided by the Central Canada Railway (CCR) which ran north from the ED&BC line just west of McLennan. Incorporated in 1913, this company, like the ED&BC, was owned by J.D. McArthur, and the Alberta government guaranteed its bonds. The line led to the decline of the Grouard-Peace River trail, and the further loss of freighting jobs. The CCR reached Peace River town in 1916 and rapidly drew settlers to the district between McLennan and Peace River. A bridge across the Peace River was completed at Peace River town in 1918, giving rise to hopes that the town would become the hub for further lines north of the river. But such rail lines were not built until the 1920s, creating a temporary imbalance in the settlement potential of the areas north and south of the Peace River. Nonetheless, when the railway reached Peace River town, local prospects seemed limitless. A few oil claims had been staked near the Vermilion Chutes, and many speculated that if oil was found, a railway would at once be built north from Athabasca. More importantly for Peace River, rumours about a possible oil strike revived in late 1917 and created a short-lived speculative frenzy in the area.[23]

Peace River town promoters were not only optimistic about petroleum development but also put great faith in the supposedly ironclad laws of locational advantage. As the *Peace River Record* editorialized in 1916, "important centres are not built by real estate manipulation and booms. They are the natural result of topographical conditions." Boosters also foretold that Peace River town would soon don Athabasca's mantle as the portal to the far north. For once, such hopes were not simply fantasies hatched by local promoters. In 1916, the Hudson's Bay Company began shipping goods to the far north by train to Peace River and from there by boat to Fort Chipewyan and Fitzgerald. To take advantage of these emerging patterns, the Peace River Development Corporation, a British company owned by Lord Rhondda (D.A. Thomas), launched a steam ship called the *D.A. Thomas* at Peace River in 1916. This ship was part of Rhondda's larger business plans for northern Alberta and the NWT, which included a tramway around the Vermilion Chutes, railway transport, radio telegraph communications, petroleum exploration and mining. The largest ship in the Mackenzie basin, it was anticipated that the *D.A. Thomas* would carry goods and passengers from Peace River to the Vermilion Chutes. Along with smaller craft, its launch increased to three the number of steam ships operating scheduled service on the Peace River, and when economic development was not forthcoming, the *D.A. Thomas* only added excess shipping capacity on the river.[24]

Steam ships on Lesser Slave Lake created faster connections between Athabasca and Grouard but mechanization also cost many people jobs freighting and portaging goods. This is the Northern Transportation Company's ship on Lesser Slave Lake in 1912. OB4386 PAA.

One of the ships competing with the *D.A. Thomas* was a Hudson's Bay Company steamboat, the *Athabasca*, formerly based in Athabasca. Indicative of how the railway exerted an impact on districts well beyond those it served directly, the *Athabasca* was taken from Athabasca by Captain Watson and pilot William Loutit over the rapids above Fort McMurray during high water in 1914. Such a dangerous journey had never been attempted, and people in Fort McMurray were astonished when the ship arrived. But the Hudson's Bay Company reasoned that given the rapid decline of river travel on the upper Athabasca River, it was better to risk smashing the ship in the rapids than to let it stand unused at Athabasca. The trip was so stressful that Watson apparently wrung the sweat from his shirt when he arrived, but, with nary a rest, the ship left the next day for Fort Chipewyan. It was taken on skids over the Vermilion Chutes the next winter to begin what proved to be a short life as a steamer on the Peace River. In 1915, the Northern Transportation Company followed this lead and took two of its ships through the rapids and based them at Fort McMurray to compete with the Hudson's Bay Company on the lower Athabasca River.[25]

The departure of the last steamer from Athabasca in 1915 added to the difficulties that the town had suffered when the ED&BC had been built directly from Edmonton to Slave Lake the year before. Its role as the portal to the north was vanishing. Shipping out of the town was now limited to cargo and passengers going down river to Fort McMurray. While substantial amounts of freight still moved along this route, it was well short of the economic activity needed to maintain the town. This trade too fell off after 1916 when the Hudson's Bay Company began shipping goods to the far north through Peace River. Athabasca was no longer the shipping point that marked the southern boundary of northern Alberta. The NWMP Superintendent at Athabasca rather plaintively remarked in early 1916 that "no one seems to come here, but all seem to go away." Indeed, the police now found Athabasca a "most inconvenient" place because "the new railways have changed the routes of travel," and in 1916 the NWMP northern headquarters were moved to Peace River. In 1917, given the "rather indifferent farming country" around Athabasca, there was only "sufficient business to warrant the existence of a comparatively small village." Indicating the town's shrinking economy, the Royal Bank closed its branch. Athabasca could no longer afford public works or street maintenance because of high tax arrears and the costs of servicing debt taken on earlier to install services. By the end of 1917, its population had dropped to 450, about one-half the houses in the town were vacant, and townspeople were demoralized. There was no traffic on the river "with the exception of dog teams carrying the mail." Unlike previous years, no scows were built in 1917.[26] By then, Athabasca was in such desperate financial shape that it was unable to pay its bond debt. In 1916, there was $121,000 in unpaid taxes, and by 1917 the town had only 17 ratepayers. Marking the levels of speculation and the collapse that had taken place, the town had already seized 71 subdivisions for tax arrears. Subsequently, Athabasca came under the control of the Municipal Finances Commission that administered the town and rescheduled its debt.[27]

During these years of crisis, Athabasca's remaining residents watched as the A&GW built slowly from Edmonton towards Fort McMurray. Like the ED&BC, the A&GW bypassed Athabasca and instead went through Lac La Biche, which it reached in 1915. The impact on Lac La Biche was immediate: businesses expanded, rival traders were better able to challenge the Hudson's Bay Company, and the A&GW opened a resort hotel. Construction was suspended for almost a year, but when it resumed north of Lac La Biche the rail line entered a land of sand hills and patches of spruce, jack pine, muskeg

*Off the tracks. The condition of the tracks on the NAR, especially during spring thaw, were often poor. Photographed near McLennan. Not Dated.* A10,177 PAA.

and swamp. The commercial potential of this long stretch was too limited to support rail traffic, a factor that affected the economy of the line for its entire existence. Indeed, even bootleggers and prostitutes could not reach the workers because of "the difficulty in getting into the country."[28]

Demonstrating its low construction standards, the A&GW laid steel over the snow during the winter of 1915. The next spring, crews had to place "trees under the ties" so trains could try and get through. While construction standards were poor, working conditions were even worse. Most of the workers laying steel were of central European origin and were paid $1.50 per day, less $1 per day for board and room and $1 per month as a "doctor's fee." But as a NWMP constable noted in 1916, frostbite (a common problem during that year's ferocious winter ) and other medical problems went untended despite the monthly medical payment. When work stopped during bad weather, the men received no wages but were charged for board and room. Some months they had almost nothing to show for their work. Performing hard physical labour in muskeg, plagued by mosquitoes in summer, and treated with contempt and brutality by their bosses, the workers went on strike in 1916 and walked back to Lac La Biche, over 200 kilometres away.[29] Nonetheless, the line neared Fort McMurray in 1917 and by 1919 had been pushed closer to the top of the Clearwater River valley. This was still about 40 kilometres from Fort McMurray, and freight was hauled from the railhead down the steep banks of the Clearwater until 1922 when the line was extended into the river valley where a new town called Waterways (now called Draper) was built.[30] To avoid the portage over the Vermilion Chutes, the Hudson's Bay Company abandoned the Peace River route to the far north in favour of the newly built A&GW through Fort McMurray. This decision dashed Peace River's immediate prospects of becoming a new pivotal centre in northern transportation.

## ▬ The Political Economy of Northern Alberta's Railways

While construction of the northern lines had been achieved, conditions were poor. Service on the ED&BC was unreliable and at times nonexistent because of shoddy construction and poor rolling stock. Ties broke and rails bent "as heavy loads pressed rails and ties down into a poorly ballasted, muddy, clay roadbed." Trains operated slowly and "heavy grain loads could only be moved in winter when the track was stable on the frozen roadbed."[31] Freight rates in 1915 during the construction phase on the ED&BC were a third higher than the highest in western Canada, and when formal rates were set the next year, the railway applied for the highest rate allowable. Although the Board of Railway Commissioners devised a somewhat lower interim set of rates, they were still high because the board ruled that the ED&BC was a "colonization road" that "in effect bears to the transcontinental systems the relationship of a branch line." These high rates soon brought complaints from residents in the Peace River country. It was observed in Spirit River in 1920 that although the ED&BC ran "through a practically level country between Edmonton and Spirit River—with the exception of the Smoky River Crossing—we have been compelled to pay mountain rates for over four years." Despite these high rates, there was no scheduled service, and trains took "from two to five times the hours to make their trips than the mileage warrants. And one imagines himself in a cat boat on a choppy sea when one is riding on this line."[32]

Conditions were even worse on the A&GW. It sometimes took over a week to reach Fort McMurray from Edmonton. By 1919, however, conditions on the line had improved sufficiently that the A&GW began carrying mail to Fort

McMurray from Edmonton, and in 1920 the last river brigade from Athabasca ran the Grand Rapids and the tramway at Grand Island was dismantled. The A&GW applied to the Department of the Interior for 875 acres for its divisional point at Waterways, justifying the amount of land requested by arguing that docks and storage facilities had to be built to handle the transhipment of freight down river. It also predicted that there would be "immense deposits of tar sands which will be shipped from here, also large consignments of salt, fish, timber and ore," and the railway would need large marshalling yards. Although the sale of public lands for divisional points was usually limited to 640 acres, the federal government granted the A&GW's request because there were "no conflicting claims" for the land.[33]

Despite these anticipated needs, the A&GW line was plagued with breakdowns and poor track continued to limit its service. Nonetheless, these problems came to be seen as part of the railway's rough-and-ready frontier character. Philip Godsell recalled his 1920 trip on the A&GW from Edmonton to Waterways as part of the romance of the north:

> The "Muskeg Limited," a conglomeration of dirty red box-cars, flat-cars, and one very rickety old-fashioned coach with a caboose tacked on to the rear, at length backed protestingly into the station. Everyone immediately made a wild dash for the nearest car, threw on his bed-roll and grub boxes, clambered aboard and used his baggage in place of a seat. The lucky ones got plush-covered berths in the coach…As the engine gave her last wheezy whistle the nondescript train, with much bumping and a good deal of noise and ostentation, commenced her swaying journey through prairie and muskeg. Twice a day there would be a brief stop for meals, then the passengers would all pile out onto the track with frying pans and tea kettles in their hands, build hurried campfires, sling on the kettles, warm up a tin of pork and beans and snatch a hasty meal. After the first fire every one knew everybody else and the artificial barriers which civilization imposes were very soon let down.[34]

Colourful or not, northern railways were a steadily escalating crisis for the provincial government. By 1919, all of the McArthur lines (the ED&BC, the A&GW and the CCR) were in almost total collapse. Alberta was twice forced to pay the interest on the ED&BC's bonds in 1919, and the federal government too subsidized its operations. The ED&BC was also in debt to many towns and villages—in 1919 it owed $10,000 in back taxes at Peace River alone. The province had to grapple with the prospect of seemingly never-ending payments to meet its earlier lavish bond guarantees. In 1919 the federal government refused to take over the northern Alberta lines and incorporate them into the Canadian National Railways (CNR), which it was then creating from the financial wreckage of the old GTP, CNoR and hundreds of smaller lines. Yet, the province was unclear about its best course of action, stating that it intended only "to take the place of the bondholders, appoint a receiver, and operate the line until the McArthur interests either can sell it or the dominion government takes over."[35] Premier Stewart was reluctant to see the lines incorporated into the CNR because this would bring them under federal jurisdiction, and ongoing provincial ambitions to direct a part of northern Alberta's new economic infrastructure led the province to persist in its own course, even though it promised to be costly.[36] Subsequently, Stewart announced that Alberta would no longer subsidize the lines unless it controlled them, and in 1920 management of the ED&BC, the CCR and the A&GW passed to the province. Alberta immediately leased the ED&BC and CCR lines to the CPR, which agreed to manage and upgrade them. The CPR also undertook to extend the railway west from Grand Prairie to Wembley. The province retained management of the A&GW and by 1925 had extended the line to a location further along the Clearwater River. This site was also named Waterways, and a spur line was constructed from the station to the river so that goods could be loaded more easily onto the boats.

## The Early Impact of the Railway

While rail service in northern Alberta evolved for the next two decades, indications of the economic change that it brought were immediately apparent. Throughout northern Alberta, railway construction brought a greater need for timber and milled lumber for ties and other uses, and subsequent population growth allowed local lumber mills to expand to meet this increased demand. In the winter of 1917–18, 160 men were working in lumber camps around Lesser Slave Lake. At the same time, expansion of local lumber operations was limited because the railway allowed importation of higher quality, seasoned lumber than could be produced by local mills. Indeed, the railway's most immediate impact on local forest resources was to increase the number of forest fires. In 1914, the Department of the Interior noted that in the past "a railway penetrating a new country was a sure indication of wholesale destruction of timber by fire." While new regulations governing railway construction supposedly lessened such catastrophes elsewhere, they were of little effect in northern Alberta. The ED&BC was among the worst offenders in western Canada; in 1914 more than half of all fires caused by railways in Alberta occurred along its lines. Conditions were so serious that the Department of the Interior asked the Board of Railway Commissioners to order the railway company to remedy the situation. After the extensive damage caused by the ED&BC, the federal government established a forest preserve along the southern shore of Lesser Slave Lake in 1917.[37]

In contrast to lumbering, the railway brought more immediate opportunities for the fishing industry in northern Alberta. By 1914, lakes around Edmonton were reaching production limits. In a pattern familiar on the prairies, depletion in southern lakes turned attention to fish resources in newly accessible areas. While many applications for fishing licences for lakes throughout northern Alberta were received by the Department of Fisheries in 1914, commercial fishing initially expanded at Lesser Slave Lake—the first area to be touched by the railway. Although rail service in 1914 was poor, it nonetheless facilitated more efficient marketing. Most commercial fishermen came from the Edmonton district and took up fishing "because they were unable to find other employment" and hoped that World War I would drive up fish prices.[38] While most were unsuccessful, corporate enterprise did better, and by 1915 commercial fishing was expanding at the east end of Lesser Slave Lake where three companies bought fish from licensed fishermen. The next year, wartime conditions stimulated rising demand and higher prices for fish. Although commercial fishing was taking place at a number of other lakes in Alberta, Lesser Slave Lake rapidly became the province's most important fishing lake. Production almost doubled over the previous year, and while most of the fish was sold in Edmonton and Calgary, some was also exported to the United States. Shipped in refrigerated cars, fish from Lesser Slave Lake could reach Chicago in 76 hours. Continued high prices led to further expansion in 1917 and improved rail service permitted increased exports. By 1919, most of Alberta's catch of lake trout and almost 60 percent of its whitefish came from Lesser Slave Lake.[39]

Both the failure of many of the small, inexperienced and poorly capitalized fishermen on Lesser Slave Lake in 1914 and the relative success of corporate activity were an early indication of the importance of adequate capitalization for successful commercial fishing in northern Alberta. Distance to market brought even higher shipping, cold storage and processing costs for northern Alberta fisheries than for those of northern Manitoba, the most important commercial fisheries on the prairies at this time. This enhanced the pressure for concentrated corporate control of capital, processing and marketing. In 1915, there were six freezers/ice houses (up from one the year before), four smoke houses (up from three the year before) and two wharves and piers at Lesser Slave Lake. Handling was also improved. Previously, "fish were shipped in sacks" and rough handling brought low prices. Consequently, local wholesalers and packers in Faust, Wagner and Joussard (then called Indiana) began to invest in better handling equipment and techniques. Fish were now packed with ice in wooden boxes for shipment. In keeping with this change, several new ice houses were constructed and about 2,400 tonnes of ice were put up in 1916.[40]

Most processing companies purchased their fish from independent fishermen, and in 1915 there were 121 men and 25 boats (including two gas ones) fishing on Lesser Slave Lake. Technically, these fishermen were free agents in that they obtained their own fishing licences, but few of them were truly independent. A processing company usually supplied nets, boats and other equipment to certain fishermen who in turn sold their catch only to that company. Although this arrangement gave the processors almost total control over the industry, most fishermen were too poor to afford the necessary equipment, let alone the facilities required to store fish so that they could take advantage of short-term price movements. Thus, they sold their production into the market immediately, regardless of price, and few earned "more than a living wage." This relationship was entrenched by the mechanization of summer commercial fishing, which unlike winter fishing, required boats, more extensive nets, refrigeration facilities and efficient transportation. While fishermen on Lesser Slave Lake remained less highly capitalized than those at Lake Wabamum where gas-powered boats were more common, an increasing number were using motor boats by 1916. This allowed them to go further out on the lake, "regardless of head winds," and to return "to the cooling plants before the catch is exposed any length of time to the weather."[41]

The increased investment in Lesser Slave Lake's fishery was enhanced and protected by the enforcement of federal fishing regulations which aimed to preserve fish stocks for commercial users. All fishing operations were licensed and closed seasons—enforced by lake patrols—were imposed during October and November. By 1917, there were so many fishing operations on the lake that the limit on whitefish was met by the end of July, making it the shortest fishing season on record. Because of the demand for licences, the federal government began to limit the allowable catch for each licence instead of restricting the number of licences as it had previously done. It also intensified efforts to restrict the activities of Native users. In 1915, Indians and Metis were forced for the first time to take out licences for domestic fishing, although they did not have to pay for them. While they could continue to catch fish for immediate consumption during the closed season, "hanging" fish to preserve it for dog food was prohibited. Apparently, this was designed to limit consumption and encourage commercial use of the resource.[42]

In the same way that the railway led to rapid expansion of Lesser Slave Lake's fishing industry, it had an immediate impact on farming in the Peace River country. Railway construction offered wage employment for residents and a market for locally produced grain, vegetables and horse feed.[43] More directly, high wartime prices led many farmers to reduce livestock production and to break more land for wheat. It also stimulated increased Euro-Canadian settlement. By 1915, the federal government was intensifying its promotion of northern settlement in general, arguing that northern areas in Europe and Asia supported millions of people and that the same latitudes in Canada could also support a "dense population." Although the growing season was short, it was noted that this was balanced by long summer days which allowed all crops to "grow and mature in a much shorter space of time" than in southern areas. By 1917 nearly every train arriving in Peace River brought more settlers, and as the Department of the Interior noted in its promotional literature that year, the completion of the railway meant that "Easily Accessible" could now be truly written "about this new and wonderful country." In 1917, the Dominion Experimental Farms confirmed its crop testing programmes in the Peace River country by making its test facilities on Donald Albright's farm near Beaverlodge permanent and by putting Albright on salary to manage the farm.[44]

Despite the federal government's promotion and the arrival of a few settlers, population growth in the Peace River country slowed during World War I because per capita enlistment of soldiers from the district was high, overseas immigration practically ceased and migration within Canada and from the United States declined. After the war, however, migration picked up. In combination, demobilization, soldier settlement schemes, high wheat prices and promotional campaigns for settlers helped stimulate migration to the Peace River country. High wartime prices allowed wheat to be grown profitably in areas far from the railway and encouraged the breaking of more land in closer-in areas. Consequently, wheat acreage increased three-fold between 1916 and 1921. By 1917, Waterhole area farmers were shipping grain to Spirit River, a trip of almost 50 kilometres that required a difficult crossing at the steep river banks at Dunvegan. Pouce Coupe farmers were also shipping grain there, an 18-hour trip that cost around 25 cents per bushel. Farming was further stimulated by the federal-provincial "cow bill" which provided farmers with easy credit for the purchase of cattle. This so stimulated imports of breeding cattle to the Peace River country that feed had to be imported at high prices from other parts of Alberta.[45]

By 1921, the number of farms in the southern Peace River country had increased to just under 3,600, almost three times the number in 1916. Occupied acreage also increased from around 330,000 to almost 880,000 acres and improved farm land increased from almost 70,000 to over 243,000 acres. The Euro-Canadian population had also increased by 6,000 people over 1916. Most of these people settled in areas where earlier settlers had already located, but the coming of the railway also pushed advance settlement further afield. Good land around Fort Vermilion now attracted a few settlers, and a handful of people were also moving into the Battle River district north of Peace River by 1920. But settlement dropped off sharply in 1921 because of post-war recession and falling wheat and cattle prices, and it did not pick up again until 1926–27.[46]

The extension of the rails to Waterways had a parallel impact on the eastern parts of northern Alberta. As the terminus of the line, Waterways (and nearby Fort McMurray) became the metropolitan centre for the Slave and lower Athabasca river districts, making it the jumping-off point to the far north that Athabasca had once been. The railway also enhanced the value of the district's mineral resources. Although petroleum retained its long-term potential, the province more immediately became involved in developing salt resources. Salt had been found as early as 1907, and by 1919 the area's MLA, Jean Coté, was lobbying for its development. The provincial government was equally enthusiastic because it wished "to stimulate and encourage by every reasonable means the development of the natural resources" along the A&GW whose bond interest it was paying. Since salt, a vital everyday commodity as well as one with important industrial applications, was then imported to Alberta from Ontario, local production was assured a ready market. A government crew drilled near the Fort McMurray townsite and penetrated nine metres into an extensive salt bed. While of commercial quality and quantity, these deposits were too far from the railhead, which was still on the height of the Clearwater River valley. Although further exploratory wells proved significant salt deposits, plans were shelved until the railway came closer.[47]

Similarly premature interest was also expressed in connection with commercial fishing on Lake Athabasca. The Fisheries Branch received several applications for licences in 1914, but as the inspector noted, they "were evidently with a future in view, as at present there is no means by which fish could be brought out at a profit." Once the railway reached the Fort McMurray district, however, the possibility of exporting fish from Lake Athabasca improved. By 1919 the Department of the Interior reported that commercial fishing was underway on Lake Athabasca, but details about it are unknown. In 1920, the R.W. Jones Company (later called Mackenzie Basin Fisheries Ltd.) planned construction of a cannery at Black Bay (where Uranium City, Saskatchewan is now located). In August 1920, about 33 workers passed through Fort Chipewyan on their way to set up "the new fishing company." Apparently no local workers were hired. While the cannery shipped several hundred cases of canned lake trout and whitefish, production was suspended because markets were difficult to develop and transportation was costly.[48] Further development of commercial fishing on Lake Athabasca did not take place until the mid 1920s.


—— **Changes in the Fur Trade**

Changing conditions in the fur trade were of greater immediate importance for the Peace-Athabasca delta than the development of a fishing industry. Both white trappers and free traders benefited from improved access and communications through Fort McMurray. The telegraph line between Edmonton and Fort McMurray that began operating in early 1915 permitted the immediate transmission of prices to buyers and reduced their risk by narrowing the time lag between their purchase of fur and its sale to wholesalers. This communications technology ensured that the Hudson's Bay Company no longer controlled current market news which had previously given it an edge over its competitors.[49]

The impact of this changing technology on northern Alberta's fur trade was overshadowed, however, by the extraordinary effect of World War I on the Canadian fur trade. In a dramatic development, the British board of trade suspended fur auctions as a wartime measure in 1914. Believing the market would collapse when sales resumed, the Hudson's Bay Company immediately instructed its traders not to buy fur during the coming winter. While it kept most of its posts open, the Bay gave its traders "absolute orders to give no credit," although some secretly violated these directives and extended credit when they could. Revillon and other traders followed suit by reducing fur purchases and closing some of their smaller posts.[50]

Not unexpectedly, fur prices fell disastrously. As elsewhere in northern Canada, Natives were caught "absolutely unprepared" and were forced into a "hand to mouth existence." At Fort Chipewyan, prices for red fox fell from $6 in 1913–14 to $1 in 1914–15; marten fell from $12 to $2; mink went from $6 to 50 cents; and muskrat fell from 50 cents to 2 cents. In a society where people had little cash or few supplies on hand, the collapse of prices led to forecasts of starvation. Missionaries, traders and police warned that while conditions would be tough for the able-bodied, they would be terrible for the handicapped, old and sick. Accordingly, they advised the government to prepare to issue relief on a wide scale.[51] In light of the looming crisis, Indian Affairs authorized the NWMP, the Hudson's Bay Company and Revillon to stockpile supplies for those in need. Soon after, the department sent a circular letter to its staff and affiliates advising that since there would likely be destitution during the coming winter, Natives should be urged to bend "their energies to the securing of *food* rather than fur."[52]

While Natives everywhere in northern Alberta experienced severe deprivation, conditions varied significantly by location. The Cree living in the swampy land west of Fort Chipewyan had a very hard winter: the goose and duck hunt the previous fall had failed and fishing had been poor. In the winter, rabbits were scarce while deep snow made hunting difficult. Similarly, the NWMP noted that there were no moose or rabbits at Hay River and starvation was likely. Although there were no rabbits in some districts, conditions in the Peace River country were somewhat better because moose were plentiful.[53] The distribution of relief reflected these variations. In early 1915 no relief was issued at Fitzgerald because moose and caribou were plentiful. At Fort Chipewyan and Fond du Lac, 152 boxes of ammunition—unaffordable because of low fur prices—were issued so people could hunt moose and caribou. At Fort Vermilion and Wabasca, relief mostly went to the old and handicapped, although at Fort McMurray, where game was presumably scarce, it was more widely distributed. In many cases, requests for relief were refused, although as Sergeant McLeod at Fort Vermilion confessed to his superior in January 1915, it was "very difficult" to deny it to children who were "in rags and tatters and really looking hungry." Most people could not buy clothes and "what they had on hand is about to fall to pieces, and while they will pull through this winter with suffering, their condition during the winter of 1915–1916 will be simply desperate."[54]

Government relief in the winter of 1914–15 showed how the state had assumed responsibility for the social costs of northern Alberta's economic system. Nonetheless, some observers concluded that the crisis would force Native people to experience a baptism by starvation in the values of the market economy. Perhaps the war had intensified Anglo-Canadian righteousness, but whatever the cause, official views about Native unwillingness to absorb capitalist ethics became harsher. While NWMP Superintendent McDonell made the familiar assertion that "the Indians are not a provident race," he anticipated that the bitterness of current conditions might transform their attitudes towards money and convince them of the need to accumulate capital. Like the keeper of a poor house, he hoped that "the inexorable terms under which they are obliged to trade now, 'nothing for nothing' may teach them the value of laying by for a rainy day. If this is once driven into them I see no reason why any of them should be really hard up, as the resources of the country are practically limitless."[55] In other cases, the crisis reinforced an old romanticism that Native people in their "natural state" were best off without Euro-Canadian material culture. One NWMP constable welcomed the collapse of fur prices because "the days of prosperity never did them [Natives] much good. Not knowing the value of money, when selling their furs at large sums, they would spend it all by giving feasts and dances." Now they were living on meat and fish and were "better off than in former years." Indeed, he thought that "if the war lasts longer, the fur market will be Nil" and people would be forced to wear deerskin which was durable and "more suitable to them than the clothing brought in by the traders."[56]

The notion that tough times would socially transform Natives—either by assimilating them to capitalist values or by forcing them to return to "traditional" and "natural" conditions—represented various streams of Euro-Canadian thought about Native people in northern Alberta. Similar reasoning, however, was not applied to Euro-Canadian homesteaders who also needed assistance. By March 1915, 63 applications for relief from rural Euro-Canadians around Athabasca had been received by the NWMP. This relief was provided by the federal Department of Immigration, or, less commonly, by the provincial Department of Health. As with Natives, each case was investigated and relief was issued as deemed appropriate. But no resentment about these demands by Euro-Canadians seems to have been expressed either publicly or privately by government officials. In this, it was significant that relief was tied to the ownership of property: in return for relief, liens were registered on the homestead.[57] These "debts" were often later forgiven by government, but land ownership—even for impoverished homesteaders—conferred dignity and social power and provided an artifice by which its owners were spared the stigma and vulnerability of charity. Those without title to land, such as Indians and most other Natives, did not enjoy such grace—a revealing indication of changing conditions in northern Alberta's social and economic life.

The impact of these new conditions was postponed, however, by a sudden rise in fur prices. The Hudson's Bay Company resumed credit in early 1915 and by the end of the year declining Russian fur exports and the booming United States economy brought increased demand for fur. In the early winter of 1915–16, traders paid "ridiculously low prices," but most people had to sell their furs to buy food. Thus, much fur had already been sold by the time prices rose. Profits were excellent for traders who had purchased fur before the price increase: fox pelts that had been bought in Fort Chipewyan in the early winter for between $1 and $1.50 sold in Edmonton for between $12 to $15 in February 1916.[58]

These higher prices were soon offered in northern Alberta by J.H. Bryan, a novice Edmonton fur buyer who appeared at Fort Chipewyan and Fond du Lac at the end of 1915. Bryan's operations were supported by New York capital, and he quickly established posts at a number of locations. His success, and the source of his capital, illustrated changes in international fur marketing. Instability in Britain had given Americans a chance to enter the field, and in 1916 fur auctions began in New York. Growing numbers of American fur buyers flooded into the Canadian north and diverted fur to auctions in the United States. Competition for fur led auction houses and brokers to offer independent fur buyers inexpensive credit, consignment deals and privileged access to current prices. This stimulated cash buying and retail competition because trappers could shop around for the best prices. While existing operations, such as the Northern Trading Company, continued to be active, new players also entered the field. In 1918, J.H. Bryan sold his fur operations to Lamson and Hubbard, one of the largest raw fur buyers in the United States, which immediately began building its own transportation facilities to free itself of the Hudson's Bay Company shipping system. With its southern portal at the railhead at Waterways, Lamson and Hubbard's transportation network spread throughout the Athabasca and Mackenzie River districts. The company had a stern wheeler (based at Fort Smith) on the Slave and Mackenzie rivers; gas boats on Lake Athabasca and Great Slave Lake; a steam tug and barges on the Liard River; two tugs, 40 or 50 freight barges and a steam ship on the Athabasca River between Fort McMurray and Fitzgerald; and crawler tractors and trailers on the Smith Portage. In 1921 it formed these operations into the Alberta and Arctic Transportation Company.[59]

This expanded transportation capacity brought falling freight rates and better access for small traders. As the end of steel, Fort McMurray quickly became an important centre for cash fur buying; buyers now came from Edmonton on the train, and every merchant in town bought furs as well. While barter remained a significant part of the trade, cash buying also increased in districts to the north. Competition was waged on economic lines, such as price and credit, by using local social and political connections, and in some cases by selling bootleg liquor. Lamson and Hubbard also encouraged white trappers in order to break the Native monopoly of trapping and to increase production. But most white trappers came north independently, and included home-steaders from the Peace River country who needed cash, a few wartime draft dodgers, and a variety of individuals who hoped to get rich quickly.[60] In what would become a familiar pattern over the next 25 years, Natives complained that many of these white trappers disrupted local economies and resources by ignoring existing trapping territories and treating fur-bearing animals merely as a resource to be mined for quick profit.[61]

Boom conditions dominated the fur trade for most of the years between 1916 and 1921. While the widespread sickness and death brought by the 'flu epidemic of 1918 temporarily stalled this boom, the trade quickly revived. Higher prices allowed Natives to purchase an expanded range of goods and to reject other work in favour of trapping.[62] For the fur trade itself, Jim Cornwall later recalled it as a time of greed and extravagant ambition fuelled by high prices and inexperienced traders. As he wrote,

> It was figured that with money and goods fur could be bought and traded at a low figure and sold at a big profit. Old and played-out terri-tory that been practically abandoned by previous traders was opened up, and was manned by discard and misfit traders who had been let out by other Companies…[W]hat these discards did with the money and goods entrusted to them is beyond belief—a book in itself. While the money lasted the fur trade was completely demoralized.[63]

By 1920, fur prices had reached unprecedented levels, but the boom collapsed in 1921, bringing a consolidation of the trade later in the decade.

— ✦ —

Although higher prices during most of World War I revived the fur trade, it was evident that older, familiar ways of life in northern Alberta would not return. Social and economic change was confirmed by the increase in white trappers and the expanding competition in the fur trade. The Hudson's Bay Company's growing abandonment by 1914 of its traditional obligations and its replacement by state initiatives for social welfare were elements in a policy that the company had extended in northern Alberta in fits and starts for over two decades. This cost the company the loyalty and respect of people who had traded with it for generations, but the company was now involved less in the fur trade and more in higher profit activities such as land speculation and international brokerage. While this demonstrated that new political and social dynamics in western Canada were changing state and corporate activity in northern life, it was only one measure of the transformation taking place.

By World War I, Canada had begun to test in a practical way northern Alberta's potential for farming, mining, fishing and other activities. Not all of these prospects would be realized in either the short- or long-term, but their pursuit would continue to shape and change life in northern Alberta in the coming years. In this transformation, the railway was a powerful agent because it permitted new economic activities in different parts of the region. In the Peace River country, the Euro-Canadian settler society that had earlier begun to develop expanded, confirming a new social complexity in northern Alberta. It helped to shift the focus of northern economic life to Edmonton and away from intermediary points such as Athabasca and Grouard. It also allowed the reorganization of patterns of Euro-Canadian settlement from more northern points such as Fort Vermilion to the more southern areas around Peace River and Grande Prairie. While this restructuring of population and economic activity in the Peace River country had clearly begun by 1909, it was only confirmed when rail connections were established. At the same time, the railway created new divisions within the Peace River country. When the Peace River had been a transportation corridor, it had united the district. After the railway, distinctions between north and south became more pronounced because the railway served each sub-region unevenly and replaced north-south connections with east-west ones. Areas south of the river benefited from rail service, while those north of the river where the rails had not yet penetrated languished.

At the same time that economic and cultural distinctions were appearing within the Peace River country, broader divergence was cutting across northern Alberta in general. The economic and social distinctions between the eastern and western parts of its economy were confirmed by the completion of the railway from Edmonton to Fort McMurray that bypassed Athabasca in favour of a direct link with Edmonton. Connections among the lower Athabasca, Lesser Slave Lake and Peace River districts were also now largely through Edmonton rather than along the Athabasca River. And while economic and social relationships between the eastern and western portions of northern Alberta were declining, settlements and towns throughout northern Alberta were beginning to be oriented into an urban system like that in the rest of the prairies. At the same time, the re-establishment of the Fort McMurray route for shipments to the far north reformulated one part of the historic route to the north by renewing it as the primary connector between southern Canada and the Mackenzie River valley and the western Arctic. But the bypassing of the Grand Rapids portage destroyed an important element in the Native, especially Metis, economy that had functioned for nearly four decades. Its passing, like its creation, was a testament to the relative interaction of social structure, technology and geography in the historical evolution of Northern Alberta.

# PART III

*An itinerant barber at Waterways gave travellers a chance to make themselves presentable. Photograph dated about 1920. A3893 PAA.*

# The Decline of
# Regional Unity
## *1920–1950*

# Getting In, Getting Out

## 7

*Transportation Developments in Northern Alberta*

THE CRACKS THAT HAD APPEARED in northern Alberta's regional unity by 1916 widened during the 1920s and 1930s. By World War II, northern Alberta functioned as two separate units—one in the east and one in the west—each with distinctive seasonal, economic and social lives. In contrast to the trapping life predominant north of Fort McMurray, Euro-Canadian farming had expanded in the Peace River country and Lesser Slave Lake and Athabasca districts. This evolution was confirmed by mining developments in the NWT and around Lake Athabasca, which reinforced the lower Athabasca River district's function as a transportation corridor to the Mackenzie River and western Arctic.

Imperial Oil's discovery of oil at Fort Norman (now Norman Wells) in 1920 was the first post-war resource boom in the Mackenzie valley, and prospectors flocked north on rumours that it was the largest oil field in the country. Men from Fort Chipewyan and other northern settlements also joined the rush to stake claims or find work at Norman Wells.[1] While this discovery did not bring the growth expected, a national gold boom (especially important in northern Quebec and Ontario) brought more prospectors to northern Alberta and the NWT later in the 1920s. Activity increased during the 1930s when the price of gold nearly doubled and production costs fell. As historian Morris Zaslow has noted, the NWT mining boom "whetted the metropolitan ambitions of the western cities and led pressure groups such as the Edmonton and Northern Alberta Chamber of Mines to lobby provincial and federal politicians" to promote northern development. Some lobbyists claimed that northern development would help in "energizing the economic system in all directions" and increase demand for western Canadian farm products. Others wanted grander benefits. In British Columbia, the Patullo government argued that the province's boundaries should be extended northward to incorporate the Yukon, and in 1939 the Alberta legislature similarly resolved that Alberta should annex almost the whole of the District of Mackenzie. As Lord Tweedsmuir remarked during his northern tour in 1937, "the future of Canada lies in its North lands."[2]

While northern mining development brought increased traffic along the Athabasca River, the Peace River country was developing in a different direction. Euro-Canadian settlement slowed there after 1920, but picked up and reached boom proportions later in the decade. It then levelled off in the 1930s in the face of the Depression. Like their predecessors, these settlers wanted to expand their economic hinterland and find easier and cheaper ways to export their produce. One popular argument held that a coast outlet, a shorter rail or highway route to Pacific ports through the mountains, was essential. Others agitated for the construction of a highway to the NWT to capitalize on its economic expansion. Such concerns were not surprising in a staple economy dependent on outside capital and distant markets.[3] Yet these attempts to devise new transportation networks were more than efforts to expand infrastructure and markets. While they were seen as a solution for many of the problems the Peace River country faced, they also expressed attitudes towards place, economy and social development central to the aspirations of people in the district.

At the same time that people were urging development of further rail and road connections, aviation also emerged as a new element in communications everywhere in northern Alberta. Despite its flexibility, air travel did not re-establish connections within northern Alberta or renew regional unity. By 1930, ancient technology such as canoes, and older technology such as steamboats, operated alongside more recently introduced technology such as railways, and beside entirely new technology such as airplanes. Each offered the potential for alternative relationships and different social and economic pursuits, and each simultaneously met particular needs relative to location of resources, patterns of settlement and geography. Economist Harold Innis concluded that the speed with which new technology was applied in northern Canada meant that "the economies of railways and mines, fur traders, prospectors, Indians, and bush pilots coexisted in a jumble, and not in neat and separate stages."[4] In part, this arose from an economy dominated by staple production in which the value of goods was always relative to their marketability. When canoes and steamships transported fur and trade goods, northern Alberta's river system had shaped the entry and exit points to the region. While fur, a light-weight, high value and easily compressed product, could be exported economically through this network, grain, livestock, minerals and petroleum from northern Alberta only gained market value through the use of different technology such as railways or by revamping older systems, such as river ship-ping. Technology was thus more than the mere application of new forms of machine power—it had relative implications for matters as disparate as regional unity, economic development, social status and employment.

## ▬ Railways and Regional Development

Following the financial collapse of the McArthur railways at the end of World War I, the province took over the lines and leased them to the CPR. During this period of state control, scheduled service became a reality, new rolling stock was purchased and lines were upgraded and extended. As settlement spread out onto the uplands and away from the rivers in the Peace River country, railway expansion continued to help connect new areas with distant markets. The railway was pushed north of the Peace River in three stages: from Peace River to Berwyn in 1921, to Whitelaw in 1924 and to Fairview in 1928. South of the river, it was extended west from Grande Prairie to Wembley in 1924 and to Hythe in 1928. These extensions totalled only about 150 kilometres, but they provided rail connections to districts that advance settlers had identified as having good farming potential. This in turn stimulated further advance settle-ment a distance from the new lines.[5]

Although it had successfully reorganized, operated and extended the northern rail system, the provincial government was reluctant to stay in the railway business. The leasing arrangement with the CPR was expensive, and when Alberta gained full ownership of the lines after various legal issues with McArthur and his bankers were resolved in 1925, it proposed selling them either to the CPR or the CNR. Each rejected the offer, forcing the province to continue operating the lines itself. In 1928, however, a deal was struck by which the CPR and CNR jointly purchased all the lines then under provincial control—the ED&BC, the CCR, the A&GW and the Pembina Valley Railway, a line built by the province from Edmonton to Barrhead in 1927. In early 1929, a subsidiary company, the Northern Alberta Railways (NAR), was created with head offices in Edmonton.[6]

The sale of Alberta's northern railways was consistent with the customary Canadian approach of providing economic infrastructure through public funding until local economic conditions made it possible for private interests to take over and run them profitably. The province's railway investment therefore ultimately served as a way of subsidizing economic growth through the private sector rather than becoming a long-term effort to manage and control the economy publicly. The province calculated in 1927 that the fair cost of replacement (minus depreciation) of the northern lines was almost $29 million. Although the NAR paid $15 million and assumed $10 million of outstanding ED&BC bonds, the province continued to pay interest and principal on almost $7.5 million of A&GW debt. While the Alberta government estimated it had lost $10 million on its railway projects, the CPR and CNR had purchased a profitable system.[7] Moreover, the sale agreement made few demands, requiring only the construction of at least 96 kilometres of new lines in the Peace River country. In 1930, the line was extended 24 kilometres from Fairview to Hines Creek, the head of a large fertile area stretching west to the British Columbia border north of the Peace River. South of the river, it was extended 79 kilometres west from Hythe to Pouce Coupe and Dawson Creek, British Columbia in 1931. This extension into another province showed a newfound flexibility. It was unlikely that rail lines under provincial ownership would have been pushed beyond Alberta's boundary, even though this would have increased the interdependency of the British Columbia and Alberta Peace River districts and entrenched Edmonton's hegemony over the Canadian north-west. The CPR and CNR privately agreed to route all NAR outbound freight equally over each other's lines—a pledge that quickly gave rise to disputes between the partners.[8]

In both the Peace River country and the lower Athabasca River districts, the NAR's high freight rates created much resentment. In the Peace River country, this was mitigated somewhat during the 1920s when a series of decisions by the Board of Railway Commissioners (prompted by farmers' demands) lowered western Canadian freight rates and equalized those to the Pacific coast. This dramatically lowered freight rates and encouraged greater use by Peace River country farmers of the port of Vancouver, which was a shorter haul than to the Lakehead. But none of these developments could obliterate geography and Peace River area farmers still faced higher shipping costs to market their goods and purchase farm equipment and supplies than other prairie farmers.[9]

*As the point where river and rail met, Waterways was a busy port in summer in the 1930s.* A10,264 PAA.

On the NAR line to Waterways, freight rates were much higher than even those to the Peace River country, and some observers claimed that they were the highest in Canada. This was partly due to price gouging, but critics—especially in the 1920s—tended to overestimate the line's profitability. Operating costs were high because the line passed over about 80 kilometres of muskeg where speeds had to be reduced, and there were several heavy grades along the line (especially at the Clearwater valley) that reduced the tonnage that could be hauled. Although weekly scheduled service was provided year-round, the population between Lac La Biche and Waterways—a distance of almost 280 kilometres—was thin and generated little traffic. By 1936, there were only a few tiny settlements along this line, and about one-third of the population on the entire stretch lived in the district around Conklin, which consisted only of two general stores and a post office. Additionally, passenger and freight traffic was seasonal. During the navigation season in summer, most cars returned empty from Waterways because there was little outgoing freight, while in winter empty cars were hauled to Waterways to bring out salt.[10]

By the early 1930s, these drawbacks still limited service on the line, but resentment about high rates was increasing. In 1932, Northern Traders Ltd. asked the Board of Railway Commissioners to investigate the NAR's rates to Waterways, but the application was withdrawn, perhaps because the Alberta government backed the NAR, which was then threatening to abandon the line.

Genuine or not, this threat was a sobering prospect since it would have forced shippers to use the more difficult and expensive river route to the NWT through Peace River and Fort Vermilion. The only group that welcomed this prospect was the Peace River Chamber of Commerce, which petitioned the Board of Railway Commissioners to force the NAR to abandon the Waterways line and divert all traffic to the far north through Peace River.[11] A short time later, however, the mining boom in the NWT brought more seasonally balanced traffic and increased tonnage passing over the line. By 1934, gold claims were being staked at Yellowknife and gold fever quickly spread. At its peak in 1938, over 30 companies were active in and around Yellowknife and 3,500 claims were staked. "Men of every description" travelled down river every day from Fort McMurray, "many of them in small boats and even on rafts with little or no provisions."[12] In 1934, gold, pitchblende and nickel-copper deposits had also been discovered at Goldfields on the north shore of the Saskatchewan side of Lake Athabasca. This spawned another mining rush through Waterways, drawing prospectors and labourers from across North America, including Fort Chipewyan and other northern points. By early 1935 claims at Goldfields were beginning to change hands, stimulating "tales of fabulously rich finds." The population of Goldfields increased from a handful of trappers and traders to about 300 by 1936 and about 1,000 by 1940. The mines were said to be as rich as those at Noranda and Rouyn and attracted major mining companies such as Consolidated Mining and Smelting Ltd. While the mine soon closed because ore grades were too low to be profitable, gold deposits at Yellowknife were under development and 300 workers were employed there by 1939. As well, silver-radium deposits at Echo Bay on Great Bear Lake in the NWT, had by then been developed by White Eagle Mines and Eldorado Gold Mines Ltd.[13].

The expanded shipping activity that these developments created for the NAR's line to Waterways renewed demands for a rate reduction. A second application to the Board of Railway Commissioners to investigate rates was made in 1934, but it too lapsed. By now, however, critics asserted that high freight rates were holding back northern mining development, and in 1936 the Alberta and North-West Chamber of Mines asked the Board to investigate the NAR's rates to Waterways. Again, the NAR threatened to abandon the line. While the NAR's general manager believed that freight volumes would probably continue to grow, he advised his superiors to try and postpone rate reductions by arguing that the upswing was only temporary. By early 1938, however, freight had increased to the point where the NAR's general manager

In the 1920s, roads in northern
Alberta, such as this one between
Smith and Slave Lake in 1928,
were impassable during
wet weather. ACA83 PAA.

admitted that the company could no longer "stave off" a rate reduction. Shipping
rates on the Athabasca River were falling because of increased competition and
traffic, and the railway had to keep in step. The mayor of Edmonton had also
now joined forces with the Chamber of Mines to press for a reduction, and the
NAR finally lowered its rates by up to 20 percent, congratulating itself publicly
that it was doing its part in assisting the expansion of northern mining.
Notwithstanding this reduction, rates were still 50 percent higher than those
on the prairies.[14] Predictably, pressure again built for further rate reductions,
and in 1947 the Board of Railway Commissioners investigated the matter. Even
when it excluded the period of wartime activity when the NAR had been
extraordinarily busy and profitable, the board found that the profit per train
mile on the Edmonton-Waterways line from 1937 to 1941 and during 1945 "was
greatly in excess" of that earned on the rest of the company's lines. In fact, the
line had "contributed considerably" to the company's overall profitability and
the board judged that rates could be lowered by up to 50 percent without
financial harm to the NAR.[15]

Railway expansion during the interwar years in the Peace River country was complemented by steady growth in its road network. In 1924 there were only 140 kilometres of improved earth roads, but by the close of the decade a provincially constructed trunk road linked Peace River (via Dunvegan) with Grande Prairie and west to the British Columbia border. Branch roads had also been built in the longest established districts and north from Peace River to Notikewin in the Battle River district. North of this, there were no roads entirely suitable for vehicle use until the 1940s. While these roads (even the most rudimentary) created links among communities and helped expand settlement and local trade, they were usually impassable during winter and in wet weather. Predictably, this led to demands for road improvement, especially gravelling. As Bishop Sovereign observed in 1935, "we never set out on a journey without an equipment of chains, ropes, a crowbar, a shovel, an axe and other similar articles. We never know when we will arrive at our destination. We never know when we will return home—all because there is no gravel on these roads."[16]

There were also loud complaints about the road between the Peace River country and Edmonton. The old trail through Athabasca and Grouard was the only road that connected the two, preserving the historical connection between Athabasca and the Peace River country. But the road was usually impassable for cars and the only practical way to reach Edmonton was by rail. Groups such as the boards of trade in Peace River and Grande Prairie strenuously lobbied for construction of a highway to Edmonton, but one was not completed until 1932. Even then, it was not fully gravelled until after World War II, making it impractical for heavy truck travel. This left the railway with nearly total control over shipping to and from the region. There was deep resentment in the Peace River country about the slowness in building and then in improving this road. Indeed, it was speculated that the Alberta government had secretly agreed to hold off such improvements as part of its sales agreement with the NAR to guarantee the railway a monopoly over transportation to the Peace River country.[17]

While the road system in the Peace River country in the interwar years was underdeveloped overall, more recently settled districts were inevitably worse off than longer established ones. Alberta's Department of Public Works was "swamped with requests" during the interwar years for road improvement in new districts everywhere in the province, but its limited budget forced it to concentrate on main (or trunk) roads leading to such newly settled areas.[18]

This policy led some communities in the Peace River country to try and build local roads themselves. By the late 1930s, a relatively good main road connected recently settled areas in the Eureka River and Worsley districts with the end of steel at Hines Creek. This only partially met local needs, however, because settlers also wanted a road that would integrate the whole district west to Fort St. John, British Columbia, then served only by a trail through the bush. In an effort to transform this trail into a more serviceable road, settlers and merchants in Fairview, Peace River and Fort St. John joined forces in 1938 and formed the Hines Creek Highway Association. The association raised money, organized volunteers to cut out the road and lobbied governments to contribute to the project. Although a rough trail halfway to the border was completed and similar progress was made on the British Columbia side, construction soon slowed. By 1940, volunteers and relief workers that the Alberta government assigned to the project were still cutting out the roadway. But the number of relief workers available for the project varied, and volunteers did not have the time, money and skill to complete such a complex undertaking. While it was evident that the road could only be completed with substantial provincial government support, Alberta was reluctant to make such a commitment in an area without extensive settlement or influential economic interests, all the while insisting that British Columbia make a reciprocal commitment. By the end of World War II, the project remained incomplete because of inadequate provincial funding and a lack of inter-provincial co-operation. In 1948, the Fort St. John Board of Trade proposed a public fund-raising campaign to build the road, but both provincial governments remained noncommittal, and Alberta continued to insist that it would build its portion of the road only when British Columbia did so on its side.[19]

## ▬ Breaking Out

### *The Coast Outlet*

The role of competing jurisdictions in stymying the construction of the Hines Creek road was even more apparent in broader efforts to revamp the transportation network connecting the Peace River country with outside markets. For many Peace River country settlers, the railway link with Edmonton was only part of what they believed was necessary to assure their economic future. Hopes that one of the transcontinental lines would be routed through the Peace River country collapsed after both the GTP and the CNoR main lines were built directly west of Edmonton. As a result, by the early 1920s many

Peace River country residents were calling for construction of a new line—a "coast outlet"—to link them directly with the Pacific coast and bypass the circuitous routes through Edmonton to Vancouver or east to the Lakehead. In 1924, during a period of doubt about the region's future, the Waterhole newspaper editorialized that while population decline and the lack of new settlers were partly due to high freight rates, the greatest problem was that Edmonton was simply too far away. Even if freight rates were lowered, they would still be high given the distance involved. Thus, the only solution was "a new and shorter outlet to a market at tidewater." Unless this was built, the Peace River country would continue to lose settlers. As the editorial melodramatically concluded, "the breath—of life—is being—cho—choked—out—of-the-north."[20]

Such conclusions reflected the problems and limitations of life in an isolated district and the view that a coast outlet promised significant advantages. As Morris Zaslow notes, it would have transformed the Peace River country from prairie Canada's "remotest farming district to the Lakehead" into one closest to an ocean port. It was popularly contended that the cost of shipping wheat would fall by 20 cents per bushel on such a route. Moreover, as Donald Albright of the Beaverlodge Experimental Substation told a Vancouver audience in 1930, such lower freight costs would help bring land into agricultural production that was now economically marginal because of high transportation costs.[21] Yet while the lack of a coast outlet was usually said to be a burden suffered by the whole of the Peace River country, various routing proposals revealed competition among different districts and the lack of a "regional" approach to the problem. Settlers north of the Grande Prairie district tended to support proposals for a line west through the mountains to Prince George and then a further 130 kilometres south to connect with the P&GE that ended at Quesnel. While these settlers further debated about which mountain pass was preferable and whether rail connections through Prince George to Vancouver or Prince Rupert were best, other people who lived in and around Grande Prairie instead supported construction of a line directly south of their district to intersect with the CNR mainline. Known as the Brule cut-off, this proposal garnered only hostility in areas lying further north. Critics in Spirit River and Peace River dismissed the Brule cut-off as of benefit only to the Grande Prairie district. Thus, while there was general agreement in the Peace River country about the need for better access to markets, there was no overall agreement or unity of purpose on how to achieve it.[22]

While the coast outlet campaign was bedevilled with sectional rivalries, greater difficulty arose because the scheme required that lines be built outside

Alberta. Initially, it was hoped that if the CPR or CNR purchased both the ED&BC in Alberta and the P&GE in British Columbia, the two would be connected as a single line. When this proved impossible, efforts were refocused on a proposition that the British Columbia government extend the P&GE from Quesnel to Prince George, and then to the British Columbia Peace River Block. The hopelessness of lobbying the British Columbia government to build railways that would directly benefit Alberta were apparent from the beginning, so efforts were made to enlist the support of people in the British Columbia Peace River Block, the Prince George district and the lower mainland. Peace River delegates first attended the annual meeting of the British Columbia boards of trade in 1921. Despite some feuding between those from Grande Prairie who wanted the Brule cut-off and those from Spirit River and Peace River who wanted a more northerly line through the mountains to Prince George, the delegates managed to have a resolution adopted urging the British Columbia government to build lines northwards. While British Columbia politicians later courted votes in the Prince George district with promises to extend the P&GE to the Peace River Block, this was a low priority for the province, which was primarily interested in dumping the debt-ridden P&GE into the lap of the federal government.[23]

To overcome the limits of provincial boundaries, Alberta's coast outlet lobbyists began to look to the federal government. Here too, they failed. While Ottawa sponsored or encouraged a number of engineering studies on the coast outlet between 1923 and 1932, all but one concluded that the project was uneconomical. This did not, however, lower expectations, and construction of northern lines elsewhere in western Canada (such as between Flin Flon and The Pas in 1927, and Manitoba's and eastern Saskatchewan's own "coast outlet" to Hudson's Bay in 1929) raised hopes, as well as resentments, in the Peace River country. While lower freight rates in the 1920s partially deflated the coast outlet campaign, it continued to be seen by many as the solution to the economic problems faced by Peace River country farmers. After 1927, the district's MP, Donald Kennedy, introduced a string of resolutions in the House of Commons demanding its construction. In his convoluted style, Prime Minister King promised in 1928 that a Pacific outlet would be built "as soon as possibly human [sic]," a promise that brought only another feasibility study.[24]

The frustrations of almost a decade of fruitless campaigning created much bitterness in the Peace River country. It was claimed by some that this apparent indifference of federal and provincial governments had contributed to the economic decline of the Peace River country in the mid 1920s by stifling development and population growth. In this climate, the assurances of politicians were increasingly met with scepticism. Edmonton's business community too was blamed for the failure of efforts to achieve the coast outlet. A resolution by the Edmonton Board of Trade in 1923 supporting the coast outlet temporarily reduced concern about the city's motives, but suspicion lingered that Edmonton's business class in fact opposed the coast outlet because they feared its construction would lessen their control over the Peace River country. In light of the paranoia and frustration that increasingly characterized the issue, the Peace River Board of Trade observed in the late 1920s that "human nature will only stand a certain limit of pet phrases and that limit had been more than reached; and an inland empire, vast in its resources and determination to more than exist, had reached its height of patience."[25]

At their most extreme, these frustrations led to calls for the creation of a separate province. This was not a unique phenomenon in Canada—secession had been proposed at various times in northern Ontario since the 1870s. In the Peace River country, it was first publicly proposed in 1927 when Charles Frederick, the editor of the *Peace River Record*, launched a nonpartisan campaign for the formation of the Peace River country and northern British Columbia (including Prince Rupert) into a separate province. This idea was endorsed by the Board of Trade in Peace River. Provincehood, it was said, would bring the coast outlet and economic growth. Significantly, the new province would not include the lower Athabasca River, which was believed not to share the frustrations or the promise of areas further west. In any case, this was not a social revolution. There were no claims that the new province would express a distinctive regionalism through a changed cultural attitude or a unique political philosophy. Instead, it was concerned almost solely with transportation— the most vital question for a community at the margins of economic and political power.[26]

While the campaign received extensive publicity everywhere, it attracted relatively few supporters. The *Peace River Record* claimed that, overall, public opinion in the Peace River country endorsed the plan, as did people in Prince Rupert which would become the sea port of the new province once the coast outlet was built. Opinion in Prince Rupert was in fact more ambivalent: the town's newspaper concluded that while provincehood was improbable, demands for it might force governments to treat their northern districts better. This view was shared by L.A. Giroux, the MLA for Grouard, who concluded that if governments immediately addressed the Peace River country's grievances, talk of secession would disappear. Otherwise, Alberta and Canada would have "another Maritimes problem on their hands." This was a reference to the broad support that the Maritime Rights Movement had enjoyed and that had forced the King government in 1927 to provide higher subsidies for the Maritime provinces, increased funding for harbours and other public works, and reduced railway freight rates. Some critics contended that Peace River secession was only a copy-cat attempt to wring concessions from Edmonton. The MLA for Peace River, Hugh Allen, called the scheme "a publicity stunt [more] than anything else," and the *Edmonton Journal* editorialized that while grievances had to be addressed, the Peace River country was not sufficiently developed to become a province. Indeed, Premier Brownlee observed that the Peace River country cost Alberta's treasury more than it contributed; a statement that the Peace River Board of Trade took as a slur since it implied that the Peace River country was "a burden."[27]

Despite such heightened rhetoric, the campaign to form a separate province quickly fell apart. While calls for secession grew from frustrations over lack of progress on transportation, feelings were not so intense that people were willing to tear the province apart over a single issue or without knowing what would follow. When Premier Brownlee observed that the Peace River country suffered only two grievances—the lack of a coast outlet and a highway to Edmonton—the *Peace River Record* sputtered that there were other grievances too. Yet, aside from the lack of long-distance telephone service, it did not detail them, and it lamely concluded that "the list of north country problems is so long" that they could not be catalogued.[28]

Enthusiasm also weakened because support for secession was unevenly distributed in the Peace River country. The campaign had been hatched in Peace River and enjoyed only limited support elsewhere. The settlement boom that was in full swing by 1928 also undercut secessionist claims that the Peace River country could not attract new settlers without a coast outlet. Yet demands for a railway to the coast did not disappear entirely. The issue remained a touchstone for an export-oriented economy, and in the 1930s federal expenditures on railways elsewhere in Canada continued to be seen as a slight to the Peace River country. As was remarked in Grande Prairie in 1932, the Hudson's Bay Railway had been built because of effective lobbying in Ottawa, and Peace River's coast outlet could be had with the same tactics. In 1937 the Board of Trade in Peace River complained about further federal expenditure on the Hudson's Bay Railway, which it said was "far beyond [the] value of the area involved." A more appropriate project, it argued, was a railway from Peace River town to Prince George, as well as one north to the Battle

River country. By this time, however, over a decade of failure had drained energy from the campaign, and its defeat was confirmed in 1937 when Sir Edward Beatty, President of the CPR, announced in Grande Prairie that the NAR would not invest in the project because of the Depression.[29]

The campaign was by this time also losing momentum because attention was shifting to the construction of a road rather than a railway. While this was not a new idea, it only became widely popular after hopes for a railway to the coast had been dashed. The coast highway campaign nonetheless drew on the same emotions, local ambitions and sense of place. Indeed, some saw it as merely another way to obtain a railway. As the Grande Prairie Board of Trade was told by coast outlet lobbyists in 1937, "railways usually follow the building of highways," and while railway construction without government or corporate support was impossible, a highway could in part be built by local people.[30]

The coast highway campaign was spearheaded by the Monkman Pass Highway Association, an organization formed in 1936 with members from both the Alberta and British Columbia Peace River country. The association promoted the construction of a highway through the Monkman Pass (south-west of Grande Prairie), whose uniform grade was said to provide the easiest route through the mountains. On the western side in British Columbia lay Hansard, a small settlement connected by highway and rail to nearby Prince George. Since Prince George was connected to Vancouver by a gravelled highway and to Prince Rupert by rail, it was reasoned that only the construction of a 240 kilometre road through the Monkman Pass as far as Hansard stood in the way of obtaining a coastal outlet.[31]

The verve and commitment of the Monkman Pass Highway Association captured the imagination and hopes of people in the southern Peace River country. It endorsed the conventional wisdom that the Peace River country's economic prosperity depended on lower transportation costs. While this was most significant for agricultural exports, a highway link with Prince George and Vancouver could also stimulate tourism, then an increasingly fashionable prospect for economic diversification in western Canada. Although the association and its supporters realized that the road could not be completed without government involvement, it assumed that volunteer effort would demonstrate the feasibility of the project and perhaps shame governments into action.[32]

In early 1937 the association announced that volunteers "were prepared to blaze a trail in the spring with or without government assistance." When spring came, Alex Monkman (after whom the pass was named) left with a crew of 15 men to cut a roadway through about 210 kilometres of bush.[33] Public meetings were held throughout the Peace River country in 1937 and 1938 to raise funds and stir up public enthusiasm for the project. Petitions endorsing it drew thousands of signatures, rallies and parades drew large crowds, and when the Grande Prairie radio station held a fund-raising "radio dance" in 1938, nearly 70 communities participated. A British Columbia auxiliary was also formed to garner political and financial support, especially in coastal cities that would benefit from future traffic over the road. By the end of 1938, 125 kilometres of the road had been cut out, and a "trail blazing" motor party travelled over the uncompleted section of the highway, coming within 45 kilometres of Hansard when snow and ice conditions drove them back. The trip was festive in its optimism and confident of its historical importance. The Beaverlodge painter, Euphemia McNaught, was among the party and recorded the landscape in a series of paintings. As Donald Albright noted, the project was "an example of determination and private initiative seldom seen elsewhere in Canada." While most people expected governments to build roads, those in the Peace River country, "by private contributions of all sorts, including labor, food and equipment, got busy and without government assistance of any sort began to build their own outlet to the Pacific." Further work in 1939 cleared the trail almost to Hansard and the whole route was cut out by early 1940.[34]

Despite its progress, the project was hamstrung by a number of factors. Strongest support for the Monkman Pass highway came from the Grande Prairie and Wembley districts in Alberta and around Pouce Coupe in British Columbia. In contrast, competing proposals for communications through the Pine or the Peace Pass, both of which were lower and free of snow for a longer period, found more support in the areas further north in the Alberta and British Columbia Peace River country. Further, the NAR opposed the construction of any highway through the mountains that would divert traffic from its lines. More importantly, the project failed to attract support from either federal or provincial governments. Even the most successful private fund-raising could only collect sufficient money to build a rough trail, and success ultimately depended on the co-operation of two provincial governments, each with different interests. Only about 24 kilometres of the trail that was broken lay in Alberta, and while the Alberta government graded and improved this short stretch, British Columbia, which had to shoulder most of the costs, was less enthusiastic. In 1938, representatives of the Monkman Pass Highway Association met in Victoria with members of the British Columbia government, but the latter refused to endorse a project they believed would create an undesirable precedent. Moreover, the British Columbia MLA for

Peace River opposed the scheme, arguing that a road should instead be built through the Peace Pass. This reflected local political priorities as well as a recognition of the natural drawbacks of the Monkman Pass. Although it was an easy grade, it was higher than competing passes and had early, heavy snowfall. In 1937 the first snowfall in the pass came at the end of September, and by May 15 it still had about 2.5 metres of packed snow that would not melt until June. Thus, while a road through the Monkman Pass was less costly to build, winter maintenance would be expensive.[35]

The lack of official support in combination with new priorities during World War II effectively doomed the project. By 1944, British Columbia had confirmed plans for a new road to connect its Peace River block to Prince George through Pine Pass—a route that best served British Columbia's interests. This dealt the Monkman Pass project its final blow. By this point too, the Alaska Highway had been completed, which drew attention away from the Monkman Pass road. A wartime project by the United States, the Alaska Highway stretched between Dawson Creek, the terminus of the NAR, and Fairbanks, Alaska, a distance of over 2,400 kilometres. While this massive construction project was not the coast outlet that been so ardently desired, it boosted Grande Prairie's economy, provided employment for many Peace River residents and enriched the NAR whose lines were upgraded to handle the thousands of workers and tonnes of material moving to the construction sites.[36]

## ▬ Looking North
### *The Grimshaw Highway*

In contrast to the schemes for a coast outlet that would lessen the costs of exporting farm produce, efforts to build a highway between Peace River town and the NWT aimed to expand the Peace River country's economic hinterland. Peace River had long thought of itself as a potential portal to the far north, even though Waterways had gained this advantage after the completion of the A&GW. The expansion of mining in the NWT in the 1930s rekindled hopes that Peace River would become the metropolitan centre for the NWT. Since it was "only" 1,200 kilometres south of Great Bear Lake, Peace River's business community anticipated significant benefits from road connections with the NWT. In 1937, the federal and provincial governments were lobbied to build a winter road from Grimshaw (at the junction of the highway to Notikewin) to the NWT. This would stimulate growth in Peace River's hinterland by bringing increased settlement and tourism to the areas north of the town and by diverting some northern shipping from Fort McMurray and Waterways.[37]

Fate was kind to these hopes. Earlier forays had indicated the potential of a winter road between Grimshaw and the NWT, and shallow water in the Athabasca delta in 1938 curtailed the shipping season and permitted barges to carry only partial loads. This in turn focussed attention on an overland route through Grimshaw to supply the mines at Yellowknife. The first tractor trains loaded with supplies and equipment left Grimshaw in the winter of 1938–39 and followed a trail along rivers and lakes for 775 kilometres. The route passed through Fort Vermilion where gas had been cached the previous year and where fresh meat was picked up for delivery in Yellowknife. After reaching Hay River, the tractor trains crossed over the ice of Great Slave Lake to Yellowknife. While slow and labourious, this winter highway was still faster than the Athabasca River route and extended the shipping season from four or five to seven or eight months.[38] Trucks and tractors had by then been improved for heavy winter use, and northern areas elsewhere in Canada were being serviced by truck transportation alone. Indeed, some claimed that the high construction and operating costs of railways made them obsolete for frontier resource development. This view enjoyed official sanction under a federal government programme that matched provincial contributions for building mining roads in areas without existing roads or railways. Although Charles Camsell, the federal deputy minister of Mines, noted that Alberta need only apply for the money, the project soon became the victim of bad blood between Ottawa and the newly elected Social Credit government in Edmonton. While Alberta's minister of Public Works, W.A. Fallow, publicly endorsed construction of a permanent winter road north of Grimshaw in 1937, he claimed that the federal government refused to co-operate, even though it had granted money to British Columbia and Saskatchewan under the same programme.[39]

In large part, these complaints about federal discrimination were exaggerated. The federal government did indeed drag its feet on the project, perhaps because of its political quarrels with Alberta, but also because it had received wildly differing cost estimates, some of which originated with the provincial government itself. Nonetheless, it was evident that the most serious barriers to the plan were home-grown. While the NAR did not oppose the road, nor did it support it because it would divert traffic from Waterways. As the general manager of the NAR informed his superiors in Montreal, while increased freight to Grimshaw might balance out the loss, freight rates to Waterways were so much higher than to Grimshaw that "on the basis of present Waterways traffic we would be losing money if any larger quantity is diverted to Grimshaw." Montreal thus advised him not to encourage the Grimshaw highway because it promised no benefit for the NAR. Moreover, while the Alberta legislature appropriated funds for the road, some members from southern Alberta criticized the plan, arguing that road construction was more pressing in their constituencies.[40]

In such a climate, it is not surprising that the Alberta legislature voted down a proposed agreement with Canada to construct a winter road from Grimshaw. By this time, frustrations with the delays over the project were reaching a high point in Peace River. In 1938 Charles Frederick and the Peace River Board of Trade again trotted out the issue of secession. As it had a decade earlier, transportation needs were said to justify the creation of a new province. Although the need for a coast outlet remained part of the secessionists' objectives, demands for the winter road to Yellowknife and scheduled air service were now the core issues. Reflecting Peace River's metropolitan ambitions, it was proposed that the boundaries of the new province include the Yukon and the western part of the NWT north to the Arctic coast and as far east as Coppermine. In other words, it would include the major areas of recent mining activity in the NWT. Again, the lower Athabasca River area (which had no proven mining prospects) was not to be part of the new province. As in the secessionist campaign of 1927–28, the proponents of a separate province expressed contempt for the party system and for politicians whose bickering was said to be holding up the construction of the northern highway. The secessionists now advocated only a limited type of government. As the *Peace River Record* editorialized, the new "province" should be governed by a nonpartisan administrative council because "we have had too much of legislative assemblies, petty premiers" and "the Gilbert and Sullivan type of emulation of the dominion parliament."[41]

The negative reception this plan found in Edmonton was dismissed by the *Record* as only outraged self-interest. Edmonton's leaders feared "that secession would mean the cutting off of all trade between Edmonton and the north. Unfortunately for us this would not be the case, since trade must follow its own channels." Nonetheless, "we have paid tribute to Edmonton and Alberta long enough. We now demand the right to work out our own destiny." Such bravado received some support in Grande Prairie, but it was most popular in Peace River, which stood to gain most from northern expansion. Without a broad base of support, however, the secession campaign of 1938 failed as had earlier ones. Attitudes elsewhere had also hardened against the creation of yet another province. British Columbia and Alberta were proposing that their provincial boundaries be extended further north, and secession naturally threatened such provincial aggrandizement. Both provincial governments thus opposed new northern provinces, which Premier Patullo of British Columbia called a "lot of nonsense" that ignored the high costs of establishing a new province. Ottawa also opposed the scheme, in part because views on government in Canada were changing. Testimony before the Rowell-Sirois commission, then inquiring into the problems and prospects of Canadian federalism during the Depression, was suggesting that Canada already had too many governments, and proposals for yet another were now even more unwelcome.[42]

One of the primary motives for a separate province soon disappeared when the Alberta government agreed in late 1938 to undertake an aerial and ground reconnaissance of the route to Yellowknife. By then, Edmonton and Yellowknife business and mining interests were pressuring both governments to co-operate and build the road. Planned for winter use only, the road started at the end of the provincial highway, 135 kilometres north of Grimshaw. A passage through the bush was cleared and graded where necessary. In January 1940, the first load of freight was dispatched over the road, and the next winter, three tractor trains (made up of sleighs towed by crawler tractors, the lead one was equipped with a snow plough and brush-cutter) made the trip from Grimshaw to Yellowknife with about 165 tonnes of freight. The trip usually took between two and five weeks. Operating 24 hours a day, off-shift workers slept in a bunkhouse, which formed part of the train. The most difficult and dangerous part of the trip was crossing Great Slave Lake where pressure ridges sometimes opened huge chasms in the ice. These were bridged with timbers carried on the sleighs.[43]

By 1946, work had begun under a federal-provincial agreement to upgrade the winter road between Grimshaw and Great Slave Lake to an all-weather highway. This became known as the Mackenzie Highway, but until its completion in 1948, all summer traffic to Great Slave Lake continued to use the river route through Waterways. While the distance to Yellowknife was about the same by land through Peace River as it was by water along the Athabasca River, the highway was the fastest route. Although extremely rough in places, the road cut the travelling time to Yellowknife to six days, roughly one-half the time needed to get there by river through Waterways. It also created year-round connections between Peace River, Keg River and Fort Vermilion, and by 1948, the road's growing importance led the NAR to consider setting up a trucking subsidiary in Grimshaw.[44]

The departure of Ryan brothers sled service from Fort McMurray
in 1928. A11,933 PAA.

## Shipping on the Lower Athabasca

Agitation in the Peace River country for railway and road extensions, as well as related concerns about the coast outlet, primarily expressed ambitions and needs relevant to its farm economy. These concerns indicated how the new society that had emerged in the district after 1916 brought with it different attitudes and a changed texture of life. In contrast, the social and economic context of communications in the district along the Athabasca River north of Fort McMurray remained firmly rooted in the needs of the fur trade, the area's geography and its historic function as Canada's corridor to the Mackenzie valley and the western Arctic.

While people from Fort Chipewyan and Fort Smith still used the winter ice to travel on the Athabasca River to Fort McMurray in the 1920s, there was little formal land communication other than winter delivery of mail by dog team. As part of the growth brought by the Norman Wells oil strike, however, a winter road for horse-drawn sleighs was built in 1922 between Fort McMurray and Fort Smith by the Ryan brothers of Fitzgerald. Since there was neither feed nor stopping places along the route, stables stocked with hay and oats brought in by river in the summer were built every 25 to 32 kilometres along the trail.[45] This winter mail road operated successfully until the late 1920s when delivery of mail by airplane made it obsolete. Even so, a new winter road between Waterways and Goldfields—a distance of almost 500 kilometres—was developed in 1938 to move freight by tractor-drawn sleighs to the mines at Goldfields. Using a roadway on the ice cleared by snowploughs, the trains followed the river to Lake Athabasca, which they then crossed to Goldfields. In its first year of operation, the company made several trips and the service was expanded further in 1939.[46] But the road was risky—loads occasionally broke through the ice on the river, and salvage was difficult, even though the water was shallow. Groups such as the Fort McMurray Board of Trade demanded that the provincial government construct an all-weather road, but the province did nothing, and the route was then abandoned in 1942 when the Goldfields mine closed.[47]

Despite these precedents, most heavy transport out of Waterways relied on ships. The great river continued to carry freight north and raw commodities south as it had since the 1800s. In the 1920s this transportation network continued to be linked to developments in the fur trade. Although the three largest trading firms in the Mackenzie basin—the Hudson's Bay Company, Lamson and Hubbard, and the Northern Trading Company—took two-thirds of fur returns in 1922, gyrations in fur prices brought changes in the trade's corporate life. Following their collapse in 1921, fur prices were uneven until they crashed again in 1927–29, and they declined further still in 1930 at the onset of the Depression.[48]

Declining fur prices in the early 1920s hurt operations such as Lamson and Hubbard, which had over-extended itself during the World War I fur boom. The company ceased operations in early 1923 and the Hudson's Bay Company purchased it the next year. Revillon too fell on hard times, and although the Hudson's Bay Company secured a controlling interest in it in 1926, the Bay attempted to suppress news of this take-over in order to preserve an aura of competition. The Northern Trading Company was also in receivership by 1925 and was reorganized with the backing of Winnipeg fur dealers as Northern Traders Ltd. Showing its continuing desperation, however, the new company was forced to borrow $200,000 in 1929 from its rival, the Hudson's Bay Company. Further decline in fur prices by 1930 brought Northern Traders Ltd. under the management of its creditors, including the Hudson's Bay Company.[49]

As a result of these corporate consolidations, the Hudson's Bay Company grip on shipping on the Athabasca River tightened. In 1924 it gained control of the Alberta and Arctic Transportation Company as part of its purchase of Lamson and Hubbard. This left practically all commercial shipping along the Athabasca River in its hands (through Mackenzie River Transport) and those of The Northern Trading Company (which the Hudson's Bay Company effec-

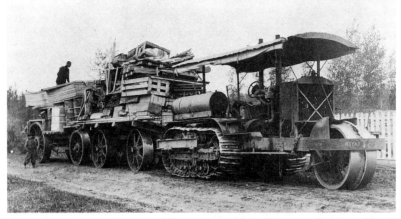

*By 1920 cartage on the Smith Portage was becoming mechanized.*
A3895 PAA.

tively controlled after 1930). Although common carrier service was also provided, these operations primarily served the fur trade. Reflecting these needs and its near monopoly, the Hudson's Bay Company did little to upgrade its transportation service or adapt it to meet the needs of mining companies in the north. As a consequence, new carriers—which used barges and tugs that could operate in shallow water and carry mining equipment and supplies more efficiently than paddle wheel steamers—emerged to serve the northern mining boom. In 1934, White Eagle Mines of Echo Bay purchased one of these companies, Northern Waterways Ltd., and renamed it the Northern Transportation Company. The next year, this company became a subsidiary of Eldorado Gold Mines Ltd., which needed better service for its radium mine on Great Bear Lake. The Northern Transportation Company also provided common carrier service, and it purchased new diesel-powered steel tugs to supplement its wooden equipment. Although ultimately unable to preserve its dominance in the face of such competition, the Hudson's Bay Company also purchased new equipment, including additional barges and motor boats—a technological shift that confirmed the gradual disappearance of local jobs cutting fire wood. By the height of the mining boom in the 1930s, the Northern Transportation Company, followed closely by the Hudson's Bay Company, dominated shipping out of Waterways, although other firms, such as McInnes Brothers (a fishing company active on Lake Athabasca), McLeod and Sons, and Goldfields

Transportation Company also provided service. Loading facilities at Waterways were gradually upgraded and the federal government constructed new wharves along the Clearwater River. By 1937, a conveyor system had been devised to transfer freight from rail cars to the boats. These developments allowed the port to handle a steadily increasing volume of goods; in 1935, almost 8,200 tonnes of freight were shipped north from Waterways, an amount that more than doubled by 1937.[50]

As had been the case since the 1880s, the major bottleneck in this northern shipping network lay at the rapids between Fitzgerald and Fort Smith. By the early 1920s there were three major firms working the portage. The most important of these was the Ryan brothers who held the contract for transhipping Hudson's Bay Company freight. In 1927, the Ryans had 20 teams of horses, three autos and two tractors on the trail. Small shippers who arrived in small scows and boats usually used "free teams, that is, teams owned by men living in Fitzgerald and Fort Smith." Most traffic arrived in early summer, but conditions on the portage were often poor. In 1923, it was so muddy and potholed that only horses could use it. While it lay wholly within Alberta and all of its traffic benefited Alberta shippers and merchants, the provincial government did little to maintain the trail because, as Premier Brownlee myopically observed in 1929, it existed "solely for the benefit of the Northwest Territories." Instead, the Ryan brothers usually maintained the trail and billed the province for the costs.[51] In 1928 they even offered to maintain it at no cost to the province in return for the right to set rates on the trail. While public opposition scuttled this particular suggestion, a similar outcry from shippers and teamsters did not prevent the province from giving the Ryan brothers an exclusive franchise for "freight for hire by means of motor vehicles" in 1931. Although prices increased under this arrangement, Alberta renewed this franchise in 1932–33. As Jim Cornwall observed, the province appeared intent on "washing it hands of the road and passing the buck of taking care of it to the shippers into the country." When demand warranted, this ensured that new routes would soon bypass the Ryan brothers' stranglehold over the trail, and in the mid 1930s the Northern Transportation Company built a new road around the rapids.[52]

Traffic through Waterways and across the Smith Portage declined at the start of World War II. In 1940, the Port Radium mines closed because of slumping radium markets and the Yellowknife gold mines closed between 1942 and 1944 because of the war. Yet this decline was short-lived. In 1942 the radium mines reopened to supply radium for the Manhattan project, and northern military projects stimulated further activity along the Athabasca

River. Following its entry into the war in 1941, the United States (in addition to the Alaska Highway) built an oil pipeline from the Norman Wells oilfield across the Mackenzie Mountains to Whitehorse. Called the CANOL project, this undertaking had a direct impact on the economy of the lower Athabasca River district. Goods and soldiers were shipped north by rail from Edmonton to Waterways and then north by barge to the construction site. About 600 United States troops were also stationed at Fitzgerald, and the United States government upgraded the old Smith portage trail and extended it north of Fort Smith. This wartime shipping boom enabled the Hudson's Bay Company to remain active even though its northern shipping operations were increasingly outdated and noncompetitive. Its river transport business had been unprofitable since the 1930s when it had faced new competitors (especially the Northern Transportation Company) and its share of freight had begun to decline. After World War II, the Northern Transportation Company, with its superior equipment, consolidated its lead over the wooden steamers, motor boats and barges of the Hudson's Bay Company fleet. The Bay would have had to purchase steel diesel-powered tugs and steel barges to remain competitive. Instead, it ended its common carrier service in 1948, although it continued to operate ships as part of its northern trading system until 1957.[53]

While traffic on the river increased after World War II with the development of pitchblende deposits at Great Bear Lake and uranium at Uranium City, growing use of airplanes and completion of the all-weather highway from Grimshaw to Hay River challenged the centrality of the Athabasca River in northern transportation. It nonetheless retained some advantages; shipping by air and even by truck was still more costly than by water, although trucks offered higher quality service through more direct, faster and less seasonal service. River transportation also continued to benefit from its corporate links with other activities. As Gordon Thiessen noted in his study of shipping in the Mackenzie basin, all the major carriers operating there after the 1930s were "tied in some way to a firm operating in another industry in the region. Each carrier has been assured of receiving a certain minimum of freight annually from the related firm." This factor had characterised shipping on the Athabasca River since the 1800s; a demonstration of how little economic diversification had occurred in the eastern parts of northern Alberta.[54]

## Northern Aviation

Airplanes challenged traditional shipping methods in northern Alberta during the interwar years. It had been evident since the 1920s that air travel could remake northern transportation by redefining the constraints of time, geography and climate. Imperial Oil's use of airplanes to reach Norman Wells marked the first use of aviation for resource projects in the far north. By 1930, planes equipped with pontoons were being used for aerial mining surveys, taking prospecting crews and other travellers to inaccessible areas and carrying mail. By the late 1920s, the RCMP was occasionally leasing or renting planes for northern work, and in 1931 the force established an "air" section. Postal service between Fort McMurray and Aklavik and intervening points began in 1929 and achieved "remarkable regularity and dispatch despite very difficult conditions" over a 2,700 kilometre route.[55] Following its dramatic growth in the late 1920s, bush flying suffered because of the economic problems of the 1930s. Although there was some growth in aviation infrastructure and service because of northern mining development, many small flyers went out of business or merged into larger companies, a process that continued during World War II when the largest companies formed Canadian Pacific Airlines.[56]

While aviation largely offered time savings in other parts of Canada that had well developed land transportation networks, it provided unique conveniences and opportunities in northern Canada. As historian Patricia Myers has shown, these advantages were reinforced by the exploits of famous Edmonton aviators like "Punch" Dickens, "Wop" May and Vic Horner. Their well-publicized assistance in arresting criminals in the far north, their flying-out of the sick for treatment, and their flying-in (often at great personal risk) of medicines during epidemics confirmed bush flying as part of the romance of the Canadian north and helped, not incidentally, to entrench and legitimize Euro-Canadian activity there. Indeed, aviation was seen as part of the Euro-Canadian triumph in northern Canada. In celebration of the arrival of an airplane from Edmonton, a 1929 editorial in the *Grande Prairie Herald* characterized the event as "more than an incident" in the history of the Peace River country. In the familiar language of progress, it was said to confirm the growing economic importance of the Peace River country and showed that the "faith of the early settlers in the ultimate success of this portion of the Dominion is beginning to be shared by people on the outside." Technological change promised wealth and historical legitimacy—as the *Herald* asserted, one reason for the economic success of the United States was "that it arrived on the scene at the beginning of the machine age. The north country is fortunate in 'arriving' at a time when the machine is the all-determining factor, so its development will naturally be rapid. The arrival of the commercial plane is one of the indications of that rapid development which is taking place, and which will be speeded up as time goes on. We are living in a great age."[57]

Such views about the impact of technological change continued to retain their currency even though planes were soon commonplace. The RCMP reported in 1929 that Natives in the NWT now looked on aviation "as a matter of course." Such acceptance was also demonstrated by entries in the daily journal of the Anglican church at Fort Chipewyan. On January 23, 1929, Bishop Lucas underlined and wrote in large script, "First Air Mail arrived to-day on its way down to [Fort] Simpson." For the rest of 1929 and most of 1930, every plane sighted flying over the town, dropping mail and landing was noted. By 1931, such entries had largely disappeared, although it was noted that Rev. Crawley had travelled to Fort McMurray in 1 hour and 8 minutes—a notation that indicated that the magic of air travel had not faded entirely.[58]

In other respects, aviation did not have as immediate an impact on the north as the public's fascination with bush flying suggested. As Patricia Myers notes, it was too costly to replace land or river transportation entirely. Nonetheless, it brought some local development. Fort McMurray became an important northern aviation centre because it was near the NAR terminus and planes apparently used the Athabasca River as a navigational marker. Other natural features further enhanced Fort McMurray's role as an aviation base. Most planes flying to the north at this time used pontoons in summer or skis in winter and used the Snye, a cross channel between the Athabasca and Clearwater rivers adjacent to the town. With placid water, and well sheltered from north and south winds, the Snye was ideal for both take-off and landing and provided safe anchoring for the planes. In 1929 James Richardson's Western Canada Airways of Winnipeg began scheduled air service from Fort McMurray to Fort Chipewyan and a number of points in the NWT, as did a rival service operated by Commercial Airways Company, which had the mail contract from Fort McMurray to the Arctic.[59]

Despite these developments, Fort McMurray's future as an aviation centre was precarious. The use of water and ice for landing and take-off meant that bush flying needed little permanent infrastructure that might direct long-term economic development towards a particular district. Indeed, it led to job losses. Bishop Breynat of the Roman Catholic church observed in 1935 that Fort Chipewyan Metis lost work transporting mail and fur in winter because of air freighting. While they "used to make a pretty good living," it was "harder for them now" because they had been forced to depend on trapping and fishing at a time of declining prices. While the Hudson's Bay Company recognized the potential advantages of airplanes, it did not purchase them for its northern Alberta operations until the late 1930s because of the realization that aircraft

*The first load of pitchblende and silver ore was shipped by airplane from Great Bear Lake to Fort McMurray in early 1936.*

A5890 PAA.

would reduce Native employment and channel money out of the local economy to the detriment of the company's trading operations.[60]

While many northern communities such as Fort Chipewyan did not have airstrips until after World War II, a rough landing field was constructed at Fort McMurray. Scheduled passenger and express service from Edmonton to Grande Prairie and Peace River also began in 1936. The federal government began constructing airfields at various centres in 1939, including Grande Prairie and Peace River, as part of a network of airports every 160 kilometres across the country. While northern aviation declined at the start of World War II, it soon picked up. Both the Alaska Highway and the CANOL project required air support and transport. Supply of material by air to Alaska was undertaken in early 1942 through the development of the Northwest Staging Route. This series of airports and landing fields between Edmonton and Alaska approximated an air route earlier surveyed by the Canadian government. The project created local employment and provided paved runways at various northern locations, including Grande Prairie and Fort McMurray. Following the war, the Canadian government reimbursed the United States government for these development costs, viewing them as building blocks for a civilian aviation system. But hopes that the Northwest Staging Route would become a permanent network collapsed because of the development of planes with greater range, which made local airstrips obsolete as refuelling stops for long-distance flights.[61]

Such consequences for local economies intensified as navigational instruments improved and the range and capacity of airplanes increased, leaving small centres with only minor distributing and servicing roles. Not everyone immediately appreciated these implications for local economic development. When lobbying the federal government to construct a new airfield in 1945, the Peace River Chamber of Commerce noted that "the post-war age is to be an aviation age and we believe that Peace River Town and airfield form a strategic centre for air routes in every direction." While communities may have benefited from rail or road communications in this way, aviation was different. John Chalmers's study of northern transportation noted that planes, operating "interchangeably on wheels or skis or pontoons, could start anywhere and go anywhere." Given these conditions, Fort McMurray failed to develop as "the transportation hub for airborne business that it had been for earthbound traffic." And, as their range and carrying capacity expanded, airplanes were increasingly based in Edmonton. This helped cement the city's hegemony over this branch of northern trade. Firms like the Hudson's Bay Company—which finally purchased two planes for its northern Alberta operations in 1939 and 1940—based its planes there, closer to wholesale and other services.[62] As in earlier years, these developments revealed how new technology often confirmed, rather than challenged, the authority of those who were already able to exert significant control and influence over northern Alberta's development.

— ✦ —

Distinctions between eastern and western districts in northern Alberta were confirmed by technological change after 1920. As the importance of the lower Athabasca River as a connecting place between southern Canada and the Mackenzie valley grew along with increased development in the NWT, the value to Canada of the Athabasca River route (both for airplanes and ships) to the north was reinforced. But while the speed and flexibility of air travel overcame distance and brought northern communities into closer touch with southern centres, this integration was double-edged. Long-distance flights made possible by technological change soon began to marginalise communities along the Athabasca River by diminishing their role in the northern communications network. By the 1950s, their economies were also being challenged as more northern traffic moved along the highway to Yellowknife through Grimshaw. Communities along the Athabasca River were losing their value to the rest of Canada, and a search for an alternate economy would dominate their evolution in the years after World War II.

The disparate development in eastern and western sections of northern Alberta sometimes brought rivalry between the two districts. Peace River's desire to dismember the old Athabasca River route to the north in search of its own place in the sun revealed such a conscious competition, but the two parts of northern Alberta more often simply went their own ways. Peace River secessionists dismissed the eastern districts of northern Alberta as irrelevant in the new future they were plotting. And although high freight rates were a burden for both the lower Athabasca River district and the Peace River country, this grievance did not bring an identity of purpose to the two sections of northern Alberta. Rather, each developed its own priorities and objectives. This was most directly shown by the campaigns in the Peace River country for a coast outlet and for connections to the NWT. The frustrations associated with these efforts were important indicators of economic and social conditions in the Peace River country. While they revealed deep divisions between different parts of the district, they were founded upon common grievances and objectives based upon the Peace River country's geography and history, its relative isolation and place as a hinterland of distant metropolitan centres, and the problems of a staple economy dependent on exports. Historian Bob Irwin has interpreted this as evidence of the development of a form of "regional identity" in the Peace River country, and concerns there about transportation clearly expressed a sense of "otherness" and definable goals and grievances, whatever local divisions may have existed. As the Peace River newspaper editorialized in 1946, "we are not baring any family skeletons when we say people living north and south of the Peace River consider themselves as separate entities" and insisted on being seen as separate places. Nonetheless, "they have always, in the past, been content to consider themselves a part of the Peace River area and as such have gained world wide publicity."[63]

While regional identity of the Peace River country was somewhat ambiguous and dependent on immediate advantage, people there did have shared interests. But whatever unique qualities it possessed, the Peace River country was by its history, culture, ambitions and economy a northern extension of prairie settlement, and its grievances were similar to those found elsewhere on the prairies. Transportation issues in the Peace River country developed within the same framework and conditions that simultaneously led other prairie farmers to insist that their regional needs and the economic barriers they faced arose from geographical, economic and political conditions. Producers wanted better integration with the national economy, and in both places people concluded that the remedy lay in additional railway lines or improved freight rates, which could be obtained through collective effort. These issues were often phrased in a language stressing regional economic and political inequality, and they were a legacy, in the prairies in general and in the Peace River country in particular, of the promotional rhetoric and advertising that had lauded the land's fertility and latent wealth and the resourcefulness and rosy future of its people. As elsewhere on the prairies, it was sometimes suggested that farm debt and an excessive reliance on wheat growing for export contributed to the problems of the Peace River country, but it was more popular to contend that all the district lacked, given its natural advantages, was better transportation. Thus, it was easy to conclude that it was politics, not geography, that blocked the fulfilment of the Peace River country's potential.

The campaigns for a coast outlet and a highway to the NWT showed how the needs and ambitions of the Peace River country had diverged from those of the eastern section of northern Alberta along the Athabasca River. The break-up of the older, larger region continued after World War II because of further economic change and parallel developments in transportation methods and routes. In 1944, the McMurray Roads Association was formed to campaign for road connections with Lac La Biche, but such a road was a low priority for the province and a highway to Fort McMurray was not operating until the mid 1960s.[64] In contrast, the province was more willing to meet the needs of the wealthier, more populous and politically influential Peace River country. Reflecting the growing importance of private cars and trucks in provincial transportation, the province officially opened the Whitecourt-Valleyview cut-off in 1955. This all-weather road gave ready access to the south Peace River from Edmonton, which provided an important alternative to the old route through Athabasca and integrated the Peace River country even more firmly into Edmonton's orbit. At the same time, province-building ambitions in British Columbia served to increase ties between the B.C. Peace River block and the rest of the province. By 1948, the Hart Highway was under construction to connect Prince George to the Peace River country through Pine Pass. As well, the P&GE was extended to Prince George in 1952 and then to Dawson Creek and Fort St. John (through Pine Pass) in 1958.[65] The coast outlet had been achieved, but only because it served British Columbia's plans for northern development, not those of the Alberta Peace River country.

# The Evolution of
# 8 Separate Societies
*Towns and Social Services*

AFTER 1920, northern Alberta's urban system evolved because of new economic and social activity. While Edmonton continued to be a common metropolitan centre for all of northern Alberta, by World War II it had increased its domination over a more fragmented northern hinterland. Northern Alberta's urban system increasingly consisted of two discrete units; one in the Peace River and Lesser Slave Lake districts and the other in the Athabasca country north of Fort McMurray. While all urban centres still served as points where national, provincial and local life and economy converged, they no longer shared connections within an overarching regional urban network. Despite the claims of boosters, in a market economy there were no permanent "natural" and geographical advantages in a town or district's location; rather, advantages were relative to factors such as transportation, market value of resources and changes in distribution of population and the deployment of capital.

Yet towns were not only economic units. They provided a focus for social life for people in surrounding areas and the highest level of medical and educational services available in the area. In part, this was the result of their concentrated population and their function as gathering points, but it was also connected, as in most parts of Canada, to the way that social services were delivered. Local governments such as incorporated towns, rural municipalities, local improvement districts, and school and hospital districts were responsible for financing and organizing schools, hospitals and other social services such as welfare. As incorporated centres, the largest towns had the highest income from property taxes to fund these services. Rural municipalities had a smaller population base from which to raise such taxes, and local improvement districts, a limited form of local government, fulfilled these duties in parts of the Peace River country with new or scattered population. Indeed, local improvement districts were the commonest form of local government in the Peace River country. In the Athabasca country, many areas had no local government of any sort.

One consequence of these conditions was that social services, especially social welfare and medical and educational services, were not uniformly available in northern Alberta. Since local government was supported almost entirely by local property taxes, a district needed a settled, property owing and tax paying population to enable it to provide social services. While pioneer districts everywhere in Alberta had difficulties providing such services, this was most often seen as only another of the temporary burdens that pioneers could expect to bear. But communities that had no prospect of ever being able to support such services locally found themselves in an untenable position since the provincial government made no effort to develop policies and programmes to meet their unique needs. This was especially important in areas with a high Aboriginal population or where geographical conditions guaranteed that future growth would be minimal. Consequently, those areas with sufficient ratepayers were able to provide needed services, others did without, and in all cases, Aboriginal people were shunted aside. This was yet another measure of the divergence in northern Alberta's culture, patterns of settlement and economic life.


## ▬ A Changing Urban Network

As commercial and social centres and railway shipping points, towns in the Peace River country with wealthy or expanding farm hinterlands grew as regional centres, while others declined as the coming of the railway reworked the configuration of existing towns and created a new urban system. The slow pace of railway construction ensured that some towns remained the head of steel for relatively long periods, enabling them to draw trade from a large area. Grande Prairie was the head of steel from 1916 until 1924, which gave it a head start in consolidating its control over a large hinterland. While Grande Prairie maintained its advantages, towns further west benefited only temporarily from the railway's extension. By 1928, when the line reached Hythe, the town experienced rapid growth, but when the line moved west to Pouce

*The first train arrived in Fairview in late 1928.* A4209 PAA.

Coupe and Dawson Creek in 1931, Hythe lost its relative advantage as the end of steel.[1]

The same process occurred north of the Peace River. As a railway terminus, Peace River became an important agricultural service and fur-buying centre for the north Peace River country and north-western Alberta. By 1923, it had four American fur buyers and a number of "outsiders" competing with the Hudson's Bay Company. As well, most local merchants bought fur and itinerant fur buyers came up periodically on the train from Edmonton. As a result, Peace River was one of the few Peace River country towns with a substantial number of Aboriginal visitors. The town's economy declined for a time after the railway was extended westward. As an official of the Alberta Provincial Police reported in 1925, "now that the railway has passed beyond Peace River the town has suffered considerably." Many businesses and services closed while those remaining found it hard to make ends meet. Some of this lost trade went to Whitelaw, which as the head of steel north of the Peace River, emerged as a rival trade centre for a large area north and west of the settlement. When the line was pushed on to Bluesky and Fairview in 1928, however, Whitelaw's influence diminished and Peace River regained some of its hinterland.[2]

The routing of rail extensions and the siting of stations around which new towns developed were particularly important influences on the urban system.

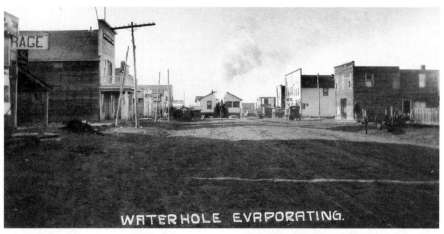

WATERHOLE EVAPORATING.

*Moving towns when they were bypassed by the railway was*
*common. In 1928 buildings at Waterhole were moved to the newly*
*created railway town of Fairview.* A4213 PAA.

Grouard's experience of being bypassed by the railway before World War I was repeated time and again in the Peace River country during the interwar years. Even though rail lines passed close by, the railway companies often ignored existing towns and hamlets and instead located stations in areas where they owned land. In some cases, this was justified because natural features affected where rail lines could go, but in other cases it was part of the railway's pursuit of profit through land development. Whatever the case, people seemed to accept such behaviour as inevitable and tried to plan accordingly. This was the case at Beaverlodge, Bluesky, and, among others, Lake Saskatoon, which were all bypassed by the railway.[3] The process was well demonstrated at Waterhole, an old stopping place on the Dunvegan-Peace River trail near the present town of Fairview. Advance settlers had moved into the area before World War I, but by the mid 1920s there was growing impatience with the slowness of railway extensions to the area. In 1921, farmers were still hauling grain long distances to the railhead. As the local chapter of the United Farmers of Alberta (UFA) noted in a petition demanding immediate completion of the line to Waterhole, hauling costs were almost equal to the sale proceeds of the grain. Thus, farmers were increasingly tempted to move to districts with better transportation. Built on leased land, "awaiting the location of a permanent townsite at a point on the yet-to-be-located railway," Waterhole nonetheless had grown into a relatively large centre of several hundred people by 1926. The main street was about a kilometre long, built up almost fully on both sides with wooden buildings. Showing the town's uncertain future, most buildings were constructed on skids.[4]

By the fall of 1928, the new town of Fairview was developing on the newly surveyed rail line about six kilometres from Waterhole. As evidence of its permanency, buildings on the main street were built on concrete foundations, and most had basements. As well, three elevators were completed and four more were planned. A few Peace River and Grande Prairie merchants established branch stores in Fairview, but most of the town's business community was made up of people from Waterhole. Most businesses felt confident about their future and located in new buildings since those in the old town were not "suitable for the modern town now building." Nonetheless, some commercial buildings were hauled from Waterhole for use as outbuildings, and a number of houses were also moved. It was a highly organized affair. A mover from Edmonton used a steam tractor to hoist buildings onto flatbed trucks, and the old town of Waterhole soon disappeared. The first train was expected in Fairview before Christmas 1928, by which time the new town's population stood at about 400. With an extensive hinterland with rich farm land, Fairview's growth was assured, and it was incorporated as a village the next year. While moving towns to suit railway company plans upset social institutions and made the boundaries of school and municipal districts less efficient, Fairview's success showed that adjustments to new conditions came relatively quickly.[5]

Unlike Fairview and other farm service centres on railway lines, Fort Vermilion's development demonstrated yet another aspect of urban growth in the Peace River country. Lacking rail or year-round highway connections, the centre continued to rely on river transport. The Hudson's Bay Company operated a motor boat service for passengers and freight, while grain was shipped by barge to the railhead at Peace River. Formal river connections between Fort Vermilion and the Peace-Athabasca delta had atrophied, and Fort Vermilion's orientation was now primarily towards the southern parts of the Peace River country with rail service. But its ongoing importance as a religious centre and the lower Peace River's major trade entrepot continued to tie it to its earlier urban function. Although the Anglicans closed their school in 1914, the Roman Catholic school and mission remained important. Thus, unlike most towns in the Peace River country, Aboriginal people continued to be a regular part of Fort Vermilion's town life. Even so, Fort Vermilion's growth depended on its role in an agrarian economy. By 1938, the town and district had about 1,500

*In 1935, spring flooding of the Clearwater River created chaos in Waterways.* A10,028 PAA.

people. A number of new settlers had arrived, and an expanding farm hinterland created economic advantages similar to those of agricultural service centres in the rest of the Peace River country. The town had a doctor, hospital (run by Roman Catholic sisters) and a number of other services. Reflecting a degree of local business organization, it also had a board of trade. After World War II, the completion of the all-weather Mackenzie Highway between Grimshaw and Great Slave Lake gave the Fort Vermilion district easier access to Peace River and stimulated economic growth. Reflecting this post-war expansion, an airstrip was built and a new high school, cinema and recreational hall were opened. The highway also brought some reorganization of urban centres in the district. Reminiscent of the railway phase, this new highway led to the creation of the new town of Manning to which buildings from North Star and Notikewin were moved.[6]

While Fort Vermilion's road connection with Peace River was significant in its development after World War II, its growth during the interwar years showed that changes in town life were not only a response to transportation infrastructure but a complex reaction to broader economic, geographic and corporate factors as well. This was also the case in the lower Athabasca district. Development of the Fort McMurray-Waterways district was affected by its function as a railhead and river shipping terminal. But further north, settlements continued to serve as administrative centres for church and state agencies and as service centres through which imports and exports flowed. As regional transportation centres in districts with large Native populations living off the land, these places retained more of their earlier character and social and economic context than farm service centres in the Peace River country that were connected with each other and to the south by roads and railways.

As in the Peace River country, rail connections to the Fort McMurray area were focussed exclusively on Edmonton. As the terminal for export shipments of fish, furs and minerals from areas further north and the import point for trappers, prospectors and other people, Waterways by the late 1920s was a busy port in summer. Partly because of pressure by major shippers such as the Hudson's Bay Company which wanted a better docking site for their river boats, the A&GW terminal at Draper (old Waterways) was moved a few kilometres further down the Clearwater River in 1925. This site was also called Waterways, and it fell short of Fort McMurray by about six kilometres.[7]

While Fort McMurray-Waterways was the portal to the north that Athabasca had once been, the location of the station at Waterways irritated many residents of Fort McMurray who recognized that this stymied their town's economic prospects. Although the two places were connected by road, it was often impassable, and Fort McMurray interests lobbied to have the railway extended into the old town. The Waterways townsite also suffered from several drawbacks that fueled these demands. Flooding and river bank erosion were serious problems, and low water in the Clearwater River in late summer sometimes prevented large river craft from approaching the terminal. Shippers were thus forced to tranship goods by shallow barges to loading platforms up to 20 kilometres away in deeper water on the Athabasca River. In 1933, the Hudson's Bay Company moved its warehouse because of river bank erosion, while low water after mid August necessitated costly transfer of goods to deeper draught river boats. The company calculated that shipping goods to the Western Arctic through Waterways was more expensive than from Vancouver through the Bering Sea, and it asserted that the extension of the line to Fort McMurray could "no longer be delayed."[8] The NAR repeatedly rejected such demands, arguing that Waterways was a better transhipment point because spring ice jams at the mouth of the Clearwater River at Fort McMurray created flooding problems and interfered with navigation. While the federal government indicated in 1929 that it was willing to build a dock at Fort McMurray if the railway was extended, the NAR refused, arguing that the government should instead stabilize the banks of the river at Waterways. The government subse-

*Waterways grew rapidly in the 1930s.* A7640 PAA.

*The Hudson's Bay Company dock at Waterways in the late 1930s.*
A12,177 PAA.

*The main street in winter, Fort McMurray, 1931.*
A11,987 PAA.

quently did as the NAR wished by dredging the river and subsidizing the railway's construction of a spur jetty upstream from the terminal to slow erosion.[9]

Despite the NAR's public statements, some observers contended that the railway's primary motive in refusing to move was to avoid being fleeced by land speculators who would hold the railway hostage when it needed to purchase land in Fort McMurray. More to the point, however, G.G. Ommanney, the CPR's Director of Development, observed in 1929 that while there were "no engineering difficulties" in extending the line, there was no "economic reason" to do so. It would create no "additional traffic for the railway" since only 10 percent of the freight handled at Waterways was forwarded to Fort McMurray. Moreover, because the line did not go into Fort McMurray, the line between Lac La Biche and Waterways apparently could be classified (under the arcane regulations governing the setting of freight rates) as an "uncompleted line" on which higher rates could be charged.[10]

As transit points for northern communications, Waterways and Fort McMurray had a unique character. Unlike farm service towns in the Peace River country, the location of the railway station at Waterways did not lead to the abandonment of the older centre of Fort McMurray. It continued to serve ongoing trade functions—the Hudson's Bay Company, for example, had stores there and at Waterways—and the merchants in the old town bought fur from places as far away as the Peace-Athabasca delta. Bush flying also added to Fort McMurray's economy. In the mid 1920s, about 200 people lived in Fort McMurray while about 300 lived in Waterways. Many of those working at Waterways lived in Fort McMurray, but the population of both towns rose and fell as people went "outside" for the winter and returned in the spring. Chipewyan men from the area and Cree from Portage La Loche also found work as dock workers, and presumably they too returned to their communities for the winter. In 1931, economic conditions declined because of the Depression, and the McMurray Board of Trade claimed that unemployment had suddenly increased. Local businesses were "up against it hard themselves" and about 25 men (a substantial portion of the permanent male work force) were unable to find work other than odd jobs.[11]

This situation turned around in the mid 1930s when expanding northern mining activity created work. Development efforts in connection with local salt and oil sands deposits further created a handful of jobs. One estimate in 1935 claimed that the floating population of both towns was now about 700. The CANOL project in 1942 further boosted employment. A secret project, the sudden arrival of 2,000 men on trains 20 minutes apart created chaos in Fort McMurray and Waterways. Employment increased just as suddenly to service the expanded population and help construct barges to ship pipeline materials north, while wages rose to levels unheard of in the district. The railway was extended a short distance towards Fort McMurray to an open area where a huge camp was set up and a special shipyard was constructed. A hospital, 400-room hotel and airfield were built, and an area was cleared where material for the pipeline was stored. These events gave Waterways a significant boost. The new airport built during the war was about 12 kilometres south-east of Waterways, which shifted air freighting away from the Snye and Fort McMurray. By 1944, the number of stores in Waterways had grown and fur buying was taking place there instead of in Fort McMurray. Indeed, one visitor described Waterways in 1944 as no longer the one street town that it had been in the mid 1930s. But when the U.S. army left as quickly as it had arrived, the economy slumped. As one resident recalled, "when they moved out of here it was just like a ghost town. Everything just died; they just moved out overnight. It seemed to me like you could hear a pin drop." By 1948, jobs were hard to find and the local Anglican minister confided that declining employment and a large transient population with few roots in the community had a negative influence on social life. As he reported, "for those who have no settled work, life is uncertain, and there is a tendency to concentrate on the material, which is understandable."[12]

In the area north of Fort McMurray, mining projects in the NWT and at Goldfields provided Natives with some wage work, and a few additional jobs were also created by the development of commercial fishing on Lake Athabasca. But hunting and trapping continued to support most people in these more northern areas. High fur prices and greater purchasing power until 1921 allowed some trappers—in a familiar pattern—to curtail trapping, while others carried on and built up credit balances with traders. Whatever the case, high prices allowed Native trappers to expand the range of consumer goods they purchased, including outboard gasoline motors for their boats. This equipment proved so useful that it quickly became a necessity. While people were also able to buy ready-made canvas tents and sewing machines in good years, trade goods sold in Fort Chipewyan in the 1920s were usually modest and included rifles, traps, some food items (mainly flour, lard, tea, and small amounts of canned fruit and jam), cloth, canvas for tents, gasoline, tobacco and some clothing. Eaton's mail order catalogues also circulated in the town and helped stimulate demand for current fashions.[13]

Uneven or falling prices in the 1920s and 1930s created difficulties for trappers, although lower fur prices in the 1930s were somewhat offset by deflation in consumer prices. Credit was still widespread, and because trappers still obtained, or least attempted to obtain, credit from more than one trader, falling prices intensified the competition among traders to collect debts in the spring. The trapping economy was further unsettled by a cyclical downturn in the late 1920s in the populations of many fur-bearing animals in northern Alberta. Competition from white trappers who were appearing in increasing numbers in parts of northern Alberta—especially in the Peace-Athabasca delta—added further difficulties.[14]

In spite of these changes, the continued centrality of trapping ensured that settlements north of Fort McMurray remained largely unchanged. As before World War I, most people in Fort Chipewyan were Metis, divided between English-speaking Anglicans and French-speaking Roman Catholics. Although everyone in the community trapped, Metis in the town mainly did so to supplement wage income. It is difficult to reconstruct ethnic boundaries along "Indian," "Metis" and "White" lines because these boundaries were relatively open, especially for Metis, but anthropologist Patricia McCormack found that many Metis described themselves as such to distinguish themselves from "Indians," whom they defined as the people who lived in the bush and trapped almost exclusively. Although "they were expressed in a racial idiom," social divisions thus appear to have been based on culture, occupation and place of residency rather than race.[15]

Fort Chipewyan also had about 25 white residents, mostly civil servants, missionaries and fur traders. There was little growth in the administrative sector of the town's economy, although an Indian Agent was stationed there in 1932. There was also some migration of people to Fort Chipewyan, which helped bring about the development of a denser urban form. Although most buildings were still irregularly spaced, they were beginning to cluster along "streets." New patterns were also apparent at the old fort. The palisades were at first replaced with fences, and in 1939 the remaining buildings were demolished and replaced with a modern retail outlet. While wartime projects did not have a direct impact on Fort Chipewyan, many townspeople found work guiding and working on the CANOL project.[16]

Fort Chipewyan's dominant character as a trade and mission centre for a large but sparsely populated hinterland meant that the seasonal rounds and nature of trapping life strongly shaped activity in the town. As shown by the field work and interviews with first Nations elders conducted by Patricia McCormack and historian Jim Parker, a band made up of 25 to 50 interrelated families and affiliates lived in log cabins in bush settlements during the winter. Women trapped for food near the bush settlements while men hunted moose or worked their traplines. While some people visited Fort Chipewyan for the Christmas celebrations and to buy a few additional supplies, traders often travelled to the bush settlements with goods. In spring, after cutting firewood for the next winter, people left to visit Fort Chipewyan for Easter and to purchase their spring supplies. They then broke into smaller family units and moved to the muskrat grounds where they lived in tents and trapped muskrats and hunted waterfowl. In summer, people hunted, fished and gathered berries in preparation for winter, and men worked for wages on the river boats or at other jobs when available. People also visited Fort Chipewyan to trade and receive their annuity payments and rations. Treaty payment time still had a festive character, just as it did in many other places in northern Alberta, and it was the only time of the year when the diverse people of the region gathered. In early July of 1931 people from as far away as Fond du Lac gathered in Fort Chipewyan for payment of the annuities. It was a time for marriages, shopping and socializing. That year, it was also a chance to enjoy the Dominion Day sports organized by the Anglican minister. Although this was "only the second time these sports have been held at Fort Chipewyan," the RCMP reported that many local people were "very skilful." After this summer visit to Fort Chipewyan, people lived in family groups in temporary camps where they put up fish for the winter and hunted moose and migrating waterfowl. Following a trip to Fort Chipewyan to trade furs and purchase the fall outfit (the most extensive purchases of the year), people returned to the bush settlements for the winter.[17]

While the same cycles of trapping life also characterized life in Fitzgerald and Fort Smith, a growing administrative sector and expanding river traffic brought increased growth to both places during the interwar years. Fitzgerald, which the English tourist Clara Vyvyan described in 1926 as a "gloomy place standing on slippery clay," had a number of warehouses by 1930, and the settlement continued to grow in the next decade because of increased shipping. By 1944, it had a hotel (an unusual thing in such settlements) and several stores. The population was said to consist of 63 Euro-Canadians and 127 Natives. Similar development occurred at the other end of the portage at Fort Smith where the federal government built new wharves between 1925 and 1929 to facilitate freight handling. Fort Smith's administrative sector also grew. The RCMP used it as a base for controlling incoming traffic and patrolling nearby Wood Buffalo Park, and in 1921 it became the headquarters for the Department of the Interior's North West Territories Branch. Tons of records and supplies were shipped from Ottawa to Fort Smith as part of the branch's creation. With a staff of 25, it administered the Mackenzie District and oversaw game regulation, the general administration of the NWT and the development of natural resources. Like Fitzgerald, Fort Smith also grew in the 1930s because of northern mining activities.[18]

## ▬ Medical and Educational Services

As increasingly important measures of standard of living during the interwar years, social and educational services in northern Alberta revealed different stages of development and growing economic and social differences within the region and between Euro-Canadian and Aboriginal communities. Before the routes of rail lines had been finalized in the Peace River country, construction of costly public facilities such as hospitals was held back. In 1920, the Alberta Medical Association noted that hospital construction there was risky because future railway development would probably change the importance of existing towns. A more persistent problem, however, was the difficulty of funding such services. While the small hospitals established in Grande Prairie and Peace

River before World War I had been welcomed as important local enhancements, it was soon found that they could not be sustained through volunteer efforts alone. Even though fund-raising was constant and unremitting in Peace River, it was impossible to operate even a modest hospital on this basis. And in Grande Prairie, there were complaints as early as 1913 that the fees at the Presbyterian hospital were too high and that its management was autocratic. This criticism also touched upon community status; as one commentator noted, church-run hospitals were suitable for pioneer areas, not for more developed places such as Grande Prairie.[19]

These early hospitals served huge districts. Other than a doctor at Lake Saskatoon and public health nurses in some outlying districts, there were no medical services west of Grande Prairie in 1920, while the hospital and three doctors in Peace River served the whole area north and west of the town. In 1918, new provincial legislation allowed the creation of municipal hospital districts in which a large area could be assessed to support a hospital. As a form of local government, hospital districts were regulated by the provincial government and received small grants, but they depended mainly on patient fees and property tax levies. Because they hoped to benefit from increased business from rural people who came to town for medical services, many town merchants tried to spearhead the formation of hospital districts that included adjacent rural areas. The most established centres (which usually meant incorporated places such as Grande Prairie and Peace River) usually won the race to be the sites where these district hospitals were located.[20]

Like their urban counterparts, rural municipal districts also tried to promote the development of medical services. Many close to large towns joined those hospital districts, but the relationship was often rocky. The whole system was administratively clumsy and inherently conflict ridden. Tensions sometimes arose because of resentment in close-by but smaller towns that had not been selected as the site for the hospital. More seriously, local governments were responsible for the hospitalization costs of indigents and any of their residents unable to pay the fees. Some local governments haggled with hospital districts over these accounts, while others were tardy or refused to pay their bills. In 1939, the neighbouring municipality of Nelson alone owed the hospital in Athabasca almost $6,500, largely for hospitalization of people on relief. Some of these arrears went back a decade.[21]

Some districts also attempted to develop their own services. Both the rural municipalities of Fairview and Spirit River tried to attract doctors through advertising. In 1918, the Fairview municipal district promised a moving allowance to any recent graduate of McGill or John Hopkins University who would move to the district, but the municipality was still shopping for a doctor several years later. In 1923, the municipal district of Spirit River went further and offered a $600 retainer to any doctor who would set up a practice, serve as the local medical health officer and carry out annual medical check-ups for school children. This arrangement proved unsatisfactory, and in 1927 a new approach was adopted—a doctor was paid an annual retainer of $4,800 and in turn agreed not to charge ratepayers any fees. While the doctor apparently soon broke the agreement, this was probably one of the first examples of a universal health care programme in Alberta. Some progress had also been made in the Fairview rural municipality by 1928 when a small hospital supported by the Women's Institute was operating at Waterhole. As had been the experience elsewhere, the Women's Institute soon found this task too onerous, and the hospital had been turned over to a board by 1936.[22]

Even the limited health care services in the Fairview and Spirit River rural municipalities depended on local taxation and were primarily designed to provide services to ratepayers. Service for others was handled on a cost recovery basis or was treated as relief. In most local improvement districts, such as those including the settlements of Hines Creek and Notikewin, low tax revenues put medical services out of reach. In 1936, the closest doctor and hospital for people in the Hines Creek district were in Fairview, 30 kilometres away over often impassable roads. Similarly, there was no hospital at Notikewin until the United Church opened one in 1937.[23] Until then, the medical needs of the people in the district were met by Dr. Mary Percy Jackson (who moved to Keg River in 1931) and a public health nurse. The province had inaugurated public health nursing in 1918 and later refined the system by adding "district nurses," specially trained public health nurses who provided a variety of medical services in remote districts. These nurses were "really junior physicians," handling the cases as they could, and sending the most serious ones to distant hospitals. In 1924, the province also set up "travelling clinics" consisting of a doctor, dentist and two nurses. For a small fee, this team provided dental care, medical examinations and minor surgical procedures for children in remote farm communities throughout the province. The province also recruited British doctors (including Dr. Mary Percy Jackson) who toured with the travelling clinics to familiarize themselves with Alberta conditions. This patchwork of medical services gradually expanded, the system became more permanent, and all of the larger towns in the Peace River country had hospitals by 1946. Nonetheless, most had waiting lists, and some, like the one at Spirit River, which opened in 1943, still served very large districts.[24]

The provision of medical services through local government probably worked well enough in areas with an adequate population and tax base and full employment. But such conditions were far from typical in newly settled districts, including those in northern Alberta. Like any programme built upon an idealization of social conditions rather than its realities, medical services could only be maintained in remote and sparsely populated districts, as in areas with nonratepaying residents, by excluding some people or by treating them as indigents. The emphasis on services for ratepayers explicitly excluded those who did not own assessable property, such as Indians, and those who did not own any land, such as many Metis. While there were successful Metis farmers, fishermen, trappers, businessmen and tradesmen, many others were impoverished, and those living close to settlements were usually the worst off because of game depletion and limited employment opportunities. Moreover, some medical problems were particularly severe among the Aboriginal population. On the reserves around Lesser Slave Lake contagious diseases such as measles and tuberculosis were widespread. Local Metis also suffered from the same illnesses (perhaps even to a greater degree than people living on the reserves), but they often went untreated, either because they had little money or because they did not always understand the treatment and control of such diseases.

In this respect, Indians were sometimes better off. Although inadequate funding was usually an impediment, Indian Affairs provided medical assistance for treaty people in some districts. A full-time nurse was stationed at Wabasca, and a travelling nurse visited the reserves around Lesser Slave Lake. The agency also kept a local doctor on retainer. In some cases, these arrangements must have been entirely inadequate; the Fort Vermilion doctor, for example, was retained on a part-time basis to deal with the whole of the north-west section of the province. Overall, Indian Affairs appropriations for health care were low and medical budgets were cut further during the 1930s. Only after World War II did the department begin to make adequate provision for health care and the construction of facilities, such as tuberculosis sanatoriums, for treatment of disease.[25]

In the lower Athabasca River district, medical services were even more rudimentary than in the least developed parts of the Peace River country. The travelling clinics did not visits areas without roads, and the doctors recruited by the province were apparently assigned only to farm communities. In almost the whole of north-east Alberta there was no local government and almost no property of assessable value. One estimate in 1935 calculated that if the total assessment in Fort Chipewyan was applied, taxes would not exceed $200. Even in Fort McMurray, conditions were poor. Before the Roman Catholic church established a hospital there in 1937, medical advice could most often only be found at the local drug store. In Fort Chipewyan, medical services were provided by the church or Indian Affairs. While it appears that health problems there were not as severe as among those Natives who lived closer to white settlements, people nonetheless required medical assistance for serious illnesses and during epidemics, such as the deadly influenza epidemic of 1928. Yet there was no government support for medical services, which were provided only by midwives, the nuns at Holy Angels convent and traditional healers. After 1932, when a medical doctor was appointed as Indian Agent, he treated everyone in the town, often performing operations in "some private dining room or house" or at the school. He also occasionally travelled to bush settlements. While all of the Indian Agents at Fort Chipewyan between 1932 and 1942 were medical doctors, later agents were not, and in 1948 it was reported that there were no professional medical services north of Fort McMurray other than a nursing sister at Fort Chipewyan.[26]

Nonratepayers in districts with organized local government could receive medical care either by paying the required fees or by qualifying for general relief. For Metis, access to medical care through welfare entangled them in a hostile system. They were ineligible for direct relief from the provincial government until 1934, and before that they had to apply for relief to the municipal district in which they lived. Each application for relief was judged individually and in public by the municipal council. While the system was demeaning for everyone, Metis were at an even greater disadvantage because they were often "shunned and suspected by the white population" and councillors were often hostile.[27] Indians were ineligible for any type of relief from local governments, and Indian Affairs distributed relief rations in times of particularly severe unemployment to prevent starvation.

Euro-Canadians too sometimes needed welfare. Such demands increased significantly during the 1930s, and most rural municipalities could not cope with the rising costs of relief. In 1935, the Municipal District of Nelson asked the provincial government to declare it "indigent for relief purposes" and to assume its responsibilities. When the province refused, the Municipal District reduced relief rates by 40 percent.[28] In 1931, the Municipal District of Fairview used road work as a form of relief. Earnings were applied to taxes or other debts owed to the municipality, a policy that tended to exclude Indians, Metis and any other resident who was not a ratepayer.[29] The province sometimes gave limited assistance to local government for such relief projects and it also distributed garden seeds, seed grain and feed to people in need. It also used the provincial Department of Public Works as a quasi-relief agency. The Alberta Provincial Police investigated people in distress and recommended those in need for work clearing brush along provincial roads or other similar tasks. In the absence of such projects, the police sometimes distributed direct relief. However, the provincial government was generally suspicious of relief in principle and usually tried to force ill-equipped local governments to shoulder these responsibilities.[30]

The limitations inherent in funding public services by means of local property taxation were equally apparent in the case of educational facilities. For places with low property assessments, public schools were difficult and at times impossible to establish. Provincial grants to support them were small and the province was unwilling to develop special programmes to deliver services in such places. These problems were not unexpected given the reliance on local taxation, and this confirmed a pattern in which only sufficiently populated districts with extensive assessable property could establish and then pay for a full range of school services.[31] While small elementary schools were operating in most districts soon after settlement, only Peace River and Grande Prairie had high schools by 1920. Few rural students attended these high schools because they had to board in town for the school term. A decade later, full high school programmes were still offered only in Peace River and Grande Prairie, although some high school courses were also available in public schools elsewhere. While rural high school districts were then being set up in Berwyn, Fairview, Spirit River and Beaverlodge, school development was generally retarded by declining local government revenues during the Depression. Well after the Depression, however, some communities, especially in the lower Athabasca River district, still found it impossible to establish and operate public schools of any type. At Fort Chipewyan, where most people were Roman Catholic, these problems were complicated by sectarianism. When Anglicans spearheaded the formation of a public school in 1945, the scheme was marred by sectarian bitterness because its organizers overtly promoted the school as an alternative to the Catholic mission school. Financial difficulties soon followed because of the village's low assessment and the difficulty of recruiting teachers during a time of high post-war demand elsewhere in the province.[32]

*Church run schools promoted cultural change among Aboriginal children. This photograph, dated 1928, is of the school room at St. Peter's Anglican school mission at Utikuma Lake. A4287 PAA.*

For Aboriginal northerners, schooling was further complicated by the divided jurisdiction based on the legal status of the pupils. As had been the case before 1920, many treaty Indian children attended school, but non-Treaty ones were often entirely excluded. In 1935, Bishop Guy of the Roman Catholic church noted that "the difficulty in the schools" in northern Alberta was that "in the same family you might have treaty Indians and non-Treaty Indians." While the residential schools did take in some Metis pupils, places for them were limited because the system was chronically underfunded. Roman Catholic priests continued to urge Indian Affairs to pay for Metis education, but they were unsuccessful. Because of racism, public schools, when available, were also usually not an alternative. As Bishop Guy observed, "some white people do not like Half-Breeds or Indians to be in their vicinity." Among other things, they feared that Metis children would spread tuberculosis. Such parental attitudes inevitably showed up in the school yard, and most Metis children in the Lesser Slave Lake district in the 1930s refused to attend the public schools where they were "ridiculed and humiliated by the white children." Peter Tompkins, one of the leaders of the Metis movement in the 1930s, argued that such discrimination hardened many Metis children against school, and since they did not have "the hitting back disposition," they were pushed aside.[33]

*These parents were visiting their children at St. Bruno's School at
Joussard. Not Dated.* OB4252 PAA.

As was the case before 1920, church-run residential schools continued to focus efforts to assimilate treaty Indians in northern Alberta. Although Indian Affairs attempted to contain it, sectarian rivalry continued unabated and perhaps even intensified as Roman Catholic schools gained in strength and numbers. By 1939 the Anglicans had only five day schools and two residential schools in northern Alberta. Its residential school in Wabasca was so dilapidated that parents feared for their children's safety because they believed the building might collapse. The Anglicans had closed their schools at Grouard, Fort Vermilion and Peace River, and the church's record of "Indian work" was said to have been one of "RETREAT, RETRENCHMENT AND DEFEAT." The Anglicans complained that the Roman Catholics had better funding, fine facilities, itinerant priests and a focussed school programme.[34] At the same time, however, it appears that financial problems in these Anglican schools reflected a tendency on the part of the Anglican church to choose to put its limited financial resources towards Euro-Canadian settlers rather than the Aboriginal population.

Government and churches alike continued to favour boarding over day schools for assimilationist and financial reasons. They also continued to endorse the wilderness-Native equation in which reliance on trapping was encouraged and life in settlements was discouraged. Bishop Breynat argued in 1935 that only rudimentary schooling was needed since "too much education is not a good thing for the Indian." And as one Anglican official confirmed in 1942, Indians were not allowed to remain in the settlements for health and moral reasons and "the Indian agents very wisely [planned] that the Indian families should leave the settlements as soon as their furs have been sold and they have gathered together their 'grub stake' for the winter." Such efforts to promote Aboriginal social isolation in order to prevent "contamination" by white society were racially motivated in their view of Aboriginal people as "noble savages" or childlike individuals requiring guidance. These tendencies also characterized the residential schools. The pupils were cut off from their families, language and culture as part of the school's assimilationist objective. Religious instruction remained prominent in the school curriculum, but in keeping with the Native-wilderness equation, Indian Affairs continued to insist that schools stress "practical" objectives, such as beadwork and sewing for girls and farming and "trades" for boys.[35]

Given their cultural objectives, residntial schools in northern Alberta, as in other parts of Canada, were often the scene of conflict. Although there were exceptions, there was much resistance to enforced schooling. While the *Indian Act* stipulated that school attendance was compulsory, many children did not attend school—in 1930 the Beaver in the Peace River country refused to be separated from their children who would have to be sent to residential schools in far away Grouard or Joussard. During the interwar years, Indian Affairs tightened the school system to enforce higher attendance, but this policy was only effectively applied around Lesser Slave Lake and other districts where Indian Agents, police and missionaries were close at hand. In 1931, the RCMP constable from Grouard helped the Indian Agent "round up school children" from the reserves along the lake for the residential school. In 1933, it was noted that people at Sturgeon Lake reserve were reluctant to send their children to school, and the next year the Indian Agent visited Wabasca to persuade parents to send their children to school. It was an ongoing struggle. In 1938 the Indian Agent reported "quite a bit of trouble with the Indians of Sucker Creek and Driftpile" reserves. Again, he relied on the RCMP to help enforce attendance.[36]

While parents could be fined or imprisoned for not sending their children to school, Indian Affairs was reluctant to take such action; assessing fines was pointless since the parents had no money, while imprisonment was costly for the department. In any case, such action would only have worsened a situation in which parental resistance, police-enforced attendance and the school environment had already created unstable conditions for many children. In 1925, "a number of the older boys" ran away from the residential school at Grouard, and the police were called in to bring them back. Running away was only one response. In 1937, a pupil set fire to the residential school at Joussard. The act was premeditated: the arsonist told some of the female pupils that he had a "dream" that "the school would burn 'Wednesday or Thursday but not later than Sunday'" and asked them if they would like the chance to go home. The girls packed up their belongings "as if they were making ready to go to their parents and relatives" for summer holidays. Following a debate on appropriate punishment, the boy was tried under the *Juvenile Delinquents Act* and sentenced to detention at the Grouard residential school until he was 18 years old.[37]

Such resistance forced the church, often reluctantly, to reexamine its whole missionary enterprise. Following his canonical visit in 1935, the Oblate's Superior General recommended that the church respect Native demands for recognition of their cultural needs.[38] Nonetheless, the schools remained committed to assimilation even though efforts to remake Aboriginal people in a Christian, Euro-Canadian pattern had been unsuccessful. Although it remains imprecisely understood, and while variations doubtless existed because of location and culture, there seems not to have been a strong polarity between traditional and Christian beliefs. In some places and circumstances, older traditions and ways of thought continued to survive and were sometimes integrated with Christian symbols and concepts. As the Anglican minister at Wabasca concluded in 1936, Christianity among the elderly had only been "superimposed on their old beliefs." When "visiting a sick man, a former 'conjuror,'" the minister noted that he had "found a fresh birch sapling laid over the roof of the house above where he lay. He was glad to have me pray with him but seemed to feel it just as well to placate the spirits also." While the missionary was confident that "our past pupils do not believe in these old ideas and that as the old people pass on they will become mere superstitions," his own evidence indicated the continuing strength of traditional beliefs within a new framework. As he noted, he had recently buried a baby whose "Christian Baptism and burial [were] keenly sought and obtained." Yet

> on a later visit I find the cross at the grave hung all over with streamers of ribbon, another pagan belief. Some of the people still go out into the bush alone to seek a spirit which visits them in a dream as a bear or an eagle. They firmly believe in the power of these spirits working through them. They are quite sure that one of our past pupils died about fifteen

months ago because a "conjuror" had put a spell on her. There is also the Feast Dance, held usually twice a year to bring good luck to the hunt. I have been invited to some of these and have always gone and injected Christian ideas when I spoke to the assembly.[39]

While the motives for these practices may have been different than this missionary presumed, they seem to indicate that Natives did not always draw rigid lines between Christian and traditional beliefs. Apparently, belief could be dual, with old and new retained for particular circumstances, as well as syncretic, from which a new reality developed.

— ✦ —

The disparities between Aboriginal and Euro-Canadian communities in northern Alberta during the interwar years became yet another element in the break-up of the functional unity of northern Alberta. Changing structures of economic life, however, contributed more directly to this fragmentation as the interlinked transportation and urban network that had created a functional unity in the Peace and Athabasca River basin after the 1880s disappeared. An urban system in the Peace River country was confirmed during the interwar years as a relationship among railways, internal communications and the local and national economy. On the lower Athabasca River, the development of Waterways as a railway terminal represented the operation of a similar dynamic, although it occurred in complete isolation from parallel developments in the Peace River country. While Fort McMurray continued to be tied to the network of older settlements further north, this was only a truncated version of the region's earlier urban system. Communications between the lower Athabasca district and the Peace River country atrophied in the absence of common conditions and facilities that would have enhanced such interaction. Growing cultural and economic differences between the two districts also limited incentives for such an interplay.

The growing disparities in social services among communities in the different parts of northern Alberta during the interwar years emerged from the view that the region's integration with Canada could be had without attention to its unique character and conditions. Instead of developing approaches and policies that respected these conditions, government assumed that integration could be promoted and would take its natural course as though there were no differences in culture and economy between northern Alberta and the rest of the province. Frontier development aimed to implant institutions and ways that were familiar and accepted in the rest of English Canada. Since medical services were largely funded by ratepayers, those who did not own property were inevitably marginalised and communities without sufficient assessable property had to go without. Travelling clinics and similar efforts by the provincial government did meet some of the needs of Euro-Canadian fringe communities in the Peace River country, but they entirely bypassed other areas such as the trapping districts along the lower Athabasca River. While the poor everywhere in Alberta suffered under this approach, its application in northern Alberta had greater consequences because it confirmed the differences between the eastern and western parts of the region and entrenched legal and racial distinctions between Aboriginals and Euro-Canadians. The same process and disparities also characterized educational services, although they were additionally complicated by their use as a vehicle for promoting cultural change among treaty Indian children.

# Farm Settlement

## 9

### The Peace River Country

AS THE PLACE where most homesteaders settled in northern Alberta after 1920, the Peace River country was shaped by the economic expansion of the late 1920s, the collapse of the 1930s and the dislocations of World War II. Settlers were first drawn by optimism, then by failure, and then as part of the post-war reconstruction of the Canadian economy. Such northern farm settlement during the interwar years was not restricted to the Peace River country, taking place across a "highly irregular, discontinuous margin of settlement traceable for some four thousand miles across the boreal forest region" of the country. In this pioneer fringe, "would-be farmers, often ill-prepared and ill-equipped for the task struggled to convert an unfamiliar and somewhat recalcitrant environment to agricultural production."[1]

Despite the arrival of new settlers, the ethnic composition of the Peace River country remained much like that in the rest of the province. While Natives made up about 5 percent of the population, about double that in the rest of Alberta, people of British descent, followed by those of Scandinavian and German origin, formed the majority of the population in older settlements such as Grande Prairie, Berwyn and Fairview. Although the British group was also largest in fringe settlements like Hines Creek in the early 1930s, people of central European descent were gaining ground quickly, making up about 27 percent of the population in comparison to about 10 percent in the longer settled Peace River country districts. Whatever their ethnic origin, most of the settlers came from other parts of North America. In 1930, it was noted that "all persons" filing in the Peace River land office had arrived from the three prairie provinces and the United States.[2]

Most of these settlers were familiar with farm life, although their experience immediately prior to settling in the north was varied. In one sample studied in 1931, 28 percent of settlers had worked only at farming before moving to the Peace River country, and almost all of the remaining 72 percent had been born on farms. While the number of married men and those with families taking out homesteads was higher than before 1920, single men continued to be over-represented, taking out over half of the homestead entries in 1929. Most settlers came individually or in family units. In 1930 it was observed that "solid colonies of persons of the same nationality are in the minority, which means that a general mixture of nationalities of all kinds has taken place. The principle object of those coming here is to find a homestead which will prove productive and very little attention has been paid to block settlement."[3]

Even so, some block settlement did occur. The most important was the further settlement of French-speaking people near McLennan between 1926 and 1930. Many of these settlers came from the Gaspé and Lac St. Jean districts in Quebec, while others came from north-east Alberta, Saskatchewan, the Ontario Clay Belt and New England. Although they were different in many ways—the New England settlers came from an urban-industrial environment while those from the prairies came from a rural-agrarian one—all were united by common language and faith. Along with the children of established farmers from the nearby Falher and Donnelly districts, these settlers extended the territory already taken up by French-speaking people. Further expansion in the 1930s took place in the area south of Falher. Although this migration of French Canadians in the late 1920s has sometimes been said to indicate that Quebec agriculture was "out of balance," Wayne Jackson has noted in his study of French Canadian settlement in the Peace River country that its impetus largely came from western Canadian missionaire-colonisateurs, not Quebec promoters. Such migration continued at a reduced rate in the 1930s and early 1940s. In 1941, the Canada Colonization Association co-operated with Bishop Langlois of Grouard to settle "interested French Canadians and other Roman Catholics in his Diocese."[4]

Another block settlement was of Mennonites in the Fort Vermilion area. In 1930, Mennonites from the prairies toured the Peace River country looking for four or five townships in an outlying district where they could establish colonies for about 1,500 people. Although they favoured the Fort St. John area in British Columbia, insufficient land was available so they turned their sights to the Carcajou area. With plans to begin settlement the next year, an advance party went north that winter to cut out roads. By 1932, a number of Mennonites were squatting on the land because they were at first unable to obtain legal title. These settlers were often viewed with disdain by Alberta's English-speaking dominant culture, and such attitudes intensified during World War II because of Mennonite pacifism.[5]

Various models have been devised by historians and geographers to explain why homesteaders located where they did. Some argue that settlers selected their land on the basis of cost; or its distance from a service town and its access to trails or railways; or because of environmental factors such as land quality, availability of water and type of vegetation. Other, more complex explanations see homestead selection as part of the development of urban-rural economic and social networks.[6] In northern Alberta, cost of land was a relatively unimportant factor in determining location because most people took homestead land. There was little unimproved land for sale because there were no railway lands for sale, and once school lands were released by the government for sale in 1928, this source of land for purchase disappeared.[7] There is evidence that proximity to a town, road or trail was important in determining where people settled in the Athabasca district, but open land that was easy to clear remained—as it had since the time of advance settlement after 1909—the most powerful influence. People with such a narrow focus were easily swayed by rumour and advertising. As Henry Leppard noted in his 1935 study of Peace River country settlement, consideration of matters such as drainage, character of soil, water supply and even transportation often did not figure in the decisions of land seekers. Many filed entries at land offices for "homesteads that they had never seen and about which they had only the most meagre information."[8] Such practices, and the attendant failure by government to restrict settlement to areas close to existing social and transportation infrastructure, led to ongoing criticism that the homestead system was inefficient and wasteful. Change came about when the province, which had taken over responsibility for homesteading from the federal government in 1930, abolished the homestead system and replaced it with a lease system in the late 1930s. This new approach brought as much criticism as the system it replaced. By then, however, settlement was winding down, although it continued intermittently in some districts in northern Alberta for several decades.

*By the late 1920s, many of the longest established farms in the*
*southern Peace country were well equipped operations that differed*
*little from farms in the southern prairies. Not dated. (ca. 1929).*
*73.62/1, PAA.*

## —— Uneven Fortunes

### *Settlement in the 1920s*

The decline in farm settlement in the Peace River country that began in 1920
lasted until 1926. High freight rates, falling wheat and livestock prices, a series
of poor crops and concerns about transportation discouraged many people
from coming and persuaded many others to leave. Soldier settlers were especially hard hit by the downturn. They had purchased land at inflated prices
immediately after the war, and high debts and falling land values forced many
of them to abandon their farms in the early 1920s. Although limited settlement
continued on the fringes of earlier settled areas, it did not begin to increase
substantially until 1927. Such declining opportunities characterized the
province as a whole, but conditions were tougher in the Peace River country
where development was more recent and farmers operated at an even greater
distance from markets. During this time of disillusionment and doubt about
the future, the population and number of farms declined and occupied acreage
fell. Nonetheless, conditions in the Peace River country were highly variable.
Well established farmers in districts with good soil and close to the railway
increased their improved acreage by clearing more land and purchasing the

farms of departing neighbours. For such farmers, the crisis of the early 1920s barely existed, and by 1928 one observer noted that the areas south of the Peace River had changed since the end of World War I from "a struggling pioneer country into well developed districts" with good farm buildings, well tilled fields and improved livestock.[9]

Homesteading in Alberta in the late 1920s was commonest in the Edmonton area, but an expanding national economy and high wheat prices also brought dramatically increased settlement in the Peace River country. Ongoing settlement schemes for World War I veterans added to this upswing. Good quality homestead land (whether treed or open) on the prairies was increasingly available only in northern Alberta. As well, towns and villages there now offered a greater range of commercial and social services than a decade before, while an expanded road and rail network offered better internal connections. In addition, freight rates had fallen by the mid 1920s, and there were spectacular crops in 1926 and 1927—"two of the most bountiful harvests ever grown in any growing area." Publicity about the area's agricultural value further encouraged optimism and advertised the Peace River country's agricultural potential.[10]

Between 1926 and 1931, the number of farms in the southern Peace River country increased from almost 2,800 to nearly 7,000, while the population grew from about 22,600 to almost 51,000. It was a heady time, especially in 1928 when a land rush developed and almost 4,400 new homesteads were filed in the Peace River and Grande Prairie land offices. Covering the whole of the Peace country in Alberta and British Columbia, these two offices accounted for about 34 percent of all homestead entries in western Canada in 1928. One report estimated that 16,000 people arrived in the Peace River country that year, which more than doubled its population over the previous year. The same year, 10,000 acres of land were cleared and 96,300 were broken. Although settlement declined somewhat in 1929, it remained high and a substantial amount of land was again cleared and broken. Following on the heels of the spectacular crops in 1926 and 1927 and an excellent one in 1928, the clearing and breaking of so much land created great optimism. Premier Brownlee forecast that the Peace River country "would provide farm homes for a million people in less than a decade" and that its production would exceed that "of all Western Canada at the present time." Edmonton civic leaders were equally confident that the expansion of northern settlement heralded future advantages for their city.[11]

Such boosterism relied on conventional thought and utilized phrases such as the "Inland Empire" and the "World's Bread Basket." In 1928, the Peace River country was described as "the Last West, and those who know it may be excused for terming it the 'Best West.' It is one of the few remaining resorts on the continent for the seeker after free lands."[12] The same rhetoric had surrounded settlement on the prairies in the previous half century, but it was additionally effective in the late 1920s because of a national romanticization of the Peace River country and northern settlement. The landscape as a metaphor for Canadian identity, as expressed by the paintings of the Group of Seven, was being reinvigorated in terms of northerness and wilderness. The Peace River country fit perfectly with these views about the wellsprings of Canadian nationhood, and they found local expression in the artwork of Euphemia McNaught of Beaverlodge who had trained at the Ontario College of Art in the 1920s under J.E.H. MacDonald and Arthur Lismer.[13] The beauty of the countryside, especially the glorious vistas of the Peace River valley, stirred the popular imagination, while the river's place in an immense water system extending to the Arctic gave people a sense that they were standing on the edge of a huge northern land. The myth of pioneers challenging an "untamed" northern land further added to the historical drama, although the Peace River country, in a contradictory impulse, was also praised because it was not all "northern" and wild. By the late 1920s extensive tracts of farm land made it a familiar and comforting landscape for southern Canadians, and the naturally occurring lightly-wooded rolling land found in some areas confirmed its pastoralism.[14]

Despite these images, most homestead land available south of the Peace River by the late 1920s was on the margins of settled areas and was relatively heavily treed. In the Grande Prairie district there was little homestead land left by 1928. In general, "the chief additions to the acreage of occupied land" south of the Peace River between 1926 and 1931 "occurred on the margins of existing settlements, in new districts, and in small scattered clearings" such as between DeBolt and Valleyview (then called Red Willow Creek) west of the Little Smoky River. By 1928, this area had about 400 farms and over 1,500 people, most of whom were very recent settlers. Around Spirit River, treed land that had been avoided by earlier settlers was now taken up, and new settlers located further west around Bonanza and south of Hythe at Lymburn. As well, increased settlement was taking place between McLennan and Peace River. But the overall scarcity of relatively open land south of the Peace River ensured that extensive settlement occurred north of the river as well. By 1930, when the railway reached Hines Creek, settlers had located in the areas north-west of Fairview. Additional settlement took place on the margins of the large plateau of arable land stretching, with some breaks, along the river west of the town of Peace River. This helped consolidate settlement in these areas and gave new settlers the advantages of existing public improvements and newly extended rail lines. In a familiar pattern, settlers searching for open land also dispersed well beyond the areas directly served by railways, settling in fringe areas such as the Fort St. John and Battle River districts that were served only by roads and trails.[15]

The Battle River district, an area totalling about 1,500 square kilometres north of Peace River, typified fringe settlement in the interwar years. The district consisted of several subregions, including both "prairie" lands and heavily timbered tracts of varying soil quality. The area around Notikewin (formerly called Battle River) was one of the first parts of the area to be settled, but in 1929 "many good souls with strong pioneer instincts" pushed almost 50 kilometres north through the bush to Keg River. This was about the time that the dominion telegraph line reached the area, and it was anticipated that settlement would extend further north within a year. The number of occupied homesteads in the Battle River district increased dramatically from about 100 in 1927 to about 800 by 1929. Other settlers were also attracted even further north to the Fort Vermilion district that contained good quality open land. By 1932 it was estimated that all the settled areas north of Peace River had about 6,000 people.[16]

While the earliest settlers in the Battle River district obtained open land, later arrivals found only land covered by small timber "impenetrably close together." People nonetheless took up these lands, "most of them bent on commercial grain farming 60 miles from a railway—where 20 miles approaches the limiting distance." In such circumstances, reports of newly available lands not only attracted settlers from outside the region but also led many who had settled these heavily treed areas to abandon their "bush farms." This proved to be a wise move for many people. As was observed in 1935, after years of falling prices and general economic downturn, most of the areas in the Battle River district with a high acreage of raw woodland had grown relatively slowly, "while a number of the younger settlements that have large acreage of prairie land have made rapid gains."[17]

Success or failure in these fringe areas often depended on the capital that incoming settlers had. While most people had very little, it was commonly believed that this would be offset by the availability of open homestead lands that could be put into production quickly. In a spurt of promotional optimism, the CPR claimed in 1930 that settlers with $500 in cash plus some farm equipment "would have an excellent start" in a fringe area since free building materials were close at hand, gardens were productive and open land could quickly be put into production. Even so, the CPR admitted that most settlers had "very limited capital, many of them having only a few dollars over the filing fee." In any case, the open land that justified low initial capitalization was almost impossible to find by 1930. In this situation, the estimate of $500 in cash plus some farm equipment was far too low to sustain a farm during the long period of clearing and breaking the land. Indeed, a more sober calculation in 1942 suggested that an intending settler needed $4,000 in cash and credit for a successful start. This amount was not significantly different from that needed a decade earlier since there was almost no change in farm income or expenses between 1930 and 1942 in the Peace River country.[18]

As a consequence of low capitalization, fringe settlers—like many farmers in similar circumstances in prairie Canada in the 1920s—trapped, worked in lumber camps, moved to towns or cities in winter to work or found jobs on construction projects during the summer to earn extra income. But in the agricultural economy of the Peace River country, relatively few wage jobs were available at the best of times, and even in 1929 wages were "at the minimum" because so many people were looking for work. The winding down of railway construction in the late 1920s, the drying-up of government funding for road work in the early 1930s, and the general economic downturn during the Depression further restricted already limited opportunities, just when many fringe settlers were setting up their farms.[19]

— **Depression and War**

While many people believed that settlement in the Peace River country would be untouched by the Depression because recent settlers constantly sent "enthusiastic reports to districts in which they formerly lived," this proved not to be the case. Immigration to Alberta fell between 1931 and 1936 because of the Depression and federal restrictions on immigration. Although homesteading continued, mainly in the Edmonton and Peace River areas, the number of homesteads filed in 1939 in the province was the lowest since 1931. Between 1931 and 1935 the number of homestead entries in the Peace River country barely exceeded cancellations and the number of farms declined overall. There was a corresponding increase in the average size of farms as migrants sold out to neighbours who remained—a familiar prairie pattern that historian James Gray called the "land-use shakedown," a cycle of settlement, abandonment and

*During the 1930s, some people from the southern prairies moved to northern Alberta where precipitation was higher and homesteads could still be found.* ACA92 PAA.

consolidation. As well, the British Columbia Peace River Block, where open lands were still available, attracted a growing number of settlers after the railway reached Dawson Creek in 1931. Even so, in the decade following 1931, the southern Peace River country's population grew by about 13.5 percent—a substantial increase for the time, even though it was far from the dramatic growth of 1928–29.[20]

Some of these incoming settlers moved north because of population pressure in their home districts. By 1935, the recently settled area around Wandering River (formerly called Muskeg Prairie) north-east of Athabasca had a population of about 700. Many of these settlers were of Ukrainian descent and came from east-central Alberta where homestead land was no longer available. More often, settlers moved north because of drought on the southern prairies. While movement off the land on the southern prairies was relatively minor during 1929–30, it began to increase after 1931, a disastrous year of drought and erosion. Many of these people moved to northern Alberta, often settling in fringe areas. Most of the settlers in the Notikewin district in 1936 had recently arrived from southern drought areas.[21] Many of these settlers arrived with little capital and quickly exhausted their savings before they could get their land into production. Others were impoverished at the start. As Bishop Sovereign of the

Anglican church observed, many arrived with "their few possessions piled on rickety wagons drawn by half-starved horses and followed by a few lean cows." As they trekked north, he watched them "with pity yet with admiration. They are no longer young; their early hopes are dead, yet they go forward bravely to make a new start." William Swift, a school inspector at Athabasca, recalled that among them was "a kind of resigned optimism characterized by the commonly displayed slogan written on the side of the conveyance, PEACE RIVER OR BUST. Occasionally they gave up and were to be observed heading south again. One case, vividly recalled, had the original sign covered by a superscription reading BUSTED."[22]

Some of this migration was sponsored by government. Alberta, like Saskatchewan, had relief programmes that encouraged farmers from southern drought areas to resettle in more northerly districts with higher precipitation.[23] Beginning in 1931, a federal-provincial-railway company scheme offered these farmers free transportation. While some moved to northern Alberta, most took land in the Red Deer and Edmonton districts, as did most of those who followed between 1933 and 1935. Alberta also reserved an extensive tract of land along the Little Smoky River that farmers could take in exchange for their dried-out lands in the south. The NAR lobbied for this programme, viewing it as a method of increasing the population in a district that produced little rail traffic.[24] Other efforts included the Relief Settlement Scheme in 1932, a "back to the land" programme sponsored by federal, provincial and municipal governments. Designed to reduce welfare costs for local governments, it placed urban families receiving relief on the land. Based on an assumption that farm life was inherently moral and regenerating, it presumed that city people of farm background were eagerly awaiting the chance to return to farming, thus reversing their earlier misguided decisions to move to the city. Consistent with this view, it was assumed that the scheme would resocialize participants and break dependency on relief since pioneering would create self-initiative and self-reliance. With "careful management," it was said, people "with few possessions" could accumulate some capital, build a home and enjoy "healthful living conditions." While most of these "back to the land" people settled on homestead land, the province also reserved land exclusively for them north-west of Peace River town.[25]

This relief settlement scheme became the centre piece of Alberta's attempts to grapple with the dislocation caused by drought and depression. If urban poverty rekindled a longing to return to farm life, there would have been increased settlement in the Peace River country where extensive arable land was available. Although the programme lasted until 1942, only a few of those participating moved north. Of the 297 families in the programme in 1933, only 27 went to the Peace River country, and in the next year, a group of 17 families from Medicine Hat settled near Driftpile. The land reservation north-west of Peace River drew few settlers because it was too remote and costly to reach. Similarly, the Little Smoky Land Reserve for dried-out farmers attracted few takers—some of those who wanted to settle there were unable to make satisfactory land trades, while others were ineligible. No one located in the area in 1934 because heavy rains made roads impassable, and only a handful of settlers had located there by 1935 when the province abandoned the project and opened the land to all homesteaders.[26]

In general, the relief settlement scheme failed because it was underfunded and because it was driven by an appeal to an idealized and unrealistic rural life. This was also a factor in why sponsored Depression settlers showed relatively little interest in the Peace River country. Most of them took homesteads closer to Edmonton and Red Deer, and while this land was often poorer than that in the Peace River country, it was less remote and offered better access to nonfarm jobs once economic conditions improved. Many of the participants returned to nonfarm employment as soon as possible, and in 1945 the provincial government admitted that the programme had offered most people only "an escape from depressing conditions" until more desirable employment came along. This increasingly became the case between 1940 and 1945 as job opportunities created by the wartime boom led to further abandonments. By 1948, almost 62 percent of participants had left their farms.[27]

Such government resettlement schemes were not unique to Alberta. In Saskatchewan most sponsored settlers took up land in partially settled wooded areas with established pioneer populations. Even though the provincial government assisted with land clearing, most settlers had little capital and had difficulty surviving until their land came into production. While the influx of government sponsored drought-area farmers was at first met with sympathy on the part of those already settled in these fringe areas, this quickly turned to "frustration and anger" when the emigrants took government road work, killed local game and did not pay taxes. By 1934, conditions in northern Saskatchewan were "chaotic" and local and provincial governments were forced to provide relief, further increasing resentments among established residents.[28]

Such tensions were less acute in northern Alberta, perhaps because the districts in which sponsored settlers located were larger and their settlement was more dispersed. Moreover, many of the areas they settled had little infrastructure and many of the people already living there had also recently arrived and were struggling with similar problems. At Hines Creek in 1936, for example, many of the area's settlers were from the dried-out south and were "absolutely broke." The whole district was undeveloped; roads were often impassable and people were so poor that barter had replaced cash.[29] Yet like Saskatchewan, Alberta's allocation of land with marginal farming value to Depression settlers created ongoing problems and demands for welfare. As well as having little or no cash, many came to their northern homesteads without livestock feed or seed grain and remained caught in a familiar cycle of poverty. Conditions in the Municipal District of Nelson near Athabasca were typical. As a woman in the district wrote in 1931, "we were blowed and dried out on our farm in Saskatchewan and we came here to homestead with horses and wagons, and we have no money to buy anything with, so we will have to get relief from somewhere." They needed clothing and, if possible, Christmas gifts, "as we didn't get anything for Christmas last year." Such conditions persisted. In 1938, it was reported that one recently arrived Depression settler lacked feed for his horses and was forced to feed them straw all winter. By spring the horses were too weak for field work.[30]

The poverty of many new settlers in the 1930s was not easily overcome. Off-farm jobs were scarce, and when they were available, wages were low. This left trapping as an important means by which one could earn extra income in fringe areas, and even though fur prices were low, this gave some people the means to get by. But in an environment of falling commodity prices and scarce wage work, demands for relief were widespread, both among drought-area farmers driven north as well as longer established farmers. Especially hard hit were poorly capitalized farmers on treed lands a distance from the railway. Shipping costs ate up an ever greater portion of their falling incomes, and resulting cash shortages also diverted capital from land clearing and higher future production and income.[31] The drying up of off-farm jobs—such a vital part of the pioneer farm economy—also added to growing economic problems. The crisis that these conditions brought was thus not only a result of under capitalization and low commodity prices, but also reflected the upsetting of the makeshifts economy that had supported many farmers during the long period needed to establish a farm and clear and break sufficient land.

While the severity of economic conditions in the 1930s led to decreased settlement in northern Alberta, World War II brought further decline. Migration from Europe and the United States stopped almost entirely, although there was some internal migration within Canada. In 1940, for instance, the

NAR and the Basilian Fathers at Mundare, Alberta co-operated to resettle people from overcrowded farming districts in east-central Alberta to the Peace River country.[32] Greatest hopes, however, were pinned on post-war immigration and an assumption that war veterans would take up homesteads after the war. The NAR reported that it had received a number of inquiries about the Peace River country from Americans working on wartime projects in northern Canada, and in 1943 the railway and the governments of Alberta and British Columbia co-operated in a campaign "to acquaint wartime residents in the north on how to settle here permanently." These anticipations were further bolstered by the assumption that farm immigration from Europe would resume once the war was over.[33] In 1944, the province gave "returning soldiers the first choice of homestead lands" and restricted homesteading for the duration of the war to "old Albertans." Governments presumed that war veterans would welcome a northern homestead as a reward for war service, and by 1944, the federal government was purchasing and "banking" farm land for veterans to help in their reestablishment and to control land prices after the war. Veterans were eligible for up to 360 acres on a 10-year lease and a cash advance for equipment and land improvements.[34]

Despite such programmes, relatively little new settlement took place in the Peace River country in 1944–45, even though land was reaching "inflationary values" in some districts. Nevertheless, in both British Columbia and Alberta, all crown land continued to be reserved for residents and for veterans. In Alberta, a resident was defined as anyone who had continuously resided in the province since the beginning of 1944.[35] Alberta held to this restriction in 1946 and 1947, which sparked criticism from the NAR and other settlement promoters. Even so, a considerable number of veterans settled on farms during this period. In 1946, 2,300 veterans were placed on the land in Alberta and 4,000 were on waiting lists. Of those receiving land in 1946, 305 took crown land in the Peace River country, while a further 660 veterans settled on farms that the federal government had purchased there earlier.[36]

By 1947, demand for land by veterans was beginning to decline. British Columbia resumed sale of crown land without restrictions, but Alberta continued to insist on a residency requirement. This provoked further criticism about unnecessary limitations on immigration, but this lack of interest in farm settlement reflected wider changes taking place in Alberta. While it had generally been believed that the province could absorb only farm immigrants, the nature of post-war immigration shifted in step with changes in the economy. By 1946, industrial workers and artisans were becoming more valued in

Alberta, indicating the emergence of different economic patterns and fore-telling the relative decline of agriculture and rural settlement as primary forces in the province's economy.[37]

## A Search for Efficiency
### The Evolution of Land Policies

The difficulties faced by pioneer settlers in northern Alberta in the interwar years provided further evidence for critics of the homestead system who argued that it had encouraged settlement without attention to proximity to towns and transportation or the suitability of soil and climate. The large number of abandoned homesteads on the prairies, including the Peace River country, was said to prove the inefficiency and waste of the system. Failures were indeed high; historian Bob Irwin has calculated a failure rate of about 50 percent in the Peace River country before 1930, and similar failure rates were seen elsewhere in northern Alberta and other areas of northern fringe settlement in Canada. While there was sometimes a tendency to blame such failings on the settlers themselves—the *Grande Prairie Herald* editorialized in 1937 that successful land settlement depended on "selective selection" of settlers—the problem was more generally considered to be the result of the way that immigration and home-steading was handled.[38]

Criticism of the homestead system was not an esoteric issue; many Canadians believed that its reform was fundamental for the country's future. A 1923 article by Donald Albright, the superintendent of the Beaverlodge exper-imental substation, typified many of these concerns from the vantage point of northern Alberta. At the outset, Albright castigated Canadians for their lack of "assertive patriotism" and for a "mercenary materialism" that eroded national purpose. People needed a higher purpose than mere "self-seeking," and Albright contended that if settlement policies were designed to promote sounder devel-opment, Canadians would discover a national purpose in the settlement of northern homestead lands. Accordingly, Canada needed to place its "own sons and daughters" rather than immigrants on the land. Race was also an element in this concern, for as Albright wrote, if Canada was to hold "her territory for the white man she must people it with the Caucasian race. Otherwise it will ultimately go by default to the yellow man across the Pacific either by infiltra-tion as at present or by conquest. 'Use or lose' is a principle which applies as inexorably in world politics as in biology."[39]

While such settlement and immigration proposals reflected contemporary thinking about the relationship among race and national coherence and purpose, Albright considered reform to be more fundamentally a matter of creating stable and rational land settlement. In his opinion, Canada needed "more homebuilders and fewer boosters; prudent producers rather than speculators and get-rich-quick parasites, such as boom times attract." But how could home-building instead of speculation be encouraged? While Albright recognized how climate and location affected northern settlement, he believed these factors only confirmed that more prudent agricultural practices and control of homesteading were necessary. As he warned, "a fine spirit it is that conquers the wilderness, but, unregulated, it speeds many to their undoing." Homesteading in general and the unique needs of northern settlement in particular required "a directing rein if it is to accomplish the maximum of development with the minimum of human privation." Thus, "every consideration of personal and economic advantage demands that settlement edge gradually into the wilderness with the frontier ever in touch with the settled area behind."[40]

Albright's critique was more inclusive than many others, perhaps because of his closeness to the problems of northern settlement. But his assumption that scattered settlement was inefficient for organizing and providing roads, social services and marketing facilities was widespread, and by the late 1920s support had grown in Canada for greater control and planning of land use. As Alberta's first planning legislation in 1929 reflected, greatest concern was expressed about urban areas. Nonetheless, it was recognized that rural land use should be controlled through planning as well. As Alberta's town planner, Horace Seymour, noted in 1930, "to allow a settler to take up land in any part of Canada that pleased his fancy at one time may have seemed a matter of romanticism— a showing forth to the whole world of the individual liberty that one could enjoy in Canada." But the consequent lack of attention to land productivity or the costs of transportation to remote areas ensured that "the result has not been an altogether happy one." Seymour also believed that land should be leased, rather than sold, to eliminate the speculation that he believed was a primary cause of dispersed settlement.[41]

Although advocates like Seymour and Albright claimed that such policies would benefit the Peace River country, it is likely that settlement would never have begun there if such policies had been in place before 1920. Nonetheless, the problems of the Depression strengthened criticism of earlier land use. As the *Edmonton Journal* editorialized in 1934, land was too valuable a resource to be squandered. "The fundamental mistake in the opening of western Canada," it argued, "was haphazard settlement" that made transportation networks expensive relative to an area's ability to support them. Moreover, it had led "tens of thousands of farmers" to try and "force a living from lands unsuited to long-term grain farming," especially in parts of southern Alberta. The disruptive resettlement of people to more suitable land had been one consequence of such methods of land distribution, and "orderly settlement" (as well as control of farming methods) would prevent waste and create permanent value.[42]

The federal government was often blamed for these problems before public lands were transferred to the province in 1930. Although it is certainly true that it promoted settlement in northern Alberta in the 1920s, such advertising was an expected function of government.[43] And while criticism of its homestead policies was often merited, the federal government was not as wantonly lax as many of its critics charged. Land was broadly classified into types (such as grazing, farm and forestry lands), and the government usually tried to close land to homesteading unless it was "fit for settlement." Nonetheless, it did not stop squatters from occupying unsurveyed land—the eviction of pioneers, even if they were squatters, would have carried a high political cost, and this effectively left one cause of dispersed settlement beyond control. At the same time, the federal government did not always jump to meet the demands of local promoters to open new land for homesteading. The Grande Prairie Board of Trade asked in 1922 that a large district south of the Wapiti be thrown open for settlement. It argued that recent "heavy fires" had cleared much of the brush, which, along with its natural "prairie patches," meant that the area could "accommodate a great many settlers" who otherwise would have to settle in areas even further from the railway. The minister of the Interior promised to reinvestigate the matter, even though an earlier survey had shown that most of the area consisted of poor farm land. This reassessment found that there was indeed little land fit for agriculture in the area—most of it was "muskeg, sand or timber land, there being only small scattered patches of land with suitable soil." The whole area could accommodate only 20 or 30 settlers, each of whom would be able to find only about 80 acres of continuous arable land. Thus, while the department would have opened the district for homesteading even though it was remote, it refused to do so because the land was not "fit for settlement."[44]

For critics of the homestead system, the transfer of natural resources to the province in 1930 raised hopes that rural land use would be planned and directed more efficiently. While Manitoba and Saskatchewan abandoned the homestead system in 1930, Alberta retained it, perhaps because the province had so much land for potential farm settlement. The provincial lands statute was similar to the federal one it replaced, except that it required a three-year residency in Alberta before one could apply for a homestead. It also reduced the length of time that a homesteader had to stay on the homestead before he or she could apply for a patent. These provisions rankled in parts of the Peace River country because they were seen to favour southern Alberta at northern Alberta's expense. The *Grande Prairie Herald* editorialized that while "there was vast room for improvement" over federal homestead provisions, the province's new rules meant "the complete stagnation" of development in the Peace River country and "a class favouritism by which the families of farmers in older settled sections of the province will be given a complete monopoly on the free lands available." The new policy would allow southern farmers to send their "sons and daughters into the Peace River country for a four month's summer holiday to possess the land, while families of worthy settlers who would be glad to come in from other provinces and other countries are barred." Indeed, Alberta was declaring that "this is not a united dominion of Canada, but a group of ten states of individual aspirations. Alberta is for Albertans only." This policy would lead to declining settlement, prevent the taking up of millions of acres of undeveloped agricultural land, and bring an end to railway extensions. The only beneficiary, the *Herald* concluded, would be the British Columbia Peace River country, "which continues to welcome immigration and development."[45]

The new legislation also enabled women for the first time to take out homesteads on the same basis as men. While the number of homesteads taken out by women skyrocketed—in the last six months of 1931 women accounted for one-third of all entries—most were "wives, sisters, and daughters of farmers" who wished to increase their land holdings. The province did not discourage this practice, seeing it as a way for farmers to consolidate their holdings and create larger and more economical farm units.[46] This indicated that the province was attempting to place its land and agricultural policies within a single framework, and this intention became more explicit in 1939 when new land legislation was adopted. Homesteading was abolished and land was made available only by lease, the terms of which varied according to land type. All land was now inspected to ensure that it was suitable for agriculture before a lease was granted. In the Peace River country, an applicant could lease up to one-half a section for 20 years, with an option to purchase after 10 years if specified land improvements were carried out. Most importantly, the applicant undertook to break one-fifth of the arable acreage in the first year. Recognizing that most settlers were poorly capitalized and that considerable time was needed to get land into production, the province (as the land owner) paid property taxes and did not charge rent during the first three years. Thereafter, rent was set at a one-eighth share of the crop, but was foregone in any year when the average yield was less than five bushels per acre.[47]

Despite its advantages in controlling and directing settlement, the lease system was not as popular as had been anticipated. For one, people were apparently afraid that their leases "would be affected by the possibility of political patronage."[48] They also complained that land inspection by provincial officials was slow, that the amount of land that had to be broken in the first year was too great and that the 10-year residency requirement before title could be secured was too long. As officials with the CNR's Department of Colonization and Agriculture noted in 1940, "to most people looking ahead, ten years is a very long period of time." People wanted immediate ownership and were reluctant to wait so long before obtaining title to their land. Such problems aside, however, CNR officials judged that the new system was "much superior to the old homestead method of land disposal in that it will make for more permanent settlement, as only suitable lands will be located on."[49]

This approach was maintained during the post-war period when Alberta continued to rationalize its land settlement policies. Reflecting a greater desire to control and direct land use and settlement, the province began moving after 1941 towards a system in which land capacity—for tillage, grazing, forestry or other uses—became the basis for land grants. Further important changes took place immediately after World War II. In 1947, land that the province considered inadequate to support a family was withdrawn from settlement. This included over half of the crown lands in the province. In 1948, "a land-classification scheme was devised which closed most of northern Alberta to agricultural settlement," except for grazing leases. Only a few areas with agricultural potential were opened when demand existed, such as near Fort Vermilion, the main area of new settlement in Alberta after about 1950. In the end, this new policy was never tested under boom conditions. Following an increase in 1946–47, there was relatively little settlement in the Peace River country, and in the 1950s the province withdrew further land from settlement. This period of inactivity ended in the mid 1960s when an optimistic agricultural outlook stimulated new settlement both north and south of the Peace River.[50]

During the interwar years, land ownership was a touchstone for a range of social, economic and political issues. Its use as part of relief programmes demonstrated its place in the provision of social welfare, and its overall function in enhancing individual and corporate capital accumulation showed its economic significance. While many people criticized the homestead system because it encouraged dispersed settlement, such settlement was simultaneously celebrated by many Canadians as evidence of freedom and a sense of adventure. So too, speculative ambitions and public enthusiasm for homesteading during boom times easily swamped more rational land policy objectives. During "the tidal wave of settlement" in the late 1920s any and all settlement was welcomed as an endorsement of the Peace River country's resources and its future.[51] Homesteading also continued to focus the social ideals of individualism and the use of public land to aid private capital accumulation. It also had powerful economic supporters. Even during the Depression, the NAR pressed the province to increase settlement in the Peace River country to stimulate traffic over its lines. Local commercial interests also demanded increased land settlement, and certain services and businesses, especially those related to farm machinery and building, often depended on new settlement for economic viability.[52]

For some people, the decline of homesteading in the 1930s not only signalled the end of the economic opportunities presented by pioneering but foretold fundamental change in the social and political character of Canadian society. Sympathizing with the theories of Frederick Jackson Turner (the American historian who had argued that the "frontier" was a process that brought democracy, innovation and individualism), the University of Alberta historian, A.L. Burt, saw the withering away of homesteading in northern Alberta as a profound social challenge. As he wrote in 1930, "the last frontier in North America is closing with the disappearance of free land up north, with the dying of the pioneer urge in our society, and with our decision to bar the doors against peasants from central and south-eastern Europe." While he recognized that homesteading would continue to take place, "we are coming to the end of the road," and he questioned if Canadian society, without pioneering and a constant stream of new arrivals, could continue to be democratic. Without homesteading, he feared that the society would become politically polarized between rich and poor, and he worried about a more rigid society developing, one that might lose "its plastic character and harden down."[53] While not all Canadians would have agreed with Burt's "frontierist" phrasing or his pessimism, they would have recognized that his concerns were significant ones for Canadian society. At least for a time, such anxieties were subsumed by the radical reshaping of Alberta's society and economy after World War II. For northern Alberta in general, and the Peace River country in particular, changes in transportation, patterns of settlement, technology, standard of living and diversification of the economy would create new and different issues and concerns.

# 10 Farming in the Peace River Country

FROM THE TIME THE FIRST BOXCAR of grain was shipped, Peace River country farmers had a love affair with wheat. Despite periodic upswings in livestock numbers and some problems with grain growing, production of cereal crops—primarily wheat and oats—remained the cornerstone of farming in the Peace River country. Such farming required suitable land and a complex transportation, marketing and mechanical infrastructure. In 1923, Donald Albright wrote that "agriculture in the Peace River country has never yet been on a permanent, stable foundation." And as geographer Henry Leppard commented in 1935, subsequent events supported this observation because the "good times" in the late 1920s and early 1930s had "without exception" occurred when world agricultural prices had soared or when railway construction or large numbers of new settlers had created temporary local markets. While many of the settlers admitted that the region had been settled "years too soon," Leppard noted that they continued to produce wheat for export in competition with wheat growers elsewhere in Canada who were "more advantageously placed."[1]

While agriculture in the Peace River country reflected the economics of farming in a district remote from markets, it was not isolated from broader currents in the agricultural history of Canada. Both federal and provincial governments played an important role in northern farm development, although they were not always successful in having their views accepted. As before 1920, both levels of government continued to facilitate agriculture by creating a framework for its development. Land surveys were ongoing after

World War I to prepare land for settlement, while the scientific classification of soils undertaken with government sponsorship encouraged more rational agricultural development. Although the federal government conducted soil surveys in forested farm areas in Saskatchewan and Alberta in 1920, systematic inventorying of soil resources began only at the end of the decade when the Alberta government financed surveys through the University of Alberta and the Alberta Research Council. These studies showed that there was less good farm land left in the Peace River country than was popularly assumed, and this assisted government in directing future settlement towards areas with the best farming potential. The federal government also provided financial support for this work, and although the Depression and then World War II slowed progress, soil surveying expanded rapidly after 1945.[2]

Government research and educational programmes also assisted agricultural development. Testing and plant breeding at the federal experimental farm at Beaverlodge and the substation at Fort Vermilion continued to help integrate northern Alberta into the Canadian economy by identifying and developing plant varieties profitable in export markets and suited to local conditions. Generally, the Beaverlodge farm aimed to find "the underlying principles requisite to an intelligent understanding of northern cropping problems." This included charting weather conditions, conducting livestock feeding experiments and distributing certified seed. Effort was also directed towards identifying and testing earlier maturing varieties of cereal and horticultural plants and crossing varieties to produce crops that would better suit local conditions. "Illustration Stations" were also operated on private farms at various locations in northern Alberta and British Columbia to field test new varieties. The Fort Vermilion substation carried out similar, but more modest, projects focussed on the particular needs of its district.[3]

The Alberta Department of Agriculture also attempted to encourage better farming practices. While it only operated for a short time, a demonstration farm built at Athabasca in 1913 helped educate farmers about sound agricultural methods and the value of livestock. In the early 1920s, the department also applied extension methods of education. It offered short courses on mixed farming in conjunction with a "demonstration train." Consisting of railway cars fitted up with farming displays, the first train visited northern Alberta in 1915 when it stopped at High Prairie, then the end of steel. Another train visited a number of centres in the Peace River country in 1921. The Department of Agriculture also appointed district agriculturalists throughout the province to provide "scientific instruction and practical self-help" and to implement the department's programmes and policies at the community level. A district agriculturalist was engaged at Grande Prairie in 1923 and others were later appointed in other locations, including a francophone to assist French-speaking settlers at Falher.[4] Such work was supplemented by private endeavour, such as the CPR Department of Immigration and Colonization. On behalf of the NAR, it ran an extension service that offered advice about farming methods and production. As one railway official argued in 1927, most farmers did not keep abreast of "modern methods" to control soil erosion and weeds, and that year the railway's extension worker visited about 500 farmers to give them information on these and other matters.[5]

## — Growing Grain in the Peace River Country

The climate of the Peace River country was a little more variable, precipitation was slightly less and the frost-free period was somewhat shorter than on the southern prairies. Rain often came in the fall and interfered with the harvest, but almost one-half of the precipitation came in May through August, making it timely for cereal crop growth. The summers were hot, and the long days in these northern latitudes effectively lengthened the growing season.[6] While some districts contained darker soils with higher humus content, many areas, especially those with heavy tree cover, tended to have heavier and slightly less productive grey-wooded soils. The latter were not as well suited to wheat, and while they benefited from forage crops that added nitrogen, they were excellent for coarse grains and livestock operations.[7]

Although climatic and soil conditions created difficulties in some years, they did not prohibit crop production similar to that in the Edmonton district and yields could be spectacular in favourable years. For farmers in the Peace River country, marketing problems often posed a greater challenge than did the natural limits on production. Shipping costs were high for all farmers, especially those in fringe communities. In 1930, the CNR estimated that "the practical limit for hauling grain" was about 16 kilometres. In theory, wheat growing areas developed within this "railway zone," while those further away specialized in feed crops (such as fodder, oats and barley) with less acreage in wheat.[8] Despite this idealized model, many farmers in fringe areas still grew considerable amounts of wheat. In addition to the already higher freight rates to national and international markets, these farmers also had to pay to have their grain moved to the railhead. While these costs had been extremely high

— Table 10-1

Farm Size, and Acreage in Wheat and Oats,
Peace River Country, 1921–1946

| | # of Occupied Farms | Acreage | Improved Acreage | | |
|---|---|---|---|---|---|
| | | | Total | Wheat | Oats |
| 1921 | 3,578 | 879,945 | 243,570 | 58,548 | 84,690 |
| 1926 | 2,796 | 857,154 | 308,232 | 128,735 | 73,001 |
| 1931 | 6,974 | 1,804,418 | 674,179 | 305,922 | 150,206 |
| 1936 | 8,671 | 2,359,863 | 942,314 | 321,495 | 234,686 |
| 1941 | 8,406 | 2,630,102 | 1,167,773 | 368,437 | 262,919 |
| 1946 | 7,134 | 2,528,902 | 1,270,354 | 421,293 | 301,902 |

Source: G.A. Willis, "Development of Transportation in the Peace River Region," 44, 51. Compiled from Census data for Census Divisions 16 and Peace River portions of Census Division 15.

in some districts in the early 1920s, they had apparently fallen by the late 1930s. Nonetheless, farmers still paid at least an additional 7 to 10 cents per bushel to truck grain to the railhead. While these costs could be absorbed when grain prices were high, they created significant problems during periods of low prices.[9]

While most acreage was in oats in the first years of settlement, wheat quickly became the major farm export from the Peace River country. As shown in Table 10-1, wheat production had gained a lead over oats by 1926, and production rose steadily, especially following the settlement boom of the late 1920s. Although it never enjoyed the dominance that it had on the southern prairies, wheat retained its primacy among the Peace River country's farm exports. In 1931, about 306,000 tonnes of wheat were exported from the Peace River country.[10] Subsequently, the volume of grain exports declined slightly relative to livestock, but from 1932 until 1946 it remained the largest export. In 1936, when grain made up 90 percent of NAR outbound freight shipments, the largest shipping points were Grande Prairie, Spirit River, Sexsmith and Dawson Creek, British Columbia. Showing that the "railway zone" in the Peace River country was larger than the ideal, grain was collected at these points from a considerable distance. Grain from Valhalla, for example, was shipped to market through Sexsmith, nearly 40 kilometres away.[11]

Despite its steady expansion, wheat farming in the Peace River country faced several problems. One of the major difficulties was that wheat varieties which met Canadian export standards matured too slowly in northern latitudes. While the development of Marquis wheat had created hopes that the Peace River country would become a great wheat-producing area like the southern plains, it was soon found that Marquis matured too slowly under northern conditions, and the harvest was often incomplete when fall rains or winter arrived. Even though colour, milling qualities and protein content had made Marquis the Canadian standard for export-quality wheat by the interwar years, Peace River country farmers were forced to grow other earlier maturing varieties. However, the colour of some of these varieties earned lower grades, while others were susceptible to certain diseases or had other shortcomings such as weak straw. Among these varieties were Garnet and Reward, introduced in 1926 and 1928 respectively. An additional problem arose when scientific studies at the University of Alberta in the late 1930s established that wheat produced on grey soils had lower quality protein than that grown on black and brown soils. While Peace River country boosters charged that these findings were biased and uninformed, this evidence reinforced the search for replacement varieties. Despite extensive testing and experimentation, the ideal wheat variety for the Peace River country had not yet been found by the end of World War II. Even so, wheat continued to be the most important cash crop in the region, and as shown in Table 10-1, acreage seeded to wheat grew steadily.[12]

Despite the growing importance of wheat, oats continued to be a significant crop. Better suited to the Peace River country's climate and soils, its use as forage and feed gave it further advantages. Since horses remained important in Peace River country farming well into the 1930s, large quantities were needed for feed. But feed oats were a low-priced commodity, and the lack of a large local cash market in combination with high shipping costs lessened their importance in farm income. Higher cash returns could be had with seed oats, and such production was boosted by the formation (with provincial government assistance) of the Peace River Co-operative Seed Growers' Association in Grande Prairie in 1928. Although involved with all types of grain, the association initially concentrated on seed oats. It operated a seed cleaning plant and helped promote the reputation and marketing of members' crops. Returns from seed sales were also enhanced through the production of registered seed oats, which steadily grew in importance in the Grande Prairie district in the 1930s. The quality of Peace River country seed oats was high, and prairie governments purchased it for distribution to drought victims on the southern prairies. In 1932, Saskatchewan purchased about 900,000 bushels, and Alberta made a substantial purchase in 1934 as well.[13]

## ▬ Mixed Farming

The production of seed oats was part of the search by Peace River country farmers for profitable alternatives to wheat. The same quest was demonstrated by seed production from forage crops such as clover, alfalfa and various types of grasses. The Beaverlodge experimental farm stressed research into forage crops in an effort to promote their use for livestock feed and soil management. More direct stimulus came from government programmes that made forage seed available to farmers at one-half the market price. Often marketed through the Peace River Co-operative Seed Growers' Association, forage crop seed production became significant in some areas in the Peace River country. By 1942, the areas around McLennan and Girouxville produced about 50 percent of Alberta's alfalfa seed. In addition to helping improve grey soils, these crops were more profitable than wheat. One estimate in 1945 claimed, seemingly with considerable exaggeration, that alfalfa seed returned $78 per acre, versus $18 per acre for milling wheat. Another popular forage crop, sweet clover, was also widely grown for seed around the towns of Peace River and Athabasca. By 1945, the latter area was touted as the largest sweet clover producing area in Canada. A sideline that developed along with forage crops was beekeeping, and by World War II the Peace River country had become an important honey producing area.[14]

The expansion of seed growing and forage crop production was a partial vindication of those who argued that the success of Peace River country farming depended on mixed farming. This assumption—so popular everywhere in Canada since the late nineteenth century—was said to have even greater merit in northern regions. The Alberta Department of Agriculture was a strong proponent of mixed farming in general, but it saw it as especially valuable for northern districts where value could be added to coarse grains and feed grade wheat by using them for local livestock production. Distance to markets and extensive grey soils in northern Alberta further justified this policy. As the department noted in 1931, "cheap grains and roughages" produced in areas remote from markets were best marketed in the "more concentrated form of beef, pork and dairy products." Such views were also endorsed by town boards of trade, newspaper editors and agricultural experts in northern Alberta. All characterized mixed farming as a route to stable economic development and expanded economic activity through processing and local use of livestock and poultry products. Moreover, as Donald Albright commented in 1923, it was also a way to stimulate local capital accumulation since "too much money is [now] sent out of the district to buy foodstuffs that are brought in from the outside."[15]

Despite such arguments about the value of mixed farming, northern farmers did not readily take on livestock as a permanent part of their farm operations. Although there was an upward trend after 1924 in hog production (and after 1930 in cattle production), farmers showed relatively little sustained enthusiasm for raising livestock and poultry. As one CPR official observed in 1930, farmers were in poor financial shape because of low wheat prices "which is the only commodity that they are interested in. Mixed farming is practically an unknown factor in the Peace River country at the present time." Although fringe areas produced more livestock than more established districts, farmers generally did not want to commit themselves to raising livestock. Instead, they turned to it during times of low grain prices or when they had damp grain that was difficult to sell. But when grain prices—and consequently feed prices—were high, farmers usually reduced their livestock and sold their grain for cash. Raising hogs and cattle was thus ancillary to grain growing and not an element in a long-range strategy of diversified farm production. High grain prices and attendant feed shortages in 1926 and 1937, for example, led to the shipment of high numbers of cattle and hogs to market.[16]

In this environment, farmers were reluctant to invest in quality breeding stock or in suitable pastures, barns and livestock equipment. "Mixed" breeds were common and cattle were often sent to market poorly finished because they had been pastured on unbroken land with little nutritional feed. Similarly, hogs were often kept in poorly constructed buildings where production suffered. As one district agriculturalist noted in 1937, Peace River country farmers treated hogs as "an in-and-out game" related to grain prices. So too, dairy cattle (which required the most expensive equipment and buildings for economical production) were usually inferior breeds. Housed in poor conditions, they were often kept only to meet the needs of the family for milk and butter.[17]

Conditions during World War II confirmed these attitudes. When British markets were cut off from Europe, hog and cattle prices rose. A wet fall in 1940 also left farmers with huge quantities of tough grain on hand. Moreover, government programmes encouraged a shift from grain to livestock production by subsidizing farmers who took land out of wheat production and converted it to forage crops or summerfallow. Consequently, large numbers of cattle and hogs were brought into the Peace River country in 1941, and the number of cattle in feedlots rose 60 percent over the year before. As agricultural economist Elizabeth Low found in 1942, under these conditions, hog raising in the Peace River country used capital more efficiently than grain growing, and greater earnings could be had with less capital and "practically the same labor." In a familiar pattern, however, livestock production began to fall when grain prices rose after 1944.[18]

The failure of livestock production to emerge as a stable element in Peace River country farming reflected a number of local and national conditions. In Canada, dairying and hog and poultry production tended to be located near large urban markets, but local markets were small in the Peace River country and export production had to compete with larger and better established operations close to the major Canadian markets. Proximity to packing plants, creameries and cold storage plants was also important for the economical production of livestock and poultry. Although there was ongoing discussion by farmers and farm advisors about the need for creameries in northern Alberta, local dairy production was too limited and uneven for them to be successful.[19] While they operated intermittently at various towns, by the early 1940s the only creameries in the Peace River country were at Grande Prairie, Valhalla and Peace River. Those in Peace River and Grande Prairie experienced uneven times, although the co-operative at Valhalla was more successful. Because the district was remote from consumer markets, a creamery was established in 1920 to process raw milk (for which there was no market) into butter that could be easily shipped to other parts of the Peace River country. It was a small operation, with butter production averaging about 45,000 kilograms per year between 1924 and 1932. A cheese factory (opened in 1939) near Debolt by local Mennonite farmers completed the dairy processing facilities in the Peace River country in the early 1940s. Similarly, while there were a few small local meat processing facilities, the closest meat packing plant was in Edmonton. Shipping livestock such a distance was costly and the animals suffered weight loss during the long haul to market. Although farmers tended to blame the railway for inadequate watering and feeding of animals during the trip to Edmonton, tests at the Beaverlodge substation showed that improved feeding practices would help the animals to withstand the trip better.[20]

The lack of local processing facilities and the problems associated with shipping livestock long distances were only two of several difficulties faced by livestock producers in the Peace River country. Heavy snow in most years made winter ranging of cattle difficult, and cattle consequently had to be kept in a barn or feedlot where they could be fed during the long winter. The huge amounts of straw and hay this required represented a highly labour-intensive undertaking. So too, limited water supply held back livestock production in many districts. Most farms obtained water from natural streams because the deep wells required in many areas were costly to dig and often produced poor quality water. Several dry years had created critical conditions by 1945 and some farmers were hauling water between 12 and 30 kilometres for their stock, a task that did little to endear livestock production to them once hog and cattle prices began to decline. Although farmers lobbied governments to construct community wells, such programmes were not practicable in areas of dispersed farm settlement. Instead, the province encouraged the construction of "dug outs," deep ponds about 3.5 metres deep, to store seasonal run-off and surface water. In 1945, the provincial department of agriculture began paying Peace River country farmers a subsidy of up to $100 for construction of dugouts to help improve "home conditions" and "assist and stabilize the livestock production" in the district.[21]

The particular difficulties of raising livestock in the Peace River country compounded the long-held prairie view that livestock were a burden on the farm. Peace River country farmers used the popular prairie term "chores" to describe the constant work and care that livestock and poultry required.[22] While this contributed to their bias towards grain farming, marketing and other local limitations made livestock production less profitable than growing grain, especially wheat. Agricultural economists B.K. Acton and C.C. Spence found in 1942 (a year of high livestock prices) that "grain growing over a period of years had been more profitable" than any other type of farming. Grain farmers, regardless of the district they lived in, had made greater financial progress than livestock farmers. This evidence indicated why farmers, despite the problems associated with growing wheat in the Peace River country, clung to it as the best means of making a living.[23]

—— **Fringe and Centre**
*Two Sides of the Farm Economy*
By World War II, significant differences between farming in fringe and longer established districts had come to characterize the Peace River country. This was demonstrated by the 1942 findings of Acton and Spence who based their

investigation on field interviews with over 400 farmers, analysis of statistical material such as census and tax returns, as well as various documentary sources. They studied the Bear Lake district as typical of those areas that had been settled immediately after 1910. By 1942 it had a stable farm economy and was "far removed from the pioneer stage."[24] It included the towns of Grande Prairie, Sexsmith, Clairmont and Wembley. At time of settlement its open dark soils required minimal clearing. Other areas in the Peace River country with these characteristics included the Spirit River, Fairview and Grimshaw districts. The fringe areas Acton and Spence studied were the Battle River, Debolt, Hines Creek, Wapiti and Lymburn districts. These areas were remote from the railway and had largely been settled during the interwar years, generally by poorly capitalized settlers. With the exception of parts of the Battle River district, these fringe districts were heavily treed and had grey-wooded soils. Historically, wheat yielded 20 bushels per acre and oats 37 bushels per acre on the darker soils in the Bear Lake district, while the grey soils in the fringe districts produced 17 bushels of wheat and 30 bushels of oats per acre.[25]

Acton and Spence showed that easy access to transportation and marketing facilities favoured the oldest communities. In the Bear Lake district, no farmer was more than 25 kilometres from a railway station, while this distance varied between about 55 and 120 kilometres in the fringe areas. While there were numerous graded market roads in the older settled district, roads in the fringe areas were often little more than trails through the bush. Better access to towns and social services such as schools and hospitals marked an important social and economic advantage of farmers in the Bear Lake district over those in the fringe areas. The Bear Lake district's soil and locational advantages were compounded by higher initial capitalization that had allowed farmers to make financial progress more quickly. Consequently, farms in the Bear Lake district were larger and averaged 429 acres, of which 70 percent, or about 300 acres, was broken. In contrast, farms in the fringe areas averaged 317 acres, of which 116 acres were broken. Not surprisingly, incomes were higher in the Bear Lake district where invested capital was over $12,000 per farm, compared to just over $4,400 in the fringe areas. In keeping with this pattern, farm homes and other buildings in the Bear Lake district were of higher quality and were better maintained, and despite their cost, many farmers also had wells. Although some of these farmers rented additional land, most, like those in the fringe, farmed only the land that they owned.[26]

Acton and Spence employed a conventional classification of farms as either commercial or subsistence. A commercial farm was one where farm production was sufficient to meet operating and living expenses, while a subsistence farm was one where income from outside the farm (usually wage labour) was essential to meet expenses. All the farms in the Bear Lake district were commercial farms, as were a majority of those in the fringe area.[27] But revealing different environments and history, commercial farms differed significantly between the two areas because those in the fringe typically emphasized livestock production. While most farmers in the Bear Lake district kept some livestock, the great majority earned most of their income from grain, especially wheat. Most also had significant acreage in oats, and only a small proportion of land was in other cereal crops (usually rye and barley) and hay. But whether they grew grain or raised livestock, the most successful farmers in both the Bear Lake district and the fringe were those with the largest amount of cleared land in crop. Regardless of location, commercial grain farms were more highly capitalized and required at least 150 acres in crop to be profitable, while farms concentrating on livestock could be profitable with only about 100 acres in crop production. While many of these commercial farms also benefited from off-farm labour, it was not as necessary for them as it was for subsistence farms. In this sense, all of these commercial farmers had moved in varying degrees beyond the pioneer economy of makeshifts.[28]

While commercial farms operated in both fringe and older established districts, Acton and Spence found subsistence farms only in the fringe. At between 177 and 241 acres (of which only between 48 and 66 acres were cleared and broken), these farms were smaller than commercial farms and had less cleared land. In general, fringe subsistence settlers had started farming with inadequate capital, and only after 12 years of farming had they begun to accumulate the amount of capital they ideally should have had when they first began farming. These subsistence farms demonstrated great variety, and it was apparent that there was a greater range of pioneer experience and tactics employed to make ends meet than in the more established districts. Acton and Spence identified three types of subsistence farms in the fringe: self-sufficient farms (where the farm produced most of the farmer's income), pensioner farms (where pensions—usually military—provided more than 50 percent of farm returns) and part-time farms, where off-farm receipts accounted for more than 50 percent of farm returns. Of these, part-time farms were the commonest type of subsistence farms.[29]

The greater diversity in pioneer experience was most graphically shown by the role that off-farm labour played in the varying net worth (the total value of all assets less liabilities) of subsistence farms. Off-farm labour accounted for about twice the increase in net worth of part-time farmers than it did for self-sufficient farmers. The pensioner group, which had almost no off-farm labour, experienced declining net worth. In the case of both part-time and self-sufficient farms, average annual outside income was equal to the average annual increase in net worth. Growth of farm capital on these types of subsistence farms thus came from wage labour, not farming.[30]

While fringe subsistence farmers still often had to go far afield to find wage work by World War II, many were now also able to find it closer to home. By 1942—when economic conditions had improved—Acton and Spence observed that people performed a wide range of off-farm work. It included predictable jobs such as custom threshing, trapping, road work, and lumbering, as well as less expected ones such as clerking in a store and working as government inspectors, minor administrators and in various skilled and semi-skilled trades. Somewhat surprisingly, subsistence farmers who had the largest farms in these fringe areas earned the highest off-farm incomes. As Acton and Spence explained, this nonfarm income enabled these farmers to purchase equipment to farm a larger acreage. This equipment in turn was used to earn nonfarm income on road construction projects or through custom farm work for neighbours. Indeed, Acton and Spence found that as the "non-farm income increased, the farm business, in itself, had a greater earning capacity." This direct correlation between increased farm net worth and increased nonfarm income was further enhanced because off-farm income also raised capital for land clearing, which in turn contributed further to the economic strength of the farm.[31]

## Farm Work

While there were many similarities in conditions on farms across the prairies, climate, lower incomes, stage of development and distance to market came together to create some differences in the Peace River country. One difference was the relative lack of power equipment on Peace country farms. While the low capitalization of many settlers in northern Alberta reinforced the economy of makeshifts during the years of clearing and breaking the land, it also restricted farm mechanization. In the interwar years, the average farm in the Peace River country had at least several teams of horses, a breaking plough and a tillage plough, several sets of different types of harrows (possibly toothed and disc types), a mower, rake, seed drill and perhaps some seed cleaning equipment such as a fanning mill. While large farms would also have had a binder

*This Fahler area family proudly showed off their horses.*
*Not Dated.* OB10878 PAA.

(to cut the grain and form it into sheaves), small farmers often shared one. Like many farmers on the southern prairies, Peace River country farmers rarely had threshing machines, and most often relied on hired custom threshing outfits. In some cases, a group of farmers co-operatively purchased a threshing machine.

Overall, Peace River country farmers relied to a greater extent on human and animal labour than was typical on prairie farms, especially in the southern parts of the plains where tractor and truck use had grown significantly by 1930.[32] This lower level of mechanization was still apparent by 1941 and it marked an important difference between farming in the Peace River country and many other parts of the prairies. Mechanization of prairie agriculture involved the creation of economical units of production, which meant that it offered fewer advantages on farms where cultivated acreage was small and incomes were low. In 1937, although tractors were being used in some parts of the Peace River country for field work, horses were more popular because they were "the most adaptable power unit for all seasons." In any case, most Peace River country farmers could not afford the high initial capital investment required for a tractor and the replacement of horse-drawn field equipment. Moreover, while horses could be maintained on farm-grown grain and forage, tractors required ongoing cash outlay for oil, gas and repairs. Thus, in the mid 1930s, horses were "not just livestock" on Peace River country farms but an

*Threshing the crop in 1923, Fort Vermilion.* OB10,729 PAA

essential source of farm power. Tractors, trucks and automobiles were too costly in a region with "good forage, poor roads and little capital."[33]

Farmers in the Peace River country nonetheless applied mechanization as far as they could given their income and type and size of operation. Steam engines were used for threshing almost from the beginning of grain farming in northern Alberta. During and after World War II, mechanization of farming increased rapidly, stimulated by the general labour shortages during the war as well as the enlistment of farmers and their children. In 1943, the district agriculturalist reported from the Peace River country that since farmers were "feeling the pinch of labour shortages," they were adopting "modern machinery and labour-saving devices." As well, higher farm commodity prices made new equipment more affordable, and the war itself provided a model—as a popular cliche expressed it, "mechanization will win the war and mechanization will win the peace." Between 1941 and 1946, the number of farms with tractors doubled in the Peace River country and began to approach the provincial average.[34]

The lower level of mechanization before World War II meant that farming in northern Alberta echoed an earlier way of Canadian rural life. But while such farming involved more physical labour, the cycles of life were much like those found elsewhere on the prairies. Work began in the very early morning and people worked throughout the day until mid evening when livestock chores were finished. No season of the year was free from work. Women attended to domestic tasks in the home, tended the garden and looked after livestock and poultry. They also often worked in the fields during seeding, harvesting and haying. Men worked equally hard. In early spring, harness and machinery were repaired in preparation for the coming summer. Seed grain was cleaned, and seeding began in late April or early May and sometimes lasted a month. From the middle of May until the end of July, ploughing, summer-fallowing and breaking new land dominated farm life. From mid July until August, the hard work of haying took over, and from mid August until mid September, the crops were cut. Threshing usually began in September and could continue until mid October or even later in those years when fall rains slowed the work. People also began to get ready for winter by insulating the house and hauling wood for fuel. By mid November the snow had come and winter tasks began: hauling grain and livestock to market, cutting wood for fuel and putting up ice for the coming summer.[35]

### —— Farming on Indian Reserves

As had been the case before World War I, some Indians living on reserves continued to see farming as a way of meeting broader economic change. In 1938 at Wabasca, for example, the Headman told Napoleon L'Heureux, the Indian Agent, that "successive failures" of trapping in the past few years had forced people "to do some farming which has helped them to get along." The band had a population of about 700, 455 of whom lived nearby in the district or on the several reserves. L'Heureux reported that:

> These Indians were trappers and making good at it; they are not lazy, are intelligent and are doing much to help themselves out of distressing circumstances. For the past three years many have turned towards agri-culture to make a living; they have made larger and better gardens; harvested more potatoes, those who could afford it have bought a cow or two which they milk; small horses have likewise been purchased and with them small fields have been tilled on which crops and oats and wheat were harvested: the wheat the Indians use for food and the oats to be fed to their horses.[36]

While these were familiar stories, farming on Indian reserves in northern Alberta did not develop significantly before 1945. Like much Euro-Canadian farming in fringe areas of the Peace River country, Indian reserve farming continued to be only one element in an economy of makeshifts. But unlike many Euro-Canadian farmers, most Indians who farmed on reserves did not move beyond a subsistence level. The poor start in farming on reserves before 1916 inhibited future success, while limited capital, the small size of arable land holdings and a lack of farm equipment further restricted the development of sustainable agricultural operations.

By the 1930s farming on most of the reserves in the Lesser Slave Agency was, to all intents and purposes, at a standstill in comparison to Euro-Canadian farming operations in the Peace River country and the Lesser Slave Lake district. At the Swan River reserve in 1933, eight people were farming 138 acres, an average of 18 acres per person. At Driftpile reserve in 1938, 481 acres were seeded by 22 Indians, or just over 21 acres per person. These operations were smaller than even the most marginal Euro-Canadian subsistence farms in the Peace River country. A few people had made more substantial progress; at Old Wives Lake—then the best arable land in the agency—255 acres were under cultivation. Of the 48 people on the reserve, three families were farming full time, and the largest farm unit had 120 acres under cultivation. By 1940, tilled land on the Lesser Slave Lake reserves had also increased, and about 800 acres at Driftpile, 500 acres at Sucker Creek and 250 acres at Swan River were seeded. At Horse Lakes, farming was far more limited, as it was at Clear Hills where the Indians were described as "progressing slowly in farming." On those reserves where cereal crops were planted, oats predominated and only a few acres of wheat were grown. Yields were often respectable, and occasionally very good. Many of the reserves also had gardens (mainly planted to potatoes), some livestock (almost exclusively cattle and horses) and poultry that supplemented crop production. Hay lands also continued to be a valuable source of income. In the 1930s they were often the reserves' greatest natural asset and formed one of the "main sources of living."[37]

Several factors contributed to the lack of expansion in reserve agriculture. While the province provided educational programmes for Euro-Canadian farmers, similar assistance was not extended to Indian farmers by the Department of Indian Affairs. In the Lesser Slave Lake agency, the Indian Agent looked after farm instruction, which meant that he was available only to those closest to the agency office. The agency clerk also served for a time as farm instructor, but as was noted in 1932, he could not adequately perform both jobs at once. More significantly, too little land was available for reserve farming. While the amount of cropped land on Indian reserves was small by any measure, most reserves, in terms of export-based prairie cereal production, were unsustainable units. The size of the reserves was fixed, totalling 640 acres for each family of five or 160 acres per person if held in severalty. This acreage included arable as well as timber, hay and waste lands. In addition, although the population on the reserves grew through natural increase and the consolidation of population as other reserves were sold, the size of the reserves remained the same. Moreover, it is now apparent that the original surveys of some of the reserves in severalty were smaller in size than had originally been stipulated.[38] But unlike Euro-Canadian farm settlers, Indians were unable to expand their land holdings. They were prohibited from homesteading and could not own land privately unless they were enfranchised and removed from treaty. Thus, while they were expected to participate in a market economy, they were denied access to the land holdings necessary to compete.

So too, the ability of Indians to acquire additional or better farm equipment was limited. Indian Affairs was generally reluctant to purchase farm equipment, and when it did so, the equipment was often inadequate. On the Lesser Slave reserves, all of the equipment on each reserve often amounted to no more than that found on a single farm in the Peace River country.[39] The Indians complained constantly about this, and the agents frequently noted in their monthly reports that new or better equipment was essential because haying, harvesting and seeding had been held up because of broken, obsolete or inadequate farm equipment. At Driftpile reserve in 1933, it was noted that the binder was in "awful shape" because it had been stored carelessly—due in part to the fact that it was unused because it was too heavy for the reserve horses to pull. As a result, Agent L'Heureux recommended that the department purchase new binders for the Driftpile and Swan River reserves because the Indians "had to wait till the White people are through with their grain to hire Binders, and by the time they have paid for twine, threshing and hire of Binders they have nothing left for their work, and they can't make their living out of farming."[40] In addition, none of the reserves had threshing machines, but custom threshing was often unsatisfactory. Custom threshers charged high rates because most of the reserves were located in isolated areas and their small and scattered fields meant that threshing equipment had to be moved constantly during the day. In many cases, the isolation of these reserves also meant that marketing farm production was impractical. At Wabasca, Agent L'Heureux recommended that the Indians raise livestock rather than grain. The small acreage in crops did not justify the purchase of harvesting equipment and the only mill in the area was at the Roman Catholic mission, where milling rates were high. Under these conditions, L'Heureux believed that stock raising was the only feasible prospect because the animals could be herded to the nearest railway terminal, nearly 150 kilometres away.[41]

The limitations of reserve farming in the interwar years reinforced the economy of makeshifts on reserves in northern Alberta. On the reserves along Lesser Slave Lake, people continued to trap and hunt as well as farm. Like Euro-Canadian fringe farmers, Indians formed a permanent local pool of casual labour. They worked on farms, on the railway, and in lumber and fish camps. As well, they sometimes worked on road crews or fought forest fires. And as was noted in 1939, the women also "occasionally tan moose and deer hides to make moccasins and gloves which they exchange at the local store for groceries and dry goods."[42] But the availability of wage work relied to a large extent on the health of the farm economy, and for much of the 1930s farm work was difficult to find. As the Lesser Slave Lake Indian Agent reported in 1934, once the crops were planted on the reserve, the Indians had little to do until haying began. During this "dull period of the year," a few people found work in the fish plant at Faust, and others travelled "as far as Grande Prairie to secure work, bushing and grubbing land." But jobs were "few and small" and wages were even lower than in the previous year and were not "in keeping with present day values." As a result, most people refused to work for such wages and returned to their reserves. By 1938, it was reported that for the first time in a number of years, "Indians could find work brush-cutting and clearing land in the Grande Prairie district and as far north as Berwyn." Jobs increased temporarily during World War II when wartime labour shortages and higher agricultural prices created some farm work for Natives.[43] But these broader changes did not always bring compensatory opportunities. The value of hay and oats, for example, declined in the 1930s as motor trucks were adopted in place of horses. By 1939, local fishing companies around Lesser Slave Lake had begun using trucks for cartage, eliminating a traditional market for fodder oats and hay from nearby reserves. Nor were the components of this economy always complementary. L'Heureux characterized trapping in 1933 as "a drawback to farming as the Indians come back home too late in the spring to work their land sufficiently and to seed in good time and the result is poor crops and frozen grain."[44] And while Euro-Canadians farmers were able either to move steadily away from an economy of makeshifts or abandon farming altogether and find work elsewhere, Indians remained firmly connected to local conditions. Thus their standard of living relative to most Euro-Canadian settlers declined, and they remained more vulnerable to the economic dislocation that became more serious during the 1940s. The mechanization of farming in the Peace River country after 1945 led to declining casual farm work at the same time that trapping incomes were falling because of low prices and disappearing wildlife.

— **Farming and Nature**

The agricultural settlement of the Peace River country brought major changes to the landscape. The land survey imposed a grid of roads replacing earlier trails, towns replaced scattered settlement patterns, land was cleared of trees and broken, and new plants were introduced. While these changes were generally welcomed as a mark of progress, it was occasionally contended that land clearing needed to be controlled. Such arguments invariably cited the erosion and environmental disaster that had befallen the southern plains after World War I. While water and soil erosion also took place in the Peace River country in the 1930s, it was never as serious as in the southern parts of the province.[45] As part of the general trend towards greater control over land settlement, the southern experience entrenched calls for controls over the destruction of naturally occurring trees and landscapes to safeguard the "future of the community."[46] Whatever merit such concerns had, they had little appeal for settlers whose objective was to eliminate trees and brush as quickly as possible and get land into production.

In the earliest years of Euro-Canadian settlement, brush lands had often been cleared by burning them in the fall. Burning heavily treed areas was less effective and ultimately saved little labour because the half-burnt timber and roots still had to be pulled out. Burning also destroyed already limited humus in grey soils as well as timber useful for building and fuel. An operator from Calgary did custom clearing with crawler tractors in the Peace River country in the late 1920s, but most settlers had too little capital to employ such services and instead cleared the land by hand. At least part of the capital brought by settlers went into land clearing, and it continued to swallow capital produced by ongoing farm production. Although new equipment was invented (sometimes in the Peace River country) to ease the task, most trees were cut by hand and roots were taken out by "that instrument of torture commonly known as a grub hoe." Though laborious, this met the needs of cash poor homesteaders. In contrast to other methods of farm expansion (such as buying or renting more land), land clearing was the most popular way of increasing crop acreage in the Peace River country. But progress was slow; in 1942, Acton and Spence found that an average of 4.5 acres per year were cleared and broken in wooded fringe districts over a 14-year period. In lighter wooded districts, such as parts of the Battle River country, about eight acres per year could be cleared and broken.[47]

These conditions changed during World War II when higher incomes and increasing use of tractors permitted faster land clearing. The war also strengthened this commitment to mechanization as a means of conquering the northern forest. The construction of the Alaska Highway had confirmed in northern Alberta an attitude prevalent everywhere in North America—any engineering project was feasible if sufficient technical resources were applied to it. By the end of World War II, higher wartime commodity prices had provided farmers with the income to use power equipment for clearing. Labour shortages and "the use of mechanized machinery in wartime for both combat and construction," caused settlers to become "more power-equipment conscious." It was claimed that over 51,000 acres of land in the Peace River country were cleared and broken in 1946, and in 1948 the estimate stood at 85,000 acres.[48]

Postwar enthusiasm for mechanized land clearing and the newfound ability to afford it were most graphically demonstrated in 1945 when the provincial government contracted the Hartman brothers of Seattle to clear and break 100,000 acres in the Peace River country using large bulldozers and other specialized equipment. This cleared land would first be made available to veterans who wanted to farm, and then to children of Alberta farmers. Any land not taken up by these two classes of settlers would be thrown open for general settlement. The project at first targeted the Wanham district (east of Spirit River), but it was anticipated that it would be expanded into other districts as well. The Wanham district was particularly suitable for this undertaking; forest fires had earlier destroyed the largest timber in many locations and the district was relatively close to highways and the railway.[49]

This land clearing project was an overt rejection of the pioneer ideal of steady and incremental farm development. It was characterized with some pride as "the most ambitious scheme of planned settlement ever attempted on the public lands of the province." Soil surveys had determined the suitability of the land for farming, and provisions were made for preservation of some woodlands. Designed as a self-liquidating project, it was linked with the lease system of homesteading that Alberta had recently adopted. Settlers signed a 10-year lease for the cleared land but did not pay any rent during the first three years. In the remaining seven years of the lease, they paid a one-third share of the crop to the government. At the end of the ten-year period, the settlers would receive

*The use of massive equipment was a feature of the Wanham land clearing project. 1950.* PA813/1 PAA.

clear title to the land and would in theory be free of debt. Public costs would be minimal because the contractor was to be paid from the income that the government received from the settler leases. This presumed that the contractor had sufficient capital and credit to meet the high costs of the project until payment was received in the last seven years of the settler's ten-year lease.[50]

The proposal—so seamless in its conception—soon became a costly headache for the provincial government. The Hartman Brothers failed to get the project underway, and a Texas firm that took over also failed to begin work. O.B. Lassiter, owner of a large contracting firm and wheat farm near Lethbridge, then became interested in the project and was given a contract to clear 100,000 acres. Using crawler tractors purchased from War Assets Disposal Corporation and huge breaking equipment of his own design, Lassiter began work in the Wanham district. By 1947, he had cleared 11,000 acres, broken 10,000 more and worked down 4,000 acres to make them ready for seeding. This land was distributed to veterans by means of a lottery. Two smaller Edmonton contractors were also given contracts to clear and break land in the same district. By now, however, Lassiter was in financial difficulty and he and the provincial government were bickering over the project. Technical problems slowed clearing and new equipment for clearing, piling and breaking had to be devised on the spot through trial and error. Recognizing that the costs of the project could not be met by the contractor alone, the province advanced Lassiter $500,000. Even then, he could not cover the high costs involved. In 1948, Lassiter was able to break only 5,000 acres while the other contractors managed to break 2,000. By now the contract had been renegotiated and the province was paying $25 per acre for clearing, breaking and final preparation of the land for farming. The project dragged on for several years. The veterans who had settled the land faced the same problems as all homesteaders did: lack of water, poor buildings, wretched roads and insufficient capital. By 1955, about 230 families were on the land, but many were in financial difficulty. As a consequence, the province was unable to collect the lease fees and recover the funds it had invested in the project.[51]

Despite its failures, the Wanham land clearing project was the apogee of the view that pioneer farming was in part a war with nature, one that could now be won more easily because of modern machinery and organization. After a tour of the project in 1948, L.L. Anthes of the Canadian Manufacturers' Association was ecstatic about the "gargantuan and revolutionary" equipment used in "this tremendous operation" that was "progressively battling nature as far as the eye could reach."[52] Whatever significance people attached to it, the Wanham project was a clear example of how farm development relied on massive environmental change. But wherever it took place, and regardless of how it was achieved, land clearing was predicated on the introduction of a new economy based on the production of crops that were not native to the region. While this process was an integral, and often inevitable, part of the historical migration of people, the movement of European peoples had been accompanied by an especially significant introduction of new plant types.[53] While the introduction of some of these plants was deliberate, unwanted ones also came with these colonists.

Defining a plant as a "weed" is arbitrary. As botanist Herbert Groh wrote in 1937 in his study of weeds in the Peace River country, "a weed" was a plant that "in some person's estimation is out of place. From the standpoint of the plant, it is always in place when it can gain a foothold and meet the competition of other plants, adapt itself to the environment and meet sufficient respite from human interference."[54] The more aggressive of these weeds choked out domesticated plants and also created harvesting difficulties because stooks containing green weeds did not dry evenly. Moreover, seed grain had to be free of weed seeds, while grain sold for milling was discounted by grain buyers if it contained weed seeds. Weeds thus lowered profits and productivity.

When the prairies had been settled by Euro-Canadians in the nineteenth century, settlers had brought many weeds with them. This was usually inadvertent—weeds were caught in parts of farm machinery and mixed with the seed and feed grain brought by the settlers. Along with native and introduced crops that managed to adapt to the newly tilled fields, weeds also prospered. The spread of introduced weeds marked the advance of settlement as surely as did trails, roads and railways, and the same process was repeated in the Peace River country. Although it was common for boosters to claim that the Peace River country was "weed free," this was an exaggeration. By 1918 it was reported that while infestations were still light, only a few fields near Spirit River were free of wild oats "despite vigorous efforts" to control them. By 1927, all weeds common to the prairies were found in the Peace River country, although they were still often localized.[55]

Before World War II, weed control in prairie Canada depended primarily on sowing clean seed, adequate cultivation and regulatory measures. In the Peace River country, it was commonly said that the physical character of the region made regulatory controls especially promising. Citing the potential of the region as a seed growing area, Donald Albright noted in 1932 that "natural barriers" that separated the districts of the Peace River country provided "an opportunity of segregating the [Peace] country from the weed filth of other parts and it might even be possible to have the Peace River country officially declared as a pure seed area, just as other areas have become purebred-sire or tuberculosis free areas." In keeping with such ambitions (and copying a practice used elsewhere on the prairies), municipal districts appointed weed inspectors who tried to control the spread of weeds. They provided information about weed control and even occasionally had weed infested fields ploughed under at the owner's expense. But the frequency with which municipal councils passed stern resolutions about their commitment to enforce weed control measures pointed to the futility of this approach. There was also some conflict over the practicality and popularity of such programmes, and in 1933, for example, the council of the Municipal District of Bear Lake defeated a motion "to instruct the weed inspector to use his full authority."[56]

Demands were also made that the provincial Department of Agriculture ensure that settlers' effects and machinery be clean of weed seeds "before shipment or before arrival in this country." Since the province pointed out that it could not make such inspections beyond its boundaries, the Municipal District of Spirit River ordered its weed inspector in 1927 to carry out such inspections before settlers' effects were allowed to be taken from the train station. In the end, there was no co-ordination between provincial and local governments to develop a uniform prevention strategy on the matter, and while some municipalities carried out "weed work," others did not, and weeds continued to spread throughout the Peace River country. By 1937, wild oats and stinkweed were well established almost everywhere. Given its relatively recent settlement, it was not surprising that "the weed population" in the Peace River country was "still more largely of native species" than was usual on the prairies. But in areas "where grain growing has been followed longest," it was noted that "the percentage is rapidly approaching that in the prairie grain belt." Even in distant Fort Vermilion, while "many of the dreaded noxious weeds" found elsewhere had not yet appeared by 1948, many common prairie weeds as well as a few native ones were prevalent in grain fields.[57]

The failure to control the spread of weeds through cultivation and regulation in part explained the eagerness with which farmers embraced the new chemical controls that appeared during World War II. Of these chemicals, 2–4–D held the greatest promise, and in the hubris of the time it was sometimes anticipated that whole species of unwanted plants could be exterminated. Almost lost in this enthusiasm for chemical controls, more cautious voices argued that chemicals could not be a substitute for good farm practices. As Herbert Groh had observed in 1937, a farmer "cannot afford to lose sight of the fact that the weed is nature's provision for reclaiming from tillage what is not being well maintained by tillage." In what could be an epigram for the history of agriculture, he noted that what the farmer "holds, he holds by virtue of wise and diligent use—the only peaceable possession possible."[58]

— ✦ —

Peace country farmers would have thought it so obvious that farming was a struggle, if not a war, with nature that it required little sustained comment. Like all farmers in western Canada, their success was predicated on changing the landscape by clearing and tilling the land and introducing new plants. The Peace River country also had other similarities with the rest of the prairies, but unique conditions—climate, soils and especially distance to market—increased the burdens faced by Peace River country farmers. To overcome these burdens, farmers there resolutely turned to grain and seed production, which they believed would offer the highest revenues as well as other lifestyle benefits. This ensured that mixed farming, the panacea promoted by the agricultural press and governments everywhere in prairie Canada, remained secondary to grain production in the Peace River country before World War II.

As in all farm communities, there were significant financial differences among farmers in the Peace River country depending on length of time they had farmed and local conditions such as soils, microclimates and initial capitalization. Farmers in the longest settled areas were able to move away relatively quickly from the makeshifts economy of the early settlement days. More recent settlers, many of whom lived in fringe communities, were not able to make this transition so rapidly, and they remained dependent on off-farm labour and debt for financial solvency. Farming on Indian reserves was constrained by too little capital and holdings that were too small, but Indians had few means to overcome these limitations because of their legal status and the rigidity of the reserve system. This provided yet another example of how the gap between Natives and Euro-Canadians, even those who were poor, continued to widen in northern Alberta during the interwar years.

# Society and
# 11 Social Life

*The Peace River Country*

F EW  E URO -C ANADIAN  SETTLERS  in
the Peace River country came with the hope of making a new culture. Instead,
they implanted familiar and comfortable relationships, institutions and
symbols of achievement. In many respects, the public culture of the region in
the interwar years did not differ significantly from that found elsewhere in
Alberta. Like the individualism that shaped economic life, the place of ethnicity
in social life, the use of time, and the regulation of public life took their reference from Canada's most influential metropolitan centres and the evolution of
Canadian and American popular culture. Yet as scholars of frontier North
American development have concluded, the mixing of local (or frontier) and
metropolitan influences was a complex interaction of culture, environment and
place.[1] In this sense, the core values of the Peace River country's dominant
culture and many of its essential elements expressed Anglo-Canadian priorities
and assumptions, and upon this foundation were grafted concerns of special
relevance to the region's particular needs, history and hopes for the future.

## —— A Pure Saxon Stock
Since the late nineteenth century, ethnicity and race, and their connection with
class, were one determinant of how power was distributed in Alberta. In this
context, the Anglo-Saxon character of the Peace River country was often cited
as a measure of the district's quality. Despite their hard work and perseverance,
those who were not Anglo-Saxon (the so-called "foreign element") were not

usually credited with the area's progress. While English-speaking immigrants were favoured overall, there was some debate (as there had been in Canada since the late nineteenth century) about the suitability of American immigrants as opposed to those who were British subjects. Nonetheless, for most observers, the nationality or place of origin of new settlers was usually overlooked if they were Anglo-Saxons. When covering the 1924 Peace River country tour of the president of the CNR, Sir Henry Thornton, *Maclean's* magazine reported that "countries are made, not by fertile lands or by desirable climates, but by the type and character of their peoples." It noted that nowhere in Canada, except possibly Prince Edward Island, was there "a purer Saxon stock" than in the Peace River country. Indeed, "Sir Henry Thornton's party were greatly struck with the superior type of the people" and they voiced their hopes that the Anglo-Saxon dominance of the district would be preserved.[2]

This idealization of the Peace River country's Anglo-Saxon character, and the determination to encourage it, reflected broader national policies. In 1924, the Three Thousand Family Programme, a joint United Kingdom-Canada scheme, was inaugurated to settle British war veterans and qualified civilian families in Canada. Similar programmes designed to strengthen the bonds of empire included the federal government's promotion in the late 1920s of British immigration to Canada through a family settlement scheme that offered low preferential passenger fares for approved British immigrants coming to work on farms or as domestics. Other projects were sponsored by some provincial governments and private agencies. While there was some resentment of these British immigrant schemes—some critics argued that efforts should instead be made to keep Canadian farmers on the land—there was greater and more persistent hostility among influential segments of the English Canadian dominant culture to non-Anglo-Saxon settlers. Nonetheless, settlement of these people increased in the Peace River country during the 1930s. While longer settled districts remained overwhelmingly Anglo-Saxon, non-Anglo-Saxons now formed slightly more than one-half of the population in fringe areas, the fastest growing parts of the region.[3] Bishop Sovereign of the Anglican church noted in 1939 that while British immigration needed to be encouraged, it was essential that the non-British people in the Peace River country be assimilated to prevent the overwhelming of "our ideals." The church was doing its part through organizations such as the Fellowship of the Maple Leaf, a church social service agency that brought out "trained and cultured British women" to work as volunteer teachers and welfare workers. Travelling on circuits, they distributed used clothing and other goods donated to the church and tutored

in the "Sunday school by post," an outreach programme that paid special attention to non-English-speaking people. Other workers served as nurses, and the
Fellowship provided some support for Dr. Mary Percy Jackson at Keg River. In
all cases, the church saw these efforts as bringing to people of "various racial
origins the culture, [and] the ideals of Anglo-Saxon life and character."[4]

Such activities demonstrated the tendency of Anglican church "mission"
work in northern Alberta to stress service to Euro-Canadian settlers rather
than Aboriginal peoples. In part, this grew from Anglican intimacy with the
country's dominant culture and its priorities, and the church viewed its mission
work as part of an effort to forge "stronger and greater links in the Imperial
Chain" and to promote Canada as a field for British immigration. As one of the
leaders of the Fellowship of the Maple Leaf noted in 1934, while the
Depression had created a crisis for British investment and trade, once
economic conditions improved, Canada would resume its role as an outlet for
surplus British capital and population.[5] The royal visit of 1939 offered another
occasion for the expression of such sentiments. The Canadian Legion and the
radio station in Grande Prairie organized tours to visit Edmonton to see the
king and queen, which, it was said, would "do much to foster a true loyalty on
the part of Canada to the higher ideals of our Empire."[6]

In such assertions of British-Canadian imperialism, French Canadians
posed a certain dilemma. While their ethnic origin sometimes caused suspicion, their British nationality demanded respect. Following the transfer of
homesteading from the federal government to the province, the first homestead
patent issued by the province went to Ernest Houde, a resident of Falher who
had been born in Quebec. There was much self-congratulation that it had gone
to a British subject. The *Edmonton Journal* noted that "without any effort to pick
them that way," all of the first patents were issued to British subjects, which
officials in the new lands and mines department saw "as a good augury for the
Britishness of Alberta."[7] But such acceptance of French Canadians was condi-
tioned by the ebb and flow of national tensions. During World War II,
deteriorating relations between French- and English-speaking Canadians over
conscription spilled into other aspects of life. In 1944, a priest from
Drummondville, Quebec appealed to French Canadians not to move to the
United States but to northern Alberta where a purely French Canadian environment could be created through block settlement. Bishop Langlois of
Grouard reportedly foresaw a second French Canadian province arising in
northern Alberta. The *Calgary Albertan* righteously responded by editorializing
that land in the Peace River country should be kept "as a heritage for our own

people, and especially for our returning soldiers," not for French Canadians who had opposed conscription. Indeed, this objective apparently formed part of the rationale for Alberta's policy that only "old Albertans" could take out homesteads in the mid 1940s.[8]

## ▬ Leisure and Public Culture

One expression of the transplanted culture of the Peace River country was the recreational activities that people enjoyed. Although time set aside for leisure was a cultural concept, the separation of work from other activities and the allocation and measurement of time it presumed were such an accepted and familiar way of viewing the world that most settlers would have found them unremarkable. In most instances, the activities that filled leisure time and provided respite from the daily routines of life in the Peace River country were those that had been transplanted by the dominant settler group. And because of its numbers, its social influence and its connection with the dominant culture in English Canada, this dominant group's institutions and practices were given legitimacy and authority as general standards for Peace River country society. Over time, these leisure time practices and opportunities evolved in step with changes taking place elsewhere in English-speaking Canada, and as part of the evolution of town and transportation networks within the Peace River country. The implanting and elaboration of recreational practices and preferences and their subsequent evolution were thus an integral, although informal, part of the settlement process.

Institutions such as schools and churches, whose purpose was to provide educational and religious services, also offered leisure opportunities as part of their overall objectives. Churches provided a range of social occasions in rural areas and towns. A survey of the registers of service for Anglican churches in the Peace River country reveals that attendance was highest at Thanksgiving, Easter and Christmas. Visits by a bishop and other dignitaries also attracted a large crowd. Yet church attendance was often poor, especially during threshing or when more appealing events competed for public attention. In 1920, only two people showed up for one service in Bluesky because of a rival baseball game, while on another occasion the minister noted in his journal: "Dunvegan picnic and sports. No one at service." Some observers blamed such choices on American immigrants. The Methodist minister at Lake Saskatoon wrote in 1922 that "in a few cases our American immigrants have been deeply religious," but "the great majority are trivial, godless, indifferent to religious needs and lacking in depth of character." Only a few observed "the claims of the Christian Sabbath," and "Sunday base-ball, berry picking in season, picnicking and autoing abound in many districts." In general, he believed that American immigrants produced "a demoralizing influence on the community."[9]

Despite their financial woes during the 1930s, schools were also important cultural and social institutions in both farm and town communities. As in other parts of the prairies, rural schools often doubled as community centres and meeting places. They offered community entertainment through concerts and sports meets, and provided a window to a wider world. Elementary school drama and music programmes benefited from competition and instruction when the first Peace River Musical Festival was held in 1924. These festivals were held alternately in Peace River and Grande Prairie, and were later held in other towns. Public attendance at these performances was usually high and the festivals attracted hundreds of school children from throughout the Peace River country who competed in drama, elocution and music. While there was some grumbling that too much school time was taken up preparing and training for the competitions, they were generally strongly endorsed as an important cultural force. They were said to create self-reliance by giving people the skill to make their own music rather than relying on the "canned" music of radios and phonographs. The music festivals were also said to bring out and develop the "musical abilities of which so many of our younger folks are possessed, but which will lie dormant in the majority of cases without this very necessary encouragement."[10]

While the festivals received a small grant from the province, most funds were raised locally and volunteers worked strenuously organizing the events. When the festival was held in Grande Prairie in 1930, "practically every home" in the town billeted between one and five competitors. During World War II, some music festivals in Alberta were cancelled and others were decentralized, but they continued to receive enthusiastic public support in the Peace River country. As Sydney Risk, the director of Drama at the University of Alberta and an adjudicator at the Grande Prairie festival, remarked in 1945, "the attitude of the people" in the Peace River country "toward their school musical and dramatic festivals is, I believe, indicative of their progressiveness."[11]

Musical and dramatic entertainment was also provided on an ongoing basis by amateur dramatic clubs, choirs and orchestras. While a few travelling variety shows appeared in the Peace River country after the railway made such tours feasible, the first chautauqua circuit to the Peace River country arrived only in 1929, and the first travelling professional dramatic troupe visited in 1932.[12]

Nonetheless, variety shows and drama had long been provided by resourceful local amateurs in many villages and towns. The Spirit River Dramatic Club was particularly ambitious; in 1920 it put on variety shows, dances and plays and borrowed funds to construct a $5,000 hall in the village. Such locally produced leisure opportunities were enhanced by commercial entertainment such as movies. At first shown by itinerant exhibitors who set up for a short time, the latest movies soon became regular features in movie theatres in all of the largest towns. While they brought Hollywood standards of glamour and style to Alberta, the provincial government censored all films to protect officially sanctioned views of morality and propriety. Sound movies had premiered in Edmonton and Calgary in late 1928 (less than two years after their premiere in New York), and the talkies arrived in the Peace River country in 1930. Some local commentators found the talkies to be superior to almost any other form of entertainment. The Grande Prairie newspaper editorialized in 1930 that "the 'talkies' embody features which are impossible in the representation of plays on the stage, such as distance, technicolor, panorama effect, etc. In a word, the talkies embody all the elements which create and hold interest. It is not too much to say that the talkies are one of the greatest inventions of the age, an invention that is bound to be even more perfect as time goes on." The public agreed. When the talkies premiered in Grande Prairie, the evening was a "wonderful success" with the cinema "packed to the doors" and a long line of people waiting for the second show. In Peace River, the cinema provided free stabling of horses and storage of cars for those coming from out of town for the inaugural show.[13]

The new technology required the renovation of old cinemas to accommodate new types of projectors, sound systems and screens. Often the renovations went well beyond technical requirements and tried to meet the new standards of glamour. In Peace River, the Boyd Theatre underwent extensive renovations in 1932. A marquee fitted with electric lights announced to the street the attractions to be found inside. The cinema had 250 seats, most of them upholstered, while the balcony had a further 80 seats, with the first row equipped with earphones for the hard of hearing. In its preview of the renovations, the *Peace River Record* breathlessly reported that the interior decorations of the theatre were "of the very best." Plaster mouldings set off the light fixtures and "the walls contain the regular false windows," curtains, flower boxes and other ornamentation. And "when finally completed, the lobby will be an attraction in itself," with "a settee, fireplace, palms and whatnots, lighted by soft and pleasing colored globes, and as the lobby is of ample size, will be much of a 'drawing

*Plenty of parking on main street helped Fairview provide a social focus for surrounding farm areas, 1941.* ACA 197 PAA.

room' type. The walls will display the heroes and heroines of the movie world in decorative frames, with space provided for advance advertising."[14]

Despite their allure, movies were only one of the commercial leisure attractions that towns offered. Bars (after the end of prohibition in 1923) and poolrooms were also popular, although both were often thought to be of dubious morality. In part, public reaction to these institutions mirrored a struggle among different groups within the province's dominant culture. In most instances, this contest was defused through the state, which regulated poolrooms and bars and censored movies. This resolution of differing social and ethical views was usually, although not always, effective. In Grande Prairie in 1923 the poolroom was closed because of complaints by local moral reformers and reopened only after a public petition. As the local newspaper noted, provincial regulation of poolrooms controlled their moral threat, and it warned that "it behoves [sic] every citizen in this town and district to watch his or her step these days, as these people [moral reformers] are out to cause trouble wherever it is possible on the slightest pretext and without the slightest provocation."[15]

Towns were often also a focus for public holidays. National celebrations, such as Victoria Day, Dominion Day, and, in French-speaking districts such as Falher, St. Jean Baptiste Day, drew a large number of visitors. Times of sociability and enjoyment, they also asserted cultural continuity and the values of the dominant groups in the area. Other groups who were less numerous, more scattered and lacking an official and formal link with national culture expressed the same motivations through local or home-based celebrations of cultural inheritance. Sports were popular during most of these holidays. The two-day sports meet at Spirit River in July 1920 drew an estimated 900 people the first day and 600 the second to enjoy horse races, foot races, sports and a dance. Both Grande Prairie and Peace River put on winter carnivals from time to time from the mid 1920s until the late 1930s. Similar to the events found in many towns and cities throughout Alberta in the interwar years, winter carnivals were an attempt to humanize winter and, not incidentally, to promote commerce during a slow business period in the year. Although they had become little more than winter sports meets by the late 1930s, those in earlier years featured sled-dog races, hockey, curling matches, dances, concerts and beauty queen pageants.[16] A wide range of other sporting events were also popular, and the most popular team sports—baseball, hockey and curling—were organized through leagues and bonspiels. Agricultural fairs also provided opportunities for sports along with other attractions. Although their number subsequently declined, fairs were held in Grande Prairie, Berwyn, Lake Saskatoon, Spirit River and Waterhole in 1931. They offered farmers an opportunity to learn the latest farming techniques and to compete for prizes with their grain, livestock and home production. While this educational role justified grants for operations and prize lists by the provincial Department of Agriculture, few fairs could survive without crowd pleasing draws such as horse races, sports and other entertainment. An official noted in 1921 that the Grande Prairie Agricultural Society planned to begin having horse races at its annual fair because the fair was "less of a success each year" and it was hoped that racing would boost attendance as it had in other places in Alberta. This strategy seemed to work; the two-day agricultural fair in Grande Prairie in 1929 drew 2,700 people on its last day. While it featured sports, horse races and a dance, the greatest attraction was the midway, provided by the Saskatchewan Amusement Company. Its electric lights gave it "a great white way appearance" and the rides included a merry-go-round, ferris wheel and a "chair-o-plane."[17]

Fraternal clubs, such as the Oddfellows and Masons established by the first Euro-Canadian settlers in the Peace River country, complemented such leisure opportunities. Masonic lodges were set up in Peace River town in 1916 and in Spirit River and Grande Prairie in 1918, while the Oddfellows had lodges in these towns as well as at Waterhole by 1920. Women's auxiliaries, the Eastern Star and Rebekahs, were organized a short time later, and both the lodges and their auxiliaries provided social connections and entertainment for members.

Related organizations such as the Great War Veterans' Association (later amalgamated into the Canadian Legion) were also active by the early 1920s. Branches of the Imperial Order Daughters of the Empire, a women's national patriotic club, were also well established in many centres. With the encouragement and assistance of the provincial government, chapters of the Women's Institute, an organization that originated in Ontario and provided educational-social opportunities for its members, were set up in many places. Youth organizations, such as the Boy Scouts and the Girl Guides, were also established in some of the larger centres by the 1920s. Service clubs, which were becoming popular everywhere in Canada, appeared in the 1920s as well. The first Elks Clubs were set up in southern Alberta in 1921, and a provincial association was established in 1928. Demonstrating that the Peace River country was in tune with the rest of the province, Elks Clubs were operating at Hythe and Grande Prairie by about 1927, and by the late 1930s they could be found in most Peace River country towns and villages. Like fraternal organizations, service clubs provided social opportunities for members through community service. Fund-raising events such as bingos and carnivals were elevated to a form of community entertainment. The carnival organized by the Elks Club in Grande Prairie in 1931 was a three-day event that began on Dominion Day, and featured parachute jumps, a midway and grandstand show, a dance and a street parade. Such events were enhanced by the fact that these service clubs often focussed on the provision of children's services like playgrounds and events such as "Kiddies' Day," a day of sports and free refreshments.[18]

While most of these organizations were located in towns and villages, they provided entertainment for both town and country people. But rural life also had its own institutions such as the United Farmers of Alberta (UFA) and United Farm Women of Alberta (UFWA), which, in addition to their political activities, offered social and entertainment opportunities. Indeed, one observer in Peace River claimed that the greatest benefit of the UFA was the "community-building spirit" and the "good fellowship" that it promoted. Other kinds of community events also became features in some areas. Near Teepee Creek (north-east of Grande Prairie) an annual rodeo was held during the early 1930s and it developed into one of the most attractive summer events in the southern Peace River country. Bucking horses, horse racing and pulling contests were the central events, but baseball, boxing, tug-of-war, bathing beauty contests (sometimes featuring men's and women's events), drinking and a dance helped draw crowds and competitors from near and far. One resident humourously recalled the story of one of these outside competitors:

All of us poor old farmers around here had on work boots and patched coveralls, but we were having a real good time. Then this great big, slim, would-be cowboy stepped up. He was from Calgary and he was going to show the locals how to ride. He was all dressed up fit to kill, and bragged around to everybody how he could ride. Now Burns had an old work horse at the time, and that horse could buck! He'd just bawl and paw when he hit the ground. Anyway, they got that horse all saddled up and that cowboy aboard and let him buck. Well, that horse went once and the horse came down, but the cowboy kept on going up and up. When he finally came down, he landed just the way he had been on the horse— and he landed hard. He picked himself up and he left and after a hearty laugh, the local riders kept on with the show. [19]

Rural social life was further enhanced by the construction of community halls that were usually supported by fund-raising events and the sale of shares to local residents. The Kerndale community near Berwyn, for example, needed a venue for social and church events, and in 1935 the assets of the UFA local were transferred to a community club for the construction of a hall. Shares at $5 apiece were subscribed either by labour or cash and entitled the member to vote at club meetings. The most popular events in the Kerndale hall were dances and socials, and in 1937 the hall was used for a total of 13 dances and one motion picture. In addition, it was rented by the "Banjo Daddy Show," which was probably an itinerant commercial variety show. By the 1950s, activity at the hall had increased to include almost two dances a month. Such events were typical. The Spirit Valley Community Association also organized dances, and its hall was used for meetings, concerts and the occasional variety show, while the grounds were often used for community sports events. But unlike the Kerndale hall, the Spirit Valley Community Association declined after World War II because of its proximity to Spirit River, which was increasingly accessible because of better roads and private transportation. As one member noted in 1951, "the people of the community are still very interested in our hall but being very close to Spirit River village the people usually go there to dance, they having better orchestras."[20]

# "The Light of Modern Times"
### The Peace River Country in the Interwar Years

The changes in life that came with Euro-Canadian settlement of the Peace River country sometimes found expression in the views and accomplishments of local individuals who epitomized popular aspirations. Three such individuals stood out during the interwar years: Herman Trelle, a prize-winning Wembley farmer; Donald Albright, the director of the Beaverlodge experimental substation; and Charles Frederick, the editor of the *Peace River Record*. Their local and provincial prominence represented a weakening of the authority of Edmonton's business and political elites to speak for the interests of the Peace River country. There had, of course, been local spokesmen (such as Alie Brick) before World War I, and Jim Cornwall in Edmonton continued to espouse northern concerns. But the defeat in 1921 of Frank Oliver as the MP for Edmonton West (the riding including the Peace River country) by an upstart UFA candidate, Donald Kennedy, marked a changing focus and orientation in the Peace River country's public life.[21] While Kennedy's defeat of Oliver was part of a broader shift in Alberta's political life, it also symbolized that the Peace River country was now producing its own advocates. Kennedy's primary concern was transportation, specifically the construction of a coast outlet, and his championing of this cause doubtless contributed to his popularity. He retained his seat until 1935.[22]

While Herman Trelle also expressed such local ambitions, he more importantly helped to vindicate the agricultural potential of the Peace River country through his success in world grain exhibitions. While there were other national and international grain show winners from the Peace River country in the interwar years—such as Robert Cochrane, John Allsop, Lloyd Rigby and W. Justyn Rigby—Herman Trelle's success was most widely discussed. Originally from the United States, he and his father took out homesteads near Lake Saskatoon in 1909. Herman soon developed an appetite for competition in national and international grain shows. With the assistance of his wife, Beatrice, he carefully selected and cleaned samples of his grain for exhibition. He won third prize for hard spring wheat at the International Grain and Hay Show in Chicago in 1923, and between 1926 and 1928 he captured a further 186 trophies and prizes for wheat, oats and peas. Of these awards, seven were world championships. Further victories included the world championship for hard spring wheat at the 1932 Chicago grain show, which he won for the third time. This victory led the *Edmonton Journal* to dub him the "wheat wizard," and his victories made him a hero in the Peace River country and to all who supported its agricultural expansion.[23]

*A 1931 portrait of Donald Albright, the prominent advocate of the Peace River country's farm potential.* A6988 PAA.

Trelle's success was especially significant in the mid 1920s when doubts were being voiced about the Peace River country's agricultural future. While he advertised Canada's agricultural industry to the world, he also validated the Peace River country's identity and future as a farming district during a time of considerable anxiety. Trelle became a household name, and the Grande Prairie Board of Trade and the City of Edmonton, among others, featured him in their promotional literature. Yet while he grew prize-winning grain, Trelle had ongoing financial difficulties. Between 1926 and 1930 the province gave him almost $2,400 in "honoraria" for his winnings at exhibitions in Chicago and Toronto. Even so, he was in serious financial trouble by 1928. Because of his symbolic importance for Alberta agriculture—and presumably to prevent the embarrassment of having the land of the Peace River country's wheat king seized in a mortgage foreclosure—the province purchased a quarter section of his land for $5,000 cash and allowed Trelle to continue farming it in return for 5 percent interest plus the property taxes. Trelle contracted tuberculosis in 1929 and since he had no money, the province paid his hospital bills, which totalled over $750. In 1932, Trelle bought more land, even though he was still in debt. When combined with "the extravagant manner in which he handles money, and in view of the further fact that he does not spend more than four or five months of the year at home," the provincial government decided to end its subsidy. But the conundrum remained; the hero of Alberta farming (he won the world wheat championship again in 1936) could not be seen to be a financial failure, and various solutions were devised to keep his financial problems from becoming public. By 1940, Trelle was being paid a monthly stipend from his assets, which were being "managed" by the CPR agency, the Canada Colonization Company.[24] Although Trelle later moved to California, the continual manoeuvring over his financial difficulties showed that his prize winnings were of considerable importance to the identity and confidence of both the province and the Peace River country.

Like Herman Trelle, Donald Albright made significant contributions to the farm life of the Peace River country through his work as the director of the Beaverlodge Dominion Experimental Farm Substation. Albright was born in Ontario and attended the Ontario College of Agriculture. From 1908 to 1913 he was the agricultural editor of the *Farmer's Advocate and Home Magazine*, but he moved in 1913 to the Peace River country along with members of his wife's family, who were part of the break-away Methodist sect, the Burnsites.[25] During the interwar years, Albright became the most prominent spokesman for Peace River country farming through his experimental work, hundreds of public addresses and the publication of numerous articles and technical reports, which created a permanent record about Peace River country agriculture and its needs and potential. But Albright was not a mindless booster. He was often critical of the practices and attitudes of Peace River country farmers, even though his admonitions and advice were always framed by a love of the place, a faith in its agricultural future and a commitment to the well-being of the average farmer. He gave talks on the local radio station and wrote a regular column for Peace River country newspapers called "Timely Hints From The Beaverlodge Station." Reflecting his moral convictions, these were always accompanied by the tag "It is a pleasure as well as a duty to serve." When forced by illness to retire in 1945, he wrote a farewell column in which he confessed that, despite a lifetime's work in plant science, his ambition had never been to breed a new, high quality, early wheat suitable for the Peace River country. Although this would have been "a very nice thing to do," he believed that its value was over-estimated. While it would have increased profits from wheat

The photographer's caption "Pushing Back the Frontier" suggests
the crude association of mechanization with "progress" that was
popular during the interwar years. A10,033 PAA.

production, it would have pushed up land costs "until the wheat grower, as a
worker, received very little more than before." For Albright, science did not exist
in splendid, arrogant isolation from society. Instead, his ambition had been to
"show how good homes could be developed and planted" in the Peace River
country, "a benefit which would weave itself into the lives and characters of the
people, conferring a boon that no economic process can filch away."[26]

Like Herman Trelle and Donald Albright, Charles Frederick came to the
Peace River country before World War I. Originally from Ontario, he decided
while working for the *Edmonton Journal* to move to Peace River Crossing to set
up his own newspaper. In 1914, he shipped his press, type, newsprint and
printing gear from Edmonton over the ED&BC's construction lines as far as
Slave Lake. From here, they were taken by scow to Grouard and then by wagon
to Peace River. This established Frederick's pioneer pedigree and the *Peace River
Record* became one of the most vigorous boosters of Peace River town and the
Peace River country. As he editorialized in 1929, the *Record's* goal was to articu-
late "a policy of the New North of Canada. It has no time for politics or party
in the partisan sense. If a movement is for the betterment of the North country
we are behind it. If it threatens the best interest of the North, this newspaper

is ready to fight against it." It was this attitude that led him to espouse the secession of the Peace River country from Alberta, as well as to devote much of his energy to local organizations such as the hospital board and the board of trade. His empire expanded when he set up a newspaper at Waterhole, and when he acquired the *Grande Prairie Herald* in the late 1920s. In 1932, a rival paper, the *Northern Tribune*, appeared in Grande Prairie, but until 1939, when he sold all of his interests and moved to California, Frederick was the most influential journalist in the Peace River country.[27]

While both Frederick and Albright were united by a common belief that agriculture held the key to the Peace River country's future, Frederick's spiky personality and his tendency to lapse into conventional boosterism marked part of the difference in the temperament and sensibility of the two men. Yet while each expressed a particular vision of the Peace River country's current conditions and needs through different methods and emphasis, both shared assumptions that were widely held in their society. Especially important was a belief in "progress," which both would have defined as the conquest of nature, the beneficent course of technological development, population growth and the implanting of a Euro-Canadian, and especially Anglo-Saxon, culture in the Peace River country. These values and assumptions were also those of the dominant culture in prairie Canada, and they demonstrated yet another element in the shared identity of Euro-Canadians in the Peace River country with those elsewhere on the prairies.

Arising from such shared definitions of progress, Euro-Canadian settlers in the Peace River country expressed an ongoing concern that their lifestyle and standard of living would reach, match, or best of all, exceed those in the longer settled parts of Canada. While this revealed an anxiety about the Peace River country's economic potential and perhaps a sense that its isolation made it seem like a backwater, faith in imminent success gave comfort in hard times. A striking aspect of reports by Anglican ministers in rural areas in the 1930s was that people, despite their difficulties, were of remarkably good humour and possessed great optimism about the future. In part, this optimism was sustained by a belief in the beneficence of technological change. As was noted in 1918 in Grande Prairie, every place had things that "attract and even force attention." While in some places it was old buildings or cities, in the Grande Prairie district it was the possibility of moving beyond "pioneer days" because of the availability of modern farm equipment. Four years earlier, such equipment had only been available from dealers in Edmonton, but now it could be purchased from local agents of "the largest corporations in the world." This was also indicative of the district's great agricultural potential, and "one can patiently watch the pioneer marks of our district descending into the darkness and making room for the light of modern times and inventions to make our district" not only the equal, but superior, to older settled districts.[28]

The long-standing appeal of these attitudes was shown a decade later when Charles Frederick wrote on the 15th anniversary of the *Peace River Record* that the Peace River country could congratulate itself on becoming like the rest of Canada. "We have already seen cross-roads develop to thriving towns, wildernesses develop into prosperous farming communities, and pack trails give way to railways" he wrote, and "the next few years will see cities growing where we now have hamlets." By 1934, on the 20th anniversary of the paper, Frederick again stressed that local identity rested on the development of local standards in step with those found elsewhere. Anxiety about the Peace River country's potential was apparently being resolved. As he wrote, conditions in Peace River 20 years earlier had been "rather primitive," without sidewalks and with "half the business places" located "in tents or log shacks." Now the town boasted solid permanent buildings. But the greatest changes had taken place in the home, where "better living conditions" had gradually come about. Local businesses now offered electric appliances, while radios kept people

in touch with news events and social life of the continent. Many of these conveniences were undreamed of twenty years ago, and yet the far flung pioneer settlement of those days not so far past is today enjoying most of the advantages of the older communities. It has been the steady march of science and the steady development of the community itself that has resulted in the happy conditions of today. In all that time there have nearly always been some who found the going hard. Yet collectively, our progress has been steady and sure.[29]

Such sentiments and the faith in science and technological change that they expressed were given an added boost three years later when the first radio station in the Peace River country was established. Radio station CFGP in Grande Prairie was described as "another big step in the march of progress" and showed that "old things were passing and a new day was being ushered in for the Peace River country. It was a time of real rejoicing. The north country's long isolation was being broken and a big agricultural inland empire was being swept into the mechanical advancement of the times."[30] The same year, a Peace River resident returned from a trip to California convinced "that people in this area are fortunately located." Prices in Peace River were lower, and "on the surface, things in California appear rosy, but like everywhere else, poverty exists and this is partially evidenced by the old cars which people operate, some so old that one might think they were driven from the ark." In this view of the world, the access by Peace River residents to the latest technology defined their advantage, success and up-to-datedness. Indeed, reports of violations of Grande Prairie's traffic bylaws in 1927 drew the comment that "the Peace River district has arrived; it is no longer in the experimental state. In common with all growing communities, it is beginning to experience its first real taste of traffic problems."[31]

While this perhaps suggested a belief that progress was inherent in technological change, it was more commonly said that progress could only be translated to everyday life and given meaning through individual initiative and the opportunities offered by the frontier. The novelist and governor general of Canada, John Buchan, lionized the settler of the Peace River country as "one of the few aristocrats left in the world. He has a right sense of the values of life, because his cosmos embraces both nature and man. I think he is the most steadfast human being now alive." A poem, published in the Peace River newspaper in 1932, called "Out Where The North Begins" by Lila McCue of High Prairie, further expressed popular sentiments about the northern farm frontier

Where you arise in the morning "before the lark,"
And your bedtime comes on before it gets dark
But the man who will work can get a good start
Out where the north begins.

And as Charles Frederick noted in his retrospective on the 20th anniversary of the *Record*, an improvement in material standards had been achieved because people had not "waited for a Santa Claus to bring it. It has come by personal and community effort which does bring results."[32]

Integral to such views was the belief that pioneering was a struggle that ended in victory over nature and adversity. As Bishop Robbins noted in his farewell address to the Anglican synod of Athabasca in 1930, he had witnessed in the past 20 years "the conquest of the prairies, the clearing of primitive forests and the conversion of hard and resisting lands into rich grain fields and prosperous farms." This had been accomplished by an "army of agricultural settlers, not with swords or guns, not in warfare of devastating weapons, but in the pursuit of peace and prosperity, each man and each woman nobly attaining victory in occupations demanding the contribution of all their brave energy and strength." Testaments of their victory were the churches, schools, railways and roads of the region, all of which held promise of a future "when industries and cities and advanced education systems will supplement the splendid story of the past pioneering years." Indeed, Robbins saw the hand of God in these developments. Just as God had supported the church in its struggle with adversity, so too, as the Peace River country passed "at last to its destiny in being brought under cultivation and development" and home to thousands of settlers, "comfort and assurance" had invariably been found "in the same conviction of the divine call."[33] As moral as well as material triumphs, these victories tended to merge into an indivisible whole. Earlier critics of the Peace River country's agricultural potential had not been forgotten nor forgiven—as Donald Albright remarked in 1930, the land that had been "disparaged" 40 years earlier by Macoun and others had successfully produced Herman Trelle's prize winning grain.[34]

These views about the past held a strong message for the present—personal struggle and deprivation brought future reward, as did faith in the promise of the Peace River country. Yet while pioneering had been a story of struggle, it had also been one of companionship. A proposal in 1934 for the formation of an "Old Timers' Association" in Peace River contended that "those who were here in the earlier years found a comradeship" that was "distinctly different" from that found in the present day.[35] Tales of adversity and comradeship also often formed part of the history of the Edson Trail which by the 1920s had become an icon for the south Peace River country's self-identity and a validation of its historical experience. Surviving the "epic" difficulties of the trail was taken as a mark of character that cast the pioneer in a heroic mould. Central in this historical memory were tales of deprivation, starvation and even death along the trail. Although one of the surveyors of the trail commented years later that "many of the stories told and published are the greatest bunk!" such myths had been fully articulated by the late 1920s.[36] Drawing an unflattering parallel with current times, the *Grande Prairie Herald* noted in 1927 that Clairmont still had many pioneers who had crossed the Edson trail "under conditions that would deter the adventurous of present times. Many and interesting are the tales of hardship and misfortune related by these old-timers, who are now the backbone and sinew of the country" and nothing could lead them "to take a trip 'outside' except under very pressing circumstances."[37] Yet even if the rigours of the north and the frontier built character, such pride was a frail defence against the blandishments of an encroaching popular culture whose movies idealized the opportunities of Hollywood and other balmy climes. It was significant that both Herman Trelle and Charles Frederick, two of the Peace River country's most famous and avid champions, later moved to California. Frederick set up a business there, and Trelle worked on a ranch. In a tragic conclusion to his life, Trelle was murdered in a dispute with a ranch hand.

Whatever their outcome, tales of pioneer struggles and material progress formed a cultural framework with which to meet contrary views. In 1932 the Grande Prairie *Northern Tribune* reprinted recollections recently printed in the *Glasgow Weekly Herald* of Reverend Wood, a missionary in the Peace River country in the 1920s. Wood drew a portrait of a rough society in which "everything was so primitive." Such a description caused few problems for contemporary readers—it was the familiar story of pioneer adversity—but the rest of Wood's recollection challenged basic elements of historical myth. In contrast to the "comradeship" of pioneer myth, Wood recalled that "British Canadians and Americans alike" disliked the "foreign element," who he characterized as "isolated and hard working; sometimes a weak, poor lot, but more often a strong hard working lot handicapped by lack of knowledge of the language and local customs." Although "a thousand things have escaped my memory," the "sum total of my impression" was "one of disappointment;" of young wives living "a life of absolute slavery to poor 'homesteader' husbands," of poor soil in places, of "eight months of snow" and cold. This challenged not only the pioneering myth but the farm potential of the Peace River country. In a rebuttal, J.B. Yule, the editor of the *Northern Tribune*, revealed in a sidebar that the newspaper had done "a little checking-up on the Rev Mr. Wood" and discovered that "he didn't just exactly fit into pioneer life. Worst of all, he lacked a sense of humor—at least of Western humor." And finally, Wood was discredited by the most powerful argument of all: the evidence of material progress that had taken place. While Wood had got lost on muddy trails, it was "the development that had taken place during the past ten years" that proved "the absolute foolishness of his remarks." Indeed, Yule noted, if Wood was "here now he wouldn't get lost so often" since the roads had improved and he "would discover that many of the people he writes so pityingly of haven't done badly at all."[38]

Even if Wood could be dismissed as a dandy incapable of pioneering, his opinion still mattered. He was a clergyman, he lived in the homeland of the dominant culture and he wrote in a prominent newspaper. His negative opinion wounded by reviving old anxieties about the region's suitability for farming and by demonstrating that not all views about progress were the same. Ultimately, however, what was most important was who had won and what the consequences of this victory were. While the progress that was so assiduously courted by Euro-Canadian settlers in the Peace River country had often led to the marginalization of Native people and at times to environmental degradation, belief in it had also sustained these settlers during difficult times by giving them a historical sense of accomplishment and hope for a wealthier, more comfortable and fulfilling future. That this was founded upon the displacement of Aboriginal people was rarely a cause for regret. A Metis, Jeanette Gray, returned to Grande Prairie in 1938 near the end of her life. She had originally come to the Grande Prairie as a child in the late 1800s and she recalled that "I used to ride horseback all over this country. I knew every inch of it and now I wouldn't know that I ever saw it. The white man came in, cut down the bush, plowed the ground and changed everything." Such change was popularly celebrated by Euro-Canadians as a sign of their triumphant occupation of the land. Gray understood the erasure of her own past differently: "if the country had been left to the Indians," she said, "there would be little change and I would feel at home."[39]

# Natives, Land

# 12          and Power

LAND OWNERSHIP had from the start of settlement in northern Alberta been the quest of most Euro-Canadian settlers. Then the most widely held form of capital, land gave its owners the power to pursue their personal priorities and offered them the possibility of economic independence, wealth and social status. Since ownership or rights to land affected the use of all resources, whether farming, mining, hunting game, fishing or trapping, control of land was of critical importance to Native people. For them, however, land rights were complicated by the ongoing vagaries of treaty interpretation.

As Euro-Canadian settlement continued in northern Alberta after World War I, Native concerns about land use increased. In response, some Native groups organized politically. While there were attempts at direct political organization among Indians before World War II, these were not successful and there was no truly independent organization in Alberta that represented their interests or spoke for them collectively.[1] Among the Metis, however, such political organization came with the formation in 1932 of the Alberta Metis Association. While it was often unable to change the course of events, the association was able to identify Metis needs, express their ambitions and grievances, and focus their identity. One of its most important objectives was to secure a land base for impoverished Metis, and its lobbying contributed to the formation in 1934 of a royal commission to inquire into Metis needs and to the subsequent establishment by the province of a network of Metis settlements.

Migration was another reaction by Natives who were increasingly confronted with the loss of their customary use of the land. Natives in the Battle River district moved further north as white settlers took up homestead lands there during the interwar years.[2] The movement of Beaver people from the Peace River country to districts further west and north in Alberta and British Columbia was perhaps also a similar response, although detailed research is needed to confirm this thesis. Metis people also continued to migrate in response to changing social and economic conditions. One well documented case concerns the migration of Metis after 1920 from Lac La Biche to the Peace-Athabasca delta. These people moved north because of depletion of fish and fur in their home district and high unemployment due in part to the decline of scow freighting between Athabasca and Fort McMurray. In some cases, Metis from Lac La Biche went north only in winter to trap, but entire families also reestablished themselves in the Peace-Athabasca delta, often alongside Chipewyan people already living there. Social integration between the two groups was often facilitated by existing family ties, but while the two groups sometimes intermarried, each tended to keep a sense of cultural distinctiveness.[3]

Some Natives also responded to these changing conditions by seeking admission to treaty. While this practice was not widespread, people continued to be admitted to treaty during the interwar years. In 1938, for example, 28 people who met the criteria of living "an Indian mode of life" and whose direct ancestors had not taken scrip were admitted to the Wabasca Band. This policy of admitting people to treaty ended in 1942. Following a study by Indian Affairs of the Lesser Slave Lake Agency band lists, about 700 people (some of them serving in the Canadian military in World War II) were struck off the band lists "on the grounds that their parents or grandparents were white or Metis." This prompted widespread criticism, and on the advice of MP Jack Sissons, an investigation was conducted by Justice W.A. Macdonald of the Alberta District Court. Macdonald concluded that "although one-third of the people in question were descended from Metis who had accepted scrip and were therefore rightly discharged from treaty," he identified about 300 people who should not have been removed from the band lists. Indian Affairs agreed to reinstate only 129 of these people, and while its rationale remains unclear, this response may have been due in part to the provincial government's reluctance to provide land (as required by the Natural Resources Transfer Agreement of 1930) for expanding existing reserves and creating new ones.[4]

Despite such problems, demands for new or enlarged reserves were ongoing during the interwar years. As before 1918, Indians requested the assignment of reserves when their treaty entitlement remained unfilled, when they judged that a reserve would help protect their interests or because new people had been admitted to treaty. While reserves had been assigned by 1920 in most of the Peace River country where agricultural settlement was occurring, reserves had not yet been set aside in most areas further north. When the question of reserves in these areas arose, Euro-Canadian priorities continued to shape the official response. When Indians renewed their request for a reserve at Fort Smith after World War I, for example, the Dominion Parks Branch of the Department of the Interior continued to oppose creation of a reserve close to the area proposed as a wood buffalo park. H.J. Bury, the supervisor of Indian Timber Land, noted in 1920 that the Chipewyan band "showed great hostility" to the proposal because "from time immemorial they had been accustomed to hunt and trap" in the area proposed for the park and they had "hunting lodges and shacks" there. The local chief argued that it would take years before band members would become familiar with "the haunts and habits of the game" in a new district.[5] Nonetheless, Wood Buffalo Park was established in 1922, and a reserve was only set aside at Fort Smith in 1941. Even then, it did not encompass all of the land that the people were entitled to by treaty. Similarly, the Cree at Lubicon Lake first asked for a reserve in 1933. In 1939, Indian Affairs recognized the band and promised a reserve, but the land survey to establish it was not completed, and further complications arose between the federal government and the Cree about band membership. The allocation of the reserve was dropped until 1952 when the province revived the issue because of inquiries about mineral leases in the area. Over four decades later, it is still a matter of often acrimonious dispute.[6]

At Fort Chipewyan, the Chipewyan and Cree bands were also asking for reserves by 1922. Indian Agent Gerald Card noted that the bands had become "somewhat hostile at the ever-increasing encroachments of white trappers on what they term 'their ground'" and saw reserves as a solution to the problem. Some of these white trappers trapped full time, while others were only trying to raise a grubstake for prospecting or homesteading. In either case, they tended to be better capitalized than Native trappers and came fully equipped with provisions, guns and traps. Since most were single or supported only a small family, they were able to spend all their time trapping and produced substantially higher catches than most Aboriginal trappers. Some also seem to have assumed that they had a type of squatter's right to trap on crown land and most showed little concern for wildlife conservation. They sometimes also used intimidation and even violence to take over districts that Natives had used for generations. For most, trapping was only a "job," while for many Natives it was both a commercial and subsistence activity. [7]

H.J. Bury noted in 1926 that the invasion of white trappers had created crises in "all the hinterland regions of Canada." Although there is evidence that the meeting of white and native trappers was not confrontational everywhere in Canada, Bury claimed that some Natives in parts of northern Alberta retaliated by burning the cabins of white trappers. He drew a sharp—and stereotypical—distinction between resource and land use by Native and white trappers. Natives, he contended, were generally "conservationists" because they trapped the same district each year, caught only prime fur, left enough animals to breed and were careful with fire in the bush. "The average white trapper," he noted, did not trap continuously in one district, but cleaned it out before moving on. In this competition for resources, Natives were often forced to adopt similar tactics and the land was stripped of its fur-bearing animals. Such problems became more extreme in the next decade. Even though fur-bearing animals and prices declined in the 1930s, the number of white trappers seems to have remained constant because there were few employment alternatives during the Depression. Moreover, at Fort Chipewyan at least, Metis in the town were forced to rely more extensively on trapping and hunting because of declining wage work. This added to the pressure on local game resources while improved access by airplanes compounded the problem. In 1929 a few sports hunters from Edmonton were using airplanes to reach Fort Chipewyan and district, and some white trappers were also said to be using bush planes to reach remote trapping grounds. [8]

The Chipewyan at Fort Chipewyan believed that they would be better able to deal with competition in the trapping grounds if they had a reserve. Although their treaty entitlement was predicated on farming, they requested a larger reserve to allow for the more extensive land use needed for trapping. They wanted a reserve in the area because "our fathers father's [sic] used to live here and we want our children to live here when we die." Chief Laviolette believed that a reserve could help reverse the damage brought by white contact; "thirty years ago it was a fine country," he wrote to the Department of Indian Affairs in 1927, "because just the Indians lived in it," but now it was ruined by over-trapping. If the Chipewyan received "some land to call our own where we can hunt and fish and grow a little potatoes" and where "the white trappers and the half breeds cannot bother us as long as we have someone here to look out for us," he believed that "the fur will come back like it was 30 years ago." He enclosed a statement of support from traders, the Roman Catholic mission and the local magistrate, and closed by saying that "this makes five letters I have had my interpriter [sic] write for me and I do hope and pray that this one is going to the right place and that you will give us our reserve."[9]

Since the area the Chipewyan wanted was swampy and suitable for little other than trapping, Indian Agent Card recommended that the reserves be assigned. Nonetheless, Ottawa dragged its feet on the matter. While provisions allowing the right to hunt in Wood Buffalo Park after 1926 temporarily reduced Cree demands for a reserve, the matter remained vital for many Chipewyan. In 1931, Indian Affairs at last surveyed a number of reserves near the south-west corner of Lake Athabasca. Since they were 34-square kilometres larger than a strict interpretation of the treaty entitlement permitted, the Alberta government balked at transferring the land to the federal government because it did not want non-Indian trappers excluded from a prime muskrat trapping area. In 1937, the province finally granted surface rights for the land but reserved water, mineral and fishing rights. Because Alberta insisted that non-Indians could trap in the area, conflict followed. As a result, the land grant did little to protect Indian livelihood from white competition, and reserves in this area were only declared in 1954.[10] Nonetheless, the surveying of reserve land near Fort Chipewyan brought changes in Indian Affairs' administration in the district. The Indian Agent at Fort Smith was also responsible for Fort Chipewyan until 1932 when an agent was stationed in the settlement. As anthropologist Patricia McCormack found, he initially had little real influence over the daily lives of local Indians because the population was scattered. Over time, however, he gained authority at the expense of traditional leaders and patterns of authority. After 1945, the agent became more powerful because more people were living permanently in the settlement and, more importantly, he recruited local wage workers for employers in other districts.[11] This was the case throughout northern Alberta. In the Lesser Slave Lake Agency, the agent still dealt primarily with people living on the reserves close to Grouard where the agency office was located. With the transfer of the agency office to the Driftpile reserve in 1931, he became more centrally placed in relation to all the reserves on the south shore of Lesser Slave Lake. Because of rail connections, he was by then also able more easily to visit other reserves in the area, as well as in the Peace River country. Reserves farther away, however, were still usually visited only as part of a circuit trip to pay annuities, a rushed trip of one or two days that provided little ongoing contact.[12]

The priority of Euro-Canadian needs in the decisions about where and when reserves were assigned was also evident in subsequent efforts to sell reserve land to Euro-Canadians. In practice, the federal government did not treat reserves as the permanent assignment of lands that had been suggested at the time of treaty negotiations. Although there was a tendency to favour the consolidation of Indians onto larger reserves where tighter control over their lives could be effected, there was also a contradictory impulse in Indian Affairs policy that anticipated a time when all Indians would be assimilated and the reserves abolished. Whatever the case, Indian Affairs typically facilitated the sale of reserve lands that were coveted by Euro-Canadian settlers. The Indians were then moved to other reserves or into areas of little interest to white settlers. As historian Sarah Carter has demonstrated, this had been the pattern on the prairies since the nineteenth century. Although there was some debate in the Indian Affairs department, sales were usually justified by "whatever arguments were expedient, no matter how contradictory." As elsewhere on the prairies, an appeal to "progress" was often used to justify the sale of reserve land in the Peace River country. In this view, unfarmed arable land was said to be "idle" while farming was deemed to be a "proper and beneficial" use of the land. As the superintendent of Indian Affairs explained in 1923 to the local MP, Donald Kennedy, the department tried to have "the excess areas" sold for agricultural use when reserves were larger "than required for Indian use, and when surrounding settlement warrants such action." Nonetheless, it was "essential" that local demand for land be gauged accurately, "as it would be a matter of dissatisfaction on the part of the Indians should large areas be released and remain unsold" because "the Indians quite naturally expect to obtain a substantial payment without delay."[13]

Sale of reserve land was allowed by the *Indian Act*, which required the agreement of the Indians concerned and their compensation with cash or other land. This legislation was periodically amended to make sales easier. By the 1920s, sales required the consent of a majority of male band members over 21 years of age—often a small part of the band's total population. In the Peace River in the interwar years, sales terms usually included an immediate cash payment, annual interest payments and promises of farm equipment or livestock, even though the latter had already been promised by the treaty but rarely delivered. Purchasers usually paid 10 percent down plus annual payments. Paid to Indian Affairs, these funds (less an administration fee) were deposited in the band's account from which the Indians were paid an annual "interest" payment. While Indian Affairs tried to collect from defaulting purchasers, the Indians suffered the consequences because payments from the band fund were not made in years when arrears could not be collected. This arrangement reflected the status of Indians as wards of the state, and demonstrated another dimension of their relationship with the Euro-Canadian dominant culture.[14]

While many reserves were sold under this paternalistic system, some Indians were successful in keeping their reserves when band members were united in pursuit of a common objective. This was demonstrated at the Swan River reserve, which the government repeatedly tried to sell over a 15-year period. One of four reserves on the south shore of Lesser Slave Lake, it had a population of 66 by 1923 and contained about 11,500 acres with excellent hay lands along the lake. While most of the reserve was suitable for farming, it had not been cleared or broken. Although the Indians owned a few cattle and horses, they made a living by trapping and hunting, selling hay and firewood, and through occasional wage labour for local farmers, businessmen and the railway. It was a successful economy of makeshifts. When the railway crossed the Swan River reserve, a station was built on land purchased from the band. The village of Kinuso (first called Swan River) subsequently grew up there, surrounded by the reserve. Like other towns, its future depended on increased white settlement, but as the Dominion Lands Agent at Grouard noted in 1916, settlement had slowed in the district because about one-third of it was "taken up with lakes, forest reserves, marsh land and Indian reservations." Thus the district was losing the competition for settlers because it offered fewer "inducements to the ordinary settler than some of the more fortunate districts, which have large areas of prairie land."[15]

In early 1923, a group of villagers petitioned the federal government stating that Kinuso's prospects were restricted because it was hemmed in by the reserve. They also argued that the reserve should be thrown open for settlement because it contained "a large proportion of land now laying idle, which is detrimental to the village and settlement." The petition was supported by the local MP, Donald Kennedy, and the provincial MLA, J.S. Coté, who had been "pressing the [Indian Affairs] Department for some action in this regard." While Indian Affairs agreed that the reserve should be sold and its residents moved to the reserve at Driftpile, a short distance west along the lake, Harold Laird, the Indian agent, disagreed. The Swan River Indians were making a satisfactory living, and although he agreed that some land at the edge of the

*This family posed for its portrait with a priest at Sucker Creek.*
*Not dated (ca. 1930s).* OB4236 PAA.

reserve could be sold, he suggested that the Indians keep control of the hay lands and lease rather than sell land nearest the village. Ignoring this advice, the Indian Commissioner in Regina recommended that the land be sold.[16]

In the interim, the band's chief, Astatchikun (also known as Felix Willier), wrote to Indian Affairs outlining his opposition to the sale. He reported that "some white people" had been secretly circulating a petition among the residents of the reserve demanding the sale of the reserve. Neither he nor his headmen had been approached by the petitioners who had gone instead "to the weak-minded" to obtain sufficient signatures to impress Indian Affairs. But Astatchikun was "absolutely against the cession of any of our Reserve" and "for all the gold in the world" would not consent to its sale. The land was essential for the Indians' future well-being because while fishing and hunting had sustained them so far, "the young ones" would have to begin farming since other opportunities were declining. Moreover, Indians from Swan River could not be accommodated at Driftpile—land there was already limited and if more people arrived, each would only "be left room enough to have a dozen bushels of potatoes a year." Moreover, "and I am sorry to say so, the worst of all is that the money we shall get from the land if sold will turn back to those heartless people who covet it and who will draw the price of it from the Indians, by the sale of intoxicating liquors and the use of night gambling." He noted that the Indian Agent, Harold Laird, had approved and encouraged the writing of his letter, and signing in Cree syllabic and English, Astatchikun concluded, "I trust your love of justice to prevent such an infamy."[17]

Infamy or not, Ottawa drew up the documents for the surrender of a portion of the Swan River reserve. Laird was instructed to call a meeting at which the sales documents could be presented for approval, but a vote could not be taken since all the young men were away hunting. This happened again in 1924 and Laird informed the Commissioner that he would try and get the Indians together the next year. Once again this meeting was not called, and the Commissioner instructed Laird "to make a serious attempt to get the Indians together and secure the surrender."[18] But in 1926 and 1927 a quorum of eligible reserve residents again could not be found, and the Indian Commissioner noted "that a special effort" had to be made on the matter. He recommended that the annuity payments not be given out the next year until after discussions about the surrender since "the Indians apparently have little interest in attending meetings once they get their money."[19]

Throughout this manoeuvring, villagers in Kinuso continued to agitate for the sale of the reserve. In 1927 Premier Brownlee added his support, and L.A. Giroux, now the local MLA, also urged the minister of the Interior to support the "opening" of the Swan River reserve, as well as the Sawridge and Sucker Creek reserves. Giroux contended that all the Indians should be consolidated at Driftpile since their reserves were "retarding the settlement" of the area and "hampering communications" among white settlers along the south shore of the lake. In a significant choice of words, he recommended that the Driftpile reserve should "at the present time not be interfered with" because it had a school and no nearby white settlers. Eventually, however, he suggested that all the Indians be removed from the area and "transferred on [sic] the [north] side of the lake behind the Grouard settlement."[20]

This pressure seems to have reinvigorated Indian Affairs' efforts. In 1928 it decided to try and secure the sale of the whole of the Swan River reserve and move its residents to Driftpile. The department noted that if the land "was sold to settlers," the sale would be "of considerable importance to the Municipality." Similar plans were also set out for the Sawridge reserve which lay to the east of Swan River, but when Laird reported that it was "not at all suitable for agricultural purposes," Ottawa's eagerness to sell it dissipated. Nonetheless, the sale of the Swan River reserve remained a priority but was deftly thwarted by the

Indians who continued to be absent at crucial times. They also avoided confrontation by stating that they now wanted better terms for the sale of the reserve, giving the appearance that they were not opposed to its possible sale. But in 1928, a meeting could not be held to discuss the sale because this time Agent Laird was absent. Apparently believing that he was incompetent or in league with the Indians, the Indian commissioner recommended that an inspector be sent "to take the surrender as I am doubtful of Mr. Laird's ability to further the interests of the Department in discussing terms with the Indians." The Indian Affairs department also considered securing the surrender of the reserve through administrative devices and suggested that it "might accept the surrender if the consent of the Indians is obtained individually, or in groups, instead of at a meeting held under the provisions of the Act. If it were possible to obtain the consent of the majority of the voting members in this way, the Inspector might make an affidavit." Since this tactic would not conform "in all respects to the provisions of the Act," it would have to be approved by Order in Council.[21]

While this subterfuge was not adopted, Inspector Murison travelled from Regina to Swan River to negotiate surrender of the reserve along with others in the Peace River country. Failing to draw a quorum at Swan River, he gave notice that another meeting would be held in two weeks. At a preliminary meeting, the Indians opposed the sale of the whole reserve but appeared favourable to surrendering the part around the village. When Inspector Murison returned, a quorum was present at the meeting, but to his surprise, the Indians "all voted against releasing any portion of their reserve." Presuming that they were incapable of setting their own priorities, Murison explained their decision by endorsing a view popularly held in Kinuso—the Indians had been "influenced" by "outsiders" against the sale. While these outsiders were not identified, Murison was all the more convinced that the reserve had to be sold. The Indians were not using the land appropriately, he wrote, because they were not farming. As well, sale of the reserve was now further justified because it would assist the department in exercising tighter control over life on the reserve. Although the Indian Agent had reported the year before that "excessive drinking, so far as he knew" was "not prevalent on the Reserves," Murison reported that

> The information which I have with regard to them as a band is that they are addicted to the use of intoxicating liquor and are immoral in their conduct. It is my opinion that it would be a good thing if the bands along the south shore of the Lesser Slave Lake could be amalgamated and

placed under close supervision. I feel that this is the only solution of the question. At present they appear to have no supervision whatever and there is practically no check with regard to their drinking and immoral habits.[22]

Despite such recommendations, Murison's failure to secure approval for the sale of the reserve led the Indian commissioner to conclude that "it might be just as well to let this matter stand for a time and the Indians may come around later on." Although the Kinuso Chamber of Commerce once again asked Indian Affairs in 1929 to sell a portion of the reserve to the village for use as a fair ground, the Indians' "emphatic refusal" confirmed the department's conclusion that the matter should rest.[23] Nonetheless, the Kinuso Chamber of Commerce and MLA Giroux continued in the early 1930s to press Ottawa (usually through Charles Stewart, the minister of the Interior and the former premier of Alberta) to obtain the surrender of the reserve. While Indian Affairs noted that it might consider the proposal later, it now refused to facilitate the sale because agricultural conditions in western Canada were poor and sale of the land to farmers was unlikely.[24] The last effort in this struggle came in 1938. The village once again wanted to purchase the land that it was by then renting from the band for a sports ground. Indian Affairs observed that the land was worth more than any other on the reserve because of its location, but it agreed to raise the matter with the band. But Chief Sowan was adamant: the land was not for sale. His reasoning disclosed the Indians' priorities and social needs—this reserve land was seen as a means of mediating Indian relationships with the surrounding society. Sowan argued that people camped at the fair grounds when visiting the reserve, as did members of the band at some times of the year. Further, "if we sell the land outright, the white people may charge us admission fees to their sports. They tried this once, and we told them the land was ours. We do not object to them having sports on this land. We enjoy going to sports ourselves." Lastly, he noted that "if we sell outright, liquor may be brought there on sports days, [but] as it is the police watch this very closely."[25]

While government and Euro-Canadian settlers failed to get their way with the reserves on Lesser Slave Lake, the results in the Peace River country were very different. By 1930 many reserves there had been broken up and their populations moved elsewhere. Even before World War I, Indian Affairs was "fending off enquiries about rumours of reserve land in the Peace River valley which would soon be placed on the market." Especially desirable was the Beaver's

Fairview reserve (No. 152), which Indian Affairs described in 1915 as resembling "a thorn in the side of that wide awake community" of settlers. Following World War I, further suggestions were made that reserves in the Peace River country be sold for soldier settlement. While Indian Affairs was not opposed to such sales in principle, it noted that there was still plenty of good homestead land available.[26] Even so, the Fairview reserve was far from forgotten. In 1928 it was described as "a choice stretch of land" of about 15,000 acres, which if "thrown open for settlement as it should be...would lend itself to rapid development," while one Indian Affairs official said it was "some of the finest farming land I have ever seen." The Beaver had two reserves, the one near the future Fairview townsite, as well as the Horse Lakes reserve (No. 152B) that had been established in 1920 near Hythe. About half of the Horse Lakes reserve was "fairly" open land and the Indians harvested hay from around the lake. By the mid 1920s, the Beaver were living on the Horse Lakes reserve as well as on nonreserve land north of Eureka River. Only a few people lived at the Fairview reserve, but there was a cemetery and annuities were also paid there, and it perhaps also served as a stopping place for travelling Beaver.[27]

In 1922, Donald Kennedy was asked by one of his constituents, who claimed to have the backing of "some three hundred settlers of the district," to help obtain the lease of the Fairview reserve for grazing purposes. Kennedy was informed that "it seems too bad to have such splendid pasture right in the centre of the district going to waste" while local farmers had too little. Although Indian Affairs was reluctant to see such fine farm land tied up by a grazing lease, it agreed that the land could be sold for more intensive farming. In 1924 it tried to arrange a meeting of the band to approve its surrender, but the meeting could not be organized and Indian Affairs did not press the matter. Since there was still homestead land available, the department saw little justification for immediate sale of reserve land in the Peace River country. For this reason, it rejected a Grande Prairie law firm's request in 1925 to purchase various reserves for group settlements "reasonably close to a railway and suitable for farming purposes" in the Waterhole, Berwyn and Peace River districts. [28]

This attitude changed with the settlement boom after 1927 and the creation of the town of Fairview and the abandonment of the Waterhole settlement in 1928. Additional pressure came from the direct involvement of powerful political figures. In 1927, Premier Brownlee wrote Indian Affairs to inquire about the possible surrender of various reserves in the Peace country. In addition to the Fairview reserve, there were nine other reserves in the Peace River town-Berwyn area, mostly small plots held in severalty. The department now decided to seek the cancellation of all except the large reserve at Old Wives Lake (No. 151A), where the population from these other reserves could be concentrated. The Indians on these reserves agreed, "providing some reasonable inducement is offered." The Beaver also agreed to the sale of the Fairview reserve, providing they received a new reserve of six sections (3,840 acres) just north of Eureka River (now Clear Hills reserve No. 152C). Thus Indian Affairs assured Premier Brownlee that it would soon be able "to place a number at least of these reserves on the market for sale and settlement." Shortly after this decision, former Premier Herbert Greenfield, by then Alberta's agent general in Britain, inquired if the Peace River country reserves could be sold for a British nonprofit block settlement scheme. Greenfield was familiar with the area—while premier, his constituency had included the Fairview Reserve. Though admitting that such a sale would be administratively convenient, Indian Affairs rejected it because there was "considerable local demand for opening of these reserves for settlement." Since local settlers expected to benefit, the department was loathe "to take any action in this matter which would result in local dissatisfaction or criticism."[29]

The surrender of the Fairview reserve went smoothly. Inspector Murison, who had come from Regina to handle it, ensured that a majority of voting members was present. Although the band numbered 140 people, the matter was decided by 22 men. Even then, Murison left nothing to chance. As he reported:

> I managed, with some effort, to gather together a majority of the voting members of this band. I engaged a man at Wembley to round up 5 members who were residing at Horse Lakes and he brought them to the Beaver Reserve, a distance of about 150 miles, but this enabled me to have a majority of the voting members at the meeting, all of whom voted unanimously in favour of the surrender...I later obtained the assent of Alfred Chatlas, the headman, and three others whose names appear on the surrender. I am attaching their declarations hereto.[30]

As part of this transaction, Indian Affairs purchased land for a reserve at Eureka River for $6.75 per acre from the Department of the Interior. This was probably about twice the land's value, but Indian Affairs approved the site because it was remote and there was little likelihood of white settlement encroaching on it. The cost of the land for the new reserve was charged against the future proceeds of sale from the Fairview reserve, and the Beaver were told that the granting of the new reserve was conditional on their agreement to release their present reserve so it could "be sold for settlement purposes and for their benefit."[31] The Beaver kept 320 acres at Fairview and were promised initial payments of $50 in both 1928 and 1929.[32]

The Cree also surrendered without contest (as a single negotiation) the reserves (most of which were small) around Berwyn and Peace River. They were then moved to the larger reserve at Old Wives Lake, and received an initial payment of $50 per person, and a further $50 the next year—the same terms that had been offered to the Beaver. This was thought to be necessary because all of the bands had contact with each other—in some cases they lived together—and "it might cause dissatisfaction" if all did not receive the same terms. Part of the proceeds of the sale were used "to buy stock, farm implements, building material etc." Because of the qualifications set for the vote, the surrender of the Cree reserves was effected by five men out of a total population of 53. Indian Affairs acknowledged that the surrendered land was "excellent farming land," open and level with no waste land. In contrast, the land at Old Wives Lake, where these people were moved, was more heavily treed, with a spring, lake and some hay lands. This, Inspector Murison reported, made it "a much more desirable reserve for Indians than the land which they have agreed to release." Paradoxically, Indian Affairs apparently agreed to supply the Indians with farm equipment with which to begin farming at Old Wives Lake.[33]

The quality of the land, its location close to the just completed railway and the settlement boom in the Peace River country created great interest in the sale of the Beaver and Cree reserves. Throughout 1928, Indian Affairs had fielded numerous public inquiries about when the land would be sold. The surrender was agreed to in the fall, and that winter the land was subdivided and made ready for sale in the spring. The sale was a major event. Indian Affairs rented the Gem Theatre in Fairview and the building was "taxed to capacity." Over 300 people attended the auction, which began at 10 a.m. and continued, with a one-hour lunch break, until 7:30 p.m. Prices were high and only a few parcels of the Beaver reserve remained unsold at the end of the day, although the sale of the Cree reserves was less immediately successful. The auction received favourable press coverage, and the department congratulated itself that the land had "been purchased by actual farmers" who had started breaking the land within days of the sale.[34]

While breaking had begun, so too had attempts to revise the terms of the purchase agreements. Purchasers paid 10 percent down in cash and were to make the next payment one year later, but they almost immediately asked that this next payment be delayed for a further six months so they could "harvest and market next year's crop before their next payment fell due." Indian Affairs sympathetically noted that the farmers had "quite truthfully" stated that breaking the land would involve "a considerable outlay of cash before they can market a bushel of grain."[35] While costs of breaking were hardly unexpected expenses, Indian Affairs agreed to this arrangement. The needs of white farmers, not the Indians, shaped its priorities.

The Beaver were paid their second cash instalment in 1929 at a gathering near Wembley. It was a festive event. Around $5,000 was paid out, and "Fletcher Bredin conducted a store in a tent, and in another tent nearby refreshments were sold." The *Grande Prairie Herald* reported that "the tents and teepees scattered throughout the woods made it easy to visualize the life of the redman when he roamed through the country free and untrammelled." Indeed, "quite a number of people from the adjoining community and town" drove out to see the spectacle of a vanishing culture.[36] And since it was believed that the Beaver had steadfastly rejected miscegenation, Dr. Grant, "an eminent anthropologist" from Ottawa, took skull measurements and blood samples as part of his research on "what diseases certain races and types are susceptible to."[37]

The reaction of the subjects to this poking, prodding and gawking was not recorded, but the next year the Beaver hired a Fairview lawyer because neither the promised farm machinery nor that year's interest payment had materialized. Indian Affairs was contemptuous, replying that "these Indians have been very fairly treated, and at the present time have no reasonable cause for complaint." The interest had not been paid for 1930 because the department was having problems collecting payments. Farming conditions were poor, and the department argued that "it would obviously be quite unfair" for it "to take any exceptional action to enforce payment." In respect to the farm equipment, Indian Affairs officials privately noted that its purchase was "optional" on the part of the department. Indeed, they suggested that it might not be supplied at all because the Indians would not look after it properly as most of them were "indolent," or had other needs, such as better housing. In its public reply to the Indians, however, the department admitted that the promised farm machinery had not been delivered, but it had to study "just what supplies of this character are really necessary."[38]

By 1931, many purchasers were still behind in their payments but argued that they had paid too much for the land and that wheat prices had fallen. At a meeting held to discuss the matter, the purchasers resolved to ask Indian Affairs to revise the purchase agreements. While admitting that the department was obligated to act as trustee for the Indians, they asked that all interest since the purchase date be waived and that payments apply only to the principal. The Municipal District of Fairview endorsed this proposal. Although Indian Affairs was sympathetic, it refused the request because it would create "a most embarrassing precedent" as a number of purchasers were making their payments. Nonetheless, the department agreed not to repossess any land for the duration of the Depression. The purchasers made the same request again in 1933 through their MP. While the department was still sympathetic, it now pointedly observed that the reserve had been sold because of "repeated demands" by the settlers and with the promise that the Indians would be paid for their land.[39] Even so, the interest rate was reduced by Order in Council, but the department did repossess some land for nonpayment of interest and principal. The whole matter was becoming increasingly confrontational, and in 1936 one farmer at Berwyn made application under the *Farmers' Creditor Arrangement Act* (part of Alberta's Depression era debt legislation) and had his purchase price reduced retroactively. This prospect raised alarm among Indian Affairs officials. Since crop prospects were good, the department exerted more pressure on the purchasers, but many refused to pay despite having promised to do so. As Inspector Christianson was informed in 1936, some purchasers "had no intention of paying for the land they were occupying." Despite political intervention in support of the farmers, the department put "a representative on the ground during harvesting and threshing operations" and managed to collect substantial arrears that year.[40] Its determination indicated that while Indian Affairs had been concerned to accommodate the interests of white farmers, it would only go so far in sacrificing Indian interests to those of Euro-Canadians.

#### ▬ Land and the Metis

The success of some Metis in farming and other occupations did not lessen the fact that there were many poor Metis. In 1934 the Metis Association of Alberta estimated that one-half of the mixed race population in Alberta who had been granted homesteads had lost them. While this failure rate was no worse than that of Euro-Canadian settlers, the consequences for Metis were graver because their employment options were more restricted. Indeed, the association estimated that about 50 percent of the mixed race population was desperately poor.[41] While many Metis in northern Alberta were good carpenters and skilful at building with logs, poverty and the lack of land ensured that their housing was usually substandard. Many lived in shacks along road allowances or on unsurveyed and other crown land not open to homesteading. Still others lived along the boundaries of Indian reserves or on the reserves themselves. Technological change had seriously eroded the economy of makeshifts that had earlier supported them and resource depletion threatened their trapping and hunting livelihood. Health care was minimal and their general lack of education gave them few alternatives. As a consequence, many Metis, especially those living near white settlements, faced very difficult circumstances by the 1930s.

As with Indians, control of land, class, status and social security framed the relationship between many Metis and the dominant society. The question of Metis status came to a head in the late 1920s when, as part of the upcoming transfer of natural resources from the federal to the provincial government, it was announced that squatter's rights would be abolished. This posed a problem for the many Metis who lived as squatters on crown lands. In 1929, a group of Metis who were squatting on a crown forest reserve near Fishing Lake in the Cold Lake district petitioned for a land grant to protect their residency. Local meetings and discussions on the matter gained wide support from other Metis in the district and from further afield. The issue also drew the attention of a local school teacher, Joseph Dion, an enfranchised Indian and a descendent of Big Bear. Dion became one of the group's leaders, and meetings in 1930 and 1931 drew increased participation. Demands quickly emerged for special land grants for Metis in the form of "reserves" or "settlements."[42]

While Metis demands centred around land ownership, the emerging movement was more than a simple quest for land. As Murray Dobbin has argued in his biography of the Metis leaders Malcolm Norris and Jim Brady, it was not just a "nationalistic" movement but was concerned with broad social and economic change for all people of Native ancestry. In 1931, councillors were elected from Metis communities in northern Alberta to organize a petition "asserting Metis demands for land, education, health care and free hunting and fishing permits." The petition garnered over 500 signatures, and following its presentation to the provincial government, the Alberta Department of Lands and Mines began an investigation of Metis living conditions. As well, a convention attended by Metis delegates from across the province was held in St. Albert in late 1932. At this meeting, L'Association des Metis d'Alberta et les Territoires du Nord-Ouest (later renamed the Metis Association of Alberta) was formed to co-ordinate and promote demands for land and justice. The association attracted wide support and by 1935 it had 41 locals with over 1,000 members. It encountered relatively little antagonism, although one of its leaders admitted the existence of opposition from some "people who are more or less trying to camouflage the fact that they…have Indian blood in their veins."[43]

A constitution was adopted that specified that anyone of First Nations ancestry (including treaty Indians) was eligible for membership. In other words, being Metis was not only a matter of biology but also involved self-definition. The constitution also provided for annual elections and set out terms for the land grants that the association was demanding. The "reserves" would be nontransferable, with title retained by the crown. It was proposed that the reserves be self-governing through a locally elected administration. Rather than being wards of the government, settlement members would elect delegates to the Metis association's central executive council that would be the supreme governing body of the settlements and "the single voice of the Metis, on and off the settlements." While the association would deal with government, local administrators would run the settlements and hire the necessary staff. Each settlement member would receive free medical treatment from a resident doctor, and schools would also be located on each reserve. Although clergy would receive land on each reserve, the association proposed that their rights be limited. This perhaps reflected a popular view among some Red River Metis that the church had betrayed them in 1885 when it sided with the government against Riel. But as one of the Metis leaders, Felix Calihoo, noted, the heart of the movement and its overriding objective was "to see that adequate provision is made for our homeless and destitute families" and to ensure their medical and educational needs. Joe Dion later called the movement "the reinstatement of the Metis race." To confirm that it was about self-identity and a new future, the meeting "abolished" the term "half-breed" (which Dion observed he had always resented) and instead adopted the term "Metis."[44]

By the time the Metis association was formed in 1932, three other individuals had joined Joseph Dion in leading the movement—Jim Brady from St. Paul, Malcolm Norris from Edmonton, and Peter Tompkins Jr., the son of the first land agent at Grouard. In his study of Alberta's Metis settlements, political scientist T.C. Pocklington noted that these leaders "were exceptional not only in their individual talents and commitment but also in the remarkable complementarity of their abilities and dispositions." A staunch Roman Catholic, Dion was the most conservative of the four and provided political respectability and linkages with the church. Norris and Brady were socialists; Norris was an accomplished orator and skilled organizer, while Brady was the movement's tactical strategist and theoretician. Tompkins, a liberal democrat, was an effective local organizer and provided an intellectual middle ground between Dion on the right and Brady and Norris on the left. The association also received support from Joseph Dechene, MLA for St. Paul, and Percy Davies, the federal MP for Athabasca, each of whom "became involved in a game of one-upmanship in championing the Metis cause and courting the Metis vote."[45]

Individuals such as Brady and Norris—the core of the Metis association's leadership—identified themselves as Red River Metis and as the natural leaders of Alberta's Metis people. The leadership was well educated, and most of the founding convention were French-speaking Metis land owners and labourers. As Murray Dobbin notes, members of the same class had been prominent in the Metis struggles of 1869–70 and 1885. But while "all classes had economic interests" in the earlier struggles, the movement in Alberta in the 1930s

> was principally in the interests of the destitute nomadic people; middle-class and working-class Metis had little economic self-interest in the struggle. Clearly, some of those Metis farmers who had been forced off the land and some Metis workers who wanted land saw the struggle as in their interests. But principally the advanced Metis were drawn to the movement by nationalist sentiment—a renewed feeling of kinship with their poorer cousins.

This motive, "based more on sympathy than self-interest," held potential danger for the movement because, as Dobbin notes, "economic interests—class differences—might lead the more advanced Metis to eventually abandon the struggle, just as many had after 1869–70 and 1885." Further threats to the cohesion of the movement lay in the heterogeneity of Alberta's mixed race community and, potentially, in the different styles and philosophies of its leaders. Yet, the overriding quest for land gave the movement unity and helped transcend ideological differences among its leaders and class differences among its members.[46]

Premier Brownlee initially stalled demands from the Metis association by claiming that the Metis were in part a federal responsibility and that the issues were complex and needed study. In early 1933, however, Joseph Dechene succeeded in having the Alberta legislature pass a resolution committing the government to consider "some plan of colonization" and to begin a study of Metis needs before the start of the next legislative session. This indicated that the Metis association had partially succeeded in shaping public debate, and during 1933 it met with provincial officials for general discussions about solutions to the problems faced by the Metis. Amidst a mounting economic and political crisis that was consuming the UFA government, and to meet the terms of the legislative assembly's resolution of 1933, the government appointed a commission of inquiry into the Metis in late 1934 under the chairmanship of Mr. Justice Albert Ewing.[47]

The commission convened in early 1935. One of its immediate tasks was to define who was Metis. Discussion at first tried to sort out what percentage of First Nations and white blood was necessary for an individual to be defined as a "Metis," but such biological approaches were quickly discarded given the complexity of Metis history. Instead, a Metis was defined as a person who had some First Nations ancestry and who lived "the life of an ordinary Indian." As Norris noted, it was "almost impossible to make any strict and definite line of distinction between the Treaty Indian and the Metis," forcing a conclusion that self-definition, as well as lifestyle, were central. The commissioners agreed and noted that "it is apparent to everyone that there are in this Province many persons of mixed blood (Indian and white) who have settled down as farmers, who are making a good living…and who do not need, nor do they desire, public assistance. The term as used in this report has no application to such men."[48] Jim Brady further contributed to this analysis by arguing that Metis in Alberta fell into two classes: a "progressive," sedentary group, and a "nomadic" one. The latter included those in the far north of the province (many of whom were not descended from Red River Metis) who lived by trapping, fishing and hunting, and people living further south who could barely support themselves.[49]

The Ewing Commission held formal hearings in Edmonton and conducted interviews in places with substantial Metis population like Athabasca, Lac La Biche and High Prairie. Missionaries, medical doctors, politicians, civil servants and members of the Metis association gave testimony about health, living conditions and social needs. While most witnesses were treated well, the commissioners were often sharp with the Metis association's representatives. The deliberations were dominated by what Ken Hatt in his study of the commission has called a "pathological model," in which "the situation of the Metis was considered analogous to an illness; reference to historical, political or economic argument was strictly discouraged." Even so, the Metis association's earlier demands for a land base were accepted with little question by the commissioners, although Ewing was unsympathetic to the association's argument that the settlements should become an "economic base for self-determination." He made it clear that "in no way was the possible granting of land related to any question of aboriginal right; it was strictly a matter of welfare."[50]

The Ewing Commission submitted its final report in early 1936. Overall, it was, as T.C. Pocklington concludes, a "shoddy" and contradictory document that employed weak evidence and ignored important aspects of Metis history and social life. It rather grudgingly admitted that many Metis suffered from poorer health and housing conditions than whites, especially in the districts around Lesser Slave Lake, Lac La Biche and St. Paul. It recommended that the province provide medical and educational services, and that northern Metis also receive free trapping and hunting licences and 320 acres of land per family. Most importantly, it recommended that two "experimental" farm colonies be created on good agricultural land close to fishing and timber resources but remote from white settlers. The commissioners emphasized that this was not a temporary relief measure but a "comprehensive scheme" that would provide a lasting solution. They rejected any suggestion that the Metis become wards of the government because this would be costly and would sap Metis initiative and self-reliance. At the same time, they recommended that the settlers not receive title to the land because they judged that the Metis had little business acumen and were unable to compete with whites. Indeed, the commissioners believed that one of the remarkable characteristics of their culture was that most Metis were not sufficiently acquisitive in Euro-Canadian terms. They did not have "the so-called 'land hunger'" and were "not desirous of becoming land owners or of settling down on land permanently and exclusively as farmers or stock growers."[51]

The assumption that the Metis were not acquisitive was basic to the Commission's recommendation that they be assimilated into white society by means of farm settlements. As the commissioners concluded, the Metis had to change their "mode of life to conform with that of the white inhabitants or...gradually disappear." Nonetheless, "a gradual initiation into the new life" was necessary and would require "a long process of education and training" led by the government. While the settlements were to be the focus for assimilation, the commissioners noted that they should be located away from whites in areas where people could at first make a living hunting, trapping and fishing. Consistent with the general Euro-Canadian view that such occupations were becoming steadily obsolete, the commissioners argued that life on segregated settlements would eventually make the Metis "more and more dependent on farming and stock raising. This is the aim and purpose of the plan." Yet the recommendation that the settlements be in remote areas was only one part of the assimilation by segregation approach. It would also, as the commission's secretary noted, forestall "dissatisfaction" by the "general public."[52] Apparently, the solution to Euro-Canadian "land hunger" could best be dealt with by the physical isolation of Natives rather than the defence of their needs and rights.

Despite its contradictions and ambiguity, the report made some important contributions. As Pocklington notes, it recognized the Metis "as a unique group in Alberta" and also proposed, "within the limits of the commissioners' paternalistic and assimilationist assumptions," some "humane steps for dealing with 'the Metis problem.'" At first, the government was not entirely committed to implementing its recommendations, and in late 1937 it approached the federal government with the suggestion that it take over responsibility for the Metis. At the time, the federal government wanted to see a trapping preserve for exclusive use by Indians created near Fort Chipewyan to protect Indian trapping territory from white competition. To this point, the province had resisted such proposals, but it now saw an opportunity to link them with the debate about the Metis. Since an Indian trapping preserve would deprive local Metis of trapping territory, A.N. Tanner, the Alberta minister of Lands and Mines, proposed that it was "an opportune time to discuss the case of our Half-Breeds" in general. Tanner proposed that "if the federal government would resume responsibility for the Half-Breed as well as for the Indian, the Province would willingly make available to the Dominion whatever lands might be required for the establishment of [trapping] reserves." Federal officials refused this offer—they had no interest in expanding federal commitments—noting that the Ewing Commission had specifically rejected any scheme making the Metis wards of the government. Nonetheless, they were eager to discuss trapping preserves, and further discussions took place in 1938. Although these brought few concrete results, they implicitly recognized that the economic and social requirements of northern Alberta Indians and Metis were not easily compartmentalized.[53]

In the meantime, and likely due in part to its failure to off-load responsibility onto the federal government, Alberta went ahead with legislation to set aside settlements for the exclusive use of Metis. By this time the Metis association was inactive; it had neglected its constituents and some of its leaders had become absorbed in personal and other political concerns. Despite this lack of public pressure, the Social Credit government (elected in 1935) was willing to act on the Ewing Commission, and in mid 1938 it hired Peter Tompkins to select tentative sites and determine the degree of Metis willingness to participate in a settlement scheme. Tompkins believed that the government's commitment was sincere; a conclusion that is endorsed by historian Alvin Finkel's judgement that it was part of Social Credit's early reformist impulse. Tompkin's view was confirmed in late 1938 when Alberta passed the *Metis Population Betterment Act*. Under this legislation, Metis were defined as people of First Nations-white ancestry who were not Indians or nontreaty Indians under the *Indian Act*. The legislation permitted the province to set aside land where Metis settlements could be established and where hunting and trapping by outsiders could be prohibited. While title to settlement land was retained by the crown, each settlement was to be run by an association made up of locally elected members. Once a settler was accepted by an association, he was allotted land and was required to construct buildings of a minimum value. Reflecting the agricultural orientation of the scheme, each settler had to clear and break two acres per year until 15 acres were cleared. Once these requirements were met, the settler received a "certificate of occupancy."[54]

The settlement associations (which later became known as councils) were required to devise bylaws and a constitution that would set out qualifications and conditions of membership for people who wanted to live in the settlement. As well, each association was "to co-operate with the minister" to develop schemes for the settlement and its social needs. This was not the co-operative system that the Metis association had recommended at the hearings of the Ewing commission. Although the province unofficially recognized the largely moribund Metis association as "representatives of the Metis population," the settlements were not politically autonomous. Provincial control was tight, and settlement councils were not corporations (as were municipal governments), and they had no rights as legal entities. Moreover, any scheme devised by a settlement council to promote the legislation had to be approved by the provincial cabinet. Nor could the local constitution and bylaws be amended without the consent of the responsible minister. The province also had the right to abolish a settlement or change its boundaries.[55]

The first settlements were established in 1938–39, and as land set aside for the exclusive use of Metis, they were unique in Canada.[56] Despite Ewing's recommendation that only two experimental settlements be set up, a number of possible sites were selected near areas where Metis already lived or had indicated they wanted to reside. Ideally, these sites had reasonably good farm land; were close to a lake with fish; had adequate fur and game and a good supply of timber suitable for building. "So far as possible," they were also to be in areas "free from interference by white settlers." By 1940, such settlements had been established at three locations in east-central Alberta around St. Paul. In

*People were lined up to make their purchases at the Metis Colony store at Keg River, 1953.* PA754/3 PAA.

northern Alberta, about eight townships were reserved for a settlement at Keg River (now called Paddle Prairie Metis Settlement), and four more were reserved at Utikuma Lake (now called Gift Lake Metis Settlement). Although they as yet had no residents, other areas were also selected. In northern Alberta, these included sites at Big Prairie—now called Peavine Metis Settlement—and East Prairie. By 1940, applications had been received from 37 heads of families at Paddle Prairie where 19 families had taken up residence and broken about 40 acres of land. At Gift Lake, the settlement's proximity to commercial fisheries at Utikuma Lake provided the settlers with an alternative to farming. Only indigent Metis were allowed to become members and relief was given in return for building roads, cutting timber for buildings and preparing the village sites. Reflecting a communal social organization at variance with typical rural settlement in Alberta, the settlements were focussed around villages. This was designed to centralize the community to facilitate general administration and the provision of schools. Each family was allotted a one-acre residential lot in the village while other lots were reserved for school and church needs. The village surveys followed "a definite plan," and roads, lanes and recreational grounds were laid out. Land close to the village was also reserved for a community farm. While minimum house sizes were specified, this regulation was at first ignored because of the need for immediate shelter. Farm land (ranging between 20 and 100 acres) was surveyed outside the village.[57]

The settlements in east-central Alberta faced difficulties because the land was sometimes poor and a number of the settlers were not interested in farming. In contrast, the settlements in northern Alberta were more successful. Although settlement life was often hard, it was markedly better than what people had previously experienced. In 1946 the Keg River settlement raised 20,000 bushels of grain, some cattle and hogs, and residents cut 100,000 feet of lumber that winter. Nonetheless, there was no provision for medical care, and Mary Percy Jackson (then living at Notikewin) charged that the province was attempting to foist this responsibility onto her and the Fellowship of the Maple Leaf. She noted that "it is one thing to look after destitute natives here in the village and another to make long trips" to Keg River. With acerbity, she noted that "the Fellowship of the Maple Leaf hardly exists to collect money to pay for drugs to be given to a settlement of half-breeds sent by the Government to an out-of-the-way place like that."[58]

At East Prairie (established slightly later than the Paddle Prairie and Gift Lake settlements), most of the settlers lived by gardening, trapping, hunting, farming and cutting timber. Most houses were built of logs, and the settlers built a school in 1945.[59] There was little formal communication among settlements, although people were clearly aware of conditions elsewhere; in 1943 a number of people from the east-central Alberta settlements moved to the more successful one at Keg River. At the same time, the province began extending its already considerable control over the settlements. In 1939, area supervisors were appointed to look after settlement business dealings and in 1940 the governing legislation was amended to redefine a Metis as a person with not less than one-quarter First Nations ancestry. This restricted membership and lessened the number of applications. Other amendments to the legislation extended other aspects of the government's already substantial authority over the settlements and gave it additional powers affecting settlement life and economy. At the same time, the government also announced that it no longer recognized the

Metis association as the representative of the Metis population. Schooling too came under tighter control. While the province had paid the full operating costs of settlement schools, it did not at first operate them. In 1945, charges that the schools were poorly run led the province to place their administration in the hands of the Department of Public Welfare.[60]

These changes showed that the Metis had not gained the freedom to organize and govern themselves as leaders like Brady and Norris had hoped. Like Indian reserves, crown ownership of land, isolation from white settlement and assimilationist intentions characterised Metis settlements policy and demonstrated that while Metis had all the rights of citizenship, their First Nations inheritance shaped government response to their circumstances. Self-government was not achieved until 1989, indicating the ongoing use of the settlements as a paternalistic welfare measure. Yet the Metis settlements became, as historian Olive Dickason phrased it, "homelands for the Metis." And as T.C. Pocklington discovered, they had a rich political life and the Metis were sometimes able to work around the limitations imposed by the legislation to promote their own interests and needs.[61]

The establishment of Metis settlements manifested one element of the complex relationship among Native people, the dominant culture and the control of land. It also had implications for self-identity. The legal status of being an "Indian" that had been extended to northern Alberta by Treaty 8 formalized distinctions within the Native community and created a new framework upon which self-identification could be articulated and even built. While the creation of the Metis association was in general terms part of a revived expression of Metis history and identity, it was also a formal articulation of legal identity first given form in northern Alberta in 1899. Although the provincial government did not recognize the existence of a Metis Aboriginal title, the crises of the Metis in the interwar years and their demands for a remedy prompted state intervention through the establishment of Metis settlements. The formation of the Metis association was one instance in which Native concerns about land were not handicapped by passivity. While this was not as clearly demonstrated by Indians in respect to pressures for the sale of reserve land, resistance at the Swan River reserve was one example of the confirmation of self-interest and identity. As well, the Beaver near Fairview also believed that an exchange of land at least better met their needs, and their demands for fulfillment of the sales agreements implied an ongoing affirmation of their self-interest. Like the demands for new reserves, these actions revealed the centrality of land in Native attempts to assert their own priorities in the new society and economy in which they now lived.

# 13 Development of Northern Resources

THE HOPES of early Canadian expansionists that northern Alberta's fish, timber, mineral and petroleum resources would bring wealth to southern investors remained largely unrealized by the end of World War II. Nonetheless, there was some expansion in certain sectors, all of which had been established to some degree during the development boom before 1920. Although each industry faced unique problems, it became apparent that fishing, mining and lumbering could prosper in northern Alberta only when they had particular advantage in southern markets. Thus, depletion in more southerly lakes in Alberta led to the development of northern fish resources, while the lack of salt production on the prairies stimulated the development of salt plants at Waterways. The opposite was also true. Adequate supplies of lumber of equal or better quality in the southern prairie markets made northern lumber uncompetitive. Similarly, competing supplies and lack of markets held back the technologically demanding and capital intensive development of the oil sands, although extensive exploration and applied research were undertaken by government.

Public involvement in oil sands development was consistent with both federal and provincial government policy, which supported the creation of infrastructure and favourable conditions for private development. Similarly, government assistance for the fishing industry took the form of fisheries regulations that favoured commercial operators and the mitigation of depletion with techniques such as fish hatcheries. In this environment, resource development was built around extractive industries producing raw or semi-processed materials. The profit earned by these operations usually accrued to owners outside the region and contributed little to local capital accumulation. Skilled labour too was often imported, and local jobs were usually part-time or short-term and contributed little to the development of a permanent skilled work force resident in the area.

## —— Fishing, 1921–1947

As before the end of World War I, development of northern fishing depended on high capitalization because distance to markets added high transportation, cold storage and processing costs to a low-value resource. The capital this required promoted corporate concentration and the integration of processing and marketing functions. Higher capitalization also stimulated expanded production. In a reinforcing cycle, increased production led to depletion of fish stocks, demanding even further capital and concentrated ownership to capture the fish that remained. State regulation of fishing (both before and after the transfer of natural resources to the province in 1930) accommodated these conditions. Subsistence fishing was discouraged in favour of commodity use, and while conservation efforts aimed to preserve fish stocks, they simultaneously ensured that "every available fish made it to market" and that existing and future investment by private fishing companies was protected and encouraged. While royalties in the form of a fur tax were paid with respect to wild fur after 1921, royalties were not collected on commercial fishing until after World War II. With only a sketchy understanding of northern fish resources and their dynamics, fisheries regulation was balanced on the razor's edge of trying to maximize production without causing depletion. Typically, the first few years of commercial fishing on a lake enjoyed extraordinary productivity, but fish matured slowly in cold northern lakes, and "when the largest fish, the big spawners, were taken, fish populations dropped quickly."[1]

The main commercial species in northern Alberta were whitefish, lake trout and pickerel. Whitefish brought the highest prices, followed closely by the other two. Prices for other fish (usually called "coarse" fish) were low and markets were limited. Since domestic markets were small relative to production, Alberta fish were exported to markets in the United States and, to a lesser extent, central Canada. Prices were generally satisfactory during the 1920s, but the Alberta industry was weak because of competition from producers in other provinces closer to markets. Falling prices and demand during the Depression intensified the vulnerability of Alberta's commercial fishery, although prices and demand for fish rose during World War II.

Existing processing facilities and improved transportation links with Edmonton ensured that commercial fishing in northern Alberta in the early 1920s remained concentrated at Lesser Slave Lake. In 1923—a year of high prices—the whitefish catch fell short of the limit by almost 10 percent. While a "phenomenal catch" in the first week "taxed the shipping facilities to the limit," the fish then scattered over the lake and fishing was poor for the rest of the season. Since it was relatively shallow, Lesser Slave Lake was vulnerable to severe storms, which further limited the catch and made speed of operations a key to profitability. These factors encouraged additional capitalization in the form of larger gas-powered boats, deeper-lying nets (which required more costly floats and leads) and expanded processing and handling facilities. A new refrigeration plant with a capacity of about 68,000 kilograms was built by the Menzies Company at Faust in 1924 at a cost of $4,000. New marketing techniques were also adopted, including the sale of filleted fish, the promotion of smoked whitefish and the shipping of fresh fish in car-lot shipments, a new practice in northern Alberta.[2]

The industry continued to be dominated by a few, relatively highly capitalized operations served by consignment or wage workers. A few private fishermen also sold fish to processors or through the United Fishermen of Faust—the only nonagricultural co-operative association in Alberta in the mid 1930s. Details about the formation of the co-operative are sketchy, but it likely developed from an effort by fishermen to free themselves from the consignment system. By 1936, the co-operative had a fish processing plant and 20 members; only a very small proportion of the several hundred fishermen working on the lake. During the Depression, an increasing number of people, including many farmers, tried to earn some income from fishing. Much of this was seasonal winter fishing (which had lower capital requirements than summer fishing) on remote lakes accessible only by winter trails. Most of this catch was "peddled" door to door in towns and cities or was sold to fur farmers. While such increased fishing led to depletion, economic desperation stimulated public demands that closed lakes be re-opened for commercial production. As one provincial official noted in 1939, these demands were "so persistent and imperative" that it was "impossible to refuse."[3]

Natives also had a similarly marginal economic role in the fishing sector. Indians could obtain free domestic fishing licences, but they had to use nets with a larger mesh than those allowed for commercial users and could not sell

*In 1935 severe floods hit the east end of Lesser Slave Lake, washing out tracks and forcing the relocation of several towns.*

A3340 PAA.

any of the fish they caught.[4] Quotas were not allocated to Indian bands because federal fisheries legislation guaranteed open access to fish resources by prohibiting "exclusive rights to any section of the population."[5] While Native domestic use of fish probably declined somewhat in the interwar years because dog teams became less common and the use of store-bought food increased, their participation in commercial fishing did not expand. At Lesser Slave Lake, Natives could not afford the deep-lying nets and gas boats required for a depleting resource. Consequently, many Natives found work as seasonal labourers at the fish plants at Faust and on the fishing boats. In 1938, the Indian Agent reported that Indians around Lesser Slave Lake had no work and faced desperate conditions. They needed better nets and equipment to "compete with the white people when the [commercial fishing] season opened." By 1948 it was reported that commercial fishing during the war had "practically destroyed" fish stocks in lakes normally fished by Natives in central and northern Alberta.[6]

Metis at Utikuma Lake found greater success in the nearby fisheries. The Metis leaders, Jim Brady and Malcolm Norris, had organized Metis fishing co-operatives in more southern districts in the late 1930s, but these projects had failed because of infighting among the co-ops, the hostility of private fish buyers and a lack of loyalty by members. At the Metis settlement at Utikuma Lake, however, government co-operation and a tighter geographical and community focus brought success. In 1941, the government allocated almost 34,000 kilograms of the commercial catch of Utikuma Lake to the Metis-run fish co-operative, The Utikuma Lake Fisheries. Private financing was secured to purchase a commercial fishing licence as well as the equipment, boxes and supplies needed for marketing the catch. A small plant was constructed for storage and packing, and coarse fish were sold locally while whitefish were exported. High prices during World War II enabled the fishery to support the whole of the colony.[7]

While Utikuma Lake supported the Metis fish co-operative, most of the industry was concentrated at several points on the south-east shore of Lesser Slave Lake, which was accessible to the railway. The geography of the industry was largely shaped by the corporate decisions of the NAR and the major processors. Faust was the most important fishing town on Lesser Slave Lake, and in 1934–35 it shipped 73 percent of the fish taken commercially from the lake. Its connection to the railway was secure and a number of fish plants were located there. The second most important centre was Widewater near the east end of the lake. Fishermen had built an ice-house there in 1924 so that they could "co-operate and ship their fish direct to Chicago, thus eliminating the middleman." By 1931 they had subdivided land purchased from the NAR, and 20 lots had been developed. The population had grown to about 70 families by 1934. By then, the industry in the town was dominated by the fish processing plants run by the large processors. There was also a small sawmill that manufactured shipping boxes. While about 19 percent of Lesser Slave Lake's catch was shipped from Widewater, it was an inconvenient shipping point because surrounding hills made access difficult and the NAR refused to upgrade the road. In 1934 the box factory closed because a larger lumber mill in the region was producing boxes at lower cost, and disaster struck in 1935 when floods destroyed the fish plants and the siding at Widewater as well as much of the track at the east end of Lesser Slave Lake. Widewater was then abandoned and the NAR established a new siding, also called Widewater, about 4 kilometres away in a location with better road access and less risk from flooding. The fish companies also moved to new Widewater or to other points a short distance further west along the lake. Fishermen were forced to follow because it was "utterly impossible" for them to market their fish independently. As one fish company executive noted, the fishermen "were entirely dependent on the buyers who furnished their nets and all equipment" and had no choice but to locate near the plants. By the end of 1937 there were three fish companies at new Widewater: W.R. Menzies Co., Taylor Fish Co. and the Burwash Fish Company. Inevitably, old Widewater declined. Although it had no services, a few people hung on in the village. By 1936, it had about 35 people, mainly living in log and "shack type" houses. Most people were poor and got by on a makeshifts economy including fishing during the season, raising a few mink (which were fed fish) and working on the railway.[8]

During the interwar years, depletion of fish in Lesser Slave Lake was an ongoing concern. As early as 1921 the Roman Catholic Bishop Guy wrote that "a very few powerful companies had taken possession" of the lake and were waging "a cruel war to the fish, which is being destroyed without discrimination."[9] In 1924 fisheries officials recommended that catch limits be reduced by one-third, and they observed the next year that "heavy fishing, larger operations and better equipment" were bringing declining whitefish production at all lakes close to the railway. The most serious conditions were at Lesser Slave Lake. By 1925–26, commercial quantities of lake trout had vanished from the lake. Whitefish too were under pressure. The limit on whitefish was reduced by over 50 percent, and while production was still high, the whitefish were smaller in size than even a few years earlier. In a common pattern in Canadian inland fisheries, attention then shifted to previously less desirable species. At Lesser Slave Lake, this meant an "enormous" increase in the production of pike. Ten years before, these fish had been unwanted, but by 1925 efforts were underway to process them into marketable forms. The fish plant at Faust began producing filleted jackfish, and the same year a smoke house was built in Edmonton to smoke filleted jackfish and whole small whitefish (likely another response to the depletion of larger fish). As the fisheries inspector reported, this expanded infrastructure allowed processing and marketing of surplus coarse fish. Proposals for manufacturing fish oil and "fish cakes" for human consumption from coarse fish varieties also attempted to maximize the lake's entire fish resources, not just preferred species that were becoming more difficult and costly to catch.[10]

During the 1930s, commercial fishing declined somewhat at Lesser Slave Lake because of poor markets. As a result, whitefish stocks in the lake improved. At the same time, the growth of fur farming in the district provided expanded local markets for coarse fish. Traditionally, fish like suckers and tullibee had been piled on the shore for use as dog food by Natives and others. While this was still the custom by 1937, it was beginning to disappear because such fish were now being sold to local fur farms. Indeed, by 1940, demand for fish as mink food was outstripping supply, and fish stocks came under even greater pressure during World War II because of rising demand in North America.[11] Although fishing was still an important industry at Lesser Slave Lake in the late 1940s—there were nine fish processing plants along the lake by 1950—depletion was again becoming a problem because of the combined impact of overfishing and declining water levels in the lake.[12]

Whitefish depletion at Lesser Slave Lake prompted the government to establish a fish hatchery at Canyon Creek in 1937. Until this time, fish plantings in Alberta had been restricted to sport fish in lakes and streams in more southern locations. It had long been popular to assume that fish depletion could be reversed by such intervention; a view that perhaps contributed to sanguine official attitudes towards depletion.[13] While just over 300 million whitefish fry and eyed eggs were planted between 1937 and 1943, the benefits were unclear. The increase in whitefish populations in the late 1930s apparently had more to do with decreased fishing and poor markets than the hatchery's efforts. Preliminary data gathered by biologist Richard Miller in 1946 at Lesser Slave Lake found that fish plantings had "no effect." He contended that natural reproduction produced about 100 times the number of fish that a lake could support, and there was consequently "enormous mortality imposed by competition for food and space." The hatchery fry and eggs were eliminated in the same manner and to the same degree, and thus "a few million hatchery produced eggs or fry fail to have any measurable effect on the fishery."[14]

As early as the 1920s, this growing pressure on whitefish at Lesser Slave Lake had led to a search for lakes that had not been fished commercially. Throughout northern Alberta, falling stocks in closer-in areas led to the expansion of commercial fishing well beyond areas easily accessible to the railway. In 1925, an ice house and storage shed were built at Peter Pond Lake (located south of La Loche, Saskatchewan) and a 125-kilometre trail was built to Cheechum, the tiny settlement on the NAR line between Lac La Biche and Waterway, from which the fish were shipped to market. Similarly, commercial fishing (including a co-operative owned by fishermen) began operating at Lake Winefred, also a considerable distance from the railway.[15]

All of these lakes quickly came under pressure—depletion was first noticed at Winefred Lake as early as 1927.[16] Attention soon turned to Lake Athabasca, the largest untouched fishing lake in Alberta. Famous for its whitefish and lake trout since the early days of the fur trade, improved rail service between Edmonton and Waterways after 1925 made commercial development of Lake Athabasca feasible. In 1926 the McInnes Fish Company moved six boats to

Lake Athabasca from Lesser Slave Lake, where it had operated since about 1915. While McInnes still had interests at lakes further south, its Lake Athabasca operations soon became most important. It had Lake Athabasca to itself until 1928 when Lake Athabasca Fisheries Ltd. (which in 1925 had purchased the cannery operations of Mackenzie Basin Fisheries Ltd. at Black Bay, Saskatchewan) built a packing plant, ice houses and lodgings at the lake and an icehouse in Waterways. In the predictable pattern of corporate concentration in the fishing industry (likely exacerbated in this case by the lake's even greater distance from markets), Lake Athabasca Fisheries Ltd. then amalgamated with three other companies (Clarke Fisheries from Lac La Biche, Johnson Fisheries Ltd., Edmonton, and the Associated Fisheries Ltd., a co-operative fishermen's association) to form the National Fish Foods Company.[17] Both McInnes and the new company operated on Lake Athabasca only during the summer. McInnes was by far the largest of the two; the limit on the lake in 1929 was 1.1 million kilograms, of which McInnes took about 790,000 kilograms. Most of this catch consisted of lake trout, much of which was shipped to Chicago. But trout prices fell in 1930, and the National Fish Company had closed its operations at Lake Athabasca by 1931. Trout prices remained low for most of the decade.[18]

The commercial fishery at Lake Athabasca employed the most advanced organizational and technical systems of the time. It was organized on a factory model and featured the integration of many different functions within a single corporate entity. The speed with which these technological developments were put in place illustrated Harold Innis's observation that the introduction of new technology and development in remote locations in twentieth century northern Canada often resembled a cyclone since "the total range of modern technology was brought at once to bear upon areas of untapped resources."[19] In the first years of operation, fishing on Lake Athabasca was sometimes suspended because the catch was so heavy that it could not be handled. More efficient equipment soon eliminated these bottlenecks, and in 1930 the limit was reached at the earliest date yet. McInnes opened offices in Waterways and living quarters for workers and a processing plant were built at Crackingstone Point on the east end of Lake Athabasca, about 130 kilometres from Fort Chipewyan. At first, fishing boats unloaded their catch at receiving depots where the fish were gutted and graded. In about 1929, additional stations were built and existing ones were moved closer to areas with the most plentiful fish stocks. As well, the size of fishing boats was increased and stronger and deeper-lying nets were used to permit operation in deeper water. Nearly half the nets had to be replaced during a season because they were destroyed during storms or by the large trout that tore through them.[20]

In preparation for shipping, the fresh fish were packed in wooden boxes with equal amounts of shaved ice. The National Fish Company had a small lumber mill near Fort Chipewyan that turned out these boxes, and McInnes had one near Waterways. Although most fish were shipped fresh, those caught late in the season were frozen, and by 1929 one of the companies had installed equipment for freezing, filleting and wrapping fish in "attractively branded" wax paper. The fish were shipped by barge to Waterways. At first, Hudson's Bay Company barges were used, but the fish companies (as NWT mining companies would later do) soon built their own transport facilities to circumvent the limits of the Bay's operations. By about 1930, McInnes had an oil-burning tug and refrigerated barges that allowed the shipment of increased loads and eliminated delays in waiting for a river steamer to arrive and tow the barges to Waterways. When the fish were landed at Waterways, they were unloaded from the barges by a conveyor system. Here, additional processing was undertaken and the paperwork for export shipments was prepared. In addition to those at Lake Athabasca, the fish companies also had freezing plants at Waterways and about 450,000 kilograms of trout were frozen there in 1929–30. Most was shipped after fishing operations had ended so that the market would not be glutted with fresh fish. At Waterways, McInnes also repacked fresh fish in larger ice-filled boxes before transferring them to refrigerated rail cars. Cold storage kept the fish just above freezing at all stages of shipment to ensure that they would be delivered to consumers "in perfect condition." Fresh fish reached Toronto or Chicago within 10 days of being caught.

Commercial fishing on Lake Athabasca broght little local economic benefit. When it had first begun, people at Fort Chipewyan had demanded that the government prevent depletion of a valuable common use resource. The Department of Fisheries responded by assuring them that while it was committed to the development of commercial fishing, it was confident that its fishing regulations would prevent depletion. These were hollow promises. By the early 1940s, fish stocks in Lake Athabasca were coming under stress and local economic benefit that might have compensated for the declining resource had not materialized. Most of the jobs created by commercial fishing on Lake Athabasca were at Waterways, the transhipment point from which the staple product was exported. There, McInnes's box factory employed about 20 workers, while the barge and ship repair yards, processing plants and administrative offices created additional jobs. Most of this was seasonal work, and many of the workers left Waterways for the winter. At Lake Athabasca, the benefits were far more limited; a situation that created much local resentment. Some local people (mainly Metis from Fort Chipewyan) found work at the fish processing camps and cutting ice during the winter, but McInnes brought most of its fishermen from Lake Winnipeg or northern Saskatchewan. Most lived at Lake Athabasca only during the summer in self-contained camps. They contributed almost nothing to the local economy since McInnes provided them with boats, equipment and supplies (including food) on credit.[21]

One beneficiary of the integration of Lake Athabasca's fish resources into the Canadian commercial orbit was the NAR, which became an ally of the Lake Athabasca fishing industry. As the CPR's director of Development, G.G. Ommanney, noted in 1929, "this fish traffic is of a most desirable character being practically all long haul express and freight business mostly to United States points such as Chicago, New York, etc." He urged the railway to co-operate with fishing interests "as far as consistently possible" to maintain and increase this profitable traffic. This policy later led the NAR to lower freight rates for fish when prices were low in the 1930s. More immediately, W. Schlater, president of McInnes Company, as well as other interested parties such as the NAR, argued that production at Lake Athabasca and other lakes could be increased "if Government co-operation can be obtained to permanently conserve and enlarge the fish supply and thereby increase the allowable annual catches." While they admitted that such increased limits might deplete the resource, they proposed that a fish hatchery be established immediately so restocking of Lake Athabasca and other lakes could begin "before depletion becomes apparent." Further, they suggested that conservation of preferred species should be undertaken by the "extermination of varieties of unmarketable fish which destroy the spawn and young of the more valuable kinds." Such "fish reduction plants" would be operated by the government, but McInnes promised to assist by catching spawn for a hatchery on Lake Athabasca and by loaning its boats free of charge. The benefits of these proposals for the fishing companies were obvious, while the railway anticipated that it too would benefit in the long term since this would enable "the annual catch limits to be raised thereby increasing the valuable long haul car-loads of freight and express traffic from this industry."[22]

Such projects were not undertaken, and the fish resources of Lake Athabasca were allowed to deplete and regenerated through natural means. This approach reached its logical conclusion during World War II. Fishing expanded during the war, and McInnes used Japanese-Canadian internees for part of its work force.[23] By 1943, depletion was becoming serious. Because most fishing operations at Lake Athabasca were on the Saskatchewan side of the lake, McInnes moved its operations to Great Slave Lake after the Saskatchewan government announced plans in 1944–45 to charge royalties on fish. Great Slave Lake had never been fished commercially, and the move was relatively easy since much of McInnes's "plant" was located on mobile barges. At first, fish was shipped from Great Slave Lake through Waterways (where McInnes's existing facilities were used), but after the Mackenzie Highway opened in 1948, it was shipped by truck.[24] By then, fish from the extreme north-west of the province was also being flown to Upper Hay River and trucked to Peace River. Although Alberta began charging royalties on fish in 1946, McInnes returned to Lake Athabasca in the early 1950s when stocks had recovered somewhat. It continued to fish the lake until 1969 when it closed its operations.[25]

## — The Lumber Industry and the Economics of Transportation

During the interwar years, the development of the lumber industry in Alberta's vast northern forests was limited. In an expression of the familiar principle of regulated open access to natural resources, both the Department of the Interior, and after 1930, the Alberta Forestry Service, required commercial lumber operators to purchase the right to cut timber on crown land. Homesteaders, however, could still take some timber without charge for building purposes if none was available on their homestead. Protection of this resource from fire also remained a priority. After the transfer of natural resources to the province, the provincial forestry service branch organized the province into two large districts. The Rocky Mountains Forest Reserve was about 37,000 square kilometres while the Northern Alberta Forest District, at almost 383,000 square kilometres, covered most of northern Alberta. The Rocky Mountains Forest Reserve was designed to protect the area for "production of timber, natural regulation of streamflow, reduction of erosion, modification of local weather conditions, game and fish conservation, and provision of an attractive area for various forms of outdoor recreation." Homesteading was prohibited in the area, and its small size enabled officials to construct trails, conduct patrols and adopt various fire protection measures. Although cost-cutting efforts by government during the Depression limited the extension of such programmes to the Northern Alberta Forest District, an official perception that it was a less valuable resource than the mountain forests further restricted programmes there. Moreover, the district included actual and potential farming areas and many parts of it were in "a state of flux between forestry and agriculture." This added to the difficulties of regulating and protecting its timber resources. Settlers who used fire to clear land increased fire hazards, and although they were required to have a permit for burning, this stipulation was almost impossible to enforce. The Department of the Interior implemented aircraft patrols out of Grande Prairie in 1928 to watch for fires, but after Alberta assumed responsibility for forests in 1930, the flights were discontinued and lookout towers were used instead.[26]

Accessibility was crucial in the exploitation of forest resources and northern sawmill operators were often at a disadvantage in comparison to those better placed in relation to provincial and national markets. Despite claims that northern Alberta's forest resources were well suited to the development of the pulp industry, the proximity of Ontario and Quebec to major North American pulp markets gave them incomparable advantages. So too, Canadian production of building lumber and shingles was dominated by high quality materials from British Columbia. While Alberta's estimated forest reserves were high, production in national terms was small, although the province's sawmills were busy turning out building lumber, timbers, shingles, railway ties and other products for local markets. This industry was concentrated in areas west and north of Red Deer and Edmonton, around Lac La Biche and in the foothills. In northern Alberta, lumbering was found mainly in areas with adequate rail access, such as the Lesser Slave Lake and Peace River districts. The industry tended to serve local needs, booming when settlement expanded and retrenching when it slowed. Lumber camps operated mainly during the winter when movement in the bush was easiest. Although wages were usually low and living conditions were rudimentary at best, the camps provided (as they did in many other parts of the province) much needed seasonal work for local home-steaders. Although Natives found some work in the camps, lumbering in the interwar years in the Lesser Slave Lake district "was predominantly a white man's occupation, except in the Dominion and Alberta Forest Services, where Indians and some Metis made up a significant proportion of trail-making and fire-fighting crews." This trend was reinforced by the growing mechanization of lumbering in the interwar years, which reduced "the value of the workman skilled only with an axe" in favour of those knowing how to use power equipment.[27]

*Trucking logs from one of the lumber camps to the*
*Chisholm Sawmill, 1937–39.* A3781 PAA.

*Logs were also floated to the Chisholm Sawmill, 1937–39.*
A3789 PAA.

Northern Alberta mills generally produced unfinished lumber. In 1929 and 1930, it was reported that there was no shingle production in northern Alberta and only very "small scale" production of treated (creosoted) and untreated poles, pilings and mine timbers. Most often, the boards, planks and other rough lumber from these small mills were marketed as they came from the mill, but some were sold to planing mills or other manufacturers for further processing into higher quality products such as siding, window sashes, door frames and finishing lumber. Ownership of the sawmills changed frequently, and most operated only part time. Once an area had been cleared of merchantable timber, the mill was moved to another location. Reports in both 1930 and 1934 noted that while there were a large number of small part-time sawmills in the territory served by the NAR, only three (including one in Edmonton) operated more or less on a full-time basis. One of these, the North West Lumber Company, was among the largest lumber concerns in Alberta. Originally owned by J.D. McArthur, the owner of the ED&BC, it operated a planing mill in Edmonton at the Dunvegan Yards (the terminal of the northern railways). While it drew timber from all of Alberta, some came from logging camps it operated around Lesser Slave Lake. Other permanent mills serving northern Alberta were the McRae mill at Faust and the Chisholm Saw Mill Ltd., which operated a planing mill at Chisholm. Over the years, Chisholm ran seasonal bush camps and small sawmills in the area close to the planing mill and around Lesser Slave Lake.[28]

While statistics on the geographical distribution of lumber production within the province in the interwar years are unavailable, northern Alberta seemingly contributed only a small percentage of provincial lumber output. In 1925, total lumber production in Alberta was 41,766 million feet board measure. The same year, the estimated cut along the ED&BC lines was about 36.5 million feet board measure.[29] Despite their relatively small scale, a few northern lumber operations in the 1920s were able to compete with producers located closer to the more densely settled parts of Alberta and Saskatchewan. Chisholm was one of these—lumber was floated along the rivers from a large forested area to its planing mill, and its direct rail link to Edmonton put its lumber within reach of markets in Alberta and Saskatchewan. Nonetheless, in common with other producers in northern Alberta, markets for the production of the Chisholm Saw Mill were upset by the combined forces of the Depression and the emergence of trucking. J.F. MacMillan, the President of Chisholm Saw Mill, observed in 1938 that the mill's operations had been satisfactory until 1930 when prices fell and trucks began to compete with railways for lumber shipments. After 1930, the Alberta market was very poor while sales in Saskatchewan were even lower. The company thus tried to sell lumber in eastern Canada and the United States, but low prices in combination with freight rates on the long haul to market reduced profits. As McMillan noted, "we have been going in the Red most every year." Moreover, he contended that profits were further squeezed because of Alberta's adoption in 1937 of minimum wages and a nine-hour day.[30]

Of the problems facing the Chisholm mill, transportation was the most serious. By the late 1930s, the company could no longer compete with Edmonton mills because of inequitable railway freight rates and competition from producers who were trucking their lumber to market. In earlier years, lumbering had taken place close to lakes, rivers and rail lines, but the use of trucks permitted lumbering in previously inaccessible areas that were closer to markets. This was especially pronounced in the Edmonton area, and northern producers lost market share in the city to these new producers. Even in closer-in districts with rail lines, trucking became increasingly popular—many lumber companies even began to use trucks to ship lumber to their branches.[31] Outraging northern Alberta producers, the railway responded by lowering freight rates to areas from which lumber was shipped by truck, but left them unchanged in those areas where there was no truck competition. These rates were set "after the particulars of the competition were taken into consideration and distance was not the controlling factor." In other words, centres with adequate road connections with Edmonton (such as in areas west and north of Red Deer) received a lower rate than did those in areas without good roads. The Chisholm mill, like other mills in northern Alberta, fell into the latter category.[32]

Although the NAR subsequently lowered freight rates for lumber coming from northern Alberta, they were still at unsatisfactory levels and the lumber companies continued to demand even lower rates. Such problems were alleviated for a time during World War II when the Canadian lumber industry boomed because of Canadian wartime needs and shortages in Britain. In Alberta, production of lumber nearly doubled between 1939 and 1942. Part of this increased production came from northern Alberta, where it created more seasonal work. Because of labour shortages, Natives were able to enter the lumber industry more easily and after the war they maintained this position. In 1941, lumber made up 3.4 percent of the total freight shipment on the NAR's Peace River lines, and by 1946 it stood at 19.3 percent. Some of this lumber came from the Hines Creek and Grande Prairie districts that by then "had

*The first salt plant near Fort McMurray failed because of its remoteness from the railhead. This photograph was taken in 1931–32, after the plant was closed.* A7599 PAA.

comparatively good road access from outlying areas where timber was cut." Lumbering also continued to expand in the Lesser Slave Lake district, and new mills were set up in a number of towns. Nonetheless, freight rates were still an issue for producers who continued to find it hard to compete with mills enjoying more favourable freight rates. While these concerns were addressed in 1948 by the Board of Railway Commissioners reduction of rates on lumber from northern Alberta, northern Alberta mills continued to operate under a handicap imposed by distance from major markets and unfavourable shipping costs.[33]

### Fort McMurray's Salt Industry

In 1924, John Gillespie, a prominent Edmonton grain trader, and a number of partners formed the Alberta Salt Company to develop the deposits located south of the Fort McMurray townsite. This was near the area where provincial drilling crews had found salt in commercial quantities in 1919–20. At that time, commercial development had not proceeded because the area was too far from the railway. Although the railway had been extended along the Clearwater River to within about 6.5 kilometres of Fort McMurray by 1925, the location chosen by Gillespie was still inconvenient. More difficulties arose because

Gillespie's site was on the other side of a steep, unstable oil sand embankment. Perhaps he assumed that once it was operating, the railway company (or its master, the provincial government) would build a spur line to the plant. Whatever the case, the mine was planned to take advantage of Alberta and Saskatchewan markets, which then imported all of their salt (estimated at 30,000 tonnes annually) from Ontario or California. The Alberta Salt Company employed the same production methods used elsewhere in North America. Water was pumped into the salt beds and the brine was pumped back to the surface and into two long narrow trays that were heated by coal-fired furnaces. Once the liquid had evaporated, the salt residue was processed for market. In 1925 the plant produced about 665 tonnes of salt, and while production increased slightly in 1926, only about 90 tonnes were manufactured in 1927, the last year of production.[34]

From the start, the Alberta Salt Company suffered because of poor transportation to the railhead at Waterways. In 1925 the provincial government built a road costing about $8,000 between the mine and Waterways. Alternately, the salt was carted to the Clearwater River at Fort McMurray where it was loaded on barges and taken the short distance to Waterways. There it was unloaded and transhipped to rail cars. Neither method was satisfactory; the road was often blocked by slumping oil sands banks, while barges were useless during times of low water in the Clearwater River and during winter. The same problems made it equally difficult to bring in coal to fire the plant's engines. These difficulties were exacerbated because the salt company, Jim Cornwall noted, used "two old barges, bought cheap" that were "not adapted for the work required of them." As a report prepared for Premier Brownlee in 1926 concluded, "the Salt Company has been very unfortunate in its choice of a site for the plant" because more accessible ones in the area "offered equal opportunities for the development of the industry." Moreover, without assured or steady supplies, wholesalers were reluctant to contract with the company for its product.[35]

These problems led Gillespie to try and persuade the provincial government to build a spur line to the mine. The cost of this extension was estimated at about $150,000 and upkeep (given the unstable terrain) would be about $15,000 per year. Although Gillespie argued that greater production and increased rail traffic would offset these costs, the provincial government was unwilling to pay for the spur line. In Canada, industrial spur lines were usually built only when a plant owner paid a deposit equal to one-half the construction costs or provided a bond of indemnity for the total amount. In addition, the manufacturer was responsible for a yearly rental fee for the tracks and equipment. While Alberta agreed to build a spur line on these terms (as well as to give the company a monopoly of salt production in the area), Gillespie was unwilling or unable to meet these requirements.[36]

Such transportation problems and the province's refusal to alleviate them convinced many Edmonton promoters that the provincial government lacked vision in promoting northern economic development. Nonetheless, the province was eager to encourage the project, but on more rational terms. Thus, it drilled test wells to identify better located salt deposits in 1927–28, and promising deposits were found only a short distance from the terminal in Waterways. Subsequently, a number of proposals were made to develop the site, but none were implemented. Interested parties were either too undercapitalized to carry the project forward, or demanded concessions that the province would not accept. Canadian Industries Ltd. of Montreal, for example, wanted an exclusive right to mine salt at Fort McMurray, a permanent exemption from royalties, no taxation for 21 years and land grants. As Premier Brownlee commented when rejecting the proposal, such concessions would have been more liberal "than we have extended to any industry that so far has been established in the Province."[37]

Further development did not take place immediately. The area was far from markets, and although salt production in Canada was dominated by plants near Windsor, Ontario, and Malagash, Nova Scotia, two small plants had also begun producing salt in Saskatchewan and Manitoba in about 1933. As the general manager of the NAR noted in 1934, the latter two plants tended "to discourage practical salt makers from investing in such an industry at Waterways or vicinity." By 1936, however, these other prairie producers had apparently failed, or at least had not achieved significant market penetration. This opened the prairie market to other regional producers and in 1936 Industrial Minerals Ltd. of Cornwall, Ontario (a firm headed by F.I. Batchelor, a former Calgary bank manager) carried out test drilling in the same area tested by provincial crews in the late 1920s. Following positive test results, the company obtained a 21-year lease from the province and began constructing a plant adjacent to the railway terminal in Waterways. C.C. Ross, the minister of Lands and Mines, called the test results "the most important strike in the province since Royalite No. 4 was brought in at Turner Valley." Industrial Minerals was in a strong position. It had few serious local competitors on the prairies, and since its operations were less than 200 metres from the railway terminal, it did not face the local transportation problems that had plagued the Alberta Salt Company a decade before. The new plant had a capacity of about

*By 1949 when this photograph of the bagging equipment at the Waterways salt plant was taken, competing salt supplies from areas closer to markets had made the Waterways plant uneconomical.*

PA-3198/4 PAA.

91 tonnes per day and used evaporation techniques similar to those previously employed by the Alberta Salt Company. The plant building was unique in Alberta; with numerous ventilating units on the roof, it looked, as one wag phrased it, like a "Turkish mosque designed by a Canadian lumberjack."[38]

Even though unit freight costs for salt from Windsor to the prairies were lower than for shipments from Waterways to Edmonton, shorter overall distance to market made salt production at Waterways competitive on the prairies.[39] By early 1938 the plant was producing about 18 tonnes of salt per day and employed 40 workers. Even so, insufficient operating capital held back plans to increase the plant's production. Consequently, a minority shareholder, the Dominion Tar and Chemicals Co. Ltd. of Montreal, took over the company later that year. Additional capital was invested to expand production, and while the older evaporation system continued in use, a new vacuum tank system with significantly higher capacity was also installed. In 1941, production doubled over the previous year to over 15,000 tonnes, and it reached 26,415 tonnes by 1945. The salt was mainly marketed in Alberta, although the company was making inroads in western Saskatchewan and eastern British Columbia as well. By this point, the salt plant, with about 55 workers, was the largest nonseasonal employer in Waterways. In 1944, however, large salt deposits were discovered during oil well testing near Elk Point, east of Edmonton. Salt was also discovered at Unity, Saskatchewan in 1946, and the firm that operated the plant at Waterways began constructing a plant there. These new supplies made the Waterways plant uneconomical and it closed in 1951. The next year, the plant was dismantled and sold for scrap. The "costs of hauling coal or fuel oil north to McMurray had made the operation of the salt plant unsound" in comparison to the more accessible supplies at Elk Point and Unity.[40]

## Mineral Development

### The Interwar Years

Even the most ardent supporters of northern development admitted that northern Alberta's mineral resources (other than petroleum) were limited. The Peace River country had no known metal deposits, although extensive deposits of nonmetallic minerals such as gypsum, coal and petroleum were apparent. In the Alberta districts of the Peace River country, development of coal reserves was limited to small operations that mined easy-to-reach outcroppings along the river banks. Such mining had been underway near Wembley since before World War I, but as one observer remarked in 1937, it provided "only a very precarious living." The abundance of coal elsewhere in Alberta ensured that coal production remained restricted to local markets. Despite a number of short-lived speculative ventures near Peace River and Slave Lake, similar problems held back petroleum development in the Peace River country. While oil exploration declined in the 1920s, it revived somewhat in the 1930s, especially in the Rolla-Pouce Coupe districts in British Columbia and along the Alberta border. Natural gas continued to dominate discoveries and dampened enthusiasm, but exploration intensified during and after World War II. By the 1950s, a growing ability to ship natural gas to distant markets by pipeline encouraged development, inaugurating a new phase in the economic life of the Peace River country.[41]

In contrast to the limited opportunities of the Peace River country, the oil sands of the Fort McMurray district prompted extensive experimentation and development efforts between 1920 and 1948. Popularly claimed to be one of the largest oil reserves in the world, efforts to exploit the oil sands were undertaken as an alliance between public and private sectors. This was further confirmed by the growing importance during the interwar years of petroleum as a source of energy. Although still small in comparison to consumption levels after World War II, its use in Canada increased rapidly in the 1920s. In Alberta, consumption of gasoline between 1923 and 1928 went from almost 55 million to about 186 million litres. Industrial application of petroleum products was also expanding rapidly.[42] But other than production from Turner Valley, Canada was dependent on imported supplies. This prompted worries about the nation's vulnerability, making petroleum a public policy issue as well as an opportunity for private investment. Internationally, forecasts of chronic shortages were common until the mid 1920s when, as historian Barry Ferguson remarked, "all too typically for the oil industry, shortages turned to surpluses and prices plummeted" because of discoveries in the United States and the Middle East. By the late 1920s, prices were falling and the market was glutted, creating a climate for yet further price declines and oversupply in the 1930s. During this time, Canada remained a net importer of oil, which sustained some interest in developing domestic supplies. These conditions helped frame efforts to develop the oil sand deposits in northern Alberta.[43]

Concerns about future petroleum supplies in conjunction with growing provincial ambitions for broader economic development prompted a meeting in 1919 at which Henry Marshall Tory, the president of the University of Alberta, J.L. Coté, by then provincial secretary, and a handful of other interested academic and government figures formed The Alberta Industrial Development Association to carry out preliminary research projects and define the scope for a permanent research agency. While a proposal for federal-provincial co-operation on research into natural resources was abandoned because President Tory (like some Alberta government figures) judged that the federal government was not enthusiastic enough about the development of Alberta's natural resources, the association actively sought provincial involvement. As Tory later phrased it, state supported research was necessary to create "the foundations of accurate knowledge upon which we can build our industries with security in the future." These and subsequent efforts led to the formation of the Scientific and Industrial Research Council of Alberta in 1921. Later called the Alberta Research Council, it was the first permanent scientific research council in Canada. The council's work emphasized research important for future economic development and for resolving technical problems that inhibited commercial development and efficient use of resources. Demonstrating a particular concern with mining and oil sands development, the Alberta Research Council was initially divided into three divisions: fuels, geology and road construction. The latter was concerned with oil sands projects, initially in respect to road paving techniques. This orientation soon expanded to include more general research into oil sands processing technology.[44]

The notion that conventional drilling could be used to strike pools of bitumen or oil near Fort McMurray continued to inspire some promoters during the 1920s. Increasingly, however, it was assumed (as Sidney Ells of the federal Mines Branch had concluded in 1913) that it was the oil sands themselves that were the valuable resource. The crudest use of this resource was for paving—either in its natural state or in a processed form. The Alberta government, several towns and cities and some private developers carried out paving experiments using oil sands during the 1920s, but all found it uneconomical or technically unsuitable. As the city of Calgary engineer reported in 1925, "at present, it is far more economical to use Californian asphalt and add our own ingredients than to use the tar sands" shipped from Waterways in a raw or semi-processed state.[45]

The apparent limitations of using oil sands as a paving material reinforced a growing assumption that techniques were needed to refine bitumen from the sand. By the early 1920s a number of commercial uses for bitumen had been developed. It could be processed into asphalt for paving, and it could also be used in manufacturing paint, varnish and a wide range of mastic and waterproofing materials. Byproducts of this processing of bitumen included gasoline, kerosene and similar substances. While the potential of the oil sands was therefore promising, important barriers remained. It was evident by this time that extraction of the bitumen needed to take place near Fort McMurray—shipping costs of unprocessed oil sands were prohibitive since the great bulk of such shipments consisted of sand that had to be separated from the bitumen and then discarded. Cost effective methods were also needed to identify areas with the richest concentrations of bitumen, to remove the "overburden" that covered them and to separate (or extract) the gummy bitumen from the sand and other unwanted materials. Research was also needed on how bitumen could be upgraded into profitable products.[46] Successful oil sands development thus had to grapple with the same problems that faced all mining operations—lengthy exploration and testing had to be followed by the necessary research, experimentation and capitalization to develop or implement a profitable method of extraction.[47] The peculiar problems of marketing petroleum products then also had to be addressed.

Recognizing the strategic economic importance of oil, the federal government maintained an ongoing interest in petroleum development. It ensured a direct role for itself in oil sands development by excluding the Horse River mineral reserve from the transfer of natural resources to the province in 1930. Thus, oil sands developments continued to involve both levels of government. The leading figures in oil sands research in the interwar years were Sidney Ells of the federal Mines Branch and Karl Clark of the Alberta Research Council. At least until the late 1920s, Ells continued to stress the potential of bitumen for paving projects. He remained in charge of federal field work in the area and ongoing surveys to identify major oil sands deposits until 1945. Clark led the scientific efforts to separate bitumen from the sands. Although he too was interested in the use of oil sands and bitumen for paving work, he correctly recognized (as Ells was slow to do) that the demand for paving asphalt could not support a commercial oil sands plant. Development thus depended, Clark reasoned, on refining gasoline and other petroleum products from the bitumen. Given the high capital costs and technological complexity of such processing, it was soon evident that any development had to be on a large scale. The estrangement that had earlier developed between Ells and Clark (and other provincial researchers) intensified and at times reached acrimonious levels. Whatever their differences, however, both sides shared a common interest in finding ways to achieve commercial development of the oil sands. To limit speculation and encourage long-term investment, the federal government ended freehold grants (with mineral rights) in 1920 and began to grant land only under leases that set out requirements for minimum investment in a plant. To avoid duplication of effort, the Alberta Research Council and the federal Mines Branch formed the Bituminous Sands Administrative Committee in 1929 to co-operate on research into the commercial utilization of the oil sands. With this two-year agreement, the federal Mines Department agreed to study mining problems (such as how to mine the oil sands and deal with overburden) while the province researched methods for extracting bitumen from the sands.[48]

This division of responsibilities reflected the fact that the primary research interest of Karl Clark and the Alberta Research Council since the early 1920s had focussed on problems associated with extraction. Clark's research built on over 40 years of scientific research and theory into methods of separating bitumen from sand and other aggregates. Technological invention tends to be incremental, and oil sands extraction technology was no different. Experiments in the 1880s by the Geological Survey of Canada in separating bitumen from sand, research in California in the 1890s on extracting petroleum from oil shales, Sidney Ells's tests at the Mellon Institute during World War I, as well as general mining technology, all provided important precedents for the use of hot water or steam to separate oil from aggregate. Although there were a host of competing theories and processes, Clark concentrated on such hot water systems. His method was to mix raw oil sand with hot water. When this mixture was heated and mixed, the bitumen came away from the sand as an oily froth that could be skimmed off. Although simple in plan, this presented a number of very complex engineering problems. Nonetheless, by 1923 Clark had designed a prototype hot water separation system and a plant based on this technique was set up at the A&GW's Dunvegan Yards the next year.[49] Despite ongoing technical problems, it demonstrated the technical feasibility of large-scale application of the hot water separation process, and as part of the federal-provincial co-operative scheme of 1929, the plant was moved to Waterways for field trials. It was also anticipated that the bitumen from this plant would be tested to see if gasoline could be refined from it. At the end of the summer's work, the plant had processed 725 tonnes of oil sands and produced about 68,000 litres of bitumen. Although a number of technical problems appeared during actual operation, the tests at the Waterways plant proved that a hot water system was the most promising method for producing bitumen from the Athabasca oil sands; a finding that became the basis for future development.[50]

In keeping with the goal of promoting commercial development, the research findings from the Waterways plant (like earlier experimental work) were publicly distributed and made freely available to commercial interests. As historian Barry Ferguson notes, while this state-sponsored research did not guarantee commercial success, it "pointed private developers to the correct methods, as well as warning of the many problems of developing the resource." Despite the project's success, further research was curtailed by the Depression. With falling government revenues, the Alberta Research Council was closed in 1933 and was not reconstituted until the early 1940s. Declining oil prices further reduced the incentive for research into methods to produce yet more petroleum. Clark became professor of Metallurgy (then an expanding field because of gold and other mining developments) at the University of Alberta, but he remained committed to oil sands research, and his previous and future

*The Abasands plant was the most ambitious attempt before World War II to exploit the petroleum riches of the oil sands near Fort McMurray. Photograph taken in 1939. A2003 PAA.*

work on perfecting techniques to process the Athabasca oil sands was a significant engineering accomplishment.[51]

The publicly sponsored research of the 1920s was not the only expression of interest in the oil sands and there were several commercial operators who applied a number of techniques to separate bitumen from sand. The only commercial operation of this period that enjoyed even marginal success was a relatively unsophisticated undertaking by Thomas Draper. Forming the McMurray Asphaltum and Oil Company in 1922, Draper tried to develop an extraction process but turned to mining oil sands for sale after a fire at his plant in 1924. An energetic promoter of paving projects, Draper established a quarry at an outcropping of oil sands at (old) Waterways (which was later renamed after him) and sold oil sands in their natural state as well as in a slightly processed form for paving and experimental projects. Karl Clark, for example, purchased oil sands from Draper for his experimental work, as did the provincial government for test paving projects.[52]

Further commercial operations did not take root until the early 1930s when M.W. (Max) Ball and a group of Denver businessmen offered to purchase the federal-provincial Waterways separation plant. The negotiations were unsuccessful, but Ball's continued interest in oil sands extraction later led him to form Canadian Northern Oil Sands Products Limited (later renamed Abasands Oils Ltd.). Financial and technical problems stymied progress until 1936 when an extraction plant and refinery were completed near Fort McMurray. This plant used a modified hot water system of extraction. Problems with the plant and the extraction process—as well as serious problems with mining techniques—prevented production until 1940. By then, Ball and his associates had invested around $700,000 in the plant. In 1941, production was stepped up and that summer the plant processed just over 17,000 tonnes of oil sands to produce about 17,000 barrels of crude oil, 1,000 barrels of gasoline and almost 8,500 barrels of diesel oil. This promising production ended when the plant burned to the ground in late 1941.[53]

By this time, the long standing transportation problems associated with marketing northern resources had been compounded because of further oil strikes at Turner Valley. This increased production glutted the petroleum market in Alberta by 1937. In this environment, expensive Fort McMurray production could not compete, especially when high freight costs were added. Abasands hoped that the war would reverse this situation and that new markets would emerge in the north because of mining ventures at Goldfields and in the NWT. Such anticipations led the company to rebuild the plant in 1942. Even though Fort McMurray petroleum was competitive at Lake Athabasca, this market dried up in 1942 with the closing of the mines at Goldfields. Moreover, Abasands production could not penetrate the more important northern markets at Yellowknife because of Imperial Oil's production from Norman Wells. Continuous water transport between Norman Wells and Yellowknife lowered shipping costs, while those for oil from Fort McMurray (which had to be transhipped at Fitzgerald) remained high. Most importantly, while Imperial Oil (which had capped its wells at Norman Wells between 1925 and 1932 because of low demand) received a five-year royalty holiday from the federal government on its Norman Wells production in 1939, Abasands was unable to obtain a similar concession.[54] Despite these difficulties, the Abasands plant gained a new lease on life in 1943 when wartime pressure for increased petroleum production in northern Canada led the federal government (in alliance with Consolidated Mining and Smelting Ltd.) to take over the plant and put it into production. Yet this plan—so generous in its optimism and financial largesse—did not bring increased production or a solution to the plant's technical problems. Since the Abasands plant was located on federal oil sands reserve land, the provincial government charged that the whole project was an affront to provincial jurisdiction over natural resources. Moreover, Alberta claimed that the project was wasteful and incompetently managed. Asserting that this "wanton plunder of provincial rights" had retarded development of the oil sands by creating the impression of insurmountable difficulties, W.A. Fallow, Alberta's minister of Public Works, demanded in 1944 that the federal government appoint a royal commission to investigate the matter. Such demands became purely academic in 1945 when—in the seemingly predictable fate of Fort McMurray oil sands operations—the plant burned.[55]

At the same time that Abasands was struggling to achieve commercial production in the 1930s, the International Bitumen Company plant owned by Bob Fitzsimmons had been operating intermittently at Bitumount, about 90 kilometres north of Fort McMurray. Fitzsimmons had drilled for oil in the 1920s in the Fort McMurray area, but he had finally concluded by 1930 that it was futile to attempt to exploit the oil sands in this manner. Clearly inspired by Clark's Waterway's plant, Fitzsimmons built a small hot water separation plant at Bitumount. He improved his process during 1931, but the plant remained a rather ramshackle and improvised operation. Lack of capital forced it to close in 1932, but after considerable efforts, Fitzsimmons raised sufficient capital to reopen it in 1937. Although plagued by breakdowns and debt, much of the plant was rebuilt and it produced several thousand litres of bitumen in 1938. Although this promising production was the first commercial production in the area, it was insufficient to keep the plant open, especially in light of the limited markets then available. By the end of the year, International Bitumen was bankrupt.[56]

In 1942, Fitzsimmons sold the plant to L.R. Champion, a Montreal financier. Champion renamed it Oil Sands Ltd. but "undertook only limited maintenance and rebuilding work during 1943 and 1944 in order to attract possible partners or buyers." During this period, the plant remained unproductive. In 1944, Champion and the Alberta government agreed to build a new plant at Bitumount. Alberta was bitter about the lack of progress at the federally controlled Abasands plant, and it hoped to succeed where Ottawa had failed. Champion, however, was unable to fulfil his obligations under the agreement, and the province took over the plant. Under the direction of the Alberta Research Council and using provincial funding, the Bitumount plant was rebuilt and a refinery constructed. Basically a test facility, this plant demonstrated that the major problems in separating bitumen from the sands had been resolved. The plant was more costly than the province had predicted, but its success and the interest it aroused led the government of Alberta to sponsor a conference in 1951 to explore ways of promoting further development of the Athabasca oil sands. This, and the resolution of technical difficulties in separation, marked the end of one phase in oil sands development efforts. Between 1947 and 1951, many new conventional oil fields (some with massive reserves) were discovered in Alberta. This predictably stalled interest in the more complex and capital intensive development of the oil sands until several decades later when prices had risen and long term supplies were believed to be in jeopardy.[57]

— ✦ —

Industrial development in northern Alberta was handicapped by the region's small domestic markets and its distance from larger markets and industrial centres. Lack of capital compounded these problems. While such conditions existed in the NWT to an even greater extent, its high value and concentrated resources such as gold and uranium compensated for these drawbacks.[58] Northern Alberta did not have such high value resources, although some of its lower value commodities found markets. The advantage for northern fish producers created by the depletion of fish in lakes in the rest of Alberta could only be seized by means of efficient and integrated production and marketing to help overcome the problems of marketing a low value perishable commodity in distant markets. While export of fish would have been impossible without rail networks (whose capital cost had been publicly supported), technological change in refrigeration and transportation expanded its scope. So too, salt production gained advantages in Alberta and prairie markets because competing production was located even further away in Ontario. Predictably, when supplies closer to markets were found on the prairies, the northern salt industry collapsed. Northern lumber production operated under the same constraints. Lumber production in more southern parts of Alberta remained high, while that from British Columbia enjoyed market advantage because of its high quality and the ease of marketing it through the national rail system. Thus, the lumber industry in northern Alberta concentrated on small local markets or else developed only in areas (such as Chisholm) from which it was possible to access wider markets. Even so, the ability to market production from these latter areas was tenuous because of changes in railway freight rates and the development of truck transportation. The same forces that affected fish, timber and salt production also had a predictable impact on oil sands development, but high capital costs and the technological complexity of extracting the resource added further barriers.

Throughout this period, government largely left these market forces untouched—there was no demonstrable benefit in fighting them, nor did government have the desire, the authority or the wealth to subsidize development or regulate the market place. In any event, no Alberta government after 1920 had a "northern policy" that might have led to a sharper focus with respect to economic development in northern Alberta. Government policy instead focussed largely on sectoral concerns (such as agriculture and transportation) that were province-wide in scope. This, of course, conferred greater benefits on certain districts, especially established rural communities. In terms of northern Alberta's industrial development, the only beneficiaries of this sectoral approach were the fishing industry, where state regulation supported commercial over subsistence fishing, and oil sands research, which benefited from provincial efforts to assist the petroleum industry by means of applied research. Such research was expected to help solve technical problems of production and outline the parameters of potential development. Beyond this, government was as yet unwilling to help capitalize oils sands development because adequate supplies of cheaper petroleum were available elsewhere in the province. In the familiar pattern whereby development of northern Alberta's resources relied on the needs and priorities of the broader economy, development of the oil sands became possible only when wider conditions and markets became favourable.

# Crisis Upon Crisis

## 14
### Trapping in Northern Alberta

In 1927, Jonas Laviolette, the Chief of the Chipewyan band, observed that Natives had been steadily impoverished because of Euro-Canadian trapping in the Fort Chipewyan district. Government did nothing about the matter, and while there were "lots of men here looking after the Buffalo" in Wood Buffalo Park, there were "none looking after us." Laviolette's complaints were not unique. While tension arising because of white competition and government wildlife policies was intense in the Peace-Athabasca delta, it was becoming a pointed issue throughout trapping districts in northern Alberta. Provincial efforts to prevent depletion of birds and animals through its game legislation were primarily based upon the assumption that wildlife was simply another commodity whose value could be enhanced by regulations to help conserve future supplies and ensure high quality production. At the same time, provincial regulations confirmed that fur and game were open access resources that any resident of the province could exploit. This position in turn had implications for treaty hunting and trapping rights. While the state enforced open access and assumed the task of controlling hunting, fishing and trapping, Indians were less able to protect their own interests in this domain. As political scientists Richard Price and Shirleen Smith have pointed out, the state "reserved to itself" the authority to determine what was meant by the hunting provisions of the treaty. Thus, it arbitrarily defined the treaty's hunting provision to include hunting for food but not for trade.[1]

All of these developments were framed by the economic and social philosophy of Euro-Canadian liberal individualism that stressed individual over collective rights and needs. This occurred against a backdrop of falling fur prices, increased competition from white trappers and the growth of fur farming. Farmed fur—an industry in part encouraged by the Alberta government—increasingly competed with wild fur and created new standards and fashions that were unattainable with wild pelts. These and other developments created stress on northern trapping life and threatened its social and economic stability. Consequently, the crisis in trapping districts, which became acute after 1927, arose from a broad base. Government interpretation of treaty rights and its wildlife regulations were crucial factors, while lower fur prices, game depletion and unrestricted competition by white trappers intensified the situation. While northern farmers also experienced economic difficulties in the 1930s, Native trappers faced more trying circumstances—their problems were not merely the product of cyclical commodity prices but of social and economic relationships as well. The Alberta government made no effort to redesign its game policies to address the social and economic problems of northern trappers, nor did it invest the revenues it earned by taxing the fur trade in rehabilitating fur resources. At the same time, while the Department of Indian Affairs also endorsed a restrictive interpretation of treaty hunting rights, it wanted to reconcile commodity and subsistence use of resources by Indians. Although the department argued that Indians were owed special consideration in wildlife regulation, it was unable to make this concern a political priority for the federal government. This failure hamstrung even its limited efforts to protect Indian hunting rights from provincial game regulation. While federal officials claimed that federal-provincial differences (because of provincial jurisdiction over game and federal jurisdiction over Indians) were "overcome by conference or agreement," it was often a convoluted process in which the needs of those without political or economic power—such as Natives—were easily set aside. These developments demonstrated one aspect of the working of Canadian federalism and how federal-provincial relations directly affected people's lives.[2]

## The State, Northern Wildlife, and the Native Economy

While it agreed that provincial efforts to conserve fur were necessary, the Department of Indian Affairs continued to argue during the interwar years that the province should also respect Indian rights to hunt for food. Even so, Indian Affairs continued to follow a "passive approach" and shied away from confronting the province over its lack of respect for treaty obligations. Nor was it able to force or convince other federal government departments to follow its lead. Wood Buffalo Park was developed by the Department of the Interior with little reference to Indian trapping needs, and the Mines Department supported white trapping as a way of grubstaking prospecting and the eventual development of northern mineral resources.[3] Indian Affairs too had its own priorities. While the Native economy was harmed by provincial policies, the federal government bore the financial costs of economic dislocation. In the late 1920s, relief costs for northern Indians doubled and they increased even further in the 1930s. Reducing costs of government was important for Euro-Canadian taxpayers, but "quite aside from this financial consideration," Indian Affairs noted in 1920 that it was "highly undesirable from the view point of adjoining white settlements that the Indian population should be permitted to become indigent." Yet ongoing reports about Indian Agents who told Indians that they could ignore closed seasons if they were starving revealed tensions within the Department about its "passive" approach and its willingness to concede juris- diction. But even though Indian Affairs was unable to establish the parameters of even this limited right to hunt during closed seasons, Indian hunters, grap- pling with unsympathetic Alberta game policies and an increasingly complex and competitive fur business, were forced to depend on the department, "both for political protection and for direct material aid, in order to remain in the field as a resident hunter providing for a family or band."[4]

The ambiguity of federal government support for the principle of Indian hunting rights and the differing priorities among government departments was in sharp contrast to the devotion of the Alberta government to the principle of open access to fur resources and its view of the fur trade as a source of govern- ment revenue. High post-war fur prices prompted it in 1921 to license fur dealers and traders and tax wild fur exported from the province. While the licensing provisions were apparently evaded by many traders until the mid 1920s, most traders immediately passed the fur tax—and often an added amount for good measure—along to trappers. The tax applied only to wild fur, not that raised on fur farms, and the levy varied according to type of fur. Only pelts that had been stamped (which proved that the tax had been collected) could legally be exported from the province. In 1923, the same year that tax rates were increased on some pelts, Alberta also instituted trapping licences. For a $2 licence, the holder gained the right to trap on crown land anywhere in the province. This unequivocally confirmed the province's commitment to regulated open access to fur resources. Indian Agent Gerald Card reported that the Indians at Fort Chipewyan claimed that the fur tax often totalled more than their annuity payments. In combination with trapping licences, this intensified Indian hostility to "the vexatious game laws imposed by the Province of Alberta." While Card believed that treaty rights made it "hardly conceivable" that Indians would be charged for trapping licences, Alberta refused to exempt Indians from this requirement. Instead, it agreed to refund, upon application, the amount of the licence fee. This technique for dealing with the taxation of Indians was accepted by the federal government.[5]

Alberta stepped up its wildlife regulation efforts in 1920 when it amended its game legislation to prohibit the taking of fur-bearing animals in forest reserves. It went even further with respect to the Lesser Slave Lake forest reserve where it banned all hunting except for "undesirable" animals such as wolves. Consequently, Indians from the four adjacent reserves were excluded from areas they had customarily hunted. The Indian Agent for the Lesser Slave Lake Agency urged Ottawa to protest this as "contrary to the promises made under Treaty No. 8," but the province held its ground, arguing that it was too difficult "to regulate without discriminating." It also contended that the hunting ban would make the forest reserve "a breeding ground" from which animals would "overflow into other areas," eventually to the benefit of "all concerned, the Indians included." While white trappers could move on, people living on these reserves did not have this option and were forced to hunt in closer-in areas north of the lake where they encroached on lands used by other Indian bands.[6]

Even though its enforcement ability was patchy, Alberta further tightened controls on hunting when it banned market hunting in 1922. While the legislation still allowed any resident north of 55 degrees to kill game (other than protected species) for food at any time of the year, nonresidents could no longer do so. Most importantly, the provisions of the *Migratory Birds Convention Act* were added to the provincial game legislation. Signed in 1916 and approved by the House of Commons the next year, this United States-Canada treaty limited hunting of insectivorous and nongame birds, swans and cranes. It also established a relatively short open season for ducks and geese and prohibited practices such as hunting from airplanes and power boats.[7]

In his study of this Convention, Dan Gottesman argues that it was "a direct product of the efforts" by "wilderness societies, naturalist clubs, zoological societies, bird watchers, professional resource managers, sportsmen's organizations and arms and ammunition manufacturers" in the United States to promote their interests. Although habitat destruction probably contributed most to the depletion of migratory birds in Canada, the Convention's appeal for Canadians lay in a recognition that hunting in the United States during migration periods

*Special barges were constructed to ship bison from Wainwright Buffalo Park to Wood Buffalo National Park in 1925.*

A4725 PAA.

also threatened Canada's bird populations. While the ban on shooting insectivorous birds was designed to assist agriculture, sport hunters were the most significant beneficiaries. As was noted in 1921, the convention ensured that game birds "will one day again figure in the sportsman's legitimate bag." And as it was argued two years later, hunting was a valuable activity for reviving the "tired business and professional man," and the open season in autumn gave Alberta hunters an "equal chance at the birds with all other sportsmen in either country."[8]

Indian hunters were granted only minor exemptions under the Convention, which was subsequently upheld by the courts as a legitimate override of treaty hunting rights. But the primacy given to sports hunting created major problems for Indians in northern Alberta where waterfowl was an important source of fresh meat in spring and summer. While it had been illegal to hunt many birds even under the "hunting for food" allowance granted to all residents of northern Alberta, this provision had rarely been enforced. Enforcement of the *Migratory Birds Convention Act*, however, began in about 1924, and despite protests by Indians, neither the provincial nor federal governments sought to tailor its provisions to northern conditions. As a consequence, the hunting season set for northern Alberta began so late in the year that birds had already started migrating before the open season began. By 1928 the open season in northern Alberta had been changed to start two weeks earlier, but the creation of a sport season restricted to the autumn remained problematic for people who hunted for food throughout the year.[9] Councillor William Whitehead and Chief Eustane Martin of the Fort Chipewyan Cree wrote in 1927 that,

> in the last three years we have been told that we can only shoot ducks for a few weeks in the Fall. We are also told that this law has been made between our country and another great country, therefore, we must NOT break that law. We, who write these words are not young men, and the Treaty that you made with us is still fresh in our memories:— "As long as the rivers flow and as long as the sun sets in the west our hunting rights would not be taken away from us." This was promised us long before our country made laws with another country which decided to allow us to shoot wildfowl in the Fall only. Are we then to starve during the summer months because the whiteman had broken his word to us?[10]

Increased protection for migratory birds was parallelled by greater efforts by the federal government to preserve the wood buffalo in the Peace-Athabasca delta. After 1911, a re-orientation in dominion parks policy began to stress minimizing human disruption of natural areas. This approach was gradually integrated into efforts to protect the wood buffalo, and by the early 1920s the Department of the Interior had resolved that the wood buffalo could best be protected by creating a national park. Despite objections by Indian Affairs and the alarm it created in the Fort Smith area, Wood Buffalo Park was established in 1922 as a protective preserve for "the only remaining wild herd of bison in America," which then numbered about 1,500 animals.[11] Totalling about 27,000 square kilometres, the park took in an area north of the Peace River extending across the NWT border. Bounded on the east by the Slave River, it included important trapping districts. Although regulations about public use were in flux for the first years of the park's existence, all Treaty 8 Indians (regardless of where they lived) were at first allowed to hunt and trap in the park. "Traditional subsistence uses" such as haying and gathering salt that did not harm the buffalo were also permitted. These uses were conditional on respect for the provisions of the Alberta and the NWT game legislation (depending on which portion of the park was involved), both of which banned the killing of buffalo and other protected species. While white trappers were immediately excluded from the park, local Metis continued to trap and hunt there until 1923 when they too were excluded, leaving hunting privileges only for Indians. Local Metis protested this ruling, and Bishop Breynat of the Roman Catholic church and O.S. Finnie, the director of the North West Territories and Yukon Branch of the Department of the Interior, endorsed their protest, arguing that Metis should be taken into treaty if necessary. Indian Affairs rejected this proposal.[12]

By 1924 the park was patrolled regularly by six rangers who enforced the hunting bans. Over the protests of zoologists who worried about the hybridization of plains and wood buffalo, over 1,600 plains buffalo from the overcrowded Buffalo National Park at Wainwright, Alberta were shipped to Wood Buffalo Park in 1925. Handled by the Edmonton entrepreneur, Jim Cornwall, the animals were shipped by rail to Waterways and by barge to the park. In the next two years, more animals were shipped north and by 1928 almost 5,600 buffalo had been transferred from Wainwright. By then they and the wood bison had begun to interbreed, which called into question the rationale for establishing the park to protect the wood buffalo as a subspecies. The intermixing also likely transmitted tuberculosis and perhaps brucellosis to the original herd.[13]

By 1926, buffalo had moved beyond the Peace River at the southern boundary of the park. Rather than seeing this overflow as a repopulation of adjacent country for the benefit of hunters, an additional 17,600 square kilometres were annexed to the south of the park to protect the expanded range. This brought the areas immediately adjacent to Fort Chipewyan into the park, which further restricted trapping in the delta and intensified pressure on adjacent nonpark land. Moreover, the NWT was by now beginning to restrict trapping by nonresidents, which put more pressure on the delta, which remained open to all comers. As Chief Jonas Laviolette noted in 1927, "all the trappers that come down the river now can't get into the Park to trap and it is hard for them to get past Fort Smith so they stop in my country and try to crowd my people out."[14]

Access for hunting in both "new" and "old" park areas, as well as the whole of the enlarged park, was governed by complicated and evolving policies in which some people were excluded while others were given access depending on prior use. By the late 1920s, however, access to the different park areas was limited to those treaty Indians who had traditionally used it. While this tended to give most treaty Cree trappers from Fort Chipewyan access to the park, only some members of the Chipewyan band had such access. In some cases, these divisions cut across family ties, and the common interests of those with park access created new social bonds in the district. Moreover, those with park access generally had higher and more stable incomes than those without. After 1928, violation of the Alberta or NWT statutes gave the government the right to cancel an individual's hunting permit in the park. Surveillance of the park was increased and efforts were made to reduce the wolf population to protect the buffalo. Arrests were made from time to time for illegal hunting. At the same time, officials began culling the herds of outcast animals, distributing the meat to local schools or those in need. This policy continued throughout the 1930s. In 1933, uniform game regulations were adopted by park authorities to eliminate the confusion that had inevitably arisen from the application of the different (and sometimes contradictory) game laws of the NWT and Alberta. The new regulations allowed the trapping of beaver (banned in Alberta) and a six-week longer open season on muskrats. People with park permits were thus able to trap outside the park during Alberta's open season, and then moved to the park to trap there for the balance of its open season. This created inequalities and added pressure on resources outside the park.[15]

Intensified efforts to protect the buffalo at a time of great hardship focussed the frustrations of people experiencing severe economic pressure. In 1926, two Cree Indians were convicted of killing buffalo; one was sentenced to six months and the other to three months in the Fort Saskatchewan jail. The trial, held in Fort Chipewyan, drew a large crowd of people who were lectured by the Justice of the Peace about the "serious nature of the crime." For their part, the Chiefs and Headmen responded that they wanted "a written contract" to confirm that "their hunting rights would not be interfered with in the New Park area." When the Justice of the Peace replied that this was the responsibility of Indian Affairs, they retorted that despite "sweet words at other meetings," their hunting rights had been ignored. They considered "this Country their Country, as they were here before the Whitemen and that they never asked the Whitemen to come and give them Treaty. They also claimed the Buffalo were here before the Whitemen and this was their Country also" and that the government was "taking up more of their hunting grounds to feed more buffalo being brought into their Country without their permission."[16]

Such developments at Wood Buffalo Park, in tandem with the migratory birds convention and the tightening of provincial wildlife regulations, reinforced a growing belief that the treaty had been a chimera. As Chief Martin and Councillor Whitehead observed in 1927, "when we think of all these happenings it makes us look back on the promises made to us when the Treaty was signed, and we feel that we are not complaining without just cause. If we live up to these laws, starvation stares us in the face, for the yearly payment of 5.00 to each one of us, and the small ration of tea, flour and salt pork, are but as nothing when our rights are interfered with as they have been in the past."[17] Even though federal initiatives to protect the wood buffalo and migratory birds brought significant restrictions on Indian hunting, the Department of Indian Affairs was either compliant or powerless to influence these developments, just as it had been in respect to other aspects of provincial wildlife policies that emphasized on the priorities and interests of Euro-Canadians.

### —— "A Business Proposition"
*Alberta's Fur Policy*

Open access to resources on crown land was seen by the "settler class" as one of its rights, and as Jim Cornwall noted in 1926, any government that granted "exclusive rights" to any one group (such as Natives) would face political trouble.[18] The provincial government's explicit discouragement of Native common and collective use of wildlife and its promotion of a system of resource use based on individual and private motivation represented the triumph of this view. Provincial government claims that this asserted the "equality" of all Albertans continued to uphold in practical terms the interests of Euro-Canadian users of game resources, especially tourist promoters and sports hunters. Sports hunting was becoming increasingly politicized and commercialized in the 1920s and in 1928 its proponents gained a province-wide voice through affiliation with the newly formed Alberta Fish and Game Association. Though they often phrased their concerns in terms of public service, these groups were primarily concerned with protecting wildlife for sport, tourism and other recreational uses. Consequently, they tended to oppose rights for subsistence and commercial hunters with whom they believed they were competing for game. Moreover, they saw the existence of different rights for subsistence hunters, even in remote districts, as establishing precedents that might apply to the whole province.[19]

Such concerns played a strong role in shaping provincial game policy and brought no benefit to northern Native trappers. As sociologist Bennet McCardle notes, while "basically subsistence hunters, dependent to some extent on a capitalist fur industry," most Natives in the interwar years combined "minimum profit with maximum conservation of resources" by following "a small-scale way of life, adapted to an economic base characterized by extreme fluctuations of supply." The province's policy towards these unique circumstances was one of indifference and, at times, hostility. As the Chief Game and Fish Guardian observed in 1923, game protection "if successfully carried out is nothing more nor less than a business proposition." In this connection, the province treated the fur trade as an enterprise in which maximum production was encouraged and use of raw materials found on crown land was regulated to ensure continued supply and open access. There were no bag limits on fur-bearing animals; conservation needs were instead promoted by setting open and closed seasons for trapping or by total hunting bans on endangered species. In this connection, the ban on trapping beaver remained in place for much of the 1920s.[20]

Compounding this situation, Native northern trappers received little in return for the taxes they paid. Neither the fur tax nor trapping licences served regulatory functions; they simply raised revenue from some of the poorest people in Alberta. By 1934–35, the province took in almost $100,000 from its taxation and licensing of the fur trade. About 80 percent of this came from the fur tax, with the balance from trapping, fur dealer and fur farm licences.[21] Before 1945, the provincial government did not use any of these revenues to assist Native trappers in marketing their furs or to regulate the activities of traders so that the trade was more socially and economically responsible. While the Alberta government established a fur auction in 1915 in Edmonton for fur taken under special permit south of the North Saskatchewan River, it was designed primarily so that farmers and part-time trappers could obtain better prices than they could get from local traders. While some northern fur made it into these auctions, the provincial government did not provide an equivalent opportunity for northern trappers to realize higher prices.[22] Nor did it implement fur-bearer restocking or stabilization programmes as did a number of other provinces, or as it did for other natural resource sectors, such as fishing and lumbering, which were important for Euro-Canadians. While it agreed in 1939 to a proposed provincial-federal fur rehabilitation programme similar to those in place in some other provinces, it demanded in return that the federal government assume financial responsibility for Metis educational and medical services in northern communities; a demand that scuttled the proposal.[23]

In contrast to its lack of fur restocking and rehabilitation programmes in northern Alberta, the provincial government sponsored a number of initiatives that benefited Euro-Canadian sports hunters in the more southerly parts of the province. During the interwar years, it implemented, often in co-operation with fish and game associations, restocking programmes for game birds and sports fish, funded programmes for the extermination of birds such as magpies and crows that threatened game birds and worked with private organizations to rehabilitate waterfowl habitats. It also generally promoted and encouraged sport hunting and fishing as recreational and tourist activities. As the federal government fur supervisor, J.L. Grew, noted in 1945, such programmes provided no benefit for northern Native trappers grappling with unprecedented challenges. Indeed, he charged that the Alberta Fish and Game Association had lobbied for an increase in the fur taxes (which helped pay for sports hunting programmes) and had been "largely instrumental in having them raised to the present rates."[24]

The only elements of provincial fur policy that benefited northern Native trappers were efforts to enhance the Alberta fur industry's reputation and standards. But for Native trappers, this was a very mixed benefit indeed. While higher fur prices assisted all trappers, this was more than offset for Natives by the overall negative impact these policies had on their livelihoods. This was especially clear-cut in the case of laws respecting muskrats, which by the 1920s made up one-half of the province's fur production. In 1920, trapping muskrats south of the North Saskatchewan River was prohibited as a conservation measure, and in 1922 the open season in northern Alberta was shortened. As Alberta's game commissioner noted, it was "conceded by all concerned that it is in the interests of the province that muskrats should not be caught before the animals properly develop and their pelts become prime."[25] This policy directly affected Native trappers, especially in the Peace-Athabasca delta where people depended on the muskrat hunt. As Chief Martin and Councillor Whitehead noted in 1927, they had not initially complained about the shorter season because at the time "the rats were not plentiful," but they knew "from experience" that the low point in the muskrat cycle had now passed and that the season could be safely extended. But George Hoadley, the minister of Agriculture and responsible for the game legislation, doubted "the practicability" of extending the open season because it would create difficulties in conserving fur-bearing animals. Most telling, however, was Hoadley's judgement that it would not assist the commercial needs of the fur industry. As he noted, "since adopting the present open season the Alberta muskrat pelt has jumped from among the lowest priced pelts in Canada to third place. In fact the Alberta muskrat pelts are crowding closely for second place on the Canadian Market. The difference in price as between pelts taken in the Fall and Spring is so great that I would be very loathe to ask for amendments to allow trapping in the Fall and early Winter."[26] In fact, further controls were introduced to enhance the value of muskrat pelts. Spearing muskrats was banned in 1927 and shooting them was prohibited the next year. As the RCMP constable at Fort Chipewyan noted, the latter regulation was "prompted by dealers outside and was aimed against ruination of pelts," but it could not be enforced and was "disregarded by all." In any case, people now shot muskrats with .22 rifles because traders had discounted pelts damaged by shotguns.[27]

#### ▬ Debates Over Access to Resources

The increased number of white trappers in northern districts during the 1920s intensified the competitive spiral that threatened the livelihood of Native trappers. For many observers, this necessitated a redefinition of who were legitimate users of wildlife. One common suggestion proposed that preserves be established where only Indians could hunt. Indians, church figures, such as Bishop Breynat, and others lobbied for this approach. The Department of Indian Affairs too supported it, arguing that hunting needed to be safeguarded by establishing hunting preserves for the exclusive use of Indians in remote areas "where other sufficient employment is not available." There were important precedents for such a system. In the NWT, all hunters were licensed and outsiders were charged a higher licence fee. By 1928, Quebec too had set aside most of its northern region as an exclusive Native trapping preserve.[28] The most significant example of a Native-centred approach, however, was in the Yukon. In 1902, the Yukon Territorial Council had applied game laws only to non-Natives, while Native hunting and trapping remained unrestricted. Historian Kenneth Coates has observed that until 1942 (when the construction of the Alaska Highway radically changed conditions in the Yukon), experience in the Yukon showed that "Native harvesting could co-exist with a small, concentrated non-Native population, and that the government could respect the need for preferential access to resources for the Indians."[29] While the same conditions existed in parts of northern Alberta, such approaches were not attempted because the provincial government refused to support them. Like later discussions over registered traplines, differences between the Alberta game branch and Indian Affairs were framed by the structures of Canadian federalism and illustrated that provincial jurisdiction over wildlife and federal responsibility for Indian welfare could not be "easily reconciled in a single set of regulations" controlled by the province and influenced by non-Indian interests.[30]

Demands for trapping preserves were at first particularly intense in the Peace-Athabasca delta where white and Native competition for resources was sharpest. In 1922, Indians at Fort Chipewyan requested that a hunting preserve for their exclusive use be established in the delta. Showing that its commitment to the trapping preserve concept was still largely rhetorical, Indian Affairs ruled that the requested area was too large and instructed Indian Agent Card to defuse the situation because "other tribes would hear of the concession and would demand similar treatment." But as Card noted two years later, the issue could not be easily side stepped. Hunting preserves had by then been established in the NWT and people at Fort Chipewyan "will want to know why they have been left out." Not recognizing the labyrinth into which they were stepping, the Indians criticized Card, arguing that he "had not urgently enough pressed their claims." In 1923, they "took up a collection, among themselves, to send a delegation to Ottawa" to deal with the issue on their own. The delegates got as far as Edmonton where they managed to meet Charles Stewart, the minister of the Interior, who reportedly "promised action along the lines asked." As Card dryly observed, "if any action has been taken, or if the issue is impossible, I would like to be in a position [to] inform them." In reply, Duncan Campbell Scott, the deputy superintendent of Indian Affairs, noted that the department had tried "to induce the Province to act in this matter but up to the present time there have been no definite results."[31]

Despite Scott's reply, there had been some progress. The creation of a hunting preserve required an agreement with the province to allocate land and develop regulations. Alberta endorsed this undertaking—perhaps the official commitment of the recently elected UFA administration to "group government" and quasi-corporatist social organization made notions about exclusive districts for use by particular groups of people a familiar, and even appealing, idea. In early 1923, George Hoadley noted that Alberta had amended its game legislation to allow the creation of trapping areas "in which the Indians would have rights over those of white trappers and in which we could possibly limit the catch of white trappers." Subsequently, Indian Affairs proposed that seven small trapping preserves be established in northern Alberta (plus one in northern British Columbia) ranging in size from 130 to 195 square kilometres, including ones around Fort Chipewyan, Lesser Slave Lake, Fort Vermilion, Fort McMurray and south of Grande Prairie.[32]

Even though they would have been too small to be of much use (a single trapline often stretched along about a 65 kilometre circuit), establishment of even these tiny preserves did not proceed. Hoadley soon grew wary of the idea;

perhaps the political costs of Euro-Canadian hostility to such a policy had been realized, or perhaps the Alberta Game Commissioner, Benjamin Lawton, who was reluctant to recognize Indian hunting rights, had influenced him.[33] Despite its bravado, Indian Affairs also dragged its feet; by late 1924 it had still not identified lands that could be set aside as preserves. By then, Gerald Card was warning his superiors in Ottawa that a preserve was "necessary for the very life" of Indians in the Peace-Athabasca delta, and that they would soon "have to be wholly maintained by the Government if a preserve for them is not set apart before the white trappers exterminate the game." The next year, when forwarding yet further Indian demands for action on the matter, he noted that tensions between Indian and white trappers were rising and causing an increased number of violent incidents on the traplines.[34]

Indian Affairs management now became somewhat more motivated. H.J. Bury, the supervisor of Indian Timber Land, noted in 1926 that unless exclusive trapping preserves were established, the Indians would be pauperized and forced to live on government hand-outs, which would rob them of initiative and turn them into mendicants. If necessary, Bury argued that Indian Affairs should pay the province to establish an exclusive hunting preserve.[35] While it recognized the serious depletion of fur-bearing animals in northern Alberta, the government of Alberta refused to agree that trapping preserves were the solution. In mid 1926, Hoadley told Indian Affairs officials that Alberta's preconditions for negotiations were that "any rights granted to the Indians will also have to be granted to the white men," and that "Indians must pay for trapping privileges" and "confine their trapping activities to the areas set aside for their own exclusive use." While these demands violated the provisions of Treaty 8 that gave Indians the right to hunt on unoccupied crown land, Indian Affairs agreed to further negotiations.[36] Indian Agents in northern Alberta were instructed to prepare maps and to report on potential trapping preserves, which were to be kept as small as possible to placate the province. In the end, seven preserves ranging between 6,500 and almost 39,000 square kilometres were proposed for northern Alberta and one was set out for British Columbia. The province, however, now upped the ante by insisting that "the selection of such areas would not in any way prevent the development of the country for the purposes of farming or mineral development." Alberta's Game Commissioner, Benjamin Lawton, also contended that the preserves proposed by the federal government were too large, and he lectured Indian Affairs that "it must be borne in mind that there are many of the homesteaders in the north country whose interests must be protected."[37]

Given Alberta's position, negotiations stalled. Although Alberta publicly supported a resolution endorsing the need for exclusive Indian trapping preserves at the 1928 federal-provincial wildlife conference (at which Lawton represented Alberta), this did not signal a change in actual policy. In any case, demands for Indian trapping preserves had never addressed the needs of all of northern Alberta's Native people. Metis in some districts had by the 1930s become wholly dependent on trapping and hunting because of declining job opportunities, and Malcolm Norris of the Metis Association argued in 1935 that Metis should be put on an equal footing with Indians in terms of trapping and hunting because their needs were the same. Indeed, one Fort Chipewyan Metis trapper wrote in 1935 that if a trapping preserve that excluded whites was not established, "it will not be long and all the Half Breeds and Indians will be on relief."[38]

This compartmentalization of northern Native society was confirmed, however, in late 1929 with the signing of the Natural Resources Transfer Agreement (NRTA) which gave control of natural resources to the prairie provinces. Like the discussions over hunting preserves, the NRTA reflected the division of powers whereby the province theoretically looked after Metis needs and the federal government those of Indians. Indian Affairs lobbied for a constitutional recognition of Indian hunting rights in the NRTA, but no one spoke for the needs of the Metis. Canada and Alberta agreed in the NRTA that provincial game laws would apply to Indians, "provided, however, that the said Indians shall have the right, which the Province hereby assures to them, of hunting, trapping and fishing game and fish for food at all seasons of the year on all unoccupied Crown lands and on any other lands to which the said Indians may have a right of access."[39] As the minister of the Interior noted, it was understood that in return for this provision, Canada would not "exercise its paramount legislative power" to "over-ride" the application of provincial game laws to Indians. The game clause in the NRTA, he noted, "merely restates the Indians' position as already set out in the various treaties."[40] While the province had gained recognition of its constitutional power over game regulation, Indian subsistence hunting and trapping rights on unoccupied crown lands had been restored and protected against provincial game laws and regulations. In keeping with this arrangement, Indian Affairs warned Indians in 1931 that "they must not, in any case, take game for commercial purposes of any kind, in any way contrary to the law and that wanton slaughter will not be tolerated." If Indians ignored these warnings, "they need not look to the department for assistance."[41]

Despite the provisions of the NRTA, the Alberta government refused to recognize a treaty-protected right to Indian subsistence hunting. It immediately attempted to limit the hunting-for-food provision by proposing that all game taken for food by Indians outside of open seasons be regulated by permits issued by the province. Indian Affairs "strongly opposed" this suggestion as "it is obvious that the purpose in mind would be to curtail the privileges at present enjoyed by the Indians."[42] But the province's newly gained constitutional control of Indian hunting on "occupied" land (on which the hunting-for-food provisions did not apply) gave it significant power. In 1931, it defined "occupied" land in a broad manner (including forest preserves, for example) in order to limit the Indian hunting provisions of the NRTA. Further, provincial officials ruled that fur-bearers were not "game" within the meaning of the agreement.[43] At the same time, the NRTA created genuine enforcement problems because the social lines between Indian and Metis were often unclear in northern Alberta. As one critic noted, since many families contained both Treaty and non-Treaty people, enforcement of one hunting law for Indians and another for non-Indians was extremely difficult.[44]

The province's position on Indian hunting rights under the NRTA was tested in 1932 when a Stoney from southern Alberta, William Wesley, was charged with killing a deer under one year of age, in violation of the game statute. Although Wesley was not from northern Alberta, the case had ramifications for Indian hunting rights everywhere in the province. He was convicted, and "in view of the constitutional point at issue," Indian Affairs engaged counsel to represent him on appeal. Mr. Justice McGillivray ruled that the NRTA's guarantee of Indians' rights to hunt for food was clear and that they had "an unrestricted right to hunt for food in those unsettled places where game may be found." While the province prophesied that Indians would now be free to "slaughter" game and reiterated its view that hunting for food should only be allowed by permit, Indian Affairs termed the decision "a complete win for the Indians."[45]

The Wesley case had both practical and symbolic implications. In 1930, news of the hunting-for-food provision of the NRTA had led the Northern Alberta Game and Fish Protective League to express "with utmost concern any such wide scope as appears to be granted Indians." The Wesley decision intensified this concern, and the Alberta Fish and Game Association unanimously passed a special resolution at its 1933 annual meeting condemning the court's ruling.[46] Reflecting the continued appeal of these concerns, the MP for the Peace River country, Donald Kennedy, termed Indian hunting rights a "live" issue in his constituency in 1935. The same year, the Alberta Fish and Game Association forwarded its earlier resolution protesting Indian hunting to Indian Affairs, along with a number of additional recommendations and allegations. The association charged that market hunting by Indians was responsible for an "alarming decrease" in big game in Alberta and that conservation programmes were necessary to protect wildlife for future generations including Natives, "resident whitemen, trappers, sportsmen" and tourists. But in the association's opinion, Natives, not whites, threatened game supplies, and it asserted that Indians had to be brought fully under provincial game laws. Because the association believed that much of this hunting took place because Indians were impoverished, it argued that "subsidies" being paid to Indians should be increased and that "all non-Treaty Indians" should "be compelled to come under the provisions of the *Indian Act*."[47] Commenting on these views, M. Christianson, inspector of Indian Agencies in Alberta, observed in a private letter to his superior at Indian Affairs that only Indians in the mountains and northern parts of the province depended on big game for food since it had been nearly wiped out elsewhere. Indians did not kill "wantonly for sport," he believed, but mainly for food, and he contended that, to the best of his knowledge, Indians in Alberta did not "peddle meat." Further, he contended that white trappers and hunters, especially in the north, were the ruthless hunters, not Natives, and he endorsed a popularly held view among Indians that due to the large number of "White people who hunt and trap now, there will be practically no game left for the generation to come."[48] The department's reply to the association was considerably more measured, and it noted that while game was a provincial responsibility, Indians had a treaty right to hunt for food. But the association refused to be mollified; as it noted in a follow-up letter to Indian Affairs, the *Wesley* case showed that whenever Indians "have been prosecuted by the authorities and fines obtained, your Department has in some cases immediately appealed the decision of the courts, which to our mind most certainly" nullified the province's conservation efforts.[49]

Despite such hyperbole, the Indian hunting provision of the NRTA and its confirmation in *Rex vs. Wesley* were not the victory for Indians that its critics suggested. Clearly, the NRTA expanded rights for Indians south of 55 degrees who had regained the right to hunt for food that they had lost under Alberta's game legislation in 1907. Treaty 8 Indians were also now unrestricted as to the type of animals they could take for food and the way they could kill them. But because the NRTA did not interfere with the application of federal game laws to Indians, they remained subject to the provisions of the *Migratory Birds*

*Photographs of trappers working their traplines are rare. This one
shows a trapper taking a break to brew some tea. Probably Fort
Smith area. Not dated.* OB1230 PAA.

*Convention Act.* At the same time, the province had gained federal recognition of
its complete control over wildlife, and while the NRTA and the *Wesley* case
established a constitutional protection for Indian hunting, it narrowed treaty
hunting rights to hunting for food only. Moreover, the province's authority to
establish legal parameters for hunting had not been impaired. In the wake of
the broad definition of "game" set out in *Rex vs. Wesley*, the province drew up
detailed regulations governing the disposal of pelts from fur-bearers killed for
food in order "to discourage any but emergency killing of furbearers for food."[50]

A growing number of precedents in other provinces, the failure of the
NRTA to address the economic needs of northern trappers, and the growing
number of white trappers in the north gave rise to further demands for exclusive hunting preserves in the 1930s. By 1934, Quebec still excluded whites from
most of its northern trapping preserves while Ontario had begun to implement
preferential status for Native trappers north of the CNR mainline. In 1938
trapping licences in the NWT were restricted to residents and their descendants, although the whole scheme was compromised because of resource
depletion, the continuing activities of resident whites and the refusal to expand
the preserves because of the objections of whites in adjacent areas. The prairie
provinces, in contrast, continued to show little commitment to protect their

northern Native hunting peoples, and Natives in northern Alberta continued to demand the establishment of exclusive trapping preserves.[51] In 1935, Indians at Little Red River, Fort Vermilion, Boyer River, Upper Hay River and Utikuma Lake, among others, all asked for trapping preserves for their exclusive use. Napoleon L'Heureux, the Lesser Slave Lake Agency Indian Agent, noted that "I have investigated and find that in most instances Indian trappers are crowded out of their traplines by white trappers who make their own laws and enforce it by threats or otherwise. It is a condition with which I have more and more to contend."[52]

In 1935, Alberta finally agreed to modify the open access system in the delta. The new game commissioner, S.H. Clark, and Inspector Christianson of Indian Affairs collaborated in establishing a trapping district south of Lake Athabasca between Wood Buffalo Park and the Saskatchewan border. The area was restricted "to those trappers already active in the area."[53] But the district had been almost completely trapped out, and the responsible Indian Agents took no interest in the project and neglected to encourage its rehabilitation as a fur-producing area. Nor were bag limits placed on trappers, and whites with trapping rights in the reserved area continued to pose problems since their aggressive behaviour and better capitalization allowed them to put out more traps. Jonas Laviolette therefore demanded in 1936 that outsiders be excluded from the delta because it was "so crowded by white people and drifters" who had taken "the best sloughs and lakes for rats, and they fight us when we go near them at all." In the now familiar appeal, he wrote that "we want a hunting Preserve for our band." Revealing that distinctions in Native status were unimportant in this case, Laviolette noted "we have no objection to native-born half-breeds of this District to trap with us, or other Indians." Permanent residency was an important factor for Laviollete because it related to how one used the resource: "knowing that the Game in our country and fur is our livelihood, we take good care of not destroying it, and we respect your laws."[54]

While Indians had always appealed to traditional knowledge of the history of the treaties to defend their hunting rights, these appeals became more pointed during this time of increasing desperation. A popular contention was that the treaty commissioners had promised that Indians would be protected from white competition—a logical conclusion in light of the treaty commissioners' assurances that game conservation would benefit Indians and that they would be able to continue to make their living as before the treaty. In 1937, Bishop Breynat obtained 21 affidavits to this effect from witnesses of Treaty 8, and Jim Cornwall also signed a similar affidavit. As sociologist Richard Daniel has noted, however, the validity of these affidavits is questionable; they were signed 38 years after the event, and, most importantly, all were identical except for Cornwall's. Rather than being 21 "separate and distinct accounts," they were probably all prepared by Breynat. Nonetheless, they marked the tensions over white competition and the persistence of Indian views that protection from white competition was in keeping with the spirit of the treaty.[55]

## ▬ Registered Traplines

Concerns about Native participation in the trapping economy were intensified in 1939 when Alberta implemented a registered trapline system. Under this approach, traplines were allocated (or "registered") to an individual who alone had the right to trap there. Like proposals for exclusive Indian trapping preserves, it involved restricting access to trapping areas. While this ended the use of regulated open access for trapping, resource use remained open in terms of residency and status and therefore still left the activities of white trappers unchallenged. Moreover, by presuming that self-interest would contribute to maximum production while still promoting conservation, it sustained the independent commodity production model favoured by the government of Alberta. As political scientist Peter Clancy has noted in his study of trapping in the NWT, it was anticipated that trappers would manage their registered lines "for long term abundance. There would be no advantage in over-harvesting on a year-to-year basis since adjacent registrations normally prevented easy movement to virgin land." For the overall success of the system, however, all registered traplines had to produce roughly equal incomes. The system also assumed detailed knowledge about the productive capacity of an area and the behaviour of fur-bearers. It indicated a shift in conservation strategies away from the "regulation" of trappers through techniques such as open and closed seasons towards a system in which species, habitats and users were all "managed" as elements within a total environment. It also structured patterns of resource use in new ways. The customary flexibility of Native trapping and the reliance on family and group rather than individual efforts were challenged because the registered trapline system restricted the geography of trapping. Further, as a type of lease, paid for by an annual registration fee, a registered trapline could be bought or sold. It thus formed a type of private property use of crown land. By curtailing open access to fur areas and individualizing resource use, it attempted to replace older communal and flexible methods of resource use with private ones mediated by the state. And by granting proprietary rights, it also served to legitimize the presence of white trappers in fur-bearing areas, further restricting Native use of wildlife on unoccupied crown land.[56]

The registered trapline system was first used in British Columbia in 1925. Alberta considered adopting it in 1929 because, as the Alberta game commissioner noted in his annual report, unrestrained competition was destroying northern fur resources and the conservation of fur supplies required "some system of regulating trapping operations." Since trappers at present could trap anywhere and use the same area trapped by others, there was "no incentive to the trapper to leave a sufficient number of any species to provide a supply for the future." The registered trapline system would eliminate these problems.[57] For the Alberta government, it was also a convenient solution. Unlike trapping preserves for exclusive Indian use, it did not presume a recognition of treaty hunting rights, nor did it challenge the principle of "equality" of all Albertans because it left white interests unimpaired.

While it was an attractive approach given Alberta's priorities, the provincial government did not immediately proceed with the registered trapline system. Regulations were drafted in 1933, but the system was not brought in until 1939. Seemingly, the province was more concerned with meeting the economic and environmental problems of the rest of the province, and in any case, it lacked the ability to administer a registered trapline system. Even when Alberta finally implemented the system in 1939, it was ill-equipped to handle it. Only a small portion of trapping districts in northern Alberta were mapped to the detail required for administering a registered trapline system. Moreover, official knowledge about patterns of local resource use and productivity was lacking. Nonetheless, by 1939 the province was experiencing increasing pressure from white trappers for protection of their lines from interlopers, and provincial game authorities had concluded that the registered trapline system would best rationalize resource use and promote conservation.[58] Under the 1939 regulations, all the territory north of township 96 (the area north of about Notikewin in the Peace River country and Fort McKay on the Athabasca River) was declared a registered trapline district. Indians had to apply for a trapline but were not required to pay registration fees, and all applications were approved by the local game guardian or RCMP officer to ensure that "no one will capitalize on the scheme to any extent." In 1941, the system was extended to all crown land north of the North Saskatchewan River.[59]

While Indian Affairs had many concerns, it did not entirely object to the registered trapline system. It hoped that it would end competition among trappers and thus stimulate "a sense of proprietorship and responsibility toward the conservation of the fur and timber resources" and help stabilize the Native economy.[60] At the same time, a contradictory impulse among some Indian Affairs officials led to tacit support, or at least indifference, to the new system, whatever its impact. Many Indian Agents saw trapping as an obsolete and discredited activity and did little to encourage its viability. As D.J. Allan, Indian Affairs superintendent of Reserves and Trusts, noted, most agents were "agriculturally minded" and viewed trapping as "merely an interruption and deterrent factor in the programme of agricultural expansion which most of them hope to impose on the Indian population."[61]

Overall, however, Indian Affairs saw more negative than positive aspects in the registered trapline system. It viewed the system as a poor substitute for exclusive hunting and trapping preserves because it did not expel whites from Indian trapping districts. As well, the department judged that it threatened Indian economic self-sufficiency and violated treaty hunting rights because registered lines were defined by Alberta as "occupied" land where Indians could not hunt for food under the terms of the NRTA.[62] While Indians in some parts of Canada apparently saw registered traplines as a positive step that helped limit non-Native encroachment, Indians in northern Alberta often opposed it. Such opposition was expressed at Fort Chipewyan, while at the Janvier Reserve near Chard, the Indian Agent reported in 1942 that people had rebelled "quite strongly" against registration that they saw as "a regimentation." Nor could people accustomed to group trapping see the sense of the system. In the Hay Lakes district in the north-west of the province, Beaver and Dene people had "very little idea of the purpose and intent of Registration, and very little idea of an individual holding."[63] Moreover, as a form of private property, registered traplines created conflict by applying concepts of legal trespass. As Inspector Schmidt of Indian Affairs noted in 1940, many Indians in the Fort Chipewyan district were "continually on the move, and when travelling, traverse—not to say trespass—other people's trap lines." Finding land that they had used for generations "given to a stranger" was a "most difficult and vexing situation" for people "born and raised in these parts."[64]

Despite such concerns, Indian Affairs could not stop Alberta from implementing the registered trapline system. Thus, it instructed its staff (partly because of earlier experience in British Columbia) to register Indian lines immediately. Otherwise, the department believed that "the whites will make a real and live effort to obtain these traplines, while our nonchalant, improvident Indians will let the chance pass by."[65] Nonchalance and improvidence were hardly the most significant barriers—the whole concept of individual trapping was still alien to many Natives in northern Alberta, while the application forms demanded sketch maps and detailed descriptions of the trapline in English. At the same time that it was urging Indians to register traplines, Indian Affairs sought administrative concessions from the province to accommodate Indian needs. In this, Indian Affairs was a supplicant. As Harold McGill, director of Indian Affairs, admitted in 1943, "the Province is under no obligation (that is, they are not compellable) to grant traplines to Indians and our attitude must therefore necessarily be co-operative."[66] Even so, given the history of white aggression towards Indian trappers, Indian Affairs attempted to have the province agree to segregate Indian lines from those of whites and Metis to minimize conflict and to allow Indians to work out their own resource use arrangements. As well, it endeavoured to persuade the province to accept prior use of land by Indians as a criteria for granting a particular trapline. Most importantly, it attempted to have the province grant "blanket permits" for registered trapping "areas" or "blocks" that could be organized on a group basis according to hereditary use, local characteristics and intra-band allocations of resources.[67] In an attempt to minimize growing conflict over trapline registration and to promote the department's objectives, J.L. Grew, the Indian Affairs fur supervisor, was assigned in 1942 to map traplines and record registrations in Alberta. Further, he was instructed to lobby the province to set areas aside for Indian traplines and to try and "obtain from the Alberta administration such concessions as he may be able to arrange" for trapping Indians.[68] While Grew optimistically reported in 1943 that he had obtained concessions "that last year appeared to be difficult of achievement," it became apparent when the province implemented the system on its own terms that Indian Affairs had achieved few of its objectives.[69]

Although the Alberta game branch toyed with the idea of issuing blanket permits, it quickly dropped this plan in order to avoid being "petitioned by other groups of Half-breeds and whites for similar privileges."[70] Thus, Indian trappers were forced to register on individual lines even though many of them had not traditionally trapped exactly the same area every year and had trapped in family or group arrangements. At Hay Lakes, such conditions were further complicated by the fact that people had also trapped in British Columbia and the NWT. Consequently, despite attempts to confine them to one jurisdiction and particular traplines, the Indians at Hay Lakes "simply followed the game and fur" and refused to limit themselves to "individual areas." This gave white trappers the opportunity to apply "to have these areas considered 'abandoned' and re-registered in their favor." These problems were made worse by poor administration. Despite the lack of adequate maps for the Hay Lakes district, the game branch insisted on using cartographic descriptions rather than natural features when approving the boundaries of traplines. Showing a devotion to procedure over practicality, the department simply drew township lines onto maps, "despite the fact that the survey into townships did not exist." Consequently, trappers had only a general idea of where their lines were located, creating further potential for conflict. Moreover, it was claimed that the people charged with enforcing the game legislation in the district and administering trapline registration "stumbled along, following the letter of the Regulations." Most were said to be local Metis, "related to half the metis in the area," who ensured that "their relations were protected and provided for at the expense of the Indian." White administrators were no better, and were said to be "so closely entangled with the 'white' interests as to be totally indifferent."[71]

Indian Affairs' failure to persuade the province to issue blanket permits was parallelled by its inability to convince the province to establish registered trapping line areas for Indians only. There was initially some support for this approach in the Alberta game branch, and the province also indicated a willingness to grant traplines to Indians in northern Alberta "by reason of prior rights." Accordingly, J.L. Grew laid out a number of "Indian areas," mainly in Treaty 6 territory.[72] But Alberta's support for Indian lines and recognition of prior rights were fleeting. White trappers apparently pressured the provincial government not to grant concessions to Indians, and in late 1943 the Game Superintendent, D.E. Forsland, confessed to Grew that he did not know "how many of these Indian areas which you laid out when you were here last summer will come into effect." He was certain, however, that "no preference will be given the Indians and they will have to take their chances with the white man and if the white man has any trapping priority then he will be the man to get the line in question." As N.E. Tanner, the Alberta minister of Lands and Mines, stated in 1945, "he would not dispossess white men to give the lines they now occupy to Indians."[73] Indeed, in a further effort to make registered trapping a universal practice in northern Alberta, the province abolished trapping licences in 1943, requiring all trappers north of the North Saskatchewan River to hold a registered trapline permit. In the Peace River country and around Edmonton, most Indians trapped only during a few weeks in the fall and spring and farmed or worked for wages during the rest of the year. Compulsory individual trapline registration did not lend itself to such a lifestyle.[74] In 1944, Alberta also moved against Indian treaty rights by demanding that Indians pay the $10 annual registered trapline fee. Apparently believing that the federal government had "unlimited money," the province threatened not to renew Indian trapline permits until the fees were paid. Although Indian Affairs strongly objected, it ultimately agreed to pay. In 1944–45 this totalled just over $7,500, about 25 percent less than that first demanded by the province.[75]

Federal concessions on fees for Indian registered traplines marked Indian Affair's ongoing inability to protect Indian interests in northern Alberta. In its 1946 game legislation, Alberta narrowly interpreted the NRTA game clause and set out procedures for disposing of pelts and hides produced from subsistence hunting. At the same time, the Alberta game branch indicated that it would allow group registered traplines, and in some places (such as Wabasca) some individual lines were changed to group ones. Even so, this remained a concession, not a right, and Alberta, unlike Ontario, Quebec and the other prairie provinces, remained committed to individual rather than group lines.[76]

**—— New Patterns**

*Post-war Adjustment and Fur Farming*

Important changes were beginning to appear in the northern trapping economy by 1946. A decline in fur prices that began at the end of World War II lasted into the 1950s. From a high of $4.50 in 1945, muskrat pelts at Fort Chipewyan dipped to $1.20 in 1949 and 43 cents in 1951. Falling incomes were offset to a degree by the extension of the Family Allowance to trapping families, "the first major social welfare scheme which was extended to status Indians."[77] Registration procedures for family allowance benefits were outlined during the annuity circuit in northern Alberta in 1945, and payments under the scheme began a short time later. Families received the allowance if their children under 16 years of age were at school or receiving "equivalent training," which included trapping. Poor Native families who previously might have sent their children to school were now able to keep them in the bush and receive the economic benefit of their labour as well as the family allowance. Children in a residential school did not receive the payments. In combination, these factors contributed to fewer school enrolments than might otherwise have been the case.[78]

Family allowances helped many people to make ends meet during the rapid inflation after World War II. As Indian Affairs' superintendent of the Athabasca agency noted in 1949, fur prices were so low that "an Indian needs a big fur catch before he can expect to take home even a small dog sleigh load of food." In these conditions, the family allowance helped to "keep the home going." The decline in real incomes made the post-war fur depression worse than that of the 1930s, which had been accompanied by deflation, and the post-war years were ones of escalating crisis for northern communities.[79] Because of increasing costs and store closures in the district, a Trappers' Union was established at Fort Chipewyan in 1946. A co-operative with about 300 members, it was designed to market furs and sell supplies at lower cost. Financed by the sale of shares to members, it was the first such co-operative in the north.[80]

Such local efforts attempted to meet the fundamental changes that had occurred in the trapping economy. By the late 1940s, local Native control over trapping and hunting had been lost because of government policies, white competition and broader social change. The most marked evidence of these changes was the increasing number of people living permanently in settlements. While there were a variety of individual reasons for the move to town, a significant factor was that a trapping life was no longer economically tenable. Consequently, as anthropologist Patricia McCormack observes in connection with Fort Chipewyan, it was not so much that people were rejecting bush life as rejecting an economy that could no longer sustain them.[81]

In addition to lower prices, the market for wild fur was also increasingly challenged by ranched fur by the 1940s. Farmed fur created a market for new colours of fur that could not be produced in the wild. By 1941, farmed fur made up about 43 percent of Alberta's fur production; an increase of about 10 percent over two years. Fur farming had begun in Alberta before World War I, and by 1915 there were 44 fur farms in Alberta; 10 of which were in northern Alberta, mainly around Lesser Slave Lake. Most of them raised fox. Young wild fox were captured in the spring and kept until fall or winter when they were pelted. This practice lasted into the early 1920s, and as had been the case earlier, "only silver, black and best crosses" were kept, and other foxes were either killed or "allowed to shift for themselves." This meant that "a large proportion of the reds and poor crosses" perished. Moreover, a "very large percentage" of the captured fox died because of improper feeding and care, causing a decline in wild fox populations and leading to the sale of "very poor pelts." In keeping with the view that state regulation should enhance the value of resources, the province imposed a closed season on fox the next year. This, it claimed, would ensure high prices and confirm Alberta's "reputation" for high quality fox pelts.[82]

A related, although less destructive form of "fur farming" at this time involved the raising of beaver and muskrat in marshy areas. These operations were little more than private trapping areas in which a wild population of animals was maintained through fencing, breeding programmes, water level stabilization and provision of adequate food. There was much public enthusiasm for this practice, and government departments and railway companies fielded numerous inquiries from people interested in receiving a free "swamp" in which to raise muskrats. Perhaps fuelled by the romanticization of the Canadian north in the 1920s, ignorance about the difficulties and costs of raising wild animals in captivity also contributed to the fantasy and escapism that characterized many of these inquiries. Both federal and provincial governments, however, were leery of granting such exclusive rights because it would be controversial with settlers who viewed open access to resources on crown lands as a right of citizenship.[83] Indeed, Benjamin Lawton, the Alberta game commissioner, believed that most applicants wanted to secure control of a suitable area, "which in all probability at present is well stocked with these animals," to have "a private trapping ground" rather a genuine fur farm. To prevent such occurrences, regulations on muskrat farm leases were developed by 1927. Although the NAR wanted to encourage such enterprises north of Lac La Biche to create traffic for its line, the government's hesitancy in regulating the disposal of marsh lands for such purposes held up development. By 1929, there were only 12 muskrat and beaver farms in Alberta, two of which were located just north of Fort McMurray. The remainder were within about 80 kilometres of Edmonton.[84]

Although interest in muskrat farms endured—Jim Cornwall proposed one near Fort Chipewyan in 1939—such approaches were increasingly replaced with more conventional ones where animals were raised in cages. By 1935 there were 534 "fur farms" in Alberta. Although some of these raised muskrats, the trend was towards fox and mink. Many of these "farms" were only a sideline to other activities, but by the late 1930s the industry became more focussed as markets for ranched fur were created and knowledge about fur animal husbandry improved. Mink were particularly suited for fur farming because they matured quickly. Those born in the spring were pelted in the early winter, in contrast to some fur-bearing animals which needed up to three years' growth. Market demand for farmed mink was enhanced by the creation of fashions for "mutations" (such as whites and pastels) that did not occur in the wild. Much of this breeding was done in the United States, but several Edmonton fur breeders introduced highly valued fur colours in the late 1930s and 1940s.[85]

The rationalization of fur farming in Alberta in the late 1930s was encouraged by the provincial government. The contrast between its lack of assistance to Native trapping and the encouragement it provided to fur farming was a graphic example of provincial priorities. In 1935, the new Social Credit administration identified fur farming as a means of diversifying the provincial economy, and it appointed a fur supervisor to administer provincial fur farm licensing and to carry on extension work with fur farmers. Although fur farms paid a licence fee to operate, the fur tax was not applied to ranched fur. In 1937–38 the province also established an Experimental Fur Farm at Oliver (near Edmonton). Working with fox and mink, the farm offered educational programmes for fur farmers and breeding experiments.[86]

Fur farms in Alberta were found mainly in the Edmonton and Calgary districts, and around Lesser Slave Lake and Lac La Biche. Feed was readily available in these districts—packing plant byproducts were used in Edmonton and Calgary, while local fish provided feed for the animals in the Lesser Slave Lake and Lac La Biche districts. Horse meat was also a popular and inexpensive feed everywhere—a gruesome indication of the shift in Alberta agriculture from horse to tractor power. Mink were being raised near the town of Slave Lake by the late 1920s, and there were mink farms in several locations at the east end of Lesser Slave Lake by the end of the 1930s. By 1939, farmed fur production in the district was valued at about $80,000 annually, and about 40 fur farmers at Faust formed an association to lobby the government for favourable treatment and educational programmes for the industry.[87] By 1945, there were approximately 60 mink farms between Slave Lake and Kinuso. At a time when average prices were around $40, one farmer in the area had developed a "platinum" strain of mink that sold for up to $150 a pelt, while another had bred a blue fox. Optimistically, it was anticipated that such new "cash crops" in combination with others would usher in "prosperity in the post-war period."[88]

Faced with the need to save money, the province closed the Experimental Fur Farm in 1940 but it maintained its extension services. According to the provincial department of agriculture, Alberta's climate was suitable for fur farming and there was plentiful inexpensive feed, especially fish and horse meat. Occasionally, the province reluctantly relaxed fishing regulations on Lesser Slave Lake so that mink farmers could obtain feed for their animals. It was also alleged that wild meat was used for mink food in northern Alberta—the RCMP at Kinuso claimed in 1939 that local mink farmers were "responsible to a great degree for the illegal hunting and fishing which is reported from time to time."[89] While these allegations were not proven, fur farms clearly required plentiful and inexpensive feed—the fur farms in the Lesser Slave Lake district, for example, consumed almost 10,000 kilograms of fish a day. Following World

War II, serious mink feed shortages developed. As the horse population declined, the cost of horse meat rose, especially when markets for horse meat opened in Europe at the end of the war. Fish and meat byproducts were also now being used by chemical manufacturers who could afford to pay higher prices than fur farmers. Fish depletion in Alberta lakes also caused a further tightening of the market. Fur prices also fell, which put further pressure on profit margins. As the Alberta Department of Agriculture reported in 1948, looming feed shortages were "a source of grave concern to the industry" because the production of horses was "practically discontinued," and this, along with the depletion of fish in northern lakes, posed a serious "menace to the future of fur farming" in Alberta.[90]

— ✦ —

The crisis faced by Native trappers in northern Alberta during the interwar years provided a clear example of how the region's integration into Canada provided few advantages for Native people. While Indian Affairs supported Indian interests by trying to establish trapping preserves, it did so, at least in part, from a desire to protect itself from the increased welfare expenditures that the destruction of Indian trapping would bring. Whatever its motives, it did not gain meaningful concessions from the province with regard to trapping preserves and other related issues. Nor was it able to create a broad consensus among federal political figures that Indian rights were a matter over which they should challenge the province. While the federal government defended its constitutional rights to regulate banking and to protect Canadian financial institutions by disallowing Alberta's Social Credit banking legislation, Indian treaty hunting rights were not considered to be worthy of equivalent effort or risk. Nor was Indian Affairs able to persuade other federal departments to endorse its support for Indian hunting rights. Even so, its efforts to obtain Indian trapping preserves and its defence of Indian interests during the implementation of the registered trapline system represented a commitment that was entirely absent on the part of the government of Alberta before 1950. Even though Native trapping and hunting were of unique social importance in northern Alberta, Alberta refused to distinguish between northern needs and those of the rest of the province in its wildlife regulations. Instead, it trumpeted a commitment to the equality of all of its residents. Through its narrow interpretation of treaty rights, and its refusal to recognize that its game laws gave advantage to mobile, more aggressive and better capitalized Euro-Canadian trappers, the provincial government effectively marginalised Native trappers. It refused to recognize that it could achieve "equality" for Native trappers by respecting their treaty rights and by curbing the activities of outsiders. This related directly to the fact that Natives lacked political power and were unable to challenge province-building priorities that contributed to their marginalization. But as Peter Clancy has observed about trapping in the NWT, "state policy [on trapping] had consequences more substantial than showing where real power lay. By rejecting systematic support for commercial [Native] trapping, the state allowed the economic force of the sectorial decline to reach its full potential. The lack of counteracting policy initiatives meant that the pattern of movement off the land would proceed absolutely."[91] So too in northern Alberta—the movement off the land in trapping districts after 1945 was in large part a direct consequence of earlier policies that had irreversibly weakened Aboriginal commercial and subsistence trapping. While trapping remained important in Aboriginal society, the social crisis that the movement off the land brought continues to affect life in many northern communities.

# PART IV

*This photograph of a Dene woman*
*was taken at Fort Smith in 1930.*
OB10,686 PAA.

# Conclusion

# Diverging Paths

# 15

NORTHERN ALBERTA'S location as a place on the way to somewhere else—to the Mackenzie River and the western Arctic, the Yukon, or northern British Columbia and Alaska—helped to shape its history. But its historical evolution as an entity in its own right and its place in the history of the prairies and Canada is also significant. By 1890, it had emerged as a regional unit in prairie Canada in part because of the corporate needs of the Hudson's Bay Company. Changes in transportation in the 1880s and the transformation of existing settlements and the creation of new ones as elements in a supporting urban system focussed the shared economy and common lifestyles of the Peace-Athabasca River basin. While these developments met specific local conditions, they were also an intimate part of the revamping of the prairie region's economy and society that followed in the wake of Canada's take-over in 1870. While corporate needs had framed the development of northern Alberta as a region, its subsequent integration with Canada ultimately led to the breakdown of its regional unity. What emerged were two smaller units—the Peace River country with its agricultural economy tied to provincial and national social and economic structures, and the lower Athabasca district whose historic fur trade economy was increasingly less relevant and no longer influential in the centres of Canadian power.

The federal government set the stage for these developments. A new place for northern Alberta within Canada fulfilled one element of Confederation's purpose to expand Canada's effective reach throughout the northern half of the continent. And while individuals such as Frank Oliver and others in Edmonton often made free with the rhetoric of local chauvinism and grievance for their own purposes, they understood that the realization of their expansionary ambitions depended on Canada. Only it could legitimize their hopes and bring them to fruition. Canada alone had the resources and ability to police and control the territory, sign a treaty with the First Nations people, and create the social and legal infrastructure to promote orderly settlement and economic development. The ability of prairie business interests, especially those in Edmonton, to influence the federal government revealed that while Ottawa could at times be remote and arrogant, it was not entirely isolated. Within the familiar partisan structures of Canadian political life, it directly assisted and promoted nascent regional interests.

Despite the professions of private expansionists, the initial restructuring of northern Alberta—in perhaps a typically Canadian fashion—waited for state involvement. But while a treaty with the region's Native people and the government institutions necessary to regulate social and economic life preconditioned development, it was presumed that such development would eventually be made real through private initiative that would be confirmed and protected by the state. Policies such as homesteading and those enforcing regulated open access to natural resources were elements in this strategy. Yet while the state often served their needs, its efforts were not only enabling devices for private interests. Federal government expansionism became more aggressive under the new Liberal government after 1897, and its attempts to control the pace and terms of development reflected a broadly active and guiding role. Its activities also had a life of their own, nurtured by the circumstances and concerns of the time. Federal efforts, such as those to control the liquor traffic and to conserve wildlife, had little to do with local needs or the concerns of expansionists, but reflected more diffuse social forces that were shaping national policy.

The scope for state activity was enlarged with the creation of the province of Alberta in 1905. This began a refinement of nation-building initiatives and sometimes encouraged their replacement with province-building ones. Within Alberta, there was significant agreement that the province should direct matters as far as it could to enhance both provincial control and the interests of its citizens. This provincial activity was constrained by limited revenues, lack of jurisdiction (most notably over natural resources before 1930) and, among other factors, by competition among different districts within the province. Yet, complementing federal government initiatives, the provincial government had adequate power to promote many of its interests and to provide infrastructure for the private sector and a forum to focus and co-ordinate its efforts. The subsidy of northern railways was the costliest and most prominent of these initiatives, but as Alberta's involvement with railways indicated, it was also sometimes drawn through a combination of vanity, provincial priorities and lack of alternatives into more direct investment.[1]

Railway policies revealed that local and province-wide economic and social interests were rarely absent from the mix of motives that shaped provincial policy. The influence of Edmonton and district in early provincial governments gave many northern expansionists a voice in provincial decision-making, as the emphasis on northern lines in Alberta's railway policies demonstrated. Southern Alberta's ongoing objections that it received scant benefit from the province's northern transportation policies reflected, however, that province-building—just as nation-building—was not without internal tensions or immune from partisan and sectoral conflict. So too, Alberta's attempts after 1930 to rationalize agricultural settlement reflected this commingling of local and provincial priorities. Extensive criticism of the homestead system's waste and inefficiency provided one motivation for change, while other incentives included the environmental and economic crisis of the Depression and the province's new-found power to legislate in such matters. A reformed land distribution system would also ideally stabilize and consolidate the farm sector, and, if successful, would contribute to the province's overall stability and growth. And as the restrictions on the granting of crown land as homesteads (and later as leases) to non-Albertans reflected, purely provincial social goals were also a factor.

The distribution and the determinants of social authority in the province added further complexity. While the Anglo-Canadian dominant culture that ruled Alberta at times harboured deep suspicions about non-Anglo-Saxons of European descent, the latter at least shared a common racial identity, could vote and own property, and were generally willing to organize their lives along the familiar lines of a capitalist market economy. In an example of how ethnicity and race had different social and political expression in different contexts, educational and social policies often aimed to assimilate non-English-speaking people at the same time that other provincial policies implicitly placed the economic needs and standards of all Euro-Canadians, regardless of ethnicity, above those of Aboriginal people. The province's dogged defence of Euro-Canadian interests in its disputes with the Department of Indian Affairs over hunting by Indians was a direct example of this viewpoint. As well, while the province extended its travelling medical clinics and public nursing programmes to fringe settlement areas with their large non-Anglo-Saxon population, it did not do so in remote districts with Aboriginal majorities. Since most of the people in northern Alberta who did not own property or pay taxes were of Aboriginal origin, it seems logical to conclude that a similarly unsympathetic attitude was reflected in the province's failure to devise specific policies for the economic and social needs of these people. In part, this was justified by divided jurisdiction, where the federal government was responsible for Indians and the province had jurisdiction over Metis. Nonetheless, when the province did act on behalf of these people, as it did with the establishment of the Metis settlements, the paternalism of its policies revealed its deeply ambivalent attitudes towards them.

While local concerns and influences were important factors in provincial policies, province-building often drew upon the models established by the federal government. The latter retained significant power, especially until 1930, and Alberta's efforts to stimulate oil sands development through its own scientific research council and its policies to stimulate farm settlement and transportation networks were similar to those employed by the federal government. Simultaneously, private interests that had earlier been aided and encouraged by both federal and provincial governments became more independent, and frustrations developed when government refused to meet their demands. This was most evident in the proposals and schemes for alternative transportation networks that absorbed so much of the energy and enthusiasm of Peace River country residents during the interwar years. These debates focussed and delineated the interests and priorities of both centre and margin, and the failure of agricultural settlers in the Peace River country to persuade government to meet their demands showed their relative lack of political and economic power. Yet their relationship with outside private and public interests was not one-directional. Many of the objectives of settlers in the Peace River country were the same as those of Edmonton's business class—economic development through railways, increased settlement, town building and expanded economic activity. Thus, Euro-Canadian settlers in northern Alberta and metropolitan capital often spoke with a single voice before World War I. These interests later diverged in some particulars, especially with respect to transportation issues, and some people in northern Alberta came to assume that Edmonton's business class was remote, exploitative and self-interested. Nonetheless, both groups continued to agree on many issues; both identified culturally with each other and wanted and needed northern Alberta's integration in the Canadian economy. When differences arose, they were not usually about ultimate goals but over the mechanics of how this integration should be pursued or the speed at which it should take place.

Settlers in the Peace River country thus reflected the hybrid character of the northern Alberta farm settlement frontier; at once dependent and independent, master and client. While employing local examples, they also drew upon a social mythology inspired by popular contemporary Euro-Canadian attitudes. An emphasis on material standards as defining success and the characterization of homesteading as a demonstration of self-initiative and self-reliance formed some of these common attributes. Those who had made it through the hardships of the Edson Trail became something of an aristocracy in the Peace River country in the interwar years and were lauded as the vanguard of its cultural and economic transformation. This attitude was reinforced by the migration to the Peace River country in those defeated by the dust bowl of the prairies. Both cases confirmed elements in the mythology of the Canadian pioneer: that the frontier tested character and that deprivation would be repaid.

Whatever complaints Euro-Canadian farm settlers in the Peace River country may have had about government failure to address their needs—and whatever sense of identity this may have revealed—the successful implanting of a farm economy there showed the success of policies that promoted development and integration. The success of this integration was revealed by the way that the identity of the Peace River country was expressed. While many of its residents were conscious of having distinctive priorities, their sense of self was not strong enough to transcend the differences that existed among its various districts. Nor did this identity become a force that motivated political life, as the failure of secessionist campaigns in the interwar years indicated. Peace River residents, in step with provincial political life, commonly supported the then popular province-wide political parties—first the Liberals, then the UFA, then Social Credit, and, most recently, the Conservatives.

In contrast to the Peace River country, the lower Athabasca River district (and other similarly placed ones such as the hunting districts north of Wabasca and those in the north-west corner of the province) became, in relative terms, underdeveloped remnants of the older region. They lacked the business and social connections with the dominant cultural and economic structures of the prairies that would have given them a voice in the new environment that was emerging. By 1939, the discontinuous development of northern Alberta's economy revealed that the lower Athabasca district's economic logic, urban system and transportation network no longer possessed the broad coherence and purpose that they had at the close of the nineteenth century. Unlike the Peace River country, new institutions and approaches had not emerged to adapt and sustain its existing economy.

The growing inequality of Aboriginal people everywhere in northern Alberta, which cut across economic and subregional lines, led to the emergence of a society in which Native and Euro-Canadians often lived in separate worlds. While they were able to resist some of the changes occurring in northern Alberta, Natives rarely could shape the policies of outside state and private agencies, nor could they successfully counter the ambitions and influence of Euro-Canadian settlers. These conditions evolved in their impact and social significance. The Native-wilderness equation that framed Indian educational policy in northern Alberta, for example, was more pragmatic than racist in the beginning. But as educational historian Robert Carney observes, when existing Indian educational programmes were maintained despite the maturation of the public school system, the "racialist overtones" of the policy became obvious.[2] And since Aboriginal people were rarely accepted as equals by Alberta's dominant cultural groups, their practical options in the face of an expanding and aggressive Euro-Canadian society were to retreat (both physically and culturally) or to resist. But nonviolent resistance was constrained by economic vulnerability and by the fact that, in practical terms, the parameters of such resistance were controlled by outside interests. Thus, Indian efforts to protect hunting rights took place within the boundaries of federal-provincial relations and how the two governments interpreted treaty rights. Although Indian Affairs at times was a defender of Indian needs—most notably through its efforts to establish hunting preserves and its attempts to modify the registered trapline system—it was sometimes also an aggressor. And while resistance in these circumstances could take direct forms, such as the refusal to send children to residential schools or to sell reserve land, it was generally limited by rules and conditions over which Indians had no control.

This picture was complicated by the fact that variations in legal status within the Native population brought different legal rights, liabilities and advantages. Because identity as mixed race and First Nations people in northern Alberta in the early 1900s was fluid, cultural differences between the two groups sometimes expressed tendencies rather than firm boundaries. Although the Metis were not culturally uniform, they came to be defined as a distinctive element in the Aboriginal community through a complex interplay of history, race and the impact of the treaty. In relative terms, however, Indian status brought certain advantages; medical care, reserves as homelands and, in theory, treaty-protected hunting and other rights. The disadvantages of Indian status were also significant; they could not vote or enjoy the ordinary benefits of citizenship, and the federal government had extensive power to regulate behaviour, land use and other basic elements of life. The Metis possessed in opposite measures the same disadvantages and advantages: while they could vote and own property, they had no legal protection of their lifestyle. In the same way that it dismissed treaty rights and Indian economic needs, the provincial government generally failed to address the needs of the Metis or to defend their unique interests. Official attention came about only after the transfer of natural resources and, most notably, after Metis organized themselves in a conventional political form through the Metis Association of Alberta. Such parallel organizations for Indians were not successful before 1945, and expression of their needs remained localized and dependent on the federal government. These distinctions—at first so artificial in many cases—over time created a basis on which new definitions of culture and self-identification for both "Indians" and "Metis" were possible.

In general, northern Alberta's integration with Canada was disastrous for the Native hunting economy. The decline of this economy was not inevitable or merely the product of forces that lay entirely beyond the influence of public policy. While little direct control was possible over fur prices, the provincial government denied possible support through marketing, conservation and allocation programmes that might have mitigated the sector's decline and supported Native economic and social equality. Rather, it treated the fur trade as merely another open access resource. Provincial policy presumed the commodification of most activities and resources that were important for Native livelihoods—trapping was just a job, fishing was just the use of a resource, income was just the product of commodity relations and resource allocation was just a function of social and economic competition. In comparison, the provincial government never took such a cavalier approach towards farmers. Their fate was never left only to the market place, and the farm sector was defended as a social and moral institution as well as an economic one with special needs and priorities. This reflected the relative economic strength of each sector, but it was also framed by a perception that Aboriginal economic and social needs were secondary to those of Euro-Canadians. It assumed that trapping was an outmoded activity in an agrarian-industrial future and that Aboriginal people were disappearing or would be assimilated. Certainly, the fur trade economy had many characteristics in common with prairie agriculture—external markets, fluctuating prices and outside capital—but it had traditionally depended on social continuity. Development after 1900 increasingly ignored the costs of disrupting social continuity in northern Alberta, even when this disruption brought relative underdevelopment to sectors of the northern economy upon which a substantial number of people depended.

The Aboriginal subsistence economy that was in place in 1900 was a complex structure. In addition to hunting, it included a range of activities that provided seasonal or supplementary income. Euro-Canadian farm settlers in the Peace River country at first also depended on this economy of makeshifts, but their goal was to escape from such conditions as soon as possible. The ambition of both public and private sectors was to create an economy that produced exports, stimulated domestic consumption of manufactured goods and created public and private wealth. This presumed the marginalization of the standards of the older economy and society. The Native subsistence economy was not capital intensive, nor did it stimulate private accumulation of capital or the commodification of social relations. This marked it as a failed economy in Euro-Canadian terms. But while this economy had been precarious at times, the mixture of hunting, trapping, labour and other activities generally sustained the social and economic needs of those who relied upon it. Although preferences for hunting over wage employment no doubt varied by location and particular group, hunting clearly formed the basis of this economy of makeshifts for most Aboriginal people and was a preferred activity for many. Thus, when the viability of this core activity was damaged, the consequences were serious indeed, and gave broader economic and technological change a disproportionate impact.

## —— Some Old Patterns and Some New Developments
### Northern Alberta Since 1950

The late 1940s marked the end of a phase in northern Alberta's history. After 1950 the railway's monopoly over goods moving to the Peace River country ended and new land policies were in place. Canada's economy and society were changing significantly, especially towards a more urban lifestyle. Development of northern resources expanded in the three decades after World War II, although settlement in the boreal forest areas of Canada declined overall. Of the settlement taking place, most occurred in the Alberta and British Columbia Peace River country. But this was not the mass movement of settlers of earlier years, and the Peace River country as a whole had lost its "frontier like appearance" by 1970. It now resembled farming districts in the rest of the prairies: log houses and crude outbuildings had been replaced with modern structures, more and varied farm equipment was common, leisure had expanded to include travel and greater mobility, and better health services, libraries and schools had been established. Towns had grown, with Grande Prairie and Peace River becoming the largest central places in the Peace River country.

Most districts now had, as they had so earnestly sought since the beginning of white settlement, all the "amenities of long-settled areas."[3]

In contrast, the situation in the eastern district of northern Alberta along the Athabasca River north of Fort McMurray and in other areas where remnants of the older hunting economy endured was considerably different. While these districts remained a "northern" place in the popular imagination, the late 1940s marked the end of a historical era for them. Trapping and hunting remained central in the lives of many Native people, but the settlements began to grow as people shifted towards a more town-oriented society and away from a hunting economy that was no longer sustainable. Fort Chipewyan, for example, increased from about 300 people in 1956 to just over 700 by 1961 and to around 1,500 in the 1970s. Social life was transformed as part of this change and a number of problems related to underemployment and poverty also emerged.[4]

Changing transportation networks also altered the linkages between the lower Athabasca River district and adjacent areas to the north and south. Distances continued to shrink with air travel, but, more significantly, use of the historic route along the Athabasca River to the far north began to decline. In 1965 the Great Slave Lake Railway went into operation to serve the Consolidated Mining and Smelting Ltd. mines at Pine Point. The first railway into the NWT, it followed the Mackenzie Highway to Hay River.[5] Much debate surrounded the routing of this railway—Fort McMurray interests wanted to see it routed along the Athabasca River, while people in the Peace River country demanded that it pass through their district, arguing that it would transform the northern Peace River country into the breadbasket of the NWT.[6]

All of these developments were evidence of the ongoing reorganization of transportation and communications networks in the wake of northern Alberta's economic and social integration with Canada. So too, social, educational and medical services improved everywhere in Alberta after the 1960s with greater provincial and federal government funding and a decreased reliance on local taxation. This was of particular benefit in northern Alberta, as it was in all areas where limited taxation and local government had previously hampered the delivery of such services. This was further enhanced by special policies and agencies, similar to those being developed in other provinces, which attempted to provide services for northern communities with small populations and limited tax revenues.[7]

Among the most important of these in northern Alberta was the Northland School Division. As historian John Chalmers noted, many northern public schools continued to face problems after World War II because of a lack of funding. To meet this problem, the Alberta government in the late 1950s established nine new school districts, each under an Official Trustee. This left untouched, however, the problems faced by the few isolated public school districts (such as at Conklin, Fort McMurray, Fort Chipewyan and Fitzgerald). Additionally, the residential schools supported by Indian Affairs faced mounting problems because of a rapid increase in the number of pupils. Some of these schools had Metis students for whom the province was responsible. While the province paid for the education of these children, this arrangement was informal, and Indian Affairs indicated "that either the Metis would have to be withdrawn from these schools or Alberta would have to enter into a firm agreement with Indian Affairs to provide for new construction and long-term operating arrangements." By this time, the province neither wanted nor was able to avoid its responsibilities for the education of Metis children. In 1960, it adopted a new policy under which every child in unorganized districts for whom it was responsible (that is, who was not an Indian) had "a right to an education as good as that available to rural children who lived in the settled and developed parts of the province." This policy contributed to the formation of the Northland School Division in late 1960. Directly administered and financed by the province, the division constructed and operated schools in places that had never before had schools or in which mission schools had struggled for years. The component districts of the Northland School Division included, among other types, isolated public schools and schools on the Metis settlements. While frustrations and failures were experienced by the Northlands School Division in succeeding years, it helped provide essential services to northern people and recognized their unique needs and experiences.[8]

These changes in social services and education occurred at the same time that northern Alberta's economy was expanding. The view of the north as a cornucopia of resources that Euro-Canadians could exploit revived after World War II, and grandiose rhetoric again came to portray a hard land and climate as a place of great richness. In 1958, the commissioners of the Royal Commission on the Development of Northern Alberta confidently drew on the hoary language of expansionism when assessing northern Alberta's resources. "There is no place in a report like this," they wrote, "for meaningless phrases such as 'boundless wealth' or 'untold resources.' The resources of Northern Alberta are great enough and near enough to development to be expressed as acres, barrels, board feet and tons." Moreover, there now existed "sufficient knowledge" about them to "speak in fairly definite terms" about their imminent exploitation.[9]

In the next two decades, such development did indeed occur, most importantly through intensified efforts to develop the region's forestry and petroleum resources. In the familiar pattern, development was shaped by external economic forces as well as declining resources in more accessible areas in southern Alberta and the rest of Canada. Provincial policies and province-building initiatives and perspectives were a further element in these development projects. Oil prices were stable for most of the 1950s and 1960s, and petroleum deposits in the southern half of Alberta were tapped. Natural gas deposits in the Alberta and British Columbia Peace River country were also developed in the 1950s for local use and export by pipeline to Vancouver. Exploration was ongoing, adding to the province's reserves and bringing predictable results for nearby communities. Among other instances of this impact, a major oil strike near Slave Lake in 1964 set off a minor local land boom.

Despite stable prices and adequate supplies of conventional oil, experimental projects concerning the oil sands expanded in the 1950s and 1960s. In 1953, a consortium called Great Canadian Oil Sands was formed between earlier oil sands promoters (including Abasands Oils) and Sun Oil Co., an aggressive United States oil company with a predilection for innovative processing and marketing ventures. Sporadic negotiations with the federal and provincial governments took place, only reaching fruition in 1964 when construction of a plant began. While the plant opened in 1968, it faced many technical and financial problems, and the venture became profitable only in the early 1980s. By this time, the company had been reorganized and changed its name to Suncor. Huge increases in oil prices in 1973–74 and again in 1979 as a result of events in the Middle East made northern reserves, especially the oil sands, increasingly valuable. Syncrude, another player in oil sands development, also appeared, in large part because of these price shocks. Like Suncor, it was a consortium whose initial success relied on complex agreements among various public and private interests. Owned by a group of private oil companies as well as the Alberta and federal governments, construction began in 1974 and the plant opened four years later. Both the Suncor and Syncrude plants were built only after extensive negotiations among public and private sectors, and after government had put in place marketing, taxation and other financial arrangements that made the massive scale, high capital costs and particular marketing needs of oil sands projects profitable.[10] Along with these developments, Fort McMurray was transformed into an urban centre with residential subdivisions spread out on both sides of the river.

Petroleum, in the post World War II years at least, dominated the politics and economy of Alberta, but the cyclical nature of this sector and the province's growing dependence on it made calls for economic diversification a familiar element in provincial political life. Through subsidies and other blandishments, the Lougheed government (elected in 1971) took an active role in encouraging such economic diversification. Despite some successes on this front, the economy was still largely dependent on oil and gas by the mid 1980s when Lougheed retired from public life. Don Getty, his successor as premier, soon faced the consequences of this dependency when oil as well as grain prices collapsed. For the public, this confirmed the need for diversification about which they had heard so much since the Lougheed years. One solution for the government lay in the province's forests, many of which were located in northern Alberta.[11]

Until the mid 1980s, Alberta's forestry policies had been relatively progressive in terms of conservation, but there had been relatively little development. A pulp mill was opened in Hinton in 1955 and another opened in Grande Prairie in about 1973. Most of the production was shipped to the United States. In 1986, new forestry policies were adopted by the provincial government. Public construction of infrastructure such as roads and bridges were combined with offers of extensive cutting rights, low timber royalties and financial assistance through loan guarantees to private companies promising to build major facilities such as pulp mills. These generous policies were designed to compensate companies for their investment in a region remote from markets, and as a result, a number of very large pulp mills were constructed in the late 1980s and early 1990s, mostly by transnational paper companies. Several of these were in northern Alberta, including Slave Lake, Athabasca and near Peace River.

Although these megaprojects were held up by the provincial government as evidence of the growing diversification of the economy, they were consistent in many respects with the historical patterns of northern Alberta's development. Northern Alberta was locked further into yet another cyclical resource sector. Moreover, given the scale of assistance provided, the number and types of jobs these forestry projects brought to northern Alberta provided relatively limited opportunities for local people. The projects also posed serious environmental challenges and prompted a highly emotional and often bitter debate among people in the affected communities. Some argued that the projects were necessary for economic development, while others contended that the environmental costs were too high. In a departure from past experience, however, a debate about the pros and cons of such development now occurred in southern Alberta as well.[12] Northern resources were once again front and centre. While southern communities had historically tended to ignore or dismiss social issues in northern Alberta out of a belief that any and all development there was beneficial, this debate about northern forestry resources demonstrated a maturing of the relationship between north and south.

# Notes

**—— Introduction**

1. Faiz Ahmed Faiz, *Poems By Faiz*, translated by V.G. Kiernan (London: George Allen and Unwin Ltd., 1971), 110.

2. *Report of the Select Committee of the Senate Appointed to Enquire into the Resources of the Great Mackenzie Basin* (Ottawa: Queen's Printer, 1888), 11.

3. The definition of what makes up the Alberta Peace River country has evolved. We define it as the districts west of McLennan to the British Columbia border and north to Fort Vermilion.

4. Carl Berger, *The Sense of Power. Studies in the Ideas of Canadian Imperialism 1867–1914* (Toronto: University of Toronto Press, 1971), 128–34.

5. Morris Zaslow, *The Opening of the Canadian North 1870–1914* (Toronto: McClelland and Stewart, 1971), xi. For a suggestive article about northerness, see David Heinimann, "Latitude Rising: Historical Continuity in Canadian Nordicity," *Journal of Canadian Studies* 28 (1993): 134–39. The limits of using the concept of northerness as an explanatory device, however, is evident in W.L. Morton, "The 'North' in Canadian Historiography," *Transactions of the Royal Society of Canada*, 4th Series, 8 (1970): 31–40.

6. There have been attempts in Canada, most notably by geographer Louis-Edmond Hamelin, to respect the relative character of northerness but still to define it as precisely as possible. Hamelin applies statistical criteria in which natural elements (such as temperature and natural vegetation cover) and human activity (such as population density and accessibility) form an incremental index of "nordicity" or "northerness." While Hamelin's index defines some places as northern that will doubtless always be seen as such, he concludes that other places have lost their nordicity. In his term, they have been "denordified." His criteria places most of Alberta north of 55 degrees (about the location of the town of Athabasca) in "northern" Canada, although he views the Peace River country as an area that has been "denordified" (Louis-Edmond Hamelin, *Canadian Nordicity: It's Your North Too* (Montreal: Harvest House, 1978), 18–46).

7. *Edmonton Bulletin*, October 4, 1884.

8. Peter McCormick, "Regionalism in Canada: Disentangling the Threads," *Journal of Canadian Studies* 24 (1989): 19; John Warkentin, "Western Canada in 1886," in *Canada's Changing Geography*, ed. R. Louis Gentilcore (Toronto: Prentice Hall of Canada Ltd., 1967), 59.

9. For discussions of regionalism, see for example, McCormick, "Regionalism in Canada: Disentangling the Threads"; R. Douglas Francis, "In Search of Prairie Myth: A Survey of the Intellectual and Cultural Historiography of Prairie Canada," *Journal of Canadian Studies* 24 (1989): 44–69; M.L. Lautt, "Sociology and the Canadian Plains" in *A Region of the Mind*, ed. Richard Allen (Regina: Canadian Plains Research Centre, 1973), 125–51; William Westfall, "On the Concept of Region in Canadian History and Literature," *Journal of Canadian Studies* 15 (1980): 3–15.

10. Kenneth Coates and William Morrison, *The Forgotten North. A History of Canada's Provincial Norths* (Toronto: James Lorimer and Co. Publishers, 1992), 33–67.

11. Chad Gaffield, "The New Regional History: Rethinking the History of the Outaouais," *Journal of Canadian Studies* 26 (1991): 64–81.

12. For example, Robert Elwin English, in his "An Economic History of Northern Alberta" (MSA thesis, University of Toronto, 1933), studied Edmonton and area as a part of "northern" Alberta.

13. For discussions and applications of similar approaches, see Christine Stansell, *City of Women: Sex and Class in New York 1789–1860* (Chicago: University of Chicago Press, 1987); Joy Parr, *The Gender of Breadwinners: Women, Men and Change in Two Industrial Towns, 1880–1950* (Toronto: University of Toronto Press, 1990); Robert A.J. McDonald, *Making Vancouver. Class, Status, and Social Boundaries, 1863–1913* (Vancouver: University of British Columbia Press, 1996); Graeme Patterson, *History and Communications, Harold Innis, Marshall McLuhan, the Interpretation of History* (Toronto: University of Toronto Press, 1990).

14. Joe Sawchuk, *The Dynamics of Native Politics. The Alberta Metis Experience* (Saskatoon: Purich Publishing, 1998), 14. For a further discussion of the term Metis, see "Introduction," in *The New Peoples*, eds. Jacqueline Peterson and Jennifer S. Brown (Winnipeg: University of Manitoba Press, 1985 ), 4–7.

## ——1

### Region and Place

1. C.S. MacKinnon, "Some Logistics of Portage La Loche (Methy)," *Prairie Forum* 5 (1980): 53.

2. John W. Ives, *A Theory of Northern Athapaskan Prehistory* (Boulder and San Francisco: Westview Press and Calgary: University of Calgary Press, 1990), 35, 56–61. A good overview on differences in "place" and environment in the Peace, Athabasca and Slave River basins is *A Report of Wisdom Synthesized from the Traditional Knowledge Component Studies* (Edmonton: Northern River Basins Study, 1996), 21–70.

3. The use of the past tense to describe the Peace-Athabasca delta is deliberate. The construction of the Bennet Dam on the upper Peace River in the late 1960s destroyed the delta's former character.

4.  In 1899, about 38 percent of those taking treaty and about 12 percent of those taking scrip lived in the Fort Chipewyan/Fort Smith area; about 21 percent and about 53 percent respectively in the Lesser Slave Lake district (including Wabasca); 21 percent and 14 percent respectively in the Fort Vermilion district (including Upper Hay River), about 7 percent and 5 percent respectively around Fort McMurray, and 12 percent and 16 percent respectively were in the Peace River country. Calculated from *Annual Report, Department of Indian Affairs for 1899*, xl–xli, *Annual Report, Department of Indian Affairs for 1900*, xlvi, and "Report of the Half-Breed Commissioners," *Annual Report, Department of the Interior for the Year 1899*, Part viii, 3. These figures are close to an 1899 NWMP estimate which stated that the total Native population of what is now northern Alberta, including Fort Smith, was 3,635, made up of 1,387 Metis and 2,248 "Indians." ("Census of Indians and Half Breeds, Athabasca District, winter 1898–99," Records of the RCMP, RG18, vol. 160, file 73, NAC).

5.  Richard Daniel, "The Spirit and Terms of Treaty Eight," in *The Spirit of the Alberta Indian Treaties*, ed. Richard Price (Montreal: Institute for Research on Public Policy, 1980), 48.

6.  Zaslow, *The Opening of the Canadian North*, 91; James Parker, *Emporium of the North. Fort Chipewyan and the Fur Trade to 1835* (Regina: Alberta Culture and Multiculturalism and Canadian Plains Research Centre, 1987), 25–36; Ives, *A Theory of Northern Athapaskan Prehistory*, 140. The Hudson's Bay Company's exclusive monopoly outside Rupert's Land ended in 1859.

7.  Daniel Francis and Michael Payne, *A Narrative History of Fort Dunvegan* (Winnipeg: Watson and Dwyer, 1993), 84; John W. Chalmers, "Missions and Schools in the Athabasca," *Alberta History* 31 (1983): 24–29.

8.  Trudy Nicks, "Native Response to the Early Fur Trade at Lesser Slave Lake," in *"Le Castor Fait Tout" Selected papers of the Fifth North American Fur Trade Conference 1985*, eds. Bruce Trigger, Toby Morantz and Louise Dechene (Montreal: St. Louis Historical Society), 278–310; Jennifer Bellman and Christopher Hanks, "Northern Metis and the Fur Trade," in *Picking Up the Threads. Metis History in the Mackenzie Basin* (N.p.: The Metis Heritage Association of the Northwest Territories, 1998), 31; Marina Devine, "The First Northern Metis," in *Picking Up the Threads. Metis History in the Mackenzie Basin* (N.p.: The Metis Heritage Association of the Northwest Territories, 1998), 26–27.

9.  Among other contributions, see Diane Payment, "Metis People in Motion," in *Picking Up the Threads. Metis History in the Mackenzie Basin* (N.p.: The Metis Heritage Association of the Northwest Territories, 1998), 69–109, and Gerhard Ens, *Homeland to Hinterland. The Changing Worlds of the Red River Metis* (Toronto: University of Toronto Press, 1996).

10. Hetherington to Officer Commanding, September 20, 1896, RG18, vol. 124, file 553, NAC; *Annual Report, NWMP [for] 1897*, 167. For a memoir of the migration to northern Alberta, see "Interview with Baptiste Bison," (1956), M4560, Loggie Collection, file 36, GAI.

11. Heather Devine, "Metis or Country-Born. The Case of the Klynes," unpublished paper presented at the Learned Societies Conference, June 6, 1997, 1–4; Joe Sawchuk, "Metis Ethnicity and its Significance for Potential Land Claims," in *Origins of the Alberta Metis: Land Claims Research Projects 1978–79* (N.p: Metis Association of Alberta, 1979), 64–71.

12. Grouard to Minister of the Interior, September 10, 1900, Records of the Department of the Interior, RG15, vol. 806, file 590,185, NAC.

13. Robert J. Carney, "The Grey Nuns and the Children of Holy Angels: Fort Chipewyan 1874–1924," in *The Uncovered Past: Roots of Northern Alberta Societies*, eds. Patricia A. McCormack and Geoffrey Ironside (Edmonton: Canadian Circumpolar Institute, Circumpolar Research Series No. 3, 1993), 110.

14. Patricia McCormack, "How The (North) West Was Won: Development and Underdevelopment in the Fort Chipewyan Region" (Ph.D. diss., University of Alberta, 1984), 80–81; James Parker, *History of the Athabasca Oil Sands Region, 1890s to 1960s. Vol. 2, Oral History* (Edmonton: Athabasca Oil Sands Environmental Research Program, Boreal Institute for Northern Studies, University of Alberta, 1980), 29.

15. Bellman and Hanks, "Northern Metis and the Fur Trade," 31; "Report of Commissioners for Treaty No. 8," in *Annual Report, Department of Indian Affairs for 1899*, xxxvii; *Annual Report, Department of Indian Affairs for 1909*, 369; Earle H. Waugh, *Dissonant Worlds. Roger Vandersteene Among the Cree* (Waterloo: Wilfrid Laurier University Press, 1996), 41; McCormack, "How The (North) West Was Won," 95.

16. Bennet McCardle, *The Rules of the Game: The Development of Government Controls Over Indian Hunting and Trapping in Treaty 8 (Alberta) to 1930* (Ottawa: Treaty and Aboriginal Rights Research (TARR) of the Indian Association of Alberta, 1976), 146–47.

17. Irene M. Spry, "The Tragedy of the Loss of the Commons in Western Canada," in *As Long As The Sun Shines and Water Flows: A Reader in Canadian Native Studies*, eds. Ian A.L. Getty and Antoine Lussier (Vancouver: University of British Columbia Press, 1983), 204.

18. Olive Patricia Dickason, *Canada's First Nations. A History of Founding Peoples from Earliest Times* (Toronto: McClelland and Stewart, 1992), 352–53.

19. "Report of Commissioners for Treaty No. 8," in *Annual Report, Department of Indian Affairs for 1899*, xxxvii; G. Neil Reddekopp, *The Creation and Surrender of the Beaver and Duncans' Bands Reserves* (Edmonton: Indian Land Claims, Alberta Aboriginal Affairs, Paper No. 2, 1996), 5.

20. McCardle, *The Rules of the Game*, 155; Elizabeth Snider, "Slavey Indians of Hay River" (Ottawa: Treaties and Historical Research Centre, 1975, typescript), 4; *Annual Report, NWMP [for] 1897*, 158, 163.

21. McCardle, *The Rules of the Game*, 155–56, 160.

22. Native independence of European technology was perhaps best illustrated by the continued preference for nonessential consumer goods such as tobacco, beads and, when available, liquor, rather than items indicating technological dependency in everyday life. (Ives, *A Theory of Northern Athapaskan Prehistory*, 154–55).

23. "Report of Commissioners for Treaty No. 8," in *Annual Report, Department of Indian Affairs for 1899*, xxxviii; David Leonard, *Delayed Frontier: The Peace River Country to 1909* (Calgary: Detselig Enterprises Ltd., 1995), 151; *Annual Report, NWMP [for] 1897*, 71; Routledge to Commissioner (Report of Patrol to Fort Simpson), April 4, 1898, RG18, vol. 1427, file 190, NAC.

24. Jean-Guy Goulet, "Religious Dualism Among Athapaskan Catholics," *Canadian Journal of Anthropology* 3 (1982): 2; Martha McCarthy, *From the Great River to the Ends of the Earth: Oblate Missions to the Dene 1847–1921* (Edmonton: University of Alberta Press, 1995), 188–90; Kerry

Abel, *Drum Songs. Glimpses of Dene History* (Montreal and Kingston: McGill-Queen's University Press, 1993), 128–43.

25. For an introduction and further references to the flavour of these debates, see for examples, John Foster, "Indian-White Relations in the Prairie West during the Fur Trade Period—A Compact?," in *The Spirit of the Alberta Indian Treaties*, ed. Richard Price (Montreal: Institute for Research on Public Policy, 1980), 181–200; Frank Tough, *'As Their Natural Resources Fail': Native Peoples and the Economic History of Northern Manitoba 1870–1930* (Vancouver: University of British Columbia Press, 1996); J.C. Yerbury, *The Subarctic Indians and the Fur Trade, 1680–1860* (Vancouver: University of British Columbia Press, 1986) and the articles in *The Subarctic Fur Trade: Native Social and Economic Adaptations*, ed. Shepard Krech III (Vancouver: University of British Columbia Press, 1984).

26. *Report of the Select Committee of the Senate Appointed to Enquire into the Resources of the Great Mackenzie Basin* (Ottawa: Queen's Printer, 1888), 162; Bellman and Hanks, "Northern Metis and the Fur Trade," 53–64; Foster, "Indian-White Relations in the Prairie West," 191.

27. Donat Levasseur, *Les Oblates de Marie Immaculée dan l'Ouest et le Nord du Canada 1845–1967* (Edmonton: University of Alberta Press, 1995), 135–37; T.C.B. Boon, *The Anglican Church from the Bay to the Rockies. A History of the Ecclesiastical Province of Rupert's Land and its Dioceses from 1820 to 1950* (Toronto: Ryerson Press, 1962), 204–38.

28. Arthur J. Ray, *The Canadian Fur Trade in the Industrial Age* (Toronto: University of Toronto Press, 1990), 5–6, 19; A.A. den Otter, "The Hudson's Bay Company's Prairie Transportation Problem, 1870–1885," in *The Developing West: Essays on Canadian History in Honor of Lewis H. Thomas*, ed. John Foster (Edmonton: University of Alberta Press, 1983), 25–47.

29. Athabasca Historical Society, David Gregory and Athabasca University, *Athabasca Landing: An Illustrated History* (Athabasca: Athabasca Historical Society, 1986), 24–32.

30. David Leonard and Victoria Lemieux, *A Fostered Dream. The Lure of the Peace River Country 1872–1914* (Calgary: Detselig Enterprises Ltd., 1992), Chapters 3 and 4. The use of Grouard, the current name, is more specific than the name Lesser Slave Lake that was often used somewhat vaguely to include a larger area than the future boundaries of Grouard (which was legally dissolved in 1944). Historically, the names of the settlement nodes in this area have been complex. In addition to Lesser Slave Lake Settlement and Slave Lake Post, other names have included St. Bernard's Mission, Stoney Point, and, simply, Slave Lake and Lesser Slave Lake. See entries in Merrily K. Aubrey, *Place Names of Alberta. Volume IV. Northern Alberta* (Calgary: Alberta Community Development, Friends of Geographical Names of Alberta Society and University of Calgary Press, 1996).

31. The phrase is Ernest Thompson Seton's. He devoted a whole chapter to mosquitoes and flies in his book, *The Arctic Prairie* (New York: Charles Scribner and Sons, 1912).

32. There are 11 rapids on the Athabasca River immediately above Fort McMurray; the most difficult being the Grand Rapids. There are seven other rapids, most between 2.5 and 3 kilometres long, plus a number of smaller ones. A difficult barrier was the Cascade, a drop of up to 2.5 metres during low water, which had to be portaged except during high water.

33. Charles Camsell, *Son of the North* (Toronto: Ryerson Press, 1954), 33–34. On the parallel use by the Hudson's Bay Company of a tramway at Grand Rapids, Manitoba, see

Martha McCarthy, *Grand Rapids, Manitoba* (Winnipeg: Manitoba Culture, Heritage and Recreation, Historic Resources, Papers in Manitoba History No. 1, 1988), 86–111.

34. Camsell, *Son of the North*, 33–34; F.J. Alcock, "Scow Brigade on the Athabasca," *Canadian Geographical Journal* 4 (1932): 97–107; [Arthur Robertson], "Journey to the Far North, 1887," Part I, *The Beaver*, Outfit 315:4 (Spring 1985), 16.

35. Mackinnon, "Some Logistics of Portage La Loche," 61–62; Archange J. Brady, *A History of Fort Chipewyan* (Westlock: Harmony Print Shop, 1994), 51–59.

36. Andrea Zubko and David Leonard, "Northern Metis and Transportation," in *Picking Up The Threads. Metis History in the Mackenzie Basin* (n.p.: Metis Heritage Association of the Northwest Territories, 1998), 212–15.

37. Emile Grouard, *Souvenirs de mes soixant Ans d'Apostolat dans l'Athabaska-Mackenzie* (Winnipeg: La Liberte, n.d.), 306; Routledge to Commissioner (Report of Patrol to Fort Simpson), April 4, 1898, RG18, vol. 1427, file 190, NAC; *Annual Report, NWMP [for] 1897*, 161.

38. Donald G. Wetherell and Irene R.A. Kmet, *Town Life. Main Street and the Evolution of Small Town Alberta* (Edmonton: The University of Alberta Press and Alberta Community Development, 1995), xiv–xv; Gilbert A. Stelter, "A Regional Framework for Urban History," *Urban History Review* 13 (1985): 193–205.

39. John W. Ives, "The Ten Thousand Years Before the Fur Trade in Northeastern Alberta," typescript for the Fort Chipewyan and Fort Vermilion Bicentennial volume, Section 1, 25; *Annual Report of the NWMP [for] 1897*, 161–64; Routledge to Commissioner (Report of Patrol to Fort Simpson), April 4, 1898, RG18, vol. 1427, file 190, NAC.

40. *Annual Report, NWMP [for] 1896*, 106; Athabasca Historical Society, *Athabasca Landing: An Illustrated History*, 30–32. In other cases, the Hudson's Bay Company did not need to purchase land in settlements, receiving it as part of its agreement with Canada in 1869. For example, it received 10 acres at Fort Chipewyan, 500 acres at Fort Vermilion and, among others, 50 acres at Dunvegan ("Deed of Surrender, Schedule C," in E.H. Oliver, *The Canadian North-West. Its Early Development and Legislative Records*, Vol. 2 (Ottawa: Government Printing Bureau, 1915, Publication of the Canadian Archives No. 9), 962).

41. Routledge to Commissioner (Report of Patrol to Fort Simpson), April 4, 1898, RG18 vol. 1427, file 190, NAC); *Annual Report, NWMP [for] 1897*, 159–160; *Annual Report, NWMP [for] 1903*, 44; Parker, *History of the Athabasca Oil Sands Region, 1890s to 1960s*, Vol. 2, Oral History, 8; D.J. Comfort, *Meeting Place of Many Waters: A History of Fort McMurray* (N.p.: n.p., 1973) Part 2, 247. The Hudson's Bay Company at Fort McKay was established in 1891.

42. J.G. McConnell, "The Fort Smith Area 1780 to 1961. An Historical Geography," (Master's thesis, University of Toronto, 1965), 44–45, 63–64; C.S. Mackinnon, "Portaging on the Slave River (Fort Smith)," *The Musk-Ox* 27 (1980): 23–25; Routledge to Commissioner (Report of Patrol to Fort Simpson), April 4, 1898, RG18, vol. 1427, file 190, NAC; *Annual Report, NWMP [for] 1897*, 161–64.

43. Snyder to Commissioner, February 28, 1898, RG18, vol. 149, file 188, NAC; *Annual Report, NWMP [for] 1897*, 168; D.R. Babcock, "Lesser Slave Lake: A Regional History" (typescript, 1978) (copy in Historic Sites Service Library, Edmonton), 261.

44. Hetherington to Officer Commanding, July 31, 1897, RG18, vol. 128, file 37, NAC; Report, Patrol to Dunvegan, Sgt. Major McDonell, February 2, 1898, RG18, vol. 1427, file

190, NAC; Griesbach to Commissioner, April 5, 1894 (report attached), RG15, vol. 686, file 328,760, NAC; *Annual Report, NWMP [for] 1897*, 70–71.

45. *Annual Report, NWMP [for] 1897*, 160, 167.

46. Raymond J.A. Huel, *Proclaiming The Gospel to the Indians and the Metis* (Edmonton: University of Alberta Press, 1996), 34–35. By the late 1890s there were four Roman Catholic schools in northern Alberta (at Fort Vermilion, Fort Chipewyan, near Peace River Crossing, and at Grouard). The Anglicans ran schools at Fort Vermilion, and Utikuma Lake. Both groups quickly established competing schools at Wabasca.

47. Parker, *History of the Athabasca Oil Sands Region*, Vol. 2, *Oral History*, 22–24; St. Luke's Centennial Historical Committee, *Unchaga Peace. The Centennial History of St. Luke's Anglican Mission* (Peace River: Valley Printers, 1977); *Annual Report, NWMP [for] 1897*, 161; Routledge to Commissioner (Report of Patrol to Fort Simpson), April 4, 1898, RG18, vol. 1427, file 190, NAC; *Annual Report, NWMP [for] 1897*, 165–66.

48. *Report of the Fourth Triennial Synod of the Diocese of Athabasca Held at Lesser Slave Lake, Athabasca, June 20, 1900* (Winnipeg: Judd Moore Printing Co., 1900), Anglican Diocese of Athabasca Papers (AP), file A220/8a, Box A.21, PAA (Bishop's Young's corrected copy); Boon, *The Anglican Church from the Bay to the Rockies*, 171.

49. *Annual Report, NWMP [for] 1897*, 71, 165–68. In the late 1890s Peace River Crossing went by various names, including the "Hudson's Bay Company Crossing," "Peace River Landing," and the "Lesser Slave Lake Portage." The settlement across the river was usually called the "Shaftesbury Settlement" but was also called the "Peace River Settlement."

50. Routledge to Commissioner (Report of Patrol to Fort Simpson), April 4, 1898, RG18, vol. 1427, file 190, NAC; Griesbach to Commissioner, May 1, 1897, RG18, vol. 128, file 37, NAC; *Annual Report of the NWMP [for] 1897*, 161–64; Griesbach to Commissioner, April 5, 1894 (report attached), RG15, vol. 686, file 328,760, NAC; Snyder to Commissioner, February 28, 1898, RG18, vol. 149, file 188, NAC; David T. Williamson, "Valleyview's first Settlers," *Alberta History* 30 (1982), 29–30.

—2

## The 1890s

1. Zaslow, *The Opening of the Canadian North*, 13–14.

2. Zaslow, *The Opening of the Canadian North*, 27–29, 87; Leonard and Lemieux, *A Fostered Dream*, 10; *Edmonton Bulletin*, July 7, 1883; In 1882 the northern parts of the prairies were organized into three districts: Athabaska, NWT and Keewatin. In 1895, the District of Athabaska was enlarged to include most of present-day Saskatchewan and Alberta north of 55 degrees (Gerald Friesen, *The Canadian Prairies, A History* (Toronto: University of Toronto Press, 1984) maps 91ff).

3. Zaslow, *The Opening of the Canadian North*, 80.

4. *Report of the Select Committee of the Senate* (1888), 13, 107. The Dominion Experimental farm in Ottawa also sent samples of Ladoga wheat to Grouard and Lac la Biche in 1888 for testing.

5. Zaslow, *The Opening of the Canadian North*, 82–91; Edward Said, *Orientalism* (New York: Vintage Books, 1979). For an application of Said's concepts to northern Canada, see D.A.

West, "Re-searching the North in Canada: An Introduction to the Canadian Northern Discourse," *Journal of Canadian Studies* 26 (1991): 108–19.

6. Dennis F.K. Madill, *Treaty Research Report: Treaty Eight* (Ottawa: Treaties and Historical Research Centre, Indian and Northern Affairs Canada, 1986), 5.

7. Rene Fumoleau, *As Long As This Land Shall Last. A History of Treaty 8 and Treaty 11, 1870–1939* (Toronto: McClelland and Stewart, n.d.), 41–43.

8. Charles W. Mathers, "A Trip to the Arctic Circle," *Alberta Historical Review* 20 (1972): 8; Thomas Court, "A Search for Oil," *Alberta Historical Review* 21 (1973): 10–12; *Annual Report, NWMP [for] 1895*, 104–5; James Parker and K.W. Tingley, *History of the Athabasca Oil Sands Region, 1890s to 1960s.* Vol. 1, *Socio-Economic Developments* (Edmonton: Oil Sands Environmental Research Program, Boreal Institute for Northern Studies, University of Alberta, 1980), 34, 66; *Edmonton Bulletin*, September 8, 1892.

9. Leonard and Lemieux, *A Fostered Dream*, 9–17; Leonard, *Delayed Frontier*, 176–79, 199; A.L. Brick, "Rev. J. Gough Brick and His Shaftesbury Mission Farm," *Alberta Historical Review* 3 (1955): 3–12; James McDougall, "The Peace River District," n.d. (1893), RG15, vol. 686, file 328,760, NAC. *Edmonton Bulletin*, September 8, 1892; *Annual Report, NWMP [for] 1897*, 168; Hetherington to Officer Commanding, July 31, 1897, RG18, vol. 128, file 37, NAC.

10. *Report of the Select Committee of the Senate* (1888), 10, 90–92.

11. Parker and Tingley, *History of the Athabasca Oil Sands Region*, Vol. 1, *Socio-Economic Development*, 66–67.

12. Zaslow, *The Opening of the Canadian North*, 57; Athabasca Historical Society, *Athabasca Landing: An Illustrated History*, 32, 36; *Annual Report of the NWMP [for] 1898*, 158–64; Routledge to Commissioner, April 4, 1898, RG18, vol. 1427, file 190, NAC.

13. Ray, *The Canadian Fur Trade in the Industrial Age*, 44; Holmes to Lt. Gov., March 30, 1894, and Pereira to Gordon, June 18, 1894, RG15, vol. 705, file 355,568, NAC.

14. William C. Wonders, "Edmonton in the Klondike Gold Rush," in *Edmonton: The Life of a City*, eds. Bob Hesketh and Frances Swripa (Edmonton: Newest Publishers, 1995), 61. Postal service was spotty and nonexistent in places until 1897 when NWMP detachments had been established in most districts. By 1900, mail was delivered by private carriers under contract, although the NWMP still delivered it in some areas (Oliver to White, August 30, 1900 and reply, September 4, 1900, RG18, vol. 206, file 147–01, NAC).

15. *Annual Report, NWMP [for] 1897*, 71; *Annual Report, NWMP [for] 1901*, 61.

16. Report, William Ogilvie, April 12, 1887, RG15, vol. 512, file 145,340, NAC; *Annual Report, NWMP [for] 1899*, 32.

17. *Annual Report, NWMP [for] 1897*, 169, 170.

18. *Annual Report, NWMP [for] 1895*, 105; *Annual Report, NWMP [for] 1897*, 165–66, 168, 170–71.

19. *Report of the Select Committee of the Senate* (1888), 13, 103–4; Janet Foster, *Working for Wildlife. The Beginning of Preservation in Canada* (Toronto: University of Toronto Press, 1978), 105–6.

20. Zaslow, *The Opening of the Canadian North*, 95; McCardle, *The Rules of the Game*, 31–38. The ban on hunting buffalo remained in effect only until 1901, but it was extended in 1902 and again in 1906 and soon became permanent.

21. Oliver to Laurier, September 11, 1896, RG18, vol. 128, file 37, NAC.

22. Hetherington to Officer Commanding, September 20, 1896, RG18, vol. 124, file 553, NAC.

23. *Annual Report, NWMP [for] 1896*, 105–6; Memo by White, September 30, 1896, RG18, vol. 128, file 37, NAC.

24. Comptroller to Commissioner, December 18, 1896, RG18, vol. 128, file 37, NAC.

25. *Annual Report, NWMP [for] 1897*, 156.

26. *Annual Report, NWMP [for] 1897*, 158.

27. *Annual Report, NWMP [for] 1897*, 166, 169.

28. *Annual Report, NWMP [for] 1897*, 162–63, 172; *Edmonton Bulletin*, July 12, 1897.

29. *Annual Report, NWMP [for] 1897*, 159, 167–72. On controlled burning, see H. Lewis, "Maskuta: The Ecology of Indian Fire in Northern Alberta," *Western Canadian Journal of Anthropology* 7 (1977): 15–52.

30. *Annual Report, NWMP [for] 1897*, 169–70.

31. *Annual Report, NWMP [for] 1897*, 165–66, 169–73, 175 (List of Prosecutions).

32. In 1897 new permanent detachments were established at Grouard and Fort Chipewyan and the next year another was established at Peace River town and a (seasonal) one was reestablished at Grand Rapids. The Fort Chipewyan detachment apparently patrolled the Smith Portage in summer.

33. Secord to Oliver, April 21, and Oliver to White, March 31, 1897, RG18, vol. 128, file 37, NAC; Correspondence, *passim*, March 1898, RG18, vol. 144, file 43, NAC; Oliver to White, March 30, 1898, RG18, vol. 151, file 236, NAC

34. Levillot to NWMP, February 3, 1897 (copy). RG18, vol. 128, file 37, NAC.

35. Hetherington to Officer Commanding, July 11, July 31 and September 14, 1897, RG18, vol. 128, file 37, NAC.

36. Report, Corporal Macdonald, *Annual Report, NWMP [for] 1897*, 200.

37. Dianne Newell, "The Importance of Information and Misinformation in the Making of the Klondike Gold Rush," *Journal of Canadian Studies* 21 (1986–87): 98–99; J.G. MacGregor, *The Klondike Rush Through Edmonton 1897–1898* (Toronto: McClelland and Stewart, 1970), 233; Wonders, "Edmonton in the Klondike Gold Rush," 65.

38. Gordon Bennett, *Yukon Transportation: A History* (Ottawa: Canadian Historic Sites Occasional Papers in Archaeology and History, No. 19, 1979), 24–27; MacGregor, *The Klondike Rush Through Edmonton*, vii–xi (maps); Leonard, *Delayed Frontier*, 165; Routledge to Commissioner (Report of Patrol to Fort Simpson), April 4, 1898, RG18, vol. 1427, file 190, NAC. Figures on the number of prospectors travelling through Edmonton are unavailable. James MacGregor estimated that 775 and 785 prospectors went north over the land route and river route respectively, but these figures appear high. He gives no evidence for his estimate (MacGregor, *The Klondike Rush Through Edmonton*, 235).

39. Grouard, *Souvenirs de mes soixante Ans*, 364; Holmes to Young, (Annual letter), December 26, 1899, AP, A.281/149, Box A.32, PAA.

40. Athabasca Historical Society, *Athabasca Landing: An Illustrated History*, 58–63; Leonard, *Delayed Frontier*, 155–56; Routledge to Commissioner (Report of Patrol to Fort Simpson), April 4, 1898, RG18, vol. 1427, file 190, NAC.

41. Holmes to Young, May 28, 1899, AP, A281/149, Box A.32, PAA; D.J. Hall, "The Half-Breed Claims Commission," *Alberta History* 25 (Spring 1977): 2.

42. *Annual Report, Department of Indian Affairs for 1900*, xviii.

## —— 3
### Treaty and Scrip in Northern Alberta

1. Fumoleau, *As Long As This Land Shall Last*, 46, 50.

2. Daniel, "The Spirit and Terms of Treaty Eight," 70; Fumoleau, *As Long As This Land Shall Last*, 59–60.

3. Extract from Report of Col. Trotter, Fort Smith Detachment, October 31, 1898, RG18, vol. 160, file 73, NAC.

4. Phillips to Officer Commanding, April 13, 1899, RG18, vol. 1435, file 76 Pt. 1, NAC; Holmes to Young, April 4 and May 28, 1899, AP, A.281/149 Box A.32, PAA.

5. *Annual Report, NWMP [for] 1897*, 173. There were many spellings of the term Windigo; a common variant in northern Alberta was Whitego.

6. Holmes to Young, April 4, June 3, and December 26, 1899, AP, A.281/149 A.32, PAA; Charles Mair, *Through The Mackenzie Basin: A Narrative of the Athabasca and Peace River Treaty Expedition of 1899* (Toronto: William Briggs, 1908), 76.

7. For views about the Windigo, see: Leo G. Waisberg, "Boreal Forest Subsistence and the Windigo: Fluctuations of Animal Populations," *Anthropologica* NS 17 (1975): 169–85; Robin Ridington, "Wechuge and Windigo: A Comparison of Cannibal Belief Among Boreal Forest Athapaskans and Algonkians," *Anthropologica* NS 18 (1976): 107–29; Robert A. Brightman, *Grateful Prey. Rock Cree Human-Animal Relationships* (Berkeley: University of California Press, 1993), 136–58.

8. Holmes to Young (annual letter), December 26, 1899, AP, A.281/1249, Box A.32, PAA.

9. Fumoleau, *As Long As This Land Shall Last*, 61–62. When land was granted in severalty, slightly more was allocated per person—160 acres as opposed to 128 on a communal reserve. The reasoning for this larger allotment was rather brutally explained by the Indian Commissioner in 1900 when he wrote that "those who settle in severalty will, in all probability, be more healthy and progressive than those on large reserves, and consequently will multiply more rapidly" and thus need more land. On large reserves, "if some families die off, such families as remain whether they multiply or not, own the whole reserve" (Laird to Secretary, December 5, 1900, Records of the Department of Indian affairs, RG10, Reel C-100099, vol. 3564, file 82 Pt. 21, NAC).

10. Daniel, "The Spirit and Terms of Treaty Eight," 69–70; Lacombe to West, July 15, 1899, West Collection, M644, GAI.

11. Routledge to Officer Commanding, December 31, 1899, RG18, vol. 1435, file 76 Pt. 1, NAC.

12. Grouard, *Souvenirs de mes soixante Ans*, 360; Holmes to Young, June 24, 1899, AP, A.281/149, Box A.32, PAA.

13. Daniel, "The Spirit and Terms of Treaty Eight," 75–76 (quoting Charles Mair).

14. Fumoleau, *As Long As This Land Shall Last*, 65; Daniel, "The Spirit and Terms of Treaty Eight," 77–79.

15. Daniel, "The Spirit and Terms of Treaty Eight," 80–81.

16. "Report of Treaty No. 8 Commissioners," in *Annual Report, Department of Indian Affairs for 1899*, xxxvi–xxxvii; *Edmonton Bulletin*, July 10, 1899.

17. Grouard, *Souvenirs de mes soixante Ans*, 368–70; Holmes to Young, June 24, 1899, AP, A.281/149, Box A.32, PAA.

18. Quoted in Fumoleau, *As Long as This Land Shall Last*, 88.

19. Daniel, "The Spirit and Terms of Treaty Eight," 85–86; Madill, *Treaty Eight*, 54–55.

20. Trudy Nicks, "Mary Anne's Dilemma: The Ethnohistory of an Ambivalent Identity," *Canadian Ethnic Studies* 17 (1985): 109.

21. Hall to Chaffey, February 28, 1898, RG15, vol. 491, file 138,557, NAC.

22. "Report of Half-Breed Commissioners," June 24, 1899 Canada Sessional Paper No. 13, vol. 34, 1900, 5.

23. Arthur J. Ray, *I Have Lived Here Since The World Began. An Illustrated History of Canada's Native People* (Toronto: Lester Publishing and Key Porter Books, 1996), 263; Joe Sawchuk, Patricia Sawchuk and Theresa Ferguson, *Metis Land Rights in Alberta: A Political History* (Edmonton: Metis Association of Alberta, 1981), 103–4.

24. D.J. Hall, "The Half-Breed Claims Commission," *Alberta History* 25 (1977): 1, 2, 5; N.O. Cote, "Grants to Half-Breeds of the Province of Manitoba and the NWT," 12 (typescript, copy in Papers of the Royal Commission on the Condition of the Halfbreed Population of the Province of Alberta (Ewing Commission), 75.75/6c, PAA). For opposing views on the Metis in Manitoba, see Thomas Flanagan, *Metis Lands in Manitoba* (Calgary: University of Calgary Press, 1991) and D.N. Sprague, *Canada and The Metis 1869–1885* (Waterloo: Wilfrid University Press, 1988).

25. "Report of Half-Breed Commissioners," 4; Mair, *Through the Mackenzie Basin*, 69.

26. Quoted in Fumoleau, *As Long As This Land Shall Last*, 107–8.

27. Zaslow, *The Opening of the Canadian North*, 225; Hall, "The Half-Breed Claims Commission," 3.

28. Fumoleau, *As Long As This Land Shall Last*, 76–77; Hall, "The Half-Breed Claims Commission," 6.

29. Sawchuk, Sawchuk and Ferguson, *Metis Land Rights in Alberta*, 131, 136.

30. Fumoleau, *As Long As This Land Shall Last*, 76.

31. Sawchuk, Sawchuk and Ferguson, *Metis Land Rights in Alberta*, 142; "Report of Half-Breed Commissioners," 4–5; Holmes to Young, September 8 and December 14, 1899, AP, A.281/149, Box A.32, PAA.

32. "Report of Half-Breed Commissioners," Table, p. 3.

33. Sawchuk, Sawchuk and Ferguson, *Metis Land Rights in Alberta*, 131, 136.

34. *Annual Report, NWMP [for]* 1909, 126; Leonard, *Delayed Frontier*, 204–5.

35. Holmes to Young, June 24, 1899, AP, A.281/149, Box A.32, PAA.

36. Deputy Minister to Comptroller, May 26, 1910, RG18, vol. 390, file 249, NAC. The most famous case involved Richard Secord. In 1921, Secord, by then a wealthy pillar of Edmonton society, was charged with "forgery of documents in the location of land procured with Half-breed scrip." The case never proceeded because Ottawa immediately amended the Criminal Code to create a three-year limitation for offenses connected with land scrip. Since Secord's alleged offence had taken place in 1903, the case was immediately dismissed. The case, and the retroactive legislation ending it, created a scandal, but both provincial and federal governments refused to respond to public outrage (Sawchuk, Sawchuk and Ferguson, *Metis Lands Rights in Alberta*, 146–51).

37. Ray, *I Have Lived Here Since the World Began*, 211–12. On Treaty 7, see the fine study, Treaty 7 Elders and Tribal Council with Walter Hildebrandt, Sarah Carter and Dorothy First

Rider, *The True Spirit and Original Intent of Treaty 7* (Kingston and Montreal: McGill-Queen's University Press, 1996).

38. Daniel, "The Spirit and Terms of Treaty Eight," 47.
39. Foster, "Indian-White Relations in the Prairie West," 183; Francis and Payne, *Fort Dunvegan*, 132.
40. Anderson to Officer Commanding Treaty Escorts, September 9, 1899, RG18, vol. 160, file 73, NAC.
41. Quoted in Fumoleau, *As Long As This Land Shall Last*, 81.
42. "Report of Treaty No. 8 Commissioners," xxxvi; Madill, *Treaty Eight*, 75.
43. Daniel, "The Spirit and Terms of Treaty Eight," 55, 88, 95.
44. "Report of Treaty No 8 Commissioners," xxxvii; Tough, *As Their Natural Resources Fail*, 173, 301.
45. Text of Treaty 8, reprinted in Fumoleau, *As Long as This Land Shall Last*, 71–72; "Report of Treaty No. 8 Commissioners," xxxvi.
46. Fumoleau, *As Long As This Land Shall Last*, 74–75; Daniel, "The Spirit and Terms of Treaty Eight," 82–85.
47. Richard T. Price and Shirleen Smith, "Treaty 8 and Traditional Livelihoods: Historical and Contemporary Perspectives," *Native Studies Review* 9 (1993–94): 60; Daniel, "The Spirit and Terms of Treaty Eight," 93. For a sample of such views, see interviews with elders, Part II, "Alberta Interpretations of the Treaties," in *The Spirit of the Alberta Indian Treaties*, ed. Richard Price, 103–60 (Montreal: Institute for Research on Public Policy, 1980).
48. Richard Daniel, *Hunting, Fishing and Trapping Rights: White Competition and the Concept of Exclusive Rights for Indians* (Edmonton: Treaty and Aboriginal Rights Research of the Indian Association of Alberta, March 1976, (typescript)), 8; McCardle, *The Rules of the Game*, 19, 88; Ray, *The Canadian Fur Trade in the Industrial Age*, 47.
49. Daniel, *Hunting, Fishing and Trapping Rights*, 9.
50. Extract of letter by McKenna, July 26, 1899, RG10, Reel C-8094, vol. 6732, file 420–2, NAC.
51. "Report of Treaty No. 8 Commissioners," xxxv–xxxvi.
52. Fumoleau, *As Long As This Land Shall Last*, 67–68.
53. Huel, *Proclaiming the Gospel*, 178.
54. Quoted in Fumoleau, *As Long As This Land Shall Last*, 68.
55. Grouard, *Souvenirs de mes soixante Ans*, 358–59.
56. Holmes to Young, April 14, 1899, June 24 and July 10, 1899, AP, A.281,/149, Box A.32, PAA.
57. Fumoleau, *As Long As This Land Shall Last*, 46.
58. Trudy Nicks and Kenneth Morgan, "Grande Cache: The Historic Development of an Indigenous Alberta Metis Population," in *Being and Becoming Metis in North America*, eds. Jacqueline Peterson and Jennifer S. Brown (Winnipeg: University of Manitoba Press, 1985), 177; Patricia Sawchuk and Jarvis Gray, "The Isolated Communities of Northern Alberta," in *The Metis and The Land in Alberta. Land Claims Research Project 1979–80* (Edmonton: Metis Association of Alberta, 1980), 278.
59. Holmes to Young, November 8, 1899. AP A.281/149, Box A.32, PAA. On white support for settling Metis claims, see for example, Hall, "The Half-Breed Claims Commission," 5.

## —4

### A Foundation for Development:

1. J.K. Rea, *The Political Economy of the Canadian North. An Interpretation of the Course of Development in the Northern Territories of Canada to the Early 1960s* (Toronto: University of Toronto Press, 1968), 58–60, 345; Leo Panich, "The Role and Nature of the Canadian State," in *The Canadian State: Political Economy and Political Power*, ed. Leo Panich (Toronto: University of Toronto Press, 1977), 6; Kenneth Coates, "The Federal Government and the Economic System of the Yukon Territory: Historical and Contemporary Aspects of Northern Development," in *For Purposes of Dominion: Essays in Honour of Morris Zaslow*, eds. Kenneth S. Coates and William R. Morrison (North York: Captus University Press Inc., 1989), 105–22.

2. *Annual Report, NWMP [for]* 1897, 158, 163; Robert W. Wright, *Economics, Enlightenment and Canadian Nationalism* (Kingston and Montreal: McGill-Queen's University Press, 1993), 25 (italics in original).

3. Zaslow, *Opening of the Canadian North*, 157–59, 181–86; Joseph Schull, *Ontario Since 1867* (Toronto: McClelland and Stewart, Ontario History Series, 1978), 146–50, 174.

4. Zaslow, *The Opening of the Canadian North*, 221–22; Morris Zaslow, *The Northward Expansion of Canada 1914–1967* (Toronto: McClelland and Stewart, 1988), 109–10.

5. J.A. Ouellette, *L'Alberta-Nord. Region de Colonisation* (Edmonton: Le Courier de L'Ouest, 1909), 7; *Grande Prairie Herald*, September 23, 1913.

6. Carl Berger, "The True North Strong and Free," in *Nationalism in Canada*, ed. Peter Russell (Toronto: McGraw-Hill Ryerson Ltd., 1966), 9–20; R. Douglas Francis, *Images of the West: Responses to the Canadian Prairies* (Saskatoon: Western Producer Prairie Books, 1989), 110–11.

7. Seton, *The Arctic Prairies*, 315–16.

8. *Canada's Fertile Northland*, 101; Armstrong to Allan, July 5, 1910, 78.099c Box 3, file 2, UCAT; Seton, *The Arctic Prairies*, 313.

9. Leonard, *Delayed Frontier*, 100–101, 236–39; A.M. Bezanson, *Sodbusters Invade the Peace* (Toronto: The Ryerson Press, 1954), 77.

10. Cameron, *The New North. Being Some Account of a Woman's Journey Through Canada to the Arctic* (New York: D. Appleton and Co., 1910), 329, 341. For similar views, see Sanders to Commissioner, August 6, 1910, RG18, vol. 1643, file 125 Pt 2, NAC.

11. Leonard and Lemieux, *A Fostered Dream*, 23–30.

12. W.A. Waiser, "A Bear Garden: James Melville Macoun and the 1904 Peace River Controversy," *Canadian Historical Review* 67 (1986): 50.

13. Pearce to Ponton, December 18, 1908, Pearce Papers, 74–169, 9/2/6/310, UAA; Waiser, "A Bear Garden," 42–43, 61.

14. *Senate Debates*, January 24, 1907; W.A. Waiser, *The New Northwest. The Photographs of the Frank Crean Expedition 1908–1909* (Saskatoon: Fifth House Publishers, 1993), 7–8. The phrase "black eye" was originally coined by Jim Cornwall about the Macoun pamphlet (Waiser, "The Bear Garden," 53).

15. *Great Mackenzie Basin. The Senate Reports of 1887–1888*, ed. Ernest Chambers (Ottawa: King's Printer, 1908); Waiser, *The New Northwest. The Photographs of the Frank Crean Expedition*, 10–11.

16. Harvey to Smart, August 24, 1900, RG18, vol. 201, file 46, NAC.

17. For this process in the Yukon and NWT, see William R. Morrison, *Showing the Flag. The Mounted Police and Canadian Sovereignty in the North 1894–1925* (Vancouver: University of British Columbia Press, 1985), 1–9.

18. *Annual Report, NWMP [for] 1915*, 228. The detachments in the Peace country were at Dunvegan, Fort Vermilion, Grande Prairie, Lake Saskatoon, Peace River, Sturgeon Lake, McLennan, Smoky River Crossing and Spirit River. In the Athabasca-Grouard corridor they were at Grouard, Athabasca, Wabasca, Slave Lake (then called Sawridge) and Smith.

19. The NWMP remained responsible for the far north parts of Alberta until 1932 when the APP was abolished. The federal police force (renamed the RCMP in 1920) then resumed its former policing role throughout the province.

20. *Annual Report, NWMP [for] 1905*, 28; *Annual Report, NWMP [for] 1910*, 40–42.

21. *Appendix, Report of the [Canada] Minister of Agriculture, Experimental Farms, Reports [for] The Year Ending March 31, 1908*, 6–7; *Annual Report, Department of the Interior for 1915*, xxxiii.

22. Leonard, *Delayed Frontier*, 234; *Annual Report, Department of the Interior for 1901–02*, xxxix; *Annual Report, Department of the Interior for 1904–05 (Dominion Lands Branch)*, 17.

23. Leonard, *Delayed Frontier*, 176; Haslett to Commissioner, June 30, 1905, RG18, vol. 299, file 454, NAC; *Annual Report of the Department of the Interior [for] 1910*, 21.

24. *Annual Report, Department of Immigration and Colonization for the Fiscal Year Ended March 31, 1919*, 28. The halls in the Peace River country were at Peace River town, Grande Prairie, Donnelly, Grouard and Spirit River.

25. *Annual Report, NWMP [for] 1908*, 121; Monthly Report, "N" Division, February 11, 1909, RG18, vol. 1611, file 2, NAC; Report "N" Division for July 1912, RG18, vol. 1664, file 2 Pt. 2, NAC.

26. Peter A. Russell, "Rhetoric of Identity: The Debate Over the Division of the North-West Territories, 1890–1905," *Journal of Canadian Studies* 20 (1985–86): 111.

27. Leonard, *Delayed Frontier*, 240–41.

28. Leonard, *Delayed Frontier*, 240–41; *Canada's Fertile Northland: A Glimpse of the Enormous Resources of Part of the Unexplored Regions of the Dominion*, ed. Ernest Chambers (Ottawa: Government Printing Bureau, 1907), 97, 99; J.G. Coté, "J.L. Coté, Surveyor," *Alberta History* 31 (1983): 30–31; *[Grande Prairie] Herald Tribune*, May 13, 1943.

29. Leonard, *A Fostered Dream*, 23; Richard Daniel, "Indian Rights and Hinterland Resources: The Case of Northern Alberta," (Master's thesis, University of Alberta, 1977), 123–26.

30. Geoff Sawyer, *A History of Lesser Slave Lake* (Edmonton: Department of Recreation and Parks, 1981), 43; L.V. Kelly, *North with Peace River Jim*, ed. Hugh Dempsey (Calgary: Glenbow Alberta Institute Historical Paper No. 2, 1972), 7; J.G. MacGregor, *From Paddle Wheels to Bucket Wheels on the Athabasca* (Toronto: McClelland and Stewart, 1974), 114; Tom Inkster, "I Remember Peace River Jim," *Alberta History* 31 (1983): 9–13.

31. John Blue, *Alberta Past and Present*, Vol. 1 (Chicago: Pioneer Historical Publishing Company, 1924), 129–30.

32. *Annual Report, NWMP [for] 1907*, 31; *Annual Report, NWMP [for] 1906*, 138; Haslett to Commissioner, June 30, 1905, RG18, vol. 299, file 454, NAC; *Annual Report, NWMP [for] 1908*, 120; Geoffrey Allan Willis, "Development of Transportation in the Peace River Region of Alberta and British Columbia—With an Evaluation of Present Day Rail and

Road Commodity Flow Patterns" (Master's thesis, University of Alberta, 1966), 31–32; Monthly Report, "N" Division, April 5, 1909, RG18, vol. 1611, file 2, NAC. On trail conditions in 1910–13, see Edward H. Carrothers, "Three Trips to Peace River Country," *Alberta Historical Review* 13 (1965): 24–29.

33. *Annual Report, NWMP [for] 1910,* 41; *Annual Report, Department of the Interior (Topographical Surveys Branch) for 1915–16,* 113; *Annual Report, Department of the Interior (Dominion Lands Branch) for 1914,* 22.

34. Bezanson, *Sodbusters Invade the Peace,* 75.

35. Morris Zaslow, "The Struggle for the Peace River Outlet: A Chapter in the History of Canadian Development," in *The West and The Nation: Essays in Honour of W.L. Morton,* eds. Carl Berger and Ramsay Cook (Toronto: McClelland and Stewart, 1976), 276; L.G. Thomas, *The Liberal Party in Alberta. A History of Politics in the Province of Alberta 1905–1921* (Toronto: University of Toronto Press, 1959), 62–63; D.R. Babcock, "Autonomy and Alienation in Alberta: Premier A.C. Rutherford," *Prairie Forum* 6 (1981): 123, 125.

36. *Annual Report, NWMP [for] 1912,* 129; Bezanson, *Sodbusters Invade the Peace,* 72.

37. On Edmonton's disproportionate political weight in the assembly, see D. Jean Rycroft and David W. Leonard, *The Electoral History of the Peace River Country of Alberta 1905–1993* (Edmonton: Alberta Legislature Assembly and Alberta Community Development, 1996), 11.

38. John Eagle, "J.D. McArthur and the Peace River Railway," *Alberta History* 28 (1981): 37; *Tenth Report of the Board of Railway Commissioners for Canada for the Year Ending March 31, 1916,* Judgement, Edmonton, Dunvegan and British Columbia Railway, March 26, 1915, 343; Robert Scott Irwin, "The Emergence of a Regional Identity: The Peace River Country, 1910–46," (Ph.D. diss. University of Alberta, 1995), 221.

39. On the scandal, see: Eva Schneider, *Ribbons of Steel. The Story of the Northern Alberta Railways* (Calgary: Detselig Enterprises Ltd., 1989), 70–74; Jay Stewart Heard, "The Alberta and Great Waterways Railway Dispute 1909–13" (Master's thesis, University of Alberta, 1990); Thomas, *The Liberal Party in Alberta,* 58–114, 206.

40. Thomas, *The Liberal Party in Alberta,* 121–24, 138; *Eleventh Report of the Board of Railway Commissioners for Canada for the Year Ending March 31, 1916,* Judgement, Edmonton, Dunvegan and British Columbia Railway, August 2, 1915, 159; Report, December 14, 1915, M2306, GAI.

41. Spry, "The Tragedy of the Loss of the Commons in Western Canada," 203–28. See also her "The Transition from a Nomadic to a Settled Economy in Western Canada, 1856–1896," *Transactions of the Royal Society of Canada,* Vol. vi, Series iv, section II, June 1968, 187–201.

42. George Altmeyer, "Three Ideas of Nature in Canada, 1893–1914," *Journal of Canadian Studies* 11 (1976): 31–33; *Calgary Herald,* June 3, 1911.

43. Altmeyer, "Three Ideas of Nature in Canada," 24, 27, 31–33. For an expression of these justifications for conservation, see C. Gordon Hewitt, "The Conservation of Wild Life in Canada in 1917: A Review," in *Report of the Ninth Annual Meeting* (Ottawa: Commission of Conservation Canada, 1918), 119.

44. Robert McCandless, *Yukon Wildlife: A Social History* (Edmonton: University of Alberta Press, 1985), 106; Dan Gottesman, "Native Hunting and the Migratory Birds Convention

Act: Historical, Political and Ideological Perspectives," *Journal of Canadian Studies* 18 (1983): 80–84.

45. *Annual Report, Department of the Interior, Report of the Director of Forestry, [for]* 1914, 102–04; *Annual Report, Department of the Interior, Report of the Inspector of Crown Timber Agencies [for]* 1909, 47.

46. *Annual Report, Department of the Interior, Report of the Director of Forestry, [for]* 1914, 102–4; Clay to Officer Commanding, August 4, 1911 and Monthly Report (Athabasca), October 4, 1909, RG18, vol. 1663, file 130, NAC; *Annual Report, Department of the Interior, Report of Superintendent of Forestry, [for]* 1910, 36.

47. Griesbach to Commissioner, April 5, 1894 (report attached), RG15, vol 686, file 328,760, NAC; *Annual Report, NWMP [for]* 1907, 32; Monthly Report (Lesser Slave Lake), March 1, 1906, RG18, vol. 315, file 206, NAC.

48. Monthly Report (Lesser Slave Lake), May 1, 1906, RG18, vol. 315, file 206, NAC; *Annual Report, NWMP [for]* 1904, 113; *Annual Report, Indian Affairs for* 1905, 188.

49. *Forty Sixth Annual Report, Department of Marine and Fisheries [for]* 1912–13, 265, 275; *Grouard News,* September 20, 1913; Tough, *As Their Natural Resources Fail,* 178–86. Concerns about Native resistance were partly based on a precedent from Lac La Biche where a closed season was imposed in 1894 but cancelled in 1896 because it was impossible to enforce and created severe hardship (Oliver to Scott, September 14, 1896 and Goudreau to Secretary, November 10, 1896, RG15, vol. 732, file 411,695, NAC).

50. McCardle, *The Rules of the Game,* 209, 245; *Annual Report, Department of Agriculture (Alberta) for* 1915, 165–66.

51. *Calgary Herald,* March 8, 1907; McCardle, *The Rules of the Game,* 246, 267.

52. Gottesman, "Native Hunting and Migratory Birds Convention Act," 75–76; McCardle, *The Rules of the Game,* 148–55; *Annual Report, Department of Agriculture (NWT) [for]* 1898, 84.

53. Seenum to Secretary, April 15, 1912, RG10, vol. 6732, file 420–2A, Reel C-8094, NAC.

54. Lawton to Pedley, March 28, 1912, RG10, vol. 6732, file 420–2A, Reel C-8094, NAC. On this issue in Manitoba, see Jean Friesen, "Grant Me Wherewith To Make My Living," in *Aboriginal Land Use in Canada: Historical and Legal Aspects,* eds. Kerry Abel and Jean Friesen (Winnipeg: University of Manitoba Press, 1995), 145–47.

55. McCardle, *The Rules of the Game,* 22, 25–26, 51–52, n.101, 127–29; Woods to Superintendent General, January 2, 1908, RG10, vol. 6732, file 420–2, Reel C-8094, NAC; McLean to Lawton, May 6, 1912, RG10, vol. 6732, file 420–2A, Reel C-8094, NAC. On hunting and animal-human relationships among one group of western Canadian Cree, see Brightman, *Grateful Prey,* 186–212.

56. Price and Smith, "Treaty 8 and Traditional Livelihoods," 64–65; Pedley to Woods, January 22, 1908, Department of the Attorney General Papers, 66.166, file 249, PAA.

57. McCardle, *The Rules of the Game,* 54–63, 103; Deputy Superintendent to Deputy Attorney General, December 16, 1907 and Seenum to Oliver, May 3, 1909 and reply, May 21, 1909 and McLean to Seenum, May 2, 1912 and McLean to Laviolette, February 13, 1913, RG10, vol. 6732, file 420–2A, Reel C-8094, NAC.

58. McCardle, *The Rules of the Game,* 245.

59. McLean to Secretary, July 24, 1900, and Chipman to Laird, October 5, 1900, RG10, vol. 6732, file 420–2, Reel C-8094, NAC.

60. Laviolette to Superintendent General, January 2, 1913 and Deputy Superintendent General to Woods, January 22, 1908, RG10, vol. 6732, file 420–2A, Reel C-8094, NAC; McCardle, *The Rules of the Game*, 54; Monthly Report, "N" Division, March 9, 1909, RG18, vol. 1611, file 2, NAC.

61. Sanders to Commissioner, August 6, 1910, RG18, vol. 1643, file 125 Pt. 2, NAC; *Annual Report, NWMP [for] 1910*, 51.

62. Deputy Minister to Secretary, September 4, 1913, RG18, vol. 444, file 310, NAC; Monthly Report (Athabasca Landing), July 7, 1911, RG18, vol. 400, file 44, NAC.

63. *Annual Report, Indian Affairs [for] 1914*, 79; Field to Officer Commanding, November 1, 1911, RG18, vol. 1664, file 2 Pt. 2, NAC; Patrol Report, Smith Landing-Fort Simpson, February 7, 1915, RG18, vol. 479, file 65, NAC.

64. Foster, *Working For Wildlife*, 115; McCardle, *The Rules of the Game*, 262; Monthly Report, "N" Division, March 9, 1909, RG18, vol. 1611, file 2, NAC. On concerns about using poison, see Field to Officer Commanding, February 5, 1907, RG18, vol. 334, file 189, NAC.

65. Seton, *The Arctic Prairies*, 320; *Canada's Fertile Northland*, 77; *Annual Report, Indian Affairs [for] 1909*, 201; *Annual Report, NWMP [for] 1907*, 124–26; Foster, *Working For Wildlife*, 110.

66. McCardle, *The Rules of the Game*, 177.

67. Monthly Report, July 7, 1911, RG18, vol. 400, file 44, NAC.

## — 5

### Northern Life and Society to 1916

1. Hurssell to Attorney General, March 5, 1903, RG18, vol. 288, file 121, NAC.

2. *Annual Report, Department of the Interior for 1900*, xxxiv-xxxv; *Annual Report, NWMP [for] 1907*, 28; *Annual Report, NWMP [for] 1908*, 122; Haslett to Commissioner, June 30, 1905, RG18, vol. 299, file 454, NAC; Perry to Comptroller, March 24, 1904 and Memo for Sifton, March 29, 1904, RG18, vol. 288, file 121, NAC.

3. Wroughton to Commissioner, May 20, 1912, RG18, vol. 427, file 325, NAC.

4. McCarthy, *From the Great River*, 85; Field to Officer Commanding, October 1, 1904, RG18, vol. 1559, file 125, NAC; Patrol Report, February 7, 1915, RG18, vol. 479, file 65, NAC. The observance of New Year's as a celebration was not mission inspired but seems to have been a fur trade and Metis tradition.

5. Field to Officer Commanding, August 15, 1905, RG18, vol. 299, file 454, NAC; *Annual Report, Department of Indian Affairs for 1901*, 201–2.

6. Field to Officer Commanding, August 15, 1905, RG18, vol. 299, file 454, NAC; Fumoleau, *As Long As This Land Shall Last*, 106; Report for July 1914, RG18, vol. 1729, file 2 Pt. 2, NAC.

7. Ray, *The Canadian Fur Trade in the Industrial Age*, 40; Monthly Report (Lesser Slave Lake), August 1, 1906, RG18, vol. 1563, file 2, NAC; West to Officer Commanding, December 5, 1902, RG18, vol. 252, file 268, NAC.

8. West to Officer Commanding, December 5, 1902, RG18, vol. 252, file 268, NAC; *Annual Report, NWMP [for] 1911*, 50, 80; Agent to Secretary, March 28, 1911, RG15, vol. 1070, file 2,122,143, NAC; Wroughton to Commissioner, June 3, 1912, RG18, vol. 416, file 3, NAC. Alberta invested over \$181,000 on construction and upkeep of the Edson Trail between 1910 and 1915 (Edson Trail, Alberta Sessional Papers, 70.414, file 23, PAA).

9. *Annual Report, NWMP [for] 1911*, 50; *Annual Report, NWMP [for] 1912*, 129; Ethel Anderson Armstrong, Circular Letter, March 24, 1913, 78.099c, Box 4, file 1, UCAT; Monthly Report, February 14, 1914, RG18, vol. 457, file 67, NAC.

10. Haslett to Commissioner, June 30, 1905 and Wilson to Officer Commanding, September 30, 1905, RG18, vol. 299, file 454, NAC; McLeod to Officer Commanding, September 20, 1912, RG18, vol. 416, file 3, NAC.

11. Monthly Report, "N" Division, June 6, 1911, RG18, vol. 400, file 44, NAC; McDonell to Commissioner, August 29, 1913, RG18, vol. 1717, file 130 Pt. 1, NAC; Parker, *History of the Athabasca Oil Sands Region*, Vol. 2, *Oral History*, 19.

12. Field to Officer Commanding, February 5, 1907, RG18, vol. 334, file 189, NAC; *Annual Report, NWMP [for] 1908*, 120; *Annual Report, NWMP [for] 1901*, 54; *Annual Report, NWMP [for] 1906*, 136. See also Patrol Report, February 10, 1908, RG18, vol. 353, file 154, NAC.

13. Howard to Courtney, May 13, 1909, RG18, vol. 1632, file 21, NAC.

14. Mackinnon, "Portaging on the Slave River," 26. See also *Annual Report, NWMP [for] 1906*, 136; Routledge to Commissioner (Report of Patrol to Fort Simpson), April 4, 1898, RG18, vol. 1427, file 190, NAC; and Biggar to Secretary, December 26, 1905, RG15, vol. 982, file 123,538A, NAC.

15. *Canada's Fertile Northland*, 109; Report, Patrol to Fort McMurray, August 20, 1912, RG18, vol. 416, file 2, NAC.

16. McDonell to Commissioner, August 29, 1913, RG18, vol. 1717, file 130 Pt. 1, NAC. By early 1913 it was not expected that the trail would be finished until the end of winter (Ibid.)

17. *Canada's Fertile Northland*, 109; John W. Chalmers, "The Muskeg Flier. The Alberta and Great Waterways Railway," in *The Land of Peter Pond*, ed. John Chalmers (Edmonton: Boreal Institute for Northern Studies, Occasional Publication No. 12, 1974), 78. Cornwall's charter was for the Athabasca Railway Company. He sold it in 1909 to an A&GW subsidiary.

18. West to Officer Commanding, December 5, 1902, RG18, vol. 252, file 268, NAC. The ship was called the *Midnight Sun*.

19. Dale Holtslander, "The Challenge of the Lesser Slave River," *Alberta History* 28 (1980): 27, 34; *Annual Report, NWMP [for] 1907*, 27.

20. Athabasca Historical Society, *Athabasca Landing: An Illustrated History*, 109–15.

21. Monthly Report, "N" Division, April 5, 1909, RG18, vol. 1611, file 2, NAC; Sawyer, *A History of Lesser Slave Lake*, 90, 100; Holtslander, "The Challenge of the Lesser Slave River," 36; Patrol Report, March 8, 1910, RG18, vol. 384, file 89, NAC; *Annual Report, NWMP [for] 1908*, 119.

22. *Annual Report, NWMP [for] 1907*, 26–27.

23. *Annual Report, NWMP [for] 1907*, 26; Patrol Report, April 17, 1908, RG18, vol. 353, file 154, NAC; Monthly Report (Lesser Slave Lake), December 1, 1907, RG18, vol. 334, file 189, NAC.

24. Michael Adas, *Machines as the Measure of Men: Science, Technology and Ideologies of Western Dominance* (Ithaca: Cornell University Press, 1989), 194–225; Sawyer, *A History of Lesser Slave Lake*, 65.

25. Monthly Report, December 1, 1906, RG18, vol. 1563, file 2, NAC; Monthly Report, "N" Division, February 11, 1909, RG18, vol. 1611, file 2, NAC; McLeod to Officer Commanding, September 14, 1914. RG18, vol. 541, file 12, NAC.

26. Athabasca Historical Society, *Athabasca Landing: An Illustrated History*, 85, 125.

27. *Annual Report, NWMP [for] 1908*, 119; *Annual Report, NWMP [for] 1909*, 127; Ray, *The Canadian Fur Trade in the Industrial Age*, 93, 103–4. In comparison, the Mackenzie River district was the company's fourth richest producing area.

28. Ray, *The Canadian Fur Trade in the Industrial Age*, 51, 61.

29. Ray, *The Canadian Fur Trade in the Industrial Age*, 70.

30. Warwick to Young, March 4, 1902, AP, A.281/309, Box A.34, PAA; Anderson to Officer Commanding, November 30, 1911, RG18, vol. 400, file 44, NAC; Monthly Report (Lesser Slave Lake), March 1907, RG18, vol. 334, file 189, NAC; *Annual Report, NWMP [for] 1901*, 59; Field to Officer Commanding, August 15, 1905, RG18, vol. 299, file 454, NAC; Patrol Report, December 11, 1914, RG18, vol. 479, file 65, NAC.

31. Patrol Report, March 24, 1915, RG18, vol. 479, file 65, NAC; McCardle, *The Rules of the Game*, 150.

32. *Annual Report, NWMP [for] 1906*, 133; Monthly Report (Lesser Slave Lake), January 1, 1907, RG18, vol. 1536, file 2, NAC.

33. Patrol Report, March 21, 1898, RG18, vol. 157, file 647, NAC; *Annual Report, Department of the Interior, Report of the Surveyor General [for] 1901–02*, 75.

34. *Annual Report, Department of the Interior [for] 1908*, 47; Field to Officer Commanding, February 5, 1907, RG18, vol. 334, file 189, NAC; Patrol Report, February 10, 1908, RG18, vol. 353, file 154, NAC.

35. Clay to Officer Commanding, May 25, 1912, RG18, vol. 416, file 3, NAC; *Annual Report, NWMP [for] 1913*, 132; *Grande Prairie Herald*, March 10, 1914.

36. On anticipation about mining, see for example, *Grouard News*, August 23, 1913 and July 15, 1915.

37. Morris Zaslow, *Reading the Rocks* (Ottawa: Macmillan Company of Canada and Department of Energy, Mines and Resources, 1975), 234.

38. Parker and Tingley, *History of the Athabasca Oil Sands Region*, Vol. 1, 34, 38, 114–15; *Canada's Fertile Northland*, 39–42, 50; *Annual Report, NWMP [for] 1912*, 206; *Annual Report, Department of the Interior, Topographical Surveys Branch [for] 1915–16*, Appendix 39, 113; Annual Report, "N" Division, October 2, 1916, RG18, vol. 1843, file "Annual Report Part 4," NAC.

39. James Parker, "The Long Technological Search," in *The Land of Peter Pond*, ed. John Chalmers (Edmonton: Boreal Institute for Northern Studies, Occasional Publication No. 12, 1974), 111.

40. Parker and Tingley, *History of the Athabasca Oil Sands Region*, Vol. 1, 37–39; Barry Ferguson, *Athabasca Oil Sands. Northern Resource Exploration 1875–1951* (Regina: Alberta Culture and Canadian Plains Research Centre, 1985), 22.

41. Parker and Tingley, *History of the Athabasca Oil Sands Region*, Vol. 1, 39–43. In addition to his professional commitment, Ells fell in love with the north, and in later years painted and wrote poems, short stories and historical vignettes about the land and its people. Some of these were published in *Northland Trails* (Toronto: Burns and MacEachern, 1956).

42. Ferguson, *Athabasca Oil Sands*, 159–60.

43. Parker and Tingley, *History of the Athabasca Oil Sands Region*, Vol. 1, 41–43.

44. *Annual Report, NWMP [for] 1904*, 113; *Annual Report, NWMP [for] 1905*, 28–29; Monthly Report (Lesser Slave Lake), November 1, 1906, RG18, vol. 1563, file 2, NAC; *Annual Report of the Department of Marine and Fisheries [for] 1906*, 51 (Table); *Annual Report of the Department of Marine and Fisheries [for] 1907*, 207; *Annual Report of the Department of Marine and Fisheries [for] 1912–13*, 265.

45. Anthony G. Gulig, "Sizing Up The Catch: Native–Newcomer Resource Competition and the Early Years of Saskatchewan's Northern Commercial Fishery," *Saskatchewan History* 47 (1995): 5; Monthly Reports (Athabasca), December 14, 1908 and January 8, 1909, RG18, vol. 353, file 154, NAC; *Annual Report, NWMP [for] 1913*, 132. In 1912–13 the total Alberta catch was 8,084 cwt. of which 1,950 cwt. was taken from Lesser Slave Lake and 1,390 cwt. from Calling Lake.

46. *Annual Report, NWMP [for] 1909*, 123, 128; *Annual Report, Department of the Interior (Report of the Surveyor General) for 1901–02*, 73; Wilson to Officer Commanding, September 30, 1905, RG18, vol. 299, file 454, NAC; *Annual Report, NWMP [for] 1906*, 133; *Annual Report, NWMP [for] 1907*, 31.

47. *Annual Report, NWMP [for] 1903*, 39; *Annual Report, Alberta Department of Agriculture for 1907*, 59; *Missions De La Congregation Des Missionnaires Oblats de Marie Immaculee*, 45e Annee No.178, Juin 1907, 167; *Annual Report, NWMP [for] 1907*, 31; *Annual Report, NWMP [for] 1908*, 118.

48. Agnes Deans Cameron, *The New North*, 337; *Annual Report, Department of the Interior, Topographical Surveys Branch for 1915–16*, 113.

49. C.A. Dawson and R.W. Murchie, *The Settlement of the Peace River Country. A Study of a Pioneer District* (Toronto: The Macmillan Company of Canada, 1934), 61; *Annual Report, Department of the Interior (Dominion Lands Branch) for 1914*, 23.

50. Carl Tracie, "Agricultural Settlement in the South Peace River Area," (Master's thesis, University of Alberta, 1967), 53; *Annual Report, Department of the Interior (Dominion Lands Branch) for 1911*, 29; Henry M. Leppard, "The Settlement of the Peace River Country," *The Geographical Review* 35 (1935): 64; Irwin, "The Emergence of A Regional Identity," 99.

51. *Annual Report, NWMP [for] 1908*, 117–18; P.L. McCormick, "Transportation and Settlement: Problems in the Expansion of the Frontier of Saskatchewan and Assiniboia in 1904," *Prairie Forum* 5 (1980): 2, 4, 14–15.

52. *Annual Report, NWMP [for] 1910*, 41; Anderson to Officer Commanding, August 29, 1909, RG18, vol. 1632, file 21, NAC; Mackenzie to Secretary, May 13, 1910, RG15, vol. 1070, file 2,1222,143, NAC.

53. For an early expression of this view, see *Missions De La Congregation Des Oblats De Marie Immaculee*, No. 159 Septembre 1902, 256.

54. Pearce to Rutherford, November 7, 1913, 74.169, 9/2/6/3/20, UAA.

55. *Annual Report, Department of the Interior (Dominion Lands Branch) for 1909*, 28; Tracie, "Agricultural Settlement in the South Peace River Area," 109. On early prairie worries about uplands, see for example, W.L. Morton, *Manitoba: A History* (Toronto: University of Toronto Press, 1957), 151–201.

56. Tracie, "Agricultural Settlement in the South Peace River Area," 19, 109a. On the preference for open land in an area north of Edmonton, see: Robin Vogelsang, "The Initial Agricultural Settlement of the Morinville-Westlock Area, Alberta," (Master's thesis,

University of Alberta, 1972), 30. See also *Grouard News*, October 7, 1915; personal communication from David Leonard. Earlier wheat varieties grown in the Peace River country were Red Fife and especially Ladoga.

57. Pearce to Harvey, March 16, 1910, 74.169, 9/2/6/3/20, UAA; Hopkins to Buchanan, June 28, 1910, UCAT, 78.099c Box 1 file 12; Edmonton Dominion Land Office to Department of the Interior, April 27, 1908 and Tompkins to Department of the Interior, December 8, 1908, RG15, vol. 1002, file 1,379,883, NAC.

58. *Annual Report, Department of the Interior (Dominion Lands Branch) for 1913*, 22; correspondence and reports, 1910–15, Agricultural Societies Branch Papers, 73.316, file 27a, PAA; *Annual Report, Alberta Department of Agriculture for 1912*, 185–87; *Grouard News*, January 9, 1914.

59. Zaslow, *The Northward Expansion of Canada*, 69.

60. Isabelle Campbell, *Grande Prairie, Capital of the Peace*, (n.p. 1968), 39, 49; *Peace River Record*, February 4, 1915; Annual Report "N" Division, October 1, 1914, RG18, vol. 1729, file 2 Pt. 2, NAC; *Annual Report, Department of the Interior (Dominion Lands Branch) for 1914*, 23.

61. Zaslow, *The Northward Expansion of Canada*, 69. The apt term and concept of "makeshifts" is from Olwen H. Hufton, *The Poor of Eighteenth Century France 1750–1789* (Oxford: Oxford University Press, 1974).

62. Ethel Anderson Armstrong, Circular Letter, March 24, 1913, 78.099c Box 4 file 1, UCAT; Annual Report, "N" Division, October 1, 1914, RG18, vol. 1729, file 2 Pt. 2, NAC; *Annual Report, NWMP [for] 1914*, 127.

63. Athabasca Historical Society, *Athabasca Landing: An Illustrated History*, 91; Dawson and Murchie, *Settlement of the Peace River Country*, 55, 66; *Annual Report, Department of the Interior (Dominion Lands Branch) for 1913*, 24.

64. Dawson and Murchie, *Settlement of the Peace River Country*, 62–63; *Annual Report, Department of the Interior for 1904–05 (Dominion Lands Branch)*, 76; Blake to Officer Commanding, September 13, 1916, RG18, vol. 1868, file 130, NAC.

65. Monthly Report, "N" Division for April 1910, May 4, 1910, RG18, vol. 384, file 89, NAC; Monthly Report (Athabasca), May 3, 1911, RG18, vol. 400, file 44, NAC; Harold Troper, "The Creek-Negroes of Oklahoma and Canadian Immigration 1909–11," *Canadian Historical Review* 53 (1972): 272–88; Stewart Grow, "The Blacks of Amber Valley—Negro Pioneering in Northern Alberta," *Canadian Ethnic Studies* 4 (1974): 25–27; Judith Hill, "Alberta's Black Settlers: A Study of Canadian Immigration Policy and Practice," (Master's thesis, University of Alberta, 1981), 78–79, 108, 127.

66. On motivations of some of these early settlers, see the various reminiscences in M4560, GAI.

67. Clay to Officer Commanding, April 25, 1910, RG18, vol. 1643, file 125 Pt 1, NAC; Leonard and Lemieux, *A Fostered Dream*, 37; typescript excerpt from Ronning autobiography, file 19, M4560, GAI; [Grande Prairie] *Northern Tribune*, August 18, 1932.

68. The first such settlement attempt in northern Alberta was the Peace River Land and Colonization Company formed in 1899 by Father J.A. Lemieux. Land was set aside by the Department of the Interior, but recruits were hard to find, the land was poor, and transportation to the district was difficult (David Leonard, "The Great Peace River Land Scandal," *Alberta History* 39 (1991): 9–16). See also *Annual Report, Department of the Interior for 1900*, xxxv.

69. *Grouard News*, August 9, 1913; Ouellette, *L'Alberta-Nord*, passim. On French Canadian migration to the prairies, see Robert Painchaud, "French Canadian Historiography and Franco-Catholic Settlement in Western Canada, 1870–1915," paper delivered at the Canadian Historical Association, May 31, 1978 (typescript). On the mixing of religious and social utopian thinking with land settlement in northern Quebec, see: Gabriel Dussault, *Le curé Labelle: Messianisme utopie et colonisation au Québec 1850–1900* (Montreal: Hurtubise HMN, 1983).

70. *Annual Report, NWMP [for] 1906*, 138.

71. While their duties included attending to the "general complaints" of the Indians, providing medical assistance and farm instruction and generally assisting the Indians to make a transition "to a more settled lifestyle," the Indian Agents could not attain such goals because travel was difficult and slow. The entries in the Lesser Slave Lake Indian Agency agent's diary reveal that he had little contact with most reserves. Although he visited close-in reserves more frequently, especially after 1916 when the railway gave easy connection along the south shore of Lesser Slave Lake, those in more distant places saw him once a year for one or two days during the flurry of activity at annuity payment time (Madill, *Treaty Eight*, 80–81; Lesser Slave Lake Indian Agency, Diaries, 1911–21, M2218, GAI).

72. Testimony, Henry Conroy (Indian Affairs Inspector, Treaty 8), *Canada's Fertile Northland*, 74; Tough, *As Their Natural Resources Fail*, 143–51.

73. Tough, *As Their Natural Resources Fail*, 143–51; Grouard to Minister of the Interior, September 10, 1900, RG15, vol. 806, file 590,185, NAC; West to Officer Commanding, October 2, 1903, RG18, vol. 1525, file 125, NAC.

74. Sawchuk, Sawchuk and Ferguson, *Metis Land Claims in Alberta*, 127.

75. West to Officer Commanding, December 5, 1902, RG18, vol. 252, file 268, NAC; Madill, *Treaty Eight*, 82–85; Stewart to Secretary, January 28, 1901, RG15, vol. 823, file 612,556, NAC; *Annual Report, Department of Indian Affairs for 1906*, 162; *Annual Report, NWMP [for] 1905*, 27. *Annual Report, NWMP [for] 1908*, 121.

76. Reddekopp, *The Creation and Surrender of the Beaver and Duncan's Bands' Reserves*, 25–28, 37–38. It appears that the land was surveyed by mistake as a reserve in common, not in severalty.

77. *Annual Report, Indian Affairs for 1910*, 189; *Annual Report, Indian Affairs for 1914*, xxx, 78; *Annual Report, Indian Affairs for 1915*, 84; *Annual Report, Indian Affairs for 1916*, 79.

78. Cory to Roche, November 21, 1913 and Memo to Scott, November 26, 1913, RG10, Reel C-9482, vol. 7997, file 191/30–11–1, NAC. For an example of ousting Indians from prospective reserve land in the British Columbia Peace River block, see, *Annual Report, Indian Affairs for 1914*, 85.

79. *Annual Report, Indian Affairs, for 1910*, 186; McLean to Secretary, November 16, 1916, RG10, vol. 7997, file 191/30–11–1, Reel 9482, NAC.

80. *Annual Report, Indian Affairs for 1900*, xl; Sarah Carter, *Lost Harvests. Prairie Indian Reserve Farmers and Government Policy* (Montreal and Kingston: McGill-Queen's University Press, 1990), 18.

81. See for example, *Annual Report, Indian Affairs for 1904*, 200; *Annual Report, Indian Affairs for 1910*, 189; *Annual Report, Indian Affairs for 1914*, 84. On Indian farming elsewhere on the prairies, see Carter, *Lost Harvests*, 45–49 and Tough, *As Their Natural Resources Fail*, 165–67.

82. *Annual Report Department of Indian Affairs for 1916*, 79; Monthly Report, February 1, 1907, RG18, vol. 1586, file 2 Pt. 2, NAC.

83. Tough, *As Their Natural Resources Fail*, 173, 204.

84. *Annual Report, Indian Affairs, for 1911*, 179.

85. See for example, *Annual Report, Indian Affairs for 1909*, 199; *Annual Report, Indian Affairs for 1910*, 186; *Annual Report, Indian Affairs for 1916*, 76.

86. Butler to Laird, November 2, 1900 and Laird to Butler, February 1, 1901, RG10, vol. 3564, file 82 Pt. 21, Reel C-10099, NAC; Anderson to Officer Commanding, July 23, 1903, RG18, vol. 1525, file 125, NAC; West to Officer Commanding, December 5, 1902, RG18, vol. 252, file 268, NAC. The Metis instructor was said to be Cunningham, who "years ago represented St. Albert in the N.W. Assembly as member."

87. *Annual Report, Indian Affairs for 1908 (Report for 1906)*, 182.

88. *Annual Report, Indian Affairs for 1908*, 185; *Annual Report, Indian Affairs for 1915*, 80; Reddekopp, *The Creation and Surrender of the Beaver and Duncan's Bands' Reserves*, 138; Daniel, "Indian Rights and Hinterland Resources," 140–41.

89. Carter, *Lost Harvests*, 12–13; Madill, *Treaty Eight*, 79. By 1912, there were eight acres in crop at Salt River and a sawmill was operating. Ambitious plans were made for the project, which was seen as potentially supplying food for Indian Affairs' requirements in the region. See *Annual Report, Indian Affairs for 1913*, 190–91 and Field to Officer Commanding, November 1, 1911, RG18, vol. 1664, file 2 Pt 2, NAC.

90. Tough, *As Their Natural Resources Fail*, 227–28, 309.

91. Macrae to Superintendent, December 7, 1900, RG10, vol. 3952, file 134, 858, Reel C-10166, NAC.

92. Indian Affairs to Secretary, November 29, 1900, RG10, vol. 3952, file 134,858, Reel C-10166, NAC; Robinson to Young, September 2, 1901, AP, A.281/250, Box A.33, PAA; Carney, "The Grey Nuns and the Children of Holy Angels," 119–20; Huel, *Proclaiming the Gospel*, 175.

93. Carney, "The Grey Nuns and the Children of Holy Angels," 117; Robert J. Carney, "Relations in Education Between the Federal and Territorial Governments and the Roman Catholic Church in the Mackenzie District, Northwest Territories, 1867–1961," (Ph.D. diss., University of Alberta, 1971), 2.

94. Joseph F. Dion, *My Tribe The Crees* (Calgary: Glenbow Museum, 1979), 157; Huel, *Proclaiming the Gospel*, 144, 175; J.R. Miller, *Shingwauk's Vision. A History of Native Residential Schools* (Toronto: University of Toronto Press, 1996), 98–100.

95. Huel, *Proclaiming the Gospel*, 98, 140–41, 148; Carney, "The Grey Nuns and the Children of Holy Angels," 110; Miller, *Shingwauk's Vision*, 89–148. There were no "industrial" schools in northern Alberta—they were being phased out just as the school system was expanding there. After 1923, all boarding schools were officially called residential schools.

96. Macrae to Superintendent, December 7, 1900 and Indian Affairs to Secretary, November 29, 1900, RG10, vol. 3952, file 134,858, Reel C-10166, NAC; *Annual Report, Indian Affairs for 1899*, 342; *Annual Report, Indian Affairs for 1901*, 433.

97. Miller, *Shingwauk's Vision*, 141; Grouard to Minister of the Interior, August 29, 1899 and Grouard to Laurier, October 1, 1900, RG10, vol. 3952, file 134,858, Reel C-10166, NAC; Huel, *Proclaiming The Gospel*, 160–61.

98. Miller, *Shingwauk's Vision*, 318–42.

99. Miller, *Shingwauk's Vision*, 15–38; Huel, *Proclaiming the Gospel*, 149.

100. *Annual Report, Indian Affairs for 1913*, 598; Robinson's Report, June 16, 1902, AP, A281/251 Box A33, PAA.

101. McCarthy, *From the Great River to the Ends of the Earth*, 163; *Annual Report, Indian Affairs for 1899*, 342; *Annual Report, Indian Affairs for 1901*, 346; Report of Synod of the Diocese of Athabasca Held at St. Peter's Mission, Lesser Slave Lake, June 6–8, 1910 Being the Seventh Triennial Synod, AP, A220/12b Box A21, PAA.

102. Ray, *I Have Lived*, 236–37.

103. Carney, "The Grey Nuns and the Children of Holy Angels," 113.

104. Huel, *Proclaiming the Gospel*, 179–85.

—— 6
## Changing Course, 1912–1921

1. Athabasca Historical Society, *Athabasca Landing: An Illustrated History*, 78; Monthly Report (Athabasca Landing), August 6, 1909, RG18, vol. 1611, file 2, NAC; Monthly Report (Athabasca Landing), June 6, 1911 and Monthly Report (Athabasca Landing), December 30, 1911, RG18, vol. 400, file 44, NAC. The line, which was later absorbed by the CNoR, began as the Edmonton and Slave Lake Railway, chartered in 1899 to build from Edmonton to Athabasca.

2. Monthly Reports (Athabasca Landing), March 12 and November 1, 1912, RG18, vol. 416, file 3, NAC; Athabasca Historical Society, *Athabasca Landing: An Illustrated History*, 104, 117; *Annual Report, NWMP [for] 1911*, 50; *Annual Report, NWMP [for] 1913*, 131.

3. Minutes, Town of Athabasca, June 2 and August 4, 1913, Town of Athabasca Papers, 70.296/1, PAA.

4. Monthly Report (Athabasca Landing), December 10, 1914, RG18, vol. 1729, file 2 Pt. 2, NAC; Patrol Report, December 4, 1914, RG18, vol. 1817, file 130, NAC; Monthly Report (Athabasca Landing), February 9, 1915, RG18, vol. 1797, file 2 Pt. 10, NAC; *Annual Report, Department of Marine and Fisheries [for] 1913–14*, 244–45 (Tables).

5. *Annual Report, NWMP [for] 1913*, 131; *Edmonton Bulletin*, September 3, 1912, quoted in Dale Holtslander, "Railway to Athabasca," *Alberta History* 26 (1978): 25.

6. Patrol Report, August 20, 1912, RG18, vol. 416, file 3, NAC; Patrol Report, January 25, 1913, RG18, vol. 1717, file 130 Pt. 1, NAC; Patrol Report, October 5, 1914, RG18, vol. 1817, file 130, NAC; Patrol Report, March 24, 1915, RG18, vol. 479, file 65, NAC; *Annual Report, NWMP [for] 1914*, 197; *Annual Report, Department of the Interior (Topographical Surveys Branch) [for] 1915–16*, Appendix No. 35, 106. For an example of realtors' hype about Fort McMurray, see "Fort McMurray. Great City of the North," *Alberta Historical Review* 7 (1959): 24.

7. Anderson to Officer Commanding, November 30, 1911, RG18, vol. 400, file 44, NAC; Monthly Report (Athabasca Landing), March 12, 1912, RG18, vol. 416, file 3, NAC.

8. Starnes to Commissioner, September 19, 1913, RG18, vol. 1710, file 74, NAC; *Annual Report, NWMP [for] 1913*, 131; *Annual Report, NWMP [for] 1912*, 128; *Grouard News*, August 12, October 12 and November 9, 1912, and May 31, 1913 and March 28, 1914.

9. Philip Godsell, *Arctic Trader. An Account of Twenty Years with the Hudson's Bay Company* (Toronto: The Macmillan Co. of Canada Ltd., 1946), 115, 118; *Annual Report, NWMP [for] 1913*, 131.

10. *Grouard News*, December 13, 1913.

11. Sanders to Commissioner, August 6, 1910, RG18, vol. 1643, file 125 Pt 2, NAC; Pamela Ann Mathewson, "The Geographical Impact of Outsiders on the Community of Fort Chipewyan, Alberta," (Master's thesis, University of Alberta, 1974), 86–88. For maps and correspondence about occupancy and improvements at Fort Chipewyan in 1919–20, see RG15, vol. 1097, file 2,602,231, NAC.

12. *Grouard: The Coming Metropolis of the Great Peace River Country, Alberta Canada* (Grouard: The Grouard Board of Trade, 1913), 12. Copy in 70.347/58, PAA.

13. Holtslander, "The Challenge of the Lesser Slave River," 36; Annual Report, "N" Division, October 1, 1914, RG18, vol. 1729, file 2 Pt. 2, NAC.

14. *Grouard News*, September 19, 1914; Starnes to Commissioner, September 19, 1913, RG18, vol. 1710, file 74, NAC; Cook to Municipal Affairs, June 5, 1914, 74.174/1032c, PAA.

15. Richard Brown, "A Town Bypassed: Grouard Alberta and the Building of the Edmonton, Dunvegan and British Columbia Railway," *The Archivist*, May-June 1990, 11; *Grouard News*, August 9, 1913, April 10 and 24, 1915.

16. Monthly Report, "N" Division, June 19, 1916, RG18, vol. 509, file 194, NAC; Assistant Commissioner to Commissioner, October 11, 1915, RG18, vol 495, file 648, NAC; Annual Report, "N" Division, October 2, 1916, RG18, vol. 1843, file "Annual Report, Pt 4," NAC; Sawyer, *A History of Lesser Slave Lake*, 95; *Annual Report, NWMP [for] 1915*, 140.

17. Schneider, *Ribbons of Steel*, 29.

18. James MacGregor, *The Land of Twelve Foot Davis* (Edmonton: Applied Art Products Ltd., 1952), 26; Leonard and Lemieux, *Lure of the Peace River Country*, 49–50; *Grande Prairie Herald*, November 3, 1914; Patrol Report, January 8, 1915, and Report (Lake Saskatoon), January 31, 1915, RG18, vol. 1817, file 130, NAC.

19. Dawson and Murchie, *The Settlement of the Peace River Country*, 36–39. See also Eric J. Holmgren, "Fort Dunvegan," *The Beaver*, Outfit 312, No. 2, (Autumn 1981): 59.

20. Extract from Report, April 21, 1915, RG18, vol. 1801, file 23, NAC; Field to Officer Commanding, March 10, 1915, Assistant Commissioner to Officer Commanding, April 6, 1915, Parry to Comptroller, June 1, 1915 and Cochrane to Officer Commanding, May 1, 1915, RG18, vol. 1850, file 23, NAC; Middleburg to Officer Commanding, March 10, 1915, RG18, vol. 1817, file 130 Pt 1, NAC.

21. Ruzicka to Officer Commanding, July 19, 1916, RG18, vol. 1850, file 23, NAC.

22. Glenda Lamont, "Migrants and Migration in Part of the South Peace River Region, Alberta," (Master's thesis, University of Alberta, 1970), 34; J.W. Judge, "Early Railroading in Northern Alberta," *Albert Historical Review* 6 (1958): 19; Monthly Report, "N" Division, June 19, 1916, RG18, vol. 509, file 1954, NAC.

23. Irwin, "The Emergence of a Regional Identity," 209–10; Monthly Report, November 9 and December 31, 1917, RG18, vol. 189, file 2-N; Monthly Report, December 31, 1917, RG18, vol. 529, file 153, NAC.

24. Camsell, *Son of the North*, 33; Annual Report, "N" Division, October 2, 1916, RG18, vol. 1843, file "Annual Report, Part 4," NAC; Evelyn Hansen, *Where Go the Boats…Navigation on the Peace 1792–1952* (Peace River: Peace River Centennial Museum, n.d.), 13–15; Report,

Patrol from Fort Chipewyan to Fort McMurray, March 24, 1915, RG18, vol. 479, file 65, NAC; *Peace River Record*, June 30, 1916. Lord Rhondda died in 1918; some of his assets were bought by the Hudson's Bay Company.

25.  *Grande Prairie Herald*, August 10, 1915; *Annual Report, NWMP [for] 1915*, 139–40; Athabasca Historical Society, *Athabasca Landing: An Illustrated History*, 148–49; *Grouard News*, March 27, 1915; General Report for July 1914, RG18, vol. 1729, file 32 Pt 2, NAC.

26.  *Annual Report, NWMP [for] 1915*, 9; *Annual Report, NWMP [for] 1916*, 143; Monthly Report, March 21, 1916, RG18, vol. 509, file 194, NAC; Deputy Minister to Reid, May 29, 1917 and Inspector to Pierre, November 26, 1917, Department of Municipal Affairs Papers, 74.174/967a, PAA.

27.  McKinnon and Co., Re: Town of Athabasca (1917); McKinnon and Co. to Wyssman, September 21, 1916, 74.174/967c, PAA; Acting Deputy Minister to Gariepy, May 3, 1918, 74.174/967a, PAA; Municipal Finances Recommendations Re: Athabasca, June 13, 1921, 74.174/968a, PAA.

28.  Edward J. McCullough and Michael Maccagno, *Lac La Biche and the Early Fur Traders* (Edmonton: Canadian Circumpolar Institute and Alberta Vocational College, Lac La Biche, Archaeological Survey of Alberta, Occasional Publication No. 29, 1991), 81–89; Schneider, *Ribbons of Steel*, 85; Field to Officer Commanding, February 1, 1916, RG18, vol. 1867, file 130, NAC.

29.  Rheault to Officer Commanding, April 4, 1916 and Field to Officer Commanding, February 1, 1916, RG18, vol. 1867, file 130, NAC; Anne B. Woywitka, "Strike at Waterways," *Alberta Historical Review* 20 (1972): 1–5.

30.  Fort McMurray Historical Society, *Timeline, Fort McMurray ca. 1700–1980* (typescript, Fort McMurray Historical Society, 1993), n.p; D.J. Comfort, *Pass The McMurray Salt Please* (Fort McMurray: n.p. 1975), 9.

31.  Colin Hatcher, *The Northern Alberta Railways*, Vol. 2 (Calgary: British Railway Modellers of North America, 1987), Introduction, n.p.

32.  *Tenth Report of the Board of Railway Commissioners for Canada for the Year Ending March 31, 1915*, Judgement, March 26, 1915, 341–43; *Eleventh Report of the Board of Railway Commissioners for Canada for the Year Ending March 31, 1916*, Judgement, Edmonton, Dunvegan and British Columbia Railway, August 2, 1916, 160; *Spirit River Echo*, April 9, 1920.

33.  Camsell, *Son of the North*, 33; Campbell to Lynch, January 22, 1915 and Lynch to Cory, January 28, 1915, RG15, vol. 1111, file 3,031,725, NAC.

34.  Godsell, *Arctic Trader*, 179–80.

35.  Thomas, *The Liberal Party in Alberta*, 190; Doherty to Pierre, August 25, 1919, 74.174/1267a, PAA; Bob Irwin, "Whose Railway Was It?," in *Edmonton: The Life of a City*, 120; *Spirit River Echo*, April 16, 1920.

36.  Thomas, *The Liberal Party in Alberta*, 190–91. In any event, former CNoR lines in Alberta, which had in total been promised even higher provincial loan guarantees than the McArthur lines, were taken into the CNR, relieving Alberta of its responsibility (Blue, *Alberta Past and Present*, vol. 1, 130).

37.  *Annual Report, NWMP [for] 1915*, 140; Patrol Report, January 29, 1918, RG18, vol. 1919, file 130, NAC; Peter J. Murphy, *History of Forest and Prairie Fire Control in Alberta* (Edmonton:

Alberta Energy and Natural Resources, 1985), 17, 191; *Annual Report, Department of the Interior (Director of Forestry) for 1914*, 101.

38. *Annual Report, Department of Marine and Fisheries [for] 1913–14*, 230, 244–45, Tables; *Annual Report, Department of Marine and Fisheries [for] 1914–15*, 229. For another example of southern resource depletion creating interest in more remote areas, see Gulig, "Sizing up the Catch," 4.

39. *Annual Report, Department of Marine and Fisheries [for] 1914–15*, 229; *Annual Report, Department of Marine and Fisheries [for] 1915–16*, 227–29; *Grouard News*, July 15, 1915; Canada, Dominion Bureau of Statistics, *Census of Industry, 1919, Fisheries Statistics 1919*, Sessional Paper No. 17d, 1921, 54–55 (Table); *Spirit River Echo*, August 30, 1918. In 1915–16, 7.5 cars (1,250 cwt.) of Lesser Slave Lake whitefish were shipped to the U.S.

40. *Annual Report, Department of Marine and Fisheries [for] 1913–14*, 238; *Annual Report, Department of Marine and Fisheries [for] 1915–16*, 227–29, 235–36, 240 (Tables).

41. *Annual Report, Department of Marine and Fisheries [for] 1913–14*, 238; *Annual Report, Department of Marine and Fisheries [for] 1915–16*, 227–29, 235–236, 240 (Tables); *Annual Report, Department of Marine and Fisheries [for] 1916–17*, 214; *Spirit River Echo*, August 30, 1918; Frank Tough, *Fisheries Economics and the Tragedy of the Commons: The Case of Manitoba's Inland Commercial Fisheries* (Discussion Paper No. 33, Department of Geography, York University, 1987), 36.

42. *Annual Report, Department of Marine and Fisheries [for] 1916–17*, 214; *Annual Report, Department of Marine and Fisheries [for] 1913–14*, 237; *Annual Report, Department of Marine and Fisheries [for] 1915–16*, 227; *Grouard News*, April 10 and September 16, 1915.

43. *Annual Report, NWMP [for] 1915*, 140; Judge, "Early Railroading in Northern Alberta," 19.

44. Patrol Report, March 4, 1916 and April 19, 1916, RG18, vol. 1867, file 130, NAC; Circular Materials Re: Peace River Country, nd. (1917), RG15, vol. 121, file 3,272,781, NAC; Monthly Report, July 6, 1917, RG18, vol. 189, file 2-N, NAC; *Annual Report, Department of the Interior [for] 1915*, xxxiii. On the history of Beaverlodge substation, see Typescripts, Loggie collection, M4560, file 2, GAI.

45. Dawson and Murchie, *Settlement of the Peace River Country*, 42, 57; *Spirit River Echo*, December 21, 1917; *Grande Prairie Herald*, April 3, 1923.

46. Tracie, "Agricultural Settlement in the South Peace River Area," 111; Leppard, "The Settlement of the Peace River Country," 64; Willis, "Development of Transportation in the Peace River Region," 31–32, 43–44, 51; Leggo to Minister, May 1, 1920, 67.303/3521, PAA.

47. Comfort, *Pass The McMurray Salt*, 9–10; "Annual Report of the Department of Railways of the Province of Alberta [for] 1927," 1; Memo, Salt Industry, September 2, 1939, 86.587/26, PAA.

48. *Annual Report, Department of Marine and Fisheries [for] 1913–14*, 230, 244–45, Tables; *Annual Report, Department of the Interior [for] 1919*, 18; Daily Journal, August 25 and November 9, 1920, AP, A13/11 Box A.E. PAA; Harvie to Deputy Minister of the Interior, February 16, 1920 and Glidden to Mitchell, May 21, 1920, RG15, vol. 1141, file 4,319,996, NAC; Morris Zaslow, "The Development of the Mackenzie Basin 1920–1940" (Ph.D. dissertation, University of Toronto, 1957), 507.

49. Ray, *The Canadian Fur Trade in the Industrial Age*, 66–67.

50. Ray, *The Canadian Fur Trade in the Industrial Age*, 97–101; Clarke to McLeod, September 10, 1914 (copy), RG18, vol. 541, file 12, NAC; *Annual Report, NWMP [for] 1915*, 148.

51. *Annual Report, NWMP [for] 1915*, 146; Monthly Report (Athabasca), February 18, 1915, Clarke to McLeod, September 10, 1914 and Morden to McLeod, September 12, 1914 (copies), RG18, vol. 541, file 12, NAC.

52. Scott to Fortescue, August 25, 1914, and Scott, circular letter (italics in original), September 21, 1914, RG18, vol. 541, file 12, NAC. On earlier distribution of relief, see West to Officer Commanding, April 9, 1903, RG18, vol. 1525, file 125, NAC and Routledge to Commissioner, September 11, 1908 and Secretary to Comptroller, December 11, 1908, RG18, vol. 362, file 573, NAC.

53. Johnson to Secretary, February 25, 1916, RG18, vol. 451, file 12, NAC; McLeod to Officer Commanding, September 14, 1914, RG18, vol. 541, file 12, NAC; Patrol Report, December 11, 1914, RG18, vol. 479, file 65, NAC.

54. Monthly Report, "N" Division, February 18, 1915 (copy), RG18 vol. 541, file 12, NAC; McLeod to Officer Commanding, January 30, 1915, RG18, vol. 479, file 65, NAC.

55. *Annual Report, NWMP [for] 1915*, 146.

56. Patrol Report, February 7, 1915 and Report, (extract) Smith Landing, December 29, 1914, RG18, vol. 479, file 65, NAC.

57. Monthly Report, "N" Division, April 21, 1915, RG18, vol. 479, file 65, NAC.

58. Patrol Report (Great Slave Lake), April 4, 1916, RG18, vol. 509, file 194, NAC; Johnson to Secretary, February 25, 1916, RG18, vol. 451, file 12, NAC.

59. Ray, *I Have Lived*, 270; Ray, *The Canadian Fur Trade in the Industrial Age*, 104, 111.

60. Ray, *The Canadian Fur Trade in the Industrial Age*, 96, 103–6, 149, 166, 223; [Jim Cornwall] Memo Re Fur Trade, n.d. [1924], Cornwall Papers, M271, GAI. On homesteaders, see: Monthly Report (Peace River), November 22, 1916, RG18, vol. 509, file 194, NAC; On draft dodgers, see Patrol Report (Peace River), February 16, 1918, RG18, vol. 1919, file 130, NAC.

61. For such complaints at Fort McKay see: Report of Patrol with Indian party, July 3, 1917, RG18, vol. 1901, file 119, NAC.

62. Annual Report, APP, "E" Division for 1918, 72.370, PAA; Parker and Tingley, *History of the Athabasca Oil Sands Region*, Vol. 1, 106.

63. Memo Re The Fur Trade, Cornwall papers, M271, GAI.

## — 7
### Getting In, Getting Out

1. Blue, *Alberta Past and Present*, Vol. 1, 307. At the same time, the federal government abandoned its opposition to signing a treaty with the Aboriginal people of the Mackenzie Valley, an action that clearly demonstrated that the far north was now seen as valuable territory. Treaty 11, signed in 1921–22, ceded all the territory from Great Slave Lake north along the Mackenzie River to the Arctic (Fumoleau, *As Long as This Land Shall Last*, 106).

2. *The Mission Field*, May 1938 (copy in AP, A.420/81, Box A.108, PAA); Zaslow, *Northward Expansion of Canada*, 9, 124, 138, 191; Jean Barman, *The West Beyond the West* (Toronto: University of Toronto Press, 1991), 263; "An Empire in the Making." The Resources and

*Opportunities of the Peace and Mackenzie River Area. Edmonton—The Gateway* (Edmonton: Town Topics Publishing Co., 1930), n.p.

3. See for example, Morris Zaslow, "The Development of the Mackenzie Basin 1920–1940."

4. Carl Berger, *The Writing of Canadian History* (Toronto: Oxford University Press, 1976), 94–98; Graeme Patterson, *History and Communications, Harold Innis, Marshall McLuhan, the Interpretation of History* (Toronto: University of Toronto Press, 1990), 79, 135.

5. The distance of these extensions was: Peace River to Berwyn, 37 kilometres; Berwyn to Whitelaw, 21 kilometres; Whitelaw to Fairview, 22 kilometres; Grande Prairie to Wembley, 24 kilometres; and Wembley to Hythe, 39 kilometres.

6. Memorandum for Neuberger, July 4, 1949, 86.587/360A, PAA; NAR Report for the Six Months Ending December 31, 1929, 86.587/706, PAA.

7. Rea, *The Political Economy of the Canadian North*, 64; *Annual Report, Department of Railways of the Province of Alberta [for] 1927* (typescript), 86.587/705, PAA; NAR, Report for the Six Months Ending December 31, 1929 (copy in 86.587/706, PAA); Irwin, "Whose Railway Was It?," 125.

8. Denzil Garrett, "The Northern Alberta Railway. A Geographical Analysis" (Master's thesis, University of Alberta, 1962), 41; Judgement, file No. 38702, Board of Railway Commissioners for Canada, *Judgements, Orders, Regulations and Rulings*, vol. 23, August 1, 1933, 158.

9. Willis, "The Development of Transportation in the Peace River Region," 47; Irwin, "The Emergence of a Regional Identity," 134. In 1920, it cost 39.6 cents per bushel to ship wheat from Grande Prairie to the Lakehead; by 1926 it cost 16.8 cents per bushel to Vancouver (Zaslow, "The Struggle for the Peace River Outlet," 279, 282).

10. Report, Board of Railway Commissioners, February 9, 1938, 86.587/265, PAA; Memo Re: Waterways Subdivision, September 18, 1946, 86.587/2812B, PAA.

11. Minister to Cartwright, February 29, 1932, General Manager to Draper, March 29, 1932 and Peace River Chamber of Commerce to Board of Railway Commissioners, December 2, 1932, 86.587/2809b, PAA; Clipping (1932) "The Water Route to Great Bear Lake…", M622, file 7, GAI.

12. Journal of the Eighteenth Session of the Synod of the Diocese of Athabasca, Peace River, June 29–30, 1938, AP, A.220/23, Box 21, PAA.

13. Zaslow, *Northward Expansion of Canada*, 102–3, 107, 114, 186; *Calgary Herald*, December 23, 1935. Goldfields was formerly called Beaver Lodge.

14. Clippings, 1934–35, General Manager to Neale, April 29, 1936, 86.587/2809a, PAA; General Manager to Hobbs, November 5, 1937, General Manager to Gilles, March 5, 1938, and clippings, June 1938, 86.587/2810b, PAA.

15. *Board of Railway Commissioners of Canada*, vol. 36, January 15, 1947 (no. 20), Judgement, file No. 38118, October 22–23, 1946, pp. 331–33.

16. *Edmonton Journal*, May 9, 1935

17. Shoubridge to Minister, March 9, 1931, 67.303/6082, PAA; Keith to Clutchey, February 26, 1930, 67.303/352, PAA; *Edmonton Journal*, February 10, 1945; *Grande Prairie Herald*, February 21, 1922 and March 23, 1928; *Peace River Record*, July 8, 1926; Willis, "Development of Transportation in the Peace River Region," 55–61.

18. Inspector to Hrycun, February 4, 1930, 67.303/10035, PAA.

19. Roadmaster to MacArthur, February 23, 1939, Agent to MacArthur, June 22, 1939, Johnston to Tye, January 30, 1940 and MacArthur to Agent, January 11, 1940 and clipping, October 13, 1948, 86.587/1244, PAA; *Peace River Record*, December 16, 1938; Shoubridge to Minister, March 9, 1931, 67.303/6082, PAA.

20. *The [Waterhole] Northern Review*, January 29, 1924.

21. Zaslow, "The Struggle for the Peace River Outlet," 274; *Maclean's*, October 1, 1924; W.D. Albright, "Settlers' Interest The Key to the Solution of Peace River Transportation Problem" (Text of speech delivered in Vancouver, March 12, 1930), Information file, "Peace River" (file 2), PAA.

22. *The [Waterhole] Northern Review*, January 29, 1924; *Spirit River Echo*, April 9, 1920; Minute Book, March 6 and 7 and April 5, 1924, and May 23, 1925, Municipal District of Spirit River Papers (microfilm), 70.237, PAA. On the feasibility of the Brule cut-off, see: Memo Re: Brule-Grande Prairie Line, January 18, 1924, 86.587/85, PAA. The Brule cut-off was also called the Obed cut-off.

23. *[Waterhole] Northern Review*, May 29, 1923 and February 5, 1924; *Spirit River Echo*, February 25, 1921; Zaslow, "The Struggle for the Peace River Outlet," 281–82.

24. *Peace River Record*, December 16, 1927; *Edmonton Journal*, November 24, 1928. On the Hudson's Bay railway, see Zaslow, *The Northward Expansion of Canada*, 38–39.

25. *Grande Prairie Herald*, February 27, 1923 and May 11, 1925; *Peace River Record*, December 27, 1927 and February 10, 1928.

26. Schull, *Ontario Since 1867*, 247; Geoffrey Weller, "Political Disaffection in the Canadian Provincial North," *Bulletin of Canadian Studies* [U.K.], 9 (1985): 72; *Peace River Record*, December 2, 1927 and February 24, 1928.

27. *Peace River Record*, December 2, 1927 and February 10 and 24, 1928; "A Province in the Making," *Maclean's*, February 1, 1928; Robert Bothwell, Ian Drummond and John English, *Canada 1900–1945* (Toronto: University of Toronto Press, 1987), 242.

28. *Peace River Record*, December 2, 1927.

29. *Edmonton Journal*, February 25, 1937 and *Grande Prairie Northern Tribune*, September 30, 1937. The lasting appeal of the coast outlet railway was shown by demands for it as late as the end of World War II. Proponents remained divided between those wanting a direct coast outlet through British Columbia and those, mainly in Grande Prairie, who continued to want the Brule cut-off. This was, however, only an echo of past struggles.

30. *[Grande Prairie] Northern Tribune*, February 18, 1937.

31. *Edmonton Journal*, February 15, 1937.

32. Sovereign to Smith, November 4, 1938, AP, A.320/1155, Box A.81, PAA

33. *[Grande Prairie] Northern Tribune*, September 19, 1935; *Edmonton Journal*, January 23 and June 11, 1937; Roadmaster to MacArthur, n.d. (1937) 86.587/1242, PAA.

34. The Monkman Pass Highway Association, Project Sheet No. 3, November 7, 1938 (copy in 86.587/1242, PAA); *Edmonton Journal*, December 20, 29 and 31, 1938, February 24, 1939 and January 20, 1940; Isabel Perry, *Euphemia McNaught: Pioneer Artist of the Peace* (Beaverlodge District Historical Association, a Reidmore Book, 1982), 42; Richard J. Chamberlain, "Monkman Pass," *The Beaver*, Outfit 312:1 (1981): 8–13.

35. *Peace River Record*, May 13, 1938; *Annual Report for the Year 1937 by the Department of Immigration and Colonization of the CPR Concerning Colonization and Land Settlement in the Peace River District*,

86.587/658, PAA; Irwin, "The Emergence of a Regional Identity," 247; *Peace River Block News*, June 2, 1938 (copy in 86.587/1242). There were three passes through which a road could be built: the Monkman Pass (elevation 1079 metres), the Pine Pass (866 metres) and the Peace Pass (577 metres).

36. *Grande Prairie Herald*, December 8, 1938; *Edmonton Journal*, February 25, 1937, January 20, 1940, May 15, 1941, February 3, 1944 and October 16, 1946. For a sampling of the extensive literature on the Alaska Highway, see *Three Northern Wartime Projects*, ed. Bob Hesketh (Edmonton: Canadian Circumpolar Institute and Edmonton and District Historical Society, Occasional Publication Series No. 28, 1996) and Kenneth Coates and William Morrison, *The Alaska Highway in World War II. The U.S. Army of Occupation in Canada's Northwest* (Norman: University of Oklahoma Press , 1992).

37. *Peace River Record Gazette*, March 1, 1946; "Peace River," n.d., Information file, "Peace River," PAA; Peace River Board of Trade to McNamara, January 18, 1932 (copy), M622, file 1, GAI.

38. *Nor'West Miner*, September 1, 1937 and November 1938; David A. Harrison, "The First Winter Road Ever," *Up Here* 6 (1990): 55–57.

39. Cornwall to Aberhart, November 30, 1937 (copy), 86.587/46b, PAA; *Nor'West Miner*, September 1, 1937; *Peace River Record*, September 17, 1937; *Edmonton Bulletin*, November 4, 1937.

40. MacArthur, Weekly Letter, August 25, 1937, Warren to MacArthur, October 2, 1937 and Clipping, April 1, 1938, 86.587/46b, PAA; *Peace River Record*, May 13, 1938.

41. Telegram Memo, April 6, 1938, 86.587/46b, PAA; *Peace River Record*, April 29, 1938.

42. *Peace River Record*, April 29, 1938; *Edmonton Journal*, April 21 and 28, 1938.

43. *Edmonton Journal*, December 19, 1938; *Peace River Record*, December 30, 1938 and December 15, 1939; Irwin, "The Emergence of a Regional Identity," 255–58; Memo, March 14, 1941, clipping and memo, February 10, 1945, and MacArthur to Mather, June 1, 1944, 86.587/46b, PAA; *Edmonton Bulletin*, February 9, 1939.

44. Report of Survey of Proposed Trucking Service, Great Slave Lake Road, July 1, 1948, 86.587/2816, PAA. The road was gradually upgraded and in the 1950s was extended around the west end of Great Slave Lake to Yellowknife (David A. Harrison, "Opening and Naming the Mackenzie Highway," *Alberta History* 38 (1990): 24–29).

45. Ryan to Robertson, June 18, 1927, 67.303/3510, PAA; MacGregor, *From Paddle Wheels to Bucket Wheels*, 163.

46. Telegrams, March 15, 1938 and February 12, 1938, file 86.587/973a, PAA; Memo re: Annual Report for 1938, 86.587/659, PAA.

47. *Edmonton Journal*, March 5, 1938 and March 9, 1939; MacGregor, *Paddle Wheels to Bucket Wheels*, 165.

48. McCardle, *The Rules of the Game*, 83; Ray, *The Canadian Fur Trade in the Industrial Age*, 116–17.

49. Ray, *The Canadian Fur Trade in the Industrial Age*, 142, 161–63. The Northern Trading Company was wound up in 1946.

50. Zaslow, *Northward Expansion of Canada*, 9. 138; Gordon G. Thiessen, "Transportation on the Mackenzie River System." (Master's thesis, University of Saskatchewan, 1962), 19–29, 31–32; Report, Board of Railway Commissioners, February 9, 1938, 86.587/265, PAA;

*Edmonton Journal*, March 14, 1938; Ommanney to Dennis, November 1, 1929, 86.587/26, PAA.

51. MacKinnon, "Portaging on the Slave River," 26–29; various correspondence, 1923–29, 67.303/3510, PAA; *Edmonton Bulletin*, June 13, 1923.

52. Ryan to Minister, February 11, 1927 and Ryan to Robertson, August 4, 1928, and Keith to O'Neill, January 27, 1933, 67.303/3510, PAA; Newson to Officer Commanding, August 12, 1933, Department of the Attorney General Papers, 82.212, file142, PAA; MacKinnon, "Portaging on the Slave River," 29–30. Cornwall to Secretary, February 27, 1932, 86.587/2809a, PAA.

53. Thiessen, "Transportation on the Mackenzie River System," 31–32; Eldorado's nationalization in 1944 gave the federal government control over the Northern Transportation Company. As a crown corporation, the company received little attention from Ottawa, other than a demand that it operate at a profit (Thiessen, 41–44).

54. Thiessen, "Transportation on the Mackenzie River System," 21–22, 31–32, 45, 114–20; *Board of Railway Commissioners of Canada*, vol. 36, January 15, 1947 (No. 20), Judgement, file No. 38118, October 22–23, 1946, pp 331–33; Edgar D. Cooke, "Boom and Bust, Bust and Boom: Fort McMurray and Waterways," in *The Land of Peter Pond*, ed. John Chalmers (Edmonton: Boreal Institute for Northern Studies, Occasional Publication No. 12, 1974), 103; MacGregor, *From Paddle Wheels to Bucket Wheels*, 167. Sovereign to Dixon, July 28, 1942, AP, A.320/718, Box A.64, PAA; Memo, Portage on Slave River, August 28, 1946, 86.587/2812B, PAA; MacKinnon, "Portaging on the Slave River," 31.

55. Patricia Myers, *Sky Riders. An Illustrated History of Aviation in Alberta 1906–1945* (Saskatoon: Fifth House, 1995), 33–58, 120–21; *A History of the Royal Canadian Mounted Police Aviation Section* (Ottawa: Information Canada, 1973), not paginated; *Report of the Postmaster General for the Year Ended March 31, 1930*, 5.

56. John W. Chalmers, "Wayfaring, Airborne and Earthbound," in *The Land of Peter Pond*, ed. John Chalmers (Edmonton: Boreal Institute for Northern Studies, Occasional Publication No. 12, 1974), 91. In 1959 CP Air northern operations were taken over by Pacific Western, a company established in Vancouver in 1945.

57. Myers, *Sky Riders*, 119–51; *Grande Prairie Herald*, March 15, 1929.

58. *Annual Report, RCMP [for] 1929*, 40; Daily Journal, St. Paul's, 1929 and 1930, passim and November 29, 1931, AP, file A.13/11, Box A.E., PAA. Philip Godsell made the same observation in his comment that the north became "air minded overnight" (Godsell, *Arctic Trader*, 307).

59. Myers, *Sky Riders*, 127; Report, Board of Railway Commissioners, February 9, 1938, 86.587/265, PAA; MacGregor, *From Paddle Wheels to Bucket Wheels*, 164–65; *Calgary Herald*, February 8, 1936.

60. Evidence and Proceedings, Ewing Commission, p.140, 75.75/9, PAA; Ray, *The Canadian Fur Trade in the Industrial Age*, 189. The company used planes in other parts of northern Canada in response to their use by competitors.

61. *Annual Report, [Canada] Department of Transport for the Fiscal Year from April 1, 1939 to March 31, 1940*, 21–22; *Annual Report, [Canada] Department of Transport for the Fiscal Year from April 1, 1941 to March 31, 1942*, 113; Charles F. O'Brien, "Northwest Staging Route," *Alberta Historical Review* 17 (1969): 15, 22.

62. Petition, Peace River Chamber of Commerce, n.d. [March 1945], copy in AP, A.320/819 Box A.68, PAA; Chalmers, "Wayfaring, Airborne and Earthbound," 89, 91; *Edmonton Journal*, November 22, 1939; O'Brien, "Northwest Staging Route," 22.

63. Irwin, "The Emergence of a Regional Identity," 269–70; *Peace River Record Gazette*, May 31, 1946.

64. Roadmaster to Deakin, August 29, 1945, Price to Perry, July 18, 1966 and Weekly Letter, March 22, 1944, 86.587/1245, PAA.

65. Barman, *The West Beyond the West*, 281.

## ——8

### The Evolution of Separate Societies

1. Dawson and Murchie, *Settlement of the Peace River Country*, 54; Leppard, "The Settlement of the Peace River Country," 68; Wetherell and Kmet, *Town Life*, 82–84; *Peace River Record*, March 1, 1946.

2. Ray, *The Canadian Fur Trade in the Industrial Age*, 148; "Annual Report 'E' Division," Peace River, December 31, 1925, 72.370, PAA; *Peace River Record*, May 7, 1925.

3. Dawson and Murchie, *Settlement of the Peace River Country*, 49–50.

4. *Spirit River Echo*, March 4, 1921; *The [Waterhole] Northern Review*, December 4, 1923 and February 5, 1924; *Peace River Record*, October 21 and November 4, 1926.

5. *Peace River Record*, October 19, 1928; Dawson and Murchie, *Settlement of the Peace River Country*, 49–50.

6. Hansen, *Where Go the Boats*, 15–17; F.H. Kitto, *The Peace River Country Canada. Its Resources and Opportunities* 1st Edition (Ottawa: Department of the Interior, 1920), 23; St Luke's Centennial Historical Committee, *Unchaga Peace*, 27–29; Crayson to Deputy Minister, April 29, 1938, Agricultural Societies of Alberta Papers, M2360, file 342, GAI.

7. Darlene Comfort, *The Abasand Fiasco* (Edmonton: Friesen Printers, 1980), 45.

8. "An Empire in the Making," n.p; Memo, May 18, 1936, 86.587/351, PAA; Manning to McLean, May 5, 1921, 67.303/10935, PAA; Reid to Warren, December 7, 1933, 86.587/86.

9. Chalmers, "The Muskeg Flier," 82; Ommanney to Dennis, November 1, 1929, 86.587/26, PAA; General Manager to Coleman, November 21, 1929, 86.587/353, PAA; Report, Board of Railway Commissioners, February 9, 1938, 86.587/265, PAA; *Edmonton Journal*, March 14, 1938.

10. James Stead, *Treasure Trek* (London: George Routledge and Sons, 1936), 114; McMurray Board of Trade to NAR, January 20, 1939, and General Manager to Devenish, January 22, 1945, 86.587/276b, PAA; Ommanney to Dennis, November 1, 1929, 86.587/26, PAA; *The Nor'West Miner*, January 1936.

11. Roth to McPherson, February 3, 1931, 67.303/10935, PAA; Hugh Mackay Ross, *The Manager's Tale* (Winnipeg: Watson and Dwyer Publishing, 1989), 26–28; Gordon Briggs, "Waterways," *The Beaver*, Outfit 270 No. 2 (September 1939): 28.

12. *The Nor'West Miner*, May and April 1935; Comfort, *The Abasand Fiasco*, 84–87; J.A. Turcotte, *Memoirs of a Jubelarian 1924–1947* (Fort McMurray: Fort McMurray Catholic Board of Education, 1985), 82; Parker, *History of the Athabasca Oil Sands Region*. Vol. 2 *Oral History*, 35; "Fort McMurray, Alberta," n.d. (ca. 1947), AP, A.1/61, Box A.2, PAA; Griffith Taylor,

"Arctic Survey III. A Mackenzie Domesday: 1944," *Canadian Journal of Economics and Political Science* 11 (1945): 199–202.

13. Ray, *The Canadian Fur Trade in the Industrial Age*, 107, 116–17, 193; McCormack, "How The (North) West Was Won," 317–31.

14. McCardle, *The Rules of the Game*, 83; Frank Jackson, *Jam in the Bedroll* (Nanaimo: Shires Books, 1979), 13–14.

15. Ray, *The Canadian Fur Trade in the Industrial Age*, 142; McCormack, "How The (North) West Was Won," 67, 84, 366, 379–81.

16. Mathewson, "The Geographical Impact of Outsiders…Fort Chipewyan," 85–88; McCormack, "How The (North) West Was Won," 253–54.

17. McCormack, "How The (North) West Was Won," 83, 316–36; Parker, *History of the Athabasca Oil Sands Region* Vol. 2, *Oral History*, 26–28; Mathewson, "The Geographical Impact of Outsiders…Fort Chipewyan," 88–91; *Annual Report, RCMP for 1931*, 107; Daily Journal, St. Paul's, July 1931, AP, file A.13/11, Box A.E., PAA. On treaty day at Wabasca, see Jack Milne, *Trading for Milady's Furs. In Service of the Hudson's Bay Company 1923–1943* (Saskatoon: Western Producer Prairie Books, 1975), 95–96.

18. Clara Vyvyan, *The Ladies, The Gwich'in, and The Rat*, eds. I.S. MacLaren and Lisa N. LaFramboise (Edmonton: University of Alberta Press, 1998), 31; Urquhart to Sovereign, June 5, 1942, AP, A.320/946, Box A.73, PAA; MacKinnon, "Portaging on the Slave River," 26, 29; "An Empire in the Making", n.p.; Zaslow, *The Northward Expansion of Canada*, 24–25; Taylor, "Arctic Survey III," 204–5.

19. Buchanan and Hunt to Manning, December 29, 1920, 78.099c, Box 5, file 5, UCAT; *Grande Prairie Herald*, December 16 and 23, 1913.

20. Buchanan and Hunt to Manning, December 29, 1920, 78.099c, Box 5, file 5, UCAT; *Grande Prairie Herald*, August 16 and 23, 1921; *Peace River Record*, October 25, 1929 and December 13, 1930; F.H. Kitto, *The Peace River Country Canada. Its Resources and Opportunities*, 3rd revised edition (Ottawa: Department of the Interior, 1930), 71.

21. Hitchins to Ward, April 26, 1939 and Hitchins to Council, August 15, 1940, MD of Nelson Papers, 68.278, file 45bo, PAA. The municipality's obligation was based on the patient's financial status at time of hospitalization, not before or after. If a patient's financial condition improved subsequently, the municipality was free to pursue him for its earlier expenditures for his hospitalization.

22. Council Minutes, July 7, 1923, July 25, 1925, February 19 and July 9, 1927, MD of Spirit River Papers, 70.237 (microfilm), PAA; Council Minutes, March 3, 1918, January 8, 1921, September 8, 1928, and February 15, 1936, MD of Fairview Papers, 70.208 (microfilm), PAA.

23. Scarth to Sweeney, February 3, 1940, Department of Agriculture Papers, 73.307, file 224, PAA; Sovereign to Corpus, December 16, 1936, AP, A.320/471, Box A.55, PAA; "Notikewin" n.d. (1936), 83.058C, Box 10, file 128, UCAT.

24. *History, Administrative Organization and Work of the Provincial Department of Public Health and Boards of Health* (Edmonton: King's Printer, 1937), 5, 9; Buchanan and Hunt to Manning, December 29, 1920, 78.099c, Box 5, file 5, UCAT; Richardson to Mackenzie, April 26, 1946, AP, A.320/624, Box A.62, PAA.

25. Report for April 1933, Lesser Slave Lake Agency, RG10, vol. 11949, Shannon No. 4, Pt. 2, NAC; Statement of Duties, N. L'Heureux, n.d. [1940], RG10, vol. 11949, Shannon No. 4, Pt. 1, NAC; Zaslow, *The Northward Expansion of Canada*, 170–73.

26. Evidence and Proceedings, Ewing Commission, 126, 138–40, 75.75/9, PAA; Memo for Ewing, May 16, 1935, 75.75/4A, PAA; Fumoleau, *As Long as This Land Shall Last*, 265; McCormack, "How The (North) West Was Won," 354–56; Gooderham to Hoey, January 12, 1948, RG10, vol. 6743, file 420-2-1-1, Reel C-8096, NAC; Parker, *History of the Athabasca Oil Sands Region*, Vol. 2. *Oral History*, 41.

27. Memo to Ewing, May 16, 1935, 75.75/4a, PAA; Evidence and Proceedings, Ewing Commission, pp. 8, 17, 62, 101, 75.75/9, PAA; Ken Hatt, "Ethnic Discourse in Alberta: Land and the Metis in the Ewing Commission," *Canadian Ethnic Studies* 17 (1985): 73–74; Extract from Report, Grouard, August 11, 1922, and Third Report, Grouard, September 11, 1922, 75.75/4c, PAA.

28. Minute Book, MD of Nelson, December 10, 1935 and April 11, 1936, 68.278, PAA.

29. Hitchins to Mills, June 9, 1923, 68.278/276, Box 28, PAA; Minutes, April 1, 1937, 70.208, Reel 1A, PAA. On Indians and relief projects, see Report for May 1936 and Report for June 1936, Lesser Slave Lake Agency, RG10, vol. 11949, Shannon No. 4, Pt. 1, NAC.

30. Deputy Minister to Cour, January 7, 1931, 67.303/12,434, PAA; *Annual Report, Alberta Department of Agriculture for 1933*, 76–77.

31. In order to establish a school district, there had to be sufficient number of pupils (usually eight), enough assessable property to pay for the operation of the school, and the consent of a majority of adults who would elect the school board. In parts of northern Alberta, the latter two requirements formed a mutually reinforcing barrier to establishing a school district and administering and paying for it (John W. Chalmers, "Schools For Our Other Indians: Education of Western Canadian Metis Children," in *The Canadian West. Social Change and Economic Development*, ed. Henry C. Klassen (Calgary: University of Calgary Comprint Publishing Company, 1977), 95–96).

32. Kitto, *The Peace River Country* (3rd revised edition, 1930), 63; William H. Swift, *Memoirs of a Frontier School Inspector in Alberta*, ed. John W. Chalmers (Edmonton: Education Society of Edmonton, Occasional Publication No. 1, 1986), 36; Gooderham to Hoey, January 12, 1948, RG10, vol. 6734, file 420-1-1-3, Reel C-8096, NAC; A.D. Fisher, "A Colonial Education System: Historical Changes in Schooling in Fort Chipewyan," *Canadian Journal of Anthropology* 2 (1981): 41.

33. Evidence and Proceedings, Ewing Commission, 27, 31, 37, 58–59, 75.75/9, PAA; Ewing Commission, Final Report(copy in 75.75, PAA), 17; *Edmonton Journal*, February 23 and 29, 1933; William D. Knill, "Schools in the Wilderness," in *On The Edge of the Shield. Fort Chipewyan and its Hinterland*, ed. John W. Chalmers (Edmonton: The Boreal Institute for Northern Studies, University of Alberta, Occasional Publication No. 7, 1971), 34.

34. Westgate to Crerar, January 28, 1942, AP, A.320/572, Box A.58, PAA; Report Concerning Indian Work, March 1939, AP, A.320/577, Box A.58, PAA.

35. Evidence and Proceedings, Ewing Commission, 144, 75.75/9, PAA; Westgate to Crerar, January 28, 1942, AP, A.320/572, Box A.58, PAA.

36. Lesser Slave Lake Indian Agent Diary, October 1931, August 1933, January 1934, M2218, GAI; Report, November 18, 1930 and L'Heureux to Christianson, September 18, 1934,

RG10, vol. 11949, Shannon No. 4, Pt. 2, NAC; Zaslow, *The Northward Expansion of Canada*, 162. In 1934, Indians at Hay Lakes asked that a residential school be established there so that their children would not have to go to school at far-away Fort Vermilion.

37. Reports for January 1937, March 1937, February 1938, and March 1938, Lesser Slave Lake Agency, RG10, vol. 11949, Shannon No. 4, Pt. 1, NAC; Indian Agent to Graham, December 19, 1925, RG10, vol. 11950, Shannon No. 7, NAC. For prewar enforcement of attendance, see Patrol Report, Lesser Slave Lake Detachment, January 30, 1914, RG18, vol. 1753, file 130 Pt. 1, NAC.

38. Huel, *Proclaiming the Gospel*, 226–39.

39. Report of Missionary Work Done During 1936, AP, A.320/1144, Box A.81, PAA.

<br>

## ——9
### Farm Settlement

1. Burke G. Vanderhill, "The Passing of the Pioneer Fringe in Western Canada," *The Geographical Review* 72 (1982): 200.

2. Dawson and Murchie, *Settlement of the Peace River Country*, 66–68; CPR, Department of Immigration and Colonization, *Annual Report 1930, Peace River Alberta*, 86.587/706, PAA; *Edmonton Journal*, August 30, 1929.

3. Dawson and Murchie, *Settlement of the Peace River Country*, 62–64; CPR, Department of Immigration and Colonization, *Annual Report 1930, Peace River, Alberta*, 86.587/706, PAA.

4. Wayne Jackson, "Ethnicity and Areal Organization Among French Canadian in the Peace River District, Alberta" (Master's thesis, University of Alberta, 1970), 22–34; [Canada Colonization Association] *Annual Report, Covering Colonization and Land Settlement Activities in the Peace River Areas of Alberta and British Columbia, March 17, 1941*, 3, 86.587/399, PAA.

5. CPR, Department of Immigration and Colonization, *Annual Report 1930, Peace River, Alberta*, 86.587/706, PAA; *Peace River Record*, September 30, 1938; Martin to Aberhart, August 24, 1942, Alberta Sessional Papers, 70.414, file 2101, PAA.

6. There is an extensive literature on this topic. See for example, Judith Wiesinger, "Modelling the Agricultural Settlement Process of Southern Manitoba, 1872–1891: Some Implications for Settlement Theory," *Prairie Forum* 10 (1985): 87–89.

7. Circular Materials Re: Peace River Country, n.d. (ca. 1917), RG15, vol. 1121, file 3,272,781, NAC. Most school lands were purchased by established farmers to expand existing holdings (Carl Tracie, "Agricultural Settlement in the South Peace River Area," 113).

8. Donald Stone, "The Process of Rural Settlement in the Athabasca Area, Alberta" (Master's thesis, University of Alberta, 1970), 170–71; Leppard, "The Settlement of the Peace River Country," 69.

9. Zaslow, *The Northward Expansion of Canada*, 46–47; W.D. Albright, "Settlers' Interest: The Key to the Solution of Peace River Transportation Problem" (Text of Speech given in Vancouver, March 12, 1930), Information file "Peace River" (file 2), PAA; E.J. Ashton, "Peace River" (typescript), November 26, 1928, 73.307/14, PAA.

10. Margaret Crawford, "A Geographic Study of the Distribution of Population Change in Alberta, 1931–1961" (Master's thesis, University of Alberta, 1962), 17; Dawson and

Murchie, *Settlement of the Peace River Country*, 45, 61; *Edmonton Journal*, December 15, 1928, October 18, 1930, August 13, 1931; Tracie, "Agricultural Settlement in the South Peace River Area," 113; Kitto, *The Peace River Country* (3rd revised edition, 1930), 31–32.

11.   Willis, "Development of Transportation in the Peace River Region," 44; Zaslow, "The Struggle for the Peace River Outlet," 283. *Edmonton Journal*, November 24, 1928; Kitto, *The Peace River Country* (3rd revised edition, 1930), 28; NAR, Report for the Six Months Ending December 31, 1929, 86.587/706, PAA; *"An Empire in the Making"*, n.p.

12.   *The [Waterhole] Northern Review*, March 4, 1928 (reprinting article from the CPR magazine, *Agricultural and Industrial Development in Canada*). See also *Peace River Record*, April 5, 1929; *Edmonton Journal*, November 24, 1928 and August 29, 1929.

13.   Dawson and Murchie, *Settlement of the Peace River Country*, 15; Isabel Perry, *Euphemia McNaught*, 21. See also T.D. Maclulich, "Reading the Land: The Wilderness Tradition in Canadian Letters," *Journal of Canadian Studies*, 20 (1985): 29–44 and Peter Larisey, "Nationalist Aspects of Lawren Harris's Aesthetics," *Bulletin*, National Gallery of Canada 23 (1974): 3–9.

14.   See for example, *Maclean's*, October 1, 1924.

15.   Leppard, "The Settlement of the Peace River Country," 65; Tracie, "Agricultural Settlement in the South Peace River Area," 57–67, 114; *Edmonton Journal*, November 24 and December 15, 1928; E.J. Ashton, "Peace River" (typescript), November 26, 1928, 73.307/14, PAA.

16.   CPR, Department of Immigration and Colonization, *Annual Report, 1930, Peace River, Alberta*, 86.587/706, PAA; Jackson, *Jam in the Bedroll*, 25; Dawson and Murchie, *Settlement of the Peace River Country*, 16; *Edmonton Journal*, December 15, 1928 and August 30, 1929.

17.   Leppard, "The Settlement of the Peace River Country," 69–71; Memo by Buchanan, n.d. (August 1934), 86.587/265B, PAA.

18.   CPR, Department of Immigration and Colonization, *Annual Report 1930, Peace River, Alberta*, 86.587/706, PAA; B.K. Acton, "A Comparison of Farms in the Grande Prairie District of Alberta 1930 and 1942," *Economic Annalist* 13 (1943): 54.

19.   CPR, Department of Immigration and Colonization, *Annual Report 1930, Peace River, Alberta*, 86.587/706, PAA. On off-farm work at Valleyview in the 1920s, see Williamson, "Valleyview's First Settlers," 34.

20.   *Edmonton Journal*, December 11, 1939; Zaslow, "The Struggle for the Peace River Outlet," 291; Garrett, "The Northern Alberta Railway. A Geographical Analysis" (Master's thesis, University of Alberta, 1962), 40; James Gray, *Men Against the Desert* (Saskatoon: Western Producer Prairie Books, 1967), 186; CPR, Department of Immigration and Colonization, *Annual Report, 1931, Peace River*, 86.587/37, PAA. On immigration policy, see Jean R. Burnet and Howard Palmer, *"Coming Canadians" An Introduction to a History of Canada's Peoples* (Toronto: Canada Department of the Secretary of State and McClelland and Stewart, 1988), 37–38.

21.   Agent to Callaghan, May 14, 1936, 85.587/351, PAA; "Notikewin," (n.d. 1936), 83.058c, Box 10, file 128, UCAT.

22.   *Annual Report, Alberta Department of Agriculture for 1933*, 76–77; *The Mission Field* May 1938, 133, copy in AP, A.420/81, Box A.108, PAA; Swift, *Memoirs of a Frontier School Inspector*, 35.

23. On Saskatchewan see: T.J.D. Powell, "Northern Settlement 1929–1935," *Saskatchewan History* 30 (1977): 81–98, and John McDonald, "Soldier Settlement and Depression Settlement in the Forest Fringe of Saskatchewan," *Prairie Forum* 6 (1981): 35–54.

24. *Annual Report, Alberta Department of Agriculture for 1932*, 48; *Annual Report, Alberta Department of Agriculture for 1933*, 53–54; *Annual Report, Alberta Department of Agriculture for 1934*, 28; *Annual Report, Alberta Department of Agriculture for 1935*, 33; CNR, Department of Colonization and Agriculture, *Land Settlement Activities, Peace River, 1934*, 86.587/37, PAA. Of the 601 families who moved in 1934, only 80 went to the Peace River country.

25. *Annual Report, Alberta Department of Agriculture for 1932*, 48; *Annual Report, Alberta Department of Agriculture for 1934*, 29; *Annual Report, Alberta Department of Agriculture for 1943*, 114; *Annual Report, Alberta Department of Agriculture for 1948*, 150. See also Department of Agriculture Papers, 67.21, file 275, PAA. Only families (not single men) with farm experience were eligible. Provided with a repayable start-up loan and a subsistence allowance, they had to participate in a personal interview and have selected a homestead that provincial officials inspected for land quality and distance from schools and transportation.

26. *Annual Report, Alberta Department of Agriculture for 1933*, 55; CNR, Department of Colonization and Agriculture, *Land Settlement Activities, Peace River, 1934*, 86.587/37, PAA; *Edmonton Journal*, June 12, 1935.

27. *Annual Report, Alberta Department of Agriculture for 1943*, 115; *Annual Report, Alberta Department of Agriculture for 1944*, 134; *Annual Report, Alberta Department of Agriculture for 1948*, 150.

28. Powell, "Northern Settlement 1929–1935," 95; Macdonald, "Soldier Settlement and Depression Settlement in the Forest Fringe," 47.

29. Sovereign to Corpus, December 16, 1936, AP, A.320/471, Box A.55, PAA; "Appeal for a Hospital," n.d. (1936), AP, A.320/373, Box A.51, PAA.

30. Whittaker to Red Cross Society, September 11, 1931, and Secretary Treasurer to Ficht, April 6, 1938, (MD of Nelson correspondence) 68.278.

31. Memo by Buchanan, n.d. (August 1934), 86.587/265B, PAA; B.K. Acton and C.C. Spence, *A Study of Pioneer Farming in the Fringe Areas of the Peace River, Alberta, 1942* (Ottawa: Department of Agriculture, Publication No. 792, Technical Bulletin No. 60, 1947), 12; *Peace River Record*, July 17, 1936.

32. CNR, Department of Colonization and Agriculture, *Land Settlement Activities, Peace River, 1940*, 86.587/399, PAA.

33. Macalister to MacArthur, April 2, 1941, 86.587/399 PAA; CNR, Department of Colonization and Agriculture, *Annual Report NAR Territory, 1943*, 86.587/399, PAA; *Edmonton Journal*, September 25, 1943.

34. Goldfinch to Sovereign, July 22, 1944, AP, A.320/1110, Box A.79, PAA; CNR, Department of Colonization and Agriculture, *Annual Report, NAR Territory, 1945*, 86.587/399, PAA. The cash advance was for up to $2,300. To receive it, a veteran had to stay on the land for 10 years.

35. [Canada Colonization Association] *Annual Report for 1945 Covering Colonization and Land Settlement Activities in the Peace River Area of Alberta and British Columbia*, and CNR, Department of Colonization and Agriculture, *Annual Report NAR Territory, 1945*, 86.587/399, PAA.

36. *Annual Report for 1946 Covering Colonization and Land Settlement Activities in the Peace River Area of Alberta and British Columbia*, 86.587/399, PAA.

37. CNR, Department of Colonization and Agriculture, *Annual Report, NAR Territory, 1946*, 86.587/399.

38. Irwin, "The Emergence of Regional Identity," 68; Athabasca Historical Society, *Athabasca Landing: An Illustrated History*, 96–103; Zaslow, *The Northward Expansion of Canada*, 56–57; *Grande Prairie Herald*, October 1, 1937.

39. *Family Herald and Weekly Star*, July 25, 1923.

40. *Family Herald and Weekly Star*, July 25, 1923. See also *Grande Prairie Herald*, April 3, 1923. Such arguments were common elsewhere on the prairies. For Manitoba, see for example, J.W. Armstrong, "Municipal Problems in Western Provinces," *Conservation of Life* 3 (No. 3, July 1917): 59–63.

41. Wetherell and Kmet, *Town Life*, 164–68; "Planning for Future Settlement," n.d. [1930], 71.4, PAA.

42. *Edmonton Journal*, January 3, 1930 and August 14, 1934.

43. Publications such as Kitto, *The Peace River Country Canada* (three printings and two editions, 1920–30) and Canada Department of the Interior, *The Lac La Biche District, Alberta. A Guide to Intending Settlers* (Ottawa: King's Printer, 1923) were examples of these promotional efforts.

44. Fitzallen to Stewart, August 24, 1922 and replies, September 22, 1922 and January 3, 1923, RG15, vol. 1,147, file 4,726,662, NAC.

45. *Edmonton Journal*, August 13, 1931; Macdonald, "Soldier Settlement and Depression Settlement in the Forest Fringe," 43; *Grande Prairie Herald*, February 13, 1931. Saskatchewan sold arable crown land to settlers, with provincial residents receiving preference, but the province restored homesteading in 1935.

46. *Edmonton Journal*, December 6, 1932. Under the former system, only widows with minor children and deserted women could file for a homestead.

47. CNR, Departments of Colonization and Agriculture, *Land Settlement Activities, Peace River 1939*, 86.587/399, PAA.

48. Buchanan to Herzer, September 14, 1939, 86.587/1244, PAA.

49. CNR, Departments of Colonization and Agriculture, *Land Settlement Activities, Peace River 1939*, 86.587/399, PAA; CNR, Department of Colonization and Agriculture, *Land Settlement Activities, Peace River, 1940*, 86.587/399, PAA.

50. *Annual Report for 1947 Covering Colonization and Land Settlement Activities in the Peace River Area of Alberta and British Columbia*, 86.587/399, PAA; Tracie, "Agricultural Settlement in the South Peace River Area," 20, 114; Vanderhill, "The Passing of the Pioneer Fringe in Western Canada," 208.

51. For example, *Peace River Record*, April 5, 1929.

52. Wetherell and Kmet, *Town Life*, 303–4.

53. A.L. Burt, "Our Dynamic Society," [University of Alberta] *The Press Bulletin*, December 12, 1930, 4.

—— 10

**Farming in the Peace River Country**

1. Leppard, "The Settlement of the Peace River Country," 62, 78.

2.  Zaslow, *Northward Expansion of Canada*, 36–37; H.C. Moss, "Mapping Our Soils. The Work of Canadian Soil Surveys," *Agricultural Institute Review* 15 (1960): 13–14.

3.  Canada Department of Agriculture, Experimental Farms Service, Dominion Experimental Station, Beaverlodge Alberta, *Progress Report 1937–1947* (Ottawa: King's Printer, 1949), 5, 14, 22–24, 85; *Report of the Minister of Agriculture, Canada, for 1925*, 24; *Report of the Minister of Agriculture, Canada, for 1926*, 125. Canada Department of Agriculture, Experimental Farms Service, Dominion Experimental Substation, Fort Vermilion, Alberta, *Progress Report, 1939–1948* (Ottawa: King's Printer, 1950), 8–29.

4.  *Grouard News*, August 5, 1915; *Spirit River Echo*, February 11 and 25, 1921; *[Grande Prairie] Northern Review*, November 27, 1923; "A Brief History of the District Agriculturalist Service" (typescript, n.d.), 73.307/226, PAA.

5.  *Annual Report for the Year 1937 by the Department of Immigration and Colonization of the CPR Concerning Colonization and Land Settlement in the Peace River District* 86.587/658, PAA.

6.  Acton and Spence, *A Study of Pioneer Farming*, 10; W.D. Albright, "Crop Growth in High Latitudes," *The Geographical Review* 23 (1933): 608–20. On grey wooded soils, see W.A. Ehrlich and William Odynsky, "Soils Developed Under Forest in the Great Plains Region," *Agricultural Institute Review* 15 (1960): 29–32. The average frost-free period on the southern prairies is 80–120 days, while in most of northern Alberta it is 60–70 days, except in the Peace River and Lesser Slave Lake districts where it is 80–90 days. For details on climate and soils, see Irwin, "The Emergence of a Regional Identity," 124–31.

7.  See for example, R.J. McFarlane, "Some Factors Contributing to the Success of Farm Operations on the Grey Wooded Soils of Alberta," *The Economic Annalist* (December 1959): 137–43.

8.  Garrett, "The Northern Alberta Railway," 37–40.

9.  Acton and Spence, *A Study of Pioneer Farming*, 23.

10. Willis, "Development of Transportation in the Peace River Region," 45.

11. Willis, "Development of Transportation in the Peace River Region," 49–51; Leppard, "The Settlement of the Peace River Country," 72; *Edmonton Journal*, March 17, 1928.

12. *Progress Report 1937–1947* [Beaverlodge], 14–15. For a good survey of issues about the use of different wheat varieties, see Irwin, "The Emergence of a Regional Identity," 136–47.

13. Irwin, "The Emergence of a Regional Identity," 147–51; *Annual Report, Alberta Department of Agriculture for 1937*, 101; Leppard, "The Settlement of the Peace River Country," 77–78; *Grande Prairie Herald*, October 19, 1928.

14. *Report of the Minister of Agriculture, Canada, for 1925*, 24; *Progress Report 1937–47* [Beaverlodge], 5; CNR, Department of Colonization and Agriculture, *Annual Report, NAR Territory, 1942*, 86.587/399, PAA; *Edmonton Journal*, October 23, 1945.

15. Zaslow, *The Northward Expansion of Canada*, 41–45; *Annual Report, Alberta Department of Agriculture for 1931*, 68; *Annual Report, Alberta Department of Agriculture for 1934*, 71; *Grande Prairie Herald*, April 3, 1923, *The [Waterhole] Northern Review*, May 1 and July 24, 1923.

16. CPR, Department of Immigration and Colonization, *Annual Report 1930, Peace River Alberta*, 86.587/706, PAA; *Annual Report, Alberta Department of Agriculture for 1926*, 27; *Annual Report, Alberta Department of Agriculture for 1934*, 71; *Annual Report, Alberta Department of Agriculture for 1937*, 101.

17. *Annual Report, Alberta Department of Agriculture for 1937*, 101; *Annual Report, Alberta Department of Agriculture for 1938*, 127. Feeding cattle on bush land required between 8 and 12 acres to support each head. (Acton and Spence, *A Study of Pioneer Farming*, 61).

18. *Annual Report, Alberta Department of Agriculture for 1941*, 82; Acton and Spence, *A Study of Pioneer Farming*, 22; Willis, "The Development of Transportation in the Peace River Country," 53; Elizabeth Low, "Profitableness of Hog Production in the Bear Lake District of Alberta," *The Economic Annalist* (August 1943): 50–52.

19. For example, *The [Waterhole] Northern Review*, April 10 and July 17, 1923; *Grande Prairie Herald*, April 8, 1932.

20. *[Grande Prairie] Northern Tribune*, August 18, 1932; Acton and Spence, *A Study of Pioneer Farming*, 11; Kitto, *The Peace River Country* (3rd revised edition, 1930), 41–42; Irwin, "The Emergence of a Regional Identity," 168–70; *Progress Report 1937–1947* [Beaverlodge], 11.

21. *Progress Report 1937–1947* [Beaverlodge], 9; *Grande Prairie Herald*, February 6, 1923; CPR Department of Immigration and Colonization, *Annual Report 1931, Peace River* 86.587/37, PAA; *Annual Report, Alberta Department of Agriculture for 1945*, 83; *Peace River District Farm Water Supply Assistance Policy* (Edmonton: Department of Agriculture, n.d. [1945]), 2.

22. See for example, *Nor'West Farmer*, December 20, 1923.

23. Acton and Spence, *A Study of Pioneer Farming*, 5, 22.

24. Acton, "A Comparison of Farms in the Grande Prairie District of Alberta 1930 and 1942," 53–56.

25. Acton and Spence, *A Study of Pioneer Farming*, 27.

26. Acton and Spence, *A Study of Pioneer Farming*, 24, 63–65, 67–71.

27. 326 farms were studied in fringe areas, of which 230 were commercial and 96 subsistence.

28. Acton and Spence, *A Study of Pioneer Farming*, 5, 30, 54, 64.

29. Acton and Spence, *A Study of Pioneer Farming*, 5, 30–31, 43.

30. Acton and Spence, *A Study of Pioneer Farming*, 36–37.

31. Acton and Spence, *A Study of Pioneer Farming*, 37–38, 62.

32. Irwin, "The Emergence of a Regional Identity," 192–95.

33. Irwin, "The Emergence of a Regional Identity," 190–95, 342 (Table); *Annual Report, Alberta Department of Agriculture for 1932*, 72–73; *Annual Report, Alberta Department of Agriculture for 1934*, 71; *Annual Report, Alberta Department of Agriculture for 1937*, 105; Leppard, "The Settlement of the Peace River Country," 72. On tractors in Alberta, see Stanley Gordon, *Agricultural Tractors in Alberta Since 1925* (Wetaskiwin: Reynolds Alberta Museum, Background Paper No. 17, 1983).

34. *Grande Prairie Herald Tribune*, October 25, 1945; *Annual Report, Alberta Department of Agriculture for 1943*, 72; Irwin, "The Emergence of a Regional Identity," 196.

35. Dawson and Murchie, *Settlement of the Peace River Country*, 40–41; Irwin, "The Emergence of a Regional Identity," 126.

36. Report for June-August 1938, RG10, vol. 11949, Shannon No. 4, Pt. 1, NAC. The Beaver at Clear Hills expressed similar thinking about the value of farming (ibid.).

37. Agency Diary, May 11, 1933, M2218, GAI; Report for April 1938, Report for June-August 1938, Report for May 1940, and L'Heureux, Statement of Duties, n.d. (1940), RG10, vol. 11949, Shannon No. 4, Pt. 1, NAC. In 1936, oats at Driftpile yielded 56 bushels per acre, a

fine yield on the reserve's acidic soil (Report for October 1936, RG10, vol. 11949, Shannon No. 4, Pt. 1, NAC).

38. Indian Agent's Diary, August 9, 1932, M2218, GAI; Reddekopp, *The Creation and Surrender of the Beaver and Duncan's Bands' Reserves*, 138.

39. In 1938, the Sawridge band had three walking ploughs, three mowers, two mechanical rakes, and disc and drag harrows. The Sucker Creek reserve also had a binder (Report for June-August 1938, RG10, vol. 11949, Shannon No. 4, Pt. 1, NAC).

40. Indian Agent's Diary, September 30, 1933 and May 1, 1934, M2218, GAI; Report for September 1933, RG10, vol. 11949, Shannon No. 4, Pt. 2, NAC.

41. Indian Agent's Diary, November 2, 1933, M2218, GAI; Report for September 1937, Report for June-August 1938 and Report for January 1941, RG10, vol. 11949, Shannon No. 4 Pt. 1, NAC; Report for April 1934, RG10, vol. 11949, Shannon No. 4 Pt. 2, NAC.

42. Diary, May 19, 1933, April 25, 1934, December 21, 1937, M2218, GAI; Reports for June and September, 1932, RG10, vol. 11949, Shannon No. 4, Pt. 2, NAC; Report for September 1939, RG10, vol. 11949, Shannon No. 4, Pt. 1, NAC.

43. Report for May 1934, Lesser Slave Lake Agency, RG10, vol. 11949, Shannon No. 4, Pt. 2, NAC; Report for June-August 1938, Report for June, July and August 1939 and Report for August 1940, Lesser Slave Lake Agency, RG10, vol. 11949, Shannon No. 4, Pt. 1, NAC.

44. Report for April 1933, RG10, vol. 11949, Shannon No. 4, Pt. 2, NAC; Report for November and December 1938 and January 1939, RG10, vol. 11949, Shannon No. 4, Pt. 1, NAC.

45. *Annual Report, Alberta Department of Agriculture for 1938*, 131.

46. See for example, *Edmonton Journal*, July 19 and August 14, 1934.

47. Irwin, "The Emergence of a Regional Identity," 183–89; Acton and Spence, *A Study of Pioneer Farming*, 26; Shouldice and McEwan to Hugill, January 4, 1937, 73.307/66, PAA; *Grande Prairie Herald*, May 9, 1927; Clipping, n.d. (ca. 1923), M622, file 7, GAI.

48. Acton and Spence, *A Study of Pioneer Farming*, 22, 26. CNR, Department of Colonization and Agriculture, Alberta, *Annual Report, NAR Territory, 1946* and *Annual Report, NAR Territory, 1948*, 86.587/399, PAA.

49. *Annual Report for 1945, Colonization and Land Settlement Activities in the Peace River Area of Alberta and British Columbia* (Canadian Colonization Association), 86.587/399, PAA; *Edmonton Journal*, October 18, 1945.

50. *Edmonton Journal*, July 27, 1945.

51. CNR, Department of Colonization and Agriculture, *Annual Report, NAR Territory, 1948*, 86.587/399; "Alberta Government Breaking Project (1947)," 86.587/84; *Edmonton Journal*, November 7, 1947, January 8 and 12, 1948, December 9, 1955.

52. L.L. Anthes, "Aboard the Friendship Train," reprint from *Industrial Canada*, December 1948, copy in 86.587/1214, PAA.

53. See for example, Alfred W. Crosby, *Ecological Imperialism. The Biological Expansion of Europe, 900–1900* (Cambridge: Cambridge University Press, 1994), 145–70.

54. Herbert Groh, *Peace-Athabaska Weeds. A Reconnaissance Appraisal* (Ottawa: Department of Agriculture Publication No. 556, 1937), 4.

55. *Spirit River Echo*, April 19, 1918; *Edmonton Journal*, November 24, 1928; "An Empire in the Making", n.p.

56. Address of Chairman, W.D. Albright to first Annual Meeting of the General Council Associated Boards of Trade, 1932, Information file, "Peace River" (folder 1), PAA; Minutes, MD of Fairview, July 9, 1927, 70.208; Minutes, MD of Spirit River, July 16, 1918, October 27, 1923, February 20, 1926, and February 19, 1927, 70.237, PAA; *[Grande Prairie] Northern Tribune*, February 23, 1933.

57. Minutes, MD of Spirit River, May 7, 1927, 72.237, PAA; *Annual Report, Alberta Department of Agriculture for 1927*, 75; *Annual Report, Alberta Department of Agriculture for 1937*, 107; Groh, *Peace-Athabaska Weeds*, 35; *Progress Report 1939–1948* [Fort Vermilion], 26.

58. Groh, *Peace-Athabaska Weeds*, 37; *Progress Report 1939–1948* [Fort Vermilion], 26.

—— 11
### Society and Social Life

1. For the application of such concepts to the history of Alberta, see Paul Voisey, *Vulcan. The Making of A Prairie Community* (Toronto: University of Toronto Press, 1988), 247–54.

2. *Maclean's*, October 1, 1924. See also *Edmonton Journal*, November 24, 1928.

3. Zaslow, *The Northward Expansion of Canada*, 47, 41; Acton and Spence, *A Study of Pioneer Farming*, 28–29 (Tables).

4. Sovereign to Andrews, June 9, 1939, AP, A.320/374, Box A./51, PAA; West to DCSS, March 1939, AP, A.320/957, Box A.73, PAA; Zonia Keywan, "Mary Percy Jackson: Pioneer Doctor," *The Beaver*, Outfit 308 No. 2 (Winter 1977): 41–47. See also Mary Percy Jackson, *Suitable for the Wilds. Letters from Northern Alberta 1929–1931*, ed. Janice Dickin McGinnis (Toronto: University of Toronto Press, 1995).

5. "Report for 1935, Fellowship of the Maple Leaf," FML to Sovereign, August 3, 1934, AP, A.320/373, Box A.51, PAA; Jackson to Sovereign, June 5, 1939, AP, A.320/600, Box A59, PAA.

6. Sovereign to Berry, March 4, 1939, AP, A.320/419, Box A53, PAA.

7. *Edmonton Journal*, January 19, 1931.

8. Clippings and typescript, AP, A.320/887, Box A.71, PAA.

9. Registers of Service, Waterhole, Griffin Creek, Bluesky, Stoney Lake, Three Lakes, Beaverlodge, AP, file A.8/5 Box AC, PAA; Reply to Questionnaire, July 11, 1922 (Lake Saskatoon), 78.099c Box 5, file 8, UCAT.

10. *Grande Prairie Herald*, February 13, 1931.

11. Grimwood to Brownlee, June 10, 1930, and clipping, file 156b and Fuller to Aberhart, May 31, 1939, file 715, PP, PAA; Sydney Risk, "From the South to the North," *Stagedoor*, vol. 3, No. 8 (May-June 1945), copy in 69-28-12, UAA.

12. *Grande Prairie Herald*, June 28, 1929; Kent to Deputy Provincial Secretary, April 8, 1932, 73.347/467, PAA; Deputy Provincial Secretary to Reap, July 12, 1932, 73.347/462.

13. *Grande Prairie Herald*, June 6 and October 17, 1930; *Spirit River Echo*, April 2, June 25 and October 8, 1920; Wetherell and Kmet, *Town Life*, 224.

14. *Peace River Record*, May 6, 1932.

15. *Grande Prairie Herald*, April 24, 1923.

16. *Spirit River Echo*, July 16, 1920; *Peace River Record*, February 3, 1928, February 20, 1931 and February 3, 1939; *Grande Prairie Herald*, February 16, 1925; *Grande Prairie Herald Tribune*, February 17, 1938.

17. *Grande Prairie Herald*, August 9 and 16, 1929; List of Exhibitions and Fairs 1931, 73.307/247, PAA; Lyne to Galbraith, March 21, 1921, Department of Agriculture Papers, 73.316, file 23b, PAA; Donald G. Wetherell and Irene R.A. Kmet, *Useful Pleasures. The Shaping of Leisure in Alberta 1896–1945* (Regina: Canadian Plains Research Centre and Alberta Culture and Multiculturalism, 1990), 311–32.

18. This information is drawn from various sources, including the *Grande Prairie Herald, Grande Prairie Northern Tribune*, and *Grande Prairie Herald Tribune*, 1920–47, *Spirit River Echo*, 1918–21 and *Peace River Record*, 1920–45. See also Wetherell and Kmet, *Useful Pleasures*, 102–17.

19. *Peace River Record*, April 11, 1919; Margaret Fraser Thibault, *The Teepee Creek Terror* (Teepee Creek: Teepee Creek Stampede Historical Society, 1978), 11.

20. Minutes, March 9, 1935 and Cash Received Accounts, 1936–57, Kerndale Community League Papers, 69.296, PAA; Financial Statements 1933–37, Spirit Valley Community Association Papers, 76.517, file 3, PAA; Edey to Registrar of Companies, September 24, 1951, 75.517/4, PAA.

21. In 1921 Kennedy defeated the incumbent Liberal in the provincial election but immediately stepped down to allow Herbert Greenfield, the new Premier, to run in a by-election. Kennedy in turn accepted the UFA nomination to run in the upcoming federal election in which he defeated Frank Oliver (Rycroft and Leonard, *Electoral History of the Peace River Country*, 20).

22. "Political Life," (typescript) n.d., Kennedy Papers, M4029, GAI. Along with Agnes McPhail and several UFA members, Kennedy became part of the Ginger Group in 1924 which split from the Progressives.

23. W.D. Albright, "Settlers' Interest: The Key to the Solution of Peace River Transportation Problem" (Speech given in Vancouver, March 12, 1930), Information file, "Peace River," (file 2), PAA; *Edmonton Journal*, December 1, 1932; *Lake Saskatoon Reflections: A Local History of Lake Saskatoon District* (Edmonton: Friesen Printers for Lake Saskatoon History Book Committee, 1980), 229.

24. Hoadley to Weir, December 8, 1930, Department of Agriculture Papers, 73.307, file 432, PAA; Longman to MacMillan, May 29, 1946, 73.302, file 3396, PAA; Craig to Hoadley, January 11, 1932, 73.307/44, PAA; Beatty to Sovereign, July 18, 1940, AP, A.320/1155, Box A.81, PAA.

25. Roger Vik, "W.D. Albright," *Alberta History* 38 (1990): 18–24; David C. Jones, *Feasting on Misfortune* (Edmonton: University of Alberta Press, 1998), 23–31.

26. *Grande Prairie Herald Tribune*, April 5, 1945.

27. *Peace River Record*, April 12, 1929; *Maclean's Magazine*, September 1, 1930; *Edmonton Journal*, June 11, 1956.

28. See for example, Annual Report, Parish of Lake Saskatoon with Wembley (1937–38), AP, A.320/1155, Box A.81, PAA; *Grande Prairie Herald*, April 23, 1918.

29. *Peace River Record*, July 19, 1929 and May 18, 1934.

30. *Grande Prairie Northern Tribune*, November 4, 1937.

31. *Peace River Record*, April 23, 1937; *Grande Prairie Herald*, July 22, 1927. The important exception to this pattern was fund raising for churches. Especially with English patrons and the Board of Religious Education in Toronto, Bishop Sovereign liked to recount tales of the Peace River country's remoteness, of the cold, of wild and dangerous animals, impassable roads and the like. Such playing to outside perception had a long history in missionary fund raising in Canada.

32. John Buchan, *Memory Hold the Door* (Toronto: The Musson Book Co. Ltd., 1940), 266–67; *Peace River Record*, February 26, 1932 and May 18, 1934.

33. Bishop's Address to Synod, 1930, AP, A220/19c, Box A.21, PAA.

34. W.D. Albright, "Settlers' Interest: The Key to the Solution of Peace River Transportation Problem," (Speech in Vancouver, March 12, 1930), Information file "Peace River," (file 2), PAA.

35. *Peace River Record*, April 13, 1934.

36. A.H. McQuarrie, "Building the Edson Trail," *Alberta Historical Review* 14 (1966): 4–5.

37. *Grande Prairie Herald*, December 16, 1927. For a recent example of this view of the Edson trail, see James MacGregor, *The Land of Twelve Foot Davis*, 27.

38. *[Grande Prairie] Northern Tribune*, August 25, 1932.

39. *[Grande Prairie] Northern Tribune*, July 14, 1938

—— 12

### Natives, Land and Power

1. The first such organization was the League of Indians of Canada, formed in 1919. Its effectiveness was limited in part because of opposition by Indian Affairs and other agencies (such as the Oblates). In 1929 the League of Indians in Western Canada was formed, but its energies were largely absorbed in dealing with the problems of the Depression. Well organized and effective Native organizations did not emerge until the 1960s (Ray, *I Have Lived*, 319).

2. Zaslow, *The Northward Expansion of Canada*, 151.

3. McCormack, "How The (North) West Was Won," 108–11, 233.

4. Report for June-August 1938, RG10, vol. 11949, Shannon No. 4, Pt. 1, NAC; Madill, *Treaty Eight*, 89–90; Daniel, "Indian Rights and Hinterland Resources," (1977), 157–58.

5. Bury to McLean, July 5, 1920, RG10, vol. 7997, file 191/30–11–1, Reel C-9482, NAC.

6. Harkin to Scott, January 28, 1920 and Bury to Scott, February 5, 1920, RG10, vol. 7997, file 191/30–11–1, Reel 9482, NAC; Fumoleau, *As Long As This Land Shall Last*, 119, 122. On the Lubicon, see: Darlene A. Fereira, *Need Not Greed: The Lubicon Lake Cree Band Land Claim in Historical Perspective* (Master's thesis, University of Alberta, 1990), 72–73; Thomas Flanagan, "Some Factors Bearing on the Origins of the Lubicon Lake Dispute," *Alberta* 2 (1990): 47–62.

7. Card to Assistant Deputy and Secretary, May 4, 1923, RG10, vol. 6732, file 420–2B, Reel C-8094, NAC; Bailey to Hoadley, June 27, 1922 and Memo for Hoadley, July 6, 1922, Department of Attorney General Papers, 75.126, file 20, PAA; Daniel, *Hunting, Fishing and Trapping Rights*, 14; McCardle, *The Rules of the Game*, 228.

8.  Ray, *The Canadian Fur Trade in the Industrial Age*, III, 205; *Annual Report, Alberta Department of Agriculture [for] 1923*, 71; Bury to Deputy Superintendent General, July 7, 1926, RG10, vol. 8093, file 420-1, Reel C-8093, NAC; *Annual Report, RCMP [for] 1930*, 35; McCardle, *The Rules of the Game*, 158–59; McCormack, "How The (North) West Was Won," 234–35; Zaslow, *The Northward Expansion of Canada*, 132–33. For findings (based on oral history) that suggest that Native-white relations in trapping areas in one part of northern Saskatchewan were not as confrontational as in other places, see: Robert Jarvenpa, "The Ubiquitous Bushman: Chipewyan-White Trapper Relations of the 1930s," in *Problems in the Prehistory of the North American Subarctic. The Athapaskan Question*, eds James Helmer, S. VanDyke and F.J. Kense (Calgary: University of Calgary Department of Archaeology, 1977), 165–185.

9.  Card to Assistant Deputy and Secretary, May 4, 1923, Laviolette to Chief of Indian Department, February 20, 1927 and Robertson to MacInnes, February 11, 1931, RG10, vol. 6732, file 420-2B, Reel C-8094, NAC.

10. McCormack, "How The (North) West Was Won," 224–32.

11. McCormack, "How The (North) West Was Won," 356–59.

12. Lesser Slave Lake Indian Agency, Diary, 1924–33, M2218, GAI.

13. Carter, *Lost Harvests*, 244–46, 250, 252; Superintendent General to Kennedy, April 27, 1923, RG10, Reel C-14813, vol. 7544, file 29,131-9 Pt. 1, NAC.

14. Carter, *Lost Harvests*, 244–45; Dickason, *Canada's First Nations*, 323–26.

15. Graham to Scott, April 3, 1923, RG10, Reel C-14813, vol. 7544, file 29,131-5 Pt. 1, NAC; *Annual Report, Department of the Interior (Dominion Lands Agent's Report, Grouard) for 1916*, 24.

16. Deputy Superintendent General to Graham, March 13, 1923 and Graham to Scott, April 3, 1923, RG10, Reel C-14813, vol. 7544, file 29,131-5 Pt. 1, NAC. Harold Laird was the son of David Laird, former Lieutenant Governor of the North-West Territories and one of the commissioners of Treaty 8.

17. Astatchikun to Scott, (received April 30, 1923), RG10, Reel C-14813, vol. 7544, file 29,131-5 Pt. 1, NAC.

18. Graham to Scott, June 1, 1923 and Graham to Secretary, May 26, 1926, RG10, Reel C-14813, vol. 7544, file 29,131-5 Pt. 1, NAC.

19. Graham to Scott, December 10, 1927, RG10, Reel C-14813, vol. 7544, file 29,131-5 Pt. 1, NAC. This tactic was likely illegal under the terms for surrenders set out in the *Indian Act* (Reddekopp, *The Creation and Surrender of the Beaver and Duncan's Bands' Reserves*, 75).

20. Giroux to Stewart, January 5, 1928 (copy), and Deputy Superintendent General to Superintendent General, December 29, 1927, RG10, Reel C-14813, vol. 7544, file 29,131-5 Pt. 1, NAC.

21. Scott to Pratt, March 11, 1928, Graham to Scott, May 25, 1928 and Scott to Caldwell, July 4, 1928, RG10, Reel C-14813, vol. 7544, file 29,131-5 Pt. 1, NAC.

22. Acting Indian Agent to Graham, January 18, 1927, RG10, vol. 11950, Shannon No. 7, NAC; Murison to Graham, October 2, 1928, RG10, Reel C-14813, vol. 7544, file 29,131-5 Pt. 1, NAC.

23. Graham to Scott, October 6, 1928, McKillop to Indian Affairs, October 10, 1929 and Graham to Scott, November 5, 1929, RG10, Reel C-14813, vol. 7544, file 29,131-5 Pt. 2, NAC.

24. Stewart to Giroux,(copy) February 14, 1930 and Scott to Baxter, January 14, 1932, RG10, Reel C-14813, vol. 7544, file 29,131–5 Pt. 2, NAC.

25. Schmidt to Secretary, August 12, 1938, RG10, Reel C-14813, vol. 7544, file 29,131–5 Pt. 2, NAC.

26. Reddekopp, *The Creation and Surrender of the Beaver and Duncan's Bands' Reserves*, 53–55, 62.

27. E.J. Ashton, "Peace River" (typescript), November 26, 1928, 73.307/14, PAA; Murison to Graham, October 2, 1928, RG10, Reel C-14813, vol. 7544, file 29,131–5 Pt. 1, NAC; Reddekopp, *The Creation and Surrender of the Beaver and Duncan's Bands' Reserves*, 59.

28. Madden to Kennedy, April 24, 1922, Lawlor and Sissons to Superintendent, March 16, 1925 and reply, April 30, 1925, RG10, Reel C-14813, vol. 7544, file 29,131–9 Pt. 1, NAC; Reddekopp, *The Creation and Surrender of the Beaver and Duncan's Bands' Reserves*, 66.

29. Deputy Superintendent General to Superintendent General, December 29, 1927; Scott to Superintendent General, February 25, 1928, RG10, Reel C-14813, vol. 7544, file 29,131–5 Pt. 1, NAC.

30. Murison to Graham, October 2, 1928, RG10, Reel C-14813, vol. 7544, file 29,131–5 Pt. 1, NAC.

31. Caldwell to Graham, July 14, 1928, RG10, Reel C-14813, vol. 7544, file 29,131–5 Pt. 1, NAC. Indian Affairs neglected to pay the Department of the Interior for the land. As was recognized in 1951, Indian Affairs did not technically have title to the land (Reddekopp, *The Creation and Surrender of the Beaver and Duncan's Bands' Reserves*, 70–71, 96).

32. Reddekopp suggests that retained land at Fairview was the only part of the reserve that was occupied in 1928. Although described as a Beaver "camping ground" used when moving between Horse Lake and Clear Hills Reserves, he notes that there was little such movement between the two locations. The balance of the Fairview land was surrendered in 1948 (Reddekopp, *The Creation and Surrender of the Beaver and Duncan's Bands' Reserves*, 94–95).

33. Graham to Scott, October 6, 1928 and Murison to Graham, October 3, 1928, RG10, Reel C-14813, vol. 7544, file 29,131–5 Pt. 1, NAC.

34. Clipping, and Murison to Graham, June 20, 1929, RG10, Reel C-14813, vol. 7544, file 29,131–5 Pt. 1, NAC.

35. Murison to Graham, June 20, 1929, RG10, Reel C-14813, vol. 7544, file 29,131–5 Pt. 1, NAC.

36. Clipping, RG10, Reel C-14813, vol. 7544, file 29,131–5 Pt. 1, NAC. The disappearing Indian was a common theme in North America. As art historian Alex Nemerov notes, in American paintings of Indians in the "old west," there was a nostalgia for the passing of the "frontier" along with an acceptance that "progress" included "a theory of social evolution that posited the disappearance of 'primitive' peoples before the inexorable advance of 'civilization.' Indians, or at least 'authentic' Indians had no existence in the present." And as he further notes, rather than viewing Aboriginal cultures as constantly adapting to changed historical circumstances, they were seen "as remnants from a stopped or dead culture of the past. As such, although they lived in the present, they belonged to a 'primitive' era that did not, nor could not, comprehend the technological and intellectual achievements of the present" (Alex Nemerov, "Doing the 'Old America' The Image of the American West 1880–1920," in *The West As America: Reinterpreting Images of the Frontier*

*1820–1920*, ed. William H. Truetten (Washington: National Museum of American Art, Published by the Smithsonian Press, 1991), 311–12).

37. Clipping, RG10, Reel C-14813, vol. 7544, file 29,131–5 Pt. 1, NAC. Grant had conducted similar research in Fort Chipewyan the previous year ( J.C. Boileau Grant, *Anthropometry of the Chipewyan and Cree Indians of Lake Athabasca* (Ottawa: National Museum of Canada, Bulletin No. 64, Anthropological Series No. 14, 1930).

38. Philmester and Dundon to Deputy Superintendent, September 25, 1930 and reply, October 1, 1930 and Graham to Scott, October 8, 1930, RG10, vol. 7544, file 29,131–5 Pt. 2, Reel C-14813, NAC.

39. Martin to Murphy, October 30, 1931, Indian Affairs to Martin, November 25, 1931, Williams to Kennedy, July 13, 1934 and L'Heureux to Caldwell, November 13, 1934, RG10, Reel C-8086, vol. 6724, file 131A–9–1, NAC.

40. McGill to Burkard, April 2, 1935, L'Heureux to Wymbs, May 14, 1936, Christianson to Secretary, August 19, 1936, Jackson to McGill, October 20, 1936 and Memo, November 25, 1936, RG10, vol. 6724, file 131A–9–1, Reel C-8086, NAC.

41. Ewing Commission, Evidence and Proceedings, 15.

42. Murray Dobbin, *The One-And-A-Half Men. The Story of Jim Brady and Malcolm Norris. Metis Patriots of the 20th Century* (Regina: Gabriel Dumont Institute, 1981), 55–56.

43. Dobbin, *The One-And-A-Half Men*, 56–59; T.C. Pocklington, *The Government and Politics of the Alberta Metis Settlements* (Regina: Canadian Plains Research Centre, 1991), 10; Evidence and Proceedings, Ewing Commission, pp. 72, 73, 75.75/9, PAA.

44. Dobbin, *The One-And-A-Half Men*, 61–63, 92; Huel, *Proclaiming the Gospel*, 212; Dion to Buck, September 10, 1940, 75.75/6A, PAA.

45. Pocklington, *The Government and Politics of the Alberta Metis Settlements*, 11.

46. Dobbin, *The One-And-A-Half Men*, 66–67; Evidence and Proceedings, Ewing Commission, pp. 54–55, 75.75/9, PAA.

47. *Edmonton Journal*, February 29, 1933; Sawchuk, Sawchuk and Ferguson, *Metis Land Rights in Alberta*, 188; Dobbin, *The One-And-A-Half Men*, 73. The other members of the commission were Dr. Edward Braithwaite and James Douglas.

48. Evidence and Proceedings, Ewing Commission, 13–14, 75.75/9, PAA; Ewing Commission, Final Report, 4.

49. Sawchuk, Sawchuk and Ferguson, *Metis Lands Rights in Alberta*, 191–92; Dobbin, *The One-And- A-Half Men*, 91.

50. Hatt, "Ethnic Discourse in Alberta," 69–70; Sawchuk, Sawchuk and Ferguson, *Metis Lands Rights in Alberta*, 192.

51. Ewing Commission, Final Report, 3 (copy in 75.75, PAA); Dickason, *Canada's First Nations*, 363.

52. Ewing Commission, Final Report, 4, 10; Rankine to Harvie, December 5, 1935, 75.75/7, PAA.

53. Pocklington, *The Government and Politics of the Alberta Metis Settlements*, 15–20; Tanner to Crerar, December 10, 1937, and reply, January 10, 1938, RG10, vol. 6733, file 420–2–1, Reel C-8095, NAC; Daniel, *Hunting, Fishing and Trapping Rights*, 37–38.

54. Sawchuk, Sawchuk and Ferguson, *Metis Lands Rights in Alberta*, 198–200; Pocklington, *The Government and Politics of the Alberta Metis Settlements*, 25; Alvin Finkel, *The Social Credit Phenomenon in Alberta* (Toronto: University of Toronto Press, 1989), 46.

55. Pocklington, *The Government and Politics of the Alberta Metis Settlements*, 25, 32.

56. In Alberta, there were two precedents, both within the tradition of religious missions. In 1866, Father Lacombe set up an agricultural settlement at St Paul des Cris, near present-day Brosseau on the North Saskatchewan River about 160 kilometres downstream from Fort Edmonton. It was abandoned in 1873 and the mission was transferred to Saddle Lake in 1876. He established another Metis settlement in 1895, called St Paul des Metis, near the present-day town of St. Paul. It lasted until 1908.

57. *Alberta Metis Settlements: A Compendium of Background Documents* (Edmonton: [Alberta] Native Affairs Secretariat, 1984), 20, 24; Knill, "Schools in the Wilderness," 37–38. At Keg River, most settlers lived in the Paddle Prairie division of the settlement; at Utikuma Lake, most were at the Gift Lake subdivision.

58. *Edmonton Journal*, October 24, 1946; Jackson to Sovereign, June 5, 1939, AP, A.320/600, Box A.59, PAA.

59. *East Prairie Metis 1939–1979. 40 Years of Determination* (n.p. 1979). For another account (but outside northern Alberta) see *Elizabeth Metis Settlement. A Local History* (Altona: Friesen Printers, 1979).

60. Dobbin, *The One-And-A-Half Men*, 126, 133–35; Pocklington, *The Government and Politics of the Alberta Metis Settlements*, 26; Sawchuk, Sawchuk and Ferguson, *Metis Lands Rights in Alberta*, 198–205; Swift to Sovereign, June 16, 1945, AP, A.320/241, Box A.47, PAA.

61. Dickason, *Canada's First Nations*, 363–64; Pocklington, *The Government and Politics of the Alberta Metis Settlements*, 38–41, 103–12.

## —— 13
### Development of Northern Resources

1. Tough, *As Their Natural Resources Fail* , 243; Gulig, "Sizing Up the Catch," 4, 7.

2. *Annual Report, Fisheries Branch, Department of Marine and Fisheries for 1923–24*, 45–46; *Annual Report, Fisheries Branch, Department of Marine and Fisheries for 1924–25*, 50; *Annual Report, Fisheries Branch, Department of Marine and Fisheries for 1925–26*, 47–48; *Pioneers of the Lakeland* (Slave Lake: Slave Lake Pioneers, 1984), 177.

3. *Annual Report, Alberta Department of Agriculture for 1939*, 47; Report of District Agriculturalists Conference, 1938, 73.307/228, PAA; *Annual Report, Fisheries Branch, Department of Marine and Fisheries for 1930–31*, 88; *Directory of Co-operative Associations in Canada 1936* (Ottawa: Department of Agriculture Publication 508, 1936), 12.

4. Gulig, "Sizing Up the Catch," 5–6; *Annual Report, Alberta Department of Agriculture for 1939*, 49.

5. Cross to Crerar, March 7, 1939, RG10, vol. 6733, file 420-2-1, Reel C-8095, NAC.

6. Report for June 1934, RG10, vol. 11949, Shannon No. 4, Pt. 2, NAC; Report for January 1938, Lesser Slave Lake Agency and Report for June-August, 1938, RG10, vol. 11949, Shannon No. 4, Pt. 1, NAC; Annual Report, Fur Supervisor, 1947–48, RG10, vol. 6743, file 420-2-1-3, Reel C-8096, NAC.

7. *Alberta's Metis Settlements: A Compendium of Background Documents* (Edmonton: Natives Affairs Secretariat, 1984), 26; Dobbin, *The One-And-A-Half Men*, 123–24.

8. *Annual Report, Fisheries Branch, Department of Marine and Fisheries for 1924–25*, 50; Burwash to Collins, June 27, 1934 and Morrison to MacArthur, November 6, 1937, 86.587/989, PAA; General Manager to McCaig, May 19, 1936 and Superintendent to Callaghan, June 16, 1935, 86.587/990a, PAA; Superintendent to Callaghan, June 7, 1937, 86.587/991, PAA. The flood of 1935 also led to the transfer of the town of Slave Lake to a new site.

9. Quoted in Gulig, "Sizing Up the Catch," 6.

10. *Annual Report, Fisheries Branch, Department of Marine and Fisheries for 1923–24*, 45; *Annual Report, Fisheries Branch, Department of Marine and Fisheries for 1924–25*, 50; *Annual Report, Fisheries Branch, Department of Marine and Fisheries for 1925–26*, 47; *Pioneers of the Lakeland*, 17.

11. Report for February 1937, RG10, vol. 11949, Shannon No. 4, Pt. 1, NAC; *Annual Report, Alberta Department of Agriculture, for 1938*, 51; *Annual Report, Alberta Department of Agriculture for 1940*, 60.

12. Gordon C. Merrill, "Human Geography of the Lesser Slave Lake Area of Alberta," *Geographical Bulletin* No. 3 (1953): 46–47.

13. For an early expression of this view about Lesser Slave Lake, see *Grouard News*, April 10, 1915.

14. Richard B. Miller, "Effectiveness of A Whitefish Hatchery," *The Journal of Wildlife Management* 10 (1946): 317–21.

15. *Annual Report, Fisheries Branch, Department of Marine and Fisheries for 1925–26*, 47–48. For similar development pressure at Wabasca see: McLaughlin to Connors, December 5, 1938, 67.303/11003, PAA.

16. *Annual Report, Fisheries Branch, Department of Marine and Fisheries for 1927–28*, 68.

17. "An Empire in the Making," n.p. On corporate developments at Black Bay, see Coté to Devereux, May 2, 1925, Caldwell to Coté April 1, 1927 and Jones to Controller, October 11, 1927, RG15, vol. 114/F, file 4,319,996, NAC. National Fish Foods Company also maintained its fishing operations at Lac La Biche and Lesser Slave Lake.

18. Cooke, "Boom and Bust, Bust and Boom," 102; Ommanney to Dennis, November 1, 1929, 86.587/26, PAA; *Annual Report, Fisheries Branch, Department of Marine and Fisheries for 1927–28*, 67. Whitefish in Lake Athabasca in the 1930s were infested with tapeworms and their sale was banned in the United States.

19. Berger, *The Writing of Canadian History*, 97.

20. This information and that in the next paragraph is from: *Annual Report, Fisheries Branch, Department of Marine and Fisheries for 1927–28*, 68; *Annual Report, Fisheries Branch, Department of Marine and Fisheries for 1928–29*, 84; *Annual Report, Fisheries Branch, Department of Marine and Fisheries for 1929–30*, 88; *Annual Report, Department of Fisheries for 1930–31*, 89; Cooke, "Boom and Bust, Bust and Boom," 102; Lynda Sturney, "Northern Alberta: McInnis Products Corporation 1926–1970," *Alberta Museums' Review* 12 (1987): 11–13; "An Empire in the Making," n.p.; Cornwall letter, June 4, 1926, 86.587/36, PAA.

21. Sturney, "McInnis Products Corporation," 2–13; McCormack, "How the (North) West Was Won," 161–63; Parker, *History of the Athabasca Oil Sands Region*, Vol. 2, Oral History, 22.

22. Ommanney to Dennis, November 1, 1929, 86.587/26, PAA; MacArthur to Gillis, January 24, 1933, 86.587/2758, PAA.

23. McCormack, "How the (North) West Was Won," 255.

24. On commercial fishing on Great Slave Lake see R.A. Jenness, *Great Slave Lake Fishing Industry* (Ottawa: Northern Co-ordination and Research Centre, Department of Northern Affairs and Natural Resources, 1963 (NCRC 63–10)), and Rea, *The Political Economy of the Canadian North*, 88.

25. Cooke, "Boom and Bust, Bust and Boom," 102; General Manager to Devenish, December 6, 1947, 86.587/46a, PAA; Huestis to Superintendent, November 29, 1946, 86.587/2758, PAA; McCormack, "How the (North) West Was Won," 256.

26. Murphy, *History of Forest and Prairie Fire Control in Alberta*, 230–36; *Annual Report, Department of the Interior, Dominion Lands Branch [for] 1929*, 85; *Annual Report, Department of the Interior, Dominion Lands Branch [for] 1930*, 83; Myers, *Sky Riders*, 100–101.

27. B.Y. Card, G.K. Hirabayashi and C.L. French, *The Metis in Alberta Society* (Edmonton: A Report on Project A (1960–63), University of Alberta Committee for Social Research, prepared for The Alberta Tuberculosis Association, 1963), 94–95; Report for May and December, 1935, RG10, vol. 11949, Shannon No. 4, Pt. 2, NAC; Report for January and March, 1937, RG10, vol. 11949, Shannon No. 4, Pt. 1, NAC. For memoirs of lumbering in the DeBolt district before World War II, see: DeBolt and District Pioneer Museum, *Sawmills Across the Smoky* (DeBolt: DeBolt and District Pioneer Museum, [1st Draft], 1977), 8–14, 18, 25.

28. General Manager to Niedermeyer, April 12, 1929 and Deakin to Callaghan, December 20, 1930 and April 7, 1934, 86.587/1292, PAA; *Edmonton Journal*, April 30, 1921.

29. Claims Investigator to Elliott, January 26, 1925, 86.587/1292, PAA; *Canada Year Book 1927–28*, 311. The same proportion was evident in 1921 (List of Sawmills [August 11, 1922] 86.587/1292, PAA).

30. McMillan to Manders, May 12, 1938, 86.587/2784a, PAA.

31. Card, Hirabayashi and French, *The Metis in Alberta Society*, 94; Memo Re: Conference, January 20, 1939, 86.587/2785b, PAA.

32. Memo by Holmes, May 3, 1938, 86.587/2784a, PAA; General Manager to Hajeck, October 24, 1938 and Gillis to MacArthur, July 6, 1938, 86.587/2784, PAA.

33. Card, Hirabayashi and French, *The Metis in Alberta Society*, 95; various correspondence 1939, 86.587/2785b, PAA; *Canada Year Book 1942*, 247; *Canada Year Book 1945*, 203; Willis, "Development of Transportation in the Peace River Region," 53–54; Hayward Lumber to Secretary, April 29, 1948, 86.587/2872, PAA; *Sawmills Across the Smoky*, 26–50.

34. Memo Re: Salt Shipments, May 28, 1926 and Gillespie to Smith, May 22, 1926, 86.587/36, PAA; *Edmonton Journal*, April 8, 1924 and November 29, 1928.

35. Letter by Cornwall, June 4, 1926, Dinning to Brownlee, June 3, 1926 and General Manager to Smith, June 22, 1932, 86.587/36, PAA.

36. Correspondence, September and December 1926, 86.587/36, PAA; *Edmonton Journal*, April 1, 1927.

37. *Edmonton Journal*, August 18 and December 29, 1927; Warren to Callaghan, July 3, 1931, 86.587/36, PAA; Brownlee to Tait, May 28, 1929, 70.414/1475, PAA.

38. General Manager to Watson, January 22, 1934, 86.587/36, PAA; Clipping, October 1936, 86.587/381b; *Edmonton Journal*, February 10, May 11 and 14, 1936, September 25 and November 23, 1937; Comfort, *Pass The McMurray Salt*, 30.

39. The freight rate on salt from Windsor to Edmonton (a distance of 2,250 miles) was 91.5 cents per 100 pounds. The rate on salt from Waterways to Edmonton, a distance of 309 miles, was 23 cents per 100 pounds.

40. *Edmonton Journal*, February 26 and November 15, 1938, March 22, 1941, November 29, 1944, December 11, 1946 and March 12, 1952; Comfort, *The Abasands Fiasco*, 128–29.

41. Kitto, *The Peace River Country* (3rd revised edition, 1930), 49; "Annual Report, Parish of Lake Saskatoon with Wembley (1937–38)," AP, A.320/1155, Box A.81, PAA; Report, 1939, Board of Industrial Relations Papers, 68.131, file 6994, PAA.

42. Parker, "The Long Technological Search," 116.

43. Ferguson, *Athabasca Oil Sands*, 35.

44. Parker and Tingley, *History of the Athabasca Oil Sands Region*, Vol. 1, 122–23; Ferguson, *Athabasca Oil Sands*, 32, 40.

45. Report on Athabaska Tar Sands, October 23, 1925, 86.587/382b, PAA.

46. Cunningham to Coleman, August 7, 1922 and Report on Athabaska Tar Sands, October 23, 1925, 86.587/382b, PAA; Ferguson, *The Athabasca Oil Sands*, 158; Parker, "The Long Technological Search," 113.

47. *Canada Year Book, 1939*, (Ottawa: King's Printer, 1940), 310.

48. Parker and Tingley, *History of the Athabasca Oil Sands Region*, Vol. 1, 46, 123; *Edmonton Journal*, May 13 and 14, 1929.

49. K.A. Clark, "Athabasca Bituminous Sands," *Fuel* 30 (1951): 49–51 (copy in 86.587/381b, PAA); Ferguson, *Athabasca Oil Sands*, 64–69, 167–211.

50. Parker, "The Long Technological Search," 115–16; Ferguson, *Athabasca Oil Sands*, 55, 93.

51. Ferguson, *Athabasca Oil Sands*, 38, 52, 56–57.

52. D.J. Comfort, "Tom Draper, Oil Sands Pioneer," *Alberta History* 25 (1977): 25–29.

53. Ferguson, *Athabasca Oil Sands*, 88–93; Telegram, December 29, 1941, 86.587/381b, PAA.

54. Parker and Tingley, *History of the Athabasca Oil Sands Region*, Vol. 1, 53–54.

55. Parker "The Long Technological Search," 117; Clippings, 1944, 86.587/381b, PAA.

56. Ferguson, *Athabasca Oil Sands*, 70–84.

57. Parker and Tingley, *History of the Athabasca Oil Sands Region*, Vol. 1, 120, 129–30; Ferguson, *Athabasca Oil Sands*, 85, 123, 128, 152; Parker "The Long Technological Search," 117–18.

58. Rea, *The Political Economy of the Canadian North*, 144–45

—— 14

**Crisis Upon Crisis**

1. Laviolette to Chief of Indian Department, February 20, 1927, RG10, vol. 6732, file 420–2B, Reel C-8094, NAC; Price and Smith, "Treaty 8 and Traditional Livelihoods," 70–73.

2. McCardle, *The Rules of the Game*, 201; "What Canada is Doing for the Hunting Indians," February 3, 1936, RG10, vol. 6731, file 420–1, Reel C-8093.

3. Ken Coates, "By The Sinews of Their Lives: Native Access to Resources in the Yukon, 1890 to 1950," in *Aboriginal Resource Use in Canada: Historical and Legal Aspects*, eds. Kerry Abel and Jean Friesen (Winnipeg: University of Manitoba Press, 1991), 184.

4. McCardle, *The Rules of the Game*, 6; Statement by Indian Affairs, Dominion and Provincial Conference, January 1928, RG10, vol. 6731, file 420-1-2, Reel C-8093, NAC.

5. Regulations Under the Game Act, October 25, 1921, *Alberta Official Gazette*, vol. 17, 1921, 960; Card to Assistant Deputy Secretary, May 4, 1923, Hoadley to McLean, June 29, 1923 and Acting Assistant Deputy Secretary to Card, July 20, 1923, RG10, vol. 6732, file 420-2B, Reel C-8094, NAC; McCardle, *The Rules of the Game*, 231-34.

6. McCardle, *The Rules of the Game*, 223-24; Laird to Assistant Deputy Secretary, November 21, 1923, and Hoadley to McLean, October 10, 1927, RG10, vol. 6732, file 420-2B, Reel C-8094, NAC.

7. Lawton to Secretary, July 14, 1922, RG10, vol. 6732, file 420-2B, Reel C-8094, NAC; McCardle, *The Rules of the Game*, 248-50; Zaslow, *The Northward Expansion of Canada*, 11. In 1942 the southern Peace River country was withdrawn from the areas where hunting for food was permitted.

8. Gottesman, "Native Hunting and the Migratory Birds Convention Act," 70; W.F. Lothian, *A History of Canada's National Parks*, Vol. 4 (Ottawa: Parks Canada, 1979), 53-54; *Good Roads*, August 1923 and July 1925; *University of Alberta Press Bulletin*, February 18, 1925; Hewitt, "The Conservation of Wildlife in Canada in 1917," 120-21.

9. McCardle, *The Rules of the Game*, 66-68, 247-50; Fumoleau, *As Long As This Land Shall Last*, 364; Lawton to Mackenzie, August 9, 1928, RG10, vol. 6731, file 420-1-4, Reel C-8093, NAC.

10. Martin and Whitehead to Scott, July 5, 1927, RG10, vol. 6732, file 420-2B, Reel C-8094, NAC.

11. Lloyd to McLean, June 9, 1921, RG10, vol. 7997, file 191/30-11-1, Reel C-9482, NAC; *Annual Report, Department of the Interior [for] 1923*, 6. Wood Buffalo Park is now famous as the nesting place of whooping cranes. These sites were not discovered until 1954 and their protection was thus not a motive for the park's creation.

12. Fumoleau, *As Long As This Land Shall Last*, 255-56; Maxwell Graham, *Canada's Wild Buffalo. Observations in the Wood Buffalo Park* (Ottawa: King's Printer, 1923), 7; McCormack, "How the (North) West Was Won," 127-31, 134-35.

13. Lothian, *A History of Canada's National Parks*, Vol. 1, 62-63; *Annual Report, Department of the Interior [for] 1928*, 122.

14. Laviolette to Chief of Indian Department, February 20, 1927, RG10, vol. 6732, file 420-2B, Reel C-8094, NAC.

15. *Annual Report, Department of the Interior [for] 1929*, 155; *Annual Report, Department of the Interior [for] 1936*, 32; McCormack, "How the (North) West Was Won," 134-38, 144-45, 214, 222, 238; Gibson to Allan, September 22, 1938 and Head to Secretary, December 30, 1937, RG10, vol. 6733, file 420-2-5, Reel C-8095, NAC.

16. McDougal to Finnie, July 3, 1926, RG10, vol. 6732, file 420-2B, Reel C-8094, NAC.

17. Martin and Whitehead to Scott, July 5, 1927, RG10, vol. 6732, file 420-2B, Reel C-8094, NAC.

18. Cornwall to Harkin, January 12, 1926, RG15, vol. 1140, file 4,283,438(4), NAC.

19. McCardle, *The Rules of the Game*, 7; Wetherell and Kmet, *Useful Pleasures*, 176.

20. McCardle, *The Rules of the Game*, 264.

21. *Calgary Herald*, March 28, 1935.

22. Ray, *The Canadian Fur Trade in the Industrial Age*, 134; *Annual Report, Alberta Department of Agriculture [for] 1934*, 48. Farmers could obtain a special permit to trap beaver or other protected animals that were damaging their property. The auctions were discontinued in 1935 when a private fur auction began operating in the city.

23. Crerar to Cross, March 21, 1939, Crerar to Tanner, May 4, 1939 and Director to Deputy Minister, May 5, 1939, RG10, vol. 6733, file 420-2-1, Reel C-8095, NAC.

24. Quoted in McCormack, "How the (North) West Was Won," 268; Wetherell and Kmet, *Useful Pleasures*, 175–77.

25. *Annual Report, Alberta Department of Agriculture [for] 1923*, 71.

26. Martin and Whitehead to Scott, July 5, 1927 and Hoadley to McLean, August 23, 1927, RG10, vol. 6732, file 420-2B, Reel C-8094, NAC.

27. Lawton to Ritchie, June 19, 1929 (copy) and Bryant to Officer Commanding, October 10, 1932, RG10, vol. 6733, file 420-2C, Reel C-8094, NAC.

28. Peter Clancy, "Game Policy in the Northwest Territories: The Shaping of Economic Position" (paper presented at the Annual Meeting, Canadian Political Science Association, June 6–8, 1983), 27–28; *Annual Report, Indian Affairs for Year Ended March 31, 1929*.

29. Coates, "The Sinews of Their Lives," 176, 186.

30. McCardle, *The Rules of the Game*, 7.

31. Card to Scott, May 22, 1924, and reply, June 10, 1924, RG10, vol. 6732, file 420-2B, Reel C-8094, NAC.

32. Hoadley to Stewart, March 6, 1923 and Scott to Stewart, November 13, 1923, RG10, vol. 6732, file 420-2B, Reel C-8094, NAC; Daniel, *Hunting, Fishing and Trapping Rights*, 24–25.

33. Hoadley to McLean, June 29, 1923, RG10, vol. 6732, file 420-2B, Reel C-8094, NAC.

34. Card to Scott, October 28, 1924, RG10, vol. 6732, file 420-2B, Reel C-8094, NAC; Daniel, *Hunting, Fishing and Trapping Rights*, 26–27.

35. Bury to Scott, July 7, 1926 and Bury to Scott, July 12, 1926, RG10, vol. 6732, file 420-2B, Reel C-8094, NAC. The province was approached about this by Duncan Campbell Scott (Scott to Hoadley, July 17, 1926, ibid.).

36. Memo for file, September 27, 1926, RG10, vol. 6732, file 420-2B, Reel C-8094, NAC.

37. Daniel, *Hunting, Fishing and Trapping Rights*, 29; Hoadley to McLean, September 24, 1927 and Lawton to McLean, October 28, 1927, RG10, vol. 6732, file 420-2B, Reel C-8094, NAC.

38. Norris to Rankine, March 13, 1935 and Mercredi to Norris, March 3, 1935 (copy), 75.75/4c, PAA; Laviolette to Minister of Agriculture, January 21, 1935, RG10, vol. 6744, file 420-6C-4, Reel C-8102, NAC.

39. Kent McNeil, *Indian Hunting, Trapping and Fishing Rights in the Prairie Provinces of Canada* (Saskatoon: University of Saskatchewan Native Law Centre, 1983), 20; MacInnes to Starnes, March 21, 1931, RG10, vol. 6731, file 420-1, Reel C-8093, NAC.

40. Murphy to Anderson, February 28, 1933, RG10, vol. 6731, file 420-2C, Reel C-8094. The federal over-ride was under S.91.24 which gave Canada jurisdiction over Indians and Indian lands. This power was apparently never exercised in the twentieth century.

41. McNeil, *Indian Hunting, Trapping and Fishing Rights in the Prairie Provinces*, 21–22; Scott, Circular Letter, May 30, 1931, RG10, vol. 6731, file 420-1, Reel C-8093, NAC.

42. Hoadley to Murphy, June 22, 1931 and Scott to Murphy, July 11, 1931, RG10, vol. 6732, file 420-2B, Reel C-8094, NAC.

43. McCardle, *The Rules of the Game*, 85–86, 241. The province defined forest preserves as "occupied" land since they had been set aside by the crown for a specific purpose and were not available for sale or lease (Gray to Craig, August 15, 1931 (copy), 75.75/6a, PAA).

44. Eben to Turner, December 27, 1946, RG10, vol. 6734, file 420–2–1–1, Reel C-8096, NAC. On judicial rulings on the meaning of "Indian" and the NRTA, see McNeil, *Indian Hunting, Trapping and Fishing Rights in the Prairie Provinces*, 24–30.

45. Hoadley to Murphy, June 23, 1932 and Memo, July 4, 1932, RG10, vol. 6733, file 420–2C, Reel C-8094, NAC.

46. Fraser to Brownlee, January 25, 1930, PP, file 59, PAA; Resolution, Cold Lake Guides Association, August 2, 1930, RG10, vol. 6732, file 420–2B, Reel C-8094, NAC; Spargo to Indian Affairs, February 6, 1935, (Resolution, October 6, 1933 attached) RG10, vol. 6733, file 420–2C, Reel C-8094 NAC; *Calgary Herald*, October 11, 1934.

47. Spargo to Indian Affairs, February 6, 1935, (Resolution, October 6, 1933 attached) and Kennedy to McGill, July 1, 1935, RG10, vol. 6733, file 420–2C, Reel C-8094, NAC.

48. Christianson to Secretary, March 5, 1935, RG10, vol. 6733, file 420–2C, Reel C-8094, NAC.

49. Spargo to MacKenzie, July 11, 1935, and reply, July 3, 1935, RG10, vol. 6733, file 420–2C, Reel C-8094, NAC

50. McCardle, *The Rules of the Game*, 94–95, 241.

51. Clancy, "Game Policy in the Northwest Territories," 37. For outlines of provincial policies, see: MacInnes to Special Game Committee, June 10, 1932, and Memo, February 23, 1934, RG10, vol. 6731, file 420–1, Reel C-8093, NAC. It seems that the white invasion of northern Ontario took place in the mid 1920s, slightly later than in Alberta (MacInnes to Special Game Committee, June 10, 1932, RG10, vol. 6731, file 420–1, Reel C-8093, NAC).

52. Extracts from Band Reports, July 1935, RG10, vol. 6731, file 420–1–4, Reel C-8093, NAC. For similar demands in 1938, see Report for June-August 1938, RG10, vol. 11949, Shannon No. 4, Pt. 1, NAC

53. Daniel, *Hunting, Fishing and Trapping Rights*, 35.

54. Grew to Allan, August 14, 1943, RG10, vol. 6743, file 420–2–2, Reel C-8095, NAC; Laviolette to Minister of Agriculture, March 31, 1936, RG10, vol. 6733, file 420–2C, Reel C-8094, NAC.

55. Daniel, *Hunting, Fishing and Trapping Rights*, 10–12.

56. Peter Clancy, "State Policy and the Native Trapper: Post-War Policy Toward Fur in the Northwest Territories," in *Aboriginal Land Use in Canada: Historical and Legal Aspects*, eds. Kerry Abel and Jean Friesen (Winnipeg: University of Manitoba Press, 1991), 195, 197; Ray, *The Canadian Fur Trade in the Industrial Age*, 117.

57. *Annual Report, Alberta Department of Agriculture for 1929*, 32.

58. Lawton to Hoadley, February 19, 1929, PP, file 15, PAA. On pressure for registered traplines, see for example, Plews to Commissioner, May 29, 1939 and Wallace to Sweeney, June 23, 1939, 67.21/325, PAA.

59. Dawn Balazs, *Transfer of Natural Resources in 1930 and Registered Traplines* (Edmonton: Treaty and Aboriginal Rights Research, Indian Association of Alberta, 1976), 12–13.

60. See for example, Grew to Allan, August 14, 1943 and Grew to Allan, March 11, 1943, RG10, vol. 6733, file 420–2–2, Reel C-8095, NAC.

61. Allan to Deputy Minister, August 19, 1943, RG10, vol. 6733, file 420-2-2, Reel C-8095, NAC.

62. Balazs, *Transfer of Natural Resources in 1930 and Registered Traplines*, 14.

63. Schmidt to Secretary, March 9, 1940 and Diary of Treaty Trip, June 20, 1942 (excerpt), RG10, vol. 6733, file 420-2-2, Reel C-8095, NAC; Report on Hay Lakes, December 19, 1948, RG10, vol. 6734, file 420-2-2-1-1, Reel C-8096, NAC; Arthur Ray, *I Have Lived Here*, 280.

64. Schmidt to Secretary, March 9, 1940, RG10, vol. 6733, file 420-2-5, Reel C-8095, NAC.

65. Schmidt to Secretary, March 9, 1940, RG10, vol. 6733, file 420-2-2, Reel C-8095, NAC.

66. McGill to Schmidt, November 11, 1943, RG10, vol. 6733, file 420-2-2, Reel C-8095, NAC.

67. Schmidt to Secretary, November 10, 1939, RG10, vol. 6733, file 420-2-2, Reel C-8095, NAC; Clancy, "State Policy and the Native Trapper," 197-98.

68. Letter from Huestis, August 19, 1942, RG10, vol. 6733, file 420-2-2, Reel C-8095, NAC; Director to Schmidt, November 11, 1943, RG10, vol. 6733, file 420-2-2, Reel C-8095, NAC; Balazs, *Transfer of Natural Resources in 1930 and Registered Traplines*, 39.

69. Grew to Allan, August 14, 1943, RG10, vol. 6733, file 420-2-2, Reel C-8095, NAC.

70. Mullen to Camsell, February 3, 1940 and Grew to Allan, January 5, 1943, RG10, vol. 6733, file 420-2-2, Reel C-8095, NAC.

71. Report on Hay Lakes, December 19, 1948, RG10, vol. 6734, file 420-2-2-1-1, Reel C-8096, NAC.

72. Grew to Allan, August 14, 1943 and January 5, 1943, RG10, vol. 6733, file 420-2-2, Reel C-8095, NAC; Balazs, *Transfer of Natural Resources in 1930 and Registered Traplines*, 61-68.

73. Forsland to Grew, October 5, 1943, Grew to Allan, January 11, 1944 and Grew to Allan, August 14, 1943, RG10, vol. 6733, file 420-2-2, Reel C-8095, NAC; Balazs, *Transfer of Natural Resources in 1930 and Registered Traplines*, 68.

74. Grew to Allan, January 5, 1943 and Grew to Skead, March 5, 1943, RG10, vol. 6733, file 420-2-2, Reel C-8095, NAC.

75. Allan to Huestis, September 5, 1944 and Allan to Deputy Minister, December 21, 1944, RG10, vol. 6734, file 420-2-2, NAC; Balazs, *Transfer of Natural Resources in 1930 and Registered Traplines*, 68-72.

76. Balazs, *Transfer of Natural Resources in 1930 and Registered Traplines*, 75-76; Conn to Skead, May 23, 1947, vol. 6743, file 420-2-2-1-1, Reel C-8096, NAC; Annual Report, Alberta Fur Supervisor, 1947-48 (typescript), RG10, vol. 6734, file 420-2-1-3, Reel C-8096, NAC.

77. McCormack, "How the (North) West Was Won," 258.

78. McCrimmon to Allan, June 2, 1945, RG10, vol. 6734, file 420-2-2, Reel C-8095, NAC; Mathewson, "The Geographical Impact of Outsiders…Fort Chipewyan," 68, 100.

79. Stewart to Gooderham, November 7, 1949, RG10, vol. 6734, file 420-2-1-3, Reel C-8096, NAC; Clancy, "State Policy and the Native Trapper," 201.

80. *Edmonton Journal*, April 11, 1946.

81. McCormack, "How The (North) West Was Won," 515-18.

82. *Edmonton Journal*, May 9, 1942; *Annual Report, Alberta Department of Agriculture for 1915*, 171; *Annual Report, Alberta Department of Agriculture for 1922*, 78; *Annual Report, Alberta Department of Agriculture for 1923*, 71.

83. On the fantasies about fur farming, see letters in RG15, vol. 1140, file 4,283,438(3A), NAC. On settlers' anticipations, see Lloyd to Williamson, July 5, 1925, and "Report of Conference on Muskrat Farming," n.d. (ca. 1927), RG15, vol. 1140, file 4,283,438(4), NAC.

84. Lawton to Harkin, December 31, 1923, RG15, vol. 1139, file 4,283,438(2), NAC; Ommanney to Dennis, November 1, 1929, 86.587/26, PAA.

85. *Annual Report, Alberta Department of Agriculture for 1933*, 48; *Annual Report, Alberta Department of Agriculture for 1935*, 43; R.W. Gillies, "History of Alberta Fur Farming" (typescript, copy at PAA, 1977), 14; *Edmonton Journal*, January 8, 1949; Wallace to Sweeney, March 16, 1939 and Sweeney to Mullen, March 21, 1939, 67.21/325, PAA.

86. *Annual Report, Alberta Department of Agriculture for 1938*, 49; D.B. Mullen, "The Game and Fish Resources of Our Province," 1939, Department of Agriculture Papers, 67.21, file 325, PAA; Conference Report, January 9–11, 1946, 73.307/3126.

87. Gillies, "A History of Alberta Fur Farming," 15–17; *[Grande Prairie] Northern Tribune*, April 13, 1939.

88. *Edmonton Journal*, October 23, 1945.

89. *Annual Report, Alberta Department of Agriculture for 1940*, 8, 58; Division file No. 39K 1350/16–95, Kinuso (June 9, 1939), 67.21/325, PAA. On fishing regulations and fur farmers, see for example, Minister to Murray, November 2, 1937, 73.307/333, PAA; Spargo to Schelfens, April 20, 1939 and Mullen to English, April 14, 1939, 67.21/325, PAA.

90. Longman to Montgomery, July 12, 1946, 72.302/3214, PAA; *Annual Report, Alberta Department of Agriculture for 1948*, 110; *Edmonton Journal*, August 9, 1947.

91. Clancy, "State Policy and the Native Trapper," 214

## ——15
### Diverging Paths

1. For a study of such provincial direct investment development policy, see Stephen G. Tomblin, "The Pacific Great Eastern Railway and W.A.C. Bennet's Defense of the North," *Journal of Canadian Studies* 24 (1989–90): 29–40.

2. Carney, "Relations in Education Between the Federal and Territorial Governments and the Roman Catholic Church," 3.

3. Vanderhill, "The Passing of the Pioneer Fringe," 217.

4. For a general discussion of social and economic change in the provincial norths during this period see Coates and Morrison, *The Forgotten North*, 97–112.

5. *Edmonton Journal*, October 17, 1967.

6. Peter Clancy, "Working on the Railway: A Case Study in Capital-State Relations," *Canadian Public Administration* 30 (1987): 450–71; Sheila Ann Brown, "The Impact of the Great Slave Lake Railway on Agricultural Land Use in the North Peace, Alberta" (Master's thesis, University of Alberta, 1971), 119–20.

7. Weller, "Political Disaffection in the Canadian Provincial North," 79–83.

8. Chalmers, "Schools For Our Other Indians," 100–103, 108.

9. *Report of the Royal Commission on the Development of Northern Alberta* (Edmonton: March 1958), 9.

10. Ferguson, *Athabasca Oil Sands*, 154–56.

11. Larry Pratt and Ian Urquhart, *The Last Great Forest. Japanese Multinationals and Alberta's Northern Forests* (Edmonton: NeWest Press, 1994), 3–5.

12. Pratt and Urquhart, *The Last Great Forest*, 14–17, 71.

# Bibliography

—— **Manuscript Collections**

GLENBOW ALBERTA INSTITUTE LIBRARY AND ARCHIVES, CALGARY
M271, Cornwall Papers.
M644, West Collection.
M2218, Lesser Slave Lake, Indian Agency Diary.
M2360, Agricultural Societies of Alberta Papers.
M4029, Kennedy Papers.
M4560, Loggie Collection.

NATIONAL ARCHIVES OF CANADA, OTTAWA
RG18, Records of the RCMP.
RG15, Records of the Department of the Interior.
RG10, Records of the Department of Indian Affairs.

PROVINCIAL ARCHIVES OF ALBERTA, EDMONTON
Information File, "Peace River."
Papers of the Anglican Diocese of Athabasca.
Premiers' Papers.
66.166, Department of Attorney General Papers.
67.21, Department of Agriculture Papers.
67.303, Department of Highways Papers.
68.131, Board of Industrial Relations Papers.
68.278, MD of Athabasca Papers.
69.296, Kerndale Community League Papers.
70.414, Alberta Sessional Papers.
70.208, MD of Fairview Papers.
70.237, MD of Spirit River Papers.
70.296, Town of Athabasca Papers.

72.302, Department of Agriculture Papers.

73.307, Department of Agriculture Papers.

73.316, Agricultural Societies Branch Papers.

74.174, Department of Municipal Affairs Papers.

74.347, Department of the Provincial Secretary Papers.

75.75, Papers of the Royal Commission on the Condition of the Halfbreed Population of the
 Province of Alberta (Ewing Commission).

75.126, Department of the Attorney General Papers.

76.517, Spirit Valley Community Association Papers.

82.212, Department of the Attorney General Papers.

86.587, Northern Alberta Railways Papers.


UNITED CHURCH ARCHIVES, TORONTO

Records of the United Church of Canada, 78.099c and 83.058c.


UNIVERSITY OF ALBERTA ARCHIVES

74.169, Pearce Papers.


GOVERNMENT PUBLICATIONS, GENERAL

Alberta. Annual Report, Department of Agriculture, 1907–1948.

[Alberta] Native Affairs Secretariat. *Alberta Metis Settlements: A Compendium of Background Documents.*
 Edmonton: 1984.

Alberta. *Report of the Royal Commission on the Development of Northern Alberta.* Edmonton: March 1958.

Canada. Annual Report, NWMP/RCMP, 1895-1-1945.

Canada. Annual Report, Department of Indian Affairs, 1899–1945.

Canada. Annual Report, Department of the Interior, 1899–1931.

Canada. Annual Report, Department of Agriculture, 1908–1947.

Canada. Annual Report, Department of Immigration and Colonization, 1919–1930.

Canada. Annual Report, Department of Transport, 1920–1942.

Canada. Annual Report, Department of Marine and Fisheries, 1906–1931.

Canada. Annual Report, Postmaster General, 1928–1930.

Canada. Department of Agriculture, Experimental Farms Service, Dominion Experimental
 Station, Beaverlodge Alberta. *Progress Report 1937–1947.* Ottawa: King's Printer, 1949.

Canada. Department of Agriculture, Experimental Farms Service, Dominion Experimental
 Substation, Fort Vermilion, Alberta. *Progress Report, 1939–1948.* Ottawa: King's Printer, 1950.

Canada. Department of the Interior. *The Lac La Biche District, Alberta. A Guide to Intending Settlers.*
 Ottawa: King's Printer, 1923.

Canada. Reports of the Board of Railway Commissioners for Canada, 1916–1946.

*Canada's Fertile Northland: A Glimpse of the Enormous Resources of Part of the Unexplored Regions of the
 Dominion,* edited by Ernest Chambers. Ottawa: Government Printing Bureau, 1907.

Dominion Bureau of Statistics. *Census of Industry, 1919, Fisheries Statistics 1919.* Canada Sessional
 Paper No. 17d, 1921.

Great Mackenzie Basin. The Senate Reports of 1887–1888, edited by Ernest Chambers.
 (Ottawa: King's Printer, 1908).

*A History of the Royal Canadian Mounted Police Aviation Section.* Ottawa: Information Canada, 1973.

Northwest Territories. Annual Report, Department of Agriculture, 1898–1904.

*Peace River District Farm Water Supply Assistance Policy.* Edmonton: Department of Agriculture, n.d. [1945].

*Report of the Select Committee of the Senate Appointed to Enquire into the Resources of the Great Mackenzie Basin.* Ottawa: Queen's Printer, 1888.

### ⸺ Newspapers and Magazines

Clippings, various topics, Legislature Library, Edmonton.

*Calgary Herald,* 1907–1911, 1935–1936.

*Edmonton Bulletin,* 1883–1899.

*Family Herald and Weekly Star,* 1923.

*Grand Prairie Herald,* 1913–1932.

[Grande Prairie] *Northern Tribune,* 1932–1939.

[Grande Prairie] *Herald Tribune,* 1939–1940, 1943–1947.

*Grouard News,* 1912–1915.

*Maclean's Magazine,* 1924.

*Missions de la Congregation des Missionnaires Oblats de Marie Immaculée,* 1900–1912.

*Nor'West Miner,* 1935–1937.

*Peace River Record,* 1915–1947.

*Spirit River Echo,* 1917–1921.

*[Waterhole] Northern Review,* 1923–1928.


### ⸺ Books and Articles

Abel, Kerry. *Drum Songs. Glimpses of Dene History.* Montreal and Kingston: McGill-Queen's University Press, 1993.

Acton, B.K. "A Comparison of Farms in the Grande Prairie District of Alberta 1930 and 1942." *Economic Annalist* 13 (1943): 53–56.

Acton, B.K., and Spence, C.C. *A Study of Pioneer Farming in the Fringe Areas of the Peace River, Alberta, 1942.* Ottawa: Department of Agriculture, Publication No. 792, Technical Bulletin No. 60, 1947.

Adas, Michael. *Machines as the Measure of Men: Science, Technology and Ideologies of Western Dominance.* Ithaca: Cornell University Press, 1989.

"Alberta Interpretations of the Treaties." In *The Spirit of the Alberta Indian Treaties,* edited by Richard Price, pp. 103–60. Montreal: Institute for Research on Public Policy, 1980. [Reprinted by The University of Alberta Press, 1999.]

*Alberta Metis Settlements: A Compendium of Background Documents.* Edmonton: [Alberta] Native Affairs Secretariat, 1984.

Albright, W.D. "Crop Growth in High Latitudes." *The Geographical Review* 23 (1933): 608–20.

Alcock, F.J. "Scow Brigade on the Athabasca." *Canadian Geographical Journal* 4 (1932): 97–107.

Altmeyer, George. "Three Ideas of Nature in Canada, 1893–1914." *Journal of Canadian Studies* 11 (1976): 21–36.

Armstrong, J.W. "Municipal Problems in Western Provinces." *Conservation of Life* 3, no. 3 (July 1917): 59–63.

Athabasca Historical Society, Gregory, David and Athabasca University. *Athabasca Landing: An Illustrated History*. Athabasca: Athabasca Historical Society, 1986.

Aubrey, Merrily K. *Place Names of Alberta. Volume IV. Northern Alberta*. Calgary: Alberta Community Development, Friends of Geographical Names of Alberta Society and University of Calgary Press, 1996.

Babcock, D.R. "Lesser Slave Lake: A Regional History." Typescript, 1978. Copy in Historic Sites Service Library, Edmonton.

———. "Autonomy and Alienation in Alberta: Premier A.C. Rutherford." *Prairie Forum* 6 (1981): 117–28.

Balazs, Dawn. *Transfer of Natural Resources in 1930 and Registered Traplines*. Edmonton: Treaty and Aboriginal Rights Research, Indian Association of Alberta, 1976.

Barman, Jean. *The West Beyond the West*. Toronto: University of Toronto Press, 1991.

Bellman, Jennifer, and Hanks, Christopher. "Northern Metis and the Fur Trade." In *Picking Up the Threads. Metis History in the Mackenzie Basin*, pp. 29–68. N.p.: The Metis Heritage Association of the Northwest Territories, 1998.

Bennett, Gordon. *Yukon Transportation: A History*. Ottawa: Canadian Historic Sites Occasional Papers in Archaeology and History, No. 19, 1979.

Berger, Carl. "The True North Strong and Free." In *Nationalism in Canada*, edited by Peter Russell, pp. 3–26. Toronto: McGraw-Hill Ryerson Ltd., 1966.

———. *The Sense of Power. Studies in the Ideas of Canadian Imperialism 1867–1914*. Toronto: University of Toronto Press, 1971.

———. *The Writing of Canadian History*. Toronto: Oxford University Press, 1976.

Bezanson, A.M. *Sodbusters Invade the Peace*. Toronto: The Ryerson Press, 1954.

Blue, John. *Alberta Past and Present*. Vol. 1. Chicago: Pioneer Historical Publishing Company, 1924.

Boon, T.C.B. *The Anglican Church from the Bay to the Rockies. A History of the Ecclesiastical Province of Rupert's Land and its Dioceses from 1820 to 1950*. Toronto: Ryerson Press, 1962.

Bothwell, Robert, Drummond, Ian and English, John. *Canada 1900–1945*. Toronto: University of Toronto Press, 1987.

Brady, Archange J. *A History of Fort Chipewyan*. Westlock: Harmony Print Shop, 1994.

Brick, A.L. "Rev. J. Gough Brick and His Shaftesbury Mission Farm." *Alberta Historical Review* 3 (1955): 3–12.

Briggs, Gordon. "Waterways." *The Beaver*, Outfit 270, no. 2 (September 1939): 28–29.

Brightman, Robert A. *Grateful Prey. Rock Cree Human-Animal Relationships*. Berkeley: University of California Press, 1993.

Brown, Richard. "A Town Bypassed: Grouard Alberta and the Building of the Edmonton, Dunvegan and British Columbia Railway." *The Archivist*, May-June 1990: 10–12.

Brown, Sheila Ann. "The Impact of the Great Slave Lake Railway on Agricultural Land Use in the North Peace, Alberta." Master's thesis, University of Alberta, 1971.

Buchan, John. *Memory Hold the Door*. Toronto: The Musson Book Co. Ltd., 1940.

Burnet, Jean R., and Palmer, Howard. *"Coming Canadians" An Introduction to a History of Canada's Peoples*. Toronto: Canada Department of the Secretary of State and McClelland and Stewart, 1988.

Burt, A.L. "Our Dynamic Society." [University of Alberta] *The Press Bulletin*, December 12, 1930, 4.

Cameron, Agnes Deans. *The New North. Being Some Account of a Woman's Journey Through Canada to the Arctic*. New York: D. Appleton and Co., 1910.

Campbell, Isabelle. *Grande Prairie, Capital of the Peace*. N.p.: n.p., 1968.

Camsell, Charles. *Son of the North*. Toronto: Ryerson Press, 1954.

Card, B.Y., Hirabayashi, G.K. and French, C.L. *The Metis in Alberta Society*. Edmonton: A Report on Project A (1960–63), University of Alberta Committee for Social Research, prepared for The Alberta Tuberculosis Association, 1963.

Carney, Robert J. "Relations in Education Between the Federal and Territorial Governments and the Roman Catholic Church in the Mackenzie District, Northwest Territories, 1867–1961." Ph.D. dissertation, University of Alberta, 1971.

———. "The Grey Nuns and the Children of Holy Angels: Fort Chipewyan 1874–1924." In *The Uncovered Past: Roots of Northern Alberta Societies*, edited by Patricia A. McCormack and Geoffrey Ironside, pp. 105–25. Edmonton: Canadian Circumpolar Institute, Circumpolar Research Series No. 3, 1993.

Carrothers, Edward H. "Three Trips to the Peace River Country." *Alberta Historical Review* 13 (1965): 24–29.

Carter, Sarah. *Lost Harvests. Prairie Indian Reserve Farmers and Government Policy*. Montreal and Kingston: McGill-Queen's University Press, 1990.

Chalmers, John W. "The Muskeg Flier. The Alberta and Great Waterways Railway." In *The Land of Peter Pond*, edited by John W. Chalmers, pp. 77–87. Edmonton: Boreal Institute for Northern Studies, Occasional Publication No. 12, 1974.

———. "Wayfaring, Airborne and Earthbound." In *The Land of Peter Pond*, edited by John W. Chalmers, pp. 89–97. Edmonton: Boreal Institute for Northern Studies, Occasional Publication No. 12, 1974.

———. "Schools For Our Other Indians: Education of Western Canadian Metis Children." In *The Canadian West. Social Change and Economic Development*, edited by Henry C. Klassen, pp. 93–109. Calgary: University of Calgary Comprint Publishing Company, 1977.

———. "Missions and Schools in the Athabasca." *Alberta History* 31 (1983): 24–29.

Chamberlain, Richard J. "Monkman Pass." *The Beaver*, Outfit 312:1 (1981): 8–13.

Clancy, Peter. "Game Policy in the Northwest Territories: The Shaping of Economic Position." Paper presented at the Annual Meeting, Canadian Political Science Association, June 6–8, 1983.

———. "Working on the Railway: A Case Study in Capital-State Relations." *Canadian Public Administration* 30 (1987): 450–71.

———. "State Policy and the Native Trapper: Post-War Policy Toward Fur in the Northwest Territories." In *Aboriginal Land Use in Canada: Historical and Legal Aspects*, edited by Kerry Abel and Jean Friesen, pp. 191–217. Winnipeg: University of Manitoba Press, 1991.

Coates, Kenneth. "The Federal Government and the Economic System of the Yukon Territory: Historical and Contemporary Aspects of Northern Development." In *For Purposes of Dominion: Essays in Honour of Morris Zaslow*, edited by Kenneth S. Coates and William R. Morrison, pp. 105–22. North York: Captus University Press Inc., 1989.

————. "By The Sinews of Their Lives: Native Access to Resources in the Yukon, 1890 to 1950." In *Aboriginal Resource Use in Canada: Historical and Legal Aspects*, edited by Kerry Abel and Jean Friesen, pp. 173–90. Winnipeg: University of Manitoba Press, 1991.

Coates, Kenneth, and Morrison, William. *The Forgotten North. A History of Canada's Provincial Norths*. Toronto: James Lorimer and Co. Publishers, 1992.

————. *The Alaska Highway in World War II. The U.S. Army of Occupation in Canada's Northwest*. Norman: University of Oklahoma Press, 1992.

Comfort, D.J. *Meeting Place of Many Waters: A History of Fort McMurray*. Parts 1 and 2. N.p.: n.p., 1973.

————. *Pass The McMurray Salt Please*. Fort McMurray: n.p., 1975.

————. "Tom Draper, Oil Sands Pioneer." *Alberta History* 25 (1977): 25–29.

————. *The Abasand Fiasco*. Edmonton: Friesen Printers, 1980.

Cooke, Edgar D. "Boom and Bust, Bust and Boom: Fort McMurray and Waterways." In *The Land of Peter Pond*, edited by John Chalmers, pp. 99–108. Edmonton: Boreal Institute for Northern Studies, Occasional Publication No. 12, 1974.

Coté, J.G. "J.L. Coté, Surveyor." *Alberta History* 31 (1983): 29–32.

Court, Thomas. "A Search for Oil." *Alberta Historical Review* 21 (1973): 10–12.

Crawford, Margaret. "A Geographic Study of the Distribution of Population Change in Alberta, 1931–1961." Master's thesis, University of Alberta, 1962.

Crosby, Alfred W. *Ecological Imperialism. The Biological Expansion of Europe, 900–1900*. Cambridge: Cambridge University Press, 1994.

Daniel, Richard. *Hunting, Fishing and Trapping Rights: White Competition and the Concept of Exclusive Rights for Indians*. Typescript. Edmonton: Treaty and Aboriginal Rights Research of the Indian Association of Alberta, March 1976.

————. "Indian Rights and Hinterland Resources: The Case of Northern Alberta." M.A. thesis, University of Alberta, 1977.

————. "The Spirit and Terms of Treaty Eight." In *The Spirit of the Alberta Indian Treaties*, edited by Richard Price, pp. 47–100. Montreal: Institute for Research on Public Policy, 1980. [Reprinted by the University of Alberta Press, 1999.]

Dawson, C.A., and Murchie, R.W. *The Settlement of the Peace River Country. A Study of a Pioneer District*. Toronto: The Macmillan Company of Canada, 1934.

DeBolt and District Pioneer Museum. *Sawmills: Across the Smokey*. (First draft of book.) DeBolt: DeBolt and District Pioneer Museum, 1977.

den Otter, A.A. "The Hudson's Bay Company's Prairie Transportation Problem, 1870–1885." In *The Developing West: Essays on Canadian History in Honor of Lewis H. Thomas*, edited by John Foster, pp. 25–47. Edmonton: University of Alberta Press, 1983.

Devine, Heather. "Metis or Country-Born. The Case of the Klynes." Unpublished paper presented at the Learned Societies Conference, June 6, 1997.

Devine, Marina. "The First Northern Metis." In *Picking Up the Threads. Metis History in the Mackenzie Basin*, pp. 5–27. N.p.: The Metis Heritage Association of the Northwest Territories, 1998.

Dickason, Olive Patricia. *Canada's First Nations. A History of Founding Peoples from Earliest Times*. Toronto: McClelland and Stewart, 1992.

Dion, Joseph F. *My Tribe The Crees*. Calgary: Glenbow Museum, 1979.

Dobbin, Murray. *The One-And-A-Half Men. The Story of Jim Brady and Malcolm Norris. Metis Patriots of the 20th Century.* Regina: Gabriel Dumont Institute, 1981.

Dussault, Gabriel. *Le curé Labelle: Messianisme utopie et colonisation au Québec 1850–1900.* Montréal: Hurtubise HMN, 1983.

Eagle, John. "J.D. McArthur and the Peace River Railway." *Alberta History* 28 (1981): 33–39.

*East Prairie Metis 1939–1979. 40 Years of Determination.* N.p.: 1979.

Ehrlich, W.A., and Odynsky, William. "Soils Developed Under Forest in the Great Plains Region." *Agricultural Institute Review* 15 (1960): 29–32.

*Elizabeth Metis Settlement. A Local History.* Altona: Friesen Printers, 1979.

Ells, Sidney. *Northland Trails.* Toronto: Burns and MacEachern, 1956.

"An Empire in the Making." *The Resources and Opportunities of the Peace and Mackenzie River Area. Edmonton—The Gateway.* Edmonton: Town Topics Publishing Co., 1930.

English, Robert Elwin. "An Economic History of Northern Alberta." MSA thesis, University of Toronto, 1933.

Ens, Gerhard. *Homeland to Hinterland. The Changing Worlds of the Red River Metis.* Toronto: University of Toronto Press, 1996.

Faiz, Faiz Ahmed. *Poems By Faiz,* translated by V.G. Kiernan. London: George Allen and Unwin Ltd., 1971.

Fereira, Darlene A. *Need Not Greed: The Lubicon Lake Cree Band Land Claim in Historical Perspective.* Master's thesis, University of Alberta, 1990.

Ferguson, Barry. *Athabasca Oil Sands. Northern Resource Exploration 1875–1951.* Regina: Alberta Culture and Canadian Plains Research Centre, 1985.

Finkel, Alvin. *The Social Credit Phenomenon in Alberta.* Toronto: University of Toronto Press, 1989.

Fisher, A.D. "A Colonial Education System: Historical Changes in Schooling in Fort Chipewyan." *Canadian Journal of Anthropology* 2 (1981): 37–44.

Flanagan, Thomas. "Some Factors Bearing on the Origins of the Lubicon Lake Dispute," *Alberta* 2 (1990): 47–62.

———. *Metis Lands in Manitoba.* Calgary: University of Calgary Press, 1991.

"Fort McMurray. Great City of the North." *Alberta Historical Review* 7 (1959): 24.

Fort McMurray Historical Society. *Timeline, Fort McMurray ca. 1700–1980.* Typescript. Fort McMurray Historical Society, 1993.

Foster, Janet. *Working for Wildlife. The Beginning of Preservation in Canada.* Toronto: University of Toronto Press, 1978.

Foster, J. E. "Indian-White Relations in the Prairie West During the Fur Trade Period—A Compact?" In *The Spirit of the Alberta Indian Treaties,* edited by Richard Price, pp. 181–200. Montreal: Institute for Research on Public Policy, 1980. [Reprinted by the University of Alberta Press, 1999.]

Francis, Daniel, and Payne, Michael. *A Narrative History of Fort Dunvegan.* Winnipeg: Watson and Dwyer, 1993.

Francis, R. Douglas. *Images of the West: Responses to the Canadian Prairies.* Saskatoon: Western Producer Prairie Books, 1989.

———. "In Search of Prairie Myth: A Survey of the Intellectual and Cultural Historiography of Prairie Canada." *Journal of Canadian Studies* 24 (1989): 44–69.

Friesen, Gerald. *The Canadian Prairies A History.* Toronto: University of Toronto Press, 1984.

———. "The Prairie West Since 1945: An Historical Survey." In *The Making of the Modern West: Western Canada Since 1945*, edited by A.W. Rasporich, pp. 1–10. Calgary: University of Calgary Press, 1984.

Fumoleau, Rene. *As Long As This Land Shall Last. A History of Treaty 8 and Treaty 11 1870–1939*. Toronto: McClelland and Stewart, n.d.

Friesen, Jean. "Grant Me Wherewith To Make My Living." In *Aboriginal Land Use in Canada: Historical and Legal Aspects*, edited by Kerry Abel and Jean Friesen, pp. 141–55. Winnipeg: University of Manitoba Press, 1995.

Gaffield, Chad. "The New Regional History: Rethinking the History of the Outaouais." *Journal of Canadian Studies* 26 (1991): 64–81.

Garrett, Denzil. "The Northern Alberta Railway. A Geographical Analysis." Master's thesis, University of Alberta, 1962.

Gillies, R.W. "History of Alberta Fur Farming." Typescript, copy at PAA. 1977.

Godsell, Philip. *Arctic Trader. An Account of Twenty Years with the Hudson's Bay Company*. Toronto: The Macmillan Co. of Canada Ltd., 1946.

Gordon, Stanley. *Agricultural Tractors in Alberta Since 1925*. Wetaskiwin: Reynolds Alberta Museum, Background Paper No. 17, 1983.

Gottesman, Dan. "Native Hunting and the Migratory Birds Convention Act: Historical, Political and Ideological Perspectives." *Journal of Canadian Studies* 18 (1983): 67–89.

Goulet, Jean-Guy. "Religious Dualism Among Athapaskan Catholics." *Canadian Journal of Anthropology* 3 (1982): 1–18.

Graham, Maxwell. *Canada's Wild Buffalo. Observations in the Wood Buffalo Park*. Ottawa: King's Printer, 1923.

Grant, J.C. Boileau. *Anthropometry of the Chipewyan and Cree Indians of Lake Athabasca*. Ottawa: National Museum of Canada, Bulletin No. 64, Anthropological Series No. 14, 1930.

Gray, James. *Men Against the Desert*. Saskatoon: Western Producer Prairie Books, 1967.

Groh, Herbert. *Peace-Athabaska Weeds. A Reconnaissance Appraisal*. Ottawa: Department of Agriculture Publication No. 556, 1937.

Grouard, Msgr. Emile. *Souvenirs de mes soixant Ans d'Apostolat dans l'Athabaska-Mackenzie*. Winnipeg: La Liberte, n.d.

*Grouard: The Coming Metropolis of the Great Peace River Country, Alberta Canada*. Grouard: The Grouard Board of Trade, 1913.

Grow, Stewart. "The Blacks of Amber Valley—Negro Pioneering in Northern Alberta." *Canadian Ethnic Studies* 4 (1974): 17–38.

Gulig, Anthony G. "Sizing Up The Catch: Native-Newcomer Resource Competition and the Early Years of Saskatchewan's Northern Commercial Fishery." *Saskatchewan History* 47 (1995): 3–11.

Hall, D.J. "The Half-Breed Claims Commission." *Alberta History* 25 (1977): 1–8.

Hamelin, Louis-Edmond. *Canadian Nordicity: It's Your North Too*. Montreal: Harvest House, 1978.

Hansen, Evelyn. *Where Go the Boats...Navigation on the Peace 1792–1952*. Peace River: Peace River Centennial Museum, n.d.

Harrison, David A. "The First Winter Road Ever." *Up Here* 6 (1990): 55–57.

———. "Opening and Naming the Mackenzie Highway." *Alberta History* 38 (1990): 24–29.

Hatcher, Colin. *The Northern Alberta Railways*. Vol. 2. Calgary: British Railway Modellers of North America, 1987.

Hatt, Ken. "Ethnic Discourse in Alberta: Land and the Metis in the Ewing Commission." *Canadian Ethnic Studies* 17 (1985): 64–79.

Heard, Jay Stewart. "The Alberta and Great Waterways Railway Dispute 1909–13." Master's thesis, University of Alberta, 1990.

Heinimann, David. "Latitude Rising: Historical Continuity in Canadian Nordicity." *Journal of Canadian Studies* 28 (1993): 134–39.

*History, Administrative Organization and Work of the Provincial Department of Public Health and Boards of Health*. Edmonton: King's Printer, 1937.

Hewitt, C. Gordon. "The Conservation of Wild Life in Canada in 1917: A Review." In *Report of the Ninth Annual Meeting*. Ottawa: Commission of Conservation Canada, 1918.

Hill, Judith. "Alberta's Black Settlers: A Study of Canadian Immigration Policy and Practice," Master's thesis, University of Alberta, 1981.

Holmgren, Eric J. "Fort Dunvegan." *The Beaver*, Outfit 312, no. 2 (Autumn 1981): 53–59.

Holtslander, Dale. "Railway to Athabasca." *Alberta History* 26 (1978): 25–28.

———. "The Challenge of the Lesser Slave River." *Alberta History* 28 (1980): 23–36.

Huel, Raymond J.A. *Proclaiming the Gospel to the Indians and the Metis*. Edmonton: University of Alberta Press, 1996.

Hufton, Olwen H. *The Poor of Eighteenth Century France 1750–1789*. Oxford: Oxford University Press, 1974.

Inkster, Tom. "I Remember Peace River Jim." *Alberta History* 31 (1983): 9–13.

Irwin, Robert Scott. "The Emergence of a Regional Identity: The Peace River Country, 1910–46." Ph.D. dissertation, University of Alberta, 1995.

———. "Whose Railway Was It?" In *Edmonton: The Life of a City*, edited by Bob Hesketh and Frances Swyripa, pp. 116–25. Edmonton: Newest Publishers, 1995.

Ives, John W. "The Ten Thousand Years Before the Fur Trade in Northeastern Alberta." In *The Uncovered Past: Roots of Northern Alberta Societies*, edited by Patricia A. McCormack and R. Geoffrey Ironsides, pp. 5–31. Edmonton: Canadian Circumpolar Institute, University of Alberta, Circumpolar Research Series No. 3, 1993.

———. *A Theory of Northern Athapaskan Prehistory*. Boulder and San Francisco: Westview Press and Calgary: University of Calgary Press, 1990.

Jackson, Frank. *Jam in the Bedroll*. Nanaimo: Shires Books, 1979.

Jackson, Mary Percy. *Suitable for the Wilds. Letters from Northern Alberta 1929–1931*. Edited by Janice Dickin McGinnis. Toronto: University of Toronto Press, 1995.

Jackson, Wayne. "Ethnicity and Areal Organization Among French Canadian in the Peace River District, Alberta." Master's thesis, University of Alberta, 1970.

Jarvenpa, Robert. "The Ubiquitous Bushman: Chipewyan-White Trapper Relations of the 1930s." In *Problems in the Prehistory of the North American Subarctic. The Athapaskan Question*, edited by James Helmer, S. VanDyke and F.J. Kense, pp. 165–85. Calgary: University of Calgary Department of Archaeology, 1977.

Jenness, R.A. *Great Slave Lake Fishing Industry*. Ottawa: Northern Co-ordination and Research Centre, Department of Northern Affairs and Natural Resources, 1963 (NCRC 63-10).

Jones, David C. *Feasting on Misfortune*. Edmonton: University of Alberta Press, 1998.

Judge, J.W. "Early Railroading in Northern Alberta." *Alberta Historical Review* 6 (1958): 12–19.

Kelly, L.V. *North with Peace River Jim*, edited by Hugh Dempsey. Calgary: Glenbow Alberta Institute Historical Paper No. 2, 1972.

Keywan, Zonia. "Mary Percy Jackson: Pioneer Doctor." *The Beaver*, Outfit 308, no. 2 (Winter 1977): 41–47.

Kitto, F.H. *The Peace River Country Canada. Its Resources and Opportunities*. 1st Edition, 1920, 3rd Revised Edition, 1930. Ottawa: Department of the Interior, 1920 and 1930.

Knill, William D. "Schools in the Wilderness." In *On The Edge of the Shield. Fort Chipewyan and its Hinterland*, edited by John W. Chalmers, pp. 30–39. Edmonton: The Boreal Institute for Northern Studies, University of Alberta, Occasional Publication No. 7, 1971.

*Lake Saskatoon Reflections: A Local History of Lake Saskatoon District*. Edmonton: Friesen Printers for Lake Saskatoon History Book Committee, 1980.

Lamont, Glenda. "Migrants and Migration in Part of the South Peace River Region, Alberta." Master's thesis, University of Alberta, 1970.

Larisey, Peter. "Nationalist Aspects of Lawren Harris's Aesthetics." *Bulletin*, National Gallery of Canada, 23 (1974): 3–9.

Lautt, M.L. "Sociology and the Canadian Plains." In *A Region of the Mind*, edited by Richard Allen, pp. 125–51. Regina: Canadian Plains Research Centre, 1973.

Leppard, Henry M. "The Settlement of the Peace River Country." *The Geographical Review* 35 (1935): 62–78.

Levasseur, Donat. *Les Oblates de Marie Immaculée dan l'Ouest et le Nord du Canada 1845–1967*. Edmonton: University of Alberta Press, 1995.

Leonard, David. "The Great Peace River Land Scandal." *Alberta History* 39 (1991): 9–16.

———. *Delayed Frontier The Peace River Country to 1909*. Calgary: Detselig Enterprises Ltd., 1995.

Leonard, David, and Lemieux, Victoria. *A Fostered Dream. The Lure of the Peace River Country 1872–1914*. Calgary: Detselig Enterprises Ltd., 1992.

Lewis, H. "Maskuta: The Ecology of Indian Fire in Northern Alberta." *Western Canadian Journal of Anthropology* 7 (1977): 15–52.

Lothian, W.F. *A History of Canada's National Parks*. Vol. 1 and Vol. 4. Ottawa: Parks Canada, 1979.

Low, Elizabeth. "Profitableness of Hog Production in the Bear Lake District of Alberta." *The Economic Annalist* (August 1943), 50–52.

MacGregor, J.G. *The Land of Twelve Foot Davis*. Edmonton: Applied Art Products Ltd., 1952.

———. *The Klondike Rush Through Edmonton 1897–1898*. Toronto: McClelland and Stewart, 1970.

———. *From Paddle Wheels to Bucket Wheels on the Athabasca*. Toronto: McClelland and Stewart, 1974.

MacKinnon, C.S. "Some Logistics of Portage La Loche (Methy)." *Prairie Forum* 5 (1980): 51–65.

———. "Portaging on the Slave River (Fort Smith)." *The Musk-Ox* 27 (1980): 21–35.

Maclulich, T.D. "Reading the Land: The Wilderness Tradition in Canadian Letters." *Journal of Canadian Studies* 20 (1985): 29–44.

McCandless, Robert. *Yukon Wildlife: A Social History*. Edmonton: University of Alberta Press, 1985.

McCardle, Bennet. *The Rules of the Game: The Development of Government Controls Over Indian Hunting and Trapping in Treaty 8 (Alberta) to 1930*. Ottawa: Treaty and Aboriginal Rights Research (TARR) of the Indian Association of Alberta, 1976.

McCarthy, Martha. *Grand Rapids, Manitoba*. Winnipeg: Manitoba Culture, Heritage and
    Recreation, Historic Resources, Papers in Manitoba History No. 1, 1988.
———. *From the Great River to the Ends of the Earth: Oblate Missions to the Dene 1847–1921*. Edmonton:
    University of Alberta Press, 1995.
McConnell, J.G. "The Fort Smith Area 1780 to 1961. An Historical Geography." Master's thesis,
    University of Toronto, 1965.
McCormack, Patricia. "How The (North) West Was Won: Development and
    Underdevelopment in the Fort Chipewyan Region." Ph.D. dissertation, University of
    Alberta, 1984.
McCormick, Peter. "Regionalism in Canada: Disentangling the Threads." *Journal of Canadian
    Studies* 24 (1989): 5–21.
McCormick, P.L. "Transportation and Settlement: Problems in the Expansion of the Frontier
    of Saskatchewan and Assiniboia in 1904." *Prairie Forum* 5 (1980): 1–18.
McCullough, Edward J., and Maccagno, Michael. *Lac La Biche and the Early Fur Traders*.
    Edmonton: Canadian Circumpolar Institute and Alberta Vocational College, Lac La
    Biche, Archaeological Survey of Alberta, Occasional Publication No. 29, 1991.
McDonald, John. "Soldier Settlement and Depression Settlement in the Forest Fringe of
    Saskatchewan." *Prairie Forum* 6 (1981): 35–54.
McDonald, Robert A.J. *Making Vancouver. Class, Status, and Social Boundaries, 1863–1913*. Vancouver:
    University of British Columbia Press, 1996.
McFarlane, R.J. "Some Factors Contributing to the Success of Farm Operations on the Grey
    Wooded Soils of Alberta." *The Economic Annalist* (December 1959): 137–43.
McNeil, Kent. *Indian Hunting, Trapping and Fishing Rights in the Prairie Provinces of Canada*. Saskatoon:
    University of Saskatchewan Native Law Centre, 1983.
McQuarrie, A.H. "Building the Edson Trail." *Alberta Historical Review* 14 (1966): 1–6.
Madill, Dennis F.K. *Treaty Research Report: Treaty Eight*. Ottawa: Treaties and Historical Research
    Centre, Indian and Northern Affairs Canada, 1986.
Mair, Charles. *Through The Mackenzie Basin: A Narrative of the Athabasca and Peace River Treaty Expedition
    of 1899*. Toronto: William Briggs, 1908. [Reissued by the University of Alberta Press and
    Edmonton & District Historical Society, 1999.]
Mathers, Charles W. "A Trip to the Arctic Circle." *Alberta Historical Review* 20 (1972): 6–15.
Mathewson, Pamela Ann. "The Geographical Impact of Outsiders on the Community of Fort
    Chipewyan, Alberta." Master's thesis, University of Alberta, 1974.
Merrill, Gordon C. "Human Geography of the Lesser Slave Lake Area of Alberta." *Geographical
    Bulletin* No. 3 (1953): 37–49.
Miller, J.R. *Shingwauk's Vision. A History of Native Residential Schools*. Toronto: University of Toronto
    Press, 1996.
Miller, Richard B. "Effectiveness of A Whitefish Hatchery." *The Journal of Wildlife Management* 10
    (1946): 317–21
Milne, Jack. *Trading for Milady's Furs. In Service of the Hudson's Bay Company 1923–1943*. Saskatoon:
    Western Producer Prairie Books, 1975.
Morrison, William R. *Showing the Flag. The Mounted Police and Canadian Sovereignty in the North,
    1894–1925*. Vancouver: University of British Columbia Press, 1985.
Morton, W.L. *Manitoba: A History*. Toronto: University of Toronto Press, 1957.

————. "The 'North' in Canadian Historiography." *Transactions of the Royal Society of Canada*, 4th Series, 8 (1970): 31–40.

Moss, H.C. "Mapping Our Soils. The Work of Canadian Soil Surveys." *Agricultural Institute Review* 15 (1960): 13–14.

Murphy, Peter J. *History of Forest and Prairie Fire Control in Alberta*. Edmonton: Alberta Energy and Natural Resources, 1985.

Myers, Patricia. *Sky Riders. An Illustrated History of Aviation in Alberta 1906–1945*. Saskatoon: Fifth House, 1995.

Nemerov, Alex. "'Doing the 'Old America'" The Image of the American West 1880–1920." In *The West As America: Reinterpreting Images of the Frontier 1820–1920*, edited by William H. Truetten, pp. 285–343. Washington: National Museum of American Art, Published by the Smithsonian Press, 1991.

Newell, Dianne. "The Importance of Information and Misinformation in the Making of the Klondike Gold Rush." *Journal of Canadian Studies* 21 (1986–87): 95–111.

Nicks, Trudy. "Mary Anne's Dilemma: The Ethnohistory of an Ambivalent Identity." *Canadian Ethnic Studies* 17 (1985): 103–14.

————. "Native Response to the Early Fur Trade at Lesser Slave Lake." In *"Le Castor Fait Tout" Selected Papers of the Fifth North American Fur Trade Conference 1985*, edited by Bruce Trigger, Toby Morantz and Louise Dechene, pp. 278–310. Montreal: St. Louis Historical Society, 1987.

Nicks, Trudy and Morgan, Kenneth. "Grande Cache: The Historic Development of an Indigenous Alberta Metis Population." In *Being and Becoming Metis in North America*, edited by Jacqueline Peterson and Jennifer S. Brown, pp. 163–81. Winnipeg: University of Manitoba Press, 1985.

O'Brien, Charles F. "Northwest Staging Route." *Alberta Historical Review* 17 (1969): 14–22.

Oliver, E.H. *The Canadian North-West. Its Early Development and Legislative Records*. Vol. 2. Ottawa: Government Printing Bureau, 1915, Publication of the Canadian Archives No. 9.

Ouellette, J.A. *L'Alberta-Nord. Region de Colonisation*. Edmonton: Le Courier de L'Ouest, 1909.

Painchaud, Robert. "French Canadian Historiography and Franco-Catholic Settlement in Western Canada, 1870–1915." Paper delivered at the Canadian Historical Association, May 31, 1978 (typescript).

Panich, Leo. "The Role and Nature of the Canadian State." In *The Canadian State: Political Economy and Political Power*, edited by Leo Panich, pp. 3–27. Toronto: University of Toronto Press, 1977.

Parker, James. "The Long Technological Search." *The Land of Peter Pond*, edited by John Chalmers, pp. 109–19. Edmonton: Boreal Institute for Northern Studies, Occasional Publication No. 12, 1974.

————. *Emporium of the North. Fort Chipewyan and the Fur Trade to 1835*. Regina: Alberta Culture and Multiculturalism and Canadian Plains Research Centre, 1987.

————. *History of the Athabasca Oil Sands Region, 1890s to 1960s. Vol. 2, Oral History*. Edmonton: Athabasca Oil Sands Environmental Research Program, Boreal Institute for Northern Studies, University of Alberta, 1980.

Parker, James and Tingley, K.W. *History of the Athabasca Oil Sands Region, 1890s to 1960s. Vol. 1, Socio-Economic Developments*. Edmonton: Oil Sands Environmental Research Program, Boreal Institute for Northern Studies, University of Alberta, 1980.

Parr, Joy. *The Gender of Breadwinners: Women, Men and Change in Two Industrial Towns, 1880–1950.* Toronto: University of Toronto Press, 1990.

Patterson, Graeme. *History and Communications, Harold Innis, Marshall McLuhan, the Interpretation of History.* Toronto: University of Toronto Press, 1990.

Payment, Diane. "Metis People in Motion." In *Picking Up the Threads. Metis History in the Mackenzie Basin,* pp. 69–109. N.p.: The Metis Heritage Association of the Northwest Territories, 1998.

Perry, Isabel. *Euphemia McNaught: Pioneer Artist of the Peace.* Beaverlodge District Historical Association, A Reidmore Book, 1982.

Peterson, Jacqueline, and Brown, Jennifer S., eds. *The New Peoples.* Winnipeg: University of Manitoba Press, 1985.

*Pioneers of the Lakeland.* Slave Lake: Slave Lake Pioneers, 1984.

Pocklington, T.C. *The Government and Politics of the Alberta Metis Settlements.* Regina: Canadian Plains Research Centre, 1991.

Powell, T.J.D. "Northern Settlement 1929–1935." *Saskatchewan History* 30 (1977): 81–98.

Pratt, Larry, and Urquhart, Ian. *The Last Great Forest. Japanese Multinationals and Alberta's Northern Forests.* Edmonton: NeWest Press, 1994.

Price, Richard T. and Smith, Shirleen. "Treaty 8 and Traditional Livelihoods: Historical and Contemporary Perspectives." *Native Studies Review* 9 (1993–94): 51–91.

Ray, Arthur J. *The Canadian Fur Trade in the Industrial Age.* Toronto: University of Toronto Press, 1990.

———. *I Have Lived Here Since The World Began. An Illustrated History of Canada's Native People.* Toronto: Lester Publishing and Key Porter Books, 1996.

Rea, J.K. *The Political Economy of the Canadian North. An Interpretation of the Course of Development in the Northern Territories of Canada to the Early 1960s.* Toronto: University of Toronto Press, 1968.

Reddekopp, Neil. *The Creation and Surrender of the Beaver and Duncans' Bands' Reserves.* Edmonton: Indian Land Claims, Alberta Aboriginal Affairs, Paper No. 2, 1996.

*A Report of Wisdom Synthesized from the Traditional Knowledge Component Studies.* Edmonton: Northern River Basins Study, 1996.

Ridington, Robin. "Wechuge and Windigo: A Comparison of Cannibal Belief Among Boreal Forest Athapaskans and Algonkians." *Anthropologica* NS 18 (1976): 107–29.

[Robertson, Arthur]. "Journey to the Far North, 1887." Part I, *The Beaver,* Outfit 315, no. 4 (Spring 1985): 11–21.

Ross, Hugh McKay. *The Manager's Tale.* Winnipeg: Watson and Dwyer Publishing, 1989.

Russell, Peter A. "Rhetoric of Identity: The Debate Over the Division of the North-West Territories, 1890–1905." *Journal of Canadian Studies* 20 (1985–86): 99–145.

Rycroft, D. Jean, and Leonard, David W. *The Electoral History of the Peace River Country of Alberta 1905–1993.* Edmonton: Alberta Legislature Assembly and Alberta Community Development, 1996.

Said, Edward. *Orientalism.* New York: Vintage Books, 1979.

Sawchuk, Joe. "Metis Ethnicity and its Significance for Potential Land Claims." In *Origins of the Alberta Metis: Land Claims Research Projects 1978–79,* pp. 64–91. N.p: Metis Association of Alberta, 1979.

———. *The Dynamics of Native Politics. The Alberta Metis Experience.* Saskatoon: Purich Publishing, 1998.

Sawchuk, Joe, Sawchuk, Patricia and Ferguson, Theresa. *Metis Land Rights in Alberta: A Political History.* Edmonton: Metis Association of Alberta, 1981.

Sawchuk, Patricia, and Gray, Jarvis. "The Isolated Communities of Northern Alberta." In *The Metis and The Land in Alberta. Land Claims Research Project 1979–80,* pp. 269–387. Edmonton: Metis Association of Alberta, 1980.

Sawyer, Geoff. *A History of Lesser Slave Lake.* Edmonton: Department of Recreation and Parks, 1981.

Schneider, Eva. *Ribbons of Steel. The Story of the Northern Alberta Railways.* Calgary: Detselig Enterprises Ltd., 1989.

Schull, Joseph. *Ontario Since 1867.* Toronto: McClelland and Stewart, Ontario History Series, 1978.

Seton, Ernest Thompson. *The Arctic Prairie.* New York: Charles Scribner and Sons, 1912.

Silver, A.I. "French Canada and the Prairie Frontier." *The Canadian Historical Review* 50 (1969): 11–36.

Snider, G. Elizabeth. "Slavey Indians of Hay River." Typescript. Ottawa: Treaties and Historical Research Centre, 1975.

Sprague, D.N. *Canada and The Metis 1869–1885.* Waterloo: Wilfrid Laurier University Press, 1988.

Spry, Irene M. "The Transition from a Nomadic to a Settled Economy in Western Canada, 1856–1896." *Transactions of the Royal Society of Canada,* Vol. vi, series iv, section II ( June 1968): 187–201.

———. "The Tragedy of the Loss of the Commons in Western Canada." In *As Long As The Sun Shines and Water Flows: A Reader in Canadian Native Studies,* edited by Ian A.L. Getty and Antoine Lussier, pp. 203–28. Vancouver: University of British Columbia Press, 1983.

St. Luke's Centennial Historical Committee. *Unchaga Peace. The Centennial History of St Luke's Anglican Mission.* Peace River: Valley Printers, 1977.

Stansell, Christine. *City of Women: Sex and Class in New York 1789–1860.* Chicago: University of Chicago Press, 1987.

Stead, James. *Treasure Trek.* London: George Routledge and Sons, 1936.

Stelter, Gilbert A. "A Regional Framework for Urban History." *Urban History Review* 13 (1985): 193–205.

Stone, Donald. "The Process of Rural Settlement in the Athabasca Area, Alberta." Master's thesis, University of Alberta, 1970.

Sturney, Lynda. "Northern Alberta: McInnis Products Corporation 1926–1970." *Alberta Museums' Review* 12 (1987): 11–13.

*The Subarctic Fur Trade: Native Social and Economic Adaptations.* Edited by Shepard Krech III. Vancouver: University of British Columbia Press, 1984.

Swift, William H. *Memoirs of a Frontier School Inspector in Alberta.* Edited by John W. Chalmers. Edmonton: Education Society of Edmonton, Occasional Publication No. 1, 1986.

Taylor, Griffith. "Arctic Survey III. A Mackenzie Domesday: 1944." *Canadian Journal of Economics and Political Science* 11 (1945): 189–233.

Thibault, Margaret Fraser. *The Teepee Creek Terror.* Teepee Creek: Teepee Creek Stampede Historical Society, 1978.

Thiessen, Gordon George. "Transportation on the Mackenzie River System." Master's thesis, University of Saskatchewan, 1962.

Thomas, L.G. *The Liberal Party in Alberta. A History of Politics in the Province of Alberta 1905–1921.* Toronto: University of Toronto Press, 1959.

*Three Northern Wartime Projects,* edited by Bob Hesketh. Edmonton: Canadian Circumpolar Institute and Edmonton and District Historical Society, Occasional Publication Series No. 28, 1996.

Tomblin, Stephen G. "The Pacific Great Eastern Railway and W.A.C. Bennet's Defense of the North." *Journal of Canadian Studies* 24 (1989–90): 29–40.

Tough, Frank. *Fisheries Economics and the Tragedy of the Commons: The Case of Manitoba's Inland Commercial Fisheries.* Discussion Paper No. 33, Department of Geography, York University, 1987.

———. *"As Their Natural Resources Fail": Native Peoples and the Economic History of Northern Manitoba 1870–1930.* Vancouver: University of British Columbia Press, 1996.

Tracie, Carl. "Agricultural Settlement in the South Peace River Area." Master's thesis, University of Alberta, 1967.

Treaty 7 Elders and Tribal Council, with Hildebrandt Walter, Carter, Sarah and First Rider, Dorothy. *The True Spirit and Original Intent of Treaty 7.* Kingston and Montreal: McGill-Queen's University Press, 1996.

Troper, Harold. "The Creek-Negroes of Oklahoma and Canadian Immigration 1909–11." *Canadian Historical Review* 53 (1972): 272–88.

Turcotte, J.A. *Memoirs of a Jubelarian 1924–1947.* Fort McMurray: Fort McMurray Catholic Board of Education, 1985.

Vanderhill, Burke G. "The Passing of the Pioneer Fringe in Western Canada." *The Geographical Review* 72 (1982): 200–217.

Vik, Roger. "W.D. Albright." *Alberta History* 38 (1990): 18–24.

Vogelsang, Robin. "The Initial Agricultural Settlement of the Morinville-Westlock Area, Alberta." Master's thesis, University of Alberta, 1972.

Voisey, Paul. *Vulcan. The Making of A Prairie Community.* Toronto: University of Toronto Press, 1988

Vyvyan, Clara. *The Ladies, The Gwich'in, and The Rat.* Edited by I.S. MacLaren and Lisa N. LaFramboise. Edmonton: University of Alberta Press, 1998.

Waisberg, Leo G. "Boreal Forest Subsistence and the Windigo: Fluctuations of Animal Populations." *Anthropologica* NS 17 (1975): 169–85.

Waiser, W.A. "A Bear Garden: James Melville Macoun and the 1904 Peace River Controversy." *Canadian Historical Review* 67 (1986): 42–61.

———. *The New Northwest. The Photographs of the Frank Crean Expedition 1908–1909.* Saskatoon: Fifth House Publishers, 1993.

Warkentin, John. "Western Canada in 1886." In *Canada's Changing Geography,* edited by R. Louis Gentilcore, pp. 56–82. Toronto: Prentice Hall of Canada Ltd., 1967.

Waugh, Earle H. *Dissonant Worlds. Roger Vandersteene Among the Cree.* Waterloo: Wilfrid Laurier University Press, 1996.

Weller, Geoffrey. "Political Disaffection in the Canadian Provincial North." *Bulletin of Canadian Studies* [U.K.] 9 (1985): 58–86.

West, D.A. "Re-searching the North in Canada: An Introduction to the Canadian Northern Discourse." *Journal of Canadian Studies* 26 (1991): 108–19.

Westfall, William. "On the Concept of Region in Canadian History and Literature." *Journal of Canadian Studies* 15 (1980): 3–15.

Wetherell, Donald G., and Kmet, Irene R.A. *Useful Pleasures. The Shaping of Leisure in Alberta 1896–1945*. Regina: Canadian Plains Research Centre and Alberta Culture and Multiculturalism, 1990.

———. *Town Life. Main Street and the Evolution of Small Town Alberta*. Edmonton: The University of Alberta Press and Alberta Community Development, 1995.

Wiesinger, Judith. "Modelling the Agricultural Settlement Process of Southern Manitoba, 1872–1891: Some Implications for Settlement Theory." *Prairie Forum* 10 (1985): 83–103.

Williamson, David T. "Valleyview's First Settlers." *Alberta History* 30 (1982): 29–35.

Willis, Geoffrey Allan. "Development of Transportation in the Peace River Region of Alberta and British Columbia—With an Evaluation of Present Day Rail and Road Commodity Flow Patterns." Master's thesis, University of Alberta, 1966.

Wonders, William C. "Edmonton in the Klondike Gold Rush." In *Edmonton: The Life of a City*, edited by Bob Hesketh and Frances Swripa, pp. 57–69. Edmonton: Newest Publishers, 1995.

Woywitka, Anne B. "Strike at Waterways." *Alberta Historical Review* 20 (1972): 1–5.

Wright, Robert W. *Economics, Enlightenment and Canadian Nationalism*. Kingston and Montreal: McGill-Queen's University Press, 1993.

Yerbury, J.C. *The Subarctic Indians and the Fur Trade, 1680–1860*. Vancouver: University of British Columbia Press, 1986.

Zaslow, Morris. "The Development of the Mackenzie Basin 1920–1940." Ph.D. dissertation, University of Toronto, 1957.

———. *The Opening of the Canadian North 1870–1914*. Toronto: McClelland and Stewart, 1971.

———. *Reading the Rocks*. Ottawa: Macmillan Company of Canada and Department of Energy, Mines and Resources, 1975.

———. "The Struggle for the Peace River Outlet: A Chapter in the Politics of Canadian Development." In *The West and The Nation: Essays in Honour of W.L. Morton*, edited by Carl Berger and Ramsay Cook, pp. 272–99. Toronto: McClelland and Stewart, 1976.

———. *The Northward Expansion of Canada 1914–1967*. Toronto: McClelland and Stewart, 1988.

Zubko, Andrea, and Leonard, David. "Northern Metis and Transportation." In *Picking Up the Threads. Metis History in the Mackenzie Basin*, pp. 203–18. N.p.: The Metis Heritage Association of the Northwest Territories, 1998.

# Index

aboriginal people, xvi, xxi, 3–5, 8–12, 19,
    23–26, 33, 36, 40–44, 46–47,
    49–72, 78–82, 96–98, 100–110,
    112–13, 117, 120–21, 135–49, 172,
    175–76, 180, 216, 219, 224–27,
    230–38, 273–77, 283, 304–31,
    335–36, 338, 344, 347, 363–88,
    391–92, 398–405, 413n4, 455n1,
    458n36. *See also* Indian status,
    Metis, *and by name of First Nations*
agriculture and farming, 24, 30–33, 40, 54,
    62, 68, 81, 83–84, 86, 92, 110,
    126–32, 138–41, 172–73, 179, 185,
    188, 213–14, 218–20, 240,
    242–46, 249–52, 255, 259–83,
    295–99, 310–11, 316, 318–20, 329,
    384, 400, 403–4, 417n4, 452n39
Alaska Highway, 200, 211, 278
Alberta and Arctic Transportation
    Company, 177, 205
Alberta and Great Waterways Railway, 94,
    125, 154, 165–69, 173, 187–88
Alberta Provincial Police, 86, 232, 424n19
Alberta Research Council, 89, 260, 353–56
Albright, Donald, 86, 172, 194, 199, 252–53,
    259, 265, 281, 295, 297–98
Amber Valley, 133–34

Anglican Church, 12, 25, 53, 55–57, 62, 69,
    148, 232, 286–87, 288. *See also*
    missions and missionaries
annuities, 54, 109–10, 226, 316
Athabasca (town), xix–xx, 6, 14–15, 18–19,
    21–22, 25–27, 31, 35, 37–38, 42,
    44, 46, 87–88, 90–91, 93–94, 97,
    109, 111, 113–17, 120, 122, 124, 126,
    128–29, 133, 151–55, 158, 163–65,
    176, 179–80, 192, 223, 228, 241,
    248, 250, 260, 264, 306, 324, 408,
    424n18
Athabasca Landing. *See* Athabasca (town)
Athabasca River, xv–xvi, xix, 3, 5, 14–19,
    21–22, 24, 31–32, 36, 40, 45, 82,
    110–14, 118, 123–24, 151, 164, 177,
    180, 185, 196, 201–2, 204–5,
    207–8, 210, 212–13, 232, 237–38,
    397, 401, 405
Athabasca Trail. *See* highways and roads
aviation, 186, 208–12, 220, 224, 344, 442n56


Battle River (town). *See* Notikewin
Battle River district, 173, 192, 198, 245, 268,
    306
Bear Lake. *See* Lac Cardinal

Beaver First Nations, 5, 8, 57, 137, 235, 306, 315–19, 330, 384

Beaver Lake, 6

Beaverlodge, 86, 128, 134, 172, 218, 232, 260, 264, 266, 297

Berwyn, 128, 187, 232, 239, 276, 292, 294, 316, 318, 320

Bezanson, A.M., 81, 92, 160

Bitumount, 359–60

Bluesky, 133, 217–18, 288

Bonanza, 244

Boyer River, 381

Brady, Jim, 321–23, 336

Breden, Fletcher, 89–90, 319

Breynat, Bishop, 57, 65, 70, 210, 235, 369, 374, 381–82

Brick, Alie, 26, 88, 90, 295

British Columbia, xix, 49, 57, 135, 185, 188, 195–96, 200–201, 203, 214, 243, 251, 260, 306, 344, 352, 360, 375–76, 383, 397; Peace River block, xix, 3, 188, 193, 195, 198–200, 214, 247, 255, 404, 407

Brownlee, John, 197, 207, 243, 313, 316, 323, 349–50

Calgary, 88, 95, 123, 133, 170, 277, 287, 290, 294, 354, 390

Calling Lake, 126, 153, 430n45

Canadian Northern Railway, 93, 111, 129, 151, 169, 193, 437n36

Canadian Pacific Railway, 13, 29, 32, 169, 187–88, 195, 198, 223, 245, 261, 265, 297

Canol Project, 208, 211, 224, 226

Canyon Creek, 339

Carcajou, 240

Central Canada Railway, 94, 163, 168–69, 187

Cheechum, 339

Chipewyan First Nations, 5, 7–9, 24, 57, 120, 224, 306–7, 370

Chisholm, 346, 360

Clairmont, 268, 302

Clark, Karl, 355–57

Clear Hills (Indian reservation), 274, 317

Clearwater River, 4, 14, 18, 167, 173, 188–89, 207, 210, 225, 347, 349

climate, 8, 15, 80–81, 129–30, 172, 261, 267, 450n6

coast outlet, 93, 186, 193–200, 440n29

Cold Lake, xx, 321

Conklin, 189, 406

Consolidated Mining and Smelting Ltd., 190, 358, 405

Cornwall, James, 45, 67, 89–91, 113–16, 123, 158, 178, 207, 295, 349, 369, 371, 381–82, 389, 424n14

Cote, Jean, 89, 123, 125, 173, 311

Cree First Nations, 5–9, 18, 24, 26, 56–57, 66, 82, 136, 175, 224, 307, 318, 369–70

Dawson Creek (B.C.), 188, 200, 214, 217, 247, 262

Debolt, 244, 266, 268

Dene, 5, 9, 11, 146, 384

Department of Indian Affairs. See government, federal

Department of the Interior. See government, federal

Depression, 1930s, 198, 209, 232, 246–50, 253–54, 257, 260, 287, 320, 334–35, 338, 346, 356, 364, 399, 401, 448n25

Dion, Joe, 142, 321–23

District of Athabaska, xix, 29, 37, 77, 85, 108, 417n2

Driftpile (Indian reservation), 235, 249, 274–75, 309, 311–13

Dunvegan, 5, 15, 23, 57, 64, 91, 129, 132, 136, 160–61, 172, 416n40, 424n18

East Prairie Metis Settlement, 328–29

Edmonton, xvi–xvii, xx, 6, 9, 13–14, 33, 35, 37, 42, 44–45, 51, 86–87, 94, 113–15,

117, 123–27, 129, 133–34, 152–53, 158, 160, 167, 170, 177–80, 185, 188, 191–94, 196, 202, 209, 211–12, 214–15, 221, 243, 246, 248–49, 266, 279, 287, 290, 295–96, 338, 340, 344, 346–47, 350, 372, 375, 386, 389–90, 398–400, 425n37

Edmonton, Dunvegan and British Columbia Railway, 94, 126, 141, 153–54, 158–63, 167–70, 187–88, 195, 298, 346

Edson, 111

Edson Trail. *See* highways and roads

Eldorado Gold Mines Ltd., 190, 206, 442n53

Ells, Sidney, 123–25, 354, 430n41

employment, 12, 24, 26, 46, 110, 112, 120–22, 133, 172, 210–11, 224–25, 246, 250, 269–70, 276, 311, 334, 336, 341–42, 344, 347, 377, 404, 408–9. *See also* freighting

epidemics, 178, 209, 231

Eureka River, 193

Euro-Canadian settlement, 77, 80–88, 91–92, 111, 128–38, 152, 179, 186, 220, 239–55, 257–58, 260, 281, 285–88, 301–2, 305–6, 310–11, 316–17, 326, 371, 376, 399–401, 404

Euro-Canadian trappers, 120, 178, 225, 307–8, 326, 375–77, 379–83, 385, 392, 465n51

Ewing Commission. *See* Royal Commission on the Condition of the Halfbreed Population of Alberta


Fairview, 32, 128, 187–88, 193, 217–19, 228–29, 232, 239, 244, 268, 316–17, 330

Falher, 131, 240, 261, 287

family allowance, 387

Faust, 171, 276, 335, 337–38, 346

fishing, 4, 9, 23–24, 26, 66–68, 97–98, 107, 110, 125–26, 138, 153, 170–75, 179,

225, 276, 310, 333–43, 360–61, 372, 390–91, 426n49, 430n45, 437n39, 460n18; and treaty rights, 98, 172, 335–36, 377. *See also* wildlife regulation

Fishing Lake, 321

Fitzgerald, 18–19, 22, 57, 86, 88, 108–9, 113, 117, 120–21, 126, 163, 175, 177, 204, 207–8, 227, 406

Fond du Lac, xix, 57, 117, 175, 177, 226

forests and forestry, 4, 25, 95–97, 122, 154, 169–70, 329, 333, 341, 343–48, 360–61, 372, 408–9

forest fires, 22, 37, 39, 41, 96–97, 343–44; controlled burning, 41, 97

Fort Assiniboine, 32

Fort Chipewyan, xix, 4–5, 7–9, 15, 18–21, 24–26, 37–38, 40, 53, 57, 69, 86, 88, 103–4, 109–10, 117, 120, 126, 137, 146–47, 158, 163–64, 174–75, 177, 185, 204, 210, 225–27, 231–32, 307–9, 326, 340–42, 365, 369–70, 374–75, 377, 384, 388–89, 405–6, 413n4, 416n40, 417n46, 419n32

Fort Fitzgerald. *See* Fitzgerald

Fort Macpherson, 45

Fort McKay, 22, 40, 123, 154

Fort McMurray, xvi, 4, 15, 18, 21–22, 24, 30, 37, 40–41, 57, 86, 88–89, 93–94, 97, 110, 112–14, 120–21, 123–25, 137–38, 151–52, 154, 164, 167–68, 173–74, 178, 180, 185, 190, 201, 204–5, 209–12, 214, 220–25, 237, 306, 348–52, 354–60, 375, 389, 405–7, 413n4. *See also* Waterways

Fort Rae, 33

Fort Resolution, 3, 21, 25–26, 33, 40, 57, 86, 104

Fort Simpson, 46, 210

Fort Smith, xvi, xix, 3–4, 9, 18–19, 22, 25–26, 40, 42, 49–50, 57, 69, 78, 88, 93, 109, 113, 135, 137, 158, 177, 204, 207, 227, 307, 309, 368, 413n4

Fort St. John, 23, 46, 56–57, 193, 214, 240, 245

Fort Vermilion, xvi, 4–5, 15, 20–21, 23, 25–26, 38, 40, 57, 81–82, 87, 91, 117, 127–29, 131, 137, 163, 175, 179, 190, 201, 203, 219–20, 230, 240, 245, 256, 260, 282, 375, 381, 411n3, 413n4, 416n40, 417n46, 424n18, 446n36

Fraser, Colin, 22, 25, 117

Frederick, Charles, 196, 202, 295, 298–99, 300–301, 303

freight rates. *See* railways

freighting, 6, 15–19, 22–23, 35, 63, 110–17, 120, 136

Friedenstal, 128, 134

fur farming, 338–39, 364, 388–91

fur trade, xv, 3, 5, 10–12, 21, 26, 38, 64, 80, 116–21, 174–79, 205, 217, 224–26, 334, 364–65, 372–74, 387–88, 403, 429n27


geological surveys, 29–32, 83–84, 122, 356

Gift Lake Metis Settlement, 328–29

Giroux, L.A., 196, 313, 315

Girouxville, 264

Goldfields, 190, 204–5, 225, 358, 439n13

government, federal, xv–xvi, 29–30, 34–37, 46–47, 77–78, 83–88, 101–6, 115, 122–25, 169, 172, 175–76, 195–96, 199, 201–2, 211–12, 221–23, 227, 237–38, 251, 259, 286, 310–20, 334, 353, 355, 359, 361, 363–64, 366–70, 374–88, 391–92, 397–98, 400, 402, 406, 465n40

government, provincial, xvi, 77–78, 88–95, 98–99, 101–6, 169, 187–89, 192, 195–97, 199, 201–2, 207, 216, 228–30, 237–38, 248–51, 254–56, 259, 260–61, 263–64, 267, 278–82, 286, 296–97, 306, 309, 321, 326, 334, 343–44, 348–50, 353–55, 359–61, 363–67, 371–92, 398–403, 406–9

Grand Rapids. *See* portages

Grand Trunk Pacific Railway, 93, 111, 169, 193

Grande Prairie, xvi, 6, 80, 82, 87, 90–91, 93–94, 111, 120, 122, 128–29, 131, 151, 160, 162, 169, 179, 187, 192, 194–95, 197–200, 202, 209, 211, 216, 219, 227–28, 232, 239, 243–44, 252, 254–55, 261–63, 266, 268, 276, 287, 289, 290–93, 299–302, 304, 347, 375, 404, 424n18, 424n24

Great Slave Lake, 4, 31, 40, 46, 49, 177, 201, 203, 343

Grimshaw, 128, 200, 268

Grimshaw Highway, 200–203, 208, 213, 220, 343, 405, 441n44

gristmills, 25, 127, 131, 275

Grouard, 15, 22–23, 25–26, 34, 40, 43–44, 46, 50–53, 56, 59–60, 72, 86–87, 91, 97, 110–11, 115–16, 122, 128, 131–32, 134–35, 143–44, 153, 155–60, 179, 192, 218, 235–36, 240, 298, 309, 313, 415n30, 417n46, 417n2, 419n32, 424n18, 424n24

Grouard, Emile, 7, 19, 45–46, 53, 56, 66, 70, 136


Hansard (town), 198–99

Hay Lakes, 384–86, 446n36

Hay River, 57, 175, 208, 343, 381, 405, 413n4

High Prairie, 128, 131, 160, 324

highways and roads, 13, 15, 23, 30, 34–35, 44, 77, 91, 111, 113–14, 128, 192–93, 197–200, 204–5, 214, 220, 230–32, 268, 278, 281, 300, 302, 347, 349, 361, 401, 428n8

Hines Creek, 188, 193, 229, 239, 244, 250, 268, 347

Hislop and Nagle, 33, 110, 113, 117–18

Holmes, George, 46, 50, 53, 56, 60–62, 70, 72

homesteading, 84, 87, 128–29, 148–49, 154, 176–77, 241, 243–44, 246, 249, 252–58, 275, 278, 287, 320, 343, 398–99, 404, 449n45

Horse Lakes (Indian reservation), 274, 316

hospitals. *See* medical services

House River, 113–14,

Hudson's Bay Company, xix, 3, 5, 8, 13–19, 21–23, 25, 27, 30, 33–34, 42, 44, 112–15, 117–18, 120, 126–27, 152–54, 158, 163–64, 167, 174–75, 177, 179, 205–8, 210–12, 217, 219, 221, 224, 397, 416n40

Hudson's Hope, 4, 15, 23

hunting, 4, 9, 23–24, 36–52, 98–106, 107, 110, 120, 126, 138, 140, 141–42, 147, 175, 185, 246, 273, 276, 310, 325, 329, 363–88, 391–92, 399, 403–5; and treaty rights, 36, 52, 54–55, 57, 66–69, 71, 100–106, 363–87, 391–92, 402

hunting preserves, 326, 374–77, 391, 402

Hythe, 187–88, 216–17, 244, 293, 316

Indian administration, xxi, 135, 231, 235, 274, 309–10, 432n71. *See also* Indian reserves, Indian status

Indian reserves, xvi, 50, 52, 54–55, 66, 71, 135–41, 230, 273–77, 283, 306–21, 330–31, 402, 420n9, 452n39, 457n32

Indian status, xxi, 57–58, 60, 64–71, 135–36, 144, 148, 230, 233, 322, 324, 327, 330, 369–70, 377, 381, 400, 402–3, 406. *See also* hunting and treaty rights

Indiana (town). *See* Joussard

Jackson, Mary Percy, 229, 287, 329

Janvier (Indian reservation), 384

Joussard, 171, 235–36

justice, administration of, 37–38, 41, 77, 85, 107–9

Keg River, 91, 203, 229, 245, 287, 328–29

Kennedy, Donald, 195, 295, 310–11, 316, 378, 454n21, 454n22

Kinoosayo, 65, 136, 140

Kinuso, 311, 313–15, 390

Klondike Gold Rush, 44–47, 65, 419n38

Lac Cardinal, 136

Lac La Biche, xix–xx, 6, 23, 40–41, 88, 93, 165, 167, 189, 214, 223, 306, 324–25, 340, 344, 389–90, 417n4, 426n49

Lacombe, Albert, 53, 55–56, 61–62, 70

Lake Athabasca, xix, 3–5, 21, 153, 173–74, 177, 185, 190, 225, 309, 339–43, 358, 381

Lake Saskatoon, 131, 218, 228, 288, 292, 295, 424n18

Lake Wabamum, 126, 171

Lake Winefred, 339

Lamson and Hubbard, 177–78, 205

land clearing, 81, 242–43, 250, 268–70, 276–80, 282, 304, 344

land policies. *See* homesteading

land surveys, 30, 87, 130, 137, 259–60

Laviolette, Alexandre, 57, 104

Laviolette, Jonas, 363, 369, 381

Lawrence, Fred, 81

Lesser Slave Lake, 4–6, 15, 23, 31, 43, 51, 58, 63, 71, 80, 82, 88, 97–98, 103–4, 109, 111, 115–18, 120–21, 125–26, 128, 136, 138–39, 151, 153, 158, 169–71, 180, 230, 235, 274, 276, 309, 311, 315, 325, 335–39, 344, 346–47, 366, 375, 381, 388, 390, 413n4, 430n45

Lesser Slave Lake Settlement. *See* Grouard

Lesser Slave River, 15, 21–22, 115

Levillot, Alicksand, 42–43

liquor, 35, 37, 41, 44, 61, 109, 113, 291, 314–15, 398

Little Red River (Athabasca River). *See* Fort McKay

Little Red River (Vermilion Chutes), 22, 57, 66, 381

Loon Lake, 5, 23,

Lubicon Lake, 307

lumbering. *See* forests and forestry

Lymburn, 244, 268


Mackenzie basin, xv, xix, 3, 5, 7, 12, 21, 30–31, 33, 79, 85, 153

Mackenzie Highway. *See* Grimshaw Highway

Mackenzie River, xix, 3–4, 12, 19, 21–22, 45–46, 82, 117, 127, 177, 180, 185, 204, 397, 429n27

Mackenzie River Transport. *See* Hudson's Bay Company

Macoun, James, 83–84, 424n14

Manitoba, 79, 81, 89, 101, 135, 170, 195, 254, 350

Manning (town), 220

McArthur, J.D., 94, 122, 163, 169, 346

McDougall and Secord, 33, 42, 115

McInnes Fish Company, 206, 339–43

McLennan, 128, 134, 160–61, 163, 240, 264, 411n3, 424n18

McNaught, Euphemia, 199, 244

mechanization, 19, 114–16, 127, 186, 209, 270–73, 275, 277–80, 299–300, 321, 340, 344, 390

medical services, 69, 131–32, 215–16, 220, 227–31, 238, 268, 321, 325, 329, 399, 402, 404–5, 444n21

Metis, xvi, xxi, 5–9, 18, 22, 24, 38, 43–44, 47, 50, 54, 57–63, 70–71, 98, 109, 113, 115–17, 135–36, 148, 156, 162, 172, 180, 210, 225, 230, 232–33, 304–6, 308, 320–30, 342, 344, 369, 372,

377–78, 385–86, 400, 402–3, 406, 413n4, 427n4

Metis Association of Alberta, 305, 321–24, 326–27, 329–30, 403

Metis settlements, 321–22, 324–30

mining and minerals, 30–32, 46–47, 49, 79, 86, 122, 179, 185–86, 190–91, 201–2, 205, 207–9, 333, 352, 360, 365. *See also* salt production

Mirror Landing, 21–22, 115, 155, 158

missions and missionaries, xix, 3, 5, 7–8, 10–11, 19, 23–26, 30, 41, 50–51, 55–56, 69–71, 109, 126, 142–48, 154, 219, 226, 231, 234, 236, 275, 417n46, 455n31, 459n56

Monkman Pass, 198–200

Moostoos, 55, 136

municipal and local government, 91, 131, 215–16, 219, 227–32, 281

Muskeg Prairie. *See* Wandering River


Native. *See* aboriginal people, Indian status, Metis *and by name of First Nations*

Natural Resources Transfer Agreement, 306, 321, 334, 344, 377–80, 384

natural resources, 4, 8–10, 35–37, 77–79, 84–85, 90, 95–96, 141, 169–70, 305, 333–34, 343, 363–64, 398. *See also by type of resource*

Norman Wells, 185, 204, 208–9, 358

Norris, Malcolm, 321–23, 336, 377

North Saskatchewan River, 13–14

North Star, 220

North West Territories (after 1905), 5, 49, 104, 185–86, 190, 200, 202, 206–7, 210, 212–13, 225, 227, 343, 358, 360, 368–70, 374, 380, 382, 392, 405

Northern Alberta Railways, 188–92, 198–203, 210, 221–23, 248, 251, 257, 261–62, 337, 339, 342, 346–47, 350, 389

Northern Traders Ltd. *See* Northern
 Trading Company
Northern Trading Company, 118, 177, 189,
 205–6
Northern Transportation Company, 90, 115,
 164, 206, 208, 442n53
northerness, xvii, 80–81, 85, 244, 389, 404–5,
 411n6
North-West Mounted Police. *See* Royal
 Canadian Mounted Police
Notikewin, 23, 192, 220, 229, 245, 247, 329

Oblates of Mary Immaculate, 5, 23, 70, 112,
 143, 236, 455n1
oil sands, 30, 123–25, 154, 333, 352–61, 400,
 407
Oliver, Frank, 33, 37, 41–42, 47, 83–84, 87,
 102, 125, 133, 295, 397
Old Wives Lake (Indian reservation), 274,
 317–18
Ontario, 79, 81, 101, 185, 196, 240, 293,
 297–98, 344, 349–51, 360, 380,
 387, 465n51

Pacific and Great Eastern Railway, 94,
 194–95, 214
Paddle Prairie Metis Settlement, 328–29
Peace-Athabasca Delta, 4, 6, 15, 21–22, 104,
 152, 224–25, 306, 373, 375–76,
 412n3
Peace Pass, 199–200
Peace River (river), 4–5, 9, 14–15, 21–22, 32,
 40, 43–44, 110–12, 122–23, 129,
 163, 179, 237
Peace River (town), xvi, 15, 23, 25–26, 32, 34,
 40, 56, 62, 87, 91, 93–94, 120,
 128–29, 131, 151, 154, 156, 158–59,
 163, 165, 168, 173, 179, 190, 192,
 194–97, 200, 202–3, 211–12, 217,
 219, 227–28, 232, 243, 245, 249,
 264, 266, 289–90, 292–93, 298,
 300–301, 316, 318, 343, 352, 404,

408, 417n46, 417n49, 419n32,
 424n18, 424n24
Peace River country, xvi–xvii, xix, 4–5, 8, 10,
 15, 23, 30–33, 35–36, 43–44, 46,
 58, 71, 80, 82, 86–87, 90–92, 111,
 114, 116–18, 121–22, 126, 128–30,
 133–34, 138–39, 153, 158, 163, 175,
 178, 180, 185–86, 192, 194, 200,
 209, 212–14, 216–20, 238–56,
 259–83, 285–304, 306–7, 309–10,
 314, 344, 386, 397, 400–401,
 404–5, 411n3, 413n4
Peace River Country Secessionism, 196–97,
 202–3, 299
Peace River Crossing. *See* Peace River (town)
Peace River Trading and Land Company,
 112, 120
Peavine Metis Settlement, 328
Peerless Lake, 5, 23
Pelican Rapids, 31–32
Pembina Valley Railway, 187
petroleum, 30–32, 89, 122–23, 163, 173, 185,
 352–53, 358, 360–61, 407–8. *See
 also* oil sands
Pine Pass, 199–200, 214
Portage La Loche, 3, 13–14, 18–19, 224
portages, 4, 13, 15–19, 21–22, 35, 37, 42, 46,
 88, 112–14, 153, 163–64, 167–68,
 177, 180, 227, 415n32, 419n32
postal services, 34, 88, 130–31, 162, 167,
 209–10, 418n14
Pouce Coupe, 128, 162, 173, 188, 199
Prairie River. *See* High Prairie
Prince George, 94, 194–95, 198, 200, 214
Prince Rupert, 196

Quebec, 79, 134, 185, 240, 287, 344, 374, 380, 387
Quesnell (town), 15, 94, 194

radio, 199, 287, 289, 297, 300
railways, xvi, 33, 45, 86, 91–95, 98, 106, 111,
 114, 125, 128–29, 131, 151–54,

158–74, 179, 187–91, 193–95, 198,
    213–14, 216–19, 220, 227, 237,
    242–47, 261–62, 266, 268, 278,
    281, 289, 300, 330, 346–51, 360,
    398, 404–5, 439n5, 439n9. *See also*
    *by company name*
rapids. *See* portages
recreation and leisure, 99, 109–10, 220,
    226–27, 288–94, 315, 343,
    366–68, 371–73, 404, 427n4
Red Deer, 96, 248–49, 344, 347
Red Willow Creek. *See* Valleyview
regionalism, xv, xviii–xix, 3, 18, 25–27, 29, 151,
    158, 179–80, 185–86, 194, 196,
    212–16, 237–38, 391, 397–99,
    400–401
Revillon Freres, 117–18, 120, 174–75, 205
river and lake transportation, xv–xvi, 3,
    13–19, 21–23, 26–27, 45, 92,
    111–16, 151–56, 158–59, 163–65,
    177, 185–87, 191, 201, 203–8, 210,
    212–13, 219–23, 227, 237, 340–41,
    343, 349, 358, 405
Roman Catholic Church, 12, 23, 25, 53,
    55–56, 62, 70–71, 142, 147–48,
    156, 232, 240, 251. *See also* mission-
    aries and missionaries *and*
    Oblates of Mary Immaculate
Round Lake. *See* McLennan
Royal Canadian Mounted Police, xvi, 29,
    35–44, 46–47, 53, 68, 78, 85–86,
    88, 104, 108–9, 113, 126, 154, 158,
    161–62, 165, 176, 209–10, 227, 235,
    418n14, 419n32, 424n18, 424n19
Royal Commission on the Condition of the
    Halfbreed Population of
    Alberta, 305, 324–27
Ryan brothers, 204, 207

salt production, 22, 89, 173, 189, 333, 348–52,
    361
Sandy Bay, 136, 139–40

Saskatchewan, xix, 29, 35, 49, 79, 89, 101, 104,
    128, 195, 201, 249–50, 254, 260,
    264, 339–40, 343, 346–47,
    349–50, 352, 449n45
sawmills. *See* forests and forestry
Sawridge. *See* Slave Lake (town)
Sawridge (Indian reservation), 313
schools, 215, 238, 268, 289, 321, 325, 330, 387;
    public, 131, 142–43, 154, 215,
    405–6, 445n31; mission and resi-
    dential, xvi, 24, 33, 54–56, 70–71,
    141–49, 234–36, 402, 417n46,
    434n95, 446n36
scrip, 50, 54, 57–63, 70–71, 135, 421n36
Secord, Richard, 42, 60, 421n36
Senate of Canada, 30–31, 84
Seton, Ernest Thompson, 80–81, 105
Sexsmith, 262, 268
Shaftesbury Settlement, 25–26, 88, 127, 136, 154
Slave Lake (town), 115, 126, 155, 158, 298, 352,
    390, 407–8, 424n18, 460n8
Slave Lake Post. *See* Grouard
Slave River (river), 3–4, 12, 18, 21–22, 40,
    112–13, 117–18, 177
Slavey First Nations, 5
Smith (town), 158, 424n18
Smith Portage. *See* portages
Smith's Landing. *See* Fitzgerald
Smoky River, 32, 128, 160–61
social welfare, 30, 33, 36, 69, 176–77, 179, 216,
    231–32, 257, 365
Sovereign, Bishop, 192, 247–48, 286, 455n31
Spirit River, 23, 128–29, 131, 162, 167, 172,
    194–95, 228–30, 244, 262, 268,
    278, 281, 290, 292, 294, 424n18,
    424n24
St. Albert, 6, 113, 321
St. Paul, 6, 134, 325, 327
Sturgeon Lake, 23, 26, 44, 51–52, 57, 98, 111,
    136, 235, 424n18
Sucker Creek, 136, 139–40, 235, 274
Swan River (Indian reservation), 139,
    274–75, 311–15, 330
Swan River (town). *See* Kinuso

Teepee Creek, 293

telegraph and telephone, 88, 120, 130, 154, 162, 174, 197

Tompkins, Peter, 233, 322–23, 326

trade goods, 10–11, 117, 120–21, 225, 414n22

trapping. *See* hunting

Treaty 6, xx, 31, 49, 58, 70, 386

Treaty 7, 55

Treaty 8, xvi, xix, 31, 49–72, 80, 85, 135, 137–43, 147, 306, 330, 366, 368, 370–71, 376–77, 379, 381–82

Treaty 11, 31, 80, 439n1

Trelle, Herman, 295–97, 303

Trout Lake, 5, 23

Turner Valley, 123–24, 350, 353, 358

Tustawits, Duncan, 56, 136, 139

United States, 96, 132, 134, 170, 177, 208–9, 211, 239, 250, 288–89, 295, 334, 337, 340–41, 347, 349, 353, 356, 366, 389

Uranium City, 174

urban systems, 20–27, 107, 109, 149, 180, 215–27, 237, 243, 288, 397, 401

Utikuma Lake, 23, 44, 50, 69, 144, 146, 328, 336–37, 381, 417n46

Valhalla, 134, 262, 266

Valleyview, 244

Vancouver, 93, 194, 198, 221, 407

Vermilion Chutes. *See* portages

Wabasca, 5–6, 15, 23, 40, 57, 110, 136–37, 175, 230, 234–36, 273, 275, 306, 387, 413n4, 417n46

Wagner (town), 171

Wandering River, 247

Wanham, 278

Waterhole, 128, 134, 172, 193, 218–19, 229, 292, 299, 316

Waterways, 167–69, 173, 177, 189, 201–4, 206–8, 220–24, 237, 340–43. *See also* Fort McMurray

weeds, 280–82

Wembley, 169, 187, 199, 268, 317, 319

White Eagle Mines, 190, 206

Whitefish Lake. *See* Utikuma Lake

Whitelaw, 217

Widewater, 337–38

wildlife regulation, 35–41, 43–44, 52, 66–69, 77, 95–106, 117, 171–72, 325, 334, 363–87, 398, 418n20

wildlife, depletion, 5, 22–23, 35–37, 40–41, 43, 96, 99, 120, 141, 170, 230, 306, 308, 321, 333, 363, 366, 372, 376, 378–79. *See also* fishing

Windigo, 51–52

Wood Buffalo, 4, 36, 40–41, 43, 68–69, 98, 104–5, 418n20

Wood Buffalo National Park, 105, 137, 227, 307, 309, 363, 365, 368–70, 381, 463n11

World War I, 132, 137, 172, 174, 242–43, 250–51

World War II, xvi, 200, 207–8, 211, 224, 226, 239, 241, 260, 265–66, 270, 276, 278, 282, 287, 306, 335–38, 342–43, 347, 358–59

Worsely, 193

Yellowknife, 190, 201, 203, 358

Yukon, 44–45, 374